395 Days

GARY G. KASTEN

To LEN
SEMPER FI

Gary Kasten

"THE HAMMER"

Trafford
PUBLISHING™

*We at Trafford believe that it is the responsibility of us all, as both individuals
and corporations, to make choices that are environmentally and socially sound.
You, in turn, are supporting this responsible conduct each time you purchase a
Trafford book, or make use of our publishing services. To find out how you are
helping, please visit www.trafford.com/responsiblepublishing.html*

*Our mission is to efficiently provide the world's finest, most comprehensive
book publishing service, enabling every author to experience success.
To find out how to publish your book, your way, and have it available
worldwide, visit us online at www.trafford.com/10510*

 **www.trafford.com**

North America & international
toll-free: 1 888 232 4444 (USA & Canada)
phone: 250 383 6864 ♦ fax: 250 383 6804 ♦ email: info@trafford.com

The United Kingdom & Europe
phone: +44 (0)1865 722 113 ♦ local rate: 0845 230 9601
facsimile: +44 (0)1865 722 868 ♦ email: info.uk@trafford.com

10 9 8 7 6 5 4

Acknowledgments

On April 1, 1968 I was released from the United States Marine Corps on the early out system. I moved back in with my parents and was waiting for college football double days to start sometime in August. I remember sitting on the front porch with my mother and having trouble trying to forget about Vietnam. I remember talking with my mother and watching cars go by, but my mind kept returning to Vietnam. I told my mother that I had to do something. I went down to the basement of our home and took out the typewriter in order to put down on paper what I had gone through in Vietnam. I wanted and needed it out of my system. I could almost see in my mind what I was going through over there. As I looked at the blank paper in the typewriter I didn't know actually where to begin, but I eventually decided to start with my first day in Vietnam.

Thanks to my father who told my brother and sister early on that it was up to us to learn how to use a typewriter. I remember that I started out using one finger, then two, and then more. By the time I got to high school I was a fairly good typist.

As I started typing, I would go into a type of trance. My fingers were typing as fast as my mind was recalling Vietnam. I had problems with spelling but I kept right on going. Each day, for the next three months I went down in the basement and wrote up to 250 pages. It really felt good to get Vietnam out of me and onto paper. Then it was time for me to go off to Drake University for double day football practice, So I shelved what I had written.

During my second year at Drake University all of the guys on the football team had to take a free lance writing course by Hank Felson. At the time, Hank Felson was a professional free lance writer who had had a few books published and had even one made into a movie. There were over two hundred students in that free lance writing course, and about twenty of us were football players. Hank Felson asked the students if anyone had or was writing a book. The guys on the football team yelled out that I had written a book. Hank Felson told me that he wanted to see me after class. When class was over he wanted to know what I wrote about. I told him that I had written about my experiences over in Vietnam, but that the book was not for people to read. He asked if my book was done and I told him I was only half way finished. He told me that if I wanted a grade in his course that I had to get it completed before the end of the semester. I remember that I went back to my dorm room and got fired back up to finish my book. In four weeks I had it completely done, and there were 430 pages, single spaced.

When I turned the book in to Hank Felson I told him that I had a lot of misspelled words, but he didn't care because he wanted to read it. It wasn't until the last day of class when Hank talked to me about my book. When the class was over and I went to him to pick up my book, he told me that both he and his wife had read the book. He was, in fact, a Marine who had fought in World War II. Hank Felson said that my book brought back memories that he had forgotten, and it had really hit home with him. He said that my book was too powerful for people to read right now, and that I should put it on the shelf for about twenty-five years and then get it published.

If it wasn't for Hank Felson I probably would have never finished the book in the first place. From one Marine to another Marine - THANKS. Also a very big thanks to the guys on the Drake University football team for letting Hank Felson even know about my book. If it wasn't for the guys on the football team informing Hank Felson about the book, I probably wouldn't be getting it published today.

Later I decided to have a few others read the book to see what they thought about it and to see if I should get the book published, including a friend's mother. The mother called me up and told me that she didn't want to sound off being harsh with me but said that I should have died in Vietnam. The college students said that my book was very good with exception of the spelling mistakes. But the final word was yes, get the book published.

After college I put the book in the closet and forgot about it for several years. I later got married to a wonderful girl, Karen Mackin from Cleveland, Ohio whom I met in Portsmouth, Ohio when we were both high school teachers. Karen read my book and she let me know there was a lot work to be done on the book. I knew that I had to get the spelling corrected so I went through the book again, this time using a computer, and corrected a lot of the words. Now the book was 550 pages long.

In the late 1990's when I was working in the post office, I asked a couple of people to read my book to see if I should publish it. A friend, Peggy Chapman, said that I should get the book published because it was really great. In a way I was glad to hear what she said but yet I was sad in that people would know just what in the hell my buddies and I had gone through over there. Thanks to Peggy Chapman for reinforcing what the people in the past have said.

I went over my book once again to make sure that I had everything in the right place, along with the guys' names in the platoon. When I finished it this time I had 624 pages.

In September of 2005 I brought a GMC truck from a salesman Tom Cranmer who was an Marine. Tom told me about Sgt. Grit and their news letters for the Marines. I went home and got on the computer to check to see if there was anything about my old outfit, 1st Battalion 9th Marines. It came up and there was an Application Form to sign up for the organization. I printed out the form and sent it in and about three weeks later I got a phone call from one of the guys in my old outfit, Ted Van Meeteren from Utah! We talked for about an hour and I told him that I had written a book about what we had gone through together. Four days later I got another phone call, this one from Charlie Horton in Oregon. I also told him that I had written a book and he told me, as well as Ted, to get the damn thing published to tell the people just what the hell all of us really went through and don't water it down. A special thanks to Ted Van Meeteren, Dale Davis, Charlie Horton and Bill Gonzales.

I went to my son Michael's English teacher Jenny Hostetler, to see if she would go over my book to check my grammar and spelling mistakes. At the time I didn't tell her that it was 624 pages long. Jenny agreed to help me, so on the last day of school I went to her class room and handed the book to her. She almost didn't want to do it because of the size of the book, but since she had already told me she would, she honored her word. She told me about her uncle who fought in the Korean War and how he never talked about it. I told Jenny that when she went through my book, she would see why guys who fought in battle didn't talk about what they went through. As she worked on the book during summer, Jenny put in the chapters as well as correcting my grammar and spelling mistakes. When she was done with a section of the book, I would write in the corrections and chapters in the computer to get it ready for publication. I want to say to Mrs. Jenny Hostetler a BIG thank you for taking her valuable time off during the summer to do this very large undertaking, Again THANKS.

I talked to Bill Gonzales on the phone and asked him if I could include some of the pictures that he took over there of the guys, patrols, buildings and huts, and places all of us had been from "The Street Without Joy", Camp Evans, Phu Bai, Dong Ha, Camp Carroll, Cam Lo Bridge, Gio Lin, Con Thein to the D.M.Z. A very special thanks to Bill Gonzales (Speedy) for giving me these pictures to be included in the book.

A special thanks to Barry Cook for his information about Trafford Publishing Company because they will be publishing the book. Trafford published the book called "Reluctant Witness" of Barry's uncle outfit, the 24th bomber group of World War II.

I want to thank all of the people who have taken the time to read my book over the years and who have wanted to see it get published.

I want to thank my parents for making me into a good and caring person.

Finally, if I've forgotten anyone, my sincere apologies.

As I was growing up, I thought my father was the meanest father on earth. Every time my younger sister or brother or myself would get into trouble he would beat us. Often the three of us would stay away from the house until he would call us for dinner. Boy, we better be there or we would get a spanking. When I was very young, about eight or nine, I would wish that my father was dead. I believe the reason my father was so hard on us was because he had spent nine years in the Army. He had done almost everything there was to do: drive and fire tanks, and be an expert in all of the weapons that the Army had at the time. He had wanted to be in a real man's army, so he joined the 11th Airborne Division and fought against the Japanese. The Japanese called the 11th Airborne, "The Devils in Baggy Pants." His buddy was Rod Serling who was on the Twilight Zone on T.V. Dad would say that the show was a nut job and that Rod Serling was a nut, but he never watched the series. Later, when he went to his first reunion of the 11th Airborne Division, he realized that Rod Serling was his buddy and that they had fought together during the war.

As I got older, every time my dad spanked me either with a board or belt, he would ask, "When the hell are you going to grow up?" The last time he beat me was when all three of us got into trouble because of my younger brother. At the time I was twelve years old. It was the first time that my dad gave all three of us an option to either lose watching T.V. for a week or taking three swats. Both my sister and brother took the no T.V. for a week, but I told him that I would take the swats. When he was finished swatting me he looked me in the eye and said that I had just became a man and that he was proud of me. He never spanked me after that.

During my senior year in high school I decided to go into the army to be a paratrooper just like my father, so I joined the Army on a ninety day delayed program. When I got out of high school, the guys who I hung out with down the street at Bill and Bob's Sporting good store told me that I should have joined the Marine Corps and played football for the Quantico Marines. So Roland (known as Stretch because of his height of 6'7"), took me to the Marine recruiter office and I joined the Marine Corps. I went from the Army to the Marine Corps in the same day. I remembered seeing the movie "The D.I." on T.V. where Jack Webb starred as the D.I. I knew that the Marines would be easier for me because of what my father had done to me as a kid growing up, such as grabbing me, being about two inches from my face while yelling at me, telling me how stupid I was, and then beating me.

When I graduated from high school the Marine recruiter told me that the only things I should know by heart before I went to boot camp on September 26, 1966 were the eleven general orders.

I did exactly what the D.I.'s wanted during the first four weeks of boot camp. I excelled over all of the other guys in the platoon during the last four weeks of boot camp. I ended up even beating my junior D.I. in one on one bayonet training, I had to figure out how to lose so that he could win. I ended up just letting him win.

On the last day of boot camp the head D.I. S/Sgt. R. P. Hellein called me into his office and while standing in front of me told me that I was the only Marine in boot camp who excelled instead of breaking during the last four weeks. He wanted to know the reason why and I told him that it was because of my father. He asked whether he was a Marine and I told him that he was an Army Paratrooper, 11th Airborne Division from W.W. II He told me that my father did one hell of a job with me and that if he went back to Vietnam that he would like to have me in his team. That really meant a lot to me since he had fought in both Korea and Vietnam.

I then went to B.I.S., Basic Infantry School, for all of us 0311's. At that time it was a two week course to get us ready for Vietnam. One evening the sergeant who was running our platoon told me that I was to set up an ambush to see how I would do up against the other platoon. He then left and went back to be with the other platoon. I told the guys that we were going to set up the ambush right here and that we were going to scare the hell out of the other platoon. I told two of the guys to take the rear door and to stay away from the main group by fifty feet, and for two other guys to take the front door and stay away the same distance. The rest of the guys told me that the sergeant knew that we are setting up the ambush here. I told them they were right. I looked around at the terrain and it was ideal for what I wanted to do. My plan was to have half of the guys on one side of the road and the other half on the opposite side. I would be in the middle so when I opened up I wanted everyone to open up at the same time. Everyone agreed. After I placed each man where I wanted them to be. We waited for the sun to go down and the other team to come into our trap.

All of the guys in my platoon were laughing and talking about what a hell of an ambush this was going to be. The sun was already down and I told all of the guys not to talk or make any noise and to be ready. We could hear the other platoon coming down the road and just as the two sergeants got about in front of me I could hear my sergeant whisper to the other sergeant that we were around here somewhere. Then I opened up and so did all of the other guys. It scared the hell out of both sergeants because they didn't know where to go and neither did the rest of the platoon. We had "killed" them all.

When it was over, our sergeant called for us to come out and he marched us back to the company area. Where he told us that we really scared the hell out of him and the other sergeant, both of whom had been in Vietnam. The sergeant told me that they were going to make me Lance/Corporal. I didn't want the rank. I didn't want to have the responsibility of taking care of other guys in combat. I was just like my father in that he didn't want the rank or the responsibility either.

Even with all of the intense training to get us ready for war I still felt that we didn't have enough training. I noticed that other guys felt like they could take on the whole world. As it got closer to our time to leave for Vietnam I knew that I still had a lot to learn about war, but the only way I could learn was to really get into the action. I remember that before I left home on leave I asked my father what I should do when I joined my outfit. He told me to look for the one guy who stays to himself and does his job without anyone else knowing what he is doing. Dad said to use all of my senses, including my sixth sense. He told me whatever I did, don't talk or make noise, always listen, and to hit the ground when the shit hits the fan. Keep my eyes on the quiet guys out in the field because they will keep you alive by their actions.

When I got to Vietnam I hoped that I would be with the best Marine outfit in Vietnam. I had heard of the 1st Marines, the 5th Marines and the 7th Marines from World War II. All of them were great outfits. I then got my orders, along with Richard McBride, that we were going to the 1st Battalion 9th Marines. I had never heard of that battalion. Soon afterwards I remember a Marine coming up to us and asking us about our assigned outfit. He told us the 1st Battalion 9th Marines was a bad ass outfit.

What we didn't know then was that back in 1965, down south somewhere in Vietnam, our outfit had killed Ho Chi Minh's son who was in charge of the V.C. in the south. Ho Chi Minh wanted the 1st Battalion 9th Marines dead and he was the one who gave us our nickname of "The Walking Dead." We had some bad ass fire fights with the N.V.A. down at Phu An, at the place called "Street Without Joy," and up at Con Thein and the D.M.Z. The N.V.A. damn near wiped us out on July 2, 1967 at Market Street and again on July 6, 1967. Ho Chi Minh almost got his wish to wipe us out.

At the end of November 1967 I was about the only one left in my platoon who didn't have a Purple Heart. One of the guys back in the rear who was a clerk asked me if I wanted a transfer and I said yes. The reason was that none of the old guys were still in my platoon and the ones who had Purples Hearts were being transferred to other companies back in the rear for the remainder of their time in Vietnam. I didn't like the games that the new officers of my platoon and company were putting on the guys such as after a fire fight having us pick up the brass (which are the shell casings), always having our rifles on safety when walking out into the bush, not firing our rifles until we got permission from the rear, policing up the area and filling in the fighting holes. As each month went by there were more and more restrictions for the infantry outfits in Vietnam.

I transferred into 3rd Division 3rd Recon and formed the first brand new outfit since World War II and that was "E" Company, Echo Company, and again I was with 2nd Platoon. We went back to Okinawa for almost thirty days to be trained as Recon. We learned to repel out of a chopper or off the side of a mountain. We had rubber boat training and river crossing, in where we lost the first guy in the company by drowning. We were taught to read a compass and map and to call in artillery. I had watched the green horns in the company go through the motions of being in the jungles while supposedly learning what to do-but all they did was play games and not take it seriously. When I did get back to Vietnam at the end of January, the team I was with, on their second patrol, got hit. I had only fourteen days left to go home.

When I first got over to Vietnam we could get the M-14 rifle dirty or muddy and the rifle would still fire. When we got the new M-16's or M-15's in April of 1967 the damn things jammed easily when they got dirty or when we would put twenty rounds into the magazine. We had lost a hell of a lot of good men because the rifle was not good in the jungles of Vietnam. It seemed like someone back in the states wanted us to experiment with the rifles to see how they performed at the cost of our lives.

I know that whatever war you were in, World War II, Korea, or Vietnam, or if you were in the Army or Marines, there will be parts of this book that will make you remember what you have done or have gone through in your outfits, and what other outfits did or didn't do to help out. You will remember you could trust the artillery to protect you with the support of the air power. There may be some small thing that will trigger something in your brain and bring you back to something that happened to you. The main thing is that your buddies who you and I have lost in war were good men who didn't deserve to die over there because of someone acting stupidly or making a mistake out in the bush, or having bad equipment. Maybe someone gave up their life for you to live, or you got orders to leave the front or the bush. I know that those memories will never leave us until we die.

Gary G. Kasten
Blanchester, Ohio
July 2007

To 2nd Platoon Charlie Company, 1st Battalion 9th Marines from March 1967 to Sept 1, 1967 and especially to five guys who have changed me into who I am today: Ted Van Meeteren and Dale Davis who made it back to the States. James Fowler, Benny Houston, George Hahner Jr., (known as Whitey), K.I.A.'s in Vietnam.

Chapter One

March 9,1967: two days before I am to leave for South Vietnam, I am just beginning to realize the naked truth of my going to war.

I am on a Marine Corps drab olive green bus heading north on the coastal highway to El Toro Air Base. Looking out the window, my mind started wondering about a young guy I had met a month earlier on a Greyhound bus going to Los Angeles, California from Ocean Side. I'd noticed that he looked like a Marine because his hair was cut so short. I had asked him whether he was a Marine and he had quietly relied, "Yes." I then had asked him if he had just come back from Vietnam, and again he had quietly replied, "Yes." From the way he had acted, so quiet and reserved, I had been afraid to ask any more questions about Vietnam. As I came back to looking out the window on the Marine Corps bus, I started wondering if I had enough training for what lay ahead. Again my mind went back to Staging Battalion and I remember working on a dummy mine with my buddy, trying to defuse it. Most of the guys that worked on the dummy mines were "killed " except for about five teams still working on them and that included us. We try to make it as real as possible and to see if we could get the pin back in the mine without it going off and killing us. We did it, and than we both help the other teams put in the pins on their mine. A strange feeling of loneliness fell upon me as I came back to the present; we were just entering the gates of El Toro Air Base.

The bus pulled in a little ways to a couple of buildings next to the airstrip that were set apart from the other buildings. As we got off the bus, a sergeant told us to pick up our two sea bags that we'd brought with us, take them to the barracks, and find a "rack" to sleep in for the next couple of nights. Then we were to report back outside to pick up our bed linens; after that we had the rest of the night off.

Heading back inside the barracks, I found a rack close to the showers so I wouldn't have to walk so far. I decided to take a good hot shower and just lie around in my rack for a while. I noticed that the other guys in the barrack were wondering what to do for the rest of the evening. Some were heading out to find a place to buy booze. Others were getting up cards and dice games to pass the evening away.

By that time, the sun was on the horizon and darkness was setting in. Lying on the rack, the empty, lonely feeling came back again, just as it had on the bus. I knew that I had to get out for a while so I decided to take a walk around and look at the base. Noticing a few stars out, I remembered the kids' verse: "Star light, star bright" but I couldn't recall the rest of the words. My sister Starr came to my mind, and I wondered if she was doing well in airline school in Kansas City. Suddenly I remembered the day when my sister and I drove to Kansas City from Cincinnati, where we had lived all of our lives. Mom had seemed more worried about my sister than about me going to Vietnam, but Dad told me to listen and keep my eyes open and my mouth shut over there.

It was very quiet and still around the base...nothing going on...I walked around aimlessly until I felt it was time to return to the barracks. When I got inside, I saw the pinochle games in full swing and everyone carrying on as though Vietnam was not on their minds. There were a few guys writing home for the last time until they knew where in Vietnam they would be. Most of these guys would never see combat. They were cooks, electricians, clerks, truck drivers, air wings. Vietnam would be just another duty station for them.

I decided to write some letters and remembered I didn't have any writing paper on me. I asked the guy in the rack above me if he could lend me some, and he gave me a few sheets, I just lay on my rack writing a girl named Jennifer, and Mom. My letters weren't even a page long...that was all I had to say in them. It seemed funny not being able to fill a page but then I'm not much of a letter writer. I decided to mail the letters the next day.

I took off my "utilities" and climbed under the covers. I couldn't sleep as my mind raced through the past. At 20 years old, there really wasn't much to my past...in the last few years, my life had centered on buddies a few years older than myself at a neighborhood sporting goods store. My mind kept jumping from one thing to another, finally centering on my parents, my brother and sister. Somehow...I dropped off to sleep.

When I got up the next morning. I knew I hadn't had a good night's sleep. After breakfast in the mess hall, the word was passed that we could do anything we wanted for the day but we could not leave the base. Tomorrow we would be leaving for South Vietnam. Since it was such a beautiful day, I decided to walk around and see a little of the base. After a few hours, I decided to call home and let my parents know that I would be leaving the next day. Spotting a phone booth, I started walking toward it. Just then a commercial plane landed and the guys that worked at the base were getting ready to welcome the plane.

After the door was opened, a few minutes passed. Finally the officers came out first and I could see the colored ribbons on their chests. Then came the enlisted men, and they all walked slowly off the plane. There were a few of the enlisted men that looked so very old and tired. A couple of them knelt down and actually kissed the ground of this country. A lot of them cried like little children, and they didn't seem able to stop the tears from coming down their faces. They all walked, almost in a single file, to a building to get their leave papers and money.

I felt a great deal of admiration for them, but I almost felt sorry for them. It seemed like such an empty homecoming. There was no band, no fanfare, to welcome them back...just a handful of people. It was almost as if no one even knew they had been gone. I wanted to thank them personally, but it didn't seem like it would make much difference coming from a... nobody like me. So turning away, once again I walked over to the phone booth.

I called home and Mom answered the phone first. I told her that I was leaving for South Vietnam tomorrow and that I would be all right. I could hear Dad on the extension. He told me that he was getting the house in tiptop shape. I could almost sense that he wanted to tell me something, but he just couldn't get it out of his mouth. I was almost ready to say goodbye when I started to cry quietly, my voice was trembling and I knew that I had to hurry and hang up. I couldn't let them know that I was afraid. I mustered my final sentence while Mom was talking, and I hung up.

I walked back to the barrack and laid down in my rack. I really felt so all alone for the first time in my whole life, and it was up to me to get myself through. I knew I had an uphill battle with myself in getting my courage up and to being the person my father had made me. As I was lying in my rack I remembered when I was in boot camp when my senior Drill Instructor, Staff Sergeant R.P. Hellein called me and told me that of all the guys in boot camp that I was the only one that they couldn't break. I then told him that my father was tougher on me than all of them. The D.I. asked if he was a Marine and I told him that he was Army and served in WWII as a para-trooper in the 11th Airborne. I then started thinking of all of the times that my father was hard on me and would beat me when I had it coming. When he would beat me he would always ask me, "When are you going to grow up?" I was glad that he had been hard on me in preparing me for being able to stand on my own two feet.

Now it was evening, and I could see that everyone was quieter today than yesterday; they were thinking of tomorrow. The barrack was starting to get like a graveyard. Then someone said, "Let's play cards," and that seemed to break up the mood. But, overall, it was still quieter than yesterday.

I got out of my clothes and hopped in my rack. After a few minutes, the guy in the top rack above me said that he was scared and that he didn't want to go. I just kept listening to him, and he was really working himself into not going. I told him that it wasn't all that bad, and that the war wasn't like it was during WWII. It seemed to calm him down a lot and then he started talking about his girl friend. He really seemed to forget about everything and after a few minutes he fell off to sleep. I knew that everyone of us es-pecially those of us who were classified as 0311, which is infantry, felt the same way.

I started thinking to myself and I knew that I was no better than anyone else and that I had to serve my country whether it was right or wrong. I believed in the flag and what it stood for, and for all of the guys who fought for it and died. I couldn't see running away from it, especially since my father had fought for this country during World War II. I wanted to show my father that he would be proud of me, his son, in fighting for liberty, and freedom.

At some point, I had dropped off to sleep with these thoughts. The next thing I knew it was morning. I heard someone yelling in the barrack, telling us to get up. We were to do anything we wanted up to 12:00 noon, but to be back in the barrack then and to get ready to leave. Once dressed, I went outside and the first thing I saw was the grand old flag, flying in the air. For some reason, the flag seemed great today, the way it was waving.

I went over to the P.X. to get something to eat. As I was waiting for my food, I could see that it was just another day for the people on this base, but for me and the other men it was the biggest day of our lives.

I went back to the barrack and took a long hot shower. As I was in the shower, I wondered if I was to be the one who would get it over there and if my life would end. I thought about when I was younger, and that I hadn't done or seen a lot of things on this earth. I graduated from high school at nineteen. Everyone in school had taken advantage of me since I had been an easy-going guy, and I didn't believe in hurting anyone's feelings. I had asked a girl in high school for a date and I was turned down. I was not too popular with the girls. I never really tried to go out with them. I was considered an outcast and I was a loner in high school even though everyone knew me. Even my school administration office caused me problems by not giving me my A.C.T. test grades back in time so I could go to college and play football on a scholarship. I felt that I wasn't wanted on this earth, except for my parents and my sister and brother. I made some friends in the Marine Corps and I was glad, but I knew that when I got over there I would have to start all over again to make new friends. I could tell that God was making it rough on me and I thought he was testing me to see whether or not I could make it.

I got dressed and a sergeant came into our barrack and told us to get our sea bags and to report outside the building. I grabbed my sea bags, and the rest of the guys jumped from their racks and quickly grabbed their gear. I just walked down the center of the aisle until I was outside. When everyone was outside with their bags, the sergeant told us to put the bags on these little trucks that would take them over to the plane when it landed.

We could see that the plane was coming, but it was flying around, giving the guys who were on it a long time to see the States from above. I knew that they wanted to get on the ground, just as we were anxious to get on the plane. Then, as the plane began its landing approach, my heart started to climb to the top of my chest. The plane finally stopped and again the officers came out first, and then the enlisted men. And again some of them kissed the ground, some cried, and still others were dazed to be back in the United States. I overheard some of the guys talking about the guys that came off the plane. They couldn't believe what they saw.

The last guy finally got off the plane and the sergeant told us that we would be boarding in a little bit. The pilots and stewardess left, a new group of pilots and stewardess boarded the plane, and after about fifteen minutes the word was passed that we were to board the plane. The officers were to board the plane first and then we were to follow by our boarding pass, and mine read 101. As I was waiting, I could feel that dead and empty feeling coming back again. All of us were quiet and were looking at the plane, which was going to take us to Vietnam. A gas truck came over and filled up the plane.

As I walked up the ladder, I knew that I would not touch the ground of the United States again for 395 days. The ground seemed so very far away from me as I looked back at it from the top of the steps. Like looking through a telescope, it seemed close enough to touch and yet so very distant. A numb and empty feeling began to settle in. As I sat down inside, I watched out the window as the rest of the guys were still getting on the plane.

After a few minutes we were finally loaded, and I watched the door of the plane close. Waiting for take-off, I thought at first that this would be only my second time in a plane. But then I caught myself and remembered that I had been in a plane three times, including this time. One of the hostesses told us to put the seat belts on and to have the chairs in an upright position for take-off. The engines of the plane began to turn over and after a short time, we were moving.

We were on the runway and the engines kept getting louder and then we took off. Everyone was quiet and looking out the windows. It seemed that everyone was thinking about home, his girl friends, wife, and friends.

The hostesses were walking back and forth and the guys were trying to look up their dresses as they went by. Some guys were grabbing them and trying to make out with them. Most of the guys were making it seem like this was going to be the last time that they would ever have fun again. Like the old saying, "Eat, drink, and be merry." Some of the guys had booze with them and were trying to get drunk. I just sat quietly thinking back over my life, though there wasn't much to think about. The only thing I ever did halfway decently was to play football for my coach and make All-City for him and my parents.

The pilot of the plane said we were flying at 48,000 feet above sea level. I hoped we wouldn't have any trouble; I sure didn't want to die in the ocean before I even got a chance to fight. The pilot said we would stop at Hawaii, but I looked out the window and saw we were chasing the sun. I knew that when we got there it would be late, and I wouldn't be able to see the island very well from the air or when we landed.

We had been in the air some five hours when the plane started to slow up. Some of the hostesses were still kissing some of the guys and having a great time in the back of the plane. The pilot got on the speaker and said that we were landing and to get our seats upright; the time was 02:30. I heard the wheel touch the ground and finally the plane stopped. One of the officers said that we had twenty minutes here and that we could go to the air terminal and walk around before we left again. Everyone jumped out of his seat and tried to get out of the plane first.

When there were just a few of us left on the plane, I got up and slowly walked out the door and down the steps to the ground. I went over to the airport terminal and walked around and then went out the front doors leading into the terminal. I looked up and down the street and there were no cars on the highway at this time. I looked around for a couple of minutes and then went back inside the terminal.

As soon as I reentered the terminal, our officers called for us to report back to the plane. Most of the guys were all over the place looking for girls and getting something to eat.

I walked back to the plane, got on board, and took the same seat I had before. Looking out the window, I watched as the rest of the men came back. I started to think about the terminal and how quiet and empty it was now except for a handful of people.

When everyone was back on board, the plane started up again, and we were off. As soon as the plane leveled off, the guys in the back of the plane were back at what they were doing before with the hostesses. I wasn't used to what I was seeing at the back of the plane, so I decided to just look out the window and try to get some sleep. I started to think of the past again and about school and the way we talked about girls. The biggest thing with all of the guys was to go out with a girl and to play with her breasts...and of course, making out in the drive-in. That was the biggest thing the guys wanted to do back at home, but they wanted to be alone with a girl. Here on the plane, the guys didn't care if anyone watched or not, and after awhile I knew that they were doing it because it might be the last time they would ever see an American girl again.

Chapter Two

My mind trailed off again and I began thinking about going to war and having to fight and kill people. I knew, too, that I would see my own buddies die in front of me. I knew it would be very real and that I had to be man enough to take it. I realized that I might be one of those who would die over there, and I started to feel that I didn't have enough training. I wished that I were back doing it all over again…but I caught myself being really scared. It seemed that only a few of us on this plane had that same feeling.

I finished daydreaming and started to fall asleep. Most of the guys were already sleeping and there were only a few in the back of the plane just talking to the hostesses. Everything around me in the plane seemed to be lifeless. As I looked out the window it seemed lifeless there too, but very peaceful.

Something woke me as the plane was coming down. The pilot announced that we were landing shortly and to make sure our seats were upright. My heart climbed to my throat, as I thought that we were landing in Vietnam. My mind was going through everything I had done in my lifetime. Soon, the pilot got back on the intercom and said we were landing in Okinawa. I then thought they were playing games with us, that there was no Vietnam and that they had made it up.

The plane landed, and as we were walking over to the terminal I could see hundreds of blue lights and some orange lights that were around the terminal. I had never seen a base as huge as this one in Okinawa. It was run by the Air Force and a great duty station away from Vietnam.

Inside the terminal the word was passed that we would get transportation in a short while, and in the meantime we were to hang around in the terminal. I didn't know what was happening. I thought that we were just stopping for a bit and then would get back up in the air and fly to South Vietnam. After we were there for a short while, I got word that the "cattle trucks" were coming. I could see the trucks coming up the road, and the word was passed for us to get in them. I climbed inside one and everyone was pushed together, leaving us no room to sit down. Everyone was disgusted about riding in them. It was the first time I had ever been in one. These were regular trailer trucks, but windows had been cut in them and benches put inside for people to sit down. A lot of the guys felt like cattle being herded to their destination.

The trucks started to move and I didn't know where in the hell they were going, but I was glad, just so we didn't get to Vietnam any sooner then we had to. We must have been in the cattle trucks for about thirty minutes when I saw a sign that said, "Welcome to Camp Hanson." By this time I felt very tired, and I wanted to find a place to go to sleep. The trucks turned to their left and went through the gates and down the main road. The camp was very quiet because everyone was sleeping. I heard someone say that it was 01:30 in the morning. The trucks turned to the right and then stopped. They told us to get out and wait, and when everyone was out of the trucks, the word was passed to go over to get our sea bags. There were two six-bys that were loaded with our sea bags. The six-by is a 2 ½ ton truck that can carry supplies or troops. They called out our names and I grabbed my two sea bags and was told to follow one of the marines to our barracks.

Once we found a rack, we were to report outside to get our linens. When we were all outside, they marched us over to where the linen was, and we received linens and our pillows. They marched us back to the barracks and told us that we were to be here for a few days, and that the mess hall was open so we could get something to eat. I made my rack and then went over to the mess hall. I couldn't believe that I was hungry and sleepy at the same time. I got to the mess hall and they gave us our food. I found a table to myself and then went over to get some milk and chocolate milk. The food was great since I hadn't eaten in about ten hours. The milk seemed to taste kind of funny…like chalk, especially the white milk.

I finished my food and went back to the barrack. I lay down for what was left of the night and fell asleep. The next thing I knew, someone was telling us to get out of the rack because we had a lot to do today. A sergeant told us to report out in the street in ten minutes because we were going somewhere. We all lined up in the street and were marched over to where the corpsmen were…for our final shots. Then they marched us to another building where we had to sign some papers to make sure that everything was in order. One of the sergeants asked if I wanted my money to go to my parents if I died over here, and I told him yes, but in a quiet and subdued voice.

When we were all finished, they marched us back to our barracks. The sergeant told us that we were free for the rest of the day, but that we weren't able to leave the base at all. I didn't do much for the rest of the day but lie around and sleep.

That evening I thought I should write a letter to my parents and let them know where I was and what I was doing. I got some papers from one of the guys from my old boot camp platoon and lay in bed writing to my parents. I told them where I was and that I was going to be here for a couple of days and then off to South Vietnam. I told them that the weather here was nice and that I had seen some old buildings that were scarred from WWII. I told them that Ryan had better do well in school and get a chance to go to college on a scholarship. I couldn't think of anything more to write so I told them goodbye and that I would give them my new address when I get to my outfit in Vietnam.

When I finished the letter to my parents, I went outside for some fresh air. It was around 19:00 hours in the evening and I had seen a group of guys dressed in their Khaki uniform with ribbons on their chests. I walked over to them to get a better look. When I got there some of them looked very old and withdrawn while others looked like they had never changed. I couldn't understand why there were two different groups of men. The ones that were withdrawn had a few more ribbons than the ones that were livelier. I decided to go back to my barrack and write a letter to Jennifer, to whom I had been writing since Staging Battalion, which was 30 days of going over infantry training and knowing all of the weapons.

A good buddy of mine in Staging Battalion had asked me to write to Jennifer because he had another girlfriend, and Jennifer was a very good pen pal to me. I wrote to Jennifer and told her about Ted and that he was doing all right, that we were going to Vietnam in a couple of days from now, and that I couldn't give her our address until we reached our final destination. For me, writing to a girl gave me a chance to be like the other guys who had girl friends to write to back home.

I finished the letter, took a good hot shower, and got in my rack. As I lay in bed, some guys were writing letters home while others in the barrack were playing cards and drinking booze. Some of the guys that came over with me were out somewhere on the base having a good time.

I somehow fell asleep until I again heard someone tell us to get out of the racks and go to chow. I got out of the rack and took a shower and then went to the chow hall. When all of us got back from the chow hall the word was passed to get out on the street. Again they marched us to a small building. The first sixty guys, including me, went inside. It was like a classroom and they told us to sit down. A Negro Marine got up and began talking to us about giving blood. After speaking for a few minutes, he stopped and showed us a LIFE Magazine with his picture inside it. He was wounded and one of the corpsman was giving him a blood transfusion out in the field in Vietnam. He stated that without the blood he would have died. The whole room was very still and every one of us wanted to give blood right then because we were all moved by his speech. The speech took only ten minutes, and a new batch of men came in while the rest of us left to give blood in the other building. When we got out in the street, they told us to let them know if we were allergic to anything. I told the corpsman that I had something back in the States that made my lips blow up for no reason. The corpsman told me that I couldn't give blood, and that if I did, I would endanger someone's life over in Vietnam. When he said that he also said it to the rest of the guys. It made me feel good that I wasn't running away or afraid to give for my fellow Marines in Vietnam. I went back to the barrack to wait for the rest of the guys to come. There were a couple of us that couldn't give, but deep down inside of me I still felt that I cheated on the rest of my buddies.

Finally, everyone was back and the word was passed to get the sea bags that were going to remain here in Okinawa. Back in the States they instructed us which sea bag to leave in Okinawa. I grabbed it and they marched us over to a different building, and there we were given a card with a number on it. They instructed us to put our names on them. After that, they came around and asked us our numbers and wrote them down on a clipboard. One of the sergeants said that we had the rest of the day to ourselves and that tomorrow we were flying to South Vietnam.

I went back to the barrack to lie down. As I did, I looked out the back and I could see an inspection going on. It was a group of Marines who were going home from Vietnam. I got back up and went out to get a better look.

When I got there, they couldn't wait to get on a plane and go home. I was glad they were going home, they had done their job, and now it was our turn. Some of them had the same look as others I had seen who were going home. Again there were the two distinct types of guys. I was hoping that I wouldn't look like those guys that looked so old and tired when I returned home, but I started to realize that being in the infantry, I would probably look like them.

I left after a couple of minutes and decided to go back to my barrack and lie down, for tomorrow was going to be a very long day...again. After a few minutes, I felt that dead and empty feeling coming back for the first time since I first got here: the realization that I was going to war and would have to kill people. I wanted to get out of my rack and run, but somehow I couldn't force myself to do it. I was too scared to do anything but wish that I was home in my own bed, with my parents and brother and sister. I wished that this was only a dream and I wanted to be back home and wake up from all of this.

Then the idea of leaving tomorrow really started sinking in, and I didn't know how to handle the reality. My mind was really racing and I couldn't think of anything specific.

Eventually I fell off to sleep but woke up early. I just lay in bed and waited for the sergeants to get us up for the last time here. I was starting to get nervous, but in a way I couldn't wait to go to Vietnam and see what it was really like. I remembered in the newspapers back in the States, the war was always on page 2 or 3 of the newspapers. But lately it was getting a lot more publicity. The war was starting to get hot, and in a way I was hoping that I could do something good for my country.

I thought of being a good Marine of whom my father could be proud. I hoped that I would be with a good outfit like my father was in World War II. I thought about him as a paratrooper in the Army fighting against the Japanese in World War II. I remembered that he said the Japanese called them, "Devils in baggy pants." I remembered how he told me he always stayed pretty much to himself in the Army. He wouldn't take any kind of rank because he didn't want to spend his time watching out for his team before his own life. He just didn't want that responsibility, and I didn't want that either. I just hoped that I could live up to my father's standards, which was very hard to do. But I felt that I could, even though I wasn't a paratrooper in the Army, but a Marine.

Someone came into the barrack and told us to get up and that we were leaving in a few hours. We were to go to chow, come back on our own, and get our stuff together to leave Camp Hanson. I went to the chow hall and ate with a couple of my buddies from boot camp. When I was finished I went back to the barrack and got my sea bag ready for the trip to South Vietnam.

The word was passed to get on the street with our sea bags because the cattle trucks were on their way to pick us up. It didn't take the trucks long. Then we were told to take our sea bags to six-bys and then to get on the cattle trucks. As soon as we were loaded, the trucks started to move. We were off, back to the big airbase where we had landed some days before. As we passed the different towns on the way to the airport, some of the buildings had bullet holes and bomb craters that were remains of World War II. There were a lot of people going about what they did in their daily chores in this country. It seemed like no one knew anything about South Vietnam or, much less, could care. It wasn't their war. It seemed that the whole world didn't care either.

We got to the airport and the word was passed to get our sea bags and take them to the waiting plane. It was a commercial airlines plane, like the one that had brought us here. When I reached the plane there were several guys motioning to us to bring our sea bags to them, for them to take care of. After I gave them my sea bag, I went over the steps that let up onto the plane. There again, we had to wait while the officers boarded first. Then they called our numbers and we got on. I couldn't wait to go. I got next to the window again. I liked sitting next to the window so I could see the country when we landed.

The engines started and we were off. A few minutes in the air the captain announced that we would be in South Vietnam in a few hours. I looked around the plane and saw that the guys were back playing with the girls. I leaned back in my seat to set some shut eye but my body and mind were too keyed up. I couldn't wait to land. I could hear in the back of the plane that the guys were getting drunk from the way they were talking. I could also hear slaps from the girls when the guys were trying to put their hands on their bodies.

Then one of the guys said, "There it is," and the whole plane got very quiet. You really could have heard a pin drop. Everyone crowded to the windows to get a better look. Then the captain of the plane got on the intercom and said that we would be landing shortly in Da Nang, South Vietnam. I couldn't believe that I was almost half way around the world. As I looked out to get a better look at what the countryside looked like, I realized how it grabbed everyone that we were finally here. The shock of actually seeing South Vietnam silenced all 300 men on the plane. I felt that each one of us felt isolated from everything.

One of the guys pointed out Freedom Hill 327 where Bob Hope performed every Christmas. It was almost like watching T.V. back at home. There didn't seem to be a war going on over here. I don't think any of us actually knew what was real or not, from the T.V. pictures of Bob Hope's show or other small filmstrips that the news media had released. To me, the hill looked just like any other hill.

The plane was making a semi circle out around Da Nang by going out to the ocean and then coming down. It was just beautiful looking at the ocean and then at the country and how green it was on this clear day. The base was huge as the plane came down and I felt the wheels touching the ground. There were rows of jet fighters in their hangers and two very large landing strips parallel with each other. The plane finally turned off to the left. Immediately two jets with bombs took off and it looked like they were going on a mission. I was starting to sense the reality of the whole thing. Everyone was playing it the way it was meant to be. There was really a war going on and we were fighting because we thought it was right.

The plane finally taxied to a stop. Outside a couple of guys in jungle uniforms pushed the steps up against the door of the plane and opened it. A gunnie sergeant about 35 years old came inside and told us that the officers were to get out first and then the rest of us. They were expecting rockets to come in at any time, so we were to get off the plane as quickly as possible and to be sure we stayed close together. The officers got up quickly and went down the steps.

It was my turn to get up and get out of the plane. As I started toward the door of the plane I could feel the heat from outside. When I got to the door of the plane I stopped and the heat and humidity were overwhelming. I started sweating and the marine at the bottom of the steps was yelling at me to move out. As I started walking down the steps, I got this strange feeling that the United States was saying to me that I was on my own and that it was up to me to get myself back in 395 days. It seemed like it had closed its doors on me and would not open them until I did my time. I was feeling alone and on my own.

A little ways off, the cattle trucks were waiting to take us somewhere. I jogged over and climbed inside one of them. I was already feeling the terrible heat, my mouth was getting dry and I wanted to get something to drink. After what seemed to be fifteen minutes, we started off. On our way to the other side of the field, the driver said that we were going over to the Marine Corps terminal to be processed. By now I was getting a little tired of being processed, flying, and driving, but never going to some place permanent.

We got to the other side and the driver told us to go inside the terminal and wait for instructions. Our sea bags were already there, and some sergeant told us to get them and follow him. The trucks started to leave and the dust was flying all over us and the area. Everything was covered with dust and it didn't look like anyone could escape from it. On the other side of the terminal they led us to a small wooden hut where he told us to wait. Everyone was dressed the same over here except for us, for our green utilities were States side. Their green utilities were thin and light and were called jungle uniforms, because of the heat and humidity.

After a couple of minutes, a marine came out of the hut and told us to go over to the side of the hut and to fill sand bags until they called our names. We started filling the sand bags when one of the clerks came out of the hut and called six names. Richard McBride and I were called first and the clerk gave each of us a manila envelop. As we got them, the clerk told us to go over to the other terminal and get on a C-130 for Phu Bai. So McBride and I followed the other four guys up to the other terminal with our sea bags. As we were heading up to the other terminal, a marine that was from here came up to me and asked what outfit we were going to. I told him that I didn't know for sure, so he asked if he could see my envelope and on the back of the envelope was 1/9. He gave it back to me and told us both good luck because we were going to need it. He told us that a lot of guys in that outfit were wounded one time or another and that the N.V.A. were always after that group of Marines. I told him that we had to leave so we could catch up with the rest of the guys that were with us. I walked back out of the terminal with McBride and the other four guys was going inside the other terminal. It was about 100 meters away. McBride and I reached the other terminal and went inside. There were a lot of men waiting for their plane to come in. I went up to one of the guys behind the counter and asked him how to get up to Phu Bai. He said that he would give me a number and that when my number was called to board the plane that would be on the opposite side from where we came in. McBride looked like an Irishman. He stood 5' 10" and had brown hair, was stocky and seemed a very reliable type of guy. There were others guys from our boot camp platoon who were left behind and were coming on the next plane to South Vietnam. As we walked toward the back of the terminal we noticed that everyone had jungle clothes on and that the six of us stuck out. Most of the Marines were carrying their rifles upside down with them in the terminal. Our states side utilities were covered with the red dust. As we were waiting for the plane to arrive, I wished that we had a rifle to protect us like most of the guys that were in the terminal.

A Marine came over to us and asked us what outfit we were assigned to. We both told him 1st Battalion 9th Marines. He was the second one that day to say good luck, because we were going to need it. I looked at McBride and said that the outfit that we were going to must really be hurting for men or that they must really lose men in combat. I knew that neither of us wanted to hear that, but it seemed that we were both destined to either get wounded or die over here. I thought to myself that if I was going to die, it better be with the best Marine outfit in the country.

Chapter Three

I could hear a loud noise outside the building; it wasn't a commercial jet but some other kind of plane. Then a voice on the loud speaker announced that everyone going to Phu Bai should listen for his number to be called. My number was called and than McBride's number was called also. We both walked out the door toward a marine taking the numbers and headed toward the C-130 aircraft. McBride and I carried our sea bags around the back of the plane and walked up the ramp into the plane. A crewman told me to put my sea bag down near the back of the plane and I then went farther into the plane and sat down. McBride sat across from me and we both put on our seat belts. I looked back to where our sea bags were and they were tying them down as well as other equipment. The crew chief then walked up and back to make sure that everyone had his seat belts on. There were four rows running the length of the C-130 and when the crew chief was finished he informed the pilot and we were off. As we were moving the rear door came up level with the floor of the plane and stopped there. The C-130 got almost to the end of the runway and was second in line to take off. We could hear the plane in front of us take off and we could hear the engines of the C-130 getting louder and still the rear door was down when we took off down the runway. As we went down the runway, we could see everything behind us and then all of us could feel the plane getting off the ground and still the rear door was down. It was really neat. We were in the air and the plane went straight up to about 600 feet and did a semi circle around and than started heading north before the rear door closed. It was like everyone was living life on the edge over here, free and careless.

It was early in the afternoon and I didn't know how long it would take to get to Phu Bai. Out the side window I could see that we were only a couple of hundred feet over the river that we were following. I was sitting facing the small window and heard a couple of pings over our heads. The plane quickly went straight up in the air again and I realized that we were being fired upon. Bullets had just missed us by a couple of feet. I didn't want to die in a plane before I saw any action. It just wasn't fair. So I prayed to God that I wouldn't have to die in this plane.

The plane started its descent again and I hoped that this time we had arrived at Phu Bai. The plane finally landed and the back door opened up. Quickly the hot air rushed back into the plane and I could feel myself trying to breathe again. Some of us got out of the plane and went over to the terminal. McBride and I grabbed our sea bags as we left the C-130. The terminal was a large building that didn't have a roof and when we got there we asked this Marine who was working there where the 1st Battalion 9th Marines were. He just pointed west to where the ground had been cleared by bulldozers and where tents were pitched all around. He seemed very unfriendly as he abruptly told us to ask the truck driver outside the hanger if he could take us there. He said that we weren't to walk over there because someone might shoot us. So McBride and I walked over to the six-by where the driver told us that he would take us there once we got on. We threw our sea bags on and then we both climbed aboard.

The dirt road was running alongside the Marine base and a lot of the South Vietnamese people either walking or riding bicycles up and down the dirt road, but I couldn't see any town or village near by. We got on the same dirt road with the people on it, and the driver didn't seem to care whether he ran over them or not. When we got to the gate of the camp, the M.P. waved us through. The truck was throwing the dust around, and the dust was landing on the tents that were next to the road. We came to a fork in the road and the truck driver stopped and told us to get out and that we were here. He didn't point; instead he just looked in the direction of our outfit. As he took off, the dust was all over us. We carried our sea bags and asked this one Marine where 1st Battalion 9th Marines was and he said that we were here. He told us that headquarters was over to the right of us and that we had better report in there first. Then we went over there and went inside; the corporal said that he would like our orders, so we handed them to him. It was hot inside and everyone there were either in T-shirts or shirtless. Clerks seemed very friendly and then one of them made a joke by saying that they now had fresh meat in the outfit. The clerks started making bets on how long we would stay over here until we either got wounded or killed. I didn't like their jokes and I knew that McBride didn't either. I thought to myself that we just got here from the States and these assholes are betting to see how long we will make it. They stopped bullshitting and told us to wait a few minutes before we went to our platoon. It took them about ten minutes and then they told me that I was assign to Charlie Company 2nd Platoon and McBride was assigned to Delta Company. The clerks then told us where our company tents were and McBride and I picked up our sea bags and got the hell out of battalion headquarters tent. They also told us where the battalion supply tent was and to get our 782 gears. The 782 gear was our combat gear that we would be carrying out in the field and it contained canteens, magazines, rifle, first aid kit, helmet, insect repellent, an E-tool which is a shovel on one end and a pick on the opposite side of the shovel, back pack, cartridge belt, a flak jacket which protected you from shrapnel, poncho which protected you from the rain, and also jungle pants a shirt and boots. As we walked to our company areas, McBride said that he had to go over to where their tents were- it was where Delta Company was. I went on over to where Charlie Company tents were and asked one of the guys there where 2nd platoon tent was. I got inside the tent and there were a couple of guys there that were just either sitting or lying on these cots. I asked the guys if this one cot was empty and they just nodded yes and I then lay the sea bag on it and went back out to where the supplies tent was and picked up my 782 gears. When I got there, McBride had arrived about the same time as me. Both of us went inside the tent and the supplies sergeant than started passing out our 782 gear and he gave us two canteens instead of one, rifle and magazines and ammo for the M-14 rifle, cartridge belt, E-tool, poncho, back pack, insect repellent, helmet, flak jacket, first aid kit and our jungle uniform and boots. The sergeant then made us sign off on the gear and then we left back to our area. I told McBride to watch himself in his new outfit and he told me the same.

I got back to the tent and went inside and could see that there was one of the other guys who had come up here with us from Da Nang. He had just got here a couple of minutes after me and he was working on getting his 782 together. I then put my 782 gears on the ground and put my rifle and magazines on my cot. I noticed that the old timers were watching both of us and after a couple of minutes one of them told both of us that we should take back half of that shit. Then the rest of them told us what to keep and what not to keep and both of us then went back to the supplies tent with the gear that the old timers told us not to take. The reason for us to take back some of the gear was because we really didn't need to carry all of that stuff and that the heat and humidity would really make us pay for it. As we were walking back to the supplies tent, I told the other new guy that my name was Gary Kasten and he told me that his name was Bill. Bill stood about 5' 10" tall; he had bark brown hair, blue eyes, and a stocky build. He also wore glasses like me. We looked somewhat like brothers. He seemed to be quiet and to himself just like me.

When we got back in the tent, we asked the old timers how to carry our 782 gears. They then told us to take our raincoat and to tie it on the back of our flak jacket. We asked them where to get the string and they told us to take the bandoleer strap and cut it into two parts and use it as string. They told us that the raincoat was used for the rain, sleeping cover at night and for carrying out the dead and wounded men. They told us to put our plastic canteens on the flak jacket also and, since we had a couple of metal canteens, to replace them with plastic ones when the guys got killed in the field. They told us to put our magazines on our cartilage belt along with our first aid pouch and to put the insect repellent on our helmet. The supply sergeant only gave us 6 magazines and the guys also told us that we would need more than six, so when someone would get killed to grab as many magazines as you can get out in the field. They told us that with metal canteens, if you get hit the shrapnel and metal from the canteens would make a bigger hole in you. They said to put our magazines on our cartilage belt with our first aid pack. The insect repellent, which was a small plastic bottle, went on our helmets. There was a black plastic band that held the camouflage cover. When we finished with the gear, we started putting the rounds into the magazines. Both Bill and I had nine magazines each and the guys told us to get more if we could out in the field. The old timers than started asking us questions about what was going on back in the States. Questions such as what were the new songs out and could we sing them, what were the new cars like, who was winning in baseball, in college football, girls, and what not. I felt a little uncomfortable talking to them because of our two different situations. They had been here so long and we were just getting here and wanted to ask them questions about over here and what to do. I could see in their faces that they had lost all contact with the United States and were trying to get back to what it was like before they themselves came here. I was glad to see that in a few days that they would be going home for good. As I looked into their tired old faces, I knew they had gone through hell over here in what they'd seen. There were a couple of them that still didn't say a word to us but just watched us. They were so thin that you could see their rib cages. They look like they weighted between 120 pounds up to 160 pounds and they were from 5'5" to 6'2". Bill and I noticed that they all had this stare about them and also that they didn't want to associate with new guys or anyone that they didn't know.

It must have been chow time because they started getting out of their cots and telling us to come with them. As some of them got up I saw that their jungle clothes were very dirty. It didn't look like they had taken a shower in weeks. There were a couple of them that didn't say a word and were like walking dead men, quiet and keeping to themselves. In a way they reminded me of the ones that I had first seen when a plane of them came in before we left the States.

I grabbed my mess gear and followed the guys to another tent and walked inside. It was really hot because of the stoves that were on. I could feel myself starting to sweat. The mess cook gave us the chow, "Rice and Spam," and we walked on. In the next tent, they had picnic tables and I sat, but before I started to eat, I took a good look around. There was a screen around the whole tent and the doors were at both ends. There was dust on the tables and also in the air. There must have been hundreds of flies around, eating the food plus walking on it. The old timers didn't bother to chase the flies even though there were a couple of flies in their food as they were eating. It made me sick, but I had to eat; I hadn't had anything since I'd left Okinawa that morning. The flies were in my food and I kept on waving my hand over the food while I ate. I thought it tasted like garbage and that a person could get sick, but no one else seemed to care.

The old timers who had been over here for awhile were eating the food as though there was nothing wrong with it. As I was watching them eat, I noticed that they didn't speak to anyone. Then another group of guys came in and sat at a different table. They were talking and laughing as though there was nothing going on. They were the clerks from our battalion that had not been out in the field. The clerks stayed away from the guys that were out in the field. The guys I was with were combat fighters and had encountered death and everything else that went along with it. When we were all finished eating, we went out the back of the tent and washed our mess gear.

When we got back I put on my new jungle clothes and jungle boots I then put my utility and Stateside boots in my sea bag and locked it back up. Bill was also changing clothes. I kept my under-pants on but took off my T-shirt. I then sat down in my cot that could easily be moved anywhere. I filled my canteens with water from outside the tent, and grabbed my cartridge belt and started putting the magazines in the pouches. I put the open part of the magazines down into the pouch so that the dust wouldn't get into them. As I looked around at the old timers, I really felt sorry for them, but I could see in their eyes that they were feeling sorry for us. Then one of the old timers came into the tent and said that he had 17 hours left and that he was going home. I started to feel sick and empty inside again and I was thinking to myself that I had 395 days to go and this guy had only 17 hours left. The old timers were happy for the Negro who had the 17 hours. I then went over to Bill and asked if he had any writing paper and he said yes. I had a pen and then lay down on the cot and began writing home. I wished that I could go home and be with my friends but I was here in Vietnam and I had to make the best of it.

I told my parents that I was in Vietnam at Phu Bai with the 1st Battalion 9th Marines, Charlie Company 2nd platoon. I told them about what I had seen and that the weather was very hot and humid and there was dust all over the place. I finished the letter and wrote the word "Free" in the upper right hand corner of the letter, which was our stamp. I asked one of the old timers across from me if we got hit here at nighttime and he said sometimes. Some of the old timers were writing letters back home while others just lay in their cots and daydreamed. It was nighttime and one of the old timers got up and turned on the light in the tent. Several minutes later someone outside was calling blackout and to close the entire tent flaps. One of the old timers close to the front of the tent and one at the rear of the tent got up and closed the flaps so that the enemy couldn't see our light.

Fatigue was setting in, but at the same time I was worried that we might get hit. The guy across from me started talking to me again and asked me where I was from. I told him that I was from Cincinnati, Ohio. I then asked him how many days he had left over here and he said that he had only fifteen days to go. I asked him what he could tell me about this outfit and what it was like. He asked if I had read anything in the papers back in the States about a company over here finding an underground hospital that the N.V.A. had built near Saigon. I told him I remembered reading something about it and seeing it on T.V.- that they had burned and killed everyone in it. He said that the N.V.A. gave us the name of "Charcoal Charlie Company." He said that Charlie Company had killed and burned everything in the tunnel complex there. He said that this took place sometime in late 1965. He also said that out battalion was the first to land in Vietnam at Da Nang and then moved down to the Mekong Delta. The outfit walked in water that was waist high and that they were always wet. He said that it was bad because it was monsoon season down there at that time. I asked him what it was like in the monsoon season and he said that I wouldn't like it at all because it would rain everyday and that the wind would blow constantly, and at night it would be very cold. He than told me that I had better get some sleep but that if we got hit, I should just hit the ground and not move. He lay on his back and in a couple of minutes was sleeping. As I then looked around, the rest of the men were sleeping, except for Bill. He was just lying in his rack having trouble trying to get some sleep. I started thinking again, and I remembered that tomorrow I would have 394 days to go. I knew that it was always going to be in the back of my mind the rest of the time over here. Somehow I fell off to sleep: my first night in Vietnam.

I heard some voices in the morning and got up and looked out the tent to see low hanging clouds. I couldn't see the sun at all. A few of the old timers said that it was time to get something to eat. I went with them in my new green jungle clothes and I felt a part of them now, except that I still had to do my time and they were done with it all and were going home. I did the same as I did the first time I went through the mess hut. I followed the old timers into the other tent and sat down to eat my food. Just then a six-by came by and the dust flew all over the place. It landed in my food, but I didn't care today. I was going to eat it any way. My friends the flies were here again and they were helping themselves to my food. I tried to eat it all before they got a chance to jump in and eat it for me; it was a losing cause.

I asked one of the old timers where I could get something to drink and he said they only had pre-sweetened Kool-Aid. I went over, dipped my cup into this very large pot, and returned to the old timers as they wished me good luck in drinking it. I took a drink, but I couldn't get it down my throat. When I did, the taste was horrible. I asked them how they could drink it and they told me that they had been here a long time and had gotten used to the damn stuff.

I didn't finish the food. Instead I went out in back. I wanted to throw it up but I couldn't, and that I was stuck with it inside of me. I looked back and I realized that the old timers were laughing at me. When they finished their chow, they came out and I went back with them to the tent. The sun was starting to climb higher in the sky and I could feel the heat and humidity rising also.

When we got back to the tent I asked one of the old timers what to do and he told me to get all of the sleep and rest I could before I went out into the field. They told Bill and me that when we did get out in the field we would not have any time to rest or sleep at nighttime. We would be walking forever out in the bush and not get much sleep. They said the way to learn how to live out there in the field was to keep quiet and listen to the squad leader and fire team leader. Both had been out in the field for sometime. There was only one of the old timers in the tent that didn't say a damn thing but I could tell that there was something else that we should know but he wouldn't speak. I got up and went over to him and sat on his cot and asked him quietly what else I should do to keep alive out in the bush. He told me to always keep my canteens full of water so that they would not make any sound. He then said to stay as far away as you can from the guy in front of you as well as the guy behind you. He also told me that if you get hit not to call for the corpsman but to get yourself back to the corpsman so that he didn't get hit also. As he was talking to me he was very deliberate. His eyes and the way he looked made me understand that I needed to listen if I wanted to live. He said that was all and good luck to both of us out in the bush. I got up and went back to my cot.

The rest of the day was lifeless; no one did anything but lie around and write letters back home. As the day went on, the heat and humidity got hotter. I noticed that by afternoon there was hardly any wind. One of the old timers came into the tent and closed the flat of the tent, and lit a candle as the sun was starting to go down. Again the day was almost gone and Bill and I just lay in our cots thinking of home.

Two more days passed and the word was given for Bill and me to report over to the clerk tent; so we reported and the clerks introduced us to the first sergeant of the battalion. He said to have our gear ready because tomorrow we were going up north to Dong Ha, the forward area of our battalion. He seemed to be a nice guy, somewhere in his forties. As Bill and I walked back over to our tent I saw McBride. When I told him that we were going to Dong Ha, he said that he was going too, and that we were going up there together. McBride was excited and so were we. I got to the tent and made sure I had everything ready to go for the next day. Back here in the rear area was very boring with nothing to do and it was good for us to get up there to our company.

I finished checking my combat gear and went outside the tent where some of the guys were sun bathing in their shorts. By now the sun was out and it was a clear day. I did notice that each day it seem to be getting hotter and hotter. I thought that I would take a walk around, and one of the old timers told me that if I was going to walk around that I had better take my rifle and magazines. As I was walking I could hear some music being played somewhere, so I followed the sound to where it was coming from. I got there and the music was coming from a wooden hut a couple of hundred meters away with two poles, flag poles, in front of it. Each pole carried a flag; on one pole the American flag and on the other pole the yellow flag with three horizontal red strips, the flag of South Vietnam. I stood a couple hundred meters away from the Marine Corps band playing music. Then I saw the American flag being lowered for the day. It was time for me to get back to my tent and to rest for the day. I realized how lonely I was over here and I just didn't know what to do, who to see, or where to go.

As I was walking back to the tent, I thought about my parents and what they were doing. I knew that I had to stop thinking about them so much and instead try to think of other things in order to keep myself busy. But I just couldn't get my mind off of them, and of course, I had nothing to keep me busy. I finally got back to the tent and saw that Bill was working on his gear. I went inside, cleaned my rifle with my toothbrush and I was ready for tomorrow. I thought that I had better start acting like a Marine and a man. I then lay down in the cot and began to drift off to sleep.

I got up early in the morning and Bill and I went with the old timers to the mess hall for the last time. When we got back the word was passed for us to saddle up and report over to the battalion tent. Bill and I grabbed hold of our gear and started out the tent and the old timers told us good luck. I could tell that they all meant it.

Bill and I walked over to the battalion tent and McBride was there also with a couple of other guys. We waited outside the battalion tent for the first sergeant to come out. When he came out, I saw that he was a heavyset man with a little gray around his ears. He had a father image about him that made us feel at ease.

He asked if we were ready and if we had all of our gear. We all said yes. And he said a truck would be coming shortly for us. In a few minutes a six-by stopped and we grabbed our combat gear and seabag and put it on the back of the six-by. Then we got on, along with the first sergeant who got inside the cab with the driver and we were off. We went out the front gate and down over to the terminal and got unloaded. Then the truck was off and the dust was all over our gear and us. I now could see why the guys in the tent told me to make sure my magazines were upside down, so that the dust wouldn't get them. We walked inside the old hanger that didn't have a roof, which was the terminal, and the first sergeant asked the Marine on duty when the plane for Dong Ha would be in. He replied that it would be down in a couple of minutes. I noticed that the Marine was very nice to the first sergeant, and I remembered how nasty he was to us when we first came up here.

The plane landed and in just a few short minutes we were on board and it was starting off again. We were in a C-130, and heading north. I knew one thing; the plane didn't stop long enough for anyone to hit us. The first sergeant said that we would be close to the D.M.Z. about 10 miles. Before I got to Vietnam I had thought that we would go down to Saigon, but boy, was I wrong. We were all very quiet on the plane and I could tell that the first sergeant noticed it. We had only been in the air about twenty-five minutes when the plane started coming down. I could feel the wheels touch the ground and the plane stop. Down went the rear door and we were told to hurry and get out. I grabbed my seabag and went out the back of the plane. I saw right away that everyone up here was very busy. There were some Marines putting up barbwire around the landing strip. There was only one runway here, and a short one at that. The first sergeant said to follow him and that we were going to where our outfit was stationed. When we got to our area, the first sergeant told one of the guys to show us to our company tents. We followed this corporal and he pointed out the tents for Delta Company first. McBride headed off to those tents. Then the corporal pointed out to where Charlie Company tents were and Bill and I headed off in the direction of the tents. Bill and I went into one of the tents and asked if this was Charlie 2nd platoon tent and they told us yes. There were five guys in the tent and we asked them if these cots were taken and they told us no. There was one guy writing home and the other three were talking. The dust was on everything up here as well.

The sides of the tent were rolled up so that the air could come in, but there wasn't any wind. There was a road out in back of the tent about twenty feet where the six-bys would be moving somewhat fast and causing the dust to fly all around the area. Both Bill and I took off our flak jackets which felt heavy and our combat gear and then went over to the company tent to report in. The clerks asked us our names and service numbers; then they said that we could go back to the tent. When we got back the guys who had been up here for a while asked Bill and me about the new songs that were out and also what was going on back at home.

Then one of them asked if we were the only ones sent here to this outfit, and we told them that five of us came up but in different companies. They also wanted to know about the sports and about the girls. I asked the guy why he wanted to know how many guys came up with us and he told me that they were short men and needed more.

These guys were very quiet and easy going and they acted so much older than they were. They were men, not boys any more. When they talked, they spoke briefly as possible and straight to the point. The heat inside the tent was not as bad as being outside having the hot sun beating down on us.

It was chow time and they told us to find any mess gear in the tent and to follow them. They told us to make sure that we took our rifles with us. We followed them and walked down one of the dirt roads and up a small hill to get to the mess tent. As we walked over to the mess tent I had dust in the mess gear; there were hot water cans where we could dip our mess gear before we got our hot chow. I went into the mess tent and got our "Rice and Spam" and went to the other tent to sit down and eat. At the end of the food line was a large pot about two feet high with the pre-sweetened Kool-Aid in it. I dipped my cup in it and only filled it half way up. There seemed to be more flies up here than down at Phu Bai. I made sure that my rifle was right next to me in the mess tent so if anything happened that I had some protection. I sat down and I was starting to get used to eating while the flies were all over me. Every time someone would come in or leave, a couple of hundred more flies would come in. I noticed that while one of the guys was eating, he would slowly raise his hand and kill a few flies that would bother him. The dead flies landed on the table next to his food, but he just let them lie there. No one really worried about being clean at all, and they seemed to have accepted the fact that they were going to be dirty all of the time. Since Bill and I had arrived we had not taken a shower since we arrived from Okinawa.

Every time the six-bys would drive by the dust would blow all over the place, including the food that we were eating. I was getting used to eating the dirty food. It didn't seem to make any difference anymore. I was changing a little each day, but I didn't know how much. When we all finished the food, we went out the back and dipped our mess gear into the garbage cans filled with hot boiling water in order to get our mess kits clean. When we were finished cleaning our mess gear we returned to our tent. The first sergeant was waiting to tell us that we would stay here for a few days before we went out into the field to join our platoon. When the first sergeant left I asked one of the guys how long he had to go before he went back to the States, and he said that he had four months to go. The others said they had either a shorter or longer time. Everyone had come at different months. A couple of them had just come back from R. & R., which was "Rest and Relaxation," out of country and the other were nursing their wounds. They told us that we had to be here for about six months before we could get, "Out of Country, R. & R." and there were three places that we could go to. They were Hawaii, Taipei, Taiwan and Bangkok, Thailand.

There were a lot of helicopters flying around and I asked one of the guys what they were doing. He said that the helicopters would carry food and water or ammo to the outfits that were out in the field. The choppers would also bring back the dead and wounded. I nodded my head to let him know that I understood. Everyone was busy all around the base, building up the defenses. I had to go to the restroom, so I asked one of the guys where the head was. One of them pointed to a little wooded hut at the end of our tents and said that was it. So I went over there taking my rifle with me. I got there and opened the door and could smell the shit that others had deposited, but

I knew that I couldn't wait any longer. There were three holes from which to pick, and I decided to take one of the end ones. I turned around and faced the opposite direction of where I was going to deposit my load, dropped my jungle pants, took a little backward step on the toe board, planted myself over the hole and did my thing. There was a four-foot screen all the way around the wooden hut that so that the wind, if there was any, would move the smell away while you were unloading into the hole. I finished and left to go back to the tent. Then I noticed some trenches which looked like the ones, used during World War I. Also, there was no grass on this base camp, just like at Phu Bai; tents were being put up everywhere. They were making this base as large as the base at Phu Bai.

I took my time in returning to the tent. When I got inside I lay on the cot and began thinking of home and what everyone was doing. Then my thoughts changed and I was thinking that just in a few days I would be fighting for my country and doing what I believed in. It was starting to get dark outside and some of the guys asked me to help put the sides of the tent down for the night. I got up and helped, and I noticed that two of the guys were lighting up candles for the rest of us to see inside the tent. I finished and went back inside. I felt a couple of mosquito bites on my arms and around my neck. I then pulled down the sleeves of my jungle shirt and put on the insect repellent. There were some mosquitoes flying around inside the tent and it sounded as if they were coming after me. One of the guys gave me a little bottle and said that it would keep the mosquitoes away and that I could keep the bottle. Now, I had two bottles so I put one in my flak jacket pocket. The liquid in the little plastic bottle was clear. I put it on my skin again around my neck and hands. When I was finished, I decided to write a couple of letters, one to my parents and the other to my pen pal Jennifer in Iowa. I told Jennifer that Ted and I got split up and he went into a different battalion and I had no idea how to get a hold of him. My body was starting to fall asleep and it was slowing down like everything else.

Time crawled as we waited around for days for something to do. There was no work assigned to us, and no sort of recreation provided. We ran out of things to talk about as boredom engulfed us. As I lay in my cot again, I could hear the generators, choppers, and jeeps around the base. In the background, some of our 105s were firing at the enemy. The air was starting to cool off some from the hot day but not much. I fell asleep and for once I had a peaceful sleep.

The next few days went by and I didn't do a damn thing but walk around and get to know the base better, where the P.X. was and the outdoor movie show. The gunny told Bill and me that we were going out to the field tomorrow. Bill and I had enough of being back at camp and it would be great to join up with the platoon. So that night Bill and I worked on cleaning our rifles with a toothbrush and making sure that our canteens were full of water. I felt the excitement of going out to the bush and meeting up with the guys in our platoon.

I got up the next morning, went to chow, and then Bill and I went back to our tent waiting word from the gunny. The gunny told us to get our gear ready and that one of the guys would take us to the chopper pad. Both of us took our seabag over to our company supply tent. Then Bill and I grabbed our gear and one of the clerks came over and told us to follow him to the chopper pad. The clerk took us about half way to the chopper pad and then told us that it was on the left side of the road and that we couldn't miss it. So Bill and I went there on our own. We both could hear the sounds of choppers. The landing pad was on a slope; there were boxes stacked up of C-rations, five-gallon cans of water, and boxes of ammo. There were about twelve guys working there, some of them were loading two choppers. An officer came over to us and we both saluted him, but he didn't return the salute. He told us to lower our hands because saluting over here was not healthy for officers; it was a sure way of dying. We both lowered our hands.

He asked us what we wanted, and we told him that we were to take a chopper out to our outfit in the field. The officer then asked what outfit was that and we told him 1/9. He told us to wait until he gave us the word to get on the chopper when it arrived. He told us to go on over to the side and wait. So Bill and I sat down and waited and watched the guys work. After several hours had gone by the lieutenant came over to us and told us that we would not be going out today. Instead we were to return to our camp and try again tomorrow. We left and went back to our company area and reported back to the gunny that we could not get out today but the lieutenant told us to try again tomorrow.

The next day came and we went to chow and when we came back to our tent, Bill and I grabbed our gear and went on over to the chopper pad. It was 06:30 in the morning and both of us were hoping that we could get out into the field today. Again the lieutenant there at the chopper pad told us to sit off to the side until he could get us on the chopper. All morning long the choppers were being filled up with supplies and then they would take off, all of the dust would blow all over the place and on us. The heat of the day didn't help much at all either. Again they told us to go back to our company area and try again tomorrow. We returned to our tent and the gunny told us that he was going with us tomorrow since he had some business to take care of in the field.

The next day, there were five of us going out to the field besides the gunny. We had been waiting for a half an hour when the gunny walked over to this small building and disappeared inside. He returned shortly and said that we would be on a chopper in just a few minutes. There were two choppers coming down just then, and they looked like a bananas with three wheels under them. They landed and lowered their back doors. There were some supplies being loaded and then one of the guys was waving to us to come over there to board the choppers. They wanted three on one and two on the other. The gunny told Bill and me to follow him, and the other two went on the other chopper. As we ran over to the choppers, I could feel my heart going up to my throat and I couldn't breathe. The heat of the chopper was throwing off on us as we boarded from the rear. Inside the chopper there were two Marines standing behind two M-60 machine guns, looking at us. They had helmets like a jet plane pilot would wear. When we were all in, the gunny told them, "Let's go." The rear door started to rise and then after a minute or so we were off. This was my first chopper ride and I was really getting scared. The chopper didn't feel to be very sturdy and I thought that it would fall apart. After a few minutes I could feel myself coming back down to normal and I was even starting to enjoy the ride.

The two machine gunners were very busy watching outside their open windows for anyone firing at us from below; they were ready if it did happen. I looked out the small window and saw a river below us that we were following for a short way. Soon we were going into the hills and boy, was the countryside beautiful. We were a couple hundred feet in the air and I couldn't see any signs of anything being destroyed over here. Then I realized that we were going to land on one of the hills below.

The chopper started going down and in a couple of seconds it landed almost on the side of the hill. The gunny told us to grab some of the supplies and the rear door opened and we came out and a couple of guys went in to pick up the rest of the supplies. Everyone was moving as fast as they could to get the chopper unloaded. The chopper took off and the other chopper then came down and the guys were moving as fast as they could getting the chopper unloaded. When the second chopper took off, the gunny told Bill and me to follow him. I looked back and knew that it would be the last time I would see that chopper. I was finally with my outfit.

2nd platoon going down south to Street Without Joy. Early April 1967. Picture by Bill Gonzales

Back at Dong Ha, from left to right: Benny Houston (Old man of 2nd platoon) and Al Quick who was later transfered to 3rd Battalion 26th Marines in May 1967. Picture by Al Quick

Taking a ten minute break, Don Horseman. Early April 1967.
Picture by Al Quick

At Dong Ha, from back row left to right: Chadwell, Frank Bignami, Don
Parillio, Dave Miller, Ted Van Meeteren, Grear, Ron Lisinski, (Ski), front
row. From left to right: Al Quick, Charlie, ?, Gary Duvall. April 1967.
Picture by Al Quick

As we followed the gunny, I noticed that we were on the side of the hill where the foliage was very thick. What looked like grass at first was not; it was taller than me and I am 6'3" tall. We followed a narrow path until the gunny stopped to talk to a guy who was sitting on the ground. By the insignia on his collar, I knew his rank was a sergeant. The gunny told the sergeant that we were assigned to 2nd Platoon Charlie. The sergeant said that they were on patrol, but that they were due back anytime. The gunny told us to wait there until they got back. So Bill and I sat down in the grass and waited for our platoon to come in off patrol.

After a half hour of waiting, a line of men began moving past us on the thin trail. The gunny told us when the last man had passed us to follow him and report to their Command Post. They all seemed to be dragging themselves to where they were going. A lot of them looked very old and there were some that weren't there that long. Some were very thin; some didn't wear jungle shirts under their flak jackets. Most of the guys looked like life had left them. They were just shells, or walking dead men, waiting for their time to go. I felt that I didn't want to end up looking like them.

Bill and I got up, not saying anything and followed the last man until we could see a couple of guys off to our right. We asked where the 2nd Platoon C.P. was, and they said that we had found it. We told them that we were assigned to this platoon. One of them was lying on his side smoking a cigarette and said that he was Lieutenant Ervin for 2nd Platoon and then asked us for our names and service numbers. Then he told the radioman to get first and second squad team leaders up there. The lieutenant then said that we looked like brothers. We told him that we weren't. After a few minutes had passed, two more men came up to us and the lieutenant told them that he was assigning these new men to them. Lieutenant Ervin was in his early twenties. He had brown hair, blue eyes, and was about 5'10" tall, and average build. He seemed sure of himself and a little cocky. Sergeant Thomas told me to follow him to his team. Sergeant Thomas had his flak jacket on but you could see how thin he was because his ribs were showing. He had been here for a while. I followed him to where he had the rest of his gear. He then began to ask me my name and service number and other information about me, and called Corporal Chadwell to come up. The sergeant then sat down to begin eating his chow and he asked me if I had eaten and I told him, "no." He told me to eat and then showed me about the heat tabs and how to use it. Corporal Chadwell arrived and Sergeant Thomas told Chadwell that I was with his team.

After a couple of minutes talking and eating, Thomas told Chadwell that he better take me over to the fighting hole. Thomas then looked at his watch and told Chadwell that it was time for the enemy to hit us. Chadwell asked him why. Thomas told him that it was Sunday and it was 18:00 hundred hours and last week the enemy hit them on Sunday at this time. Then

Chadwell told me to follow him on over to the fighting hole and when we got about ten feet from the fighting hole, we could hear thumping noises in the distance. Chadwell quickly jumped into the hole with the other guys that were around; I just watched the other guys get into the hole and then I jumped in. The only trouble was that the hole was only 12 inches deep and there were about five of us trying to get to the bottom of that fighting hole. We could hear the rounds coming toward us from the other side of the hill. Then just as fast as it started it was over. I was scared to death and was hoping that it was over for good.

Thomas came over to us and told us to stay right next to the fighting hole because he felt the enemy was not done with us just yet. The guys got out of the hole and two of us got out our E-tool and started digging the hole deeper. The ground was almost like cement. After a little bit I asked one of them if I could have the E-tool and I got in and started digging the hole deeper. After a couple of minutes the word was passed for the corpsman to go up to where the wounded men were at. Then after about fifteen minutes all of us could hear the thumping sounds again and this time I was on the bottom of the hole and the rest of the guys were jumping in. We could hear the rounds hitting the front of our hill again since we were on the back side. But then the rounds were walking toward us. I could feel that some of the guys wanted to get up and run but there was nowhere to run to. Then one of the guys started saying The Lord's Prayer out loud and I began saying it to myself. All of us could hear the rounds hitting close to us and getting closer. As the shells were hitting the ground, we could feel the ground shake. The shells were getting even closer to us; it felt like they were coming right for us and all of us knew that the next round would get us. All of a sudden we could hear the next round. It was coming straight toward us and there was nothing any of us could do, or anywhere to go. I never in my whole life felt so helpless and now it looked like my life was going to be over. All of us got very quiet and then as the shell was coming down on us, it missed us and hit the ground below us by about ten feet. We could hear a couple of more rounds coming but they were hitting well below us. Then, all of a sudden it was over again.

For the next couple of seconds, none of us could move, but we kept on listening to hear any more mortars that might be coming at us. We got out of the fighting hole without saying a word to each other. I just sat there not knowing what to think or do. Again we heard someone call for the corpsman up. I was hoping that no one in our outfit got killed. Someone said to get the tubes ready, and soon we started pumping our mortar rounds back at the enemy. I couldn't figure out how they knew what hill the enemy was on. We started digging the hole deeper again. I didn't realize that I had blisters on my hands from digging the fighting hole until I felt blood running down the handle of the E-tool. One of the guys told me to get out and let the rest of us dig the hole. I could still hear the 60mm mortars firing at the enemy and I was hoping that we were hitting them like they had hit us. As I sat next to the hole I could feel myself getting very tired. It was dark out now and one of the guys said that it was going on 21:30 and then our mortar teams stopped firing. Everything got very quiet.

The word was being passed that a couple of guys in our platoon had gotten wounded and the chopper was coming for them. I heard there were a couple of the guys that were serious and needed to be evacuated out of here by chopper. About a half hour later we could hear a chopper coming in the distance and I hoped that they could find us. It was totally dark and the sun was gone for the day. As the chopper was getting closer to us, Sergeant Thomas told Chadwell to take his team down the hill a short way to make sure that the enemy didn't sneak up on us. There were four of us in the fire team and Chadwell told us to get our gear and that we were going down the hill. I grabbed my gear and followed Chadwell down the hill and he pointed to each of us where we were to be. He looked at me and pointed for me to stay where I was and he went a little farther away from me, but each of us could see each other in case something would happen to us when the chopper came.

There were a few trees in front of me that were about one to two inches thick and the brush was very thick so it was very hard to see anything. I was scared and nervous and I tried to listen as well as I could to hear if anyone was sneaking up on me. I could hear the chopper above us making a lot of noise; it was difficult to hear anything. It seemed like minutes were going by slowly, and everything moved in slow motion. I was getting very tired and I wanted to get some sleep, but I realized that I might be up all night. Now I could see why the guys that were back in the rear told us to rest as much as we could, because out in the bush you were not going to get a good night's sleep at all.

What seemed like a long time was only about 45 minutes and before I knew it, the chopper left. I couldn't tell if the chopper had landed or not but I hoped that he had. Chadwell then looked at me and pointed back up the hill and I was glad. I then looked at the other guy and pointed at him that we were moving back up the hill. We got back up the hill and I told the other guys that I was glad that they had gotten the wounded. One of the guys from another fire team came over to us and said that the chopper did not land. They were afraid that the enemy might hit them when they landed. They didn't want to get hit and be stuck out here in the field with the rest of us.

We got back to our fighting hole and Sgt. Thomas told me that I had better go and get some sleep for what was left of the night and that I had third watch which was an hour long. I got out my poncho and covered myself up and the next thing I knew someone was kicking me at the bottom of my foot and told me that it was my turn. I got up and sat next to the fighting hole with my rifle across my lap. As I sat there I was thinking about the wounded men and hoping that they would make it to the morning to get medievac. This was my first time standing night watch and I could tell that this night was rough. I hoped that we wouldn't get hit again today. My hour was done and I then woke up the next guy in my fire team. I went back to my poncho and covered myself up and tried to fall off to sleep.

The next thing I knew someone kicked me at the bottom of my boot and told me that it was time to get up. I got up without making a sound. The other men were rolling up their ponchos, so I did the same. I tied it back on my flak jacket. It was cool this morning and that the sun was not out, there were only clouds. Chadwell told me that I better get something to eat before we left. About an hour went by and the word was passed that we were moving out.

I got my gear ready and just sat there on the ground waiting for Chadwell to tell me to saddle up. I was watching the rest of the old timers to see how they were handling themselves out in the field. None of them said a word to each other but made sure that they had everything ready to move out when the word came. As I was sitting there, my mind raced back to wishing that I had had more combat training back in the States. But then, I remembered that everything I was trained for back there didn't really relate to what to do over here. Back in the States you would be out in the field all day and than would go back to the barracks and have a good night sleep...not here. Now, I knew why my father told me to pay attention to the old timers over here because they would keep me alive. I knew that I would be learning everyday over here on how to keep alive and hopefully make it back to the States.

This day was going to be my first full day in the field. I felt that it was to test me for all the days to come, whether I would be a damn good Marine or not. I was going to make sure I did my best everyday. As I was sitting there, I felt that last night was the worst night that I had gone through. I knew now that the rest of the nights over here weren't going to be easy at all. The word was passed that the choppers were coming for the wounded men.

The sun was just then rising above the hills and clouds, and I was surprised to learn that we had beat the sun up, tired as we were. The word was passed quietly that we were moving out in a little bit and to saddle up. Sergeant Thomas came over to me and told me that I was going to be the radioman for his squad. I told him that I didn't know anything about the radio; he said neither did anyone else. Thomas said that he wanted everyone to be able to work the radio in case everyone in the team got wounded or killed. I agreed to give it a try. Corporal Chadwell brought the radio over to the fighting hole that we had dug the night before and handed it to me.

The radio was on a pack board the length of a man's back. It also had an extra battery in case the other one failed. The battery alone weighed five pounds in addition to the 25-pound radio itself, not counting the pack board. I adjusted the straps and put it on my back. It didn't feel too bad because my shoulders were carrying the weight of the radio. I told Sgt. Thomas that I was ready and I asked what our call sign was. He said that we're Charlie 2-1; our platoon call sign was Charlie 2. I asked what it meant and he explained that "Charlie" meant Charlie Company, the 2 meant 2nd Platoon and the 1 meant 1st Squad. When someone called us, I was told to answer, "This is Charlie 2-1, over;" when calling someone, I was to say their name first and then ours. They would know who was calling them. Thomas told me that I was to be behind him and that if they called us to let him know and he would help me out until I got used to it.

I had the handset in my left hand and Thomas told me to hook it to my flak jacket pocket so that I didn't have to hold it all of the time. It made it a lot easier for me to hold my rifle. Then I heard on the radio, "Charlie 2-1, Charlie 2-1, over." I grabbed the handset and pressed in on the side of the handle and said "This is Charlie 2-1, over." The person at the other end told me that we were going to be the point squad and to start moving out. I told Sgt. Thomas, who then told Chadwell his team was point and the other fire team would be behind us. They started going out on the small trail that I had been on when I had arrived last night. Sgt. Thomas followed the last guy of the 1st fire team and I was right behind him and then the 2nd fire team. As we were moving out, there were four guys sleeping on the ground close to one another with a poncho that covered them. I asked Sgt. Thomas why they were not getting up and moving out with the rest of us. Thomas told me that since the chopper didn't land last night that they had died during the night and that the corpsman couldn't do a damn thing to save them. I could feel myself getting sick because I had just walked past them and there was nothing anyone could do for them now. I could feel the hate rising up inside of me because the chopper didn't come down and pick these guys up. We started to go down the hill and I was glad to get off of it. As we got to the bottom of the hill, we started back up on another hill. There was already a group of Marines there. As we walked past them, my old buddy from boot camp, McBride, waved but we didn't say a word to each other. I noticed that he was as tired as I was. Sgt. Thomas looked back at me to see how I was doing.

We walked up and down the hills for what seemed to be a couple of hours, and then I heard on the radio that we were to stop for ten; I told Thomas and he passed it on up to the point team and we stopped. I then got off the trail and sat down looking and listening around me. We could feel the heat of the sun raising the temperature and humidity. The clouds were gone now and the skies were blue. I was starting to feel the pack board digging into my back and shoulders. I looked down the hill that we were on and there was a dry creek bed. The trees made it hard to see for a long distance but then it make it hard for the enemy to see us.

As we were sitting there, each one of us was facing outward, and every other man faced the opposite direction of the guy in front of him. Sgt. Thomas looked at his watch and told us to get up and that we were moving out and he told me to call Charlie 2 and inform them. I got on the radio and called, "Charlie 2, Charlie 2, this is Charlie 2-1, we are moving out, over." "Charlie 2, roger that, Charlie 2-1 over." Thomas then told the 2nd fire team to take the point and that the 1st fire team was to be behind us. The second fire team was moving up and as they passed us they made sure that they were not too close to each other.

As soon as the last man passed, Thomas then got behind him and I got up and followed and we passed the guys in my fire team and then they got in behind me. I was trying to figure out which way we were going north, south, east or west. I couldn't tell because of the hills and the thick foliage. We were starting to come out in a clearing and it looked as if we were going to be out of the hills for good. The hills were low rolling and ranging from about five to ten feet high with small bushes on them, no more than a foot or two feet high. I looked back and the last big hill was about 1000 meters back and off to my left side. Our battalion was in a staggered column.

About two hundred meters in front of me were two Marines taking moving pictures of us coming out of the hills. They had on jungle clothes but I couldn't tell whether they were from some T.V. network or what. Then the point team stopped and the word was passed back to Sgt. Thomas that they were next to a river. Sgt. Thomas told me to call back to Charlie 2 and tell them that we had reached the river. Charlie 2 called me back and informed me that the point team was to check out the river. I passed on the information to Sgt. Thomas and he walked up to the point team and had them check out the area around the river. Then the point team crossed the river and I hoped that nothing was going to happen to them. It seemed like a half hour went by and finally the word came back that it was all right to cross the river. Then Charlie 2 called us and said that we were to cover the rest of the guys until they were finished taking a bath in the river. I passed the word on to Sgt. Thomas and he then told both fire team leaders where to put the men and cover the company on this side of the river. The position for each man was approximately 10 meters apart, facing back in the direction of where we had come from.

The rest of the company moved out and took a bath in the river. Most of them in the company were old looking and tired, and very dirty. Thomas put me about twenty feet from the river and in the middle of all the guys in our squad. A lot of the others guys were having fun bathing in the river. It looked like we were going to be here for a good while. All of us in the squad sat down and watched to make sure that the enemy did not sneak up on us.

Then I heard someone calling me on the radio and I then called Sgt.

Thomas over. The voice on the radio said, "Charlie 2-1, Charlie 2-1, this is Charlie 2 over." Sgt. Thomas grabbed the radio and told me that our squad could go bathing in the river. There was another squad that was taking our place while we went bathing. As the other squad took our positions, our squad then went to the river. I went over to the edge of the river and took off the radio and my combat gear. I then took off my boots and the only thing I had on was my jungle pants. I got up and went into the river which was only about two feet deep. I sat down about half way in the middle of the river.

The river was at least 40 meters wide. I could feel the cold water against the hot sun and it really felt good touching my legs and lower body. I then leaned down so that the water was up to my neck and I could almost feel the pain in my shoulders starting to leave where the straps had dug in. The lieutenant in our platoon told us that we had ten minutes and then we would be moving out. I dunked my head with my whole body under water. I held my breath for as long as I could to try to escape from the hot sun. I did this several times and it felt very refreshing. I began rubbing all over my body to get the dust and oil off of me. I sat there for five more minutes enjoying the running water going past me. I felt like all of the worry of the world was gone while I sat there in the water. I knew that it was time to get out so I got up and walked back to where my gear was. The rest of the guys in the squad were also starting to get out of the water.

I put on my combat gear and the radio and the rest of the guys were also getting their gear on as well. Sgt. Thomas told the squad to cross the river to the other side with the rest of the company. When we got to the other side of the river, Sgt. Thomas told us to spread out and to cover the squad that was on the other side of the river. They were then coming across the river. After they got across the company then moved out. Sgt. Thomas asked me how I was doing and I told him that I was all right for now. We traveled about 2000 meters and the word was passed to stop. Up in front of us the company was making a large perimeter. The landscape was very flat and there were only a couple of trees in the middle. The word was passed that the Company C.P. would be at the trees. Sgt. Thomas then told both fire team leaders where their teams were to be in the perimeter. As I took off my gear with Chadwell's fire team, I looked around and asked Chadwell, "Is this our front line?" and he said, "Yes." It wasn't like all of the wars before this where you had a straight line and you knew where the enemy was and what ground he had. Here the line was a 360-degree circle that was made for the day and it was the ground that we owned until we left; then it was anyone's ground. Now, the guy on our right and the guy on our left as well as the guy behind us was our protection and only protection against the enemy out in the field. It just didn't make any sense. I had thought that once you took the ground, you kept it, it was yours. Or if you lose the ground from the enemy, it was theirs.

It was around 12:00 and the sun was making the temperature rise even higher. Some of the guys got out their E-tools and were digging their fighting holes for the day. As I was watching, the word was passed again that we were going to have hot chow out here in the field. This really made the guys happy. In the distance there were two trucks coming our way and I knew that the food was coming. When the two trucks arrived, one of the trucks had the food and the other truck had P.X. supplies for us to buy, if we wanted to. I didn't have any money on me and the guys that had been here had what they called "Military Money" that they got paid with. Small tables were being set up so the hot food that was in the large cans could be set on them. Then the guys were told to get their food. I went over with my rifle and saw that they had paper plates for us to use. I went through the line and there was fried chicken, potato chips, bread, cake, and kool-aid or coffee. When they were finished giving me my food, I went back to my fighting gear, sat down and began to eat. The chicken was cold but it was better than not having any food at all. About ten minutes had passed and in the sky a small black cloud was coming our way from the west. They put the small tables back on the truck and took off back to Dong Ha.

I started talking with the guys in my fire team; there were only four of us, me, Chadwell, Charlie and Ted Van Meeteren. Chadwell was the fire team leader and he stood 6'0" tall and had a little bit of a Southern drawl. He wasn't as thin as Sgt. Thomas, but he had been here for a good while. Charlie was about 5'7" tall and was a little on the stocky side. He said that he had been here a couple of months now. Van Meeteren was about 6'2" and had been here for awhile and told me that I could call him Van. They really tried to make me feel at home. Chadwell asked me where I was from back in the States and I told him that I was from Cincinnati, Ohio. And he started laughing and told me that he lived fifty miles up the Ohio River in Maysville, Kentucky. He said what a small world this was. As we were talking, the small black round cloud was getting closer to us and now it seemed to be getting larger. The wind was starting to pick up and it was unusual at this time of day to have any wind at all. All of us were looking at the round black cloud that was getting closer to us and around the black cloud the skies were blue as far as we could see in any direction. The wind was picking up and the round black cloud was almost over us and the wind was really blowing. The guys grabbed their gear to keep it from blowing away. The wind was moving about 40 to 50 miles an hour and still getting stronger. I had the radio pack lying on top of my gear. Now the black cloud was over us and the wind was moving about 80 to 90 miles an hour. My gear was sliding along the ground and I was starting to move with the wind as well. The wind had moved me about ten feet and then it started slowing down and started to rain, not hard, for a couple of minutes. Then it stopped raining and the winds were back down to around 40 to 50 miles an hour and the raindrops started coming down again and it changed into small hailstones. The hailstones were really hitting us but at least our flak jacket and helmet kept the hailstones from hurting us. Our arms were the only things besides our legs that were getting hit by them. It lasted about five minutes and then the winds started dying down and the hailstones stopped as quickly as they came and the round black cloud moved eastward toward the hills that we had just left.

All of us were picking up our fighting gear that the winds had moved. It took a couple of minutes for the Company to gather up the gear. The sun was back out and boy did the heat and humidity climb back up quickly. I sat down with my gear and tried to relax as much as I could with Van Meeteren, Charlie and Chadwell. We heard that the lieutenant wanted all three squad leaders up to the C.P. I had a funny feeling that something was up and I looked at Chadwell and he knew as well. Chadwell said that it looked like we were going to move out. I had hoped that I could rest for the remainder of the day, but it didn't look as if that was possible.

Meanwhile, word was passed that there was mail call. I knew that I wouldn't have any letters. I asked Chadwell when the last time they got mail in the field. He told me that it was ten days ago. As everyone had received their mail, each of them sat down alone near his gear and just looked at the envelopes addressed to them from their folks, friends, and girlfriends back at home. As I watched each of the guys slowly open up their letters, I felt terribly all alone. I wished that I had some letters, but I knew it would take some time before the letters would catch up with me. I could imagine now how my father must have felt when he was shipped over seas in the Pacific. No one around me was saying anything because they were all absorbed with reading their letters. Oh God, I wished I had just one letter to read…just one, to ease the pain. But I knew I had to be like everyone else and wait awhile for my first letters to arrive. I sat down and just looked into the sky, wishing that I wasn't here. I never really knew how much a letter really meant to me until now. I didn't care if it said, "Hi and Goodbye," as long as I had a piece of mail addressed to me.

After about twenty minutes, Thomas came back and said that we were going back to the hills. He said that we would be leaving in an hour. The guys in our squad were voicing their opinions by groaning and moaning. But we did as we were told. The hour was up and we got our combat gear on; I picked up the radio and looked at Thomas and told him that I was ready. Only our platoon was moving out, while the rest of the company was to remain here. I thought to myself that our platoon seemed to get all of the shit details. Lieutenant Ervin said that we were going back to the last hill we had come from to see what we could observe.

Sgt. Thomas told the two fire team leaders that our squad had point again. Charlie 2 called me and told us to move out. Thomas then told

Chadwell's team to move out first and then he looked at me and told me to call Charlie 6 that we were leaving the "I.P." When I finished telling Charlie 6 the information, I than asked Thomas what, "I.P.' meant. He told me that I.P. meant "Immediate Position." Gradually, I was learning some new things on the radio and understanding it better.

We arrived back at the river where we were earlier and the lieutenant told me on the radio that our squad was to cross the river first. I told Thomas and he told the second fire team to take the point and cross the river. The first man started crossing the river while the rest of us watched. When he got about half way across, the next man moved out and when the second man got half way the first man was on the other side and the third men started out. The rest of the squad moved out the same way. When it was Sgt. Thomas's turn to go and I waited until he was about half way and I started going across. I could feel the loneliness of being all alone in the middle of the river as I was crossing it. If I got hit in the middle of the river I knew there was only one who could help me and that was me. But, I made it safely and moved to the position where Thomas pointed out for me to watch for the enemy.

When the whole platoon was finally across the river we moved out again. There was a hill about 1500 meters from where we were and I hoped that it was the one that we were heading for. We kept moving in that same direction. The hill didn't seem to be very tall from where we were.

We finally reached the bottom of the hill and it was high. One of the guys found a path leading to the top. It was steep in some places and was causing us problems. We finally reached the top and the lieutenant came up and told Sgt. Thomas to take his men over to the northwest part of the hill. Thomas told me to follow him again while he told the fire team leaders where to put their fire teams. Then Thomas told me to get with my fire team. Chadwell pointed out a bunch of stubby bushes that we would dig next to. I took off the radio, got out my E-tool, and started digging out our fighting hole for the night. Each of us took turns in digging out our hole. It took only half an hour since the ground was not as hard as the other hill I had landed on in the chopper. I could still feel the pain in my hands from the other night's digging. Chadwell than told Charlie, Van and me that we were finished with digging the hole. Chadwell told us what watch we had for the night. He said that we would be on an hour and off until our second watch later in the night.

Chadwell told me that we were finishing up an operation called, "Prairie II." I asked him why they named the operation and he said it was for record keeping in knowing what operations we all had been on. We didn't start our watch until 22:00 hundred and my first watch was at 24:00 hundred and again at 03:00 hundred. After each of my watches, I was to wake up Charlie by kicking him at the bottom of his feet. I also made sure that I had my fighting gear ready so that I didn't have to reach or search for it. We put up out little sticks for our fields of fire so that we had interlocking fire from the other fighting holes. The sun was down now and I made sure that my rifle was next to me with a round in the chamber and the magazine locked and loaded. As I reached for my poncho, I noticed that the mosquitoes were out after us that night. I grabbed the mosquito repellent from my helmet and covered my arms and the back of my head with it. The mosquitoes were still biting me through my jungle uniform, since it was very thin. I then took off my flak jacket that I'd had on all day except when I went swimming earlier. I turned my flak jacket around and took off the poncho. I then opened up the poncho and covered myself up so that the mosquitoes wouldn't bite me. There was a cool breeze coming from the west and the heat of the day was slowly leaving. The rest of the guys were also bedding down for the night, with the exception of the guys who had first watch. As I lay down, I went over what I had done and seen for the day. I sure had done one hell of a lot of walking up and down hills. And it seemed like forever getting out of them. My mind went on and I remembered the river and the cold water all over me while I was bathing as well as the hot sun beating down on us. The temperature had to have been in the 90's. I remembered the straps of the radio digging into my shoulders and back and how tired my feet were from walking so much. I remembered the hot food and mail, and how the guys were excited about reading their letters, and that strange black cloud that had come over us and how it had blown me almost off my feet. It sure was some first day in the field.

The next thing I knew, I felt a kick at the bottom of my foot. I quickly got up and Charlie whispered to me that it was my turn. He gave me a watch and the handset of the radio and told me that it was all mine, but before he settled down for the night I asked him if they always kicked the bottom of the guys' feet and he said, "Yes." He told me if I didn't, some of them would either knife or shoot me if I touched them anywhere else on their body. I just nodded and he dropped off to sleep. It was dark and I realized I was watching out for these guys in my fire team as well as the guys that were up at this time with me in our perimeter. I felt that I was finally doing something good, and it felt great inside. I looked down and on each side of me to make sure that the enemy was not creeping up the hill. When I looked at the clock, it was only 00:15 and I still had forty-five minutes to go. I looked up into the sky and I couldn't believe how many stars were out and how quiet. My mind was thinking of home and also here where I was, now. At 00:30 on the radio the platoon radioman called, "Charlie 2-1, Charlie 2-1, if all secure, press your handset twice, if not, press it once," so I pressed the handset twice and I could hear the platoon radioman call for our other squad and saying the same thing to them. The platoon radioman sounded like he was real loud-he wasn't, but it made you think that he was, on the radio. I then started thinking about my father doing the same thing I was doing...watching. But he did it against the Japanese, and I was doing it against the North Vietnamese. I remembered that he only talked a couple of times about the war against the Japanese and how nasty they were against the paratroopers. I looked at my watch and my hour was almost up. Then the platoon radioman called me again and asked the same thing he had before and I pressed my handset twice. I kicked Chadwell at the bottom of his foot and he got up and I handed him the handset and watch and I then got under my poncho and tried to get some sleep. I could feel my body being very relaxed and the next thing, I was off to sleep.

The next thing I knew Charlie was kicking me at the bottom of my foot again and I got up quickly. Again he gave me the watch and the handset of the radio to me. I sat next to the fighting hole with my rifle across my lap. I started thinking back to the previous night and the young guys who were wounded badly by the mortar fire. They had died senselessly because the chopper refused to land. It seemed like the chopper pilots were only worried about themselves. They had a safe place to sleep when they got back to the base and they didn't care about the men out in the field with no cover. The more I thought about it, the angrier I became. I made a pledge to myself to shoot down the next chopper that refused to land for the wounded men. I grew even angrier and more bitter as I remembered how the men had just laid on the ground covered by their ponchos and they never got a chance to get the hell off that hill. At least the dead men were going home instead of staying on that hill forever.

My thoughts were interrupted as the platoon radioman called, "Charlie 2-1, Charlie 2-1, if all secure, press your handset twice, if not press it once." I then pressed twice on the handset and I knew that my watch was half over. The next thirty minutes went slowly and the radioman called me on the phone again and I pressed it twice. I got up and kicked Chadwell again and gave him the watch and handset. As I went back to my poncho, Chadwell got up and went on over to the fighting hole and sat down and watched and listened. As I got under my poncho, I started thinking about how nice it would be to receive some letters from home. I never realized how lonely a person could be when you are out of touch with people you love. Then the next thing, I was off sleeping.

The sun was coming up and I could feel the sun hitting me. Charlie told me it was time to get up and get my gear ready. I took my poncho and rolled it up for the day and tied it on the back of my flak jacket. The clouds had covered the sky again so that the sun could not get through, and it was a light gray color. I noticed that the guys were starting up their breakfast of C-rations. I got out a heat tab and looked at what I had and cooked it. After I finished, I was still hungry, but I knew that if I ate everything up now I wouldn't have anything later. I would just have to eat very little and get used to it and fast. We all just lay around until about noon when the word was passed that we were getting a package and for the squad leaders to come to the C.P. Charlie told me that from now on to use my sock to carry my C-rations and I could tie it on the back of my flak jacket as well. It made a lot of sense and when we got back to Dong Ha, I would get my seabag and get one of my green socks.

When Sgt. Thomas came back he had candy and cigarettes, apples and milk. I couldn't figure out who would send milk out in the field. After Thomas made sure that we all received an equal share, he said that we were going out on an ambush for the night at the bottom of the hill. He went on to say that we all had better try to lie around and get some sleep during the day. By about 12:00 noon, the clouds were leaving and the blue skies and sun took over. The temperature started rising as well as the humidity. Charlie and I took his poncho and made a cover so that the sun would not hit us. It gave us some shade so we could just lie on the ground and try to get as much rest as we could before we went out on the ambush. The rest of the guys in the platoon were doing the same thing with their ponchos to keep the sun from cooking them. The day seemed very long and I wanted to do something besides just lie around and do nothing. As the hours were creeping by slowly, I was feeling all alone, home sick, but starting to feel that Charlie, Van, and Chadwell were accepting me. I didn't know the guys in the other fire team as well as the guys in the platoon. I'd seen them but I didn't know their names. As I looked around everyone was sitting with their shirts off, writing letters home or sitting next to their fighting holes or under their ponchos doing nothing. Charlie, Van, and Chadwell and I were talking about what was going on back in the States and how we felt that we were so far away from there. Just talking about back home and cars seem to take our minds off of this place that we were in. All of the guys in the platoon were talking or thinking about home and what they were going to do when they got there. Finally evening came and pretty soon we would be leaving for the ambush. Chadwell looked at his watch and said that it was time for chow and to get as much rest as we could before we left for the ambush. From noon to now there was no wind, but the temperature was very hot and humid. Yesterday we walked for hours for most of the day and today we stayed in one place doing nothing. Sgt. Thomas came over to me and told me that I would be carrying the radio on the ambush. I just nodded to him and he then went back to the other fire team.

We had a couple of hours to go before the sun started going down for the day. Charlie, Chadwell, Van and I just lay on the ground and tried to rest as much as we could. The sun was almost gone when Thomas told us to saddle up; it was time to leave. I grabbed my gear and put the radio on my back and we went off. We walked past the C.P. group and they told us good luck. We got to the trail that had brought us up here and started back down it. We walked past the last man on the hill and they just nodded to us. We could see in their faces that they were concerned about all of us, even though they didn't know me that well. As we were walking down the hill I thought about how close our platoon really was. It gave me a good feeling. The hill made it hard for the enemy to see us and I knew that we would be able to set up the ambush. When we reached the bottom of the hill, Sgt. Thomas started pointing out where we were going to set up. The two fire team leaders took over from there in placing their men for the night. The trail made a fork down next to the little streambed. There were little bushes on each side of the trail and we set up just behind one row of them.

The guys took off some of their gear but were very quiet about doing so. Thomas had me in the middle of the ambush because of the radio. Thomas told both fire team leaders who had what watch for the night. I took off the pack with the radio on it and put the radio on squelch so the enemy would not hear it. I took off the rest of my combat gear and got out my poncho. I made sure that my rifle was ready in case I needed it. Thomas told me that I had fifth watch for the night. I lay down and hoped that we could hit the enemy and get back at them for what they had done to us the other night.

I felt someone kick me at the bottom of my foot, and I quickly got up and took the handset and watch. As I listened and watched, I prayed that the enemy would come by and that we could get back at them. It was really hard to see because of the blackness and the guys next to me. I was a little scared but I had to really stay focused on what I was doing, hoping that I could see or hear them coming. I heard the C.P. calling me on the radio both times and I knew that my hour was up. I kicked the man next to me at the bottom of his foot and handed him the handset and watch. I then lay down quietly and covered myself up with my poncho, I could hear the mosquitoes flying around and they were really working on me. I wanted to slap them but couldn't because I knew that if I did that it would give away our position. Somehow I fell off to sleep.

I felt someone kick me and whispered to me to get up and get my gear on and that we were moving out. I grabbed my poncho and started rolling it up in the dark; the sky was still very dark and something must be up for us to leave at this time. I started looking for the radio and finally I got it and Thomas whispered to me and asked if I was ready and I told him yes. Thomas then told me to call Charlie 2 and to let them know that Charlie 2-1 was coming back up the hill. When I finished talking to the platoon radioman I then told Thomas and he pointed to one of the guys and we headed back up the hill. It seemed like we were making too much noise getting back up. We reached the top of the hill and went back to our fighting holes. I laid my gear down and we had about an hour and a half before the sun came up.

Chadwell told me that I had the watch and then to wake up Charlie for the last half hour. I woke up Charlie and gave him the watch and radio; he had the last watch and he just smiled because it was only for a half hour. The sun came out first and then the gray clouds covered the sun for most of the morning until around noon. I must have gotten up around 08:00 hundred and just laid around. Chadwell was telling Charlie and me that we needed more men in our platoon and that the whole battalion was very short handed. I asked Chadwell how many men were supposed to be in a platoon and he said, "Full strength is 56 men including the C.P. group," and I asked him "How many do we have now?" and he said that we had something like 44 men. Chadwell told me that there were supposed to be four men in a fire team and three fire teams in a squad and we had only two fire teams. Chadwell also said that we were to have three squads of riflemen with three fire teams each, one machine gun squad of two four man teams and a four man mortar team. It was about 12:00 hundred, noon time and the gray clouds were leaving and we could see that the sun was coming out and all of us knew that today would be hotter than yesterday. It seemed like it was getting hotter everyday. I asked Chadwell, "Does it get hotter than this going into the summer?" and he said, "It is just starting to get hot out." The day went by very slowly and again we were to observe to see if the enemy was moving about. All of us took turns watching and listening for the enemy while the rest stayed under the ponchos and tried to keep cool, which was impossible.

The next day came and we were all up around 05:00 hundred in the morning. The word was passed that we were leaving the hill and being picked up by the six-bys. I was getting used to talking on the radio, although I had never been trained on it in the Marine Corps. I got my gear on and we moved out around 10:30 in the morning. Our platoon walked down the hill and back to the river and we crossed it again. In a way, we all knew that the enemy was nowhere in sight. We finally got back to the rest of the company and were told that the trucks wouldn't be here for a while.

Our platoon radioman came over to me and talked to me about the radio and showed me everything about how to work it and the different call signs that they were using. Such as I.P., O.P., L.P., crossing a river, stream, hill, etc. He told me what O.P mean which was Observation Post, and L.P. was Listening Post plus the company call sign which was Charlie 6 and the Captain was Charlie 6 Axel. He told me that when we got back, he would get me a small book and I could write down all of the information that a radioman needed to have. Then he told me that I was to be calm on the radio at all times and not to get excited. I told him thanks, and he got up and left. He was as tall as me but he looked like he weighed about 170 pounds, he had blue eyes and brown hair. He seemed very nice and was very good on the radio by being really relaxed when he was talking. I remembered that he said to me before he left that I was getting calm on the radio when I talked.

That meant a lot to me.

Finally in the distance, we could see the six-bys coming. We couldn't wait to get out of the field and back to the rear. The six-bys stopped and we saddled up and walked over to the dirt road. They told us to board the trucks and that we were moving out. I got on one of the trucks with my fire team. Sgt. Thomas also got on the same truck and walked up to the back of the cab and laid his rifle over it. When everyone was on board, we made sure that our rifles were pointing outboard so if the enemy was shooting at us that we were ready to return fire. Then the trucks started off, following the lead truck; they all turned around and started heading south. Soon we came to a village and the Vietnamese people came out on both sides of the road; they were asking for "chop-chop," which meant food. Some of the kids and young girls were trying to sell us bread and soda pop. American soda pop at that, for twenty-five cents. I asked Charlie how they got the soda and he said, "From the Black Market." I remembered hearing back in the States that the people over here could poison the food and drink without you knowing how they did it. I didn't buy anything from them but there were a few of the guys who did. There were still other guys that were giving the people our C-rations. We were moving slowly through the vill. For the first time I came close to the straw huts and the way the people lived. The huts had four walls that were made out of straw. The people would raise up a wall so that the air would pass through. Inside of the huts was not much of anything. There were no chairs; their beds were made out of bamboo sticks and they had a little shrine where they prayed. They had nothing to compare to the people back home. The front yards were very small, only about thirty feet long and twenty feet wide. I could smell the shit from the water buffaloes that were kept in their yards. There were a couple of huts that looked like stores, because there was a lot of merchandise inside. The people were very small and looked undernourished. The name of the village was Cam Lo.

The lead truck turned right and ahead of us was a Marine guard at a T-shaped intersection directing our convoy. When our truck got to the Marine, he pointed for our truck to turn right. Our trucks were heading toward the bridge, which was 100 meters away. There were two sandbag bunkers on each side of the bridge as well as on the other side of the bridge. As we went past, I saw that the Marines who were guarding the bridge were bored as hell. A little way further the lead truck took a left. This time we all followed it. The road changed from a dirt road to a black top road but it still was only wide enough for one way traffic. The trucks stayed about four-truck lengths away from one another.

As we rode along, I thought about what the platoon radioman told me about the different reports on medievac, spot reports, arty mission, W.I.A. and K.I.A. reports and the many different code words, enemy squad was called, "Spider." He also explained to me the call signs for each platoon and our officers. For example, 1st Platoon was Charlie 1, 2nd Platoon was Charlie 2 and 3rd Platoon was Charlie 3. Our company call sign was Charlie 6 for the company radioman and to talk to the captain, his call sign was Charlie 6 Axel.

One of the guys in the truck said that we would be at Dong Ha in a little bit and that he couldn't wait to get some sleep. But just before the trucks got to the camp, they took a right turn onto another black top road that led west and the name of this highway was, "Highway 9." We traveled about four more miles until we saw a small stream about 300 meters below us on the right of the road and a huge mountain called, "Dong Ha Mountain." On the left side of the road there was a gravel road leading to the top of the hill that we were heading toward. The hill was small compared to Dong Ha Mountain across from it. The six-bys were moving very slowly because of the grade, but we did make it. Then the word was passed to get out and to line up in our platoons from outside the gate. I went with my fire team and we all gathered to form our platoons. I got a chance to see the guys that were in 2nd Platoon and as well as they got a look at me. The lieutenant told the platoon that we would be here for awhile. It was a Marine Camp but I couldn't tell how big it was. We walked through the gate and saw a sign overhead that said, "Welcome to Camp Carroll." When we got inside, the lieutenant told us that we were going to have perimeter watch. Our squad was to have fighting holes numbered 42 to 49 in the northwest part of the base. The lieutenant said that the holes were numbered and that we wouldn't have any trouble finding them. As Sgt. Thomas told the fire team leaders which fighting holes they had, I went with Chadwell.

I took off the radio, and boy did it feel good to get it off. I put my fighting gear in the bunker that had been built with sandbags. I was glad that I didn't have to dig another hole. After I got myself together. I knew I'd get a chance to let my hands heal before we went out in the field again. I grabbed my rifle and broke it down so I could clean it. I didn't have a chance in the field for fear that the enemy might attack at any time. But I had the time now to clean her and after a few minutes of using my toothbrush on my rifle to get the dust off, I put her back together.

I looked out in front of our bunker and the concertina wire was out around the base. There were two rolls of concertina wire next to each other and another one on top of the two to make it harder for the enemy to get into the perimeter. There were two sandbags on top of each other in front of the bunker about fifty feet but just short of the concertina wire. In front of the two sandbags was a device that was in a half moon shape, green in color, with a cord that led back to the bunker where we were. I asked Corporal Chadwell what it was and he said that it was a claymore mine. I had heard about them back in the States when I was going through training but never saw one. Chadwell told me that there were 700 BB's inside of it. It had a killing radius of 150 yards in front of it and a back blast of 100 yards behind it. That's why we had sandbags behind them. To protect our own men.

On this hill the ground was more of a red color than the other hills that we had been on. On those hills the ground was brown-red in color with gravel mixed in with it. The other fighting bunker was only twenty meters away. Then Charlie asked if I had a nickname and I told him that in high school I had been called, "Hammer." He asked how I got the name "Hammer" and I told them that it was connected with my playing football in the ninth grade. I got the name one day before the song came out called, "If I had a Hammer," and it stuck with me from then on. I told them that when I played football, I would get someone hurt on the other team every time I played. The nickname also stayed with me in high school football. I had broken a kid's back, but I didn't find out about it until the next year. I told coach that I didn't do it on purpose. I hit this halfback and he flew up in the air and landed on his back over the quarterback who was throwing the ball. Then Charlie told the other guys that they should call me, "The Hammer." I really felt at home and being accepted as one of them, for good. Charlie was a Lance Corporal and usually the point man for the team. Charlie was a very, very friendly guy, short and stocky with brown hair and blue eyes. Then there was Van, who was from Salt Lake City, Utah. Van was a preacher but he only performed baptisms. Van was 6'2" tall and thin and also had blue eyes. He was with the other fire team in our squad but was moved into our fire team. He didn't say much but he would talk to you if you talked to him first.

I started thinking about the one guy I had seen on the truck when we were coming up here to Camp Carroll. He was a machine gunner in our platoon. I remembered that he was whistling on the truck by himself and having the M-60 machine gun ready in case we got hit. I then asked Charlie if he remembered the machine gunner in our platoon and he asked, "Which one?" and I told him, "The Negro," and he said that his name was Maxwell and that he liked being a loner. I then went back to thinking about Maxwell and that there was something about him that I liked. I remembered that I started whistling a different tune and he looked at me with a strange look. I remembered that both of us had a slight smile on both of our faces. By the way he handled himself, he wanted no part of anyone, white or black.

The sun was getting hotter with the humidity climbing as well. The platoon seemed like nice guys and easy to get along with. I hadn't had the chance yet to meet the whole platoon, but I hoped to in time to meet them all. I asked Charlie, "When does a person have the chance to shave?" He said that they all dry shave in the field because they didn't have soap or they didn't shave at all because it took too much time. Besides, the enemy could smell soap out in the field for miles as well as how bad your B.O. was but there was really nothing you could do about it. I told him thanks, and that it was the only question I had right then. I remembered out in the field how the guys that smoked would cup their hands together so that the lighted end of the cigarette would not show during the daytime or nighttime, and when they blew out the smoke that they would blow downward toward the ground. At nighttime they would get into the fighting hole and smoke inside of them. The only time they would smoke in the outfit was if we were setting up for the day or night. We would never smoke on patrols.

The word was passed that it was time for chow and to find some mess gear. We looked in our fighting bunker and there were a couple of them lying around so all of us grabbed them and went over to the mess tent. The other men from our platoon were walking over to the tents that were only 200 meters away from the perimeter. I could smell the hot food and I couldn't wait to get to it. I was hoping that we would get steaks. When we got in line they were feeding us "Rice and Spam." We all went through and into the other tent, and I noticed that they didn't have any screens around the tent to keep the flies out. It didn't make any difference anymore to me. There just wasn't any use in chasing them away. There were just too many of them to combat. After I ate, I went over to see Bill and his team, and got a chance to meet some more of the guys in our platoon. I told them that they could call me Hammer if they wanted to.

It was going on evening and the Sgt Thomas told us that both fire teams could have one man stand watch during the night and that the rest of us could get somewhat of a good night sleep. We had stayed there a couple of days and each time we went to chow they fed us rice every meal. These past couple of days gave me a chance for my blisters to heal. As these days were going by slowly I was thinking about what it was like being fired upon by the enemy and wondered if I would be able to take it under fire. I could take being mortared and in some ways I knew that I could take a fire fight. It was really on my mind and I asked Charlie and Chadwell what it was like in a firefight. Both of them said that it was like hell opening up and when the firing was over it would get very, very quiet and still. The other thing was that you couldn't see the little sons of bitches. It seemed that it was harder than the fire fight itself, the quietness and wondering if they were coming again. Charlie said that the palms of his hands would sweat and his mouth would be very dry. Chadwell said that his hands didn't sweat but he just didn't like it when the fighting was over because he didn't know if they were going to attack or leave without a sound. The quietness after the firefight was the killer to him as well as most of the guys.

Sgt. Thomas came by our two fire teams and said that we were moving out this morning and to get our fighting gear on. Thomas told Chadwell and the other fire team leader that we were going to watch a bridge. About twenty minutes later a couple of other fire teams from our company came and took over our fighting bunkers. Sgt. Thomas told us to get over to the six-bys, which were between the mess tents and the company tents and to get on them. The rest of the company was not going, just our platoon. I looked over to Chadwell, but before I could say anything he said that we always get the shit details from Lieutenant Ervin and that I should always expect the unexpected from our platoon. Chadwell said in his southern drawl that our squad was always the point team for our platoon, our company, and our battalion, whenever we were all together going on an operation. I wanted to be with the best, but I didn't want to be in the spotlight to be shot at by the enemy.

We went down the hill, took a left on Highway 9 and drove west. We had only gone about a mile and a half when the trucks stopped. The Marines from the other outfit said it was about time someone relieved them. They wanted to get on the trucks and get out of this damn place. We got out and they asked us who we were, and we told them that we were from 1/9 Charlie Company, 2nd platoon. (1/9 meant 1st Battalion 9th Marines.) They quickly got on the trucks and said that the place was all ours. The six-bys moved out going east to Camp Hill and the lieutenant called for the three-squad leaders. He told them where they were to be positioned. He pointed out where the C.P. or Command Post would be, on the other side of the road away from the river. Thomas came back and said that we had this side of the bridge and second squad had the other side of the bridge.

I pointed to a fighting hole at the far end of the bridge and asked Thomas if that was ours. He said yes, and I informed him that I was going there. I went over to the fighting hole with the radio on my back and sat down with the rest of the guys in our squad. The bridge was only 30 meters long and we were the only ones on the west side of the bridge. I took off the radio and looked back on the other side of the bridge where the rest of the fighting holes were on both sides of the road. To the right of our fighting hole there was a big drop of about three hundred feet down into a lake fed by the river. I noticed how green the vegetation and the steep hills were around us, all except for the plants near the road, which were covered with dust. I took off the rest of my fighting gear and set it up so I could use it in a hurry if I had to. The rest of the guys were doing the same thing. It was like no one had to tell us what to do first when we set up in the field. Lieutenant Ervin always made sure that we had on our flak jackets when we were standing our watch in the fighting holes. No one in the platoon wanted to wear the damn things because they were heavy and hot. If we were not on watch, the rest of the guys took the damn things off.

After a few hours, I saw that the bridge was used by the six-bys, either filled with supplies or empty going west to Khe Sanh or coming east to Dong Ha. Every time they came past, the dust from the sides of the road would blow all over the vegetation and us. I knew I wasn't going to like sitting here and having these damn trucks coming and going and kicking up the dust around us. The heat of the sun and the hot air didn't help either.

The next day came and it was even hotter than the day before. I kept looking at the big blue lake below us, wishing that Lieutenant Ervin would say that we could go swimming. Finally, around noontime, the lieutenant passed the word that two guys from each fire team could go swimming while the other guys would stand guard duty at the bridge. Thomas told me that I could go with Charlie, Bill and Van to the lake. We walked down the steep slope. When we got to the bottom, I laid my rifle and magazines down close to the edge of the water in case I needed them quickly. As I jumped in, I saw that a few of the guys were already in the water from our platoon. We were like little kids swimming around. The guys up at the road were watching and I knew that they wanted to come down, but they had to wait their turn. The water was cold like the time I was in the river. It seemed strange that the water would be cold when it was so hot out. It felt great to get the dust out of my hair and my clothes. One of the guys told me that I'd better not wear any underpants, especially white, so I threw them away in the bush. I was just like the rest of the guys since no one wore any skivvies. I took my jungle pants and shirt and washed both of them and then lay them out to dry while I was swimming.

I had spent about 45 minutes in the water and I'd had enough. The guy that told me about the skivvies was a Negro. I asked him his name and he said that his name was Benny Houston. He was about 5'9" and seemed to have a good outlook in life and was nice. Benny was called the "Old Man" of the platoon. He was 27 years old. This was the first time I had ever talked to him. Benny and I walked up the hill together. He told me that I should grow a mustache, and that it would make me look good. I thought about it as we were walking back up the hill. I told him that I would think about it, and he said that he would trim my mustache for me when it was time. We reached the road and I went back to the fighting hole and told Sgt. Thomas that he could go. As I sat there next to the bunker, I thought about Benny and what he said about me growing a mustache and I looked at Charlie and he had his mustache and so did some of the other guys in our platoon.

I asked one of the guys about Benny and Charlie said that everyone in the whole company knew him. He said that everyone thought of him as the father of Second Platoon. Benny was married and had two kids, a boy and a girl, and was from Chicago, Illinois. The rest of the company also thought of Benny as the father of the company.

The next several days we went swimming everyday and then the word was passed that we were moving out again, but we didn't know where. I was still trying to find out which direction was west, south, east and north. The trucks came with replacements and we boarded the six-bys. When we got back to Camp Carroll they told us not to get off the trucks because we were going with the rest of the company on an operation. The rest of the men got on the trucks and they started off down Camp Carroll and onto Highway 9 going east this time. When we got to Highway 1, we turned left and went north. As we were riding up there we all watched the countryside in case we got hit. Everyone was sitting on the floor of the trucks. Soon we passed a village off to our right side and some of the kids asked for chop-chop. A few of the guys threw food cans for them. A few minutes later the trucks stopped and the word was passed to get off them. We were moving out as soon as we could. As we got off the trucks, we were next to a strip which was only 200 meters wide and as long as the eye could see, looking west. I heard some of the guys say that we were at "The Strip." I didn't know what it meant, but I didn't care. The Strip was McNamara's line between Gio Lin near the coast and 16000 meters west toward Con Thein. The strip was right next to the D.M.Z. The company was moving west toward the mountains, which were a great distance away.

Chapter Four

We were on the south side of The Strip and walking parallel with it, going west. We followed it for a while and then turned south on a one-way dirt road. No one was using this road because some plants were growing on it. We stayed on this road for about twenty minutes until the word was passed that we were to set up in a large clearing surrounded by hedgerows. I noticed that the hedgerows separated each of the rectangular shaped fields.

As we were digging in for the day, I realized that I had to go to the bathroom, so I asked Chadwell where I could go. He pointed outside of the perimeter to the hedgerow and said that I'd better take my rifle and E-tool. Then I remembered that I didn't have any paper to wipe myself. But who in the world would have or take paper with them out in the field? Then as I was about to leave, one of the guys told me that he had some paper that I could use. He threw it to me and I left. As I walked out there, I dug a small hole and did my thing, and when I was finished I covered it back up so that the smell would not escape. As I walked back I felt that my body was changing to the climate because I had just had the runs. When I got back to the fighting hole, I had to go again. So I went back to the hedgerow and dug another hole and let the rest come out. I made sure that I didn't have to come back anymore and then headed back for the final time. When I got back to the guys, I asked one of them if there was some way to stop the shits, and he said to eat a lot of peanut butter. The next day came and the word was passed that we were moving out again, so we all packed our gear and left. We were walking east and south and north and west and it seemed that we were waiting for the enemy to come to us. I could hear nothing on the radio and everything around us was very quiet.

We stayed south of The Strip for about four days, and I had the runs the entire time. The word was passed that we were moving out and going back where the trucks had dropped us off the first day. When we got there some of the guys were sitting on either side of the road waiting for the trucks to come. I sat down with them and waited for just a few minutes until the six-bys arrived. The six-bys came up Highway 1 and turned around and stopped for us to get on. They told us to get aboard and that the trucks were getting us out. I realized then that I didn't have the runs anymore, so it looked as if my body had gotten adjusted to the heat and humidity. Van told me on the other side of the strip was the D.M.Z. When Van said that, I got a little nervous inside but tried not to show it to the other guys.

We were going south to the camp and soon there it was-Dong Ha-but we went past the base and kept going straight south. No one knew where we were going; I thought that it must be another operation. The guys wanted to go back to the bridge to go swimming, but it was not to be.

My ass was starting to hurt from the long ride that we were taking. It was a little over an hour before we were told to get off. It looked like we were nowhere. There was sand all around. Soon we started walking east, this time toward the ocean, and the terrain was starting to change into low rolling hills. Then we started going north and the hills were getting larger. The word was passed that we were setting up that night on one of the hills.

The next day came and we were patrolling more new ground that we had not been to. We walked through some rice paddies and then word was passed that we were going to take a ten-minute break. Chadwell told me to check myself for leeches; the rest of the guys were dropping their pants and checking all over themselves, and I did the same to make sure there weren't any leeches on me.

It was going on evening and the terrain was flat. I didn't have the radio to take with me this time because Thomas was making sure that all of the guys in the squad knew how to work it. The terrain was hilly with small bushes but there was nowhere anyone could hide.

When I got up the next day, I felt something heavy on the side of my right leg just above my combat boot. There was also a large spot of blood on the inside of my jungle pants. I knew that I had a leech on me, but I decided not to look at it until I saw the corpsman. I walked over to the corpsman, still feeling the leech hitting my leg as I walked. I told Doc Marsh, the corpsman, that I had a leech and he told me to come over to where his gear was. When I got there, Doc Marsh pulled up my pant leg and said, "Oh, my God…he's a big one." The leech was about 16 inches long and was sucking the blood out of me at both ends. It was about two inches thick and as green as it could be. Doc Marsh put some salt on it but it didn't move or come off. A few of the guys were passing the word around that Hammer had a leech on him. About six of the guys came over and they made all kinds of faces. They kept saying they were glad that it wasn't them. I told Marsh to get the damn thing off me because it was drinking all of my blood. Marsh was taking his good old time in trying to get the leech off of me. One of the guys said to burn it off, and I agreed. Doc Marsh got out a lighter, put the flame up high, and started burning the leech at one end. One end of the leech came off and Doc Marsh then started burning off the other end, and finally the leech dropped to the ground. Doc Marsh was going to put the flame right on it but one of the guys stopped him. He said we should get some grass, set the leech in the middle of it and set it on fire. I told the guys that when it blew up they should catch my blood. The guys got a laugh out of that. Then we heard a pop and the leech had blown up for good. There were two circular holes in my leg about an half inch in diameter, and the blood was pouring out slowly. Doc Marsh asked me why I hadn't felt it during my two watches during the night and I told him that I didn't feel anything at those times.

As I walked back, I couldn't believe that I'd had a leech on me, and I couldn't figure out how he got on me. I then looked at my pants leg and saw that at the bottom of the pants were two strings hanging out. There were two holes where the string came out of and I figured it had gotten inside there and waited until sometime during the night to attack me.

Several more days passed and we were back in the hills, but they were no way near as big as the ones up north. All of us were getting very, very low on water and each day seemed to get hotter than the day before. It was bad enough for us not to be able to drink during the day but when night came we could only have a sip. As we were setting up for the night, word was passed that we'd gotten a Sunday pack. I remembered the first couple of days when I was out in the field that we had gotten a Sunday pack on the hill watching for the N.V.A. Later that night I saw Sgt. Thomas coming from the C.P. group, carrying something in his hands. He called for the two fire team leaders and gave them what he was carrying. They in turn passed the stuff out to all of us. Chadwell asked me if I smoked and I told him that I didn't and that I would take candy in its place. He gave us each equal amounts and then we passed between ourselves what we wanted or didn't want.

The next day came and the sun was getting even hotter than the day before. All of us in the company were running out of water. What water we had was very hot in the canteens and we couldn't drink it. During the end of our patrolling the area for the day, Maxwell, Speedy and the radioman from one of our machine gun teams remembered that there was a well close to us. They left the platoon while all of us started to set up for the day. As all of us were digging in for the night, Maxwell, Speedy, and the radioman came back with cold water. They passed the word to the rest of us in the company that they remembered that there was a well about fifty meters from us. The rest of the guys went on over to the well to drink the cold water but Lieutenant Ervin told us that we all couldn't go but that we could send one guy from each of the fire teams with the canteens to get them filled. I told Sgt. Thomas that I was going to take the canteens over to the well and that I would be back. After I gathered the canteens from the guys in the fire team, I then went on over to the stream. I pulled on the rope and the bucket came up and I drank from the bucket and boy, was the water ice cold. It really felt great going down my throat. When I had my fill of the water I then filled the canteens up and headed back to the team.

A few more days passed and as night fell we were setting up on a hill that we had been on before. We had all finished digging our holes for the night when I heard a single shot being fired at us. The word was passed that one of the guys got shot in the balls. As soon as I heard that I started to laugh along with the rest of the guys in the platoon, even though we were expecting the enemy to attack us. The sun was gone and I couldn't believe that the enemy had been lucky enough to hit him. But as I looked back to where he got hit at the very top of the hill, I could tell that a person could form a good silhouette against the sky.

About twenty minutes later, the word was passed that the guy had gotten a bullet through both legs and that it had missed his balls all together. I was really glad that he didn't get hit there. Then the word was passed that they needed four guys to make a large square. They picked our squad and I was one of the lucky ones. I couldn't figure out why they wanted us to make the square. The gunny came over to me and gave me a flashlight and told me to stay here. Chadwell told me that it was our lieutenant who told Captain Curd that we would do it like every other shit detail that came up. I was getting to dislike the lieutenant for offering us to do every shit detail. Why not the other platoons? Then the gunny went over to where the other guys were and placed them with a flashlight. The hill that we were on was not a steep hill but a gradual climb. The rest of the company protected us while we were out on the side of the hill in the open for anyone to hit us four. Captain Curd came over and told us when we heard the chopper to turn on the flashlights and point them straight upward to the sky. It took about twenty minutes until I heard a chopper coming. I turned on the flashlight above my head and made sure that the light was going straight up into the sky. I didn't feel like getting hit, but boy did I feel like I was a big target for the enemy. I hoped that the enemy would not hit us. As the chopper was coming down, I couldn't hear anything while they were loading the wounded guy. I could feel that empty and lonely feeling coming over me again as I stood my night watches. As the chopper left, I quickly turned off the flashlight. I wondered what the wounded Marine would say when he got back home to his parents about getting wounded, especially when he was putting on his jungle pants on with both legs high in the air. I gave the flashlight back to the gunny who had given it to me earlier. I then went back to our fighting hole and felt a little safe there. Chadwell then told us what watch we had, which we had to stand twice every night in the field. I got out my poncho and covered myself and while lying on the ground next to my rifle, I wondered what my parents were doing and what my friends from high school were doing as well. I could feel that empty and lonely feeling coming over me again and I hoped that in time it would go away and not hurt so much.

When the next morning came, I went with several guys to get water. Some of the guys in my fire team asked me if I could fill up their canteens for them. I said that it was all right and that I would do it. One of the guys gave me his belt and I put all of the canteens on it and then I went down off the hill with the other guys who were getting water for their buddies. There was a hut and a couple of people living in there; behind their hut there was a well and we got the canteens filled up there. For the first time, I hoped that we would get hit and that the rest of the guys would come down off the hill to help us. But nothing happened and when we were finished with the canteens we all went back up the hill.

When we got back up the hill, the word was passed that we were getting picked up by the trucks and were going somewhere else. I was getting tired of walking around and not getting hit. I wanted to change the day a little by getting into a firefight. The other guys were in the same mood I was in, I thought.

We walked a little way until we reached one hill that had booby traps and we were to stay on the trail that overlooked a church. We went down to the church and walked around the outside. The French had built it when they were here. When we got to the other side of the church, we saw thirteen marble statues of all of the apostles and Christ. They were all so beautiful, I couldn't believe my eyes, and I wanted to go inside the church to see what it looked like. We walked in a staggered column between the statues. There was a dirt road out in front of the church. As I looked at each of the statues, I saw they were all made of white marble and all stood about 13 feet high on pedestals, which were 4 feet high themselves. The path from the church to the dirt road out in front was 150 meters away. We got to the dirt road and walked up it until the rest of the company was there. The word was passed that we were to stop and get off the dirt road until the trucks came. I went over to the side of the dirt road and sat down. I looked at my jungle pants and I saw that they were very dirty, and so was I. I got out my canteen and started drinking my water; it was cool. I looked back at the church as I was drinking the water there were people coming out of the church. I looked behind me and saw a water buffalo in the yard. Chadwell told me that we were at Quang Tri City and the people down here were all right.

As the people from the church were walking up the road to their homes, they were smiling at us. We all just sat there looking at how clean they were and how dirty we were. As most of the people went by, I noticed one girl walking up the middle of the street toward me. I stopped drinking water and I couldn't keep my eyes off of her. She was just beautiful. Then Chadwell said out loud, "Look at that," and everyone in our outfit just stopped what they were doing and all eyes were on her. She had on white high-heeled shoes, and a white and pink flowered silk dress, which had an opening on each side that reached from the waist down to the ankles. She was wearing a white silk pair of pants and she had a little pink and white flowered umbrella, which was open. To really top it off she had long black hair down to her waist and her skin was almost white. She was half French and Vietnamese. The way she walked was like she was walking on air and it looked like the dust of the road never moved as she moved down the middle of the street. She moved very lightly and had a lot of grace. She was looking at all of us, and I just sat there with my mouth slightly open and couldn't take my eyes off of her or even move. Then one of the Vietnamese people, a man, told her something and she stopped. I heard a jeep coming, and a Vietnamese guy that was driving it got her inside. It was just wonderful to watch her move as she got into the jeep. She didn't try to show herself off, it just seemed to be natural for her. After she left I thought about the girls I knew back in the States, and the only ones that would come close to her would be the ones that you would read about in books, never in real life. She was just out of this world, the way she moved and looked. I knew that the people back in the States wouldn't believe it if I told them. They would think I was crazy or just making it up. Then the trucks came and as we climbed aboard and moved out, I was looking for her, hoping to see her just one more time. But I couldn't find her and as we left the town I looked at myself again. I couldn't believe how dirty I was and I was embarrassed to have had that young lady look at me. But it was over, and I knew that I wouldn't see anything that good for a long time. I asked Chadwell again what city was this and he said, "Quang Tri City." The trucks took us back to Camp Carroll and we got the same bunkers we'd had before.

The next day the word was passed that we were going to get paid. I was called over to the lieutenant's bunker and the lieutenant was sitting at a small table. The officer asked me my name and service number I said, "Gary Kasten-my service number is 2304479," and he said that I had $300.00 coming. I looked at the money he gave me and it wasn't the kind that you would get back in the States. The money was printed on different colors of paper and the largest bill was a twenty. He gave me all twenty dollars bills.

On the following day the word was passed that we were moving out again, back into the field. The word was either passed by the company or Battalion C.P. The trucks came and we were told to saddle up. They had brought some new replacements for us who were already in the six-bys. Benny was carrying the radio and he put it on one of the six-bys. He came over to me and said I was looking good on the mustache and that it would be soon time for him to trim it. By this time they had informed us that we didn't have to use the clumsy pack board with the radio anymore. I was happy about that and it was a lot easier to carry. The six-bys turned around and we headed back east on Highway 9 toward Dong Ha and then back up north. We went up Highway 1 which went east a little bit and then back up north and got off. This road was also blacktop but went straight north. Now I could tell where north, south, east and west were. They were taking us back up in the hills we were in when I first landed in the field. I hoped we didn't have to go to the same place. The six-bys turned onto a dirt road that led us east into the village. When we got to the vill, the rest of the battalion was there waiting for us, and when we got off Captain Curd called for Lieutenant Ervin. Everyone in the platoon knew right off that we were going to be the lead platoon for the whole battalion again. I knew that our squad would be the point squad for our platoon. The six-bys turned around and went back to where they came from. I remembered back in the rear Lieutenant Ervin would want to be your buddy but when we would go out into the field he didn't want any part of what we said to him. If we didn't have bars on our collar we didn't know what we were talking about. Whatever he said was it and our opinions didn't mean a damn thing to him.

As we were waiting for the lieutenant to come back and tell us that we had point for the battalion, the Marines that were stationed at the bridge were watching us as closely as the people from the village. Some of the young kids were selling miniature loaves of Vietnamese bread; some of the guys were buying the bread and eating it. I was next to Chadwell and even he brought two loaves and gave me one. He said that it was all right because the people here liked the Marines. So I grabbed it, told him thanks, and took a bite. The taste was very different, as though it was lacking something. I asked Chadwell why the bread tasted funny and he said that they didn't use baking soda.

One of the new guys asked some of the other guys in our company where we were headed and they told him that we were going to Phu An. Then one of the guys, Charlie, said, "Oh, no, no... not there again." He was starting to get the shakes. I went over to him and asked him why he was nervous and he said that when they had tried to get there once before, they ran into a N.V.A. regiment. I asked Charlie how many of us didn't come out at that time and he said a few didn't make it. I was getting scared a little and I almost didn't want to go. The not knowing of what it was like there was scaring me. Thomas came over to me and told me to go back to where the radio was and pick it up from Benny. Then Lieutenant Ervin came back and went straight to Thomas. I knew that we were going to be the point team for the battalion. I put the radio on my back and saw that the rest of the guys in our squad were getting their gear on. Before Thomas was finished with the lieutenant and saw that we were already moving up front, he said, "You guys know when we are getting the shit details," and we all just grinned.

As we walked up to the front of the rest of the battalion in a staggered column, the guys from the other companies were telling us good luck. I noticed it in their faces that they were glad that 2nd Platoon Charlie took the point and in a way they seemed secure with us out in front of them. Charlie was the point man for the whole battalion. He walked up the dirt road until the word was passed to stop. We went up the road about 200 meters before we stopped.

As I sat down again with the radio on my back without the pack-board, I remembered what Charlie had said about the last time they walked down this road leading into Phu An and running into a N.V.A. Regiment. I could feel the butterflies in my stomach and I was hoping that we would not hit them. I couldn't figure out why we were sitting here, but the word was passed not to move out yet. It must have been a half-hour before I heard on the radio that we were to move out. I told Thomas and he waved at the point man, Charlie, to move out. The guys said that there was a lot of blood from the dead and wounded on this dirt road since the last time they came back. One of the guys said that it was about 7000 meters from here. The guys in front of me were walking about fifty yards apart in a staggered column. Then Thomas moved out and he told me to be about 25 feet from him in case something came across the radio.

As we were moving, I could hear the big guns from somewhere firing up in Phu An. Van Meeteren, who was behind me, said that it was the 175mm guns from the Army at Camp Carroll firing for us. The rounds were passing us to their destination, and as they passed they sounded like a freight car coming in sideways. I was glad that I wasn't at the other end receiving those rounds.

Soon I started to get the shakes and butterflies like I never had before in my life. It was never like this when I played football in high school, or at least it wasn't this bad. I knew the other guys were hoping that we would not run into the N.V.A. again and have such a hell of a firefight on our hands. They were all concentrating on what was around them by listening to the noises in the surrounding area. Back in the distance was the village about a thousand meters up the road and on the right side was a Marine base being built. They had 105s and 155s up there on the hill and the bulldozers had buried all of the grass.

In a short time, about 45 minutes later, we were far away from everyone and everything got very quiet. I heard on the radio that they were calling me and I answered, "This is Charlie 2-1, over." The voice on the radio asked me if we had seen the tiger and pig yet. I then asked Thomas if we saw the tiger and pig and he told me that they hadn't come up yet. Thomas then told me that the tiger was a tank and the pig was the Ontos. The Ontos is a track vehicle with six 106 rifles on it, three on each side with two men in it, a driver and a loader. I called back and told them that they had not gotten here yet.

The word was passed on the radio that we were to stop and that 3rd Platoon would take over as the point for a while. I passed the message up to Sgt. Thomas and he walked up to the next guy and told him to pass the word to stop. I then got off the dirt road and faced outward toward the hills that surrounded the road. The guys who were on the other side of the road were facing the other direction. I heard a noise that sounded like a tank and soon it came into view. The tank was following 3rd Platoon as they were going past us. They were gesturing quietly with their hands and mouths that they were going to take the honors of being point for us. I grinned and watched them go past. As the tank passed I thought that the gooks would be crazy for trying to hit us. Then I realized that the guys were starting to move and I got up and started with them. I made sure that my rifle was facing my side of the dirt road so that I could protect this side while the guys on the other side protected their side.

The dirt road wiggled around the top of the hills, and the bush was only about a foot high and there was hardly any cover if the enemy wanted to attack us but I knew that they were not that stupid. The radio straps were starting to dig into my shoulders through my flak jacket, and it seemed that I had traveled a little longer than the first time I'd carried the radio. As I was walking and keeping my eyes moving, I could see on the dirt road blood that had been spilled before from this outfit. Then I heard the Ontos coming up the road. Now I felt that we were very strong and powerful, and I was even hoping that the N.V.A would be stupid enough to hit us. I wanted to get back at them for what they had done to us before. I just couldn't get it out of my mind. The weather, of course, was getting hotter and more humid everyday.

The sun was starting to go down and my stomach was starting to moan for food. Then the word was passed to stop and Captain Curd and his C.P. group moved up to the point platoon. We waited for a few minutes and then the word was passed for the rest of the men to move up as well. Captain Curd was telling our point man that we were to go to our right and set up part of the 360 degree perimeter. We got off the road and Lieutenant Ervin quickly came up and directed the squad leaders where to put their squads. I realized that the more I saw of Lieutenant Ervin, the more I didn't like the way he acted to the squad leaders as well as to the men in our platoon. He always made sure that he was the boss and had the last word.

We took our positions on the hill and Thomas told me that I was to go back to my fire team and stay with them for the night. I found my fire team and took off the radio. I got my E-tool and started helping Charlie, Van, and Chadwell in digging our fighting hole. We had the hole down about three feet and it was good enough for the night. Chadwell said that we had better make our dinner before the sun went completely down. Already there wasn't going to be too much light left and we had to hurry up and get our food cooked. I got my C-rations out of the sock I had tied to my radio, got into the fighting hole and started up my fire with the heat tab, a blue tablet wrapped in cellophane, which I opened and lit with a match in a B-3 ration can which I had just opened. It only took a few minutes to cook my food, and soon I was eating my lunch and dinner as one. The other guys were doing the same thing. The mosquitoes were out and they were really biting us. When we were all finished eating we put on our insect repellent. It did a little good, but not much.

Chadwell then gave us our times for watch, and of course we had to watch twice, one hour each time during the night. I got my poncho and covered myself up with it so that the mosquitoes wouldn't bite me and began to think about home and how my parents were. I couldn't believe that I was starting to get homesick and wanted to be home. Then my mind traveled on and I was thinking about Stretch, the gunsmith that worked at Bill and Bob Sporting Goods Store in my hometown, Groesbeck, Ohio, a little town just outside of Cincinnati. I remembered how Stretch had told me to join the Marine Corps so that I could play football at Quantico. He said that I had a good chance of making it and that I could get into college or get a chance to play Pro Football from there. But instead of playing football at Quantico, I was playing football with the gooks, trying to stay alive. I knew that Stretch never thought that I would be here and that his intention was to see me play football at Quantico. I knew if I got back that I would raise a little hell with him. I had worked for Stretch in the shop sanding down the gunstocks and refinishing them. I had learned a lot from Stretch; his first name was Roland, but everyone called him Stretch because he stood 6'6" tall.

The night was clear and there were a lot of stars, and it seemed cooler than the night before. I heard Chadwell tell Charlie that first watch was on. As I lay there on the ground listening to the sounds around us, I was thinking that tomorrow would be my first actual firefight. I somehow fell off to sleep and then I felt someone kick me at the bottom of my foot; Van gave me the watch and whispered to me that it was my turn. I got up and walked over to the hole, which was only a couple of feet away and sat on the edge of the fighting hole with the radio in it. As I was looking at the stars I had a strange feeling of being all alone in the world. I then had this feeling that I didn't want to die and I was afraid of death. I looked back and saw Van getting under his poncho and going off to sleep. I realized that since I'd joined my outfit that I hadn't had a chance to sleep all night but once since I'd been with my platoon out in the field. I looked around and saw that everyone was sleeping except a few of us that were sitting on the edges of our fighting holes watching and listening in case the enemy came. Something inside of me was telling me that tomorrow was going to be the biggest day of my life besides the first night when I arrived in the field, and that I hoped that I would be able to pull my weight. My mind was racing about everything: home, parents, brother, sister, friends from school and some of the guys that I had met in the Marine Corps. After I clicked the handset twice for the second time on my watch, I got up and kicked Charlie at the bottom of his foot and whispered to him that it was his turn and gave the watch and handset to him. I grabbed my poncho and again covered myself up and tried to get some sleep. It seemed that this time in the night the mosquitoes were not out as much.

Van again kicked me at the bottom of my foot and whispered to me that it was my turn again. I got up and went over to the fighting hole-this was my last watch for the night. I knew that when my watch was over I had to get all of them up for the day. I looked at the watch and the time was 04:02 in the morning. The sky was still very dark. I sat there thinking about what today would be like for all of us. Some of the guys that were sleeping were tossing and turning. I hoped that I was ready for it. I just hoped that I could handle what I had to do. I didn't want the guys in the platoon to think that I was yellow and couldn't do my job. At 04:30 on the radio, the platoon radioman called me and told me if all was secure, to press my handset twice and I did. At this time the sky was starting to get light. About 04:45, the skies were getting even lighter out and it was almost any time for the sun to come up for the day. Then the platoon radioman called me for the last time and asked if all secure; I pressed twice and then let the guys sleep a little longer, about fifteen more minutes. Some of the guys were getting up before 05:00 and were starting up their little fires to heat their food. The sun was barely coming up now and almost everyone was getting up around the perimeter, including Charlie and Van. It was so quiet and peaceful at this time of the day, even the weather was cool and felt nice. I started cooking breakfast out of the C-ration can, Ham and Eggs. After I ate, I grabbed my gear and made sure that I was ready. Charlie was next to me and he said that Phu An wasn't too far from here. Charlie seemed a little more quiet today then other days in the field. Even Chadwell and Van seemed to be to themselves as well. The mood of the whole battalion was the same as the guys in my fire team. The sky was blue and the sun was just peeking over the hills. Word was passed that the tank and Ontos were to go back. We could hear them turning over their engines and began to move back from where they had come from the day before. As I was looking at the guys in the fire team, I realized that everyone was putting on their game faces for what lay ahead.

Chapter Five

Charlie didn't look like he was afraid and the feeling was coming over me as well. As I looked around the guys in our platoon, I could almost feel the tightness among the guys as well as the whole battalion. All of us had a job to do and we were going to do it the best way we all knew how. We all knew in the fire team that they would be calling us up to take point, again. Word was passed that Alpha Company was to take point and our company would be behind them and then Bravo and Delta Company. Alpha Company was walking past us and we were gathering next to the dirt road wishing the guys luck. As Alpha Company walked past us in a staggered column, they seemed to be ready for what was ahead of us and started going down to Phu An.. Then Lieutenant Ervin quickly came up and told us that we were next. Sergeant Thomas told our other fire team that they were to go first and then us. We got to the bottom of the hill when all of a sudden, holy hell broke loose. I could hear the A.K 47 rifles firing on the other side of the stream that we were about to cross. I stopped and squatted and was waiting for word to move up to where the firing was. I could feel myself being scared for the first time in my whole life; I mean really scared. The firing went on for about fifteen minutes and it didn't seem to slow down at all. Charlie was next to me and he said he knew that it was coming, and the N.V.A. had been waiting for us this time. I knew that we were in for it. On the radio that I was carrying I heard that Charlie Company was to go over to the other side of the stream and pick up the dead and wounded. Sgt. Thomas then told some of us to help Alpha Company. I got up and told Sgt. Thomas that I was going to help out in getting the dead and wounded guys. I took off the radio and handed it to Thomas. The rest of the guys from our company were to stay here in case they were needed or if the enemy attacked us. Chadwell, Van, Charlie and I went over to the other side of the stream and walked about twenty feet when one of the wounded guys walked back to us. He fell on the dirt road and Charlie and I grabbed him and walked with him back up the top of the hill. When we got him back there, Captain Curd said to put him with the other wounded and dead on the side of the road that we just came down from. We laid him down and then I saw four of the guys carrying another wounded guy. But this time as they laid him down, they covered his face and body with his poncho. I knew that he was dead. I walked over to where he was and saw one arm and hand sticking out of the poncho. His arm had turned yellowish and it was making me sick. I turned away and felt that I wanted to vomit, but I couldn't. I told myself that I had to go back and do my job and help. I wanted to hide and not go back. Sergeant Thomas was watching me from a distance

Charlie and I as well as the other guys started walking back down the hill and as I walked past Sergeant Thomas he told me not to think about it. I couldn't help thinking about the dead guy; they were still bringing back the dead and wounded. We reached the bottom of the hill and crossed the twenty-foot stream. I felt the cold water on my legs as we walked over to the other side. When I got to the other side again there was blood all over the dirt road where the enemy had killed and wounded our sister company. The fighting was still going on but farther away from us. I walked up the road that had a little incline and on the edge of the road was a hedgerow that followed along the dirt road. We were getting closer to where the fighting was. I was walking very slowly, trying to look through the hedgerow to see if I could see the enemy. I then took the safety off my M-14 rifle, ready to fire for the first time in my life with real ammo. I then remembered the first night in the field when they hit us with mortar rounds and how it made me mad that we couldn't fight back, but now we could do something by firing back at them.

As I was walking up the road I saw the packs that the guys had left behind. I walked about 100 meters, then saw someone in the bushes, I turned and was about to fire my rifle when I saw that it was a wounded Marine. I heard a couple of rounds coming toward me and I knelt down and fired back at the hedgerow that was about 200 meters away. I went over where the wounded Marine was in the hedgerow and we both fired our rifles at the enemy. A couple of Marines were coming near us and I gestured to them that we had a wounded man here. They came up to where I was firing back at the hedgerow. I kept on firing down close to the ground because the enemy had to be low also. When they got the wounded man down the road a little way, I stopped firing and listened for any more return fire. The enemy was not firing at all and I hoped that I had gotten him. I helped the other men carry the guy back, and as we got up the hill again, I saw that a lot of guys were wounded and a few were killed. The ones that were dead were on the edge of the dirt road and the wounded were being treated by the corpsmen at the top of the hill that we had been on the night before.

The word was being passed that the choppers were coming and we needed the guys that were around to help get the wounded men on the choppers. I saw the choppers coming and only two at a time were coming down. The word was passed to get the wounded men out first and then the dead. I helped in getting one of the wounded guys on the chopper. As I got back Sgt. Thomas called me over and told me to get with my fire team. I remembered that there were some guys getting off the choppers as we were putting on the wounded guys. Then the word was passed that the short timers were the ones that were coming back out to help us. These were the guys that had less than fifteen days to go before their tour was up before they were to go home. I could not believe how tight this outfit was, the old guys caring for the young guys out in the field.

I went back to the radio, and I just sat next to the road listening to what was going to happen next. Soon I heard the word being passed around asking if we had gotten everyone out of there. A few minutes someone from Alpha Company asked where Sergeant Singleton was. Someone else from the same platoon said that he had saved the guys in his squad.

Everyone knew that Singleton had to still be in there, with the N.V.A. The Battalion Commander said that Charlie Company was going in there to get him but, before we did, he called for air strikes, so we all waited for the jets to come. We waited for about an hour when the F-4 Phantom jets, two of them, finally arrived to help us. They made a pass first, a couple of hundred feet above us and went high in the air and came almost straight down. One of the guys said that they were using the 20mm cannons that were on the planes. It sounded like a heavy swarm of bees. They made about five or six passes each and unloaded everything they had. Then they began to leave and I knew that it was our turn to go back in there.

Two hours had passed and I heard on the radio that Charlie 6 was calling Charlie 2 and I told Sgt. Thomas that the captain was calling Ervin. We both knew without a word that we were going to be the point squad for the battalion. I looked at Thomas and I noticed that he was a little on the nervous side. It was the first time that Thomas showed himself as being scared. In a way, I was hoping to be the point squad going back in there, but this time I didn't feel as scared as when the fire fight went on earlier. I felt that I could handle myself now under fire. Sgt. Thomas passed the word to the rest of the guys in our squad to go and that we had the honors of being the point squad going in looking for Sgt. Singleton. I could hear the 2nd Platoon radioman calling me and I told him that we were already on our way and that we were moving up to be the point team. Sgt. Thomas told Chadwell that his team had the point, that Thomas and I were behind them, and then our other fire team. We started out in a staggered column and the guys that we passed were telling us good luck and to watch ourselves. It seemed to me that even though we didn't know each other from the other companies that all of them cared. I felt really secure by them caring about us. I was getting the butterflies again because of being the point for the whole battalion. I was thinking of the guys that were wounded and the ones that were dead. I hoped that we didn't get it like them, but I knew that it was our turn now. We crossed the stream and started up the road that led into Phu An.

Chapter Six

We had walked about 200 meters when the word was passed to stop and wait for the rest of the company to move up to us. As we waited, all of us were watching everything out in front of us and it seemed so very quiet, like something was going to explode soon. We could see a wide-open large field to our left. Then the word was passed that on our right side would be 1st Platoon and on our left side would be 3rd Platoon. Behind 1st Platoon was to be Bravo Company and behind 3rd Platoon was to be Alpha Company and Delta Company to cover our rear. As the other two platoons got on line with us the word was passed to move out into the wide-open field. I heard on the radio to keep a sharp eye out for the sergeant. I used my hands to tell Sgt. Thomas to move out slowly and he relayed it to the rest of the guys with his hands.

As we walked up into the wide-open field we could see that there were hedgerows on each side. We reached the hedgerow that was in front of us and went through it and again there was another wide-open field. We had walked about 300 meters into the open field when our squad found the dead sergeant. I walked over to where Sgt. Thomas was and the guys in our squad put Sgt. Singleton into the poncho. We were right on the edge of the next hedgerow; there were dead N.V.A all around the dead sergeant. It looked like he took a hell of a lot of them with him. There were a couple of guys that were taking pictures of the dead N.V.A. I just kept my eyes and ears open out in front of me in case I heard the enemy. I was about two feet from one of the dead N.V.A soldiers whose head was gone. There were thousands of flies eating his flesh, but it didn't make me sick like my buddies who had died. There were five or six other N.V.A. with the N.V.A. whose head was gone in a fighting hole that were also dead. It made me feel good to see the beheaded N.V.A., the satisfaction of getting back at them. I then moved over to where the dead sergeant was and helped carry him out with the help of Bignami, Van and Quick. I got on the radio and told Charlie 2 that we had found Sergeant Singleton and were getting ready to leave. I could feel the hairs on my back standing straight up and it was too damn quiet. Frank Bignami, Al Quick, Van and I grabbed the dead sergeant and without a word started moving back to where we had come.

We got on this very small trail leading back to the rest of the battalion. We must have walked about twenty feet when all hell broke loose again, but this time it sounded louder than before. As soon as the firing started all of us dropped the dead sergeant on the trail and ourselves to the ground.

Sgt. Thomas was in front of us and he started digging with both his hands and feet into the small trail. I couldn't believe what I was seeing. His head was trying to get lower than his body. I had the phone next to my ear and nothing was going on or anyone was saying anything. The N.V.A. were firing from where we just left. It looked like we were in a very large U-shaped ambush. Our whole battalion was in the ambush. The only place that the enemy did not fire from was from the rear. I looked back to see what the other guys in my fire team were doing. The dead sergeant was on the trail behind me and the rest of the guys were off the trail firing in the directions that the enemy was. Van and Quick were behind the dead sergeant and off the trail firing their rifles at the N.V.A. Quick was between Sgt. Singleton and a banana tree to kept from getting shot at from the N.V.A. who was shooting at him but the rounds were going into the banana tree and Sgt. Singleton. Van got up and was about ten feet away from the N.V.A. that was firing at us and before the N.V.A. could put another clip into his AK-47 Van killed him. At this same time Van also saved Captain Curd and the gunny lives besides Quick. Sgt. Thomas, called back to me without looking and told me to listen on the radio and to see what or if there were any instructions. I was firing my rifle off to the right side and away from Bignami. Bignami was next to the hedgerow shooting at the N.V.A. that were near by. I stopped firing and told Thomas, "O.K" and kept the phone next to my ear. I could hear the rounds flying over my head and on each side of me. I kept my head next to the ground and as I lay there, I wanted like hell to get up and run out of there as fast as my legs could take me. I knew that I had to get off the trail. But I knew that if I got up that I would be a dead man. It took a lot of courage to maintain my composure and it was very, very hard. I looked around to see if I could fire back at the enemy and the only place was off to the right side and back at the hedgerow. I fired off a couple of rounds and Thomas told me to listen to the radio and to quit firing. I looked at Thomas and he was still trying to dig a hole with his hands and feet. He wouldn't fire his rifle at all. Still there was no word on the radio. What seemed like an hour was only twenty-five minutes.

As I lay there listening to the radio, a round from the enemy hit my helmet and grazed it. Then a couple of seconds later I felt this strange feeling, starting from my toes and running up the back of my legs and body to the top of my head. It felt like there was someone lying on top of me. I could almost feel the warmth of it while it was over me and it was telling me that nothing was going to happen to me over here. I felt that I was back home in a movie theater in the front row watching what was going on. This feeling stayed with me for a couple of minutes and I felt secure inside. It again told me that nothing was going to happen to me in Vietnam. The next thing, I felt like it got up off of me and left but was near by.

With the phone next to my ear, I heard the company radioman tell the three platoons to get back by fire teams to the dirt road. I told Thomas that the company radioman had said that all fire teams were to get back to the dirt road and then to the stream on their own. Thomas told me to tell the guys behind me to get Sergeant Singleton and that we were getting out of there before we got cut off for good. I got up and grabbed the poncho and the rest of the team grabbed the other three corners of the poncho and we started heading back. Thomas took off quickly and headed back to where the rest of the battalion was. The four of us moved the best we could carrying Sergeant Singleton on the trail leading back to Delta Company. We couldn't use our rifles because we had only one free hand. The fighting didn't slow down at all and it seemed that the enemy was moving. There were other fire teams leap frogging back to where we had come. As we were moving back on the small trail, the arm of Sergeant Singleton was hitting me in the back of my calf muscle. The four of us finally reached the hedgerow with Sergeant Singleton. There were other teams that were in the open field behind us still leap frogging back. Delta Company was in the hedgerow next to the road that lead to the stream. All we had was the open field in front of us, then we would reach Delta Company. Thomas was moving out faster than us and the next thing he was gone. We made sure that Sergeant Singleton was going home, even if we got hit ourselves. When we got though the hedgerow into the next open field, the enemy wasn't firing. The fire teams that were on the other side of the hedgerow that we had gone though were still getting hit. The arm of Sergeant Singleton was still hitting me in the back of my leg and I was getting this sick feeling of him hitting me. I wanted to ask him to stop but I knew that he would not be able to since he was dead.

We were in the middle of the open field when I heard on the radio that the 105s were going to give us cover fire to get out. I told the guys with me that our 105s were getting ready to fire where we had been. We could hear the rounds hitting into the other open field where there were only a couple of fire teams left and I was hoping that they had gotten out of there before the rounds hit. We finally got to the dirt road and walked back to the stream with Sergeant Singleton. Then the rifles and machine guns firing from the enemy stopped and all anyone could hear was our artillery firing. We finally reached the stream and crossed it with Sergeant Singleton. As we crossed the stream, we kept the body of Sergeant Singleton above the ice cold water, and it really felt cold. The jagged rocks that were in the stream made it that much more difficult to cross with Sergeant Singleton. As we got to the other side, four other guys from Sergeant Singleton's squad came up to us and carried him to a safe place for the chopper to take him out. Bignami, Van and Quick went back to where Charlie Company was.

The Sergeant's squad was carrying their Sergeant Singleton back up the hill. My arms and hands were tired from carrying the sergeant from where we found him to the stream. It was difficult to carry someone under fire for a great distant without getting hit ourselves. I was glad that I had been one of the guys to carry him out. Sergeant Singleton received the MEDAL OF HONOR for saving his squad that day. I felt very good about it. I could feel my whole body being drained from this firefight that we had been in all day. It was still going on. Captain Curd was here at the stream with his C.P. group, making sure that all of the fire teams got back.

A lieutenant with a handle-bar mustache came over to me and asked if I had seen a sniper. I told him no. I asked the lieutenant if I could go with him and he said that I'd better ask the captain first. I went over to the captain, waited until he finished talking to a couple of guys, then I asked him if I could go with the lieutenant to look for the sniper. The captain said that he needed a radioman because his radioman was not here and he needed me. I told the captain that I wasn't that good on the radio and that I was still learning. He then told me that this would be great on the job training under fire. I went back to the lieutenant and told him that the captain wanted me here and that I was to be his radioman. So the lieutenant took off into the bush on the other side of the stream. As I watched him leave, I wished that I could have gone with him. I went back to the captain and he told me that my call sign was Charlie 6. One of the squads called Charlie 6, which was me, and said that one of the guys had lost one leg and the other one was just hanging on from one of our own 105 rounds that had just hit. I informed the captain and he told the other radioman to call for a chopper with a doctor. Our 105s were still firing at the area we had been. The other radioman was very calm on the radio when calling for the chopper and doctor. The same squad called again and this time I tried to relax when I talked. They told me that they were setting up relay teams of four men about every thirty yards in getting the wounded man back to the stream. They told me on the radio that they were about 300 meters away. The captain came over to me and asked what was happening and I told him that they were setting up relay teams of four men all the way to the stream. Then I heard that the chopper with the doctor came and he was coming down the hill to us at the stream. The sun was down with a little light left, and it was going on evening. Our artillery rounds were still going over our heads while the relay teams were carrying the wounded guy. The captain then told me to get on the radio and asked if there was anyone left besides the relay teams with the wounded guy. I called Charlie 1, Charlie 2 and Charlie 3 to make sure that they had everyone accounted for. The radioman called and told me that the name of the wounded guy was Richard Strouse from 2nd platoon Charlie Co's mortar team.

The doctor arrived and was next to the captain waiting for the wounded man. All of us at the stream saw the relay team coming toward us. The strain on all of the faces of the guys was evident. The stream seemed to be running faster than earlier. They slowly got into the stream with Strouse and at the same time they kept talking to him. A couple of us got into the stream to help out the relay team so that Strouse wouldn't get any water on him. I could feel the jagged rocks under the water. The water was much colder than before. I grabbed onto the poncho with the other guys that came in to help and one of the guys slipped into the water but kept the poncho from going down. We got Strouse to the other side of the stream and laid him down and the rest of the guys there came up to where Strouse was and grabbed their ponchos and covered the doctor and the wounded guy so that no one could see the flash lights, The rest of us just sat around waiting to hear how the wounded guy was. Several more guys came over to help out in making sure that the ponchos covered the doctor and wounded man. It must have been about ten minutes later when the doctor came out of the cover and told the captain that there was nothing he could do out here but to get him back to the rear. The doctor said that he couldn't operate here and said that the guys that had wrapped his legs up and talked to him all the way back did one hell of a job by keeping him alive. He said that he had never seen a bunch of guys in an outfit disregard their own lives and run under fire from our artillery and the N.V.A. firing at them while keeping Richard Strouse alive.

The doctor said that Strouse was going to make it but they had better get him out before night set in, since he had lost a lot of blood. Captain Curd told the other radioman to call for a chopper and to get the doc and the wounded man out as soon as possible. The radioman went to work on the radio and after a couple of minutes said that the chopper was here and that we better hurry up and get him up the hill. There were six guys and they picked the wounded guy up and carried him back up the hill. They were still talking to him and making sure that he stayed awake until they got him back to the hospital. I was never so glad to hear that he was going to make it back. I got up and all of us went back up the hill and I could feel myself getting tired and being drained.

We got up to the top of the hill and the captain told me to go back to my team and that his radioman was back now. Everyone had the same fighting holes they had the night before. My fire team was eating. When I got to them, they were tired and exhausted and they told me that they were glad to see me back. I took off the radio and slowly sat down. I then looked at what I had to eat and I didn't feel like eating much so the only thing I ate were some cookies and candy. All of us could hear the chopper coming and all of us grabbed our rifles and got ready in case we got fired upon. It must have been ten minutes until the chopper landed and they put Strouse and Doc on the chopper and it quickly left heading south. Charlie and Van Meeteren were with Strouse when he got hit by our 105s. They helped in bandaging his legs and by talking to him kept him alive. Ted Van Meeteren told me that he saved Captain Curd's ass when we were heading back with Sergeant Singleton.

I then looked over to the other hole and saw Sergeant Thomas and I remembered back down there earlier when we were carrying out Sergeant Singleton that Thomas had been digging a hole with his hands and feet. He wouldn't even fire his rifle. Deep down inside of me I knew that I couldn't trust him in a firefight for any kind of support. I took off the rest of my fighting gear and I could feel the weight of the day lifting off my shoulders. I was never so tired in my whole life; even two a day football practices couldn't hold a candle to this day. I knew that I had aged today; I just didn't have the spark of being lively anymore. I could feel the fatigue setting in now and I wanted to get a good night's sleep but I knew that it was not to be. I knew now that the only people that cared about us were the guys that went through what we had gone through today. I remembered earlier today when the short timers came out to help us out, even dying in making sure that all of us got out alive. Today had seemed like eternity, I thought that it would never end. Chadwell told me that I had third watch, I asked Charlie what time it was, and he said 19:45. I then got out my poncho and covered myself and tried to get some sleep.

As I lay there, I didn't feel like talking to anyone. I could tell that everyone else felt the same way. I looked at Charlie and he knew how I felt and that there was nothing anyone could do for any of us. My body was very tired but it wouldn't unwind. I was thinking about what had happened and what I had done by helping carry Sergeant Singleton with the rest of our fire team and about when Strouse only had one leg just hanging on with the other leg totally gone. I was so proud of all the guys that made up the relay teams, talking to him under fire just keeping him alive and most of all disregarding their own lives. I remembered Sergeant Singleton's arm hitting the back of my calf muscle while carrying him and when we laid him down and his arm turned a little yellowish. I was glad that we got him out of there and for him to be able to go home. I remembered before we all went back in to get him that a couple of the guys in his squad said that he gave up his life by charging the enemy position so that his squad would make it back out alive. I then quickly thought of Sergeant Thomas and I knew that he wouldn't save his squad-but his squad would end up saving his ass.

Chapter Seven

The next thing I knew, Van kicked me at the bottom of my foot, and I got up slowly. Van realized that I hadn't slept at all because I was thinking about what had happened earlier. I went over to the radio and heard someone say, "If all secured, press your handset twice, if not, press it once." So I pressed it twice and heard the platoon radioman call our other squad to see if they were all right. As I was sitting next to the fighting hole I looked around and everyone was covered by their ponchos. It reminded me of earlier when we carried the dead and wounded men out. There were a few of the guys who were moving around in their ponchos and having trouble trying to sleep. I knew that the enemy wasn't going to hit us tonight because of the fighting that we had with them yesterday. The N.V.A. had enough of the 1st Battalion 9th Marines for awhile. I was really proud of all the guys in this battalion in watching each other's backs during the fire fight. I remembered a couple of the guys telling Strouse that he better not go to sleep or die after we carried his ass to the doc. Then I remembered that strange feeling I had that covered my whole body telling me that nothing was going to happen to me over here and that I could do whatever I wanted. I didn't want to tell anyone for fear that they would laugh at me. And beside that, who would ever believe me in the first place? It was still hard for me to understand it. I took off my helmet and I looked at it and could feel where the bullet had dented it. I thought that a bullet hit me when I was lying on the path with Sergeant Singleton. As I looked around I knew that there was one good thing about this battalion and that was all of the guys looked out for one another and also made sure that everyone would go back home, even if they died or were wounded. It was an unwritten rule in this battalion that everyone would be taken care of and no one would ever be left out in the field for the enemy to have. I knew that I felt good in case if I died that the guys would make sure that I made it back to the States. My watch was over and I waited for the platoon radioman to call me to see if I was secure or not. I kicked Chadwell and he got up and took over the watch.

As I lay down, I could tell that I was ready for sleep and as I looked up at the sky I could see all of those stars again. The next thing I knew I was off to sleep. I thought that I'd just closed my eyes when Van kicked me at the bottom of my foot and I got up. I couldn't believe it went that fast. I got up and went over to the radio and sat down. As I sat there watching and listening, I went over what I had done yesterday and I hoped that we didn't have to go through this again but I knew deep down inside of me we would. I didn't like losing guys I knew and how much it hurt inside when someone in your outfit dies. It was like a part of you dies as well. Now, I knew why my father never talked about what he did out in the jungles when he fought against the Japanese. My hour was up and I woke up Chadwell and whispered to him that it was his turn. I went back to my poncho and covered myself up and made sure that he was at the fighting hole before I went off to sleep.

The next thing I knew Chadwell got us all up and said it was time to get something to eat. I could tell that we were going back into Phu An but no one said anything, but I knew that it was on everyone's mind. As we all ate, no one said a word. After all of us were finished with eating, the word was passed to saddle up and that we were moving out. We all rolled up our ponchos and got ready to go back into Phu An but the word was passed that we were going back to Cam Lo. I knew that had to be the village where we bought the bread. Charlie said that it was a nice 7,000 meters to walk back, the same way we came on the dirty, dusty road. The spirit of the guys was flying, just happy to get the hell out of here. But in the back of my mind I knew that we had some unfinished business yet to do. I picked up my helmet and I noticed where the bullet had put a nick in it. I remembered that the dead sergeant who we carried out had six bullets in him when we found him.

Then the word was passed to saddle up and to get on the road in a staggered column. As the battalion got on the road, the word was 2nd platoon Charlie Co. was to be the rear security as we left. As I got on the road behind Van in a staggered column, I saw our platoon sergeant was right behind me. He had gray hair and he was somewhere in his early 40's. We started moving out and I could feel the platoon sergeant breathing down my neck. I didn't like it with him being so close to me. Then the next thing was he started to mouth off to me by telling me that I was too far from the guy in front of me but as I got closer he then would tell me that I was too close. I was starting to get a little pissed with him. A couple of minutes passed; he was coming up to me and as he got close I pointed my rifle at him from the hip and he got the message that I wasn't going to take any more shit from him. He then went on past me and up to the platoon C.P. group. That was the one and only time I ever saw him in our platoon.

Chapter Eight

After a while we were getting close to the artillery base. They were busy building up their defenses, next to the village called Cam Lo. I knew that we had made it back safely. As we walked through the village and got to the bridge the word was passed to get off the road and to wait for the trucks to pick us up. As I sat down on the edge of the dusty road I looked at myself and I couldn't believe my jungle pants. Instead of being green, they were now almost brown and some of the dirt was rubbed in with my sweat. I looked like I needed a bath and that included my jungle clothes. I didn't wear my jungle shirt during the day because of the heat but I would wear it during the night to keep the mosquitoes from biting me. After about an hour, the six-bys were on their way and we were to make sure that we had everything ready. No one got up but just sat there waiting for the trucks. Finally they arrived and the word was passed that we were to get on them. The trucks took us back to Camp Carroll and when we got there Lieutenant Ervin told the squad leaders that we had the same fighting holes as before. The old platoon sergeant got his orders to go home and I was very happy that he was gone. I knew that if he had stayed that I would have beaten the hell out of him.

The next day came and the word was passed that we were going to trade in our M-14 rifle for the new M-16s. I didn't want to turn in my rifle because I felt very secure with it. I didn't know a damn thing about the new rifle. One of the sergeants who came from our C.P. group called us up and told us to bring our rifles and magazines with us. He then said that we were going over to pick up our new rifles and magazines and to get into platoon formation and most of us were laughing and carrying on like kids. He than told us his name and it was Sergeant Tony Lefefe and that he was the new platoon sergeant. He then called, "Right face;" and we turned right and he then said, "Walk." What we didn't know that there had been a disagreement between Sgt. Thomas and Sgt. Lefefe about who was to be the next platoon sergeant and Lefefe won out. When we got to the tent, the sergeants were waiting for us and then we got into a single file and each of us turned in our M-14 rifle and magazines and received eight magazines and the new M-16s. We were on the backside of Camp Carroll and there was a small rifle range that had been made up for us. The distance from the target to us was only fifty feet. They also gave us a box of ammo each and told us to put only ten rounds in our magazine. We sat around and loaded up the magazine with the ammo and after a couple of minutes the sergeant showed us how easy it was for us to open it up. Then they showed us how to fire the rifle and the rounds came out the right side of the rifle. Us left-handed guys had to make sure that our right arm was directly below the bottom part of the rifle so that the rounds were not hitting our arm. We got into a prone position and fired a single shot at our targets. We made our adjustments by turning the sight up or down and left or right. Once we got our sights corrected, they told us to put the selector on fully automatic, and we shot a short burst. The rifle hardly moved and the longer we fired automatic, it still hardly moved. We then fired upright and as I fired the rifle one round at a time with my right arm under the rifle, the rounds were still hitting my right arm. I knew that I would have to turn the rifle on its side so that the rounds wouldn't hit my arm. We fired all of the rounds that they gave us and they told us that we were finished and now experts. I could tell that there was a very light kick to the rifle, not like the M-14s. When I was done firing my new rifle, my right arm had a few shell marks.

I was finished with knowing my new rifle and sat down and waited for the rest of the guys to get the feel of their new rifles and of course lining up their sights. Sgt. Lefefe than told everyone to get in platoon formation and that he was going to take us back to our area. He then said, "Left face!" and as we turned to our left, he then said, "Walk," and the guys in the platoon including me all laughed again. We then walked back to the area and as we did, there were four of the Army 175mm guns. They had a very long barrel, and were very large. When we got back Sgt. Lefefe then told us, "Dismiss!" and our fire team went back to our fighting hole. We then wanted to clean our new rifles since we had just fired them and none of us had a clue what to do; so a couple of us went over to our corpsman, Doc Marsh, who did carry the M-16 rifle and asked him. We asked Doc how to break down the M-16 and he showed us how it was done. He said, "There are two pins on the left side near the trigger. Push them through the rifle to the other side." Then Doc Marsh said that was it, and boy how easy, it was a lot simpler than the M-14. Doc Marsh was the only corpsman who carried any kind of weapon in the company. There was only one corpsman per platoon and a company corpsman.

We then went back and showed the rest of the guys in our fire team what to do. I got out my toothbrush that I had in my left pocket in my flak jacket and cleaned my rifle. After I was finished I put oil on the rifle and one of the guys from the platoon passed the word not to put too much oil, just a little bit. Too much oil would jam the rifle. So I wiped away most of the oil with my jungle shirt. I started putting the rounds in all eight of my magazines as I was taking the ammo out of the bandoleers. In each of the bandoleers were six pockets that had paper boxes that carried 20 rounds in each. When I was finished I wanted to see if I could put the magazines in the bandoleers and it worked, so I put all of my magazines except for the one in the rifle and I was ready. Then someone said to only put in about 18 rounds in the magazines-if you put in twenty it could jam. What the hell kind of weapons are these? I took out three rounds to be on the safe side. I told Charlie, Van and Chadwell about putting the magazines in the bandoleers and they were also doing the same thing. Charlie had a couple of ammo pouches on his belt and he could put three of the magazines in each of them. All of us knew that eight magazines were not enough for us out in the bush. We all knew when we got in a fire fight with the N.V.A. The only time to pick up extra magazines would be lying around the dead men.

The next day came and the word was passed that we were going out again. But again, we didn't know where we were going. I gathered my fighting gear and put on my two bandoleers around my neck and across my body. One of the guys in our outfit was not going with us because his brother was over here and he had been told that he was leaving Vietnam. We could see in his eyes that he wanted to go with us but that just wasn't possible. I was glad that he was able to go home alive. He was taking pictures of us climbing onto the trucks. As I sat in the truck I remembered that he had taken a picture of me a few days before, coming from the mess hut.

As the trucks were starting to move out, the word was passed that we were going east and then down south on Highway 1. But we didn't know how far down south. I could hear the rest of the guys say they were glad that we didn't have to go back up to Phu An. There were a few of the guys who knew where we were going, but they wouldn't say. We traveled for a long time and all of us were getting sore asses from traveling. We were going past a lot of small villages along the side of Highway 1. As we passed, the children would run along the side of the highway next to the trucks, asking for chop-chop. Again some of the guys would throw "Ham and Mother fuckers" at them, which were lima beans and ham that a lot of the guys didn't like. The children were four to eight years old and very thin and most had hardly anything to wear, just shorts and sandals. They looked like they hadn't eaten for some time. The majority of us gave our C-rations which consisted of about three days worth of food. The people seemed to be very friendly down here and there didn't seem like there was much of a war going on in this area. The countryside was a little different too. The soil was getting more sandy, not like that hard clay dirt that was up north near the D.M.Z.

There was a bridge in front of us and some soldiers were watching it; they were ARVN, South Vietnamese Army. As we got closer, the bridge looked like a railroad bridge instead of a bridge for cars and trucks. It was made completely out of steel. The six-bys were making a sharp left to go on the one way bridge. As we were going over the bridge, I noticed that the ARVN guys were small compared to us in size and weight. They were very small and very thin. They were eating rice and a couple of them smiled as we drove by. We were coming into a town and the buildings were made out of concrete. Outside the town, the countryside was sandy on the left side of the road that was near the ocean and on the right side of the road, there were small rolling hills with very small bushes on them.

It must have been twenty minutes later when the trucks stopped on Highway 1. We got off the trucks and walked into the small rolling hills that were right of Highway 1, which was west. We must have walked about 2000 meters and we came up on a military base. Chadwell told me that it was Camp Evans. We got inside the camp and waited for about fifteen minutes when Thomas came over to us and said to follow him and he then showed us where we were going to be for the night. Thomas took us back outside the gate and our platoon set up a perimeter. Chadwell was told that this was our spot and to dig in for the night. The base was on a very wide hill; it wasn't very tall. We had been digging for about half an hour when word was passed that we were getting mail. The ground was not as hard as the ground up north. There were a couple of six-bys coming down from up north and they then turned left onto a dirt road that let into Camp Evans. As they came into the camp, on one of the trucks there were different colored sacks of orange, yellow and red plus C-rations cases. All of us knew that we were going to get mail today.

I sat down next to the fighting hole we had dug and I told Charlie that I hoped that I had mail this time and he looked at me and knew that I needed to hear from home. It was getting on around 14:00 hundred hours, when one of the guys from our C.P. group called for the squad leaders up to the C.P. to get their mail. As I sat there waiting for the mail to come, I started thinking that I had been in Vietnam almost 30 days. Thomas came back from the C.P. group with his hands full of mail and boxes and he then started calling out the names of the guys in the squad. Then he called, "Hammer," and started passing out about ten letters to me. I went back to the fighting hole and sat down, looked at the letters and saw that all of these letters were addressed to my last duty station back in the States. The first letter I opened was from my mother. All of the rest of the letters were from her except for one, which was from Jennifer. Mom started the letters off by saying, "Hi, Sweetie, How are you? Everyone is fine back at home." She would then go on to say what Ryan and Starr were doing. After I had read all of my mom's letters I then opened up Jennifer's letter and she was still talking about Ted. Ted was the guy that got me to write to her as a pen pal. In her letter, she asked me to watch over him when we got to Vietnam. When I was finished with her letter I knew that I had to let her know that they sent him to another outfit and I had no idea where he was. As I sat there with all of these letters, it felt great to have someone back in the States to write me. I noticed that there was some new men that had joined our outfit. The rest of the guys were still reading their letters and thinking of home. One of the new guys

was James Fowler who was with me in boot camp and all the way through
Staging Battalion. He was one of about seventeen men who was left behind
for the next plane to take over to Vietnam. He saw me and came over and
said that he was assigned to the squad I was with. I told him that he looked
great and he said that I looked like I had lost a lot of weight. James also said
that I looked tired and I told him that I was. James could tell that I had seen
some shit over here, but was afraid to ask. I quickly asked him how it was
back in the States and he said that everything was the same. I could sense
that he wanted to ask me questions about what it was like over here. I told
James that I was glad to see him. James picked up my spirits.

I asked James how many guys had come with him to this outfit and he
said that there were five of them. Then James said that the Army had steak
and fruit cocktail waiting for us. By now the sun was almost gone and the
word was passed that we were going to get some hot chow. As James and I
were going to the mess tent, I thought how he sounded like Gomer Pyle on
T.V. back in the States. I told James that I really liked hearing his voice...he
just smiled.

As we got to the Army tent, it was dark outside and getting very difficult
to see where we were going. We went inside the tent which had a couple of
lights. As we went through, we picked up paper plates then were asked how
many steaks we wanted; when they asked me I said, "two steaks." I went to
the next guy serving and he handed out fruit cocktail and put it on the side
of the steaks as well as on part of them. We went out the back of the tent in
the darkness, trying to find a place to sit and eat. They didn't give us anything to cut the steaks with and no fork or spoons to eat the fruit cocktail.
I had to use my hands to eat the fruit cocktail and steaks. My hands were
not very clean but I didn't give a damn, I was going to make sure I ate it all.
When I finished eating the first steak, I knew I was going to have a little
trouble eating the second one, but I was determined to eat it too. I finished
the fruit cocktail and one of the army cooks came out of the tent and said
there were more steaks if we wanted them. I decided to go back and take a
couple more steaks back with me to my fighting hole. The Army cooks told
us they were sorry that they didn't have anything else for us to eat. All of us
in our platoon for the first time in Vietnam had steaks to eat and we were
thankful to the Army for feeding us. As I got my steaks, I went back out
and got James and we went back to our fighting hole. The darkness made it
difficult to find our area. We walked back outside the gate of the camp and
finally made it to our position.

James told me that he would see me tomorrow and went over to his fire
team. Chadwell gave us our watches for the night. On both of my watches
I keep thinking about James and I hoped that nothing would happen to
him on his first night out in the field. He was a kind of guy who shouldn't
be over here in the first place. He was one of the easiest going, and nicest

guys anyone could ever meet. I remembered back in I.T.R. when we were on leave and all of us went to Oceanside and in the middle of town the guys would play a game with James by hiding from him. I remembered I was walking down the street by myself and one of the guys said that James was coming this way and to hide from him. I had ducked in between two buildings and I'd watched James walk past me from the other side of the street. As he walked past, I realized then that no one wanted to be around him because he talked like Gomer Pyle. I came out from between the buildings and walked over to James and we walked down the street together. I remembered the look on his face when I came up to him and asked him where he was going. He really felt rejected by the other guys. He told me in his slow southern voice that he was looking for the guys but couldn't find them anywhere. I told him that I would walk with him if he didn't mind. As we were walking I had asked James how many brothers and sisters he had, and he said that he had six brothers and one sister. As we were walking I could tell that he was feeling better. On both of my watches I had thought about James and I hoped that the guys wouldn't do what the guys back in the States did to him. It is bad enough trying to fit in with the guys over here when you first come over from the States. I hoped that they would make him feel a part of the outfit.

Morning came and everyone was just lying or sitting around doing nothing, James came over to me and I saw that he was very nervous. He sat down and asked me what I was thinking about as we were sitting next to the fighting hole. I told James that I was thinking about nothing. Then James looked at me and asked me what it was like in a firefight. I just looked into his eyes. I just couldn't tell him what it was really like, and I said that he didn't have to worry about it, it was no big deal. Then I told him that it wasn't all that bad and that he wouldn't have any problems in getting through it. As he looked at me he knew that it must be very bad when the shit hit the fan because of the way I looked at him. He was showing me that he believed me, which I knew he didn't.

During the middle part of the day, the word was passed that we were going out on an operation. I told James to make sure that his rifle was clean and ready for tonight. He just nodded and went to work on his fighting gear. He had everything that they gave him when they passed out the 782 gears. During the rest of the day, most of the guys sat around and read their mail that we had gotten yesterday. A couple of the guys in our platoon received boxes sent to them from back in the States. I went over to Chadwell who was talking to one of the guys from the machine gun team called "Ski," short for his Polish name, Lisinski. In his box he had cans of soups, crackers, cheese, and other goodies. I decided to write a letter to my parents asking them to send me canned goods so I could eat them instead of the C-rations. I then went back to where my gear was and wrote a letter to my parents and told them to send me goodies. On the outside of the letter in the upper right corner where you put a stamp all we had to do was write the word, "FREE," I was told that the letter could be mailed anywhere in the United States.

It was going on evening when Sgt. Thomas came over to me and said that I would be with our platoon mortar team carrying their 60mm mortars. Sgt. Thomas loaned me to them because they were short of men. I asked Thomas if he could get someone else because I wanted to be with James Fowler and keep an eye out for him in the field. Thomas said that James had to learn just like everyone else over here and I knew that I could not argue with him on that point. I then told Thomas that I would do it, carrying the mortars. Thomas told me that he would watch over James. Then I started thinking about Sergeant Singleton and being on the trail with the rounds hitting near us and Thomas didn't even shoot his rifle at the enemy. The only thing Thomas did was try to dig a hole with his hands and feet. I had a strange feeling that he would not watch over James if we got hit. I went over to the mortar team and told them that I would be carrying the ammo for them. Gary Sneed said that I would be carrying 10 rounds of 60mm on a pack board. I told Sneed that I would be back when we moved out. Upon returning to my fighting hole I saw Ski who asked me if I wanted some cheese and I said, "yes." He had this tube of cheese and told me to stick out my hand and he squeezed the tube of cheese into the palm of my hand. He said that he had to get rid of the stuff before we went on patrol.

I then sat down next to James and told him that he better get some rest before we went out. I lay down and could still feel the hot sun beating down on us. I knew that I had to get all the rest I could so that I was ready to carry the mortar rounds. I lay there thinking about everything including James Fowler and hoping that nothing would happen to him on his first night in the field. I heard one of the guys say that there were four South Vietnamese soldiers going with us tonight. They were going to take over as the point team for the company. I looked at James and saw that he was getting nervous; I told him that everything was going to be all right, and that nothing was going to happen. He told me that God was watching over him, and he felt secure.

The sun was almost gone and that night was coming on fast. I knew that it wouldn't be too long before we would be moving out. Before I knew it, it was 23:00 hundred hours and the word was passed that we would be moving out in a little bit. It was really dark out; there were a few mosquitoes around but not many. I told James to stay close to Thomas, and that I had to go on over to the mortar team. I got over to the mortar team and Sneed had the pack board ready for me and I then put the pack board on my back. As everyone was getting himself ready, most of us thought that this was one of the dumbest things we had ever done: to leave at nighttime on an operation knowing that we would be making all kinds of noises out there. I knew that all of us were wondering who had come up with this idea and thought it was Capt. Reed. Captain Reed had replaced Captain Curd who had gotten wounded. Captain Reed wanted us to be the first outfit to have a night operation in all of Vietnam.

The word was passed to move out and to keep quiet, which was a joke, and not make too much noise. We started moving out and I could hear the guys making all kinds of noises because of the darkness. I looked down as I was walking to see if I could see the ground and I couldn't. I couldn't even see my legs and feet. I thought to myself, how stupid this was because the enemy could hear us walking in the field. Again I wondered whoever it was that wanted us to go out on an operation at night time had to have some screws loose.

As we were walking, I thought about James again. After a few hours of walking and no rest, I could hear several guys fall into a rice paddy. We had gotten into the rice paddies and were walking on the dikes that were in between the paddies, which were very narrow. I couldn't believe that I hadn't fallen yet, with all that 60mm mortar rounds that I was carrying. No sooner had I thought about it when I fell off the path and into the rice paddies up to my knees in mud and having trouble trying to get out of there. As I tried to move my legs in the mud, I could hear the sucking sound of it trying to keep me in the paddy. I could just barely see the guy in front of me and one of the guys behind me was helping me to get out of the paddy. As I got out, there was a red light a couple of hundred meters ahead. I started out again and hoped that I could find the guys who were in front of me. A couple of minutes went past and one of the guys who was in front of me came back and whispered to me that we were almost out of the paddies. Behind me I could still hear guys falling into the paddies because of the darkness.

When everyone got out of the rice paddies the word was passed that we would stop for a few hours before moving out again. I stayed with the mortar team. I then took off the pack board and the rest of my fighting gear and took out my poncho and covered myself up and tried to get some sleep. It was 04:30 in the morning when we had stopped. As I lay there, I started thinking about James and how he was doing his first night in the field. In about an hour the sun would be coming up and a new day would begin. No sooner had I closed my eyes than the word was passed to get ready to move out. I got up and rolled my poncho and tied it on the back of my flak jacket and got all of my gear ready to move out. The sun was just barely coming up, itself.

The platoon started moving out again and as we did, all of us could see that the terrain was changing from the rice paddies to flat land with small bushes about a foot high and the ground was changing to sand. I looked back at James who was a short distance from me and realized that he was very tired his first night out in the field. I was happy just to see James. We had walked all morning without rest and finally word was passed for us to stop awhile. I took off my pack board and sat down in the sand. In front of me were six guys who were walking much farther ahead of the platoon. It looked as though they were looking for something. After a little bit they came back to the platoon and passed the word that there were booby traps in front of us. Then the word was passed that in a little bit we were going to move out but to make sure that we had a lot of space between the guy in front of us and also not to round the corners but to square the corners. If we rounded the corner, we would be stepping on the booby traps, so we had to square the corners by doing a 90 degree turn. We started moving out again and I made sure that I was one hundred feet behind the guy in front of me. I looked back and saw that the guys behind me did the same thing. As we were walking we made sure that we were walking in the same footsteps of the guys in front of us.

We walked for about four more hours when the word was passed to stop. There were four vehicles coming toward us with several guys on them. As they got closer to us some of the guys said that it was first platoon Charlie Company. They went past us and were going somewhere in a hurry. After they past us, the word was passed to move out again.

Chapter Nine

Our platoon was going to be a blocking force when we got close to the village. We moved out for another half an hour and then we were told to set up for the night. The time was around 14:30 and Lieutenant Ervin called up the squad leaders and told them where to make the perimeter. I was to stay with the mortar team so I didn't have to go back to my fire team. The corporal of the mortar team told me that we would dig our hole here, almost next to the one lane sandy road. As we dug the hole, we were about three and a half feet down when water came up to the surface, so we filled the hole up with sand until we didn't see any water. The mortar team also dug another hole about eighteen inches deep for the mortar tube and set the tube up for the evening. We hadn't eaten all day and after I finished my fighting hole I sat down and ate my chow by myself.

After a few minutes, Lefefe made rounds to each of the fighting holes and told the guys that there were booby traps about fifty feet from us on the little knoll. After I finished eating, I went over to see how James was doing and how he was handling himself out in the field. As I sat next to James, I looked at my hands and remembered my first time out in the field when my hands were bleeding from digging into the side of the hill that we were on. James had heard that a few more booby traps had been found around us and that the engineers were disengaging them. He and I were talking about boot camp days and we were having a great time reminiscing. I stayed with James until it was time for me to get back to my fighting hole. Again I told James that nothing was going to happen and to keep his head down. As I got up and walked away, I thought I had done one good thing in that I made James forget about the war and had him relax for a short time. I reminded Sgt. Thomas to keep his promise about keeping an eye out for James. Thomas knew that I knew he was scared to fire his rifle in a firefight.

The sun was going down now and it was time to get back. As I got back to my hole, I kept on thinking about James, hoping that nothing would happen. I made sure that I had my fighting gear ready to put on if we had to leave this place quickly. It was really getting dark out and it was like last night, pitch black. There were no stars out as well as no moon; everything was just black and quiet. At least we were a blocking force and didn't have to march out again in the dark. I was just lying on the ground, resting, and didn't have to stand watch since I was with the mortar team. I knew that the stars and moon would not be out until around 02:00 when we could at least see a little. I thought to myself that James made it through his first 24 hours out in the bush. I knew that the guys in our fire team would keep an eye out for James, especially Charlie, Chadwell, Quick and Van.

It was around 22:30 hours and in the distance we could hear A.K.- 47s firing and then the word was passed to saddle up and that we were moving out. One of our sister platoons was getting hit. I got my gear on and the mortar pack and the word was passed to get on the road. I walked over to the road, which was about ten feet from me and the rest of the mortar team was ready to go. Everyone of us was having trouble getting to the road because of the darkness. When everyone was on the road the next word was passed to fix bayonets. I couldn't believe it: fix bayonets. I got out my bayonet and put it on the end of my M-16. I started thinking; "What is going on?" Then the word was passed to hold on to the guy in front of you, on his shoulder. Then we started out in a double file toward the fighting. We moved out holding onto the guy in front of us, in two lines the trucks tires had made down the sandy road to the vill. Starting out we sounded like a herd of elephants, making all of that noise.

I held on to the guy in front of me while holding my rifle straight up with my other hand so I wouldn't stab the guy. We sounded like a chain gang going down this sandy road in pitch black out where you couldn't see your hand in front of your nose. As we moved down the road, we saw a small fire in the distance and as we got closer I saw that it was one of our vehicles that had gotten hit by a R.P.G round. A R.P.G. round is a shoulder held rocket that the North Vietnamese Regular used against our vehicles. I remembered that both 1st Platoon and 3rd Platoons had the Otters and were riding them earlier. The Otter is a track vehicle that only carry supplies or men. Then the word was passed to stop and in a couple of minutes, another vehicle came up with guys sitting on top of it as well as inside and Captain Reed said he was going to go around and hit them from the left side while we went down the sandy road to the vill. We started moving out again and the stars were starting to come out, but still there weren't that many out to help us seeing where we were going. About one hundred meters down the road, the word was passed that the mortar team was to set up here on the side of the road. I went with them and Sneed started setting up the mortar tube and were waiting for instructions. I took off the pack board and Sneed told me to open up a couple of the rounds that were inside the canisters. I gave them the rounds and asked Sneed if I could go back to my fire team and he said yes.

I got up and started down the road, and saw that there were a few dead men in the middle of it. One of the guys was running toward me and asked if he could have my rifle, I told him, "No." He started screaming that these damn rifles didn't work and kept on yelling. I hoped that my rifle wouldn't jam.

As I was running up to where the fighting was, I heard something and hit the ground. As soon as I hit the ground I knew that the sand went right up into the magazine and into the rifle. I knew that the rifle wouldn't work, so I broke it open in the dark and got out my tooth brush that I kept in my flak jacket pocket and started cleaning it. I could hear the sand as I brushed my rifle with the toothbrush. I couldn't tell if I was getting all of the sand out of my rifle and it was difficult with all of the darkness. When I finished, I moved the bolt a few times to hear if there was anything that was stopping it from moving. It was still so damn dark out that I couldn't tell if the rifle was clean or not. Then I put in the magazine and put a round in the chamber. I got up and went down the road, and this time I ran into Lieutenant Ervin who said to help get the wounded out. Lieutenant Ervin and his radioman were with some of the dead and wounded men, and that he was making his C.P. there in the middle of the sandy road. I knew that he was not going anywhere; he didn't want to be with the rest of our platoon fighting down in the vill. I saw one of the wounded guys and I picked him up and carried him back to the lieutenant. There were a few guys who were also carrying the wounded and dead men back and putting them down on the road where the lieutenant was. I went back down the road and again, ran into a guy trying to carry one of the wounded men and I helped him get the guy back to the rest of the wounded men. Again, I started back down the road so I could get into the action and help out. We had lost a lot of men, and the battle was still going on but there was not much firing of rifles from either side down at the vill. I came across another Otter and I saw that it had gotten a direct hit from a R.P.G. round. I saw another wounded man walking back and I helped him back to the other dead and wounded men.

Lieutenant Ervin told me that I was to stay and protect the wounded men. By now the moon was out and the sky was getting a little lighter than before but not much. Lieutenant Ervin told another guy in our platoon to stay back and protect the wounded men, also. When the guys brought back the dead and wounded, they would run back down into the battle. Both of us got out our E-tool and started digging a hole about 18 inches deep in the middle of the road and put the wounded men in the hole so the enemy couldn't hit them above ground. We got all of them under ground level and Lieutenant Ervin told us that he heard that the enemy was coming around us to hit us from the rear area. Lieutenant Ervin told both of us to go back up the road about a hundred meters and protect our rear door. As we were setting up, I asked the other guy his name and he said Michael Poisson but everyone called him "Poison." He had a M-79 grenade launcher that looked like a shotgun but the barrel was about 3 inches in diameter. He was carrying a pouch that held about 50 rounds. The M-79 was a single shot piece, like a shot gun.

Both of us then lay down close to the ground so that the enemy could not see our silhouettes. I told Poison to watch from nine to twelve o'clock and I would watch from twelve to three o'clock. As we watched, we could see about twenty feet in front of us. I thought about James Fowler and how he was doing and I hoped that Sergeant Thomas was watching over him. About fifteen minutes had passed and I could tell there was something on Poison's mind. We could hear that the firing was dying down even more. Both of us knew that the N.V.A were coming around the back door. I looked at him and asked what was wrong and he didn't say anything. I asked again and he still remained quiet. I told him that I was going to see the lieutenant and that I would be right back.

I finally reached Lieutenant Ervin and asked him if he could send a couple more men back to watch the rear door with us and he said that he had none and it was up to us to hold them off on our own. Then our Platoon radioman said out loud, "Oh…MY GOD" and then looked at the lieutenant and said that the enemy had just killed Captain Reed and that they were after the Captain's radioman John Pantaleon. Our platoon radioman said that he could hear the rounds as they hit the Captain's radioman Pantaleon and that his last words were, "Oh…Please God… Help…Me." After that, there was only silence on the radio. We all knew that they were both dead and that there was nothing any of us could do. Our platoon radioman got up and walked off the road to vomit, and I knew that I had better get back to Poison who was watching the back door. I quietly returned to Poison and told him how it was with the Captain and his radioman getting killed, that the enemy could be coming at any time and to really keep an eye out. I told Poison that we were the only ones to watch the back door and it was up to both of us to take on the enemy if they came because we were not getting any help. He was ready, and I couldn't wait for the enemy to come so I could get back at them. Both of us were hoping that they would try to sneak around and come in from the back door.

We both kept our heads moving all of the time making sure that the enemy didn't come up on us. As I watched and listened, I could tell that my senses had been getting sharper each day and night. After a couple of minutes, I asked the guy what his name was again and he said, "Poison." I asked if this was his real name and he said, "Yes." He quickly asked me what my name was and I told him that the guys called me "Hammer." He said that it sounded like a good nickname for me. Again I asked him how he got the nickname of "Poison" and he said that he could tell if the guys in the platoon would get killed or wounded and he didn't want to know many of the guys because of it. He said that four of the guys in second squad had gotten killed and he had known that they would and it was eating at him. He told me that he just wanted to be all alone so that he wouldn't see what the future held for the guys in the platoon. I couldn't believe what he was saying, the guys not wanting to be close to him. It was bad enough trying to make it out of Vietnam alive let alone being lonely over here by yourself. I then told him that it was bullshit, and that he could not keep himself alone and away from the guys in the platoon. It was just too hard to stay to yourself and not have any friends. I told him that I would be glad to be his friend and then he had a little smile on his face. I told him that he could talk to me any time and that it was not his fault that the guys died next to him in combat, but it was their time to go. He just happened to be in the right place in the wrong time when they got it. I had picked up his spirits and told him he was not a jinx to anyone in the platoon and it seemed to relax him a little.

It was getting lighter out and I knew that morning would finally come to end the longest night I had ever gone through, again. The firing stopped and everything got very quiet. I didn't like it when it got very quiet after the battle, for it meant that it might start up again at anytime. I really started to watch and so did Poison. I could feel the sweat coming down my face and my palms. We watched for about forty-five minutes until the sun came up. Then Poison and I got up and walked back to where the rest of the dead and wounded men. Everyone was exhausted and wanted to rest. The battle was finally over and fatigue was starting to settle in on all of us. None of us had had more than an hour of sleep, which had been at the beginning of the night.

Some of the guys in our outfit were coming back from the vill, so I asked them if they had seen James Fowler and none of them knew where he was. Finally, I saw Sergeant Thomas walking back by himself and asked, "Where's James Fowler?" He then looked at me and said that James was killed during the night. I told Thomas, "You told me that you would watch over him." Thomas then said that they had gotten separated when they got down into the vill. I just looked at him, looking straight into his eyes to see if he was telling the truth. As I looked into his eyes, I knew that he had gotten scared and hid somewhere by himself. As he was talking to me, all I could do was just look into his eyes. I was hoping that he hadn't lost James because of his weak leadership under combat. But, deep inside of me, I knew that he only looked out for his own skin. I knew from this day on that I would never trust the son of a bitch, forever. I looked at the dead bodies that were on the road and they were all covered up from head to foot in their ponchos. I had this lonely feeling of emptiness deep inside of me. I remembered the last thing that James had said before we went into the battle was that God was with him. Only the second full day in the field and James had gotten killed. I remembered from boot camp that he was from Oklahoma and had six brothers. It seemed that the nicest guys die young. Sergeant Thomas then slowly left without a word. I went over to my fire team and asked them how they were doing and they said that it was a hell of a mess down there in the vill.

When Thomas walked away from me, he knew that I couldn't trust him with anyone because I knew just what kind of a man he really was. I lost all respect for him and I also knew that I would never rely on him backing us up at all. I hoped that he would get his orders soon so he could go home and get the hell out of the field. Thomas really buffaloed a lot of guys in our platoon. If the guys saw what I had seen of him out in the field, they wouldn't trust him either.

Quick said when they first got down to the vill that when they came up to someone that they had to turn that person around and get as close to his face as possible to see if he was a Marine or N.V.A. - and then we used our bayonets on them. Van said that James was shot in the head early last night when we first got into the vill. I then asked Van where in the hell was Thomas and he said that he didn't see him anywhere. Everyone was separated from each other and it was dark as hell everywhere. I told Charlie that James Fowler had gotten killed and he said that he was only one of two from our platoon that had gotten killed. The other new guy got it also. Chadwell said that there were only a few of us from our platoon who had gotten wounded and killed. I asked the guys if they had seen Thomas and James and they said that they didn't see them at all. They told me that it was very difficult to know where everyone was and that included the enemy.

The lieutenant told our platoon to set up a perimeter around the dead and wounded men. I went with my fire team and we set up about eighty feet away. We sat down and now it was somewhere between 07:00 and 08:00 in the morning. The word was passed that we had captured two N.V.A. soldiers who were being brought back with what was left of our company. Most of the guys from our platoon were all right, but 1st Platoon as well as 3rd Platoon really lost a lot of men. One of the sergeants from 1st Platoon got up and started running down the road, asking for a rifle. Soon he was yelling for a rifle and someone gave him one. Looking down the road, I saw they were bringing back one of the prisoners. There was a Marine on each side of the prisoner and the sergeant came up to about ten feet from the prisoner and opened up on him with all the rounds that were in the magazine. Then the sergeant started going down the road looking for the other prisoner. Lieutenant Ervin told the guys to stop the sergeant from killing the other prisoner when he came. When the sergeant saw the other prisoner he didn't have any more ammo so he jumped on the prisoner and started choking him. The rest of the guys were trying to get him off the prisoner and finally got them separated and held the sergeant down until the prisoner was gone. In a way I was hoping that the sergeant would kill the other prisoner. We could hear the sergeant yelling out to kill the little S.O.B.

I asked Chadwell, Charlie and Van if they had ever gone out on a night operation and they all told me that this was the first time ever in Vietnam. They said that the captain wanted to have a night operation so he could show everyone that it could be done. I told them that the captain got just what he deserved. I felt for the captain's radioman Pantaleon for being killed because of this stupid operation that our captain had wanted to do. Then the word was passed that we had 22 K.I.A.'s (killed in action) and 28 W.I.A's (wounded in action), and one of them was James Fowler who was one of two K.I.A.'s from our platoon. In the back of my mind, I knew that Sergeant Thomas wasn't telling me the whole truth about what had happened last night. But I knew that I would never know what really happened to James.

As we were waiting for the choppers to come to pick up the dead and wounded men, I started thinking back to boot camp and that our Drill Instructor wasn't lying when he said that we would lose a lot of guys from our Boot Camp Platoon. I was also wondering about McBride and how he was doing in Delta Company. I had this empty and lonely feeling and it wouldn't leave. Then someone said that the choppers were coming and to get ready getting the dead and wounded men out. One of the guys said that there would be two choppers at a time and to be ready to take out the wounded men first. The first two choppers came down and a new captain got off of one of the choppers; the guys loaded both choppers with wounded men. The name of the new captain was Hutchinson, and he would be taking over Charlie Company. None of us guys in the company gave a damn about the captain. The rest of the choppers came in pairs of twos and we finally loaded the rest of the choppers with the prisoner and the dead men.

The word was passed that we were moving out and as I looked around I saw that a lot of us were just drained. I could tell deep down inside of me that I was not afraid to die over here. It seemed that death was nothing to fear. As far as I knew, the United States was on a different planet than us here in Vietnam. Somehow the word was passed that there were only about twenty some guys each in first and third platoons that had come out of this battle. Most of the guys from both the 1st Platoon and 3rd Platoon died in the Otters. The word was passed to move out. We must have walked about 2000 meters when the orders came to stop. Sergeant Thomas was staying away from me and I was glad. I sat down slowly and began thinking about James; my body was somehow numb from what had happened and I knew that I had to get a hold of myself. I could feel the tears running slowly down my face. Then Benny Houston came up to where I was and he told me to take it easy and that there was nothing anyone could do. He also told me not to think about it and that I had a long way to go over here in Vietnam. I looked up at him and said that I didn't care anymore what happened to me now. He said to not talk like that because I didn't know what I was saying. He then told me to let it all out and to get it off my chest. The tears came down even harder. Benny patted my shoulder and then quietly walked back to his team. Benny knew that I had to get through this on my own. I just couldn't believe that James got shot in the head. It was hard for me to understand why.

Chapter Ten

The word was passed that we were moving out again. I got up and started walking again and I could feel the intense heat coming off the sand that was everywhere. I knew that it was going to be another very long hot day. As we were walking, Lefefe came up to me and told me that I was too slow and to move it up. Lefefe came up to me a couple of more times and was either telling me that I was too far away or too close. As he came up, I told him if he said one word that I was going to give it to him. He just smiled a little and walked up to our C.P. group. I knew right then what he was doing to me: he was getting my mind off of my buddy James who got killed. He was trying to get me to stay focused on what I was doing. I knew that Sergeant Lefefe was all right, and could tell that he cared about everyone in the platoon. I wanted to tell Sergeant Lefefe that I was O.K. and that he didn't have to worry about me but I knew that he already knew. The word was passed that we would stop here for the day.

It was mid afternoon and we just had to get some rest and food. We dug our fighting holes for the night and got our ponchos out and used our E-tools as posts and made cover from the sun. Benny Houston came over to me and said that my mustache needed a trim. I got up and we went back to his fighting hole and he trimmed my mustache for the first time. It only took him about two minutes and he said that it was starting to take shape. I told Benny that I really appreciated what he had done for me earlier. He told me that he would have done it to anyone in our platoon and that we needed each other over here. I knew that what he said was right in that we all needed each other if we were to survive. I got up and nodded to him, and said that I had better return to my fighting hole.

As I walked back to my hole, I saw Bill who was also growing a mustache. I walked over to him and said that his mustache was looking great and he told me the same. He was changing himself by being quiet and not saying much to anyone after what we had seen in our short time here. When I got back to my fighting hole James was still on my mind and I knew that I couldn't do anything for James and that I missed him..

The word was passed that the guys in our company had captured a V.C. (Viet Cong subject), and the Company C. P. wanted to interrogate him. After about half an hour we heard they were going to let him go. A lot of us jumped to our feet because we couldn't believe the Company C.P. group was going to let the guy go. After about half an hour the Company C.P. group let the V.C. go and as he was leaving, most of us could tell that he was counting his steps from the C.P. group to where he was going. Some of the guys were telling the Company C.P. that the V.C. was counting his steps as he was walking away, but the Company C. P. didn't do a damn thing.

Now I knew that there was no way to talk to the officers in this outfit about anything out in the field. The officers knew everything and they were not going to listen to any of us enlisted men. The officers seemed to know everything and acted almost the same way. I just wondered if we were ever going to get a captain who had his shit together.

The sun was very hot and the sand was reflecting the heat off the ground. I decided to get under the poncho where our fighting hole was and sat in the bottom of the hole. I could feel the coolness of the ground and it was making me relax for the first time in a long time. I wanted to drink some water but my canteens were very hot and I knew that it wouldn't be until late at night before I could drink my water. I just sat there not saying a word to anyone and most of the guys were just sitting or lying around and not saying a thing. It must have been half an hour or so when we heard a pumping sound. All of us guys started getting to our holes because we knew what was coming: mortars from the enemy. I raised my hand and grabbed the radio that was standing next to the hole and brought it down into the hole. Charlie, Van and Chadwell also got on the edge of our fighting hole and we could hear that the mortar rounds were hitting where the Company C.P. was. The rounds were really coming in on the Company C.P. and they were really getting hit hard. A lot of us were thinking to ourselves that they deserved to get hit. We all hoped that from now on that the Company C.P. would listen to us enlisted men. I knew that the new captain learned from this and I hoped that he wouldn't make the same mistake twice. From the top of our fighting hole we could see where the firing was coming from. Our mortar teams were firing in the direction of the enemy and hitting all around them. It seemed as if it took only ten minutes for the whole thing to be over with. There was a thin hedgerow that was very close to the village where the V.C. were firing their mortar tube.

I heard on the radio that Captain Hutchinson called for our platoon, so I got out of my hole and started to get my gear ready. I knew that Lieutenant Ervin would call for our squad to go out there. I then called over to Sgt. Thomas and told him that the captain called for our platoon. On the radio our lieutenant called for Sergeant Francis up to our Platoon C.P. I then passed it on to Sergeant Thomas and he in turn informed Francis. About five minutes had passed and Sergeant Francis came past me and told me to get the radio ready for his squad and that one of the guys would be over to get it. Benny Houston was walking over to me and asked for the radio and I gave it to him and told Benny to watch himself. Benny said that they were going over to where they fired the mortar tube to see if the V.C. were still there. I told Benny to watch out for himself again and he smiled and nodded to me and the rest of the 2nd squad walked past us going over to where the enemy was. As 2nd squad left, Francis took the point with Johnson, Poison and Benny behind Francis. The 2nd fire team was behind Benny and Bill was the last guy in the squad. All of us could see that they were walking in a zigzag pattern going out to the V.C. mortar tube. They were about a good 800 meters away from us.

I went over to the Platoon C.P. to talk with Chico, who was our new 2nd platoon corpsman. I asked where Doc. Marsh was and he told me that he was now the Company Corpsman. Chico was a Mexican from California; he stood about 5'10" tall and weighed about 160 lbs. As we were sitting there talking about nothing of importance, we heard an explosion out where the 2nd squad was. We got up and looked in the direction of 2nd squad and were waiting for Benny to call back to 2nd Platoon. Sergeant Lefefe came over to us and asked if we could see anything out there where they were. I said, "No," in a soft quiet voice hoping that no one was hurt. A few minutes had passed, which seemed like a half an hour, and the rest of us went over to the platoon radioman to hear what had happened. We knew that someone must have stepped on a booby trap and that the guys were working on him out there and we knew that Benny would be on the radio to let us know how they were doing with the wounded man.

Lefefe asked the radioman if he had heard anything yet from 2nd squad and the radioman only shook his head, "No." After a good twenty minutes our platoon radioman started talking to 2nd squad and when he was finished he looked at Lieutenant Ervin and Sergeant Lefefe and told them that "Character Hotel" was dead and Sergeant Francis told him that one of his legs was blown off. Sergeant Francis was very calm on the radio but we could hear his voice breaking up. We all knew who Character Hotel was: Benny Houston, the old man of 2nd Platoon. The word was passed throughout 2nd platoon and a silence fell over the whole platoon. I started thinking that he was 27 years old and had two children and was from Chicago. It was a couple of hours earlier that he had trimmed my mustache. I felt that Benny would be alive if only the captain hadn't released the V.C. They fired their mortar tube at our Company C.P. and 2nd squad had to go out there looking for the V.C.

We could see in the distance that they were coming back to the perimeter and that four of them were carrying Benny in the poncho. They followed their steps coming back into the perimeter and I went over to Benny. As I got there where he was lying on the ground, the rest of the guys from 2nd Platoon came over to him and gave their last respects to Benny. I looked inside the poncho and he looked like he was asleep in that blood-soaked poncho. One of his legs was gone and the other one was torn up. It showed on each of their faces how much he had affected this platoon. I just couldn't believe that he was gone. I could feel the numb feeling coming over me again and I couldn't understand why God had taken him. I said a short prayer for both Benny and James. The tears were coming down my face again. Most of the guys had tears in their eyes as well. Benny really kept 2nd platoon together, being older than the rest of us.

I went over to Bill and Poison who had gone out with them and asked what had happened out there. Poison said that the first three of them stepped over the trip wire and Benny was the only guy to step on the trip wire which set off the booby trap. He said that none of the three of them had seen the damn wire. Bill was the last guy and when the booby trap went off everyone froze, but it was too late for Benny. Bill said that they all tried at first to stop the bleeding and kept talking to Benny to keep him awake but despite everything they did, they could see that Benny was slipping fast. They had both legs wrapped and kept talking to Benny so that they could get him back to the company but everything was in vain. As I looked at Francis, Johnson and Poison they were really taking it very hard because they had done everything they could do to try to keep Benny from dying out there. They went on over to their position and sat down together not saying a word to anyone. I knew that it hurt them bad in losing Benny.

Captain Hutchinson called in for a chopper to pick up Benny and we were told when the chopper came that we were moving out again. Everyone in the platoon came over and gave their last respects to the old man of 2nd platoon. I then walked on over to my fighting hole and slowly got on my gear. I was still numb and I couldn't get away from it. As we were waiting for the chopper two black guys came over to see Benny and looked inside the poncho where Benny was lying and started calling all of us in 2nd platoon all kinds of names. They were telling us that we didn't give a damn about Benny and that he was just another Nigger to us. If it was a white guy, he would be alive and not dead. I just looked at them and they were trying like hell to get themselves out of the field, to get on the chopper with Benny and to be back in the rear where it was safe. A few minutes later a banana-shaped chopper came and our squad went over to unload it. When it was time to put Benny in the chopper both Negroes wouldn't or didn't want to pick Benny up to put him into the chopper. I couldn't believe what I was hearing from these guys and yet they didn't have the guts to help carry Benny on to the chopper for him to go home. When we had the chopper unloaded, four of the guys from our platoon picked up Benny and put him into the chopper. It really pissed me off that these guys wouldn't help pick up Benny and put him on the chopper. The chopper lifted up into the air and I was glad that Benny was able to go home. As for the two Negroes, they were also on the chopper. I sure was going to miss Benny because he had made the black and white guys work together as one unit. Now that Benny was gone, the Negroes in our company would not work with the rest of us. The supplies had been dispersed throughout the company. I got back to the fighting hole and the word was passed that we had 6000 meters to go before we would get picked up by the six-bys on Highway 1.

As we were walking, I started crying and the hot sun didn't help out at all. I felt my boots sinking about six to eight inches into the sand. After about an hour, Lefefe came up to me to see if I was all right. I just nodded, and he rejoined the C.P. group. I couldn't figure out why he was so concerned about me. He didn't know me that well and I didn't know him but I knew that someone had told him that I was close to both James and Benny. We were leaving the sandy part of the region and re-entering the area of hard ground again. As we walked a little way, we were told that we were coming into a vill, and we were going to sweep through it. As we got closer to the vill, the word was passed that there were booby traps on the path leading into the vill. These booby traps were "foot traps" to disable a person out in the field. We were on one of the trails that led into the vill and one of the guys in front of me pointed to the ground and said that there was a foot trap with bamboo in the bottom with very sharp ends and 5 inch rusty nails on all four sides that were on an angle pointing downward. I remembered learning back in the States that the enemy would poison the bamboo stakes as well as the rusty nails so when you stepped inside of it that you would receive the main purpose to get you out of the field for a short while.

We came into a large clearing just in front of the vill and the word was passed that we were to get on line for the sweep through the vill. As we were getting on line, the word was passed to fix bayonets. When the other two platoons got on line with us, the word was passed to move out slowly. There were some pineapple plants and palm trees around the vill. There was no one outside of the huts. This was the first time we had gotten on line for a sweep through the vill. It seemed to me that we were doing a lot of first times stuff over here. As we were checking inside each of the huts, the people inside each hut were scared to death of us as we moved through. By the look on the mama-sans' and children's faces, we could tell that they couldn't wait for us to leave their village. We were coming to the end of the vill and we did not see a thing. When the whole company finally got through the vill, the captain told all three platoons that we were going to leave in three staggered columns into the rice paddies. Our platoon covered the right side of the company and 3rd Platoon had the left side and 1st Platoon with the Company C.P. was in the middle.

The rice paddies were about 600 meters long and we finally were out of them. When the last guys from all three staggered columns got out of the rice paddies the word was passed to take a ten-minute break. When the break was over we got up and still moved out in three staggered columns. The ground was still flat and there were hardly any trees around. We must have moved out for about forty-five minutes later when the word was passed to take another break. Then a few minutes later Sergeant Lefefe came over to me and said that he was going to save my life. I looked up and slowly asked how…and then he gave me a "Lifesaver." He handed me a red lifesaver and asked me what I thought about that. I looked at him and just smiled and then told him, "Thanks." He then left and didn't come back to see how I was doing.

The word was passed that we were moving out and that the trucks were coming. I told Chadwell that we were moving out and he in turn passed it back to the rest of the guys behind us. As we started moving out, the other two sister platoons came toward us. We must have walked about 400 meters to reach the blacktop highway, which was Highway 1. We crossed the road and started up north on Highway 1 until everyone in the company was next to the road. The word was passed to stop and wait for the six-bys to come. As I was sitting on the side of the highway waiting, Chadwell came over to me and told me that we had come through a place called "Street Without Joy." Chadwell told me there was a French author who was here twenty years ago when the French Army was fighting the V.C. and N.V.A. He wrote about what happened here with the French Army and also about the booby traps. He came back twenty years later and went with the 1st Battalion 9th Marines before I joined the outfit and stepped on a booby trap and died. The name of his book was called, "Street Without Joy," but this time he ended up getting killed.

I looked up the highway and saw about four or five kids coming down from a vill about 400 meters away. The kids were from 6 to 10 years old; one of the boys came over to us and just looked at us. Then one of the guys asked the boy if he could get us some water and he understood and said that he would be right back. We watched the boy go back up to the vill and in a couple of minutes he came back with some kind of a container holding the water in it. The guy that asked for the water got it first and then the boy brought it down to us. All of the guys were telling the rest of the kids that they needed water also. The next thing we knew the rest of the kids were running back to the vill and brought back different containers filled with water and gave it to us. The little boy made another trip back to the vill and this time handed me the container filled with water. I could feel how cold the water was going down my throat. The water felt so good going down that it refreshed me. The little boy just stared at me as I drank the water and didn't say a word. As I looked into his eyes I could see he felt good about giving us the water. The little boy then passed it on to the rest of the guys in my fire team. As I was watching the kids passing out the water there were even more kids coming down from the vill with containers filled with water for all of the guys in our company. The kids felt like they were doing something great in getting the water for the guys; you could see it in their faces. The guys were grateful and were giving the kids C-rations in return. The sun was really heating up and the humidity was also climbing. Everyone was taken care of by the children and then they sat around the guys talking to us and telling us that, "Marines are number 1 and Ho Chi Minh Number 10." It seemed that all of the kids really cared about us Marines and were glad that we were here to protect them if for only a little bit. When the little boy was finished, he came back over to me and sat down and started talking to us. The guys in our fire team were having a good time with him but we could see that the six-bys were coming down the road and that it was almost time to for us to leave. All of us in the fire team got out a can of C-rations and gave it to the boy and told him thanks for the water. The six-bys went past us and went down the road a little ways and turned around and came back. They stopped in front of the company and the word was passed to get on the trucks.

As I climbed aboard the truck and sat down, I just looked at the children and saw that some of the younger kids didn't have any clothes on at all and they looked like they were between the ages of 3 and 4. The older kids had on shorts and shirts with the exception of some of the boys who only had on shorts because of the heat. As the trucks started up the engines some of the kids walked back up to the vill where they lived. The guys were still giving the kids C-rations although not one kid had asked for the food. All of us knew that they needed the food because they looked so old and very thin. Then the trucks started to move and the guys waved to the kids. The kids waved back saying, "MARINES NUMBER 1," as we passed. We could see a couple of the kids in the vill smoking cigarettes. I remembered that a couple of the guys asked the kids if they saw the N.V.A. and V.C. and the kids told us that they had come through two days before us. The kids told us that the N.V.A. were heading back up north from here.

The six-bys were taking us back up north and after a couple of minutes I started thinking about James and Benny. As the six-bys were heading north on Highway 1, I saw that they were taking us back to Dong Ha. We went inside the gate and over to our company area where I had been when I first arrived here in Dong Ha. The six-bys stopped and we were told to get out. Then the word was passed to follow the C.P. group and that we were going to a new area where our battalion was going to be. When we got there, there were no tents but only a large open field. A bulldozer came over to our area and cleared the ground of the small bushes and even out the ground so we could put up the tents even though we didn't have any tents at this time. After about twenty minutes the bulldozer left and there were two six-bys coming with our tents and we were going to put them up. The six-bys arrived and we unloaded them and Captain Hutchinson showed us where the tents for each platoon were to be. Alpha, Bravo, and Delta Company already had their tents up and were watching us. We put up our tents and put the cots inside of them. We rolled up the sides of the tents so that the air could move through, so it wouldn't be so damn hot inside of them. It took us about forty minutes to get the tents up and get the cots inside. When we were finished the word was passed that we had the rest of the day off. I then got on the cot and just lay there trying to get some sleep. Most of the guys were doing the same except for a few who were starting up a football game.

A couple of minutes later Frank Bignami came over to the tent and asked any of the guys if they wanted to play a football game. The guys in the tent decided no and then Frank came over to me and said that they needed me and I told Frank that if I played that I would get someone hurt. He told me that it was only going to be two-hand tag against the other platoon. He kept insisting that I should play and I finally agreed. I got off the cot and went over to where they were getting ready to play the game. The guys in my platoon told me that I should be a blocker for them. I told them that it was all right with me. Our platoon had the ball first. The guys were really getting into this game. We got on line with the runners behind us and told the other platoon that we were ready, but instead of kicking the ball they threw it to us. We made about fifteen yards and then we got into a huddle and I just listened to the play calling; I was laughing and went up to the line to block. Across from me was a tall kid and he was telling me that he was going to kill our platoon and I told him that we were only playing tag, not tackling. When the ball was snapped, he hit me with his forearm and went in to really try to hurt some of the guys on our team. As we walked past each other, I told him that he better knock it off. On the next two plays he was still using the forearm on me and hurting the shorter guys in our platoon. When we got back in our huddle, I told Don Horseman to run the ball over me and the guy across from me was going to get his fucking ass kicked. When I got on the line, I got myself ready to really lay into this son of a bitch. If he wanted to hurt people, then it was time for me to kick his ass for good. As the ball was snapped, I really hit him with my forearm and set the son of a bitch right on his ass as Horseman ran right past him. As he was getting up he told me that that's not fair. I told him that he better get ready again because I was really going to lay into his ass again. The next couple of times, he wanted no part of me and my platoon. The other team would put two guys on me and I would still kick both of their asses. As we got into the huddle, the guys in my platoon told me that they were glad that I was in 2nd platoon and not on another platoon. The score of the game was not even close after I started hurting the other team. After about half an hour, I told the guys that this was going to be the last play for me and that we were going to make a power sweep play and that I was going to be the lead blocker and that the runner should run right behind me. As I pulled around with the runner behind me, I was knocking everyone out of the way and there was one guy left and he came at me and I lifted him straight up into the air and he ended up landing on his ass. Everyone on both teams laughed like hell and all of us felt sorry for his ass since he landed right on it. I then left and another guy from our platoon took over for me and I went back to the tent.

When I got to the tent, I went over to my cot to lie down. The guys told me that they couldn't believe how I handled the other platoon by myself. They told me that I better play football for the Quantico Marines when I got back to the States. They all told me that they would kick my ass if I didn't try out for the team. I just looked at them and they all knew that they couldn't kick my ass after they saw me kicking the hell out of the other platoon. I told all of the guys that I would try out for the Quantico Marines Football Team when I got back to the States. As I lay in the cot, my mind started thinking of James and Benny and wished they had been here to see me in the football game.

The guys in the tent told me their names: George Hahner, known as Whitey; Don Parrillo; and a big guy almost as big as me named Grear who carried a M-79 grenade launcher. Then I met two of the machine gunners in our platoon besides Maxwell and their names were Bill Gonzales (known as Speedy) and Kenny Fulton. The rest of the guys were playing the football game. Kenny said that he was from Dayton, Ohio. I then told Kenny that I was from Cincinnati. He said that he was really from Kettering, Ohio. And I told him that I had a cousin who lived in Kettering. I asked him what high school he had gone to and Kenny said, "Kettering High School." I told him that my cousin went to the same high school. When I told him my cousin's name, which was Kenny Castor, he said that he knew Kenny in High School. I told Kenny what a very small world it really is and he agreed.

Chapter Eleven

The word was passed that we were getting mail and I was looking forward to seeing if the letters had my outfit's name on the address. So far I had been getting mail from the other duty stations before they came to Vietnam. Chadwell came into our tent and passed out the letters to all of us. I didn't have any boxes this time from my mother. I remembered that she was sending a box a week to me. Chadwell gave me about six letters and again most were from my mother. The addresses on the letters were still catching up with me. After I read the letters, the word was passed that it was time to eat. It was going on around 17:30 hours and I grabbed my mess gear and went on over to the mess tent. Again the cooks served us rice. After we were finished and as we walked back to the tents for the evening, the word was passed that we were going to get two cans of beer each. When we got back to the tents, the word was passed that it was time to walk over to the supply tent and we were to get the cans of beer there. All of us got up and went on over to the tent and they passed out two cans to each of us. I could feel that the beer cans were warm. As I was walking back, Doc Chico came over and walked back with me. We got back to the tent and sat down on the cot and opened up the cans of beer. It was the first time I had ever drunk beer with the exception of the time when I was a little kid and my grandfather gave me a beer and it made me very sick. I remembered that my head was spinning around and that the taste of the beer was horrible. I remembered that I ended up in my grandfather's bed with one hell of a lot of pain in my stomach with a spinning head. And now I was about to drink beer, warm beer at that, and I knew that I wasn't going to like the taste. I didn't want the other guys in the outfit to think that I was not a beer drinker. Chico and I started drinking the warm beer and we were drinking as much of it as we could at a time. After we both drank the first beer in about two minutes, I could feel myself getting dizzy but I opened up the second beer. Chico did the same and as he opened up the can a couple of the guys came over to us and gave us their second can of beer saying they didn't want it because it was warm. I thought to myself that German people drank warm beer. I didn't care for the taste but I started drinking the second can with Chico. As we were drinking the second can, both of us started feeling great. Neither of us was feeling any pain at all. Other guys started giving both of us their cans of beer until we both had about 12 cans each.

One of the guys came into the tent and said that he had a large can of ice cream and wanted to know if we wanted any. Chico and I got up and walked over to the guy who was outside the tent and he gave us the can of ice cream. Both Chico and I used our hands to dish out the ice cream. It was really great and it was better than the beer that we had been drinking. After we finished off the ice cream Chico told me that he had a surprise. As we went back to the tent, Chico told me that he would be right back. He went over to his tent, which was the Platoon C.P. tent, and came back with his medical bag and a C-ration can. Chico told me to sit on the ground and he sat next to me. He then told me to watch. He shook the C-ration can and after about thirty seconds he let out a frog that was inside of it. The frog started jumping sideways and it was the funniest thing that I have ever seen. Chico put the frog back into the C-ration can and shook it up a couple of more times and each time the frog would jump sideways like it was drunk. Then Chico told me to wait, this would be really funny. He then got his medical bag and opened it up and got out a needle, filled it up with some kind of fluid, then grabbed the frog and he put the needle up its ass. Chico then told me to watch the frog. As we watched, the frog didn't move at all and then after a minute, bubbles were coming out of its ass. There were more bubbles and then the insides of the frog started coming out. I looked at Chico and said, "Is that what you do when you don't have anything else to do?" Chico said, "Yep." I started laughing and couldn't believe that both of us were having a great time. Chico got up and said that he had to leave and hoped that I had a great time and I told him that I did.

I could tell by the way he walked that he was still drunk. There were a few beer cans left but I didn't feel like drinking any more beer. I got up and got into my cot and went off to sleep. The next thing I knew someone kicked my cot and told me to get up, that we were going out to the field again. My mouth was very dry from the beers last night. I went outside the tent to the water bag and took a long drink. I came back and got on my gear and all of us just sat in the tent until the six-bys came.

The six-bys arrived and the word was passed to get on the trucks. Only our platoon was leaving and the other two platoons were staying here. Then Chadwell told us that we were going to Cam Lo Bridge and that we would be there for awhile.

The trucks went up north on Highway 1 and about ten minutes later we turned off the highway to the other black top road that went straight north. It was about fifteen minutes later that the six-bys turned right off the blacktop road onto the dirt road that led into Cam Lo.

The village and the bridge were just in front of us; the six-bys stopped just before the bridge. All of us got out and Lieutenant Ervin called for the three-squad leaders. The rest of us just sat down next to the road. The six-bys then went over the bridge and went into the vill and turned around and stopped on the other side of the bridge. The Marines that were already here got on the six-bys and the trucks started off going back to Dong Ha. The three-squad leaders went back to their squads. Thomas told us that 1st squad had south of the bridge from the river to the road and 2nd squad had north of the bridge, from the road to the river. 3rd squad had the other side of the bridge with the C.P. group that had the cement building that was next to the river. 3rd squad and the C.P. group got up and went over to the other side of the bridge and I was glad that Lieutenant Ervin was as far away from us as possible. Lieutenant Ervin had Dave Mullins machine gun team on our side of the bridge and Ron Lisinski's machine gun team on the other side with the lieutenant and 3rd squad. All of us felt that each day that went by when we were out in the field that we just couldn't stand Lieutenant Ervin, hearing or looking at the bastard. He was becoming a real asshole and he really made us think of him that way. He always volunteered the platoon for everything in the company when we were out in the field. He didn't care about any of the guys in his platoon, only himself. He was trying to make a big name for himself.

Thomas came over to Chadwell and told him that his fire team had the fighting bunker next to the river and the southwest corner. Chadwell then told us that Charlie and Smithy would be with him next to the river and Van, Grear, and I would be at the fighting bunker at the southwest corner. I looked at Chadwell and told him the reason why he wanted the fighting bunker next to the river was so he could go swimming first. All of us were laughing and Charlie said, "Why not?" We all then went over to the two fighting bunkers and Van, Grear, and I took off our gear. We could tell that this place needed to be fixed up better than this. Van said that it looked like we better fix up the bunker first, which was in front of the fighting hole. We put our fighting gear inside the bunker and then it started to rain. All of us got our ponchos and put them on to keep from getting soaked. It rained for about forty-five minutes before it stopped and then the heat and humidity shot straight up again. As we waited for the rains to stop, I asked Van where he came from back in the States. Van told me that he was from Salt Lake City, that he was a preacher and that his job was to perform baptism in his church. Van was a little strange in the way he talked and acted, but for some reason I liked him. There was something about him I couldn't put my finger on but I felt that he knew what the hell he was doing over here. I knew that I could trust him with my life.

The rain stopped and both of us took off our ponchos and we decided to get something to eat before we started on the fighting hole. After we ate, all of us started working on our bunker. It was going on around 13:00 hundred hours and two little boys from the village came over to us and they asked us if they could help us and I told them no but Van said that it was all right and that they could fill the sand bags for us. Van asked the boys how old they were and the oldest one said that he was six and his brother was five years old. As Van and I worked on the bunker the two brothers were hard at work filling up the sand bags. Grear and Smithy went on over to Chadwell and helped them work on their bunker. It was going on 16:30 hours and Van and I told the boys that we were finished for the day and the two brothers asked us for some C-rations and Van gave them a couple of cans of food. They were very happy to get the C-rations from us. As they were leaving, they said that they would be back tomorrow to help again. Both of us then got our fighting gear in the fighting hole and had everything ready for the night watches. Chadwell came over to us and said that Lieutenant Ervin told him to pick up a couple of cases of C-rations. Van and I went over to the other side of the bridge to get them. When we got to the other side of the bridge, we saw one of the guys digging a deep hole. We got our C-rations and then went on over to where Lloyd was; he was the one that was digging the hole. Lloyd was with 2nd squad. Van asked him why in hell was he digging the square hole and Lloyd told us that he was caught at his fighting hole without his helmet and flak jacket by Lieutenant Ervin. Then Lloyd yelled out, "I hate this green Mother Fucker." Both Van and I started laughing. Lloyd again yelled out again and said, "I hate this Fuckin' place." We both knew that Lloyd wanted the lieutenant to hear him. Van said that it had to be eight feet deep and how was he going to get out of the hole? Again Lloyd didn't really give a damn. As Van and I walked back to our fighting hole we could still hear Lloyd yelling out in the bottom of the hole, "I hate this green Mother Fucker," and the both of us were laughing like hell going back. Van knew that tonight was going to be hard in the sense that there were only three of us to stand watch for the night. Van said that it was going to be a little rough for the three of us because we would be a little tired from working all day and standing watch for the night.

The two of us decided to eat around 17:00 hours and to get some sleep right after dinner. Both of us just lay on the ground next to the fighting hole and tried to get some sleep in. It was hard to do with the heat and humidity. It was nighttime and Van told me that it was my turn to watch. I got up and went over to the fighting hole and as I sat on the edge, I started thinking about James Fowler and Benny Houston. I wished that both of them were still alive and here with the rest of the guys in the platoon. I could still feel the emptiness deep inside of me of losing both James and Benny but there was nothing I could do. I knew that for the rest of my life, I would always be thinking of both of these guys. We didn't have the radio so all we had was the watch to keep time. How quiet it was here at the bridge and all of the stars were out tonight. As I looked at the watch, I saw that it was time to get Grear up for his turn. I went over to him and kicked him at the bottom of his foot and he got up and quietly went on over to the hole. I gave him the watch and he just shook his head. I laid down and after what seemed like minutes of sleeping, Van kicked me and it was my turn again and he gave me the watch. As I sat next to the fighting hole watching out in front of me, I could feel my body tire from working all day yesterday on the fighting hole. I wasn't looking forward to working on the bunker today. My hour was up and it was time to wake up Grear for his turn. It was 05:00 and both Van and I let Grear sleep in the bunker because he was the last guy to stand watch. We started working on filling the sandbags when we heard Grear yelling for us to help him. Both of us stopped what we were doing and went over to the bunker and the one side of the wall had caved in on him and he was telling us to help him get out of there. As we were taking the sandbags off of him we were both laughing. When he finally got out, both Van and I just kept on laughing. Grear didn't see the humor in it.

Chapter Twelve

It was around 08:00 in the morning and Van, Grear and I had just finished breakfast and the two Vietnamese brothers came over to our hole with
a couple of kids. I knew that we didn't have a lot of C-rations for most of the
kids so Van told them that only three of them could help and that was all.
The rest of them left and went on over to the other holes to see if they could
help the other guys. Van had the three boys fill up the sand bags and Van,
Grear and I worked on the bunker and made it a lot bigger and deeper. This
took us a couple of days to finish. On the last day of working on our bunker
we gave the boys C-rations and one of them had a sandbag with something
in it. I asked the boy to come over to me because I wanted to see what was
inside of the sandbag and when I grabbed the sandbag, it was our food. I
looked inside it and saw that he had stolen more C-rations cans without us
knowing it. I looked at Van and he just shook his head a little and said to let
him go. I gave the sandbag back to the kid and they left without a word. He
knew that he was in trouble but after I gave him the sandbag back to him
with the C-rations in it, I knew that he was going to be a life long friend.

The next day came and the boys came back again and we told them that
we were finished working and that there was nothing for them to do. The
two boys came back and they asked Van and me about the world and the
United States. I remembered back when I was in high school in history class
the teacher said, "If you were in a different country and the children would
ask you about the United States what would you say about the U.S.?" I didn't
know how to start or what I should say. I looked at Van and I let him do
the talking. After a little while Van and I asked the two boys their names
and the oldest one said that he was Tu and his brother was Thi. Van and I
told about the kids in the United States and what they did. Their eyes got
very large and we could see that they wished that they lived there. We told
them about Christmas, Easter, and the other holidays. We told them that
our schools back in the United States were about two and three stories high
and had many classrooms. The boys told us that they only had one room
and that their school was on the other side of the bridge and almost in the
middle of the village.

When Van and I talked about freedom to the kids, we could see that
they never had freedom to do what they wanted to do or say what they
wanted to say without the fear of being tortured. The two brothers said they
wanted to come the United States to experience freedom. Van and I knew
that everyday these kids were just trying to survive in their country. As the

two brothers left I felt so sorry for them because they would never know how good life can be without war. I just didn't know if they would make it through this war.

Chico was giving out a sick call every morning around 09:00 to the village people, offer them help if they needed it. Most of the people that saw Chico were the young teenage girls from the village. For the first couple of days, Lieutenant Ervin told all of us that we could not go swimming at all. Then word was passed that we could go swimming in the river for two hours each day but there must be two guys on duty while the rest were in the river. Chadwell came over and told Van, Grear, Quick, and me if we wanted to go swimming that we could go and that Charlie, Smithy and he would stand watch. It was going on around 12:00 noon and Van grabbed a rubber lady and took a towel with him. Grear and I just took a towel and went with Van to the other side of the road and down the side to the river. We had passed Mullin's machine gun team which was next to the road and he was letting two of his men go down to the river. When we got there Van took everything off except his jungle pants. He laid the rubber lady into the water and he then got on top of it and started floating around. I took off all of my clothes and laid my rifle next to the shore so I could get to it quickly in case we got hit. There were already a couple of the guys in the river having fun. It must have been about half an hour later that a couple of teenage girls were on the bridge watching us. The guys were waving at the girls to come down and join them and the next thing I knew the girls were in the water having fun with the guys. They had the girls on their shoulders and the girls were trying to get the other girl to fall off the shoulders of the guy that was carrying her. It was the first time that I had ever seen the guys really having fun and smiling. I could feel the coolness of the water hitting my body and it felt great against the hot sun. I pretty much stayed to myself. I would take a deep breath and go under the water as long as I could to escape from the heat and humidity. I thought about James and Benny and wished that they were still alive. I had a bar of soap and started washing my body and after I did that I grabbed my jungle pants and shirt and washed both of them with the bar of soap. I laid them down so that the heat from the sun would dry them out fast. Van was on the rubber lady just floating around and relaxing. The rest of the guys that were down on the river were having a great time and I could see it on their faces. I was getting tired and it was time for me to get out and let the other guys get into the river and have fun. I climbed out of the river and put on my jungle pants and boots. I looked over to where the girls and guys were having fun and none of the guys were having sex with the girls. Since the guys were naked and the girls weren't, they were playing tag and still playing king of the mountain. Van was still in the water and he told me that he would be coming out in a little bit and I told him that I was going to let the other guys come on down and I'd stand watch.

When I got back to my bunker, I told Chadwell and Charlie to get on over to the river and that I would watch. I told Chadwell that Van, Quick and Grear would be there in a couple of minutes. Chadwell, Smithy and Charlie then went over to the river and as they left, I started thinking about the people here in the village. I noticed that there were no men in the village at all from the ages of 14 to 60. I knew that the enemy must have them or they were in the Army of South Vietnam.

A couple more days passed and I went swimming, everyday. Then the word was passed that we were going on a squad patrol around the village. It was going on around 09:00 in the morning that we were going. I grabbed my gear and Sgt. Thomas came over to me and told me that I would be carrying the radio. A couple of minutes passed and Chadwell came over with Charlie and he told us to come with them. All of us walked over to the bridge and to the other side. Chadwell told us to sit down and wait for Sgt. Thomas to come out of the C.P. bunker. We were talking to some of the guys from 3rd squad who were on this side of the river with the C.P. group and they were not very happy being close to our lieutenant. I saw Whitey and his rifle which had a Playboy pennant attached to it. I told Whitey that I liked it. The pennant was about 9 inches long and at it widest point about 3 inches. It was all black except for the bunny and lettering, which were white. He had the pennant on the rifle of his.

Thomas came out of the bunker and told us to saddle up and as we got to our feet, the other guys were telling us to watch ourselves. Thomas told Chadwell that his team had point and that the other fire team was behind us. Charlie took point and behind him was Van, Chadwell, Grear, Thomas and then me and the other fire team Quick and Smithy. Charlie started moving, I then called the C.P. and told them that we were leaving the I.P. We walked down the road heading east through the village. We reached the T in the road and still headed east going out of the village. The people in the village were waving at us as we left. We moved about 2000 meters and Thomas told us to stop and then passed the word that we were going to go north for about 1000 meters, but before we left, to go north and to change point team. Thomas told us to take a ten-minute break. Thomas then told the guys to start moving out and I was to call back to the C.P. and let them know that we were at Checkpoint 1 and moving out. We reached Checkpoint 2 and I then called it in to the C.P. Thomas told us that we were now going to go about 2000 meters to the west. As we started heading west, the vill was off to our left side and we were angling toward the edge of the vill. The Artillery base on our right side on the hill was just outside of the vill. As we were getting closer to the vill, we could see the dirt road that was leading north from the village and past the artillery base. When we got to the dirt road, Thomas told us to go south on the road into the vill. I called the C.P. and told them that we were at Checkpoint 3. I knew that we were almost done with the patrol and it wouldn't be long before we got back to our bunker and rested for the day. When we got into the vill Thomas told us to take a ten minute break. I saw what looked like a schoolhouse and walked on over to it. The building was made up of cement walls with a straw roof. There were bullet holes all around the building. I went inside to see what it was like. When I got inside I couldn't believe what I saw. There was only one chalkboard and it was half broken. There were a few chairs for the kids to sit in and only a couple of books that were just lying around. The roof had holes in it from being hit by small mortar rounds.

I remembered when I was a little kid how I didn't want to go to school and all of us kids wished that we didn't have to go. We always looked forward to snow days. I also remembered that when I was in high school we had books, paper, pencil, pens, and a new high school building to go to. I realized how lucky we are in the whole world to be able to go to school and have great teachers and to be able to further our education.

Van came over to the school building and the both of us just looked at what these kids had, nothing. I heard Sgt. Thomas call for me and I went back outside and went on over to the dirt road. The chickens and water buffaloes were in the different yards of the vill. We started moving out toward the T in the road. Again, the people of the village were waving to us and they all had smiles on their faces knowing that we were here protecting them. We got to the intersection and went west which led to the bridge. I got on the radio and told them that we were at Checkpoint 4 and heading for the C.P., which was 100-meters away. We reached the bridge and I called in for the last time to the C.P. that we had arrived. I then went with my fire team back to our bunker. When I reached my bunker, Van, Grear and I took off our fighting gear and started getting something to eat. It was going on around 17:45 and we hadn't eaten all day.

About an hour after we had eaten, Van, Grear and I saw that Sgt. Thomas was coming over to our bunker with a new man. Thomas told us that we were getting a new man in our fire team and his name was Chuck Knight. Thomas told us to make sure that Chadwell knew about the new guy. Thomas left and we told Chuck to take off his gear and to take it easy. I called for Chadwell to come over and Charlie also came with him. Chuck Knight introduced himself to all of us and we all told him our names and I used my nickname, "Hammer." We asked him where he came from back in the States and he said that he came from Lebanon, Missouri, near Kansas City. As he was talking to us, he was a little nervous and Charlie and Van told him that we were in a safe place. Chuck said that he came from 2nd squad and had joined us at Camp Evans with James Fowler. All of us were making him feel at home and part of the unit. Chuck made me think of James Fowler a little and I was hoping that nothing would happen to Chuck, especially in this outfit. Chadwell left to see Sgt. Thomas and to get some more information on Chuck. When Chadwell came back he told us that there were about four or five new men that had come into our platoon. Chadwell told us that 2nd squad also picked up a new man by the name of Dale Davis. Chadwell said there would be two fighting holes during night watch duty. During the daytime our squad would watch only one fighting hole. The bunker that was next to the river would not be used during the nighttime but only during the day in case we got hit.

I knew that all of us were making Chuck feel at home but at the same time we didn't really want to know much about his personal life. We then started asking him questions about what was going on back at home, the new songs, cars, and sports, just the standard questions. Tonight it looked like we were going to have only two watches but only an hour each time, which was great. Chuck had all of the 782 gears that he was issued back in the rear to take out into the field. None of us could understand why the guys back in the rear would make the new men carry all of that shit out in the field. Chadwell told him when we got back to the rear to get rid of half that shit, because the weather would be getting hotter everyday through summer. The only thing that Chuck liked to talk about back at home was fishing and hunting.

I found myself talking like the guys that had been here for a while. I noticed that I had changed just like the old timers. I could see that I had been losing weight and steadily getting thinner. My jungle clothes were now changing from green to a faded green with brown mixed in with it. My jungle boots were not black but only the raw leather showing, which was somewhat brown.

Charlie was talking and telling us that all he needed was another Purple Heart and he was going home for good. Chuck asked him how many Purple Hearts he had and Charlie said that he had two so far and only needed one more to get out of Vietnam. Charlie said that he got shot by the enemy one time and the other time by our own troops. Charlie said they were coming back in from a L.P. to the lines when the guys shot at him thinking that he was the enemy. I looked at Charlie and told him if he wasn't so damn short that the guys would have not mistaken him as the enemy. All of us were laughing and having a great time. Then Charlie said that the only other way of getting out of here is to have two forty-eight hours Purple Hearts. Charlie said that you have to be in the hospital for over forty-eight hours two times to be eligible to go home. Charlie said that all he needed was one more and he said that he didn't mind if he got it in the arm or leg, just so he would get that third Purple Heart. In a way, all of us were hoping that he would get wounded lightly so that he could get the hell out of this place. At least he would make it back alive. At the same time we all didn't want to see him get hit.

I asked Charlie where he got hit and he said that he got it in the arm and on the side of his neck. I could see the scar on the side of his neck. Charlie said that our troops shot him in the neck.

A couple more days went by and the word was being passed that we would be leaving soon. At the vill we got to know the people here and felt how close all of us were to each other. Around 10:00 in the morning one of the new guys, Dale Davis, came over to us and told us that we were moving out and to get our fighting gear ready. Dale told us that we were going to Phu An, I said in a very slow and soft voice, "Oh, no…not there again." Dale heard me and asked if it was a bad place. I just looked at him and said that there was nothing to worry about. He then left to pass the word on to the rest of the guys in our platoon.

I was thinking to myself about the last time we were there trying to reach Phu An and didn't quite make it. I remembered carrying out Sergeant Singleton and Strouse who lost one leg and the other leg just hanging on while the relay teams kept the guy alive by talking to him. And of course, the huge U-shaped ambush that the N.V.A. had against our battalion. I got my fighting gear ready by putting it on top of the bunker and waited for the word to come down to get on the road. Van was making sure that his gear was ready as well as Quick, Grear, Charlie, Smithy, Chadwell and me. Chuck didn't know what to expect and none of us said a word to him. Chuck was getting scared because we were not saying anything. All of us were making sure that we were ready. He knew that something big was coming down. It was going to be my second time going down there and for the older guys it was their third time. I was hoping that this time we would be able to reach Phu An and get the N.V.A. out of there for good.

I told Van and Chuck that I was going to see a couple of the guys on the other side of the bridge for a little bit. As I was walking to the dirt road, I almost stepped on a snake, which was a 5 pacer, and it was moving very fast in the grass. I went back to the bunker and told Van and he grabbed an E-tool and both of us went back to see if we could kill the snake. Both of us looked around but the snake was long gone. We then went back to the bunker where Chuck was sitting. We could hear Sgt. Thomas calling for us to get on the dirt road. I put on my gear plus the radio and went on over to the dirt road. I told Chuck that we had a few hours of humping before we got there. As we got to the dirt road Thomas told us to get into a staggered column and when everyone was on the dirt road, we moved out to the other side of the bridge and walked up about fifty meters and were told to get off the road and wait. I went off to the side of the dirt road and the village people came out and the kids were talking to us and telling us not to go but to stay. Then the word was passed that we were waiting for the rest of the battalion to come. It was about twenty minutes and we could see that the six-bys were coming this way. The trucks went past us and turned at the T in the road and the troops got out of the trucks and got into a staggered column. One of the six-bys came back with Marines in it and they were taking over guarding the bridge from us. They were not from our battalion.

The word was passed that Captain Hutchinson wanted our lieutenant up. All of us knew that we were going to be the point team again for the battalion. As we watched, the lieutenant walked up to where the captain was. All of the guys would have loved to shoot the son of a bitch in the back if they could. A couple of minutes went by when the word was passed on the radio that our squad was called up to be the point team again. I told Thomas that they wanted us up to the front of the column and that we were to be the point squad again. Thomas told Chadwell that his team was point and as we moved out in a staggered column, the rest of the guys in our battalion were telling us, "Go get them." All of us were laughing as we moved up in a staggered column. I really didn't like walking the next three hours just to get to Phu An. Bravo Company was not with us on this operation-it was only Alpha and Delta Companies.

We reached the front of the battalion and I called back on the radio to our platoon that we were moving out. As I looked back, the rest of the guys who were sitting down on the road were getting up and ready to move. A lot of the village people were telling us there were a lot of N.V.A. down there waiting for us again. The village people didn't want our platoon to go down there but to stay here and protect them. As we walked farther away from the village heading north to Phu An, I looked back and the people were still waving to us. I was hoping that we wouldn't get hit hard like we had the last time we went down there. About a 1000 meters out the word was passed that Alpha Company was to be on our left flank. Once they got out there, we started moving out again down the road to Phu An. We finally reached the last hill before going down to the stream that led into Phu An. Alpha Company had to go around and set up as a blocking force and Charlie Company was going to drive them into Alpha Company. Delta Company was going to remain behind Charlie Company. The word was passed on the radio that we were to stay on the hill for the night and that tomorrow we would be going into Phu An.

We got the same old fighting holes we had the last time we were here. I stood my two watches and both times thought about going to Phu An. I was hoping that this time we would be able to get the N.V.A. out of there for good. I could feel the loneliness coming over me but I also knew that nothing was going to happen to me. I could almost feel something that was with me and watching over me, again. I said a little prayer for the new guys who joined our outfit as well as the old timers that they would not get hit or killed. In a way it seemed like life was very hard on all of us, and that it was up to us to get ourselves out alive. I wasn't thinking about home as much as when I first got here and the other thing was that I wasn't afraid of death anymore. Inside of me death was the very last thing on my mind.

Dong Ha, Forward battalion area of the 1ˢᵗ Battalion 9ᵗʰ Marines. March 1967 – picture by Bill Gonzales

Charlie Company on patrol just south of Quang Tri City. Early April 1967 – picture by Bill Gonzales

Charlie company out of water for three days, Maxwell, (Speedy) Bill
Gonzales, and the radioman remembered the Well when we were here
before. Frank Bignami receiving water from the woman who lived there.
April 1967 – picture by Bill Gonzales

On patrol down at "Street Without Joy," looking back is Gary Duvall who
was later killed at "Market Street" in the D.M.Z. April 1967.
– picture by Bill Gonzales

Cam Lo Bridge, white building is the platoon C.P. We protected the
bridge for about a week. Early May 1967. – picture by Bill Gonzales

Cam Lo Bridge, Jerry Vizer youngest guy in the platoon (17 years old).
Vizer was later killed up at Con Thein. May 1967
– picture by Bill Gonzales

Cam Lo Bridge, left is Platoon Sergeant Tony Lefefe and right is Grear who was transferred to 3rd Battalion 3rd Marines shortly after this picture was taken. Early May 1967.

Cam Lo Bridge, from left to right is Charlie, Gary Kasten (Hammer), and Chadwell, my fire team leader. Early May 1967.

It was going on morning and I could hear that it was time for everyone to get up and eat before we went into Phu An. I got up and looked around and everyone was working on cooking their food. All of the guys were very quiet and thinking to themselves about what lay ahead. It was 06:30 and the word was passed to saddle up and that we were moving out. As I was getting my gear on, I could hear in the distance some vehicles coming our way from Cam Lo Bridge. They were our tanks, four of them. In a way I was glad and in another way I wished that they were not with us. The sound of the tanks made it very difficult to hear the enemy. The tanks finally arrived and the lieutenant told us that we were taking point again for the company. I knew as well as the rest of the guys in our squad that we had the honors of being the point team for the whole battalion. The lieutenant told us that Alpha Company was being the blocking force so that the enemy could not escape. Delta Company was in reserve in case we needed them. Thomas came over to me and told Chadwell that his team had point again for the company. Thomas told me to stay with my fire team and that he would be close by.

Chadwell told Charlie to take the point this time, followed by me, Chadwell and then Chuck in that order. Behind our team was Van, Quick, Sgt. Thomas, Grear and Smithy. We started moving out in a staggered column down off the hill by following the same dirt road that led down to the stream. The rest of the guys in our platoon and the sister platoons were telling us to watch ourselves. I could hear the tanks starting up their engines and they didn't leave until our platoon was down the hill before they left. As we reached the bottom of the hill, the stream was right in front of us and yet I could feel that the enemy was not around here. We were moving out very slowly and making sure that the enemy was not hiding in the hedgerows that were on both sides of the road. I knew that down the dirt road about 100 meters was an open field off to our left side and I knew that was where we were going. We moved down the road slowly until Charlie reached the open field off to our left side and I called back to the C.P. and told them that we had reached the open field and were heading toward it. We followed the tire path that led into the open field that went to the vill, off the dirt road. The word was passed to stop and I could hear on the radio that we were going to have flanks out on both sides of us. Third squad had one fire team on our right side of the platoon and the other fire team on the left side of the platoon about 100 meters away from our main column.

I remembered this very large open field which was about 500 meters long with the hedgerows on both sides of us and in front. It was about 300 meters wide. We reached the hedgerow in front of us and I remembered that it was not very wide going through it. We got into the next open field, which was about 500 meters long and about 300 meters wide. As our whole company got into the open area with the tanks, I remembered that we found the dead sergeant from Alpha Company up ahead just in front of the hedge-row. We reached it and the word was passed from the C.P. to stop. Then the word was passed that the whole company, including the tanks, was to get on line and that we were going to sweep through the village which was just in front of us about 200 meters. It took us about twenty minutes until we got everyone on line including the tanks and then the word was passed to move out. The tanks then opened up with their fifty caliber machines guns into the hedgerow. We were almost side-by-side and the bushes were very thick. All of the guys were also firing their rifles into the hedgerow. It was almost damn near impossible to see the guy on the right or left side of you. I could hear the tanks still firing their fifty and once in awhile they would open up with their 90 mm. For some reason I had gotten out a little too far in front and Dale Davis from 2nd squad yelled as hard as he could, "Hammer duck." As soon as I heard "Hammer duck," I dropped down in a prone position and both tanks opened up with their 90mm on me. I couldn't hear a damn thing at this time. My ears were ringing from the 90s and I could only see what was happening and I got up and started moving out again. I started to get scared because I couldn't hear a damn thing, just the ringing in my ears. I was hoping that it would quickly leave so I could be able to hear with the rest of the guys. I was firing my rifle on semi-automatic in front of me.

There was an opening up in front of us and as all of us, including the tanks, came out of the hedgerow. In front of me was a thin hedgerow that was about five feet wide leading to the village and new fighting holes dug by the N.V.A. I could almost sense that the enemy was watching us and didn't want any part of us at this time. The N.V.A. didn't go where we wanted them to go which was to Alpha Company so they could cut them down. There were palm trees around the vill as well as pineapple plants. As we were getting closer to the vill, everyone was watching each other. Some of the guys were taking pictures of the place while others were taking out their lighters lighting up the straw off the roofs of the huts. I came up against a bunker that was next to a hut and I then took out a grenade and pulled the pin and at the same time Van Meeteren also pulled the pin from his grenade and both of us from both sides of the bunker threw the grenades into it. We then called, "Fire in the hole!" and after a couple of seconds they went off. If there was anyone inside of the bunker, they were dead.

We had completely gone past the village and the word was passed to go back through the vill. We were going to set up in the last large clearing before we went into Phu An. As we went back Captain Hutchinson called for the lieutenants from the three platoons and told them where they were to set up their platoons. The captain had two of the tanks on the west side and the other two tanks on the east side of the hedgerows. Lieutenant Ervin came back and told us that we had the east side of the perimeter and part of the north. Next to our fire team was one of the tanks and in a way it felt good to have something that big next to us with all that firepower.

Chadwell told us our watches for the night and on my first time at watch I could hear the tanks starting up their engines for about fifteen minutes and then turn them off. The tank didn't really make a lot of noise but it helped the enemy know just where we were. I could still feel the enemy watching us but they didn't want to hit us. There was a smell about the place that all of us didn't like here and knew that the N.V.A. were watching us. I still could feel myself being very edgy and the rest of the guys felt the same way with the exception of the new guys. I was glad that the enemy didn't hit us and that the new guys got through this without getting wounded or killed. When my watch was over, I kicked the bottom of Charlie's foot and he took over. I then lay down but I couldn't really sleep, I could still smell that strange odor near us. I just lay there waiting for my next turn to watch and after three hours it was my turn. I got up and I could tell that the rest of the guys were not sleeping as well, with the exception of the new guys. Everyone in our company knew that the N.V.A. were getting ready to hit us. It seemed that the N.V.A. always wanted it on their terms and still the N.V.A. knew that if and when they did hit us that we could still kick the living hell out of them.

Morning came and the word was passed that we were going back to Cam Lo Bridge. The guys in the tanks were very happy to get the hell out of this place and didn't want to be around the 1st Battalion 9th Marines as well. They had heard about some of the firefights that we had with the N.V.A. The word was passed that the tanks were leaving at 05:30 and that all of us were to be on 100 percent alert in case the enemy was going to hit us while the tanks left. At 05:30 the tanks started up and they all moved back to where they came from. All of us were watching to see if we were going to get hit but still no firing from the enemy. Word was passed to eat and that we were moving out at 06:30 back to Cam Lo Bridge.

It was 06:30 and the 1st platoon had point, followed by 3rd Platoon and then 2nd Platoon. We moved back to the large clearing and then back to the dirt road. When we got to the dirt road we did not go back to Cam Lo Bridge. Alpha and Delta Company went to different areas as well. Charlie Company headed due east for about 4000 meters and the terrain was changing into a very large flat area with thin hedgerows. We were coming into another vill and someone told us that the name of this place was Phu Ox. It was even smaller than Phu An with no one around. We ended up on another dirt road that lead through the vill and on the left side was a small Catholic church that was about 75 meters from the road. The word was passed that we were going to stay here for tonight.

The Catholic church was on the end of the small vill. The captain had the whole company move down the road about 100 meters from the church and we moved left into the open field which had a hedgerow only on the north side. As we were setting up the perimeter, our platoon had the north side and part of the west side. Our fire team was about fifty meters from the hedgerow and we started digging our fighting hole. It was getting close to 17:00 hundred hours and almost time for food. Thomas came over to us and said that our squad was going out on a ambush tonight.

At 20:00 hundred hours, the word was passed to saddle up. As we were getting our gear on, some of the guys from our platoon came over to take over our fighting holes for the night. I picked up the radio and made sure that it was working before we left. Thomas told the squad to move out. I got on the radio and told the C.P. that we were leaving the I.P. and to pass the word to the rest of the guys in the platoon that we were leaving the perimeter. Thomas looked back at me and I told him that I had already called the C.P. We were going straight out in front of our position heading north. We reached the hedgerow and went through it. It was not very thick and then we were in another wide field and another hedgerow, which was about 150 meters in front of us. We moved up to the edge of the hedgerow and Thomas pointed to all of us that we were going to stay here for the night. Thomas then showed each of us where he wanted the guys to be and that the radio was going to be in the center of us. Thomas had Van on the end, then Charlie, Chuck, Chadwell, me, Parrillo, Quick, Smithy, Grear, and Thomas. Thomas whispered to us not to wake him unless we heard something. Everyone took off their gear as quietly as possible and we were right next to each other. I then called on the radio back to our platoon and told them that we had reached our L.P. I heard the platoon radioman say, "Affirmative, over." I then took off the radio and turned one of the knobs on "squelch" so that the enemy could not heard the radio. I then got out my poncho and the rest of the guys were doing the same. I made sure that I had my gear ready to put on if we had to get out in a hurry. I took the radio and moved it more to the left side of me so that the guys could hear the C.P. call us every half hour during the night.

Chadwell shook me and I got up and he handed me the radio. He then lay back down and I sat up and put my rifle across my lap. I looked up and all of the stars were out. I could also hear some of the crickets making their sounds. I knew that the enemy was not around and as I sat there I took off my high school ring. I looked at it and though what my high school did to me; I decided to bury the ring here in Vietnam. I wanted no part of my high school. I remembered when I came home on leave at Christmas time. I received a letter from my high school that I had scored very well on my SAT and could have gotten a scholarship to North Texas State University to play football; now I was playing football with the N.V.A. I remembered going to school and telling off the administration for what they had done to me by keeping the SAT test from me. One of the counselors put the test score on the shelf and forgot about where he put it.

The half hour was up and I could hear the radioman call me - if all secure to press my handset twice - which I did. I only had a half hour more to go for the night. As I was listening and trying to see out in front of me as well as on both sides of me, I could tell that my senses were getting very keen. I started thinking about my father and when he fought against the Japanese. I knew that I was going through the same ordeal as he had. I remembered him saying that one night when he was on night watch, he heard a Japanese running through their lines and he and five other guys pulled their pins from their grenades and threw them at the Japanese and in the morning they found the him dead. I heard the radioman call for me and I pressed the handset twice to let them know that we were all right. I then shook Parrillo and he got up and I handed the radio to him and he shook his head at me to let me know that he was awake. I covered myself up and went back to sleep.

The next thing I knew someone shook me and whispered to me to get up and to wake up the next guy. It was getting close for the sun to come up. I shook the guy next to me and I started rolling up my poncho and tied it on the back of my flak jacket. I started getting my gear on and the last thing I put on was the radio. Thomas told us to go back to the hedgerow in front of our company position and to stop there. Grear took point and all of us moved out in a single file but staying at least 30 feet away from each other. When we all reached the hedgerow, Thomas told Grear to get ready to fire the green pop-up. Thomas then told me to call the platoon and tell them that we were ready to come back in. I called the platoon and told them that we were ready to come back in and the platoon radioman told me to pop the flare. I nodded to Thomas to fire the pop-up and he told Grear to fire it on a 45-degree angle toward the company area. Grear hit the bottom of the green pop-up with the heel of his hand and it went off. I then called on the radio back to the platoon and asked them what color they saw. They said, "Green." I told the platoon radioman, "Affirmative." About five minutes went by before the platoon radioman called back to me. The platoon radioman told us to come on in. I told Thomas that it was all right to go on in. Grear got up and started going through the hedgerow. As we got to the other side, the guys on the perimeter were watching us very closely to make sure that we were not the enemy. I felt really scared about coming back in and not knowing if my own troops would fire on us. I just hoped that they had passed the word around the perimeter that we were coming back in and not to shoot. Now, I could see why our own troops shot Charlie in the past. If they didn't get the word that the team was coming back in, it was easy for the guys on the perimeter to open up.

We did some patrols east and south of the Strip for the next couple of days and all of us could tell that there were no N.V.A. around. Each day that we went on the patrol we would come across a pipe in the ground that ice cold water was coming out of. The pipe was about an inch in diameter and I made sure that I got a long drink from it. It was the only time during the day that most of us got to drink water during these very hot days. We came up to the edge of The Strip which was also called, "McNamara's Wall" where the Seabees bulldozed a strip 200 meter wide and about 15000 meters long, from Con Thein to Gio Lin. The strip went east to west between these two outposts.

The word was passed that we were leaving and heading back down south. The whole company got ready to leave and we started back down the road through the vill heading west. We were in the rolling hills that didn't have any trees or bushes on them. As we were going up on one of the hills, the guys were turning left when they got to the top of the hill. It was the dirt road that led back to Cam Lo Bridge. The word was passed to get into a staggered column when we reached the road.

When we finally reached the outskirts of Cam Lo vill, the six-bys were waiting for us. As we got into the vill the mama-sans and kids came out and were happy to see us, especially us guys from 2nd platoon. Lieutenant Ervin told us to get on two of the six-bys and to get ready to leave. We boarded the trucks and sat down and while we sat, the kids came up to us and wanted us to stay but we told them that we had to go somewhere else. The trucks started up the engines and started off going toward the bridge and heading west back to the black top highway, which was about two miles away. We turned left onto the black top road and headed straight south. The lead truck turned into Dong Ha and as each of the trucks went inside the gate we took out the round in our rifle chamber and put the rifles on "safe."

The trucks took us over to where our battalion was stationed here in Dong Ha. We got off the trucks and they left. I went over to our tent and took off my fighting gear and radio and turned the radio off to save the batteries. Chadwell got word from Thomas that on the side of the hill was a place for us to take a shower. They were going to start it up in about half an hour from now and if we wanted to take a shower to make sure that we got there at that time. I sat down on my cot and grabbed my sea-bag and took out a bar of soap and a towel. I took off my jungle shirt and then took off my socks. Some of the guys from our company were heading on up to the showers. I got up and grabbed the bar of soap and towel and headed on up to the shower.

They had a huge tub about fifteen feet in diameter that held the water and on the outside of the tub was the pump that pumped the water into a single pipe that went up to about seven feet into the air and then branched off into two pipes that went about twenty feet long with holes in each line for the water to come out. I took off my jungle pants and boots and got under one of the pipes that was above me and on the ground were pallets for the floor so that we didn't get our feet muddy. The pump started and in a couple of minutes the water was coming out and the water was warm. I washed myself with the bar of soap and it really felt great to take a shower for the first time. There weren't any girls around to see that all of us were having a great time and that we were all naked and out in the open. I couldn't believe how thin all of us were when we took off all of our clothing. I was finished and went on over to where my jungle pants and boots were and put them on and went back to the tent.

When I got back to the tent and to my cot, I took out my razor and dry shaved. When I shaved under my nose I thought about Benny and that he trimmed my mustache that day when he stepped on the booby trap. Then my mind thought about James as well. I didn't want to have a mustache because it made me think of Benny. I could still feel the pain of losing him and not being able to talk with him. He was the only black guy in the whole battalion who talked to both the black guys and white guys and made sure that everyone got along together. I remembered what he told me that the black guys didn't want to be close to the white guys. It was difficult for him to make them understand that. I started thinking about Maxwell and how much of a loner he was, even with the black guys. Maxwell stayed close to his machine gun team and no one else. When I finished dry shaving, I just lay in my cot thinking about this place and the guys in our platoon, and battalion. In one of the tents the blacks guys were singing Motown songs and one of the black guys couldn't carry a tune. All of them told him to get away and do something else. I couldn't believe they would do that to another black guy. All of the white guys in our battalion didn't give a damn if the blacks stayed to themselves but the black guys chasing one of their own away just because he couldn't carry a tune was low down. They didn't want any part of him, making it quite clear that they didn't want him with them. The black guy didn't want the white guys to know that he was not one of the brothers. I knew that deep down in my heart that we needed each other if all of us were going to survive, regardless if we were black or white. I looked over in our tent and Maxwell didn't want any part of the blacks singing their soul music. I looked outside my tent and there were only a very few Negroes that stayed away from the blacks that were together when we got back to the rear.

Chapter Thirteen

The word was passed that we were going to have mail call. I was like everyone else, I couldn't wait for the mail to come here from the outside world. Thomas came into the tent and handed out the letters and again I had about ten letters that had my outfit's name on the address. There were no boxes for me yet but I knew that Mom would not fail me. I knew that it would take a little longer for the boxes to get over here. After I took my time in reading my mother's letters, it was time for chow and I got out of the cot and went on over to the mess tent. I hoped that they would feed us steak, like the Army did back at Camp Evans. However, I saw they were feeding us Rice and Spam and at the end of the chow line was the huge bucket of, Pre-sweetened Kool-aid. I passed on the Kool-aid and took water instead. After chow I went back to the tent and sat down on the cot thinking that the only time we were going to get any steaks in our battalion area was when our outfit was out in the bush. The only people that were getting the steaks were the cooks and clerks in our battalion area. These clerks and cooks would write home and tell how bad it was and what they are going through over here. They would listen to us when we would be back in the rear, and then tell their friends and family back at home how bad they are having it over here.

One of the guys came into the tent and told us that they were going to show a movie on the other side of the mess tent. He told us that the movie would start around 20:00 hundred hours, if we wanted to go. As the sun was going down, I decided to go on over to where the movie was going to be seen. I walked behind the mess tent and a bunch of benches set up for the troops to watch the outdoor movie. Poison was with a couple of the guys in our platoon. I was glad that the guys didn't stay away from him and he was being welcomed back into the platoon. The movie started and it was a Western. As the movie started the loneliness came over me. I tried not to think about it while I was watching the movie, but it was still with me. When the movie was over, I got up and went back to the tent to get some sleep in for the whole night. As I sat down on the cot, the dust flew up in the air from the dirt road. Every cot in each of the tents in the battalion was covered with dust.

Some of the guys were playing poker and having a good time. I just lay in my cot and went off to sleep. I could hear some of the guys talking about going to the mess tent, so I got up and went on over to the mess tent and after I was finished with the chow, I went back to the tent. The word was passed that we were going out on another operation. I gathered all of my combat gear and all of us waited for the word to saddle up. Chuck Knight turned in half of the 782 gear that he didn't need. He didn't want to burn up out there in the hot sun and humidity. The rest of the new guys did the same thing by turning in some of their 782 gear. I grabbed the radio and turned it back on to see if the battery was going bad and it was. I grabbed the extra battery and put it into the radio and took the old one and trashed it. I then went over to Thomas and told him that I needed another battery for the radio. Thomas told me that he would get me one. Thomas came back into the tent and gave me the extra battery and then told us that our new squad leader was Chadwell and that Van was taking over the fire team. Thomas said that he was now a short timer and that he was not going back out in the field. I was thinking in a way that I was glad that Chadwell was taking over and Van was the fire team leader. I didn't have to worry about Thomas not doing his job out in the bush, because I knew that he was more afraid than all of us.

The six-bys arrived and the word was passed to get on the trucks. When I got on the six-by, I looked at Thomas and I could tell that he was glad that he was not going out with us. I knew that if we hit the shit that he couldn't fire his rifle. The rest of the guys in our squad knew it also. After everyone got onto the trucks and sat down, the six-bys started off. We got to the front gate of the base and turned right onto Highway 1 heading south to Quang Tri City. We reached the city and the word was passed to get off. The trucks turned around and headed back up north to Dong Ha. Chadwell came over to me and said to give the radio to Chuck so he knew how to use the radio. I handed the radio to Chuck and told him that our call sign was Charlie 2-1 and our platoon call sign was Charlie 2. Chuck then gave me the case of C-rations. He told me and Chadwell that he was glad he didn't have to carry all of the 782 gears that were issued to him. We both looked at him and said that the radio wasn't a picnic to carry and he was going to find it out. The day was starting to get hotter by the minute and all of us knew that we were going to do a lot of humping in the hills.

The company started moving through the city in a staggered column. As we got to the end of the city, the dirt road went down off this large hill that we were on. In the distance we could see that it went right back up into another large hill. There were a couple of us in the company that were carrying the cases of C-rations. There was a hut off to our right side about 60 feet from the road and a mama-san was calling to us Marines with the cases of C-rations. Next to her was her daughter who looked like she was about sixteen and mama-san was saying, "You boom boom for chop chop." The mama-san kept saying it to us and I couldn't believe what I was hearing. She was very desperate in letting us have her daughter for the C-rations. It was just so hard to believe that this was happening. I remembered the war movies that I had seen when I was a kid and how the people were very hungry and would do anything to get food and that included giving their daughters. I thought that it was made up but to see it in real life was so very hard to believe.

We reached the top of the other hill and we could see many low, rolling hills with bushes that were about two to four feet high. We stayed on the dirt road for about 3000 more meters and then got off the road and walked around the hills for another 2000 meters. We got word that we were setting up on one of the hills for the night. As we were digging our fighting holes, Chadwell went on over to the C.P. group and Lieutenant Ervin informed Chadwell about what was out here. Chadwell came back and told us in the squad that S-2 said that there were 10,000 N.V.A. out here and that they were going to attack Quang Tri City and our company of less than 135 men were to hold off 10,000 N.V.A. Chadwell looked at all of us in the squad of eight men and laughed and said, "No big deal, we can handle 10,000 N.V.A" All of us began to laugh. We were getting used to going up against very large numbers of N.V.A. but they would somehow retreat and not hit us, if they knew that 1st Battalion 9th Marines were in the area.

Van told us what watch we had for the night and the rest of us bedded down. All of us stood our two watches and when morning came, one of the guys in our squad told the rest of us that he took a can of bacon and a can of powdered eggs from the mess hall and we were going to eat good today. The next three days went by and we moved all over the rolling hills and couldn't find the enemy. On the fourth day, 3rd platoon set up for an ambush just off the dirt road for the night. It must have been around 03:15 when we heard one hell of a lot of rifles and machines guns going off. It sounded like the Fourth of July. All of us were up and the word was passed that we might be going out there where 3rd platoon was. After about twenty minutes the word was passed that we were staying here until morning and then we were going on over to where 3rd platoon was. Captain Hutchinson told 3rd platoon not to leave their positions until we got to them before they went down the hill and look to see if there were any dead enemy lying around. The sun was starting to come up and the word was passed to saddle up.

We reached 3rd platoon, which was 500 meters away, and they left and went down the hill while we gave them cover. We could see 3rd platoon down at the bottom of the hill looking around for the enemy. It was about half an hour later when they came back and they said there were a lot of blood trails and a few straw and plastic hats lying around. It looked like 3rd platoon kicked the hell out of the N.V.A. and somehow they recovered their dead soldiers so that we wouldn't know how many of them we killed.

The word was passed to move out and that 2nd platoon was to take point. Captain Hutchinson told Lieutenant Ervin that we were to move out in a staggered column on this dirt road for a short while. Chadwell told Van that our fire team had point and Van told Chuck Knight to take point, then me, and then Grear. We went about 1000 meters and then we were getting sniper fire on our left side of the dirt road. I was on the right side of the road and Chuck who was point was on the left side and I asked Chuck if he could see the snipers and he said no. I was in a prone position and I knew that the enemy had to be almost as high up as us. There were two or three rounds from an AK-47 that just missed my right elbow by about 2 inches. I told Chuck that I was going to move across the road to get a better chance of firing my rifle at them. Chuck said, "Go!" and I got up and went across the road and got right back down in a prone position and started firing my rifle again. There were only three of us firing our rifles while the rest of the company just watched. No sooner had I gotten back down into the prone position when another two to three rounds from the AK-47 just missed me by an inch. I could tell that this guy was really trying to get me. I kept on firing my rifle at the places where I thought the enemy was. I knew one thing: he had to be almost right in front of me because of the rounds that hit right in front of my right elbow. There was a large bush that looked like it was about four feet high and about three feet wide. I told Chuck that I was firing at the large bush and that it had to be the only place for the sniper to fire his rifle from.

After about ten minutes, Chuck and I knew that the sniper must have left or we had gotten him because we were not getting any more return fire. The word was passed that we were going back on the road and that Grear and I were to be rear point guys for the company. We moved back about sixty meters; we were going down off the hill and the road went back up on the next hill. Grear and I stayed back from the rest of the guys about 100 feet to protect the rest of the column. We were still moving in a staggered column. When Grear and I reached the bottom of the hill again, we heard only two rounds coming at the company. It was hard for Grear and me to see where the rounds came from but I knew that the sniper was trying to piss us off and to make sure that we were having a bad day. The sniper fired his rifle a couple of more times and that was all we heard from him for the rest of the day.

We were moving to the southwest and it was new territory for us. The next day came and as we were patrolling the area, the word was passed there were booby traps around. Shortly after we got word, all of us heard an explosion. The word was passed that Poison was the one that had stepped on the booby trap. One of the guys in the platoon said that Johnson was wounded as well. I remembered what Poisson had said to me a while back that the guys called him "Poison" because if you were around him that you would get either killed or wounded. Well, I knew they couldn't call him poison now. We waited for the chopper to come to pick them up and to get them back to the med station. After they were gone, Captain Hutchinson

called for flanks on each side of our staggered column. All of us in the
company were out of water and the next couple of days were going to be
very rough on all of us. The sun and humidity wasn't helping us at all. In
the distance was a very large hill and I knew we were heading for it. We
finally reached the big hill and set up our perimeter around it, the Captain's
C.P. group was at the top of the hill. Chadwell told us that we didn't have
time to dig our fighting hole for the night and that we were going to go out
on an ambush. It got to be around 20:00 hundred hours and Chadwell told
us to get our gear on and that we were moving out. We went to the bottom
of the hill and moved about 200 meters to where there was a small trail and
we set up for the ambush.

The next thing I knew, Chuck kicked me at the bottom of my foot and
told me to get my gear on, we were moving back to our company. I knew
that something big was going on. We moved out and reached the bottom
of the hill. Chadwell told Charlie to get ready to fire the green pop up.
Chadwell told Chuck to call the platoon and let them know that we were
ready to come back into the perimeter. We waited for a couple of minutes
and Chadwell told Charlie to fire the green pop up. Chuck got back on the
radio and asked the C.P. what color the pop up was. They told us "green"
and Chuck said, "yes" so the word was passed to come on in. We got inside
the perimeter and our lieutenant told us to be ready to leave if we had to. He
told us that 2nd Battalion 4th Marines were getting hit up at Con Thein. We
knew that it must be very bad for us to come back in from our ambush.

It was around 01:00 and the whole company was on 100 percent alert
in case we were needed up north to help out 2nd Battalion 4th Marines. Our
squad was setting near the top of the hill with no cover. In the distance we
heard a pumping sound, and I knew the enemy was shooting at us with their
mortars. Chuck was about ten feet from me-he got up and was about to run
to the perimeter. I got up and tackled him. I told Chuck not to move and
to stay as close to the ground as possible. I laid on top of him to make sure
he didn't get up. Being on top of Chuck made him feel a little better. I was
over him and could feel his body getting calm. He knew that if anything
would happen to him that it was going to happen to me first. The rounds
were hitting all around us and I could feel him shaking underneath me.
The shrapnel was hitting all around us but I didn't say a word to Chuck. I
whispered to him to just listen and we could tell if the rounds were coming
at us or not. The ground was shaking around us but the rounds were missing us by about thirty feet. I hoped that no one in our company got hit by
the mortar rounds. It lasted for about twenty minutes and then it got quiet.
I told Chuck that being on the side of the hill the shrapnel would fly over
us. I knew that I could tell if we were going to get it or not by the way they
were dropping in on us.

Chapter Fourteen

When it was over, I got off of Chuck and he then asked me how I knew that they were mortars and I told him that my first night in the field we had gotten hit by mortar rounds from the N.V.A. and that we had lost four men. I knew that he would never forget the sounds of what a mortar round sounded like from now on. I listened to hear if anyone had gotten hit and the word was passed that everyone was all right. I then told Chuck that the first two months are dangerous for anybody coming over here because we were still thinking about home, girlfriends, cars and sports. I said to him that he has to concentrate at all times when we were in the field or back at the base camps, and not to let his guard down for one minute. Everyone in the whole company stayed up for the whole night. We were still on "Standby" to help 2nd Battalion 4th Marines up at Con Thein.

Morning came and still no word about us to stand down in case we had to go to Con Thein. I hoped the Marines up there were not getting hit hard, but no one knew what they were going through. It was around 10:00 in the morning that the word was passed that the 2nd Battalion 4th Marines didn't need any help. Then the word was passed that we would stay here for the rest of the day and our squad dug our fighting holes and that one guy from each fire team was to gather all of their water canteens and get them filled up with water. I told Van Meeteren that I would go and get the water while they dug the fighting hole. I collected all of the canteens and went down off the hill and followed the other guys in our company to the water. There was a hut and a mama-san with her family and it was the first time that I had seen a mama-san helping Marines. The woman was in her thirties, and I could almost sense that she wanted no part of us and I knew that she was a V.C. but there was nothing any of us could do about it. After I filled up the water from the well, I went back up the hill and gave the canteens back to the guys. The rest of the day all of us just sat around doing nothing. It was great getting the ice cold water from the well and everyone of us was drinking like crazy. All of us knew that we would be out of water in a couple of days from now. As the day rolled on, all of the guys would take a trip to the well and drink the cold water because of the heat and humidity. The water in our canteens were already hot and we couldn't drink from them. It seemed that each day would go by and every night we were being beaten down by the enemy, by the weather, and lack of men in our battalion.

A couple of days passed and we were going back on the hill where Poison had stepped on the booby trap. We were to put out flanks and our

C.P. called for 1st squad to send out one of our fire teams. Chadwell called for the 2nd fire team to go out on the flanks. It was Grear, Dale Davis, Smithy and Quick. They were on the side of the hill and then we moved out. The flanks were about fifty feet away from our staggered column. All of us made sure that we didn't trip any trip wire. We got about halfway through the hill when Dale stepped on a booby trap and I watched him go straight down like his feet had just gotten cut from underneath him. There was another explosion and a couple of more guys stepped on the booby traps. Then the word was passed not to move but stay where we were. Dale got up and yelled out, "I'm pissed," and then started walking again and Grear came up to him and made him stop, before he stepped on another booby trap. Everyone in the column stopped and all of us waited until they took care of Dale as well as the other guys. The word was passed to stay on the trail and not to get off of it because the guys could see the booby traps all over this hill. Grear told us that Dale had got it in the legs and one of his arms but he was not that bad. I then started out to where Dale was, which was about fifty feet from me, and the guys were telling me not to go but I went through the minefield and reached Dale. I told Grear that I would carry him back to where the corpsman was so he could make sure that he was all right. I carried him through the minefield and back on the trail, and sat him down; Chico came over and started taking care of Dale.

As soon as Chico began checking out Dale, we heard another explosion behind us and we knew that another guy had gotten it. The word was passed again that no one was to move, but to stay put. It was about fifteen minutes while the corpsmen took care of all the wounded guys. Somehow Lieutenant Ervin was off the trail talking to our three squad leaders, Chadwell, Francis, and Von Bargen about thirty feet from us. The word was passed that our lieutenant wanted character, "Kilo up" to be the platoon radioman. Kilo is the first letter of the last name and that was me and my last name was Kasten. I started walking up to the lieutenant; I could hear Chuck coming up behind me and he told me that the lieutenant called for Knight to be the platoon radioman, I looked at him and told him that the lieutenant wanted me. Chuck and I argued for a couple of minutes and said that the lieutenant didn't call for Hammer. Chuck finally told me that he had walked farther then me and that he wasn't going to go back from where he came from. It was just too damn hot and humid out to be walking around for no reason.

I finally gave in and he said that nothing was going to happen now because he had walked so far to get to the lieutenant. Chuck finally got behind the lieutenant while the three squad leaders were facing Lieutenant Ervin and I could hear the lieutenant tell Chuck that he was the new platoon radioman. Chuck got the radio and was behind the lieutenant about five feet. I could almost hear what was going on; the lieutenant was telling the three squad leaders which squad was to be first, second and third when we started out. The three squad leaders were telling the lieutenant there was a booby trap right in front of him and he told them that they didn't know what the hell they were talking about. Just before the lieutenant took the first step, all three squad leaders quickly moved away about ten feet from the lieutenant. Then the lieutenant took that first step and he set the booby trap off. The smoke went up as he fell to the ground, yelling like crazy. Chuck also fell to the ground and I knew that he also got it too. Some of the guys in our platoon picked up Chuck and carried him on over to the trail. Lieutenant Ervin walked over to the trail with the rest of us except for the flanks and sat down waiting for the platoon corpsman to help him. Word was passed that the flanks were to come back in.

Our regular platoon radioman had come down with heat stroke. Chico was now working on the wounds of both Dale and Chuck but he refused to help the lieutenant. Captain Hutchinson came up to see just what was going on. Lieutenant Ervin was lying on the ground and yelling for the corpsman to help him but still Chico refused. Captain Hutchinson told his radioman to call up the company corpsman who was Marsh, who used to be our platoon corpsman. When he saw our lieutenant on the ground bleeding in the legs, Marsh almost didn't want to help the lieutenant but the captain gave him an order and he did it. We got everyone ready to move out and to get off this hill. Then we would call in for choppers to get the wounded and some of the guys that were coming down with heat stroke out of here. It was really getting hot out and the humidity was even getting worse. Again most of us had little water but it was too damn hot to drink.

Captain Hutchinson then told us to pick up the wounded and the heat stroke guys. The guys in our platoon picked up everyone except for Lieutenant Ervin and Captain Hutchinson ordered all of us in the platoon to pick up the lieutenant but not one of us moved to lift a hand. Captain Hutchinson could see in our eyes for the first time that our lieutenant treated us like shit and now he was getting it right back in his face. Captain Hutchinson then called for four guys from another platoon to carry the lieutenant. All of us couldn't believe that the lieutenant was crying like a little baby. Even the captain couldn't believe what he was seeing. I really think that the lieutenant did one hell of a job of making the captain and us believe that he was one tough lieutenant and that he could take anything out here in the field. Well...the captain found out that the lieutenant was really a pussy.

Captain Hutchinson told us to move out and Sgt. Lefefe told our platoon to move out and off this hill. We followed the trail that led off the hill and then we moved off to our left side into a large clearing that was flat. As we were getting close to the open field there were bushes that were about two to three feet high. I helped carry Chuck and we lifted him high into the air so that the bushes would not scratch him. The four guys from the other platoon didn't pick up the lieutenant as high, but they made sure that he could feel the bushes scratching him. He was really crying like a little kid. I knew that all of us were glad that he had gotten what he deserved. We laid Chuck on the ground and he started talking to me and wanted me to take care of his 38 pistol. He told me to take care of it for him and I tried not to take it but he insisted. I finally gave in and took his 38 pistol. I then took out my canteen and gave what water I had to Chuck. The rest of the guys were giving what water they had to the guys that were wounded and who had heat stroke. No one in our platoon gave any water to the lieutenant. After about half an hour the choppers came and we got them on the choppers and they were gone, including the lieutenant.

Chapter Fifteen

The word was passed to saddle up and that we were getting out. We moved back to Quang Tri City and walked through the city to the other side. The six-bys were not there and then the word was passed that the six-bys would be coming in about fifteen minutes. All of the guys in the company sat down along the side of the dirt road. There was this pale yellow building that was built by the French and it was another Catholic church. One of the guys from our company got up and took off his combat gear but took his rifle and went on over to the church and started going inside. One of the sergeants from our other platoons told him not to go inside the church. All of us in the company were watching the guy to see if he was going inside the church or not. But he kept on going and went inside the church to pray. I heard one of the guys say that it was Sunday and then a couple of the guys got up and also took off their combat gear but carried their rifles and went inside the church. Then the rest of us got up and took off our combat gear and carried our rifles with us and went inside the church to pray as well. The sergeant was telling all of us not to go inside but none of us listened to him.

Inside the church, the guys had their rifles next to them while each of them prayed by themselves. Everyone of us sat by ourselves with their rifles and prayed alone. I went to one of the old style long chairs about ten feet long and put my rifle next to me and I then sat down. This was the first time since I had been in Vietnam that I had gone to church. A couple of minutes went by and the lieutenants from the other two platoons and Captain Hutchinson came in also and they prayed by themselves as well. I then turned back and just looked at the altar; it had a cross of Jesus that was about six feet tall. I just stared at the cross and I could almost feel what Jesus must have gone through when they put him on the cross. Jesus must have felt so all alone in the whole world the last few hours on the cross before he died. Here I was in a strange land protecting people against the N.V.A., who were killing them. I then started saying the 23rd Psalm:

> The Lord is my shepherd; I shall not want.
> He maketh me to lie down in green pastures;
> He leadeth me beside the still waters.
> He restoreth my soul; he leadeth me in the
> Paths of righteousness for his name's sake.
> Yea, through I walk through the valley of the

Shadow of death, I will fear no evil; for
Thou art with me; thy rod and thy staff they
Comfort me.
Thou preparest a table before me in the presence
Of mine enemies; thou anointest my head with
Oil; my cup runneth over.
Surely goodness and mercy shall follow me all
The days of my life; and I will dwell in the
House of the Lord for ever.

I finished my prayer with tears in my eyes. I then asked God to take care of Benny Houston, James Fowler, Sergeant Singleton and the other guys in our battalion who had died and take them into His kingdom. I then asked God to take care of Chuck Knight, Dale Davis, Poisson, and Johnson and the other guys that had been wounded from the booby traps and heat stroke, earlier today. I could feel the pain of losing those guys that had died over here and the loneliness began to come over me. I could almost feel that all of us in the company were making sure that we were making peace with God so when the time came that it was our turn to go, we were ready. Slowly each of us left the church and went outside. I wiped away my tears and slowly got up and grabbed my rifle and quietly went outside the church and went back to where the rest of my gear was. I took one last look at the cross that Jesus was on and it made me think of my church back at home. As I put on my fighting gear, I was still thinking of my church back at home, and how I had spent a lot of time at church helping my pastor.

The six-bys began coming down the dirt road and one of the sergeants went inside the church and told the rest of the guys including the captain that the trucks were coming. The guys coming out of the church quickly grabbed their gear. The trucks then turned around and faced north and Captain Hutchinson told us to get on the trucks. As I got on the truck, I sat down and just looked at the pale yellow church. The six-bys started out and we headed north on Highway 1. The lead truck went into Dong Ha and arrived at our battalion area. The word was passed that we were going to be here for only a couple of days and that we were going to get a new lieutenant. The word was also passed that some of the guys were being transferred to another battalion over here and that some of their people were going to be in our battalion. A couple of hours had passed when the word came down for Grear, Al Quick, Jim Von Bargen and a couple of other guys from our platoon plus guys from our company that were going to either the 3rd Battalion 3rd Marines or the 26th Marines. They were to get all of their gear and sea-bags ready and wait for the six-bys to take them.

About half an hour later, two six-bys came with guys from the 3rd Battalion 3rd Marines and they got off the trucks with their gear and seabags and our buddies got onto the trucks and we wished them good luck with their new outfits. We waved goodbye to them as they left and we told the new guys where our tent was and introduced ourselves to each other. We got only a couple of guys and the rest of the guys went to 1st and 3rd platoons. It was going on evening and the word was passed that we were going to have a company formation. All of us got out of the tents and into platoon formation. Captain Hutchinson said a couple of words and then introduced 2nd Platoon to our new lieutenant and his name was Frank Libutti. The captain then told the 1st and 3rd Platoons they were dismissed and that 2nd Platoon was to stay where we were. Captain Hutchinson left with the rest of the company and we stayed with our new lieutenant and he told us that he wanted us to go out on a couple of small patrols to make sure that we had good spacing between us when we were out in the field. None of us could believe what we had just heard from the new lieutenant. Here we go again with another asshole telling us how we should handle ourselves out in the bush. We could tell that he didn't trust us either, just like our last lieutenant. We all knew that he was digging a grave for himself. Here we had a green lieutenant and he thinks that we don't know what the hell to do out in the bush. It was like a slap in the face to all of us. The new lieutenant then told us that we were dismissed. We went back to our tents. None of us liked what he had said to us.

When we got back to the tents, the guys weren't saying a thing. I could tell that all of us were not getting a break with the officers who took over our platoon. It seemed like we were getting these green lieutenants that thought they knew everything about what to do out in the field. I just lay down on my cot and wished that for once we could get a lieutenant that would listen to his men and not act like he knew everything; that we could have a lieutenant that would listen to us and value what we had to say out in the field. I somehow fell off to sleep and the next day came.

Chapter Sixteen

We got up and went to chow and when we got back, there were some new men that had joined our platoon. There were six new men and of the six were two that the older guys in the platoon knew before I had come to the outfit. Whitey, Chadwell, Van, Francis, Lefefe and others called out their names; Corporal Sullivan and Corporal Boni and the rest of the old timers went over to where they were and started talking to them. The guys were asking them about their thirty days of leave. They told the guys that it was great in Hawaii. Boni and Sullivan told them that they lived it up and got drunk almost everyday. They were glad to be back but still they really didn't want to be here but still be on leave. Sullivan told me that they had enlisted for another six months over here to be with the platoon and help out us new men. I couldn't believe that they would enlist for another six months. Charlie told me that the reason why they enlisted was that they had more than two more years to serve in the Marine Corps and they would have to make another thirteen-month tour again before they got out. This way they only had to do six months and there was no way for them to make another thirteen-month tour. I told Charlie that it didn't seem right, but it seemed to be the smart thing to do.

The word was passed to get our gear on and that we were going on a patrol. I grabbed the radio and turned it back on and tested it to make sure that it was working all right. Two six-bys came and the lieutenant told us to get on the trucks. We boarded the trucks and they moved back out to the main entrance. The six-bys turned left and we headed north but only about 1000 meters and the word was passed to get off the trucks. Lieutenant Libutti was telling Sgt. Lefefe what he wanted the platoon to do. Lefefe then told the platoon that we were going to move out heading west in a staggered column and that the lieutenant wanted to see if we were doing it right. So the word was passed to move out and as we walked in a staggered column, the lieutenant made sure that all of us were doing what he wanted by having good spacing between us. We went about 1000 meters and then we headed south toward Dong Ha base. I could hear on the radio that we were to stop and to put out flanks. Corporal Sullivan's fire team had one of the flanks and 2nd squad had one of their fire teams out there on the flanks as well. We traveled about 800 meters and then we turned and headed east to Highway 1. On the radio the word was passed that we were to get into a single file and with flanks out. The area that we were doing this practice patrol on was clear and you could see only small bushes that were about one to two feet high. There were no trees around at all. The heat of the day was getting to the lieutenant and we could tell that he had enough of practicing. The lieutenant carried more gear than us and was finding out that there was no way for him to take all of the 782 gear on an operation.

When we got to the road the word was passed to head back into the camp. We walked through the main gate and went to our battalion area. When we reached the tent, the guys were really pissed off with Lieutenant Libutti for this senseless waste of time. The rest of Charlie Company watched us drag our sorry asses to our tents. I was thinking to myself that we were not back in the States where we would go out and then come back in and rest for a couple of days-this was Vietnam. I got to my cot and took off the radio and then turned it off so I could save the battery. I knew that if we went on any more practice patrols that he would really get all of us pissed off for sure and someone would shoot him in the back when we were out in the bush. We had the rest of the day to ourselves. I heard a couple of the guys say that they were testing Lieutenant Libutti to see if he knew what the hell he was doing out there. They were laughing and said that he was as green as they come and he couldn't handle live fire under combat. We all knew that it was up to Sgt. Lefefe to keep this platoon from getting killed. Most of us just laid in our cots and slept for the rest of the day.

The next morning came and we went to chow and when we got back the word was passed that we were going out on another operation. Again we didn't know where, but we would know for sure when we got outside the main gate of Dong Ha. All of us cleaned our rifles and made sure that we had plenty of water in our canteens. We passed out the C-rations and I put my cans of C-rations in my sock. The six-bys came and stopped in our area and the word was passed to board the trucks. Our whole company got on the trucks and all of us made sure we were settled before the trucks took off. Then the trucks started off and headed back up north again.

I knew that there were only two ways for us to go and if we stayed on Highway 1 we would be going to The Strip and if we went straight north off of Highway 1 we were going to only one place and that was Phu An. We were coming up on the road where we either went northeast on Highway 1 or straight north to Cam Lo Bridge. The six-bys went straight north to Cam Lo Bridge.

After about fifteen minutes the lead trucks turned off the highway onto the dirt road that was leading straight east into Cam Lo Bridge. The six-bys stopped just past the bridge and the word was to get off the trucks and get into a staggered column. All of us got off the trucks and then they started up and went through the vill and turned around and headed back to Dong Ha. We sat down on the edge of the dirt road and waited for the officers to give the word on what we were doing. The officers were in the middle of the road discussing which platoons were to go and in what order. Some of the kids were having fun with the Marines that had the bridge detail. As I sat and waited for the word to pass to move out, one of the two little Vietnamese brothers that helped us here when we had had the bridge detail came up to Van and me and told us not to go and that there were a lot of N.V.A. up there in Phu An.

After about half an hour, the word was passed to get up and that we were moving out. I got up and as I did the little boy grabbed my hand and held on to it. I looked down at him and he was crying without making a sound. The tears were slowly running down his face. I looked over to Van and the other brother was telling Van not to go as well. The guys were starting to move out and as I started to walk, the little boy walked next to me. After a couple of minutes of holding my hand and still telling me not to go, he knew that I had to and he finally let go without a word. The mama-sans coming out of their huts passed out bread that they had just made or waved at us. I looked back and the little boy was still standing in the street, waving. I could feel the warmth from the kids and mama-sans. The people of the vill really cared for us and I remembered that a couple of us gave them some of our C-rations as we left. The people from the vill knew that there was a very large N.V.A. force down at Phu An waiting for us and they didn't want us to go, knowing what was about to happen.

We stayed in a staggered column all the way to the last hill before it went down to the stream and then into Phu An. We set up our perimeter on the last hill and our squad had the northeast section of the perimeter. We dug our fighting holes and settled in for the evening. No one said a word and all of us knew that tomorrow was going to be a very long day for us, I hoped that no one would get killed. No one in our company was saying a word to each other and I knew that most of the guys were praying to God. None of us in the company said a word but only thought about what tomorrow was going to be. The word was passed that the squad leaders were told to report to the C.P. Chadwell got up and went on over to where Lieutenant Libutti was and after about ten minutes came back and told us that the rest of our battalion was going to be a blocking force so that the enemy could not escape. When Chadwell was done talking, he looked at all of us and said that we better get some rest because we were going to need it. Chadwell told me that our new platoon radioman was Boni. I just nodded and didn't care if I was the platoon radioman or not; at least I was still with my fire team.

I stood my first watch; as I looked around our perimeter I saw the guys that were also watching out in front of their positions. While the other guys were sleeping. I could feel or sense that the enemy was down there waiting for us to come. At least we knew that they were down there because the people from Cam Lo had told us. I thought about Chuck and how he was doing with the wounds that he had received from our last lieutenant. My mind went back to thinking that when morning comes we would hit the

N.V.A. in Phu An. I could sense that all of us in the battalion wanted to hit them very hard and take over Phu An for good. My watch was up and I then woke up Charlie and gave him the radio and watch. I got under my poncho and could feel that the night air was getting cooler. It seemed even though the days were getting hotter, all of us were getting used to the heat and humidity. The next thing I knew, I was off to sleep and Chadwell woke me up and told me that it was my turn again. I got up and I was the last watch for the night before the sun came up. The last half hour of my watch, the guys were getting up on their own and knew that today was going to be hell on earth. As the guys were getting up they started cooking their food and staying to themselves. As the guys looked at each other, they knew what the other guy was thinking. For some reason I could feel the closeness in our company as well as our battalion, even with our stupid officers leading us.

I watched the stars slowly disappear in the skies. By 04:45 the skies were starting to get lighter and the sun would soon be coming up. At 05:00 hundred in the morning the platoon radioman called me for the last time and I clicked on the handset twice and finished my watch. I kicked the guys at the bottom of their feet so they could get up and start their breakfast. The other guys in the company were also waking up the rest of their men as well. No one said a word and I could tell that all of us were thinking about Phu An. After about an hour, I rolled up my poncho and got my gear ready for the day. The word was passed that we were getting ready to move out. Our C.P. called me and told me that our squad was to take point going into Phu An. I told Chadwell and he told Van that we had the point team and to get the guys ready to move out. Everyone in our company was going on over to the dirt road. Van told us to move out and Chadwell told me to stay with my fire team. Chadwell didn't want the radioman next to him because the enemy would always try to shoot the radioman first and the guy in front of him. Van told me that I was the third guy in the fire team and that he was behind me. As I walked toward the dirt road, I took the antenna and bent it down so that it would not stand up into the air for the enemy to see. When we got to the dirt road, we started down it in a staggered column and the rest of the guys in the company were telling us to watch ourselves. I could feel the butterflies in my stomach and could also sense that the enemy was waiting for us. We got down to the bottom of the hill and crossed the stream: I could feel that the enemy was watching. We started up the road on the other side of the stream and walked about 100 meters and we knew that there was the tire path that went off to the left to the village in a large open field about another 200 meters ahead. When we got to the large open field, I called back to the C.P. and told them that we had reached it. They told us to keep on going. We followed the tire tracks that went through the middle of the open field heading northwest. The hedgerow was in front of all of us. We tried to listen for any sound of the enemy. We were still in a staggered column. We were about 40 feet from each other and 40 feet behind the guy in front of us. We went though the hedgerow and were in the second large open field and still not a sound or smell from the enemy. We carefully walked up to the second hedgerow and on the radio the C.P. called me and told us to stop when we got to the hedgerow. I passed the word up to the point man in our fire team. There was this concrete building on the edge of the village. We stopped and got on one knee and faced outward in the staggered column. A couple of minutes later Lieutenant Libutti came up and told us that Captain Hutchinson wanted us to be on the east side but on the other side of the hedgerow that surrounded the field. I remembered that we had found the dead Sergeant Singleton back a little way to the right of us next to the hedgerow when we were here the last time.

Chadwell came up to Van and told him to take his fire team off to the right side from where we were. I followed Van with the rest of the guys in our fire team over to the hedgerow that was on our right side. This part of the hedgerow was very thin compared to the rest of the hedgerows there. There was a fence but it was broken and the only part of the fence that was still up were the posts. Van told us to dig our fighting hole here and we took off our gear and while two of the guys were digging, Van and I watched the area in front of us facing east. We could still feel that the enemy was watching us but they hadn't opened up on us. I looked around the perimeter and saw that the guys were digging the fighting holes very deep in case we got hit. The ground was very easy to dig and it didn't take long to finish the holes. Captain Hutchinson took his C.P. group and had them in the cement building that was north facing Phu An. The rest of the companies took part of the perimeter from the north, west and the south connecting to our platoon.

It was going on around 10:00 and Captain Hutchinson passed the word that the tanks were coming in for support. The tanks didn't arrive until around 11:00 and Captain Hutchinson told them that they would cover the west and east side of the perimeter. The lieutenant of the tanks hoped that we would get into a fire fight with the N.V.A. He heard that when the 1st Battalion 9th Marines was in a fire fight that all hell broke loose and wanted to see what it was really like. We could hear the lieutenant yell out to the N.V.A. to bring it on. We knew that when it started that he would not want to be around when the shit hit the fan, just like the last time we were here with the tanks and they were happy to get the hell out of this place in a hurry. We then put up our little sticks to mark our field of fire so that we had interlocking fire from the fighting hole on our left and right sides. This way we didn't end up shooting our buddies as well. The word was passed that we were going to get re-supplied around 12:30. All of us kept our eyes open and no one said anything. Captain Hutchinson's C.P. was inside the cement building.

The word was passed that the choppers were coming in with food and ammo for the 60mm mortar teams. All of us got to our fighting holes and watched. We knew that if the N.V.A. was going to hit us it was when the choppers came. There were about ten guys from one of the platoons that were going to get the supplies from the choppers when they came. We could hear them coming and we knew that it would not be too long before they arrived. Then two of the choppers came in from the west and landed in the middle of the open field and the guys ran over to them and unloaded both choppers and started leaving. I looked back to see how the guys were doing. The last guy that was leaving the area was carrying a couple cases of C-rations. The blond-headed guy must have taken ten steps and the last chopper was about 100 feet in the air when all of a sudden without any warning a mortar round hit right where the chopper had landed. The explosion knocked the blond-headed guy to the ground. Then he got up and ran as fast as he could to where his buddies were with the C-ration cases.

The N.V.A. were really hitting us with their 60mm mortars at the northern part of our perimeter, especially where the cement building was because that was where the Company C.P. was. All of us were in our fighting holes waiting for the N.V.A. to attack us. The mortar rounds were also hitting near the tanks as well. The N.V.A. were really firing their mortar tubes at us and were not letting up at all. About ten minutes passed and I could hear on the radio "Hammer, up!" to the Platoon C.P. I told Van that our C.P. group wanted me and I would be back. I got up as one of our mortar teams was firing back at the enemy. I went back about 100 feet on the inside of our perimeter going south and Boni passed me going to where the guys were on the perimeter, telling me that I was the platoon radioman and he wanted no part of it. I couldn't believe that Boni didn't want any part of the radio and now he was giving it to me.

The radio was sitting on the ground upright about twenty feet from the hedgerow next to the hole. I couldn't see where Lieutenant Libutti was. As I got closer to the hole, I saw Lieutenant Libutti at the bottom of the hole with his hands and arms covering his head. I quickly thought to myself that a couple of days ago he was checking on us to see if we were doing it right out in the field and here he is in the bottom of the hole with his hands and arms covering his head. I then sat down on the edge of the fighting hole and held the handset next to my ear to hear if there was anything going on but heard nothing. I watched one mortar team that was next to the cement building really firing their tube like crazy back at the N.V.A. I could almost hear one of the black guys telling the other mortar teams the coordinates. It seemed that the fighting was between their mortar teams and our mortar teams. I looked over to one tank that was about 75 feet from me and the lieutenant was firing his fifty cal. machine gun. There were no AK-47s firing at all. Lieutenant Libutti looked up at me and told me to get in and I told him that I was all right where I was. I had my right leg in the hole and my left was outside of the hole. I looked at the lieutenant and he was really scared and didn't know what the hell to do. All of the guys knew how Lieutenant Libutti was going to handle himself once he was under fire: scared shitless. I knew what he was going through and yet he and many others like him wanted to lead men into battle. He finally realized this was for real. It was the real thing...life or death. His eyes were big and he didn't want to die, just like the rest of us. I told the lieutenant in a calm voice that I would take care of things up here for him. About twenty minutes passed and the firing of the mortar tubes from both sides didn't let up as I watched the black guys next to the concrete building firing their tube. The next thing that happened was the enemy got lucky and hit the base-plate of their mortar tube. All four of the black guys were dead in a blink of an eye-they were all dead. I said out loud, "Oh...My God." Lieutenant Libutti looked up to me and thought that we were getting overrun and I looked down at him and said that it was nothing and to stay down. There were a few rounds that hit the concrete building as well and I knew that our captain and his C.P. group got wiped out. A couple more minutes passed and the firing was starting to slow down from the N.V.A.'s mortar tubes. Our 60s mortar tubes were still giving it back to the N.V.A. Two of the corpsman went over to where the black mortar team had been and were checking them out. There was nothing they could do for them. I still couldn't believe that one moment they were alive and the next moment they were all dead.

There were a few rounds that came close to me but just missed the tanks. I looked at one of the guys that was on the top of the tank behind the 50 cal. machine gun. His flak jacket looked like strips of paper on his back and I couldn't believe that he hadn't gotten hit. The flak jacket saved his life. Ten more minutes had passed and there was no firing from either side. Everything got very quiet and I got on the radio and told my two squads to keep a sharp eye out for the enemy. All of us in the company knew that this was the time for them to attack us. I could feel myself shaking a little but I didn't want the lieutenant to know. I was like all of the other old timers in that we hated the quietness after the battle. I felt that it was worse than the battle itself. Not a word was on the radio and I then told the two squads to check to see if everyone was all right. This was the first time I shook and I knew that it was because I had to make sure that everyone in the platoon thought that our C.P. was on top of everything, even though our lieutenant was scared to death. Sgt. Lefefe was no where to be found, since he was the platoon sergeant. Lefefe never came up to see how the lieutenant was at this time but was on the line with the guys. The lieutenant from the tanks sat down on the tank and started to shake. I knew that he got his wish to get into a battle with the N.V.A. with our outfit. I knew that he wouldn't want to go though this again.

Then the word was being passed around by mouth that the captain was alive and that all of his radiomen were wounded. Captain Hutchinson was on the perimeter with the guys while the mortar rounds were coming in. He was making sure that the guys were ready for the ground attack if it came. I knew that Bill was in the building with all of the other radiomen in the company when it got hit, he was only wounded with the rest of them. I heard on the radio that we were going to pull back and get the dead and wounded out. I told Lieutenant Libutti and he got up out of the hole and told me not to say anything to the guys. I could see in his eyes that he was just plain scared and didn't want any of the guys in the platoon to know and that included Lefefe. Libutti told me to get the guys ready to pull back. I got on the radio and passed the word to the two squads and to make sure they told the other squad without the radio to get ready to move out and that we were moving back.

One of the tanks went up to where the black mortar team had been and the guys were putting them on the tank to take back. The wounded guys were on the other tanks. The word was passed to move out; I didn't hear a word on the radio from any of the other platoon or company C.P. It was like I was the only radioman in the company which I was. We moved back to the dirt road that led to the stream. When we got to the dirt road, Captain Hutchinson told me to stay there and that the rest of the company was going across the road into another large field to set up a perimeter for the dead and wounded men. This was where we were going to have the choppers pick up the dead and wounded men. Two of the tanks had the wounded men and took them across the open field and got them off; then the tanks made a perimeter to protect them. The tank with the dead men on it came right up to where I was and stopped next to the road. The captain told me that I was the only radioman in the company that had not gotten wounded. Captain Hutchinson told me to call in for the medievac choppers. He pointed to the radio and as I looked, there were six radios. He told me this was the only one that he cared about and to disregard the others. The next thing I knew, there were news reporters from N.B.C, A.B.C. and C.B.S. and a few others agencies. I had no idea where they came from. When the tank came up and stopped with the dead men they were like vultures taking pictures of them. I went over to them and told them if they took one more picture that I was going to kill them. At first they didn't believe me until I pointed my rifle at them. A couple of the dead men didn't have any clothes because the shrapnel had cut their clothes off. The newsmen didn't care one thing about the dead men, they just wanted a great picture so they could look great so they could tell the American people that we got our asses kicked by the N.V.A. I went back to where the rest of the radios were and knelt down and started calling in for the choppers to pick up the dead and wounded men. They told me that it would be about half an hour from now for them to come. I then informed Captain Hutchinson and he nodded.

The choppers were coming and I told the captain that the choppers were on the way. The captain told the guys to get the smoke ready for the choppers so they knew where to land. Captain Hutchinson went on over to where the wounded men were and told the guys there to get ready to load them onto the choppers. The captain told me to tell the choppers to come in from the southwest and leave northeast. As we waited for the choppers to come, it started to rain-not very hard. It rained for about ten minutes and then it stopped just as quickly as it had started. The sun was back out and we could feel the heat and humidity rising. I could hear the chopper calling me on the radio and they said that they were close. I then told the choppers to come in from the southwest and leave northeast. When I could hear them, I told the captain to pop the smoke and I then asked the pilot what color the smoke was and he said "red" and I told him "affirmative." The choppers were coming down and they loaded up the wounded men first on the CH-34s. As soon as they left I could hear more of them and I told the captain to pop the smoke and we repeated the process about ten times.

All of the wounded and dead men were put onto the choppers and were gone. It took Captain Hutchinson and me about an hour to get all of the wounded and dead men out. A couple of minutes later, Captain Hutchinson came over to me and told me to go back to my platoon. I just nodded to him and left. The captain told the tanks to go and they left as well. The tanks were very happy to get the hell away from us. I got back to my platoon and looked to see where the lieutenant was. As I was walking over to where Libutti was, Van said that Chadwell and Charlie were gone and that they were going home. I could hear the tanks starting up their engines and they then went back down the dirt road that led to the stream and on down to Cam Lo Bridge. I heard on the radio that the company was to saddle up and to get ready to move out. I passed the word on to the lieutenant and he told Lefefe to get the platoon ready to move out. We were going back to Phu An. We got to the first large open field and the word was passed that we were setting up here for the rest of the day. We were going to be the blocking force for the battalion. Our platoon covered part of the north side and almost all of the east side of the perimeter. Lieutenant Libutti told me that we would have our hole here about 50 feet from the perimeter and about 100 meters from the company C.P.

I got out my E-tool and dug our hole. I was finished in about forty-five minutes. I started eating my food for the evening. I stayed to myself and tried to unwind after what we had gone through. I thought about Bill and I hoped that he wasn't real bad. I remembered that Bill and I looked almost alike when we first joined 2nd platoon together. I remembered what the captain said that Bill was not seriously wounded. It hurt to see guys I knew getting wounded or killed. After I finished my meal, Lieutenant Libutti told me to call on the radio for the squad leaders to our C.P. I called on the radio and informed the two squad leaders the lieutenant wanted them to go to the C.P. and make sure they told the other squad leader as well. When they got to the C.P., Lieutenant Libutti told them that we would be here for a couple of days and that we were being a blocking force for our other companies. Libutti told the squad leaders to make sure that everyone had their C-rations for the next couple of days when we got supplies this afternoon. The three squad leaders, Bignami, Francis, Sullivan and Lefefe just listened to the lieutenant. He told them that he would listen to them out in the bush but he would make the final word and they were dismissed. The squad leaders got up and left without saying a word. The squad leaders still didn't trust Lieutenant Libutti because he still hadn't proven himself, and hadn't shown them that he could handle himself under fire. Lefefe went back to where our corpsman was and pretty much stayed away from the lieutenant until Libutti called for him.

After they left and Lefefe went back to his hole with the corpsman, Lieutenant Libutti looked at me and said that he wanted to talk to me. I thought to myself, now what? Both of us went over to our hole and he then began to say thanks for not telling the guys that he was at the bottom of the hole while the mortar attack was going on. Lieutenant Libutti then asked me what would it take for the guys in the platoon to follow him as a leader. I couldn't believe what I was hearing from him. Lieutenant Libutti started telling me that he was married and went to one of the military colleges on the east coast. As he was talking, I thought about my father because he didn't want to take care of the guys in his outfit in World War II. He just didn't want that responsibility hanging over his head. I knew deep down inside of me that I didn't want to have the responsibility of taking care of the lieutenant and the whole platoon. I just didn't want it, but I knew that Lieutenant Libutti was asking me for my help.

I thought that if I taught the lieutenant how to lead his men without acting like a prick and to get the men to trust him that we could have a great platoon and I wouldn't have to have the responsibility of taking care of the whole platoon after a couple of weeks. I thought about it and then looked at the lieutenant and told him that I would teach him everything I knew and how to trust his men and believe in them. I knew that I was really asking a hell of a lot of myself to teach the lieutenant. I told him that "Right now, they don't trust you, Lieutenant Libutti; you have already pissed off the guys with your patrols that we had when you first came to us. Whatever they told you back in the States on how to handle your platoon over here will not work. You can throw the book away." I then told him that I would tell him what he did wrong during the day when the guys were not around if he messed up. I knew that I had to tell him when he screwed up and I didn't care if I hurt his feelings. I then told him that after two weeks out in the field that he would be on his own and not to ask me how he was doing. Libutti looked at me and told me that he understood and said don't be afraid of telling him off. I told him that I wouldn't be, he would know. I told him that it started today. I said that he took his first step by talking and listening to me. I also told him to pay attention to Sgt. Lefefe as well. Right now, even he doesn't trust you to lead the men in this platoon. I then told him if he wanted to make a great impression on the guys in a hurry, to make sure he checked on all of them each evening when we set up in the field and telling them that they were doing great out in the bush and showing that he cared. I also told him never to tell the guys what to do out in the field, they already know. This would help in winning them over quickly.

When we were finished, I knew that he was going to be a damn good officer of this platoon. He was man enough to ask me for help in commanding a Marine platoon here in Vietnam. The lieutenant took his first step to becoming a Marine officer in this outfit. The rest of the day went by waiting to see if the N.V.A. were coming to us. It was going on evening and as I watched the lieutenant doing his stuff in the C.P., Lieutenant Libutti told Lefefe and the corpsman what time their watches were for the night. Libutti said that I had the last watch and that I had better get some sleep in. When he was finished talking to me about what time my watch was, he asked me how he was doing and I told him that he was doing a shitty job with the guys. He looked at me and couldn't understand what he had done wrong for the day. I then told him, "Did you go around the perimeter and check on each of the guys in the platoon to see how they were doing?" He quickly got up and went on over to the perimeter and checked on the guys. Sgt. Lefefe saw what the lieutenant was doing but just stayed where he was at. I knew that what the lieutenant was doing may have Lefefe gotten closer to the lieutenant. The lieutenant came back and took the first watch. I told him that he had to call the two squads with the radio every half hour to hear if they were all right or not. I told him what to say on the radio and that the captain would call us every hour to see if our platoon was all right for the night. I got out my poncho and lay down. The lieutenant looked at me to see if he did it right his first day. I looked around our perimeter and the guys were at their fighting holes, watching. I felt a lot safer because I was not on the perimeter but inside of it.

Chapter Seventeen

Lefefe kicked me at the bottom of my foot and told me that it was time. I got up and went over to the radio and sat down. As I sat there, I thought about the day before and the dead and wounded guys in our company. I then thought about Bill because he had come over with me on the plane and both of us went to 2nd Platoon Charlie Company. Then he got the job of being the captain radioman. I remembered the captain asking me my name and I told him that everyone in my platoon called me, "Hammer." . I remembered the blond guy walking away from the chopper with the case of C-rations and a couple of seconds later a mortar round hit right where the chopper had landed but was about 100 feet in the air when the round hit. I started thinking about the black guys in the mortar team that were firing their mortar tube and calling out the coordinates to the other mortar teams but it was time to call the two squads on the radio to see if they were all right. Both squads clicked two times on their handsets and I went back to thinking of the day again. I remembered Captain Hutchinson calling for me to call in for the medievac choppers to get the dead and wounded men out of here. Plus, the damn newsmen that were with our company and taking those pictures. How insensitive they were by taking those pictures of the dead men! I could feel the loneliness coming over me and I knew that the guys in the platoon were going to stay away from me now that I was the platoon radioman sucking up to Lieutenant Libutti. I didn't like the idea that I was going to end up being a loner in this outfit and at the same time, I was going to teach Lieutenant Libutti about being a damn good Marine in our platoon and getting the guys to back him up out in the field. I knew that whatever I did, I was damned by the guys but they wouldn't know what I was doing for them. I remembered kneeling in the puddle of water when it rained for about ten minutes waiting for the medievac choppers.

It was getting close to calling the two squads again on the radio. I called them and again both of them gave me the two clicks on the handsets, I waited for the company radioman to call me and I in turn pressed my handset twice and I was finished with my watch. I then got up and went over to where the lieutenant was and kicked him at the bottom of his foot. He quickly got up; he wasn't used to getting up for the night watch. It was his first time ever to stand radio watch. I then lay down and the next thing I knew it was time for me to get up again. I went over to the radio and just looked around and I could tell that the enemy had left Phu An and I knew that it was ours. But still I knew that I wasn't going to let my guard down at all. My watch was over and the sun was coming up and I looked over to Lieutenant Libutti and he was still sleeping and none of us in the C.P. group woke him up. I started cooking my food and I knew that the smell of the food would wake him up. Lieutenant Libutti finally got up and without saying a word cooked his food. After he was finished he came over to me and said that he was going to check on the guys in the platoon and get to know them. I told him that he better show them he cared for them and made sure that they were fine…with small talk. He left and inspected our perimeter and came back and said that some of the guys had responded but not all of them. I told him he still had a long way to go before all of them would trust him with their lives, especially when we got into a fire fight with the N.V.A. and he would have to stand up and be with the guys when the shit hit the fan. The rest of the day went by doing nothing. I didn't like these kinds of days doing nothing or going on patrols. This waiting around for the enemy was crazy.

The next day came and the company radioman called me and said that the captain wanted to see the lieutenant and me at the company C.P. I told Libutti that the captain wanted to see us now. We walked over to the captain with our rifles and he told Libutti that we were going on an 8000-meter patrol and that we were going to take an Artillery F.O. Lieutenant and his radioman on the patrol with us. (The Arty F.O. means Artillery Field Officer.) The captain then showed both lieutenants the route that we were to take and when he was finished he then told them that they were dismissed. As we started going back to our platoon, the captain called for me to stay; he wanted to talk to me. After everyone was gone and there was no one around us, Captain Hutchinson told me to take care of my lieutenant out there in the field. He than said, "Hammer, do you understand me?" I looked at him and smiled and he knew that I would take care of my green lieutenant. I knew that Captain Hutchinson cared for Libutti and wanted nothing to happen to him. Lieutenant Libutti showed the captain that he was eager to learn what to do out here in the field.

As I walked back to the lieutenant, he was telling Sgt. Lefefe and the squad leaders what we were doing today. Lefefe then went over to 3rd squad and told them that they were taking the point for this patrol. I got on my gear, put the radio on by back and everyone was ready to move out. I knew that I had to watch myself by not interfering and hopefully Libutti kept himself calm on this patrol with the Arty F.O. Lieutenant with us. I knew that I couldn't say anything in front of the Arty F.O. Lieutenant to help Libutti. I had a bad feeling about taking the Arty F.O. Lieutenant with us. We were starting to leave the perimeter and I called on the radio to the company radioman that we were leaving the I.P. I hoped that Lefefe would help a lot in making sure that everything ran smoothly within the platoon. Lieutenant Libutti looked back at me and told me to call on the radio that we were leaving the perimeter and I just nodded.

We walked back to the dirt road that led to the stream and as we crossed it, I wanted to fill up my canteens since they were empty. We went up the hill and went about 1000 meters when the word was passed back to us that the point team had found the small trail that led off the dirt road heading east. I called back to the company radioman and told him that we were at Checkpoint 1. So far everything had gone well. The platoon started walking down the side of the hill to the bottom and when we got to the bottom of the hill, we were still following the small path and the word was passed to stop. A couple of minutes passed and the word was that the point team had found a Chi Con grenade in the mud. There were also footprints that were fresh on the trail. The day was getting very hot and humid already. It was somewhere around 10:00 in the morning. Libutti passed the word up to the point team to move out slow and to keep their eyes open. We traveled about another 200 meters and I heard an explosion. Everyone knelt down where they were; all of us were watching the hills around us. The best thing was that the hills were all bare and it was easy to see if the enemy was on them. Then the word was passed back to Libutti that we had one wounded guy but he was not bad and the N.V.A. had gotten away. I knew that I had to get the information on the wounded guy in our platoon and then to call it back to the company. Libutti and I went up to the point team with Lefefe and the corpsman. The Arty F.O. lieutenant and his radioman also came up to the wounded guy. When we got to the point team, I got the name of the wounded guy and his service number and where he got hit from the grenade. When I got all of the information, I asked Libutti if he wanted me to call in for a chopper and he said yes. Lefefe then told the guys to set up a perimeter for the chopper so we could get the wounded guy out. Doc Chico bandaged the guy up and then we moved him up on the side of the hill off the trail that we were on. A couple of the guys got out one of their ponchos and held it over the guy so that he didn't get heat stoke as well.

The rest of the platoon was setting up the perimeter and I got on the radio and told the company radioman that we had a wounded guy and that we needed a chopper to medievac him out of here. I gave the company radioman the information of the wounded guy and he told me that the chopper was on its way. I knew that the captain was listening to what was going on with us. I got out my radio book and looked up the frequency for the medievac choppers and I didn't have it in my book. I went over to the F.O. radioman and asked him if he had the medievac frequency and he said yes. I wrote it down in pencil and waited for the chopper to come. As we waited, the corpsman came over to me and asked if I had any water and I checked my three canteens and I told him no. I thought that I had one of my canteens full but I didn't. I told Doc to check with Maxwell and I knew that if anyone in the platoon had any water that he would. The company radioman called me and told me that the chopper was on it way and to expect it in half an hour. I then told the company radioman that I was changing frequency so I could call in the chopper. I passed the word on to Lieutenant Libutti and he told Lefefe to get ready to pop the smoke. I could hear the chopper coming and he was coming up from the south and heading northeast to us.

I told the company radioman that I was changing frequency and that I would be back on the air in twenty. The guys put up a poncho over the wounded guy so that the sun would not hit him. I went over to Maxwell to see if he had any water for sure and he looked at me and shook his head and said that he didn't have a drop. Maxwell said that he would have given the water to me and only me if he had it. I knew that he would have given me the water but I was surprised that even he didn't have any water either. I went back to the wounded guy and saw the chopper coming; I then called the chopper and told him that we were at his "two o'clock." Whatever direction the chopper was going was always his 12:00 o'clock. That way he knew where we were. He was getting close to us and I told him that we were getting ready to pop the smoke and I called over to Lefefe to "Pop it." Lefefe then popped the smoke and it was "red" and the pilot then called me and said that it was red and I told him "affirmative." I told him to come in from the south and go out to the northwest.

The chopper came down and the guys in the platoon picked up the guy and carried him over to it. All of us could feel the heat moving around with the dust in the air. I could tell that this was going to be a very, very hot and humid day. The chopper lifted and went out going northwest like I told him. I then changed my frequency and called back to the company radioman that I was back on the air.

The F.O. Lieutenant was telling Lieutenant Libutti that we needed to take a short cut and that we would not be able to finish this patrol. I could tell that he was scared and he wanted to go back to where the rest of the company was. Lefefe and I both didn't say a word and just listened to the F.O. lieutenant trying to convince Lieutenant Libutti on how to run his platoon. Lieutenant Libutti told Lefefe to tell the guys that we were moving out, heading east on this small trail that we were following. I was glad that Libutti didn't listen to the A.O. lieutenant. As we were walking, the F.O. Lieutenant was still talking to Lieutenant Libutti and was trying like hell to make him change his mind. We traveled about 2000 meters and the word was passed that some of the guys were coming down with heat stroke. Lieutenant Libutti told Lefefe that we would stop here and rest for a little bit. As the guys sat down where they were, there was no place for us to get out from under the sun. We were in a very wide low area and the hills were about 800 meters apart, north and south. Libutti then got out his map and looked to see just where we were. He knew that we had to be going up north very soon. None of the guys in the platoon had a drop of water in their canteens. The trail that we were following was about half way up the side of the hill. Lefefe got up and came over to me and looked at someone out across the field looking northeast of us on the edge of our perimeter. I looked to see what the hell he was looking at and I noticed that there was an N.V.A. sitting on a large rock facing north. There was this tree that was next to me and I picked up my rifle and was getting ready to shoot at the N.V.A. when Lefefe told me that the N.V.A. was his. Lefefe rested the rifle on the branch of the tree and took aim and fired his rifle. The tracer round which was red went right over the N.V.A.'s right shoulder and boy did he get up and run like hell into the heavy foliage. You could follow the bullet as it left the rifle to where it was going because it gave off a red light. All of us started laughing at Lefefe and boy was he mad as hell for missing him. The word got around to the whole platoon and everyone got a big laugh out of it. I knew that Lefefe was embarrassed and he should be for missing the N.V.A.

Libutti told me we were going to go north from here and to tell the captain's radioman that we were at Checkpoint 2. I got on the radio and while I was telling the radioman that we were at Checkpoint 2, Libutti told Lefefe to get the point team heading north. As we started out, I knew that we were going to go where the N.V.A. had been sitting on that large rock. We went around the large rock and there were a lot of small thin trees that were about twenty feet high and about an inch to two inches in diameter. We were moving like a snake going in between the trees in a single file. It was some 20 degrees cooler with the shade of the leaves that were over us and keeping the sun from beating down on us. It really felt great after being out in the sun. The word was passed to stop and Lieutenant Libutti to come up. Lieutenant Libutti, Sgt. Lefefe and I went up to where the guys wanted the lieutenant. When we got there, there were two N.V.A backpacks full of supplies. Most of the supplies were from the University of California at Berkeley. They were medical supplies to help the N.V.A. Lieutenant Libutti told the guys to pick up the packs and that we would take them back with us. Libutti looked at me and I could tell that he wanted to see if I was behind him and I just nodded slightly.

Lefefe then told the point team to move out; we were still heading through the thin trees when about fifteen minutes later, all hell broke loose. I could hear our M-16s firing as well as hearing some of our grenades going off. Then the word was passed to turn around and get the hell out. All of us turned around and started running as fast as we could. Some of the guys who were up near the front of the platoon were running faster then the rest of us. I started to laugh as I was running but at the same time I was scared like the rest of the guys. It was hard for me to move because of the radio and the trees grabbing my radio as I was running. When we got back out into the sun, the heat and humidity hit each and everyone of us and took our breath away. It felt like the temperature went from 70 to 120 degrees in a second. We went back to the other side of the valley where we were before going north. Lefefe told the guys to make a perimeter and to rest here. As I got back to the tree where Lefefe had shot at the N.V.A. a little while ago, I could feel the hot sun beating down on me and I didn't have any water to drink. The rest of the guys were feeling the effects of the heat and humidity. The word was passed that a couple of the guys were coming down with heat stroke. Doc Chico was going over to the guys and trying to help them, but there was nothing he could do without water. Doc Chico laid them down and the only thing he could do was fan them to try to cool them down which was impossible.

Lieutenant Libutti asked the Arty F.O. lieutenant for a fire mission he said that he could order one. Lieutenant Libutti then gave him the coordinates and the F.O. Lieutenant told his radioman that he needed a fire mission. A couple of minutes later his radioman told us that a "Willie Peter round" was on its way. Lefefe told the guys in the platoon to watch for the white smoke of the Willie Peter round. The round landed where the trees were and the lieutenant told his radioman to add 100 meters and fire for effect. Then in a couple of minutes, I could hear the rounds from the 105s firing from Cam Lo Bridge. Boy, were they letting the N.V.A. have it! I got on the radio and told our company radioman that we were having a fire mission on a N.V.A. bunker complex that we had found.

After about thirty minutes, the 105s stopped firing on the position. The guys in the platoon were telling us at the C.P. that more of them were coming down with heat stroke and Doc Chico was trying to take care of them. Lieutenant Libutti told me that we now had six guys down with heat stroke and that he wanted me to call in for choppers to get them out of here and also for some water for the rest of us. I then got on the radio and called the company radioman and told him that we had six guys down with heat stroke and also we needed water for the rest of the guys in the platoon. The company radioman told me that he would get back to me as soon as he reported this to the captain. A couple of minutes passed and the company radioman called me back and told me that the choppers would not be on their way for a little while. He said that he would call me when they were on their way to us. I then passed the word on to my lieutenant and said that I was going on over to Doc Chico and see if I could help him with the guys that had heat stroke. I told Lefefe to listen to the radio and let me know when the choppers were on their way. I took off most of my gear and only took my rifle with me and I walked on over to where Chico was trying to take care of the guys. It seemed that the sun with the heat and humidity were getting worse by the minute and it was very hard just to walk around.

The guys were all lying down on the ground with no cover from the sun. Chico asked me again if I had any water and I told him no. He then said that the guys were really burning up and that we needed water fast. I then told him that there was a stream about fifty feet from us and he told me that it was polluted and not good to drink. I told him that it was still water and that I was going to get it for the guys. I asked him if it was all right to pour the water on them to try to get their body temperatures down a little. He said that it would help a lot. I then walked over to the stream and there was fungus growing on the top of the water. I took off my helmet and separated the helmet liner from the outside shell. I took my hand and moved the fungus away and then dipped both the helmet and liner into the water and got them both filled up and went back to where the guys were lying on the ground and slowly poured the water over the ones who really needed it. As the water hit them on their chests, they flopped around like fish out of water. Some of them had their eyes rolled up where you could only see the white part. I went back a second time and again poured water over them: Dale Davis, and Ted Van Meeteren were two of the worst. A couple of them wanted to drink the water themselves. I told them not to drink the water while I was pouring it over them. As I went back and forth from the stream to the guys, the rest of the guys in the platoon were watching me work my ass off. I just finished giving the guys the water and then Doc Chico was getting light-headed and started weaving back and forth. I quickly ran back to the stream and got some more water and this time I threw the water on him and said to him that he couldn't get heat stroke on the guys who he was trying to take care of. I could feel myself getting light headed but I tried to stay focused on keeping them alive until the choppers came. Every time I poured the water on the guys they still flopped around like fish. I knew that the guys had to get out of there quickly and under shade, but there was none. I kept putting water on them: they really needed to get the hell out of the sun before they all ended up dying. I knew that our whole platoon was in very bad shape at this time. With six guys down and the rest of the guys being close to coming down with heat stroke, I knew that the N.V.A. could wipe us out if they knew the shape that our platoon was in. I was hoping that Lefefe would call me and tell me the choppers were coming, but I kept going back and forth from the stream pouring the dirty water over the guys so they wouldn't die.

It was a little over an hour later when Lefefe called me back and told me that the choppers were on their way. I was glad they were coming; I knew all of us in the platoon were really getting hit very hard from the heat and humidity. It was very hard just to breathe with the humidity, heat and the sun on all of us. I could hear the Arty F.O. Lieutenant still getting on my lieutenant and telling him what he should do next. Finally, I could hear the two choppers coming and we passed the word around the perimeter to keep a sharp eye out for any snipers. Lefefe got out a smoke grenade and was ready when I gave him the word to pop it. A few of the guys went over to the guys who had heat stroke, to help carry them to the choppers. Then the choppers started coming in from the southwest. I called the company and told them that I was changing frequency in order to call in the choppers and that I would be off the air for fifteen. I then turned the knob on the radio to a different frequency for the choppers and I told them we were at their one o'clock. I could see them moving to one o'clock and I told them that they were not too far from us. The pilot told me to pop the smoke and I told Lefefe to pop it. Lefefe popped the smoke and the pilot said, "purple" and I told him "negative" and then the pilot said "green" and I told him "affirmative." I told him to come down from the southeast and go out to the west.

The first chopper came down while the other chopper was giving us protection from above. As the first chopper landed, the guys walked them to the chopper; at the same time, the door gunner was passing out a couple of five gallon cans of water. I had Dale Davis, one of the heat stroke guys, holding onto my radio while we were walking over to the first chopper. Dale was really hanging onto me and I could feel him dragging me down. I was almost carrying him to the chopper. As I got him on it and the chopper went up off the ground about fifteen feet, it came back down and the door gunner pushed out two of the guys before it landed. They fell to the ground like a couple of sacks of potatoes. I couldn't believed that this asshole threw the guys off the chopper before it landed so they could get up into the air. I wanted to shoot the bastard. It took off and this time went up into the air without any trouble. A minute later the other chopper came down and I helped get the two guys who were Van and Davis onto the chopper while the door gunner gave us a couple of cans of water for the platoon. Then the chopper lifted up into the air and the guys were gone.

Lefefe opened up one of the five-gallon cans of water and each of us took a drink from it. The water was very hot and wet but I only took a small drink. I didn't drink any more because it was very hot but it also had a bad taste. I had enough of the water and the rest of the guys drank what they could of the water. Whatever water was left, we poured it out onto the ground. I then went over to Lieutenant Libutti and the F.O. Lieutenant was still trying to tell Libutti how to run this patrol. I then changed the frequency back to our company. I got on the radio and told the company radioman that 2nd platoon was back on the air. As I told the company radioman that I was back on the air, I knew that the captain had to hear the argument between Lieutenant Libutti and the Arty F.O. Lieutenant in the background. It was around 15:30 hours and knew that we couldn't finish this patrol and I knew that Libutti realized it also. Lieutenant Libutti called Sgt. Lefefe and me and told both of us that we were heading back the way we came in here. We were heading back to our company. As Lieutenant Libutti was telling us this, the F.O. Lieutenant was really making a big deal of the decision that Lieutenant Libutti had made. The Arty F.O. Lieutenant wanted to make a short cut so we could get back sooner. I got on the radio and told the company radioman of the decision and as I was talking, I knew that the company radioman and captain could hear the F.O. Lieutenant making a hell of a lot of noise in the background.

Lefefe told the rest of the guys that we were heading back the way we came in here. All of us knew that we couldn't finish the patrol even if we had to. We had lost seven men on the patrol and our platoon was now down to about thirty men. None of us could have fought the N.V.A. if we had to; we were all drained from the weather. The point man started moving west back on the small trail that had led us here. We rounded our way back to the top of the hill. We finally made it to the dirt road and started down it until it went down to the stream. When we reached the stream, each of the guys dipped his hands into the icy cold water and drank it. I did the same and it tasted a hell of a lot better than the five gallon cans of water that they had sent out to us. Those cans were sitting out in the hot sun all day at the chopper pad and they didn't care if the water was hot or not, they didn't care back in the rear. Most of the guys had to carry the empty cans back with us to the company. We were getting very close to the company perimeter and I got on the radio and told them that we were coming in and not to shoot. The company radioman told us to come on in and I then passed the word to Lieutenant Libutti and he passed it on to Lefefe and on up to the point team. We walked like we were dead men and didn't even care if we got hit. As we reached the perimeter and took our fighting holes, the guys took off their gear in slow motion and got under their ponchos so that the sun would not hit them. I went over to our hole and slowly took off the radio and then the rest of the gear and sat down. Lieutenant Libutti came over and he also was taking off his gear very slowly. The look on his face said it all. He just had had it with the Arty F.O. Lieutenant. This was the hardest day of his life over here. I knew that the F.O. Lieutenant was still on his mind. The Arty F.O. Lieutenant left and headed over to the company C.P. with his radioman. I knew that the bastard was going to tell Captain Hutchinson a lie about Lieutenant Libutti. I knew that he was going to make Libutti out as incompetent.

I looked at Libutti and told him that he did damn good out there and not to worry about the F.O. Lieutenant. The company radioman called me on the radio and said that the captain wanted to see Libutti. I then told Libutti that the captain wanted to talk to him. As he got up, I told him to tell the captain just what the hell the Arty F.O. Lieutenant was trying to do. The company C.P. was about fifty feet from our platoon C.P. About twenty minutes later Libutti came back and I could tell something big happened at the company C.P. Libutti told me that the captain wanted to see me. I then got up and as I walked on over to the captain, I was getting pissed. The captain was by himself and said, "Hammer, what the HELL was going on out there?" I asked him, "What do you mean, sir?" And he said, "Between the two lieutenants." The captain said that he could hear them arguing in the background when I was talking to the company radioman. I told the captain to get rid of that son-of-a-bitch F.O. Lieutenant because he was trying to show my lieutenant how to run his platoon and also he told Libutti that he didn't know what the hell he was doing out there. I said the F.O. Lieutenant wanted me to tell you what he wanted to do out here behind my lieutenant's back. I told him that I didn't take orders from him. I told the captain that Lieutenant Libutti did a damn good job out there with his platoon considering listening to that asshole F.O. Lieutenant who had wanted to run his platoon for him. I also told the captain that the F.O. Lieutenant was trying to get our platoon sergeant to go along with him about Libutti not capable of leading a platoon. I told the captain I hoped that our platoon never saw that son-of-a-bitch again and if we did he might get a bullet in the back from our platoon. The captain knew that I had gone through hell on this patrol. Captain Hutchinson looked right into my eyes and knew that I was sticking up for Lieutenant Libutti and he knew that Libutti had done one hell of a job out there in running this platoon and doing all the right stuff. The captain told me to go back and that I was to be off the radio for a couple of days. I told him that I was all right and I asked him if he was finished with me and he said, "Yes, Hammer." The captain told me not to tell Libutti what we had talked about. I just nodded my head and slowly walked back to where my lieutenant was.

I got back to Libutti and he asked me what the captain wanted and I told him that it was nothing and Libutti asked if the captain wanted to know how he did out there, right? I then told Libutti that it was about the radio and not him whatsoever. I then sat down and I told the lieutenant that I was going to take a little rest if he didn't mind. I could feel my body being drained and my mind was drained as well. Lieutenant Libutti got up and walked on over to our perimeter to see how the guys were doing. I just didn't feel like eating at all. After a couple of hours I told Libutti that I was going to go back down to the stream to fill up my canteens, all three of them. I took my rifle and went down to the stream and filled up the canteens of mine and the lieutenant.

It was going on evening and the sun was almost gone and I just sat at the hole thinking about what had gone on this day. I wanted to be with my fire team, to be with the guys and to relax. This job of being the platoon radioman is a very lonely job in that everyone thinks you are kissing up to the lieutenant and getting a lot of goodies.

I had first watch for the night and everyone in the C.P. was settling down for the night. Libutti came over to me before he covered himself up. I knew what he was about to say and before he said his first word, I told him that he did one hell of a job out there and the platoon watched how he handled himself with that Arty F.O. Lieutenant. I also told him that I was glad that he checked on the guys when we got back inside the company perimeter. He then went back to where his poncho was and covered himself up. I could still feel the fatigue from the patrol but I was feeling a little better mentally. I knew that I was taking on one hell of a job by helping out my lieutenant so that the guys in the platoon would accept him. I could tell that the lieutenant really appreciated what I was trying to do for him. I looked over to where he was and knew that he had the longest day of his life over here and he had aged quite a bit. I started thinking about the guys who had heat stoke and how they were doing. Morning came and the whole day, all of us in the 2nd platoon just took it easy. Most of the guys were feeling better than day before. Everyone of us didn't move at all during the day and stayed out of the sun. Most of the guys tried to sleep most of the day but the heat and humidity made it hard on all of us.

On the radio the captain called for the lieutenants from his three platoons for a meeting. I knew that we were getting ready to move out again. Lefefe came over to me and he could tell that we were going to leave this area very soon. Finally Libutti came back from the meeting and he told me to get the squad leaders up to the C.P. I got on the radio and called 2nd and 3rd squad leaders and told them to make sure that they informed the 1st squad leader to come with them. When they got to the C.P. the lieutenant told them that we were moving out in a little bit and that we would be getting on the tanks with Alpha Company and that we were heading west about 2000 meters and setting up there for a couple of days. Libutti told the squad leaders to tell the guys to saddle up and wait for the tanks to come. Libutti came over to me and said that the captain didn't want me on the radio for two days. I went over to our hole and started putting on my gear with the exception of not putting the heavy radio on my back. Boni became the platoon radioman for the next couple of days. Lefefe came over to me with Doc Chico and none of us said a word. Lefefe got his orders for Out of Country R. & R. He was staying with the company and would be leaving sometime this evening. The lieutenant got on his gear and all of us just waited for the tanks with Alpha Company to come by and pick us up.

We could hear the tanks coming; there were four of them. Finally they arrived and the word was passed to get on the tanks. I went with the lieutenant and he told me to get on this tank and that he would be on the other tank. Two other guys from our platoon got on the tank with me that also had guys from Alpha Company on it. Everyone in our company was on the tanks and the word was passed that we were moving out. The tanks started off again, heading due west. About twenty minutes had passed and then the tanks stopped for a couple of minutes. I looked to see if anyone had gotten off the tanks but it was hard to see because the sun was almost gone for the day. I couldn't tell and the next thing the tanks started off again. Ten minutes had passed and then the tanks stopped and everyone got off. I asked one of the lieutenants from Alpha Company if he knew where Charlie Company was and he said back where the tanks had stopped before. I told him, "Thanks," and the two other guys that were with me followed me. I told them that I knew where the platoon was. We started walking back to where we had come from by following the tanks tracks.

I told the two guys who were with me to follow me because I knew where our platoon was. The two guys were scared and nervous. The sun was down now and it was getting dark. I then followed the path of the tanks going back east. The ground where the tanks had gone over was chewed up by the tracks. I told the guys to keep their eyes open and listen for the enemy if they were around. I went about to where the tanks had stopped the first time and I could hear someone digging. I then pointed to the two guys that we were going off to our right to the hedgerow. When I got to the hedgerow, I raised my hand to stop and I could hear someone call out, "Who goes there?" I then replied that it was, "Hammer, and I am looking for 2nd platoon." The Marine told me to come on in and I told him that there were "Three of us coming into the perimeter and don't shoot." I then pointed to the two guys to come on up to me and we then went on through the hedgerow and into the perimeter. When I got into the perimeter, I asked the guys where 2nd platoon was and they told me that they were over to the left of them. I told them thanks and we went on over to where 2nd platoon was digging in.

We walked on over to where we could see 2nd platoon and the two guys left and went on over to where their fire team was digging their fighting hole. Lieutenant Libutti was digging our C.P. hole and I told the lieutenant that I would finish digging the hole. Boni was with the radio and didn't say a word to anyone. I could tell that he was not happy to be the platoon radioman and Libutti told him to go back to his team. It didn't really take long since the ground was really soft. When I finished digging the hole, the lieutenant told me that he was glad that I got back safely.

Libutti looked at me and told me that he had really messed things up out on the patrol the other day. He was blaming himself for getting one man wounded from a grenade and for six guys getting heat stroke. He was making himself believe that he was the cause of what had happened out there on the patrol. I stopped him right there and told him that he was not the cause of the guy getting wounded and the six guys coming down with heat stroke. He felt that he made the wrong decisions. I then changed my tone with the lieutenant and told him not to say another stupid thing about the patrol and him causing the problems out there. I was getting pissed at him and told him that he did one hell of a job of being the officer and leading his men out of trouble. I told him that damn F.O. Lieutenant was trying to run the platoon and telling him just how to run this patrol. I told him that the F.O. lieutenant had no right in trying to tell him how to run his platoon,

The next time a F.O. Lieutenant wants to run his platoon, he better shove his foot up his ass and quick and take charge of the situation and make damn clear he understood it. Lieutenant Libutti knew that he pushed the wrong buttons with me and in a way was glad because what I told him was the truth. I knew that he wanted to hear me say it to him. I told him that this conversation was over with and that, I better not "Ever" hear him bring this up again. I said that, "You're doing the right thing for this platoon. Now go and get some sleep in before it's your watch."

It was 21:00 hundred hours and I had the first watch. Lieutenant Libutti covered himself up with his poncho. I went on over to the hole where the radio was and sat down. About twenty feet away was a very large tree that was about 60 feet high. I could hear the mosquitoes and they were out in force. As I sat there next to the radio, I started to cry a little and I knew that trying to help the lieutenant and with Lefefe to run this platoon was just too much. I knew that I couldn't let all of this get to me and that I had to be very strong. I knew that I couldn't show how I felt out in the field with the lieutenant and the guys in our platoon. My watch was over and I kicked Lefefe's foot for him to stand the radio watch for our platoon. I then went over to my gear and I covered myself in my poncho so that the mosquitoes would not bite me. I stood my second watch of the night and morning came and I got up and had my chow. I sat next to the radio all day in case the captain wanted the lieutenant.

I knew deep down inside of me that I had a lot of responsibility for this platoon and the lieutenant. And to top it off, I didn't want the damn responsibility. All I wanted to do was take care of myself and no one else. The company radioman called me and told me that Charlie 6 Axial wanted Charlie 2 Axial. I told the lieutenant that the captain wanted to talk to him. He got up and went on over to the captain and after a little while he came back and said that we were going on an ambush, and that we were going to take the F.O. with us again. I just looked at Libutti and he could tell that I didn't want the F.O. lieutenant running his platoon. Libutti then told me to get the squad leaders up for a briefing. I got my gear ready and Libutti told the three-squad leaders and Lefefe about the ambush that we were going to do. Libutti then told them that we were leaving at 17:00 hundred hours. He dismissed them and my squad leader, Bignami, just looked at me as though I was a traitor. He wanted no part of me or even to talk to me. It didn't take long for the guys to hate me.

It was getting very close to 17:00 hundred hours and the guys from the other platoons came over and took our positions while we went on this little ambush. I knew that the captain was really making my lieutenant learn a lot in a very short time. The F.O. lieutenant came over to our C.P. and told Libutti that he and his radioman were ready. It was not the F.O. lieutenant we had the other day. It looked like the captain got rid of the son-of-a-bitch.

Libutti then passed the word up to the point team to move out heading south. We were in a staggered column and moving out. Some of the guys were telling us to watch out for ourselves. We moved out about 500 meters and the point team stopped and passed the word back that they had hit the dirt road. Libutti then went up to the point team and told me to stay where I was. He came back and told me to tell the captain that we were at Checkpoint 1 and moving out. As we got on the dirt road we were going the same way as the road...southwest. We had gone about 1500 meters and there was a large hill off to our left side and Libutti told me that we were at Checkpoint 2 and to let the captain know. Libutti told Lefefe to have the point team head up the hill. We reached the top and Libutti told me to dig our hole in the middle. Libutti told the squad leaders to position their men off the top but on the side of the hill so when the sun went down it would be hard for the enemy to see up except for the C.P. group. Us guys in the C.P. group had to stay low or the N.V.A. could shoot at us. Our C.P. group was the 60 mortar team, Doc, me, and the lieutenant.

We were on top of the hill itself. The F.O. lieutenant and his radioman were about fifteen feet away from us and they were behaving themselves. It was starting to get dark and it was time to stop digging the hole. Libutti told me that he was going to check on the guys around the perimeter and to make sure they were settling down for the night. I thought that he was doing a good job of showing the guys that he was right there with them and that he cared for them. He came back and we did have some cover up on the top of the hill in that the bushes were about three to four feet high. I told the lieutenant that I would take the first watch and that he would be second and then Doc. He agreed - and Libutti's eyes were very tired. I stood my watch and called the squads that had the radios, which was 1st squad and 2nd squad, every half hour. My time was up but I decided that I would let the lieutenant sleep for half the night. I couldn't believe that I was not tired at all.

It was going on around 01:00 and was time to call the two squads; "Charlie 2-1, Charlie 2-1, if all secured press your handset twice, if not once." Then I got two presses from the handset. I then called for "Charlie 2-2, Charlie 2-2, if all secured, press your handset twice if not, once." I didn't get anything on the radio. I called again and still I didn't get any response. I knew that someone was sleeping on his watch. I called to Charlie 6 that I would be off the air for ten. I got up and took my rifle with me and I went over to the perimeter and I heard one of the guys whisper for me to halt and I whispered to him that it was Hammer and that I was coming. He whispered back to me to come on in and when I got to him I asked where 2nd squad was and he told me off to the left. I told him that I would be coming back from there in a little bit and not to shoot me. He nodded and I went over to the next hole. Someone was sitting upright next to the hole and the rest of the guys in the fire team were all sleeping about ten feet from the fighting hole. The guy that was at the fighting hole with the radio next to him and the handset in his hand was sleeping in a sitting position. I shook the hell out of him and boy did he jump. His eyes got very large and he was scared to death. I then whispered to him that if he was that tired to let one of the other guys take his watch. He insisted that he would not do it again. I told him that he better not. I then left and went back the way I came so I wouldn't get shot. I got to the next hole and I went back to my hole where my radio was. I looked down at my watch; it was 01:30 and time to call again. I first called the company radioman that I was back on the air. I then called 1st squad and I got two clicks on the handset and I then called 2nd squad. I didn't get a response; I called two more times and still no response; I then went over to the perimeter again. The guy from 1st squad said, "Not again!" and I said, "Yes, again." I went on over to the hole and again the radioman was sitting upright next to the hole holding the handset in his hand. This time I kicked him very hard at the bottom of his foot and I also woke up one of the guys from the fire team as well. The guy was telling me that he was all right and that he would not do it again and I told him that he better get someone else to stand his watch if he was that tired. The other guy came over and asked what the hell was going on and I told him that the radioman was sleeping on his watch. The guy insisted that he would not do it again and I told him that if he did that I was going to cut his throat. I looked him right into his eyes and he could see that I meant it. The other guy went back to sleep and I told the guy again that I would cut his throat the next time. I left and went back to my radio. When I got back there I had ten minutes before I called both squads again.

It was 02:00 and time to call the two squads. I called 1st squad and said if they were secured to press their handset twice and they did. I then called, "Charlie 2-2, if all secure, press your handset twice, if not, press it once." I got nothing. I thought to myself he better not be asleep. I again called 2nd squad and repeated what I had just said to them, and still no answer. I then got on the radio and told Charlie 6 that I would be off the air for ten. I then grabbed my bayonet and was really pissed at this asshole. He was going to get what he deserved. I went over to the perimeter and the guy from 1st squad saw that I was pissed and I had the bayonet in my hand. He told me "Easy!" as I went over to the hole and there he was still sitting there, sleeping like a baby with no worries in the world. I walked up to him and he was really in a deep sleep. I then knelt down and took my bayonet and started on the right side of his throat by his ear and lightly cut his skin and only a little bit of blood came out. He didn't even feel my bayonet cutting his skin and didn't move at all. He was still sleeping and I then took the point of the bayonet and stuck it right at his Adam's apple. I started pushing it into his throat and still he didn't move. As I was going deeper into his throat he quickly got up and I then grabbed the back of his neck so that he wouldn't get away. I wanted him to know what it was like having a bayonet going into his throat. His eyes got as large as a silver dollar and he started shaking. I then whispered to him that, "I should kill you right now." He was trying to talk but the bayonet was keeping him from saying a word. A couple of the guys woke up and could see that I had my bayonet in his throat and told me to let him go. I told them that this was the third time that he had fallen off to sleep on me while he was on watch. One of them looked at the watch and told me that they would take care of it and for me to take it easy. One of the guys whispered out his name and they said, "Hughart."

I finally let go and the guys told me that they would take care of it and that it would never happen again. I told them, "I hope not." I went back to my hole and I got on the radio and told Charlie 6 that I was back on the air. This time I could tell that it was Captain Hutchinson on the radio and asked what the hell was going on out there and I told him that there was no problem and that everything was all right.

The rest of the night went along without a problem and I knew that the guy was a new guy that had just come over from the States because I had never seen him before. I started thinking about when I first came over here and how tired and sleepy I was when I first came. I knew that I had to back off and give the new guy a chance. I thought to myself that I gave him three chances in one night to get himself squared away. I knew when we got back to the company I had to come up with a reason why I had to go off the air. I knew that I would tell my lieutenant and the captain that the battery went dead on one of the squad's radios.

The sun was starting to come up and the lieutenant and Sgt. Lefefe got up and both of them came over to me and wanted to know why I didn't get them up for radio watch. I told both of them that I didn't feel tired and that I wanted to make sure that they were rested. Both of them told me thanks and I then got Libutti alone and told him that if the captain wanted to know if he had stood radio watch to tell him yes. I also told Libutti that one of the squad radios had gone dead and that the new guy didn't know that it had gone out and I had to change the battery.

After all of us ate, the lieutenant told us that we were going back to where the company was. I got my gear on and we headed back. Just before we got to the company perimeter, I called the company radioman and told them that we were coming in from the south and to tell the guys not to shoot us. We waited until we got word to come on in and they told me that we could come in. I passed the word to the lieutenant and he then passed it on to Lefefe and he passed it on to the point team to move out. We reached the perimeter and went back to our fighting holes. The guys that had heat stroke a couple of days ago were waiting for us. They were glad to be back with the rest of us. They told us that the wounded guy was being rotated back home, that his 395 days were up. He had finished his tour of duty in Vietnam. I was glad for him because he was going home alive.

The rest of the day went by while the whole company stayed where we were. The word was passed that Alpha Company and we were to be the blocking force for the rest of the battalion. Around 13:00 hundred hours the captain called me over to his C.P. I told Libutti that the captain wanted to see me and I told him that if the captain asked him if he had stood his radio watch for the night to say "Yes" and he understood. I got over to where the captain was and he asked me what the hell had been going on out there in the field. I told the captain that one of the squad radio batteries went out and the new guy that took watch didn't know it. He didn't know that I was going to call him every half hour. I told him that I replaced the battery with a new one. Then the captain said, "Lieutenant Libutti did not stand his radio watch and I want to know why." I then told the captain, "Lieutenant Libutti did stand his radio watch last night." The captain said that he knew that the lieutenant was sleeping out there in the field. I kept on insisting to the captain that Libutti stood his radio watch because I was the one that woke him up. Then Captain Hutchinson started shaking his head and he knew that I was not going to tell him the truth and then told me that he wanted to see the lieutenant. Captain Hutchinson had a smile on his face as I left him. When I got back to our C.P. I then told Libutti that he wanted to know why he didn't stand his radio watch last night and I told him that I woke you up both times. Lieutenant Libutti said "O.K." The lieutenant came back and didn't say a word at first, then said the captain had asked him the question but quickly dropped it. Both of us got a little laugh out of it. Libutti said that he appreciated what I did for them last night by letting them sleep. I told Libutti that I couldn't sleep at all and now I was going to get some sleep during the day. Everyone in the platoon just sat at their fighting holes in case the enemy came to us.

The next morning came and Alpha Company was moving past us going east and then they turned and headed north. It must have been fifteen minutes later that all hell broke loose. All of us in Charlie Company got our fighting gear on and waited for word to come down that Alpha Company needed us. On the radio, the company radioman told us that all of us were moving out to help Alpha Company. Captain Hutchinson came over to Lieutenant Libutti and told him that our platoon was to swing around from the side and hit the enemy from the left flank, if we could.

Libutti then told the squad leaders in the platoon to head north from here on the road. As we headed north, we could hear the firing from our right side. We must have moved about 300 meters and then the word was passed to move east. There was a wooden fence with barbed wire - only two strands. We were on the left side of the fence, and there was good cover for us with the trees on this side. On the other side of the fence was a very long field of tall grass that was about two and a half feet tall. The field was a good 100 meters wide until you could see the tree line on the other side. All of us knew that they had to have a machine gun nest watching out for their flanks.

We moved about 200 meters and I came across a couple of pineapple plants and there was a good sized pineapple inside it. I then took out my bayonet and cut it. Just before I cut the pineapple, Dale Davis looked back and saw that I had taken out my bayonet and he thought that we were going to have hand-to-hand combat with the N.V.A. He then turned around and kept on moving. I was holding onto the pineapple and then the word was passed to stop. I sat down and started trimming the pineapple with my bayonet. The lieutenant looked back at me and told me to get rid of the pineapple and I told the lieutenant, "I haven't eaten." Lieutenant Libutti told me, "Hammer, you don't have time for that and put the damn thing down." I then dropped it and the lieutenant told the point team to go into the field of tall grass, but to watch themselves.

The point team started out going into the grassy field and about half way into it the N.V.A. opened up with their machine guns. All of us hit the deck and waited for instructions. The word was passed from the point team that one of the guys was wounded but not seriously. They got back and the machine gun was still firing. The rounds were going over our heads by about a foot. Some of the rounds were hitting the trees that were protecting us. Some of the guys from the point team came back and had opened up on the machine gun nest. They knew where to fire their rifles at the enemy machine gun. Most of us couldn't fire our rifles because we could have hit the point team in our platoon. The word came back that the wounded guy just got grazed across the chest. The round came inside his flak jacket from the side and just cut the skin a little.

The company radioman told me that they were sending a tank to help us with the machine gun nest. I passed the word on to Libutti, and he then passed it onto the rest of the platoon. The machine gun nest stopped firing and they could hear a tank coming in their direction. The tank arrived where I was lying on my back and Lieutenant Libutti told the lieutenant of the tank where the enemy was. The tank then turned toward the field and moved up to the fence and opened up with its fifty cal. I knew one thing: I sure as hell didn't want to be on the other side receiving the fifty caliber rounds. It must have been ten minutes and Libutti told Lefefe to move out toward the machine gun nest. This time the enemy had a lot more fire coming at us and I knew that they moved a lot more N.V.A. to cover their flank. It just wasn't a machine gun nest that was firing; there were AK-47s rifles firing as well. They didn't want us to overrun them. We knew that we were not that strong to accomplish our mission and the lieutenant didn't want any more of us getting hit. In a way we did help out Alpha Company by making the enemy move a lot of their men away from them and hitting us instead.

The company radioman told us to retreat with the tank and that they were going to call in artillery on the N.V.A. I then passed the word to the lieutenant and as I did, the tank started to retreat as well. Libutti told the guys that we were to go back to where we had come from. We moved out and went back about 300 meters and then stopped. We would hear the 105s, 155s and the 175mm from Camp Carroll and Cam Lo firing their artillery and the rounds sounded like a freight train coming in sideways. We could hear them hitting the enemy lines. We stayed there for about half an hour. Word was passed to move back to where we had been the other day so that we wouldn't get hit by our artillery rounds.

As we moved back to our perimeter, the guys were very tired from the heat and humidity as well as trying to get around the enemy. It was around 16:00 hundred hours and Captain Hutchinson told Libutti that our platoon was to go down about 600 meters and to pick up our supplies. Libutti told the platoon to saddle up and that we were heading west for 600 meters. When we got there we set up a perimeter and waited for the choppers to come with the supplies. I changed the radio frequency and waited just like the rest of the platoon. The sound of the choppers came and I got on the radio and told them that we were at their three o'clock and as they changed directions I told the guys to pop the smoke. The pilot told me the color and I confirmed it; I told him to come in from the south and go out to the west. Both choppers landed and dropped off the C-rations and ammo cases. The guys gathered up all of the supplies and I then changed the radio frequency back to our company frequency and told them we were on our way back to the company.

As we were going back to the company perimeter, I thought that what the captain did (to have us go down 600 meters away), was a great idea in case the enemy fired mortar rounds. The company would not get hit like the last time we had when we were being supplied within the company at Phu An. I knew that Captain Hutchinson was learning fast himself not to make the same mistake twice. The more I saw and talked to Captain Hutchinson, the more I could trust him because he really cared for his three platoons. Besides that, I really liked Captain Hutchinson. He made sure all of the small details were being corrected out in the field. When we got inside the company perimeter, we took the supplies on over to the Company C.P. and the captain had the X.O. 1st Lieutenant Dixon passed out the ammo and C-rations to the three platoons. We went back to our part of the perimeter and I, with the rest of our C.P., took off our gear and sat around trying to rest. I looked around at our platoon and I noticed that we were getting very small as a platoon. The squads were to have three fire teams each and we had a fire team and a half each. We needed men in our platoon as well as for the whole battalion. It looked like we had around thirty men in our platoon. Our platoon was to have fifty-six men. Every evening, Lieutenant Libutti would go around and check on the guys at their fighting holes. Sgt. Lefefe was still on R. and R. and I couldn't wait for him to return to help me with the lieutenant. After Lieutenant Libutti did his rounds with the troops, he would then come over to me and sit down and ask me how he was doing before he would go to sleep. I would say the same thing, "You're doing what an officer is supposed to do. You're listening to the squad leaders as well as the guys in the platoon." I knew that he wanted me to say more but none of us in the platoon hardly talked about anything because of the weather over here, being so damn hot and humid. I knew that I couldn't say too much now; I didn't want him to rely on me and his two weeks were almost up. I knew that I had to start separating us a little each day now. He was still a little green but it was leaving him and he was starting to feel comfortable as an officer. I knew that he was winning over the guys in the platoon and they were warming up to him.

Two days had passed; word was that we were moving due north in the morning to an outpost called Con Thein. Sergeant Lefefe finally came back off of R. & R. and the guys were happy to see him. Lefefe made the rounds and then reported to the lieutenant and even Libutti was glad to see him as well. Lefefe could tell that the lieutenant had changed in the week and knew that he had seen more shit and was listening to the squad leaders. Lefefe knew that I had been working on the lieutenant on being a fine officer for 2nd platoon. It looked like we had finally got the N.V.A. to leave Phu An and the surrounding areas. It was the last night in the field that I told Lieutenant Libutti that this was the last time for him to ask me how he was doing. His two weeks were up. I told him that he had done a great job in conducting himself as a good officer in front of the men and treated the men as Marines. He took the time to listen to what they had to say out in the field. He was starting to realize that he could handle himself in combat. I also told him that he had made himself close to the guys in the platoon by checking on them every morning and just before night time. I also told him that he didn't need to rely on me any more and that he could handle himself well out in the field. Lieutenant Libutti was about to say something to me but I cut him off. I didn't want to hear a damn thing from him from now on about how he was doing out in the field. I also told him that Sgt. Lefefe was coming around to him and that he was seeing a very big difference in the way he talked to him and also listened to his advice. I then told him that it was my turn on the radio and that he better get some sleep in before it was his turn. He still wanted to say something to me but I wouldn't let him speak. I knew that he wanted to thank me for all that I had done for him in becoming a damn good Marine officer in this platoon. He then covered himself up and I just looked at him and I then prayed to God that it was up to Him to watch over my lieutenant from now on. I prayed that nothing would happen to him while he was over here, but with this outfit it seemed that everyone was either getting killed or wounded.

As I was sitting next to the hole with the radio next to me, I could tell that I had gotten close to the lieutenant…very close. I then looked around the perimeter and most of the guys were covered up by their ponchos. I hoped that Sgt. Lefefe would work with the lieutenant in making us a great platoon. I was glad now that I dropped some of the responsibility and could worry a little more about myself. I was still the platoon radioman and in some ways I wanted to be back with my squad and just take care of myself. Morning came and the word was passed that we were moving out in the morning heading north from here. I got all of my gear on and waited for the word from the captain for our platoon to move out.

Lieutenant Libutti was coming back from talking with the captain. Libutti told me that when we moved out, that both of our sister platoons would be on each side of us and behind us would be the tanks. Alpha Company would be next to our sister platoon that would be on our right side. Libutti looked at me and said that I was the main radioman for our sister platoons as well as all of Alpha Company - what I said everyone had to do. Libutti then told Lefefe to get the guys to move out and that we would go a little ways and then have our platoon on line. We moved out in a staggered column and about 100 meters, Libutti told me to tell the squad radiomen to stop and to get on line. First and second squads were on my left side and third and machine gun squads were to be on my right side. I then sat down while 1st Platoon went on our right side and 3rd Platoon on our left side. All of them got on line as well. The tanks lined up behind us. Then Alpha Company got on line on our right side as well. Then each platoon as well as the Alpha Company radioman called me and told me that all of them were on line to 2nd platoon. I then called Charlie 6 who was behind us with the tanks and they told me to pass the word on to everyone to move out. I passed the word out to both platoons and Alpha Company and we started moving. We must have traveled about 100 meters when the company radioman called me and told me that we had a wounded guy in our platoon. I knew that none of us heard any shots. I passed the word to Lieutenant Libutti and he said for me to stop the rest of the platoons and Alpha Company. I had everyone stop until we found out what had happened. Charlie Company's radioman said that the wounded man was character, "Papa." (Character means person, Papa is the person last name.) The only person I knew it could be was Parrillo and then the radioman said that one of the tanks had knocked over one of the palm trees and it had hit Parrillo. I then passed the word on to Lieutenant Libutti about what had happened and they had him on one of the tanks. Lieutenant Libutti told me to pass the word on to the platoons and Alpha Company that we were moving out. I looked back and the tanks were still knocking down some of the palm trees that were in the way. The guys were now far away from the palm trees that were falling to the ground.

We had moved about 400 meters and the word was being passed back to me that they had found a tunnel. Charlie 6 called and told me to pass the word on to both platoons and Alpha Company to blow up the tunnels if they came across them. We walked through Phu An and kept on walking north. There were no people around at all and all of us could tell that no one had lived here for some time. As we were going past the small vill, one of the guys came over to me and handed me a steel box and he said that they found it in one of the tunnels. I opened it up and there were papers written in Vietnamese. The papers might be very important but we needed someone who could read Vietnamese to know how important these papers were. I gave the box to Lieutenant Libutti and he made sure that it got back to Captain Hutchinson. We got past the vill and we started to move up on a large hill. Charlie 6 called me and told me to stop the platoons and Alpha Company. I then told everyone to stop and Captain Hutchinson came up to us and told us to move out in a staggered column with flanks out on both sides. The captain radioman then took over and told the other platoons in Charlie Company to get behind 2nd Platoon and then Alpha Company behind them. Lefefe then told the squads which fire teams he wanted out on the flanks. Lefefe waved his arm and the platoon started moving up the side of the very large hill. It was not steep but it wasn't too bad of a climb. We went another 200 meters and the point team came across a dirt road that was going along the side of the hill, east to west. The company radioman told me when we hit the dirt road to stay on it and head west until we got the rest of the company and Alpha Company on the road. The guys moved about 100 meters on the road and still stayed in a staggered column when word was passed to stop. The guys knelt down on each side of the dirt road. We waited for the rest of the company to get on the road. There was something coming down off the hill heading toward us. It was a very small vehicle that had a 106 mm recoilless rifle on it with two Marines. That was all that could get onto that vehicle. They rode past us and went east on the dirt road heading down to the bottom of the hill going around Phu An. They looked like they were taking a Sunday drive. Then the company radioman told me to move out, heading up the hill on the dirt road. The point team started moving out and as we were heading to the top of the hill, we saw an old CH-34 chopper that had gotten shot down some time before and it was stripped clean-only the shell of the chopper remained. When we got past the chopper, the dirt road went right and led straight to the top of a large hill. At the top was this large camp with only one strain of concertina wire around. It had three knolls inside it. Each of the knolls were about another sixty feet higher. One of the guys said that this was Con Thein, Hill of Angels. The word was passed to me that we were to move off to the side of the dirt road and to set up our perimeter on the south side of the strip. I passed the word on to the lieutenant and he had Lefefe start setting up part of the perimeter so that the other two platoons of Charlie Company would cover the rest of our perimeter. As Alpha Company came up, they went to the west side of the camp and set up their perimeter.

I was very tired and I took off the radio and sat down. There were new men that were assigned to our platoon who had been waiting for us to get here. Lieutenant Libutti came over to me and he said that I was off the radio and that I needed to be with my fire team. He told me that Michael Bradley was going to be the radioman for our platoon. He knew that I had had it and that I needed to be with the guys again. Libutti told me to report back to my fire team. I got up and walked on over to where the fire team was and told them that I was back. Van, and Smithy were happy to see me back. There were some new faces in the squad as well. Van told me that one of the new guys was Robbins in our fire team. Van said that Smithy would go to the 2nd fire team which there were only two of; now it would make three. Van picked up Hughart a couple of days before from second squad. I asked Van who our squad leader and he said that it was Frank Bignami.

The guys in the fire team were digging the fighting hole and we were facing south from the strip. The edge of the strip was about twenty feet from us and was hard to see through the line of trees and heavy brush that was next to the strip. Bignami came over to us after he had talked with Lieutenant Libutti and said that we would be taking over Con Thein tomorrow. I looked around and most of the guys were out in the open, being on the strip with no cover. The guys were making sure that the fighting holes were deep.

It was going on evening and the sun was starting to go down. Van told us what watch we had for the night and of course we all had two one-hour watches. I lay down and covered myself up and was not too far away from the fighting hole in case we got hit. The rest of the guys in the company did the same thing. As I covered myself up with the poncho I could feel that someone was watching us. The feeling of someone watching us was very strong and it was very hard for me to get any sleep. I could tell one of the guys was coming over to me and I got up before he was going to kick me. I got up and went on over to the fighting hole and he went on over to where his poncho was and lay down. As I sat there looking south and along the edge of the strip leading to the east of us, I wanted to get up and go on over to the hedgerow in front of me and look for the enemy. I still had that feeling they were watching us. I also had something strong inside of me telling me to go out there to the hedgerow and look for the enemy. But I knew that if I did that there would be no one here watching over the guys that were sleeping and it would leave a hole for the enemy to come on in and kill the guys in our squad. The night seemed to be very dark and cold, even though it wasn't cold out at all. My turn for watch was over and I then woke up Van and he took over. I could see in his face that he had the same feeling as I had about someone watching us. I whispered to him and told him that I didn't hear a sound out there but I could feel them watching us. Van nodded to me and I then lay down and covered myself up.

I did my second watch for the night and still I had that feeling that they were watching us but they didn't want to give us a fight. My watch was over and again I woke up Robbins and he took over. The next thing, I felt the heat from the sun hitting me on my face. I knew that it was early morning and around 05:10 hours. I got up and everyone else was getting up. I could tell that the N.V.A. had stopped watching us during the night. We cooked our C-rations and waited for word to come, to take over Con Thein from the 4th Marines.

The word was passed to saddle up and that we were moving into Con Thein. All of us got up and we moved to where the gate was that led into Con Thein. It was on the dirt road that we had come up yesterday. As we were outside the gate waiting for them to open it up, the word was passed to wait for the 4th Marines to leave first. We waited for about half an hour. Then the guys started coming out and as they were walking past us in a staggered column, going down that dirt road, they were telling us to keep our eyes on the Green Berets that were on the middle knoll. The guys from 2nd Battalion 4th Marines were telling us that the night they almost got over run, the Green Berets sat at the top of their knoll watching the Marines get the hell kicked out of them. They were telling us that they didn't lift a hand to help them. The guys from 2/4 recovered their fighting holes from the N.V.A. on their own. That was the night that we were on stand-by. The guys from 2/4 said to keep a sharp eye out on those "BASTARDS" up there. Every man from 2nd Battalion 4th Marines told us that the "GREEN BERETS" were not worth a damn. A couple of the Marines were telling us to keep our eyes out at night time especially, because they would see some-one flashing a light to the west into the mountains. The last of the men from 2nd Battalion 4th Marines left and they told us to move inside and Libutti would tell us where we were to be stationed. Lieutenant Libutti showed all of the fire teams what bunker and fighting holes we had. He looked at me but did not say a word to me in front of the guys. I could tell he had missed me being around him. I was glad that he was showing the guys he knew what the hell he was doing.

As I was taking off my fighting gear, Bignami came over to us and told us more about what had happened to the 4th Marines that night we were on stand-by to help them if they needed it. Bignami said that it started about 22:30 hours and that the N.V.A. were coming through the lines from the west side where the South Vietnamese Mountain Yard were guarding that part of the perimeter. The 4th Marines protected the north, east and south part of the perimeter. The N.V.A. were going from fighting hole to fighting hole killing the Marines. There were two Marine troop carriers that carried about twenty men in them and the N.V.A. threw a satchel charge and killed the guys inside the vehicles. What was left of 2/4 regained the perimeter and forced the N.V.A. back out. Bignami said they did it all on their own without anyone helping them, especially the Green Berets. Bignami told us to make sure that we kept one eye out on the Green Berets that were above us on the middle knoll. We were getting to dislike the Green Berets here at Con Thein and I was like the rest of the guys starting to hate them.

I remembered the bitterness on the faces of the guys from 2nd Battalion 4th Marines because they wanted to kill the Green Berets for not helping them. I remembered back when I was in high school that there was a song that a Green Beret had made; I liked it very much. The song was about how tough they were and that there were only a few of them, but they could take on the world. Now, from what I heard from the guys from the 4th Marines, my expectation of the Green Berets wasn't worth a damn. I couldn't trust them in a firefight after what I had heard.

Our fighting hole was about twenty feet in front of our bunker; there was a road between our bunker and the fighting hole. In front of the fighting hole was only one strand of concertina wire. It was about thirty feet away. There were also two claymore mines for each hole. The claymore is 6 inches by 12 inches in a half moon shape with 700 BBs inside it with a cord that led back to the fighting hole for us to squeeze the trigger and it would go off. I looked over to the east side of us and there was a small landing strip for a single prop plane to land. I looked behind us and the three knolls were about forty feet higher than our part of the hill. Then word was passed that we were getting mail and that it would be here sometime during the day. I got out my rifle and started cleaning it with my toothbrush. It was about 13:00 hundred hours and I could hear a six-by coming up the hill. As the six-by was going inside the gate, I saw the bright yellow, orange and red sacks of mail. I knew that it would be another hour before we got word to pick up our mail.

It was well over two weeks since we had mail. Bignami came over to me and told me that I better get on over to the C.P. and that I had better get someone to help me carry my mail back. I asked one of the guys, Dale Davis, if he would help me and I remembered him as one of the guys with heat stroke who I had also carried out of the minefield. He got up and went with me on over to the C.P. and there was a pile of small boxes that were 12 inches by 12 inches square. When I got to the C.P., Lefefe told me the pile that was on the ground was all mine. At the top of the pile were about thirty letters for me as well. Lefefe gave Dale his bundles of letters and Dale came over and helped me carry the eight boxes. We got back to the bunker and I told him thanks and that I would give him something in a little while. Dale left and went back to his bunker, which was next to mine. All of the guys sat by themselves to read their letters. There were quite a few letters for each of the guys. I then looked at my letters and lined them up by their postmarks and read the oldest letters first from my mother. There was only one letter from my father. It was the first time he had written to me and I made damn sure that it was the last letter I opened. The only guys that didn't get a letter were the new men.

Most of the letters were from my mother and it was nice in the way she wrote to me. I had a letter from my brother and sister and they seemed to be doing well, also. Starr told me that she met a young guy by the name of Michael Caldwell who was in the Air Force and that they were going steady. She mentioned that they might get married. I was glad for her and I just hoped that he was a good man for her. I was finished with all of the letters and I then had one more - my father's. I was really glad that he had written me and I knew that whatever he wrote, it meant a hell of a lot. I slowly opened it up and I then unfolded the letter and started reading.

Hi Son,

How are you? And how is everything going with you? We are all fine as can be. And we all miss you. There is not much to write about because Mother does all of the writing.

I'm out of anything to write Gary so I guess I'll close for now. Wishing you the best of of everything.

Love,
Dad, Mom, Ryan.

P.S. I pray the good lord watches over you and protects you and your friends.

After I was finished with his letter I could tell that he knew what I was going through and it meant a lot for me to get this letter from him. I could sense that he was trying to make me think that everything was normal at home and that he was keeping everything under control. I then started opening up the boxes that Mom had sent me and I wanted to see what was inside.

I opened up the first box and Mom had a couple of cans of Campbell's Vegetable Beef soup, a can of Fruit Cocktail, can of Pears, Crackers, Cheese and other small cans of goodies. I opened up the rest of the boxes and I decided to give some of my stuff to the guys in my fire team. I went on over to Dale Davis and gave him some of the goodies that I had received from my Mother. Dale told me to say "Thanks to Ma Hammer." I then passed out the rest of the stuff to the guys in my team. I heated up the can of Vegetable

Beef soup and just couldn't wait to eat it. When it was done cooking, I took my time in eating it and boy was it good. It really hit the spot.

One of the guys had received a newspaper called, "Stars and Stripes." When he was finished, he let the rest of us read it. It was the first time I had seen the newspaper since I had been over here. I started reading it and the first page was like any newspaper back at home telling the big news around the world and the big news back in the States. The sports section was coming up and I wanted to know what was going on with baseball and how the Cincinnati Reds were doing early in the season. There was some news on NBA Basketball but most of the sports news was on baseball, since it was baseball season. I got to the last page and it told of the guys that had gotten killed during the week and what branch they were in. Most were Army and Marines. Bignami told me that they put in the K.I.A. in the paper at the end of every issue but the paper only came out once a week. I was hoping that I wouldn't see anyone I knew in the paper. I could feel the sorrow coming over me as I looked at the names. All of these guys dying at an early age and missing out on going out with girls, getting married, having kids, going out with the guys, and someday being grandparents. All of their lives being cut short for keeping the rest of the kids back at home safe and happy.

I gave the paper to one of the other guys so that he could read it. I then just sat there thinking of the guys who had died this past week and the sorrow that was inside of me. The only other people that would feel the sorrow would be the guy's family members, mother and father, and if he had any brothers and sisters plus his relatives.

It was going on around 19:30 hours and as all of us were getting ready for the night, staying close to our bunker and fighting holes, we heard an explosion that was just behind us and all of us hit the ground. About two seconds after the explosion we heard another explosion and then it got very quiet. We knew that it was not any incoming rounds or we would have heard it coming in on us. The rest of the night was quiet and then morning came and the word was passed in the platoon that Gerard Vizer had walked into a mine field that was behind us. All of us in the platoon were pissed and wanted to know why the Green Berets hadn't told us about the mine field that was behind us. Van said that Vizer was picking up the small parachutes that were lying in the mine field and when he stepped on the mine and fell, the upper part of his body had set off the second mine and it took part of his face off. All of us looked at each other and we hadn't known that there was a minefield behind us. All of us had a question and that was why hadn't someone told us that there was a mine field behind us. Van said that Vizer was the youngest guy in our platoon and that he was seventeen years of age. He had been with our platoon for a good long while and that he was getting short in going home. Van said that the guys from our platoon were in the mine field picking up Vizer now.

All of the guys in the platoon stayed where they were and looked behind to see what the hell was going on. There were about five guys in our platoon in the minefield to get the body of our buddy. It must have been about half an hour later that we got word that it was the seventeen-year-old in our platoon for sure. The word was passed that he stepped on the mine and it blew off both legs when he fell. His head hit another mine and blew off his head. All of us knew that it was very fast and quick and he didn't know what hit him, thank God. What was left of his body the guys put into a poncho and covered it up and got it out of the minefield so that he could go back home to be buried. Some of the guys in the platoon told me that he was very quiet and everyone liked him a lot. He wasn't very tall, only 5' 7" and weighed around 120 pounds. He lied about his age so he could join the Marine Corps and fight for his country. The guys said that he wanted to be over here and fight against the Communists. Everyone in the platoon was pissed about what had happened to Vizer because we hadn't been told about the mine field behind us. In front of us was only one strand of concertina wire, behind us was a mine field, and on top of the knoll were the great Green Berets whom we were protecting.

It was going on around 19:00 hundred hours and one of the guys from the C.P. group came over to us and told us there was going to be an officer to talk to us about the minefield behind us and to see if we had been told about it. The guy got up and left and went to the next fighting hole to tell them the same thing he told us. I looked up to where the C.P. position was, which was facing east looking at the strip and Lieutenant Libutti, and he looked at me from a distance. I could tell that he was unaware that the guy hadn't passed the word on to the platoon as well. The same guy that was going from fighting hole to fighting hole was trying to cover his ass.

He didn't want the lieutenant to know that he was doing this, covering his own ass. I knew that Libutti thought that the word was passed to the platoon that there was a minefield behind us.

It was nighttime and I was doing my first watch of the night. It was very quiet and peaceful out and the stars were out at this time. I started thinking about the seventeen year old, the youngest guy in our platoon that had just stepped on a mine. I remembered that one of the guys said that Hughart was going to write a letter to Vizer's sister and was hoping to go out with her when he got back to the States. Vizer would show some of the guys how beautiful his sister was. I couldn't believe that one of the guys was only thinking for himself disregarding what had happened to Vizer. I couldn't believe how low a person could get. I then started thinking about the oldest guy in our platoon, Benny Houston, who also had stepped on a booby trap. James Fowler came into my mind and just having known these guys was really getting to me. I then started thinking about Charlie and that he got his third Purple Heart and he was going back home. It made me feel good inside but still it hurt thinking about Benny, James and the guys in our battalion that had given their lives. I started thinking about Sergeant Singleton and how he gave up his life for his squad by saving them and giving up his life for them. And how our whole battalion went back in and we picked up the sergeant and ended up in a large U-Shape ambush by the N.V.A. and that we had to call in artillery ourselves. Then I thought about the relay teams in carrying the wounded guy from our platoon; his name was Strouse; he had lost one leg and the other leg had just hung on. Being under fire from our own artillery and the N.V.A. small arms fire, we got him out of there and saved his life. I felt great about this outfit but at the same time realized how much sorrow all of us had gone through in seeing our buddies getting wounded and killed.

I did my two watches for the night and when it was going on morning, I ate some of the food that my mother sent me. At 10:30 in the morning the word was passed that the Green Berets were going to have an airdrop from a C-130. This was how they were getting their own supplies - by airdrop. At noon we all could hear a C-130 plane circling around overhead and then it went west toward the mountains and then turned around and headed back to Con Thein, going east. As the C-130 was getting close to us, we could see that it was going to fly over the southern part of the base camp. It was close to being overhead and then the supplies were pushed out the back of the plane and the supplies had parachutes on them. The C-130 was at least 1000 feet in the air as it went overhead, heading east along the southern side of The Strip; then it headed south.

I looked up and could see that there was a 50-gallon drum coming down toward me. The drum was swinging back and forth. I sat on top of my bunker and the rest of the guys went to other bunkers to get out of the way. I wasn't going to move - I was standing my ground. The drum was about 100 feet above me when I knew that I had to get inside the bunker before it hit. I waited as long as I could before I went into the bunker and a couple of seconds later the 50-gallon drum hit outside; I then went out to see how close it had hit. It had landed right next to the bunker. I took out my bayonet and cut the strings from the parachute and I rolled it up and put it into the bunker and covered it up with a couple of sand bags. I then went back outside and sat back down on top of the bunker and waited for the Green Berets to come and pick up their 50-gallon drum. It took about five minutes and a jeep came down from the middle knoll toward me and stopped about thirty feet away. A sergeant got out and came over and asked me where the parachute was and I told him that I didn't know. I then told him, "I went inside the bunker and waited for the drum to hit and when I came out the parachute was not anywhere to be found." He kept on insisting that I had it and I kept telling him that I didn't know where it was. He was getting upset and his voice was changing, getting very nasty with me and I kept calm while he was almost screaming at me. The sergeant was as tall as me and he then told me, "I'm going to kick your ass if you don't give me that parachute." I then got up off the bunker and told him, "It will be a cold day in hell before anyone kicks my ass, you son-of-a-bitch." I then told him, "If you think you're man enough to kick this boy's ass… let's get it on." He really pissed me off. I was changing into my father because I was not that easy - going guy but someone you didn't want to tangle with.

Then behind the sergeant came his captain and he asked his sergeant what the hell was going on here. The sergeant told the captain that I took the parachute and I wasn't going to give it back to him. The captain told me to give it up. I told the captain the same thing I had told the sergeant and that I was inside the bunker when the drum hit. I waited a couple of minutes before I came out and when I did the parachute was not here, only the drum. The sergeant told the captain that I was lying and his captain was believing his sergeant over me. The captain then demanded that I turn over the parachute and as the captain was getting nasty with me. I knew that I was not going to give up the parachute at all. The captain was believing his sergeant and disregarded what I had been telling both of them. I knew now that I wasn't going to give up the parachute to these sons-of-bitches. I told the captain to go to hell and that I didn't have his damn parachute, for the last time. A couple of minutes passed and Captain Hutchinson came over and asked what the hell was going on and the Green Beret Captain told my captain that I had their parachute and that they wanted it back. Captain Hutchinson then asked me if I had the parachute and I replied, "Sir, I went into my bunker when the 50-gallon drum hit and I waited inside for a couple of minutes before I came out and when I did there was no parachute around." I kept telling them that I don't know where the parachute was and I didn't have it. I told the captain that if the sergeant didn't stop - bad mouthing me that I was going to kick his ass for good. Captain Hutchinson could see that I was really pissed at both of them and he knew that hell would freeze over before I would give them the parachute, if I had it.

Captain Hutchinson then calmly told the Green Beret Captain that his Marine didn't have it…he didn't have it. The Green Beret Captain then started getting nasty with Captain Hutchinson and that did it. I could see that Captain Hutchinson wasn't going to take that shit from the Army Captain. Both captains really got into it and I just looked at the sergeant and was shaking my head that he better not do anything. After a couple of minutes, Captain Hutchinson told the Green Beret Captain that his ass would be off of this outpost in 24 to 48 hours from now and it was going to be an all Marine outpost. The Green Beret Captain said that he was going to call General Westmoreland about this and that we were going to be gone. Captain Hutchinson then said, "We'll see who leaves here." They finally took the 50-gallon drum and put it into the jeep and went back up to the top of the middle knoll. As they were leaving, they were still pissed at both of us and both Captain Hutchinson and I didn't move one inch.

The Green Berets were gone. Both of us watched them leave and then Captain Hutchinson said that he wanted to see me in his bunker. Then he said, "Hammer, where is that parachute? I want it." I told him that I really didn't have it and he said, "I know you do." I told Captain Hutchinson that it was mine and that I was going to use it as my blanket at nighttime while we were here. Captain Hutchinson said that he wanted it for his bunker. He said that I was to bring it to his bunker in ten minutes and that he would be waiting for me. When I got there to his bunker with the parachute, I walked down the steps. When I got to the bottom of the steps, off to the side was the radioman at his station. I then looked around his bunker and it could hold about twenty guys. I noticed the parachutes that were hanging on three of the walls. I knew that he wanted my parachute to cover the fourth sandbag wall. He said that he would give me a full Sunday box with everything in it. I told him that he had to do better than that for the parachute. Then Captain Hutchinson said that he would give me two Sunday boxes for the parachute. I looked at him and said that it was still not enough. After a couple of minutes, Captain Hutchinson said that he would give me two and a half boxes of Sunday Packs and I then agreed to the two and a half boxes of Sunday packs. As I looked at the captain radioman he was smiling at the both of us. I knew that he got a big charge out of us playing each other over the parachute. As I left the bunker, the radioman went back to listening on the radio for any messages. I then handed the parachute to Captain Hutchinson. There were ten Sunday boxes stacked up next to the radioman and I grabbed two and a half boxes with me. The captain said, "Hammer, you are something." I told the captain, "Thanks for covering up for me against the Green Berets. You're still the best damn captain we've had in this company." I made sure that I made him feel wanted by this company. I knew that he really cared for me and made sure that I got off the radio for awhile. He knew that I had gone through hell taking care of the green lieutenant. I turned around and went back to where the guys were at our bunker and I then passed out the half box Sunday pack to the squad. Their faces showed that it was Christmas and they were really happy with getting the smokes and candy. I then went over to the C.P. and gave two boxes to the C.P for the rest of the platoon. I gave both boxes to Lieutenant Libutti and told him to pass out one box now and the other box later to the guys. He didn't ask me where I got it and I was hoping that he wouldn't. I was trying to make him look good in front of the guys in the platoon. I went back to my bunker and sat on top of the bunker for the rest of the day. I made sure that no one in the platoon knew that I had made a deal with the captain and also how the platoon got the Sunday packs. The only one that knew was Lieutenant Libutti and I told him to keep it to himself. I told the squad that

I found a Sunday pack and it was only half full of goodies.

As I sat on the bunker, there were two batteries of 105s artillery rifles, each battery consisting of four guns each. They were on the south side of the base with their guns facing north into North Vietnam. Evening came and we took our two watches again. As I did my watch, my mind went over what had happened the past couple of days. I noticed that I was not thinking of home as I had when I first came over here and now home seemed like a dream. I could tell that all of us were depending on each other to survive and to make it back home. I started thinking about the Green Berets and the sergeant telling me he wanted the parachute and the way he said it to me. I knew that I would have been like my father if I had grabbed the sergeant and that he wouldn't be standing at all. I would have kicked the shit out of him like my father. I remembered when I was a little boy and Dad had stopped the car at a red light. He got out of the car and went inside a bar for a pack of cigarettes. When he came back out the light was still red but this guy came up behind dad and said a couple of words and the next thing Dad hit the guy three times and the guy fell to the street. Dad got back in the car and drove off. Dad was Golden Gloves in six States as a teenager, plus being a paratrooper in World War II. Growing up with my father was very tough on us kids. But I was glad that my captain came over and bailed me out. Now, I was hoping that Captain Hutchinson would be able to get the Green Berets off this hill for good.

Morning came and Frank Bignami came over and told us to saddle up and that we were going with the engineers to check on the dirt road that led to Con Thein from Phu An. As we moved over to the gate, our whole platoon got in a staggered column to protect the engineers. Frank told Van that we were going out on the flank and Van told me that I was to be the point man on the flank; he had no one with any experience but me. The three engineers were starting out the gate. I got to the gate then went out off the road about fifty yards to the right. There were a lot of trees and bushes around, and it was hard to tell if the enemy was there waiting for us as we walked parallel with the road. The engineers were waving their mine sweeping gear back and forth as they moved along the dirt road. We finally reached the bottom of the hill, after an hour on the road, close to Phu An. There was the stream and the word was passed that we could wash ourselves if we wanted to. I knew that it was the same stream that we had crossed going into Phu An. This part of the stream was behind Phu An. There were a couple of us who decided to wash ourselves. I could feel the cold water touching my skin but I decided to wash anyway. The longer I stayed in the stream the colder the water got and I knew that I couldn't take it much more. The other guys didn't stay in as long as me. I finally got out. There were a couple of more guys that washed themselves but only their faces. I filled up my canteens and I was ready to go back up to Con Thein.

I started to feel a light pain under one of my teeth on the left side as I got my gear on. It seemed to come and go. The word was passed to saddle up and that we were going back. We walked back in a staggered column up the hill of Con Thein. We got inside the gate and our fire team went back to our bunker and just laid around for the rest of the day. The word was passed that we would be going on a mine sweeping detail every fourth day. All of us knew that we were going to be here for a little while. One of the guys from our squad came over to us and told us he was going to be with our fire team. Van asked him his name and he said that it was Hughart. I remembered seeing him in one of the squads but when? Hughart told us that while we were on the patrol with the minesweepers that an officer came and only talked to the company C.P. about what had happened to the guy in our platoon who had stepped in the minefield. He said that the officer got all the information and left.

Around 09:30 choppers came toward us carrying bulldozers. The choppers were landing the bulldozers on the strip next to Con Thein. A couple of hours later, the word was passed to saddle up and that our platoon and third platoon were going out on The Strip to watch over the Seabees while they cleared the strip wider from 200 meters to 600 meters. I looked east down The Strip. They were making the strip wider at that end as well and they were coming toward us. We moved out and our platoon covered the south side of The Strip while the 3rd Platoon covered the Seabees on the north side of The Strip heading east. Libutti had us in a long line in the woods parallel with The Strip and we faced south to make sure that the enemy would not knock off the Seabees. I would, once in awhile, look back at the Seabees and they had one of them riding shotgun on each of the bulldozers. As I sat on the edge of The Strip at times my jaw had a sharp pain like my tooth hurt, but it didn't last long. It was going on around 16:30 hours and the word was passed to saddle up and that we were going back to Con Thein. We moved back with the bulldozers, inside Con Thein. The word was passed that we could take it easy for the rest of the day.

Hughart told us that he knew Vizer in our platoon who had stepped into the minefield behind us and that he was writing to his sister. Hughart said that they had been good friends and that the Vizer was going to have Hughart go out with his sister when they got back to the States. All of us in the fire team just looked at him and couldn't believe that Hughart was more interested in going out with the guy's sister. Hughart told us that she was a knock - out and showed us the picture of the girl. It was the way he was talking that made us think that all he wanted was to meet the guy's sister and to hell with Vizer and what had happened to him. The more he talked the more we started disliking him. All of us knew that he was only out for himself and didn't care about the rest of us. Hughart then sat down and started writing the letter to the girl. The rest of us stayed away from him and didn't say a word. Hughart stood about 5' 9" tall and weighed about 150 pounds. I remembered seeing him in our platoon before but I couldn't remember where.

Van told us what time we had our watch for the night. I stood my first watch and I was thinking about what Hughart was saying. I just couldn't believe that he was interested in the guy's sister and didn't give a damn about the young guy that had died. I just hoped that he didn't get that chance to meet her. My watch was up and I then woke up Robbins. I got kicked at the bottom of my foot and went over to the fighting hole and everything was very quiet. I looked behind me up at the middle knoll at the Green Berets and a flashlight was going on and off pointing west into the mountains. I grabbed my rifle and was ready to pull the trigger. At the same time a couple of other guys around the camp opened up on the flashlight with me. Everyone got up but we told them that it was nothing. The guys went back to sleep. Morning came and Van came over to me and asked what the hell went on during the night and I told him that someone up at the Green Beret's knoll was flashing a light into the mountains west of us. I made sure that they didn't do it again.

Van told me that someone was changing the times on the watch and I asked him what the hell was he talking about. Van said that somehow we were off one hour and that he had stood an extra hour before the sun came up. I told Van that it had to be Hughart because we knew that it wasn't Robbins in our fire team. Van told me that he was going to change the order of times tonight and that he was going to have Hughart in between us and told me to wake him up when I took over each time. Van had another watch so only he and I knew of the other watch for the night. That day we went out and patrolled for the Seabees again until 16:30 hours, and again we had the rest of the day to ourselves. Again I had that pain in my jaw but it only lasted a couple of minutes each time. Night came and Van told us which watch we had for the night. Robbins took the first watch then Van, Hughart and then me. I had the last watch. Hughart woke me up and I took over. When Hughart gave me the watch I waited for him to go to sleep and I then woke up Van and told him that I was now on watch and he looked at his watch and said that I had a half hour before it was my time to stand watch. We both knew now for sure that it was Hughart that was turning up the watch. I looked a couple of times behind me to make sure that the flashlight on the knoll didn't go on. My watch was over and I then woke up Robbins and gave him the watch. Robbins then got up and went over to the fighting hole and when he was finished he woke up Van and again it was time for Hughart watch. It was my time for my second watch for the night and I knew that within my hour I should see the sun come up. The first half hour went by and of course it was still dark and I knew that within the next fifteen minutes the night sky should start getting lighter. As it got close to

05:00 in the morning, it was still dark out. I went on over to Van and woke him up. He looked at his watch and compared it to mine which was 05:00; his watch read 04:00. We knew that Hughart was moving the clock up so he only stood watch for half an hour and not the full hour, both times. Both of us went over to where Hughart was sleeping inside the bunker and kicked the bottom of his foot very hard. Both Van and I told Hughart that if he ever changed the watch again that we were going to kick the living hell of him. When Hughart got up I remembered who he was; he was the same guy that I had put the bayonet to a couple of weeks ago because he couldn't stay awake. Van looked at me and said I was pale and white looking and asked if I was alright. I told him yes but inside of me I was feeling a lot of pain in my head as well as having a headache. Hughart's eyes got very large and he knew that the next time we were going to beat the hell out of him. He shook his head and he told us that he would never do it again. Both of us told him that he better not…or else. I couldn't believed that we ended up with this asshole.

It was almost time to go out and protect the Seabees on The Strip. I grabbed my gear and again I could feel the pain coming back under my teeth on the left side of my jaw. We watched as the Seabees moved the woods farther away and we came across a 500-pound bomb that was dropped but had not gone off. I couldn't believe how big it was; I just kept looking at how big it really was. As I sat out there on the edge of The Strip watching the Seabees knock down the trees and plow back the ground, I could feel the pain coming and going from my jaw. It seemed like it was just under one tooth but it also made me feel that the tooth was in pain also. I was getting used to the heat and humidity and I knew that I had lost a lot of weight. It was time to saddle up and to get back to Con Thein. So far we had gone about 2000 meters along The Strip. We got back inside and Frank came over to us and said that we were going on a L.P. for the night. I got back to our bunker and I just lay down and could feel the pain leaving me. I didn't feel like eating and as evening came the word was passed to get ready to move out. Frank came over to me and said to get the radio and to let him know when I was ready. I went over to the other squad and took the radio. I checked it and called the C.P. and told them we were getting ready to leave the I.P. I went on over to Frank and told him that I was ready and he looked at me and asked me if I was all right and I said that I was. He was concerned about me and told the squad to move out. It was 21:00 when we started moving out. We headed out in front of our position zigzagging through the single strand of concertina wire. We headed south into the tree line about 600 meters and stop for the night. I got on the radio and told our C.P. that we are at Checkpoint 1. The platoon radioman said to me, "Affirmative."

I put the radio on squelch so that it didn't make a sound in the woods. I then lay down and the pain left a little. All of us knew that we were the early warning signal for the rest of the guys at Con Thein, we were expendable. Van whispered to me that I had the fifth watch for the night and he asked me if I was all right, and I just nodded my head. He could tell that I was in a lot of pain and I was trying to hide it from them but they could tell. I tried to relax but I knew that tonight was going to be very rough on me. I didn't think that I could make it to the morning. It was my turn to stand watch and I hoped that the enemy would take the night off themselves. The pain was now taking over my whole head and I was getting a big headache. My time was up and I woke up the next guy. The next thing I knew was that someone was waking me up and telling me to saddle up and that we were going back in. I knew that it had to be around 02:00 and something was up. I went on over to the radio and Frank told me not to call the C.P. and that we were going back in. We then started back into the perimeter and hoped that the guys wouldn't shoot us. I could feel the pain getting worse with each step. My head was pounding and now part of my body was in pain. I also noticed that my eyelids were hurting me each time I blinked. I got over to our bunker and slowly took off the gear and Van and Frank both told me to see Doc Chico in the morning. They both told me to try to get some sleep for now. I didn't look good at all and they were very concerned about me. I slowly went on over to the C.P. and called for Chico to see me. A new corpsman came out and he told me that his name was Dodson. Dodson then asked me what was wrong with me. I told him how it started out with a pain in my jaw on the left side just under one of my teeth. Now, I was having very sharp pain all over my body as well as when I was blinking my eyes. Dodson then told me to lie down on one of the bunkers and not to move.

I lay on top of one of the bunkers that was facing east toward the strip. Dodson told me he had nothing for me and didn't know what I had. I needed rest and not to move. Dodson said there was no way for them to move me because of the pain. I was going to have to remain here until the pain left. He said that all of my nerves were on fire. A couple of hours passed and I could hear in the distance, 152 rounds coming in on us from North Vietnam. The Marines got out of their bunkers and started firing their two batteries of 105s back at the N.V.A. into North Vietnam. They fired their guns as fast as they could load them. They looked like they were having fun giving it back at them. Everyone got inside their bunker and I couldn't move. I tried but the pain was unbearable throughout my body, including my legs. I knew that I had to stay right where I was. I could hear the shrapnel flying around and a couple of the guys who were in the bunker that I was lying on came out and put their flak jackets over my body and legs when the rounds were not coming in. The flak jackets were giving me more pain but I didn't care. I rather have the pain of their flak jackets than getting hit by a 152 round. I turned my head a little and boy the pain shot right through my whole body and the guys in the bunkers were watching me. The shrapnel was flying all around and hitting the sandbags around me. The guys were really worried about me being out on top of the bunker while they were inside and there was nothing they could do to move me because of the pain. The shelling lasted about forty-five minutes, with our two batteries of 105s still firing on the North Vietnamese. They fired about another twenty rounds apiece. The Marines artillerymen were really firing their rifles as fast as they could load them. I have never seen Marines loading those guns that fast. The Marine Artillery men stopped firing and took a rest. When it was over the quietness came over the camp. The artillerymen were having a great time in firing their 105s back at the N.V.A. in North Vietnam. The guys came out of their bunkers and came over to me to see how I was doing. I told them thanks for putting their flak jackets over my body. They told me that they didn't want anything to happen to the Hammer.

That night, I somehow fell off to sleep for a little bit but then I would wake up and feel the pain when I would move a little. When I blinked my eyelids, the pain was unbearable. The pain was not letting up and was still at the same level as when the corpsman told me to lay on this bunker. The next day came and around 09:30 our platoon had to go out and protect the Seabees on the strip. The guys took their flak jackets off me and told me to take care. They would see me later during the day. I could hear them leaving and going out on the strip. I didn't feel like eating or drinking again. And as I lay there on top of the bunker, I would think about myself being in Boot Camp and what my head D.I. S/Sgt. R. Hellein said about me. I remembered that he called me into his office the day before we graduated from boot camp and what he said to me. Staff Sergeant Hellein told me that I really excelled the last four weeks in boot camp and that I made one hell of a Marine. It made me feel great inside when he said it to me. He asked me if my father was in the military and I told him that he was an Army Paratrooper in World War II and fought against the Japanese. My father would always grabbed me when I did something wrong. I would be about two inches from his face when he talked to me when he wanted to get a point across. He would scare the living hell out of me when I was at a very young age. I told the D.I. that they did the same thing my father had done to me when I grew up. The head D.I. said that my dad would have made one hell of a D.I. in the Marine Corps and I agreed with him. He told me that if he went back to Vietnam that he would have me in his squad. He said I could handle myself under fire. He told me that I was dismissed and as I left his office I really felt great. I met all of his expectation and I knew my father had played one hell of a big part in it. Now, I knew why my father was hard on me, because life is hard. I knew that he didn't think that I would be going to war but I am glad that he was hard on me.

Chapter Eighteen

It was around 17:00 hours when the platoon came back and the guys took off their flak jackets and covered me up with them for the evening and nighttime. The flak jackets that the guys put over me would cause me to really get hot. It was bad enough being hot and humid out and to have the extra flak jackets make it even hotter. The next day came and the N.V.A. started shelling us again. As soon as we started getting hit our two batteries of 105s started shelling back at the N.V.A. It seemed to be a contest on who was going to outlast whom. The rounds again were hitting all over the place and the shrapnel was hitting all around me. The guys would call out to me to see how I was doing and I told them that I was just hanging around. On the fourth day, I could move a little and sit up but only for about ten minutes and I had to lie back down before the pain would come back. I could blink my eyelids now without any pain, but I could really feel how weak I was all over my body. We were getting a few more new men into our outfit.

The guys were coming back in from the strip everyday around 15:30 now. The Seabees were getting about to the half way point on the strip. A couple days had passed and the guys just came in around 15:30 and as soon as they got to their bunkers, all of us could hear the N.V.A. artillery rounds coming. The guys quickly took off their flak jackets and covered me while they all got inside the bunkers. The Marine batteries were waiting for them and they started firing back. The Marine 105s were really pumping out the artillery rounds to the N.V.A. It lasted for about forty-five minutes and it was over with for the day. Most of the guys from our platoon came over to where I was sitting up. Boni, Sullivan, Whitey, Van, Robbins, Horton, Moore, Speedy, Fulton, Lisinski, Lugar, Hughart, Smithy, Bignami, Francis, and a couple of others were all talking when one of the guys from our platoon came over to us and said that we were going out on a small patrol tomorrow. I remembered him because he had been with us since Cam Lo Bridge. He had that southern drawl when he talked; it was Dale Davis. As he left, Sullivan and Boni, especially Boni, told the rest of the guys that Dale looked and talked like a shit bird. The guy was about twenty feet walking away and I knew that he heard them saying things about him. I got pissed off and told the guys, "One of these days, he will probably save your lives." I remembered how the guys in boot camp treated James Fowler. Most of them stopped laughing but a couple of them didn't really care; Boni was the main one. I went after the guy and told him that I would like to be his friend and I asked him his name and he said that it was "Dale Davis." He said that he was from Ft. Worth, Texas. Dale stood about 5' 10" tall and I told him that I had to get back and lie down and I would see him later. I went back to the guys and I looked at them and I told them that it was uncalled for. I looked into their eyes because they were wrong in laughing at the guy and making fun of his Southern drawl. They stayed around for another half hour and went back to make sure their gear was ready to go out on the small patrol. I could tell that the pain was coming back and I had to lie back down for awhile. Doc Dodson came over to me to see how I was doing and I asked him if he had any idea what the hell I had and he said that he really didn't know. The only thing he did know was that I couldn't stand up for a long time or sit up for long periods. He said that I could not be medivaced because we didn't have many guys in our platoon.

All of the guys were getting serious now since they were going back out on the strip for the day. They were told that they would watch the Seabees, and then do a small patrol to see if the N.V.A were around. I knew what kind of man Boni was; he was just like Sgt. Thomas in that he didn't have any guts. The only reason why Boni extended six months was because of Sullivan. He followed Sullivan where ever he went out in the field - he wanted to be next to him in case the shit hit the fan. I remembered when he gave up the platoon radio so he could be next to Sullivan so that Sullivan would save his lazy ass. I wondered if Sullivan knew?

Dodson came over and checked on me everyday and said that I was getting stronger and that it would be a couple of more days before I could hopefully stand on my feet for good. I could feel myself getting stronger but I could only stand for a short while before the pain would come back. The next day came and again around 17:00 hundred hours the N.V.A. started shelling us again and the guys put their flak jackets over me again. The rounds were hitting on top of the three knolls and on the north and south side of Con Thein. It lasted for about half an hour and then our 105s opened back up on them for about the same amount of time. It was nice to see that the Green Berets were getting hit more than us.

The next day came and it was around 10:00 in the morning when Jerry Moore came over to me and asked if I could be his radioman for the fire team that he was going to take out that evening on a L.P. I asked Jerry when he had made fire team leader and he said a couple of days ago. I told Jerry that I was still too weak and could only take a few steps before I started getting the pain back in my whole body. I knew there was something wrong as he walked away. I couldn't understand why he would come to me to go out with him on this L.P. for the night. I really was feeling bad that I couldn't help him. Deep down inside of me I knew that I had to go out with him on this L.P. I knew that I had to lie down now for the rest of the day and save as much energy so I would go out with him. As the day went by, I still couldn't eat anything and I then started getting my combat gear ready for the night. I didn't say anything to anyone; that included, Bignami, Van and Doc Dodson.

It was going on evening and was getting close for Jerry Moore to get ready for the L.P. Again he came over to me to see how I was feeling and he told me that, "You're the only guy in this damn outfit that I can trust and the best friend I have." I then told Jerry thanks, and I wished that I could go, but the way I was feeling…I would not be much help to him. Again he turned and walked away slowly with his head down and I knew that I had to go with him for sure. I laid back down and tried not to do anything until it was time for them to leave. I just hoped that I was doing the right thing for him and not become a burden out there.

I then ate a little and that was it; Jerry's team was heading toward the bunker that I had been lying on for the past week. I got up and I told Jerry that I was going with them, but I don't know how much help I could give him. He had a smile and said that Boni was carrying the radio, I remembered when we went to Phu An and we got hit, that Boni called me up to take over the platoon radio because he wanted no part of it. I had a feeling that he would cause a problem out there for Jerry. I couldn't understand why Jerry was the fire team leader and Boni was a corporal and was taking orders from a PFC. I was behind Jerry and we headed out on the east side of the perimeter of Con Thein. I made sure that the rest of the guys in the platoon didn't know that I was on the L.P. for the night. We zigzagged on the north side of the strip to about 500 meters on the strip itself. The pain came back with each step but I didn't want Jerry to know it. He looked back at me and said "This is where we will be for the night." I lay down and covered myself up and Jerry told me that I had first watch. Boni came over to me and gave me the radio and I put it on squelch so that the enemy couldn't hear the sound. I got on the radio and told the C.P. that we were at our position. I knew that the C.P. knew my voice and that I would be in trouble when I got back tomorrow morning, but I didn't give a damn. Right now my buddy needed me for the night and so did the rest of the guys in his fire team. I was a little worried about Boni because I knew that he would do something to mess things up out here on this L.P.

Jerry looked at me and could see that I was in pain and I told him that I could make it for the night. I had the first watch. The platoon radioman called me every half hour and I responded back to them by pressing my handset twice. My watch was over and I then woke up the next guy and gave him the radio. As I was lying on the ground, I could feel my whole body getting the shakes. After the second watch, I woke up the next guy and covered myself up with my poncho and tried to relax as much as I could so that the pain would leave. I just hoped that the pain would settle down until we left in the morning to go back into Con Thein. A couple of hours passed and it started to rain for about five minutes. I was awake; the drops felt as though

Dong Ha, From left to right:Michael Bradley, Denny Lugar, Ron Francis,
Dick Boni, David Mullins, Randy. Morning of July 2, 1967
– picture by Bill Gonzales

2nd platoon on patrol just southeast of Phu An. Started out with 24 guys in
the platoon. Ended up with 17 men, one wounded and six with heat stroke.
The day was extremely hot and humid, 120 degrees, no one had water in
the platoon. CH-34 with water cans. May 1967. – picture by Bill Gonzales

From left to right – Dick Boni, Sergeant Thomas (who received orders to go home) and Frank Bignami, who later became my squad leader. May 1967.

N.V.A. bunker just south of Con Thein. May 1967.
– picture by Bill Gonzales

At Dong Ha, From left to right Gonzales, Doc., ?, Randy, Blissard, ?, ?, Jackson. Down in front Baker. Early June 1967. – Picture by Bill Gonzales

At Phu Ox, From left to right: Bill Gonzales (Speedy), Ron Lisinski (Ski), Kenny Fulton: one of the machine gun teams. Early June 1967 – picture by Bill Gonzales

At Phu Ox, Catholic church was used as the Company C.P. Early June
1967 – picture by Bill Gonzales

Keeley unloading supplies, later became 2nd platoon radioman. Early June
1967 – picture by Bill Gonzales

someone was hitting me with golf balls. It was only a few drops but they were big ones and after about half an hour later someone touched me on my shoulder. Jerry whispered to me that the radio wasn't working. I looked at Jerry and whispered, "What the hell do you mean the radio doesn't work?" He said that the last half hour we did not hear anything from the platoon and that the radio was dead. I got up and I could really feel the blood racing into my head but at the same time I could also feel the pain coming back as well. I went on over to the radio and Boni was playing around with it. He was telling Jerry that we needed to get back to Con Thein, now. I whispered to Boni, get the hell away from the radio I'll get it fixed. The battery as well as the hand set were wet from the rain because someone hadn't wrapped the radio in plastic like he was supposed to do when it rained…Boni. I knew for sure that Boni was behind all of the problems and making sure Jerry was unfit to be a fire team leader. Jerry had all of the guys up at this time and Boni was telling Jerry that we had to get back to Con Thein. I changed the battery and still I couldn't hear anything. I grabbed the handset and took it apart in the dark and dried all of the pieces inside by blowing all of the water off the different parts and put it back together. Then the radio started working. We were back on, but when I called for our platoon I didn't get any answer. Now what? I knew that someone had changed the frequency and that was Boni. Boni was whispering to Jerry that we had to get back to Con Thein. I finally got a hold of the platoon after changing the frequency a few times in the dark without any light. I told them at the platoon that our battery was dead and that all was secured out here. I told Jerry that we were in good shape and I went on over to Boni and whispered to him that if he messed with the radio that I was going to cut all of his fingers off. I told him that if he made Jerry go through hell again that he had to deal with me and I would beat the living hell out of him. When I was finished talking to Boni, I asked him…"You understand me?" He shook his head and went back to his poncho.

I went back to Jerry and told him that everything was going to be all right for the rest of the night and that Boni would not be giving him any more trouble. The other guys in the fire team were scared and I told Jerry to tell them that everything was all right and to get some sleep. I just couldn't believe that Boni was scaring the rest of the guys in the team and doing a great job in doing so. He was really making Jerry Moore look like he didn't know what the hell to do out in the bush. I was really in a lot of pain now and knew that morning had to come quickly. I could hear the guys changing their watches during the rest of the night. I tried like hell to relax and let the pain leave, but it retreated slowly. I couldn't sleep and all I could do was try to relax and hopefully morning would come fast. Then Jerry touched my shoulder and said, "Hammer, it's time to get up and time to get the hell out of here." I asked Jerry if he had the pop-ups and he said, "Yes." He asked me to get on the radio and to get us back into Con Thein. I called the platoon and told them that we were coming back in and that we were ready to shoot the pop-up. I waited for the platoon radioman to give me the green light. Then he gave me the word and I told Jerry to go and have them pop it. It was green and the radioman told me "green" and I said "affirmative" and he told me to come on in. I told Jerry that we could go on in. Jerry and the rest of the guys could see that I was shaking like a leaf. I looked at Boni and he was still talking to the guys about not trusting Jerry Moore. I gave him a dirty look and he shut up. Jerry told them to move out and head back to Con Thein and again we zigzagged back to Con Thein.

We got back inside the perimeter. I headed back to my bunker where my fire team was. As soon as I got to the bunker and took off my gear, Captain Hutchinson called for me to see him. I slowly walked on over to his bunker and went down inside. Captain Hutchinson asked me what was I doing on this L.P. and why wasn't I resting. I told the captain that my buddy needed me on his first patrol as a fire team leader and I was glad that I did go even though I was still in pain. I told the captain that one of the guys, an old timer, was trying to discredit Moore. He said, "Your lieutenant wants to see you also." I knew that he could see that I was in pain and told me to get out and see Libutti. I went on over to my lieutenant and he looked at me and wanted to know why I went out and didn't tell anyone that I was going on this L.P. I told the lieutenant that if I did say anything that he and the Doc wouldn't let me go. I didn't say a word after that and I could tell that he understood and told me to get the hell back and get off my feet. As I was walking back, Dodson came over to me and asked how I was and I told him that I was in a lot of pain and that I had to get off my feet so that the pain would leave. He walked back with me to the bunker and I laid down for the rest of the day. Later the platoon went out to protect the Seabees on the strip. The next couple of days went by and I was feeling stronger and still I knew that it would not be too long before I could be with the guys in protecting the Seabees. We got hit again from the N.V.A. and again our 105s were firing back.

As the next couple of days passed, every time I got up, my head would spin for a couple of minutes before I would be all right. I could feel myself getting stronger but still I couldn't do most of the simple things like going on a patrol or walking for a great distance. I remembered a couple of days ago when Dale Davis came over to us and told us that we were going out on a patrol and how the guys, especially Boni and Sullivan, made fun of the way he talked and how the rest of the guys followed them by laughing at Dale. It really made me mad again how Boni tried to screw up the radio for Moore to discredit him, making him think that he could not do the fire team leader's job. He almost had Moore thinking to himself that he couldn't do the job. Thank goodness that I had gone along with them and made sure

Moore knew that he did a damn good job of being a fire team leader out there. I remembered that I told Moore to be a lot tougher on those guys that were trying to screw him over and not to take their shit. I noticed that most of the guys in the platoon had their own buddies whom they stayed close to most of the time. The guys would be together but most of the time, they wouldn't say a word because just being next to each other made them feel good inside. There were a few of us like Charlie Horton, Jerry Moore, me, Dale Davis, Van, Bignami, Bradley, Speedy, that tried to get along with everyone in the platoon. We had good squad leaders, and older guys like Frank Bignami, Ted Van Meeteren, Francis, Whitey, Lugar, Sullivan in our platoon and a damn good lieutenant and platoon sergeant. I knew that Van was keeping an eye out as well as me on Hughart to make sure that he didn't change the time on the watch at nighttime. The guys were tired from watching the Seabees working out there on the strip, sitting there on the edge and making sure that they didn't get hit from the N.V.A.

A few more days had gone by and Dodson checked on me each day, I told him that I believed that I was all right and that I was ready to go back to my fire team. Again, I asked Dodson just what the hell did I have. He wasn't sure but it could have been stress. The word was passed that the Green Berets were leaving Con Thein for good. It took almost two weeks for them to leave. The word got around to all of the guys that were here, including Alpha Company. The next day came and around 08:00 hundred in the morning they were getting their gear into the vehicles that they had, which were Jeeps. Some of the guys were cheering them for leaving and glad to see them go on as they left the camp. Some of the guys were telling the Green Berets that this base now belonged to the Marine Corps. It didn't take them long to leave and now Con Thein belonged to us completely. If it wasn't for the guys from 2nd Battalion 4th Marines that fought and died here retaking Con Thein about a month ago, this place would still be in the hands of the Green Berets. This base deserved to be for the Marines only. I was very proud of Captain Hutchinson because he was the one that really got them out and off the base by talking to General Westmoreland. I knew that the guys didn't know what had happened behind the scenes. A couple of guys had said that they also cut the strings off the parachute to have them as blankets in their bunker and never gave them back to the Green Berets as well. I just smiled to myself and was glad that they did the same as I did but I gave up mine to the captain.

The next day came and I saddled up with the guys for the first time and went out protecting the Seabees that were clearing The Strip heading east. I had a little pain but I didn't want to be left behind in case we got hit out there on The Strip. Doc Dodson would come over to see how I was doing and he said that I still looked a little under the weather and that I might not be going out tomorrow. The next day Doc Dodson came over to me to see if I looked all right and he let me go with the rest of the guys. As each day went by, we moved farther east. One evening about 20:00 our company could hear motor rounds being hit on the edge of The Strip between Con Thein and the north side of the strip itself. We couldn't figure out what the hell was going on out there. Then the word was passed that we were going out there tomorrow to see if we could find anything. That morning we saddled up and headed off to the north part of The Strip where the road went due east to Market Street. The road was north of The Strip by about 1000 meters heading east. As we looked around there was some fighting equipment but that was it. Even the N.V.A. wasn't around. So the rest of the day we patrolled on over to Market Street which was half way between Con Thein and Gio Lin. We then headed back to Con Thein for the day. About a week went by and there was another Marine outfit that was taking over Con Thein and we knew that we would not be coming back again. We moved east on the south side of The Strip and we were to go about 8000 meters which was half way between Con Thein and Gio Lin. The word was passed that Alpha Company was being hit by the N.V.A. and that we were to help our sister company. As we traveled east along the south side of The Strip (but not on the strip itself), we got to a place where it dipped down slowly about 100 meters and there were rice paddies on The Strip but they were half dry. We moved past the rice paddies and started going back up again where we couldn't see them and the word was passed to stop. Captain Hutchinson came over to Lieutenant Libutti and they talked for a little bit and then the captain went back to his C.P. group. Lieutenant Libutti then called Corporal Bignami and told him that his squad had the point. Frank came back and told Van that his fire team was to take the point going across The Strip. Bignami didn't have much of a pick between the two fire teams because there were two of us that knew what to do out in the bush. That was Van and me. Van then called us over to him and he said that Hammer was to take the point and then Hughart, Smithy and then him. Just before I was ready to leave, Van told me to make sure that I zigzagged going across The Strip. I told him that I planned on doing that.

The word was passed for the machine gun teams to come up and to give us protection as we moved across The Strip to the north side. Kenny Fulton, Maxwell, Duvall, Speedy Gonzales, Philip Ritivan, Lisinski and the rest of their teams began setting up the machine guns. Lisinski and Maxwell got behind their machine guns and looked at me and told me that they were ready to protect me. I then got up and I looked back and Lieutenant Libutti was watching me; he was concerned about me and I gave him a little smile and then started moving out very slowly on The Strip. As I started moving out, I leaned over a little so that I didn't make myself a big target for the enemy, since I am 6' 3." I was looking ahead at the tree line, which was next to The Strip itself and all of that brush where the N.V.A. could be hiding behind where the bull dozers had pushed up the brush next to The Strip. I could feel the butterflies in my stomach and hoped that the N.V.A. was not on the north side watching us. I knew that if I got hit that there was no place to hide out on the strip itself since everything was flat. I made sure that I zigzagged moving across The Strip. The Strip was now 600 meters wide and I could still feel the butterflies in my stomach. In a way I wished now that it was back to 200 meters. It seemed that every step that I made was like it would be forever getting to the north side of The Strip. I looked back to see how far the guys were behind me and they were staying as far away from me as well as each other. I knew that if I got hit that I was strictly on my own and that I had to get myself back to Doc Dodson, somehow. Each step felt like eternity.

As I got closer to the north side of The Strip, I knew that the enemy was not here and I felt a little safer. I finally reached the edge of The Strip and then went about 50 yards and headed for a bomb crater. I then set up there watching while the rest of the guys came across The Strip. Frank finally got up to me and was telling the rest of the guys to spread it out and to keep a sharp eye out. There was another crater and some of the guys got into it also. Finally the rest of the company came over and the word was passed to move out still heading northeast.

I got up and was still the point man, I was heading northeast. About 600 meters in this very large open area was a dirt road that was going north and south. When I reached the dirt road the word was passed to stop and I knelt down, keeping a sharp eye out in front of me. I was watching straight ahead. The rest of the guys were in a staggered column behind me and were facing outward on each side of me. There were two buildings that were damaged by the war and no village people around. The two buildings were about 200 meters from the dirt road that was going north and south, but the buildings were east of the road. I knew that we were in the heart of the D.M.Z. Anything north of the strip was the D.M.Z. About 100 meters on my left side was another dirt road and it started going straight west parallel with The Strip to Con Thein. The road that went west connected with the road that went north and south.

Lieutenant Libutti and Sgt. Lefefe came up to me and said to head off toward the two buildings; we were going to set up a blocking force for Alpha Company. I got up and started walking east in the field of tall grass that was about eighteen inches high toward the two bombed out buildings. I crossed the road that headed north and south and went past it toward the two buildings. When I reached the buildings, I knelt down and Van came up with the rest of the fire team to where I was and our company set up a perimeter there at the buildings. I could hear no firing from either Alpha Company or from the N.V.A. I was facing north and about 300 meters away, there were trees and a lot of brush. I could feel the heat of the day rising again; it seemed days like this were hotter than the days we would get hit. It must have been about half an hour later that we heard two jets flying over us and they were coming in from the west and going out to the east. The Marines jets, Phantom 4s, made a couple of passes and on the third pass the first jet dropped two canisters of napalm at the enemy in the tree line that was about 500 meters from us. As those two exploded, the second jet came over about the same height, which was 300 meters, and it, too, dropped two canisters of napalm at the enemy. The enemy was screaming and yelling and we could also feel the heat from the napalm coming at us. The air was being sucked into the flames and the temperature rose higher than the heat and humidity from the sun. Still there was no firing of rifles from anyone. The flames were a bright white, yellow, orange, and red and followed by a very large black puff of smoke. The jets made another pass with napalm and after that they opened up with their 20 mm. cannons. Everyone was ready and still the enemy did not come our way. I knew that what was left of them had gone back to the river and on over into North Vietnam. One of the jets then went out to sea and came back over The Strip. When he got over us he went straight up into the sky and then came back down and at the last moment pulled out and then left to give us a show. It was great, and the guys got a kick out of it.

At 15:30 hours, the word was passed that we were moving out and heading back to Con Thein. All of us got up and the word was passed that third squad was to take point and our squad was to be behind the Platoon C.P. group. We headed back to the dirt road that was going north and south. The point squad went up the dirt road, north to where the other dirt road went west toward Con Thein, parallel with The Strip. Alpha Company was coming down the dirt road that led north; they were coming south toward us from the D.M.Z. As we were passing each other, they were telling us that they heard on the radio Hanoi Hannah telling the guys of the 1st Battalion 9th Marines that we were going to get wiped out. One of the guys said that they were playing three rock and roll songs for our battalion. As our company was heading west in a staggered column on the dirt road I remembered when I first came to Da Nang, this Marine came over to McBride and me and asked us what outfit were we going to. I remembered giving him my envelope and he looked on the back of it and it had 1/9 and he said, "That is a bad ass outfit over here." and then he told us, "Good Luck, you're going to need it."

There in front of us was a huge tree that had to be about four to five feet in diameter and when we had gone past it, we headed southwest to The Strip. When we got to the edge of The Strip the word was passed to walk on the edge to Con Thein. Around 17:00 hundred hours we moved back into the perimeter of Con Thein itself. The other outfit went out on a patrol for a couple of days. We got our old bunkers and we settled in for the night and

At Phu Ox Charlie Horton. Early June 1967 – picture by Bill Gonzales

At Phu Ox, dead N.V.A. shot in the head by a fifty cal. Early June 1967 – picture by Bill Gonzales

At Phu Ox, Bill Gonzales with N.V.A. skull with bullet hole. Early June 1967 – picture by Bill Gonzales

At Phu Ox, Charles Sullivan, later was killed on June 30th on Operation Buffalo. Early June 1967 – picture by Bill Gonzales

D.M.Z. near Market Street. From left to right Pulan, George Hahner (Whitey), Denny Lugar, Short Round, Dodge, Kenny Fulton, Ron Lisinski (Ski). Late June 1967– picture by Bill Gonzales

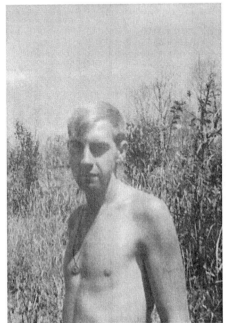

D.M.Z. near Market Street. Jerry Moore Late June 1967 – picture by Bill Gonzales

Con Thein on The Strip from left to right: ?, George Hahner (Whitey) with his Playboy pennant, Frank Bignami, and Dick Boni. June 1967

Between Con Thein and Gio Lin in the middle of The Strip at its lowest point. May 1967 – picture by Bill Gonzales

Operation Buffalo, at Market Street Charlie Company. Early July 1967. – picture by Bill Gonzales

I got my times for my night watches. Hughart was still having trouble in standing his watch and each night Van and I would raise holy hell with him. Hughart said that he really had trouble trying to stay awake; he just couldn't do it. The next day came and around 10:30 there was an observation plane flying about a good 1000 meters high and about 8000 meters from us in the D.M.Z. We could hear firing from the N.V.A. in the D.M.Z. at the plane. As all of us were watching what was going on, we knew that either Alpha Company or us might have to go out there and get the pilot if his plane went down. We could hear that the engine was starting to miss and we all knew that he better get the hell out of there fast. The plane was heading back to our position, coming in from the southwest, and I remembered the small landing strip for this kind of plane. He flew over us and went southwest and came around and started getting lower and lower to land on The Strip. As he was coming down I knew that this would be a great time for the enemy to hit us with their artillery from North Vietnam. All of us got our flak jackets on and got to our bunkers or fighting holes. The plane landed safely and the pilot was all right.

Doc Dodson came over to my bunker and said that I was going back to the rear for the doctors to check on me. I told Doc that I was all right but he told me that the lieutenant wanted to make sure that I was all right, also. Dodson said that the six-by would be coming later today and to make sure that I got on it when the word was passed for me to go. It was about two hours later when I heard a six-by coming up the hill to Con Thein. The word was passed for Hammer to get on the truck. The guys were taking off the supplies and as soon as they did, I got on the truck and sat down. There were a couple of other guys that also got on the six-by and we started leaving heading back down the dirt road heading south. Some of the guys were happy to see me go and they were telling me to have a good time back in the rear. As we wound around the hill of Con Thein, we came into Phu An. Everything was changing and it didn't look the same as when we were here the last time. We got to the stream and the Seabees had put two large galvanized tubes that let the water pass through. They were 24 inches in diameter and filled in between and around the pipes was dirt. As we got to the other side of the stream, the Seabees cut into the hill so that it was not as deep as before when we had walked down it.

Everything was changing fast and it was not the same as before. As we got closer to Cam Lo Bridge, we saw the artillery base on the left side of the road was even larger than before and it was now well-fortified with three strands of concertina wire, the new German type of concertina wire. As we went into Cam Lo Bridge, the village people were very secure with the artillery base and of course the Marines that took care of the bridge itself. The mama-sans were waving at us as we passed through the vill. The kids were hanging around the Marines at the bridge and having fun with them as they had when we were here. I told the driver that when we got to Dong Ha to drop me off at the 1st Battalion 9th Marines area, if he could. He pulled into the Camp and took me close to the area of the 1st Battalion 9th Marines. He stopped the truck and told me to go on over the hill and our area was on the right side of the dirt road. I got off and slowly walked on over to the area. As I was getting close to our battalion area, I saw that the tents were being replaced with, "hardbacks." These were buildings that were made out of plywood, with screens to keep out the flying insects at nighttime and mosquitoes as well as flies during the day time. I saw our area and I went on over to our tent and I took off my fighting gear and put it on the cot and went over to the company clerk tent and told them that I was here to see a doctor and that I was going to go back out to the bush. The first sergeant came over to me and said I was not going out to the bush until the doctor released me. I asked the first sergeant where the medical tent was and he told me over between Alpha and Bravo Company. I went over to where Alpha and Bravo Company were and asked one of the guys there where the Battalion Aid station was and he pointed to the tent and I told him thanks.

I walked inside the Battalion Aid station and said that I was to report to them. A doctor came over to me and asked what was wrong. I told him my symptoms and how it first started, having pain all over my body as well as my teeth aching and my eyelids hurting every time I blinked. He asked me how I was now and I told him that I was all right and I wanted to get back out in the field with the rest of my buddies. He said he wanted me to stay one more day before he would release me and that he wanted to see me again tomorrow. I then got up and started leaving the tent and there were about fifteen Negro Marines from our battalion in the Battalion Aid Station. There was nothing wrong with them but they were complaining about every little thing. I could see that there wasn't anything wrong with them. They just didn't want to go out in the field with the rest of the guys. They didn't have the guts to fight against the N.V.A. I knew deep down inside of me that they couldn't be trusted when the shit hit the fan. I made sure that I saw the first sergeant and I told him that the doctor wanted to see me tomorrow and that he would release me so I could go back out to the bush.

I went back to my tent and lay down on my cot and was thinking of the Negroes that were at sick call. I knew that if they were out in the field they wouldn't help anyone and that included themselves. I looked at the new guys in the tent that were going out in the field soon. I didn't say anything to them, I just wanted to be left alone. In the other tent next to mine, I could hear a record player playing and the songs were all Motown. It sounded like there were three or four Negroes singing along with the music. I looked over to the other tent since the sides were up and another Negro joined them and started singing along with them and after a couple of minutes they were yelling at him to go and that he couldn't sing and they didn't want any part of his ass, even if he was a Negro. This was almost the same thing a couple of months ago when I was back in the rear. I watched as he slowly walked away from them, rejected because they didn't really give a damn about him, even if he was a Negro like them. I couldn't believe that they would chase him away. Being back here in the rear they were all safe. I could tell that he was really hurt because they told him he couldn't sing with them. They didn't want any part of him at all, all because he couldn't keep a rhythm. I then started thinking about Maxwell in our platoon and I remembered that he didn't want to be around Negroes, Whites or anyone but by himself. Maxwell was a loner. I knew that I was the only one he would talk to but I was it besides his machine gun team. I knew that if Maxwell saw what had happened back here, he would have probably kicked their asses for being the way they were.

I heard that the showers were being turned on and that we had fifteen minutes to get there if we wanted to take a shower. I got up and I took off my jungle shirt and boots and socks. I put on my boots and I grabbed a bar of soap and towel from my seabag and headed up to the side of the hill, took a shower out in the open, naked as can be. I started thinking if the girls were here they would love this, seeing all of these naked guys out in the open taking a shower. I had a little smile on my face and went back to washing myself and it felt great taking off all of the dirt that was on my body. After about five minutes, I put on my brown jungle pants and boots and walked back to the tent. It was evening and I went to chow and again they were serving Rice and Spam. I only ate a little Spam and never took the rice that they gave. Now I know why my father never ate rice when he came back from W.W II in the Pacific. The rest of the evening I just lay in my cot and stayed to myself. I knew that I was going to have a good night's sleep and that I didn't have to stand two watches. I knew that Van might have trouble with Hughart during the night watches but I also knew that the other guys would be making sure that he didn't turn up the watch.

The next day came and I went on over to the Battalion Aid Station. As I walked inside the tent, I saw there were again eight to twelve Negroes in sick bay waiting to be taken care of. I waited for about ten minutes and the doctor told me to follow him and he checked me over and asked how I was and I told him that I was feeling better and stronger each day. I would like to go back out in the field with my platoon. He looked at me and said that I could go and I told him that if he didn't let me go that I would have gone anyways. He shook his head and smiled a little and told me good luck. I left and went back to the company tent and I told the first sergeant that the doctor released me and that I can go back out in the field. The first sergeant told me that I could go back out tomorrow and to take the new guys out with me. I then left and went back to my tent. I laid down in my cot and some of the guys had on the radio station with Rock and Roll music. A couple of the guys said that one of the stations that had Hanoi Hannah on were playing three songs to the 1st Battalion 9th Marines everyday. I asked the guys just what songs was she playing and they said that the first song was NO WHERE TO RUN , NO WHERE TO HIDE, the second song was WE GOT TO GET OUT OF THIS PLACE, and the third song was what they were going to do to us, WIPEOUT. I told the new guys not to worry and that she was using propaganda. I knew that Ho Chi Minh really wanted us to be a "WIPEOUT." One of the new guys told me that there was a P.X at the top of the hill and that he was going there. I told him that I would go with him. We walked up the hill and when we got there at the top, there was a long wooden building, 60 feet by 40 feet, and they were only letting five guys go in at a time. There were also "Doggies" in line with us, "Doggie" is a slang word for Army. After a couple of minutes we went inside and I couldn't believe they had stacked up cans of different juices such as orange juice, pineapple juice, grape juices, different soda pops, candy and cigarettes. I asked the guy with me if he would help me carry some of this stuff back to our tent and he said that he would. I started buying the different juices, candy and cigarettes for the guys out in the bush. We took them back to the tent. I laid the goodies on the cot next to me and I grabbed some sandbags that were empty and started filling them up with the goodies. I knew that the guys would be happy to see this stuff. Later that day the first sergeant came into the tent and told the green horns that they would be going out tomorrow and to follow me. He came over to me and told me that I can't take this stuff out in the field and I told him, who is going to stop me? He just looked at me and I told him that the guys need this stuff and that I was going to take it out regardless of who tried to stop me...they better not. He had a little smile on his face and knew that this would help them out a lot out there in the field. He said that there was an order that, "NO ONE CAN TAKE GOODIES OUT IN THE FIELD." He knew that I was going to take it out there regardless of what the orders were.

The next morning came and we went on over to the chow tent and came back. The first sergeant told me that the six-by was on its way and to get the green horns ready to go. I told the green horns to get their gear ready and that the six-by was on its way, and to get ready to board it. The truck came into the area and turned around and then stopped. I grabbed the goodies and put it on the truck. I told the green horns to get on the truck and to sit down. I went on over to the first sergeant and asked him if there was anything he wanted me to say to Captain Hutchinson and he said no. The first sergeant told me to take care of the green horns and I told him that I would. He then turned around and went back into the tent. I went on over to the truck and got on and sat down and told the driver that we were ready and he took off. When we got out the front gate I put a round in the chamber of my rifle and put it on semi-automatic. The rest of the new guys watched what I did and did the same. We headed back up north and I thought that we would be going to Cam Lo but the truck stayed on Highway 1 and we headed to Gio Lin which was the other outpost up on the strip at the other end of Con Thein. On the side of Highway 1, there were rice paddies. Some of the females were working in the paddies putting down the rice plants into the water. They all had black pajamas on and they were rolled up above the kneecap so that the leeches didn't stick on them as well. I was always moving my eyes to make sure that the enemy wasn't firing at us. The green horns were enjoying the ride as though they were state side and there was no war going on. I saw some of them were really scared and didn't know what to do if we got hit. I tried to put them at ease by the way I looked, care-free. I could tell that it helped a little but that was the best I was going to do for them. I just wanted no part of them because I didn't know if they could handle themselves in a fire fight, especially in my outfit.

The six-by was going through the vill, and as we slowly passed, the silent mama-sans inside their huts definitely gave us cold looks. Getting closer to Gio Lin, the six-by went right onto the southern part of the strip which was just in front of the base. We were heading west and there was a two wheel dirt path heading due west parallel with the strip about 100 feet south. We traveled about 1000 meters and the six-by stopped and I told the guys to get off the truck. Our company was just outside the base on the southern part of the strip, I told one of the green horns to help me with the sandbags of goodies. There were six sandbags, and the guys from my platoon came over to me and said, "O.K. Hammer what did you bring us?" I told them that when I got to the platoon I would pass out the goodies. We walked on over to where our platoon was and the six-by left, going back the way it came. I told the green horns to follow me on over to where the platoon C.P. was and had them report to the lieutenant. I got back to where Van, Davis, Horton, Moore, Speedy, Maxwell, Bignami and the rest of the guys in the platoon were and started passing out the goodies, to the guys that smoked first. I passed out ten cartons of Winston and ten cartons of Marlboro. Each guy got a carton of smokes. I then passed out the candy and juices to all of the guys in the platoon, even to the assholes. There weren't that many of us besides the green horns that came out with me.

When I had finished passing out the goodies, Dale began writing a letter to his girl back in the States. He told me how much he loved her and was expecting to marry her when he got back. I told Dale that he better not get his hopes on her too high and she might not wait the 395 days before he came home. I told Dale that a girl back in the States couldn't wait for a guy to come back from Vietnam because there were so many guys around home for her. Dale told me that she was going to college after all of the trouble they had with her parents when they were in high school. Dale said that her parents didn't want her to go out with him and that they would meet down the block so that her parents wouldn't know that they were together. He really had fallen in love with her and I just hoped that she would be faithful to him. I knew that a girl being in college would see a lot of guys and her going out with just one of them would screw with her mind. I just hoped for Dale's sake that she would be true to him.

I got up and told Dale that I would be back and that I was going on over to see Whitey. Whitey told me, "Thanks for the goodies," and I told him that "It was the least I could do to all of you rejects." He started laughing and then started talking about his sister Midge and how she would take care of him and cover up for him from his parents, especially on the weekends where he would go out drinking with his buddies. He really loved and cared for his sister a lot. I told Whitey that I had to get back to my fighting hole but as I got up I started thinking about my sister. I told Whitey that I had a sister too and she would do anything for me as well. He nodded his head and understood that we both had sisters that would do anything for us.

During both of my watches that night I thought about my two closest buddies who I hung around with in high school, Bruce Knox and Ted Grogen. I remembered the times we had together in high school. Bruce Knox was a trainer on our football team and after every game he and I would go to Burger King and have a Double Whopper or a fish sandwich. On the weekend we would all go out to the movies. Bruce Knox was going to school to be a police officer for the City of Cincinnati. Ted had signed up to go into the Coast Guard and became a medic. And here I was in Vietnam fighting against the Communists.

Morning came and the word was passed that 2nd Platoon was going to go west until we hit the dirt road that led north to The Strip. The rest of the company was also saddling up but they were going to move out also as a blocking force for our platoon. We moved out following due west until we got to the dirt road and the word was passed to move north and cross The Strip. The rest of the company made a blocking force up against the southern edge of The Strip. The company followed the southern edge of The Strip while we went west following the dirt road. When we got to the road that went north and south, Van pointed to me to head north. Our platoon was to make the N.V.A. retreat back to The Strip and the rest of Charlie Company would take them out. The N.V.A. was nowhere to be seen and I went up the road going north to The Strip. When I reached The Strip Van informed me I was to go across The Strip.

We stayed in a staggered file and crossed The Strip and when we got to the other side the word was passed to stop. Lieutenant Libutti came up and told Francis that his squad was to take point. Cpl. Francis came over to one of his fire teams and told Whitey to take point for the platoon. He nodded his head and started up to where we were and started moving out on the dirt road going north. I told Whitey to watch himself. As we moved about

200 meters north, I could hear the Marine Corps Hymn being played with feeling and intensity inside my head. It seemed that I couldn't hear anything around me but the song in my head. It got louder and louder as I walked. Off to my left side there were the two bomb craters; to the east were the two building that were shelled by both us and the N.V.A. about 200 meters from the road. I knew that we were at Market Street. About 300 meters down the road was the cross road that headed due west to Con Thein. We were to keep on going down the road, heading north. All of us were taking our time and the hairs on my back started standing up as I walked down this very large hill. The Marine Corps Hymn was starting to get softer inside my head. The dirt road was heading downward into the D.M.Z.

I remembered before where Alpha Company got hit by the N.V.A. when the jets dropped napalm on them. The guys were really staying as far apart as possible. I was moving my head around and keeping a very sharp eye out on everything around me. I could feel how proud I was to be a Marine but right now was a bad place to be a proud Marine. We went about half way down the hill; on both sides of the road the banks were about ten feet high. The music was still playing in my head; it wasn't as loud as before but it wouldn't leave. Our platoon started heading west. We walked up the bank and there was a small field with hedgerows around it. Our whole platoon got inside the small field and the word was passed to make a perimeter for the company. When everyone was in the company perimeter, the captain said that we would be here for a short time. All of us knelt down but we all were watching out in front of ourselves. We didn't like being here and all of us could feel that the N.V.A. was watching us but they didn't want to hit us. As I kept watch, the Marine Corps Hymn finally left me and now I could hear the sounds around me. There was something about being here that made all of us up tight. Everyone of us was listening and not talking at all while we stayed here.

After thirty minutes, Libutti told our squad that we were to take the rear point for the platoon. 3rd squad took point heading north again. The rest of the company followed 2nd Platoon. We were going even farther down the hill and we came across a stream. It was about fifty feet wide and about 18 inches deep. When we got to the other side, something told us that we were in North Vietnam. One of the guys said that we had just crossed the Ben Hai River and now we were on their land. We were hoping that they would hit us but they still were just watching us very closely. Our platoon made it look like we were a company - sized outfit. We started traveling east about 500 meters, came across the dirt road again and headed back south. We crossed the river again and slowly headed back up the same hill. As I went up the hill, I knelt down and stopped a little to hear if anyone was walking around us. I would then get up and move out again, stopping every fifteen steps to listen for the enemy.

Our platoon finally reached Market Street and the word was passed to take another break. After the break we moved out and went to the edge of The Strip. Our platoon had the northern part of the company perimeter. We set up a perimeter for the day and the word was passed that Hammer was to move to 2nd squad because they were short of men. I grabbed my gear and went on over to the squad leader, who was Corporal Sullivan. We were so short of men in our platoon that they were moving the experienced guys around between the three squads. He told me that he was glad to have me in his team. He told me that they were going out on an ambush for the night and he wanted me to be the rear point man. There were a couple of green horns in the squad and they were hoping to see some action and the rest of us old timers didn't say a damn thing to them. Sullivan looked at me and I shook my head about the green horns. Sullivan told them that they would soon see action and they wouldn't like it. A couple of hours passed then it was time to move out on the ambush. Sullivan came over to me and said to make sure that I had both red and green star clusters with me. Dale Davis and Charlie Horton were in second squad and had a little experience besides Sullivan and myself.

We moved out and headed for the two bombed out buildings and there was a small hedgerow next to the building that only had bushes. It really looked like a great spot for hitting the N.V.A. Corporal Sullivan used his hands to tell where everyone should be. I was to protect the one end and he protected the other end of the team. Sullivan pointed to each man and gave each guy a number and that number was the time he was on watch for the night. I slowly took off my gear quietly so as not to make any sound. The green horns were making a little sound but didn't realize how bad it really was up here just north of The Strip. After a little more than half the night went by, it was my turn to stand watch. I could hear the insects but I could feel that the enemy was watching us. It seemed that when we were on the north side of The Strip that the N.V.A. didn't like us to be in their territory - this was their grounds. When my watch was over, I woke up the next guy and gave him the watch and handset from the radio. I then started to lie down. The guy I told to take over also lay down. I got up and he looked at me and said that he was awake and I kicked him hard at the bottom of his foot and he then woke up for good. He couldn't believe that he had the watch and radio in his hands. He whispered that he was awake and that I could get some sleep. Morning came and Sullivan woke me up and said that it was time for us to get back to the platoon. Sullivan got on the radio and called to the platoon that we were ready to come back in and were waiting for them to tell us to pop our flare. After a couple of minutes the word was passed and I popped the flare, which was green. They told us to come on in and we slowly moved back to our platoon. When we got back into the platoon perimeter the rest of the company was gone but our platoon was to stay here for the day.

The word was passed that the rest of our company was crossing The Strip and that we were going to go to Con Thein for supplies. The Strip was finally finished by the engineers and it was now 600 meters wide from Con Thein to Gio Lin. Closer to Con Thein, the Marines had strung three strands of concertina wire around the whole perimeter. It was going to be a lot harder for the N.V.A. to take over this outpost. We crossed The Strip and went to the south side of the base so that we could get re-supplied. As we were getting our supplies the guys there told us that everyday on the radio Hanoi Hannah was saying that the 1st Battalion 9th Marines were going to get wiped out. One of the guys said that we were going to get wiped out on May 23rd. The Marines told us that they were still playing the same three rock and roll songs for our battalion. This really made us guys pissed off. There was no way that they were going to wipe us off the map. The other Marines that were there at Con Thein were somewhat sorry for us because of what the N.V.A. was going to do to us. They were happy that they were not in the 1st Battalion 9th Marines and didn't want to be around us when the N.V.A. did attack us. We could tell that they wanted us to get our supplies and get the hell away from Con Thein.

The word was passed that the six-bys were coming to take us back to Dong Ha. It was about an hour when we heard the six-bys coming for our company. All of us boarded the six-bys and they took us back to Dong Ha. We could see that the countryside was changing very fast here. The old shell of a CH-34 that was about 200 meters from Con Thein was no longer there. The road was much wider and very dusty as we went to Cam Lo. We finally got back to Dong Ha and as we went through the gate, all of us took out our magazines and put the rifle on safe so that they would not fire. The trucks took us to our area and all of us got off the trucks. We went to our tents and most of the guys got into their cot and tried to get some sleep, but the day was another hot and humid one. It was around 16:30 and the word was passed for all of us in Charlie Company to get into formation. We were complaining as we got into platoon formation. Captain Hutchinson and the three Second Lieutenants from each of our platoons told all of us guys to follow them. We went behind the clerk's tent and there was a small trailer with ice cold beer and ice to keep it cold. Captain Hutchinson told the whole company to get two beers each and that it was on all on the officers from Charlie Company. All of us grabbed the two beers and sat around and drank them. It was the first time that any officers in this outfit had done anything for us guys. When all of us were finished with the beer, we headed back to our tents and most of the guys laid in their cots to get some sleep. When I got back to the tent, Speedy was cleaning his machine gun while sitting in his cot. He was making sure that the machine gun was ready when we would be going back out into the bush. Speedy had his camera on his cot and I had taken a lot of pictures of the guys in our platoon back in the rear and also out into the bush. It was time for chow and most of us guys didn't go to chow, so we took out our C-rations and cooked the food inside our tent. We knew that they would have rice for us and none of us wanted the damn stuff. The rest of the evening the guys got out their writing gear and wrote home, while the rest of the guys were sleeping for the night.

Morning came and around 09:00 the word was passed that we were going back out into the bush. All of us got our gear on and just sat around until the six-bys came. They arrived and we got on the trucks, which took us back up to Cam Lo. When we got there we were told to get off the trucks and get in a staggered column. We were headed up the road to Phu An and Con Thein.

When we got to the bottom of the hill - where Phu An was - we stayed there for two days and patrolled around the area which the N.V.A. had given up for good. We headed south into the hills that went to Cam Lo but we only went about 2000 meters. I had a little scratch on my right wrist. It was nothing at first and I didn't make any bones about it at the time. We got back on the road that went to Cam Lo in a staggered column but only went about half way there. We patrolled around the hills for a few days and as each day went by the little scratch got a little bigger from the dust and dirt that was thrown up in the air by the six-bys running back and forth from Con Thein and Cam Lo. As we moved north on the dirt road in a staggered column the six-bys continued kicking up the dust around us as they passed, which was flying all around and settling down on us. My right hand was starting to swell up twice its size. When we stopped for a ten-minute break, I went up to Doc Chico and showed him my right hand and he asked me why I hadn't shown it to him earlier. I told him that it wasn't swollen then. He got out a bottle of peroxide and poured it over the cut, which was now about the side of a half dollar. He told me that he wanted to see me everyday after we got done with the patrols. Boy, when he poured it over the cut, I was about to jump like hell. I wanted to call him every name in the book but I didn't; he just smiled at me when he poured it over my hand. He would then say that it hurt him more than me. I looked at him and said that I was the one that was feeling the pain when he poured the peroxide. He just smiled.

We stayed for another day and then started heading northeast. We went about 4000 meters and hit a dirt road and I remembered it from before and knew that we were going to Phu Ox. This dirt road also led to Market Street on the other side of The Strip. We walked down the dirt road that was leading north to The Strip and came into Phu Ox and the small church on the left side of the road. When we got past the church, we headed east for about 500 meters and stopped for the day. The company set up the perimeter and I quickly dug our fighting hole and told the guys that I was going on over to see some of the other guys in our platoon. I saw Whitey and he told me that they had made up a song for being over here. Whitey asked if I would like to hear it and I said yes, of course. This is how the song went: to the tune of "Sitting in My La La, Waiting for My Ya Ya."

Riding on a six-by, going down to Phu Bai.
Uh Huh, Uh Huh
Riding on a six-by, going down to Phu Bai.
Uh Huh, Uh Huh
It may sound funny, but I don't believe I'm going home.
When I hear that Arty, I know that it's no party
Uh Huh, Uh Huh
When I hear that Arty, I know that it's no party
Uh Huh, Uh Huh
It may sound funny, but I don't believe I'm going home.
When I hear those mortars, I want to get my orders.
Uh Huh, Uh Huh
When I hear those mortars, I want to get my orders
Uh Huh, Uh Huh.
It may sound funny, but I don't believe I'm going home.
When I hear that Recoil, it puts me in a turmoil.
Uh Huh, Uh Huh
When I hear that Recoil, it puts me in a turmoil
Uh Huh, Uh Huh
It may sound funny, but I don't believe I'm going home.
My heart slips, when we go across the strip
Uh Huh, Uh Huh
My heart slips, when we go across the strip
Uh Huh, Uh Huh.
It may sound funny, but I don't believe I'm going home...

The guys that wrote the song sang it to me. When they finished, I knew that they had put a lot of thought into the words. I knew the words were true and in a way each of us knew that we weren't going home. This war had changed each and every one of us. None of us were happy-go-lucky guys any more but only trying to survive this war so we could hopefully go home if that was possible. I saw on the faces of the guys in our platoon; how old all of us looked, and how much life has been drained from our bodies. It seemed that all of us had accepted what might happen. Whitey then asked me what I thought of the song and I told him that it hit home for every one of us in this outfit. I told Whitey that I hoped that we would be able to make our 395 days so we could go home. Whitey just nodded and I told him that I better get back. I went on over to Doc Dodson and had him pour the peroxide on my hand. It was very hard not to have any tears while he poured it. I told him that he look liked he was having fun.

The next day came and we saddled up and moved westward in a staggered column back toward Con Thein. We got about 2000 meters and set up on the south side but off The Strip about 400 meters. The word was being passed that from now on we were to police up the area just before we left from now on. Now, that was a little too much bullshit for over here. What did they want us to do, make the countryside beautiful? The rest of the guys were upset about the new orders. One of the guys passed the word that the North Vietnamese Regulars were going to wipe us out tomorrow because it was May the 23rd. All of us just laughed because the battalion was in four different locations. It would be very hard for them to try to wipe us all out. We were talking about what we had been hearing about Hanoi Hannah and what she and her people were going to do to us. I knew that we would welcome a good fight with the N.V.A. and hopefully that they would not run away as they usually did. All of us knew that the N.V.A. were afraid of our battalion. We knew that if they hit us that they had to have 10 N.V.A.'s to 1 of us from 1/9 to hit us on their terms. The word was passed to keep a real sharp eye out for the next couple of days in case they decided to hit us.

It was time again for my visit with the doc. I just hated it, that I had to see Doc Chico everyday, but I was glad that it was only one time a day. When I got over to the C.P. Dodson was waiting for me and had that bottle of peroxide. As he was pouring the liquid over my hand, I dropped down to my knees again and boy did it burn inside. He wrapped my hand and I asked him why they couldn't send me back to the rear and he told me that there weren't that many of us in our platoon. Doc Dodson said that there were only 24 of us all together in the platoon. As I left, Lieutenant Libutti was talking to a new guy in our platoon named Stuckey and wanted him to take a fire team; Corporal Stuckey said that he wanted to learn what was going on over here first before he took the job. Libutti concurred and said after thirty days that he would have a fire team. I didn't talk to the guy since he was new and a corporal and Libutti wanted him to take over a fire team. At least he wasn't stupid in taking the fire team before learning what to do out in the field. He had never been in a fire fight and if and when he did, would he be able to help out the rest of the guys in the battle or hide?

We stayed here for a couple of days and the word was passed that we would be moving out again. My hand was not getting any better because of the dust but again, it was not getting any worse. I just hated going to see Dodson everyday for him to look at it and pour the peroxide over my hand. We only had 24 guys left in our platoon, and six of them were green horns, making eighteen guys with combat experience. I remembered there were 44 of us when I joined and now there were 24. Each of the fire teams were down to three guys with the exception of the machine gun teams and mortar team, which had four guys each.

As we moved out heading east again, the pain in my right hand was not really bad but it made me think about it while we were on the patrol. I was glad in one way that I was left - handed in shooting my rifle. I wished that someone would cut off my right hand because of the pain that I was having. The word was passed that 2nd platoon was to take point, and that Hammer was to take point. I walked up to the front of the column and Libutti told me where I was to go and to follow this trail that led north until I hit the dirt road. He then told me to watch myself and I nodded and started out. We moved out in a single column to make it look like we had a lot of guys in our outfit to see if we could get the N.V.A. to open up on us. As I was point, there were a lot of places for the N.V.A. to hit us. There was no cover at all for us, but still I kept on moving out. I must have traveled about 1500 meters when I started to come across combat gear left behind from another Marine outfit that got hit here a week earlier. There were water bottles that had holes in them and combat gear that was cut up pretty bad. From the way everything looked, the N.V.A. had had a field day with one of the Marine outfits. There were no bodies around and then I hit the dirt road. I stopped and passed the word back that I was at the dirt road waiting for my next instruction. The word was passed to move up the road in a staggered column until we reached Fu Ox. I started moving out heading north to Fu Ox toward the vill. There was even more combat gear of both Marines and N.V.A. on the road.

As I came into the small vill I could smell rotten flesh. The smell of rotten human flesh is very hard to describe, I would rather smell shit or rotten eggs than human flesh. The bodies had been lying somewhere out in the open with the sun beating down on them for over a week. I could tell that I was just past the small vill. I looked back and saw we were still in a staggered column. The Catholic church was on the left side of the road. Just in front of me on the road was what looked like a body but it was flattened out. The hedgerow was just past the church and I remembered the field that we had set up in before. The word was passed for me to stop. As I knelt down, I could really smell the rotten flesh, but I couldn't tell where the smell was coming from; it was not the body that was on the road. I knew that it was close to me but still I didn't know where. Libutti came up and told me to head into the large open field on the left side. As I moved out toward the open field, Bradley came up to me and told me to set up here facing north toward the hedgerow about fifty feet from me. We were setting up our perimeter around the church. Captain Hutchinson was coming up and went right on over to the church and he passed the word that the church was to be his Company C.P. I got up and Libutti was right behind me and told me to set up where I had set up before when we were here. I took off my gear and was told that Dale Davis and I were to be in one fighting hole. Dale got out his E-tool and started digging the fighting hole for us. He told me not to dig and that he would take care of it while I took care of my right hand. After a couple of hours, I knew that it was time for me to see Dodson so he could pour the peroxide on my hand. Lefefe and the platoon radioman Bradley were watching me and they both told me they were glad that it wasn't them. Again I dropped to the ground, as the pain was unbearable. Again Dodson covered the cut up so that the dust would not get into it. My right hand was twice the size as my left hand but it was not getting any larger, thanks to Doc Dodson.

When I got back to Dale, he told me about the dead N.V.A. that was on the road. Dale said that a N.V.A. soldier got out on the road and was shooting at a tank. Our tank just ran over the stupid ass. I started laughing because I couldn't believe that this guy was that stupid in getting in front of the tank and shooting at it before it ran over him. The N.V.A. had to be on dope to stand out in front of a tank to get run over. I had a funny feeling that the tank didn't run over the guy one time but several times. I asked Dale if he had smelled the rotten flesh that was next to the road when we came up and he said yes. He said that the dead body of the N.V.A. was in the hedgerow a couple of feet from the N.V.A. that was on the road. I told him that I wanted to see just where, and went on over to the body. I looked into the hedgerow, which only had bushes, and there he was. You could see that the N.V.A. had gotten shot in the face and part of his face was caved in. The N.V.A.'s body had deteriorated quite a bit. There were flies all over his body and especially around his head. The smell of a dead human is unbelievable and I knew that I had to get away from the dead N.V.A. I'd rather smell shit, farts or rotten eggs than smell this. I went back to my fighting hole and sat down with Dale. Dale said that we needed to get out of the sun and to try to keep cool. Everyday was hot but we really hadn't thought about it that much because we were getting used to it. It seemed that the hottest part of the day was from 10:00 to 15:00 each day. Dale and I got a couple of sticks from the trees and used them to hold up our poncho for the day. The rest of the guys in our company were doing the same thing, trying to stay out of the hot sun. Dale would take out a cigarette, light it up and blow the smoke into our fighting hole. This was one way to make sure that the smoke didn't travel very far.

The word was passed that we would be here for awhile since the N.V.A. were after us. We were only going to have small patrols, L.P. and ambushes only and try to draw the enemy in on us. The word was passed that there were to be two guys per fighting hole and to try to get some sleep in during the day when we were not on patrols. Dale and I were under the poncho sitting in our fighting hole watching and dozing off if we could. Dale and I ate and started taking down the poncho for the night and got ourselves ready for our watches. Most of the day, we didn't feel like talking because of the heat and humidity. I told Dale that it would be stupid to be on for one hour and off one hour. Dale said, "Let's go for two hours and see what happens." I agreed and I told him that I would take first watch. Dale got under his poncho and I sat in the fighting hole watching and listening for the enemy. I knew that our whole company would be going through hell for these next days. How long, no one knew. I looked at my watch and it was going on midnight and I knew that I had to get Dale up. I kicked Dale at the bottom of his foot and he got up and I told him that I was finished for now. He got up and went into the fighting hole. I went over to my poncho, which was next to the fighting hole itself, got under it and felt off to sleep. The next thing I knew, Dale kicked me at the bottom of my foot and told me that it was my turn. I slid into the fighting hole and looked at the watch and it was 03:00 in the morning. Dale lay down and was off to sleep fast. I stayed up for the last three hours of the night. When morning came I took my poncho and used it as our cover for the day. I let Dale sleep as long as he could. I looked over to the other fighting hole and he was doing the same thing that I was doing, letting his buddy sleep as long as he could before the heat of the sun would make it unbearable to sleep any longer.

Today was the 23rd of May and we were to get hit by the N.V.A. and wiped out. I knew that it was on everyone's mind so all of us were keeping a sharp eye out for the enemy if they did come. Most of us thought that it would be stupid for them to hit us after telling us what day they were coming to get us. I could almost feel that the N.V.A. was not around and of course the day was starting to get very warm and I knew that it was going to be another very hot day. Around 13:00 it was time for me to see Doc. I could tell that the swelling was going down and my hand was starting to heal. Dodson was standing with the bottle in his hand and he looked at my hand and wrist to see how it was coming and then poured the peroxide on my hand. Again I tried not to fall on my knees, but I ended up there anyway. When he was finished, he told me that it was looking good and that it won't be long before it was healed. When I got back to our position Dale was working on our fighting hole by putting banana leaves for our cover instead of us using our poncho. The banana leaves were a hell of a lot better than the poncho because they kept the heat of the sun from reaching us underneath it. The other guys around the perimeter were doing the same thing in making their position bearable by using the banana leaves as a roof over their fighting holes. That evening Van came over to me and said that Dale and I were going with him and Smithy out on a L.P. for the night. Ted said that each of us would stand one two hour watch for the night. I knew that all of us were really beat and that we all needed sleep. It was like we just didn't give a damn if they hit us or not at this time. When it was time to go, I grabbed the radio and called our platoon C.P. and told them that we were leaving for the night. The time was 20:45 when we left the perimeter. Van took the point and I was right behind him. We went out about 500 meters and up against the hedgerow. We were the early warning system for the rest of the company in case the N.V.A. decided to hit the company. We were expendable. There were three L.P.'s out each night from our company while we were there. There was also one ambush that the company had out each night. When it was my turn to watch, Van made sure that I was awake before he laid down. As I sat there looking out around, I could almost see the N.V.A. walking out in front of me about 1000 meters - but I just wasn't sure. I couldn't tell if my eyes were playing tricks on me. I knew that I was beat and it was very hard on each of us to know if we were seeing things. The time seemed to go by very slow and it was very quiet. Every half hour the platoon radioman would call me and if all secure, I pressed my handset twice. Finally my time was up and I shook Dale and handed him the watch and handset to him and before I covered myself up, I made sure that Dale was awake. Then someone woke me up and said that it was time to go back in. I got on the radio and called our C.P. and said that we were coming back in and the radioman informed me to shoot the flare. I told Van and he shot the green pop-up and they confirmed that it was green and told us to come on in. As we were walking back, I just hoped that the guys on the perimeter wouldn't think that we were the N.V.A. As we got to the perimeter we could see that the guys that were on watch were half asleep and half awake. When we got back to our fighting hole, both Dale and I got under the banana leaves and went back to sleep.

At noon, I got up and told Dale that I was going to see some of the other guys in the platoon to see how they were holding up. I went over to the road and Maxwell and his machine gun team, Philip Ritivan, Randy and the fourth guy were playing cards using an old C-ration box for a table. Maxwell asked me if I had any C-rations and I told him that I didn't have a damn thing. Maxwell said they have been digging up the old fighting holes here but we didn't leave any food the last time we were here. The machine gun was pointing down the road which was north. I left and talked with the rest of the guys in the platoon, Whitey, Horton, Moore, Van Lugar, Bignami and our other machine gun team of Lisinski, Fulton, Speedy Gonzales and the other guy in their team. All of the guys were asking me if I had any C-rations on me and I told them that I was in the same boat as them. Later that day when I went back to my fighting hole, Dale was changing our cover by using more banana leaves. He put on the last branch and as he put it on the top, he ran away so that it wouldn't fall down. I asked him why he ran away and he told me that this was the second time he had put the branches on top but when he put on the last one the whole thing came down. Dale looked at me and said that this was the way to put on the last branch by laying it down gently and run like hell away from it. I started laughing. It was funny. I told Dale that I hoped that they called in for re-supplies because our food situation was getting very, very low. We hadn't had anything to eat now for five days and counting. Everyone in the company wanted something to do so that we wouldn't have to think about food. The word was passed that 2nd platoon was going on a short patrol. All of us saddled up and waited for the platoon C.P. to call us. The guys from the other platoons came over and took our positions before we left. The word was passed to get on the dirt road. When we got there, 3rd squad took point and we headed east. There were open fields with thin hedgerows around them. We could tell if the enemy was in the hedgerows. We must have gone about 1000 meters and then headed north toward The Strip. When we got very close to The Strip, we headed west going parallel with it. Again we could tell that the enemy was not around. We came up to the dirt road that led north and south and we went back south to where the rest of the company was. When we got back to the perimeter we went back to our fighting positions. We took our gear off and got under the banana leaves that Dale made and it was good to get out from under the sun. The next couple of days went by very slowly and now none of us had food. The captain had been calling for a food drop but the other Marine outfits were getting hit. The heat from the sun and the humidity made us feel like not eating during the day. The only thing we had was the small stream that ran thought part of our perimeter. At least we had water to drink.

That night we could almost see the N.V.A. about 800 meters to the north of us walking around our perimeter but making sure there was a lot of cover between us. We couldn't shoot them because of the trees and bushes that gave them much of their cover. That morning, as everyone got up, we all knew that the N.V.A. was watching us but they were not going to hit us. The word was passed that Captain Hutchinson was calling in re-supplies but they would not be able to supply us again because the N.V.A. was hitting other Marine outfits at this time. The procedure was to supply the outfits that were getting hit before they would supply the ones that were not getting hit. We all knew in our company that the N.V.A. was trying like hell to starve us out if they could. I told Dale that I was going to see Maxwell and the other guys to see how they were doing. As I left, some of the guys were digging up the fighting holes that had been made here before when we were here. They were looking to see if there were any cans of food that had been thrown into them. Most of the guys gave up digging. I went over to see Maxwell's machine gun team and how they were doing. I filled up my canteen and I asked Maxwell how he was doing. He said that we needed food. Maxwell had a Hawaiian guy in his fire team named Philip Ritivan and I couldn't believe what he was doing. They were all small guys from 5' 7" to 5' 10"in his gun team. Philip was with the other guys trying to catch the crabs that were in the stream. Maxwell said that they had these little crabs and the guys were catching them and eating them. I laughed and told Maxwell that we didn't have to worry about water, we got plenty of that.

Maxwell just smiled and said yes we do. I told him that I was going back.

I got up and remembered that I wanted to see Kenny Fulton also. I then told Maxwell that I was going over to see the other gun team of Kenny, Speedy, Bowman and Ski. They were on the other side of the road in the open field west of them. I walked on over to where Ski was and they were just sitting around doing nothing like the rest of the guys in the company. I talked to Ski and the guys for about ten minutes and told them that I had to get back. I asked Ski how the food situation was over on this side of the woods and he said very poor. He said that they were eating some bugs and roots from the trees. I left and went back to see how Dale was doing at the hole. He was under the banana leaves smoking a cigarette.

I went under the banana leaves to get out of the hot sun and sat in the hole with Dale, not saying anything. I waited for him to say something first. After a few of minutes Dale told me he was thinking about his girl back in the States. From the way he was talking, I knew he was really in love with her. I could tell that his whole world revolved around her. He wanted to talk more about her so I asked him how they met and that started him talking. He said that they knew each other in high school and they had been dating since the ninth grade. Dale said that her parents didn't want her going out with him. She would sneak out and meet Dale down the street almost every night. Dale said that this went on for four years. I asked Dale what she was doing now and he said that she was in college. Dale said that when he got back they were going to get married. I then asked him what if she ran into a guy in college and didn't want to get married to him and he said that it would not happen. Dale said that she really loved him as much as he loved her. I then told Dale that I didn't think she really knew what the hell he was going through over here. He didn't say a word. I said that I hoped she would not write you a Dear John letter. Something deep down inside of me knew that it might happen. I knew that it would devastate him. From the way he was talking I could tell that he was not getting as many letters from her in the past month. She had been writing him almost everyday and now it was almost once a week. I prayed that she would be true to him. We stopped talking and just sat there looking out in front of our position and there was nothing for either of us to eat today. We hadn't had any mail for a while and I knew that it was eating at him that he hadn't had a letter from her in some time. The only thing we had was water and we had plenty of that. About an hour went by and I told Dale that I was going to dig up some roots to eat. I remembered back in boot camp they told us that if we didn't have any food we could eat bugs, roots or anything that moved. I then went on over to one of the trees that was close by and dug up some roots for us.

When I came back with some roots to eat, Dale was still thinking about his girl. I hoped there were a lot of letters from her when we did get mail. Being hungry wasn't the worst thing over here; it was not getting any mail that made all of us down in the dumps. It was amazing how our spirits would rise when all of us got mail and how much our spirits dropped when we didn't get mail for two weeks. I told Dale not to think about her now and he said that it was hard not to. Dale then told me that he got three letters a week from her and I told him that when we did get mail that he would be reading all day long. Dale told me that I was one hell of a friend over here and that he loved my "Ma Hammer goodies" when I got them. Boy, did Dale have a big grin on his face when he said it. Dale also told me that it was nice of me to write to his parents telling them that their son was all right and that his injuries were not that bad. I told Dale that I didn't want to write any more letters to his parents. Dale just laughed and said that he would try not to get hit anymore or get heat stroke. I gave Dale a couple of roots and both of us ate them. Dale told me that he might end up growing roots and end up being a tree one of these days. I told him that I would be next to him growing roots also.

I told Dale that I was going to see Whitey and see how he was doing. As I was walking away, I envied Dale because he had a girlfriend back at home and I didn't have a girl. I only had a couple of good buddies back home in Ted and Bruce. I finally reached Whitey's fighting hole and talked with him and asked him where he came from and he told me that he came from Chi town, which was Chicago. Whitey always seemed to have a smile on his face. As he was talking I realized one thing about all of the guys over here. It was about how and what they were going to do when they got back to the States. All of the guys in our outfit - when they or if they - made it back to the States, were going to treat the girls like ladies and show them a great time by treating them with respect. All of the guys were going to get their sport cars and cruise around town and get a good job and make money. I could tell that all of us knew just what to do when we made it back to the States. But the States seemed so far off in a fantasy world and we were here where someone was trying to take our lives away from us. None of us wanted to be here but our country called us and we were doing the best we could. Right now Hanoi Hannah was telling us they were going to wipe us off the map. I knew that the people back in the States were going about their business of going to work, school, college, and daily routines and not really thinking about what the hell we were going through. It seemed like the people back in the States really never thought about us or even cared at all. After a little bit, I told Whitey that I was going back to my fighting hole for the evening. I saw Ted Van Meeteren, Frank Bignami, Smithy, Hughart, Robbins, Jerry Moore, Charlie Horton, Lugar, Boni, Ron Francis, Stuckey, Sullivan, Keeley, and Davis at their holes and most of them were trying not to move and stay under shade from the sun. I looked over to our C.P. group and Bradley was at the platoon radio and Libutti and Lefefe were also under cover from the sun.

I got back when the sun was starting to go down and the heat was starting to let up. Dale told me that he had first watch and that I better get some sleep. I fell off to sleep and of course my turn was in the middle of the night. I could tell Dale was giving me a somewhat decent night of sleep. I took the rest of the night, so that he could sleep. As I stood my watch my mind would think of the guys that had died and how much all of us missed those guys; I just thought of Benny Houston being the oldest guy in our platoon and how he watched over all of the guys and made sure we took care of each other. And then the youngest guy, Gerald Vizer whom no one had told of the mine field that was behind us up at Con Thein. Then I thought about Hughart who said that he was going to write to Vizer's sister and try to get a date with her when he got back from Vietnam. I thought about James Fowler how he got killed the second night in the field. I knew that Thomas hadn't taken care of him during the night when James got shot in the head. Then I thought about Chuck Knight and how our last lieutenant stepped on the booby trap and both of them were wounded. Lieutenant Ervin was crying and needed help and not one of us guys including the corpsman helped him. I had Chuck's 38 cal. pistol in my seabag and if I made it back home I would send it to him. I stopped thinking about the guys and looked up into the sky and there were so many stars out that it looked like they were almost on top of each other. I then started thinking about if I was doing the same thing my father did during W.W. II in the Philippines, fighting against the Japanese, looking up into the sky and seeing all of those stars. I looked at the watch and it was going on 02:30 in the morning. I knew that Van was having all kinds of hell keeping Hughart to stand his watch at night time. I could feel my body wanting to go to sleep but I had to stay up as long as I could. I looked at the watch and it was going on 04:00 and I knew that I couldn't stay awake any longer and woke up Dale. I gave him the watch and got under my poncho and fell off to sleep fast. It was very hard to try to sleep during the day because of the sun and heat.

The next day came and Dale and I were going to see a couple of guys that were next to the road. We asked the guys in the next fighting hole to watch our position and said that we would be back in an hour. Dale and I walked on over to the fighting hole and there were about eight of us there talking about nothing. After a couple of minutes we all heard a chicken. We could see that it was by the church and was heading our way. All of us were very hungry and we all agreed to surround the chicken and kill it for food when it got closer to us. The guys grabbed the bamboo sticks and cut off some of the small branches and had them ready to hit the chicken. One of the guys said that we should surround the chicken and on the count of three we would hit it at the same time. As they encircled the chicken and started closing in on it slowly, the rest of the guys in the company that were near by were watching and hoping that they would get it. The closer they got to the chicken, my mouth started to water. The rest of the guys were thinking about having chicken for the day. The chicken looked very good although it was very thin - but for us it looked very fat. Then one of the guys, without saying a word but only using his fingers, started counting: one finger, two fingers and then three fingers, and they all hit each other at the same time with the bamboo sticks and the chicken quickly ran away. A couple of the guys ran after it but it really took off fast. I started laughing as well as the other guys. Then the captain came out of the church and told us to leave that chicken alone and to behave ourselves. Captain Hutchinson had a smile on his face and he was laughing at us for trying to get that chicken. When a couple of guys said, "but Captain..." he cut them off. He knew that all of us were hungry and we really needed to get re-supplied.

All of the guys that had watched them were all laughing, including the guys that went after the chicken. We all got a good laugh out of it but still we were all hungry. It sure would have been nice to get that chicken. Dale and I told the rest of the guys that we were going back to our fighting hole. I couldn't believe the guys; they couldn't get that chicken! Everyone was holding their breath, hoping that they would get it. I knew to myself that I would always remember this, as long as I lived.

As evening was coming on we could see in the distance the enemy walking around but it was very hard to get a shot off at them because of the vegetation. We all knew what they were trying to do. Everyday now they were trying to starve us out by hitting other Marine outfits in the field. We all knew that the Marines back in the rear knew that also. As night closed in on us, I took the first watch so that Dale could get some sleep. I stayed up as long as I could so that he would only have one watch for the night. Each night was taking a toll on us since there were not that many of us in the Company. The 1st platoon had something like 22 men and 3rd platoon had something like 26 guys. Morning came and again all of us just lay around doing nothing. Some of the guys would write letters but most of the time we just stayed where our fighting holes were and either daydreamed or talked about our past. It was really getting to all of us now that we needed food and quickly. I could feel the walls of my stomach rubbing up against themselves. Eating the roots, grass and small insects just wasn't getting it.

I went on over to see our corpsman and he looked at my hand. The swelling was down and it was looking very good. He poured the peroxide on my hand and it was not stinging at all. He said that I was all right and I didn't have to do this anymore. It was more than a whole week of him doing this to me, pouring the peroxide on my hand. I then left him and went back to my fighting hole. Lieutenant Libutti looked at me and I just nodded to him that I was all right and he wanted to talk to me but decided not to. The word was passed that it was our turn for a patrol around Phu Ox. Again the other platoons took over our holes and we saddled up and got on over to the road. Libutti told us that we were going to go south on the road for about 500 meters and then head east for about 1500 meters, than north about 1500 meters and then back here. The heat and humidity was climbing and all of us knew that it was going to be a very long, hot and humid day. As we moved out, we moved out slowly because of the heat. All of us knew that we couldn't move fast or we would all end up with heat stroke. It took us about six hours to do this patrol. When we got back to the rest of the company, we slowly went to our holes. As I looked at the rest of the guys going to their holes, I saw that we were really in bad shape. The guys seemed to not care anymore. I took off my gear and decided to see Lieutenant Libutti to see if and when we were ever going to get re-supplied.

I was thinking of Libutti and I knew that he was doing a good job and that our platoon was really together; all of us were very close. I decided to go back and talk to the lieutenant about when we were going to get re-supplied. I asked Libutti when he thought we would be getting re-supplied and he said that the N.V.A. were hitting the other Marine outfits in the field. That's why we are not on the priority list back in the rear to get the supplies. When the other outfits were taken care of, then they would send out the supplies to us. The N.V.A. knew that whatever outfit out in the field was being hit that they had top priority in getting food and ammo. I told him that they were doing a great job of it and all of us were starving. Libutti told me to just hang in there and I told him that I was all right but the other guys may not be. I then left and went back to my fighting hole.

Evening was coming and again it was going to be another very long night. Dale was very tired and the night watches were taking their toll on all of the guys in the company, as well as me. I told Dale that I had first watch, and that I would wake him up later. I knew that I had to stay awake as long as I could before I would pass out. Dale really needed a good night's sleep. It was around 22:00 hundred hours and as I looked up there were thousands of stars all over the sky. As I looked at the stars, I got a very cold feeling that someone was watching us. I knew that the enemy was out there and I went over to the fighting hole on my right side and told the guy I was going out in front to the hedgerow to look around and not to shoot me. I then went over to the fighting hole on our left side and told them the same thing. I took only my rifle and magazines with me. I started out in front of our position heading toward the hedgerow which was only about thirty yards in front of me. When I reached the hedgerow, I slowly and quietly moved into it so I could get a better chance of hearing or seeing the N.V.A. As I sat there for a couple of minutes, I could feel the hairs on my back rise up and knew they were out in front of me but were not closing in on us, just watching our perimeter. I could even smell them. I couldn't see them, but I knew they were out there.

I looked back at our perimeter and each of our fighting holes was very clearly seen because the stars were out. I knew that the enemy could see us very well because we were right out in the open. We were hoping that they would attack our positions since they knew right where we were. I stayed there for about ten minutes to see if I could hear them but still no movement at all from them. Some of the stars were disappearing and the moon as well. I knew that it was time to get back to my fighting hole before it would be too dark and the guys would be shooting at me. When I got back to the perimeter I went over to both fighting holes on each side of us and told them that I was back and I couldn't see them but I could smell them. I went back to my fighting hole where Dale was still sleeping. I got into our fighting hole so it would be very hard for the N.V.A. to see me, thinking that a Marine was asleep at his watch. There were now less stars out and it was very hard to see the hedgerow, which was only thirty yards in front of us. I knew that it would be very difficult for the enemy to keep an eye out on us now that it had gotten darker. As the night moved on, I thought I could make it through the night without sleep but I knew that was impossible. I looked at my watch and it was going on around 04:30 and I knew that I could make it until the sun came up. When it was daylight and the sun had not gotten over the trees, I laid on the ground and thought that if I made it the twelve hours of night time staying alive, then I had to try to make the twelve hours of daytime staying alive. This was everyday and there was no letting up. This would go on until the end of our tour of duty, if we made it through our 395 days. As I laid there, I looked up into the sky and now all of the stars were gone and it was really black. I couldn't see more than a couple of feet in front of me. It seemed to be the worst time of the night for everyone, even for the N.V.A. as the rest of the night went by and it was getting closer to morning. At around 04:00, Dale woke me up. The darkness of the night was slowly disappearing and soon the sun would be coming up.

As the sun came up hitting Dale in the face, he jumped up and wanted to know why I didn't wake him up for watch and I told him that he looked so peaceful sleeping that I couldn't make myself wake him up from his beauty sleep. Boy, did he get mad at me for staying up all night. I knew that if I had gotten him up during the night for his watch that he would still be sleeping. Even though his eyes would be open, he would still be asleep. I told Dale that I couldn't sleep and at least one of us would be sharp for the day.

It was going on around 11:30 in the morning and the word was passed that 2nd Platoon was going out on a patrol and to saddle up. They told us to get on the dirt road and that we were heading north toward The Strip. We started moving out in a staggered column and it felt great just to do something rather then stay around here and do nothing. We moved up the road for about 600 meters and the point team stopped and said that they were next to The Strip. The word was passed to head east toward Gio Lin along the side of The Strip. As the rest of us came up to the road before we turned to our right heading east, we could see an Ontos on the side of the road that had been hit by an R.P.G. round by the N.V.A. The vehicle was stripped of everything and the only thing left was the shell of the vehicle itself. We walked east for a while and the word was passed to rest for ten. As we rested, all of us knew that the enemy was not anywhere around us, east of the road leading to Gio Lin. The heat of the sun and humidity were going back up, but it seemed that we were getting used to it. Most of us took a drink out of our canteen before the canteens could get very hot. All of us knew that we would not be able to drink again until we got back and poured out the water and put cold water from the stream back into the canteens. We went for about 3000 meters and headed south for about twenty minutes and the word was passed to head back west. It was around 17:00 hundred hours when we got back to the perimeter with the rest of the company.

As we moved into the company perimeter, the guys from the other platoons were waving at us and asked us if we had a nice time and we told them that the walk was great for the body. Everyone was cracking jokes at each other. They wished that they could have gone on the patrol and not just lie around doing nothing. Just doing nothing made the day drag on so slowly. Dale and I went back to our fighting hole and slowly took off our fighting gear and Dale told me that he would go and get our canteens filled back up. I only gave Dale one of my canteens and he also took one canteen himself. I told Dale that the other two canteens could cool down on their own. Again today there was no re-supply and it didn't hurt since we had water and it was more important to have water than not to have water. All of us knew that we could live without food for a longer while.

The word was passed that the lieutenant wanted to see me. I told Dale that I would be back and I went on over to where the C.P. was. When I got there the lieutenant told me that I was up for R. and R. out-of-country. Libutti said there were three places to go but only two of them were open and they were Thailand or Formosa, China. I told Libutti that I would go to Formosa, China, which was Taipei, Taiwan. Libutti said that I would be going at the end of the month, June. I went back to my fighting hole and when I got there Dale was gone and Charlie Horton was there. I asked Charlie what happened to Dale and he said that Dale was moved on over to the 2nd squad for now. Charlie said that I was now back in 1st squad. In our platoon everyone was being changed to different squads. Frank Bignami was now my squad leader, not Sullivan. Van was still a fire team leader but he had different guys. It really didn't make a damn bit of difference with the guys. Our platoon only had 24 guys in it and there was only one fire team in each squad that had only four guys in it, and the other fire teams had three guys in it. The rest of the day dragged on and again there was nothing to do but think about what new songs that were out and what the new cars looked like. For some of the guys just thinking about their girls was very hard on them. Again thinking about food was really getting to all of us. I told Charlie that I was going on R. and R. next month and that I was going to Taipei. Charlie looked at me and said that I really needed the rest. Charlie told me the only time all of us had to worry about getting killed was in our first two months, in the middle of our tour after our out-of-country R. and R. for thirty days, and our last two months, because we were thinking about going home and not paying attention to what we were doing out in the field.

The next day came and the word was passed that we were going out on a patrol. The whole company got out on the dirt road and started out in a staggered column heading north to the strip. We went about half way up the road and the word was passed to stop and that 2nd Platoon was to put out flanks. Bignami called me and told me that I was to be the point man on the left side of the column and Horton was to be behind me. I then moved out to the left side of the column; Dale Davis was the point man on the right side. I was about 100 yards from the main column and the word was passed to move out. Captain Hutchinson looked at both Dale and me and waved his hand to move out. We still headed up the road and then the captain pointed to us that we were moving to the east, off the road. The Strip was right in front of us, about fifty feet ahead. I looked back and Horton was about 100 yards behind me and Van was about 100 yards behind Charlie. We were going parallel again with The Strip but did not cross it. We could feel that the enemy was watching us and studying what we did out in the field.

About an hour went by and the main column had stopped for a ten minute break. I knelt down and faced outward. There was a water pipe sticking out the side of the small rise in the ground and clean water was pouring out. I went on over to it and starting drinking it and boy, was it very cold. I drank as much as my body could hold. I then took out one of my canteens and emptied it and filled it up with the cold water. I kept it there and let the water keep the plastic cool as well. I went back to watching outward. I looked back at Charlie and pointed to him when he came up to it to drink it, by using my hands for him to understand. He nodded his head and looked back at Van and also told him. The main column was getting up and started heading east. A couple of more minutes passed and again Captain Hutchinson pointed to us out on the flanks to start heading south again. We headed south for about half an hour and then headed west back to Phu Ox. We did this for the next couple of days, doing the same routines, hoping that the N.V.A. would hit us. On the third day after doing the patrol and heading back to Phu Ox, the captain told Libutti that we were to go down south from the vill and set up a perimeter for the choppers to drop off mail and supplies. The word got around and everyone in the company was really looking forward to getting the C-rations and mail.

We went back about 500 meters, going south on the road to an open field and set up there waiting for the choppers to come. There was a small open field on the left side, which was east of the road, and we set up our perimeter waiting for the re-supplies to come. It was about forty-five minutes later and we could hear the sounds of the choppers coming. They really sounded great and we couldn't wait for them to land. It had been at least fourteen days since we got re-supplied and about ten of those days when we didn't have any food at all, just water. The first chopper landed with the C-rations and ammo. Then the next chopper landed with the yellow and orange bags of mail. Only a couple of guys stayed on the perimeter and all the rest of us went over to where the supplies were and I helped carry one of the cases of C-rations. Then all of us moved back to the vill and went on over to the Captain's C.P. (the church) and dropped off the supplies there and then went back to our perimeter and waited for the C-rations and mail to come to us.

I got word that the corpsman wanted to see my hand. I went on over to Doc Dodson and as he looked at it he said that it looked like it was starting to swell up again and he again poured the peroxide over the cut and it only burned a little. He said that he wanted to see it again tomorrow morning to make sure that the swelling went back down. I went back to the fighting hole and Charlie told me that the food was here as well as our letters. The only thing on my mind was the food and Charlie was cooking his food and I was right along with him. I opened up a can of ham and a can of cheese and I mixed them together and heated them up. There were only three pieces of ham that were about 2 1/2 inches in diameter each. I ate the first piece and started eating the second one and I was half way finished when I couldn't eat anymore. I was full. I couldn't believe how much my stomach had shrunk and I couldn't eat anymore. I knew that from now on no one was going to pass out their food to anyone else when we went out in the field. I could hear some of the guys say that they were going to eat ham and mother and not give it away.

I then went to my letters and one of the letters was very thick, about two inches. It was from my buddy Ted's sister who was still in school. There were also two letters from Jennifer and the rest of the letters were from my Mother. I decided to open up the letter from Diana Grogan first. Diana and my brother Ryan had gotten all of the kids in my school to put their names on the letter in support of what we were doing. She told me that everyone was looking forward to seeing me come back home. I looked at all of the names and I knew most of them except for the sophomores. I laid the letter in my lap and Charlie looked at me and asked about the letter. I told Charlie that the kids back in my high school were behind us over here. Charlie said that it was very nice of them to write their names on the letter. I just nodded my head and agreed with Charlie. It was starting to get dark and I decided to read the rest of the letters the next day. I told Charlie that I was going to see Dale and see if he got any letters from his girl. When I got there, he was reading her letters and I asked him, "Are you happy now?" and he was all smiles. I went back to my fighting hole and got ready for our night watches.

The next morning came. Around 09:00 hundred one of the guys had a little transistor radio and a couple of us were listening to Hanoi Hannah's rock and roll station. Then she came on and told the guys from the 1st Battalion 9th Marines that she was dedicating three songs for us. She told us the first song was, "Nowhere to Run, Nowhere to Hide" and then played it and when it was over she told us that the next song was, "We Got to Get Out of This Place" and then played it and when that song was over she said that this song is what the N.V.A. was going to do to us and she played, "WIPE OUT." One of the guys said they had been playing these songs everyday for us. When the song was over she got on the radio and said that we would be wiped out in the month of June. The guys said they wished that they would hit us so we would have something to do. These milk runs were boring and all of us knew that the N.V.A. were watching us but would not hit us. What they were trying to do was starve us. That didn't work and now they were telling us that they were going to wipe us out. We damn near wiped out the N.V.A.'s best outfit, the 324th Bravo Regiment, back in Oct. 1966. Boni, Sullivan, Van, Thomas, Chadwell, Lefefe, Francis, Lisinski, Horseman, Bradley, Maxwell and a couple of others in our platoon were there at the time. Only Boni and Sullivan extended for another six months over here.

The word was passed that we were going out on our standard patrol for the day hoping that the enemy would hit us. We patrolled the southern side of The Strip while Delta Company had the north side of The Strip. Bravo Company was back at Dong Ha and Alpha Company was up at Con Thein. Another week went by and still nothing was happening. We were getting re-supplied every fourth day out in the field.

The third week of June Delta Company started getting hit on the north side of the strip. Delta Company asked for us to help them. We saddled up and moved down the dirt road in a staggered column to the strip and when we got to the edge of The Strip, the captain told 2nd Platoon to come across last. As our platoon got closer to The Strip we were still in a staggered column going across as we went. We finally reached the other side but the N.V.A. were nowhere near us. We were going down the road still heading toward Market Street where the two bombed out buildings were. We could hear some firing but it was still farther down the hill. We reached the cross roads and Captain Hutchinson had the company heading off to where the two bombed out buildings were, which was about 200 meters from the road, east. We reached the buildings and the captain told us to make a perimeter and to dig in. Delta Company was trying to force the N.V.A. back to us. We were to be a blocking force. Charlie and I got out our E-tools and started digging the fighting hole deep. The ground was not hard, thank God, and it only took about twenty minutes. Charlie and I were facing north and we fixed our field of fire and then took our grenades and straightened out the pins so it would be easier to pull them. The firing stopped and everything got quiet. All of us were ready but still nothing was coming our way. I remembered that Alpha Company got hit here a while ago when we used napalm on them. It was only about 300 to 400 meters from us. It must have been about an hour later that Delta Company came back from the north. As the guys walked past us, they were telling us good luck and to watch ourselves. They said that the enemy was behind them. Delta Company got to the dirt road and headed south to The Strip itself and then headed back to Con Thein.

After Delta Company passed us, all of us were ready for the N.V.A.. attack. We all knew that tonight might be the night they would try something. I told Charlie to get some sleep in, but he just laid on the ground right next to the fighting hole and had his rifle ready. It was evening and the sun was down but there was still light out and I knew that we had to get some rest in before night time. We did our cooking in the bottom of the hole so that the enemy could not smell the food. I kept a watch for a couple of hours and I asked Charlie to take over when it was around 22:00. He got up and I lay down also next to the fighting hole. The word was passed that we were to go on 100% watch. All of us knew that if they hit us it would be just before the sun went down or just before the sun came up. Charlie and I sat on the edge of the fighting hole with our rifles in our hands. It was almost dark out and Lieutenant Libutti came by to see how we were doing and told us to stay low in our fighting hole so that the N.V.A. couldn't see where we were when the moon and stars were out. Libutti then left to check on the rest of the perimeter.

Part of our perimeter was in with the hedgerow, which was east and south. Us guys that had the north and west side of the perimeter were right out in the open in the field. All of us knew that during the night when the stars came out with the moon that the N.V.A. could see us very well. Around 23:00 hundred hours, the stars and moon were coming out. It was time for all of us to get into the fighting holes so that the enemy could not see our outlines. Charlie Horton and I got into the fighting hole and really kept a very sharp eye out to make sure that they didn't come up on us. We knew that it would be dangerous for the N.V.A. to walk out there in the open field at this time. I could feel the hairs standing straight up on my back and I knew that they were looking for us but did not know actually where we were. I looked on both sides of me and with a little light from the stars and moon I couldn't see the other fighting positions on both sides of us. All of us were keeping very low in our fighting holes. I knew that the N.V.A. weren't going to be stupid by walking out there in the open fields. After a couple of hours went by, the moon and the stars started leaving. It was now getting darker.

Then we heard someone coming from the right side of the perimeter whispering for Hammer. I whispered to him to stop and asked who it was and he whispered back that it was Lefefe. I told him to come on in and he quietly came over to us. I told Lefefe that this was a bad time for him to be going around the perimeter to see if we were on watch. I told him that we could smell them out there. Lefefe asked if we were all right and I told him that we were just fine. He said that he was going over to the next hole and wanted to know who was there and where. I told him that it was Van and pointed to where his hole was. Lefefe told me to keep a sharp eye out. Both Charlie and I looked at each other and whispered to him, "What the hell you think we're doing?" He got out of the hole and quietly went on over to the next hole. A couple of minutes went by and Lieutenant Libutti came over to each of our fighting holes to see how we were doing. It was getting close for the sun to come up and we knew that this was another good time for the N.V.A to hit us - but they didn't. Finally the sun came up and the word was passed that we were getting ready to move out. We knew that by being very low during the night when the stars and moon were out that they couldn't tell where our perimeter was. We got out our E-tools and covered up the fighting holes so that the enemy would not use them against us when we left.

The word was passed that we were moving out. We were going back to the crossroads. When we got there, we went straight west and when we got to the giant tree the word was passed to go south to The Strip. When we got to The Strip, we moved to the edge going east. We reached the dirt road that led north to Market Street again. It was going on around 14:30 hours. The word was passed that we were going to set up on the edge of The Strip for the day. There was no place to get out of the sun so some of the guys got some sticks as poles and tied their ponchos on the poles to get out of the sun. The whole company rested for the day because we were up all night. The heat and humidity was really cracking down on us; all of us had our flak jackets off as well as our jungle shirts. I went on over to see some of the guys when I came across Boni, Sullivan, Bignami and Van. Sullivan showed one of the guys where the button was to press the camera to take a picture. Sullivan was cleaning his .45 cal pistol on The Strip. I went on over to see Dale and went back to my fighting hole. As I walked back, I could see that all of us were very, very thin. The shorter guys that were from 5' 7" to 5"10" weighed about 110 lbs. The few tall guys like Robbins, Van and me weighed about 150 lbs. I really didn't think about it until I was walking back to Charlie. I told Charlie that I was going to try to get some sleep but the heat of the sun was very hot. There was no breeze and the only thing we had was our poncho over us.

Just being on the strip itself made a lot of us feel uneasy. I didn't care if the enemy hit us or not. We were all very tired being up all night and now the sun was taking its toll on all of us. There was no easing up at all for us. I somehow fell off to sleep, if you want to call it that; most of the guys were sleeping under the protection of their ponchos. The rest of the day dragged on slowly and then it was going on evening. Charlie told me that he knew that he was going to get hit. I didn't respond to what he had just said to me. Charlie looked at me and didn't say anything more about it. I told Charlie that I didn't want to hear it and he told me that he had to tell me about it. I told Charlie that I cared for all of the guys in the platoon and right now I didn't want to hear it. I started thinking about Chuck Knight and that he had also told me that he was going to get wounded. I just didn't want anything to happen to any of these guys. I really wasn't ready to hear anything that Charlie was going to tell me. I just hoped that the feeling he had would just go away and that he would not have to tell me.

It was time for our night watch and Charlie said that he would take the first watch and that I better get some sleep. All of the guys put on their jungle shirts and flak jackets so that the mosquitoes wouldn't bite us, since we were so very thin. I took my poncho off the sticks that we used for cover from the sun and now was going to use it as my blanket for the night. I put my rifle next to me and made sure that I was right next to the hole. Charlie was about a couple of feet from me watching out in front of us. A couple of hours passed and Charlie woke me up and told me that it was my turn. I got up and took over. Charlie then covered himself up and was right next to our hole. I sat up and had my feet in the fighting hole. The sky was dark. I knew that this was a good time for them to try to sneak up on us if they wanted to. Charlie stayed up for two hours. We had The Strip on the south side of the perimeter so we knew that the N.V.A. only had three places to attack us from and it was from the east, north or west. Our platoon had most of the southern part of the perimeter.

As I was listening to see if the N.V.A. were sneaking up on us, I started thinking about what Charlie had said to me about getting hit. I remembered when Jerry Moore asked me to help him when they made him a fire team leader and Boni made all kinds of trouble for him, making him think that he couldn't handle the job. Charlie seemed to be one hell of a nice guy and one hell of a Marine. He would do anything for any one of the guys in the platoon. I just didn't want anything to happen to him. It seemed that all of the guys that I got to know in this platoon either got wounded or killed. I started thinking about death and that it didn't scare me anymore about dying. It seemed to be the least thing on my mind in the field. I could tell that none of us were afraid about dying anymore. I knew that those of us that did die were dying for our buddies in our outfit, not for our country and flag, but for each other. Our Country didn't give a damn for us and we knew it. I knew that if I made it back to the States that no one would ever understand that we die for each other and not for our country or flag. I could still feel something watching over me and I just didn't want anyone to know about it. I knew that the guys would think that I was crazy.

The stars were starting to come out and the skies were getting a little lighter. In front of my position, I could see very far. All of us could still feel that the N.V.A. were very close by, watching our company. Finally morning came and we ate our food. There was not a cloud in the sky as usual. All of us made sure that the M-16, were clean and we hoped that they would not jam on us if we fired our rifles. Around 09:00 hundred, the word was passed to saddle up because we were going on a patrol. The captain told Libutti that our platoon had rear security on this patrol. We started down the dirt road to Market Street, which was north. When we got to the crossroads, the lead platoon was heading east toward the two bombed out buildings. As we were getting close to the building we started heading north again to where we had napalmed the N.V.A. when Alpha Company got in a little trouble with them. When we got to the tree line we headed west toward the dirt road. All of us were uneasy. We knew they were here but wouldn't show themselves. When we hit the road, we got into a staggered column and started going down toward the river. As the banks of the road got higher, Captain Hutchinson called out for flanks before we went any farther. We moved out for another 100 meters and then headed west into another large open field. Captain Hutchinson had a feeling that the N.V.A was around and didn't want them to have the upper hand. The captain passed the word that we were going to stay here for a while, so we made our perimeter very close to the hedgerow so that the N.V.A. didn't sneak up on us. Most of the guys started digging shallow fighting holes next to the hedgerow.

As the outfit settled in for the day, everyone had everything ready in case the N.V.A. tried to hit us. All of us had the hedgerows for protection. As we sat there looking out in front of our positions, no one talked. All eyes and ears were on 100 percent alert. Charlie asked me if I knew that there were about 500,000 N.V.A. in the D.M.Z. and I said to him. "Is that all?" I asked Charlie how in the world he knew and he said that he read it in the Stars and Stripes. I looked at Charlie and told him there was a little over 80 of us in our company and we were supposed to make sure that they didn't come over to South Vietnam. Charlie said that the odds were in our favor and both of us laughed. I started thinking about what it must have been like for the guys being surrounded in the Alamo back in 1849. Both of us kept a sharp eye out as well as listening to hear if they were coming for us. All of us knew that Bravo Company had the south side of The Strip and were patrolling that area. They would be the only guys that could help us in case we got hit and they had about 90 some guys themselves. All of us listened for any sounds of movement by the N.V.A. All of us knew that our company could not make a mistake out here or they would overrun us. Captain Hutchinson knew that he couldn't give the N.V.A. a chance to wipe us out.

It was going on around 15:30, the word was passed to saddle up and we were moving out. Libutti came over to Charlie and me and told us to be the rear security for the company. We started out in a staggered column again and were still heading west. I told Charlie that we wouldn't move until the last guy was about 100 meters from us. As we watched the company moved out both Charlie and I listened to see if anyone was coming up behind us. Charlie looked at me and said that it was time to move out because they were about 100 meters from us. We both started moving out very quietly and as we walked we tried to hear if they were following us. We tried not to make a lot of noise with our steps. The company then turned south toward the strip. Charlie and I still kept our distance from the company as we went back up the hill. I knew that it would be a foolish thing for the N.V.A. to attack us while we were going back up the hill. Captain Hutchinson made sure that he used the terrain in our favor so the N.V.A. couldn't make their attack on us. The company reached the road that was going from Market Street, west toward Con Thein, still heading south for about 400 meters and the word was passed to stop and to dig in for the day.

Charlie and I finally arrived and set up on the southern part of the perimeter. Charlie got out the E-tool and started digging the hole; I told him that I would take over went he got tired. After a couple of minutes, I told Charlie that I was going to take over. The rest of the guys were making sure that their holes were deep enough. We finally dug our hole and made sure that we had everything ready for nighttime. We had our field of fire marked with the fighting holes on each side of us. We took out our grenades and put them on the ledge of our fighting hole, then we ate and again Charlie got the feeling about getting wounded out in the field. I told Charlie that I would be next to him and I was not going to take the R. & R. but I would make sure that he wouldn't get wounded. He looked at me and told me that I better take the R. & R. He told me that he was all right but he wanted me to go on R & R. Night came and they didn't hit us. All of us knew that they were close by but still, they didn't want to hit us.

Morning came; I decided to go over to where Libutti was and told him that I didn't want to take R & R because there were some things I had to do. Libutti looked at me and asked me why. I tried to give him an excuse but I could tell that it wasn't going to fly with him. He told me it was not up to him if I didn't want to go but I had to talk to the captain. I then asked Libutti if he would talk to the captain on my behalf and said he would try. Libutti told me that he would get back to me on this. I went back to my fighting hole. When I got there, Charlie Horton was cleaning his rifle and I thought that I had better do the same. Neither of us said a word but just kept busy to ourselves. Most of the guys were doing the same thing and were staying to themselves. For some reason, everyone of us knew for sure that the N.V.A. was here and they wouldn't attack. We could almost smell them being close to us. Some of the guys were in the fighting holes, smoking or writing a letter home. A couple of hours went by and the word was passed that Captain Hutchinson wanted to see me. I got up and went on over to the company C.P. and the captain was lying on his side. He asked me why I didn't want to go on R & R , I told him that one of the guys in my fire team felt very strongly that he was going to get wounded. If I were around, he would not get hit. He shook his head and told me that I was going on R & R. and that my buddy would say the same thing: go on R & R. Captain Hutchinson told me there was no way that I could get out of it. I would be going in a couple of days and that this discussion was closed. He said I would be on the chopper when the time came. Captain Hutchinson said there was nothing more to talk about and that I better get back to my fighting hole. As I turned around to leave he said, "Hammer, it is your turn for R & R and you're going, and you are to have a good time; that's an order." I told him that I wanted to be here in case we got hit by the N.V.A. Captain Hutchinson said that Charlie Company was going back to Dong Ha in a couple of days from now. I slowly walked away and went back to my fighting hole, Lieutenant Libutti saw me and he said almost the same thing the captain said, that I deserved going on R & R., I needed the rest. I reached my fighting hole and Charlie Horton asked me what the hell the captain wanted and I told him that I would be leaving in a couple of days from now. Horton then said, "GOOD," that I deserved it, and he was happy that I was going.

Two more days passed and we had been patrolling the north side of The Strip for almost a week. We hadn't been supplied now in a week. As usual, we were always short of water and food. What water we had in our canteens we couldn't drink because it was hot. The only time to drink was around 04:30 in the morning. All of us could tell the N.V.A. were around but we couldn't see or hear them but we could smell them. I asked Charlie if he still had that feeling and he told me that it was gone and he was all right. I knew he was lying, but I knew that he wanted me to go on my R & R. The company set up each night at a different location so that the N.V.A. wouldn't have a fix on us when we did set up for the night.

It was time for the company to set up for the evening and we hit the dirt road that went west from Market Street to Con Thein; we headed south for about 200 meters and set up for the night in the open field with small bushes. Captain Hutchinson made sure that there was a lot of open ground between us and the hedgerows. We were about 1000 meters from Market Street. All of us made sure that our fighting holes were dug deep. Around 20:00 hundred hours, word was passed that there was an ambush team going out for the night and part of 2nd Platoon was going to take over their part of the perimeter while they were gone. The squad headed north of our position about 500 meters over the hill that we were on. Horton and I got up and they showed us where to go and take up their positions on the perimeter. Horton and I set up in one of their fighting holes facing east toward Market Street. I took first watch and after a couple of hours, I woke up Charlie and he took over. It was around 02:30 in the morning, when Holy Hell broke loose. I quickly got up and hit the fighting hole with Charlie in it and we were ready for the attack. After a couple of minutes we heard firing from both the M-16s The AK-47s died down quickly; only the M-16s were firing for the next ten minutes. It lasted for about fifteen minutes and then everything got very quiet. Horton and I saw someone checking each of the fighting positions along the perimeter heading toward us - it was Lieutenant Libutti. When he got to our position he told us that the ambush team hit the N.V.A. and that we were to be on 100 percent alert until morning. Libutti told us that he had to check on the rest of the platoon and he got up and went on over to the next hole. I could feel my body getting excited and Horton felt the same way. We were hoping that they would hit us. We were ready for them. We had our grenades ready and all we had to do was pull the pins. As the next couple of hours went by, there was no attack. Everything around us was very quiet and still. As the hours went by our bodies got tired waiting for the N.V.A. and we knew they were not coming. The sun was starting to come up and I told Charlie to get some sleep. It was about half an hour later after the sun came up that the ambush team came back in. Charlie got up and we went back to our fighting hole, which was facing southeast in our perimeter. I told Charlie to go and get some sleep before it got really hot today.

Word was passed that we were going to stay here for the day and to get in our rest. Being up most of the night took its toll on the whole company. Captain Hutchinson knew that if we went on patrol that the company would not be very sharp if we got hit. So he made the decision for the whole company to stay here and rest for the day, which was unusual for us. Our company was well under strength and here we were in the middle of The Strip and in the D.M.Z. hoping that the N.V.A. would attack us. At least we had our fighting holes dug and were in a great place if the enemy did hit us - we would be able to see them coming from a good distance away. Charlie told me to go and get in whatever sleep I could. The sun was really warming up fast and all of us knew that it was again another very hot and humid day. As I was lying on the ground and trying to sleep, I could hear some of the guys talking and even walking around. Everyone in the company had their jungle shirt off because of the heat and humidity as usual. After a couple of hours I told Charlie that it was his turn and I watched while he tried to get some sleep. Corporal Bignami who was our squad leader came over to see how we were doing and the both of us said that we were peachy; he left with a smile on his face. Our platoon had only 24 guys in it and everyone was making sure that their spirits were up. I went on over to see Dale and he was doing fine as could be. Dale told me that he was glad that I was leaving for R. and R. Dale told me that when I come back to make sure I had goodies for all the guys in the platoon. I left him and went back to Charlie, but before I got there I saw Jerry Moore and asked him how he was doing and he nodded his head and smiled. I could tell that the guys must be giving him hell since he acted as a fire team leader. I knew that Boni was still talking behind his back.

The rest of the day went by very slowly. All of us knew now that the enemy was getting ready to attack us, but when? This waiting game was really getting to all of the guys in the company. The ambush team had hit the N.V.A. good last night. It seemed the N.V.A. was trying to make it on their terms instead of ours. The N.V.A. was waiting for us to make a mistake and then they would hit us but good. So far we were not going to make any mistakes out here. There were a couple of guys taking pictures with their 35mm cameras. Speedy was one of those guys taking pictures of the guys in the platoon. There were some guys writing letters home but most of us were just watching out in front of our positions to make sure that the enemy

didn't attack us. As the sun got lower in the sky, most of the guys were trying to get some sleep before the night came.

The word came that we were going to have the same ambush team go
out again. I knew that the captain wanted the same ambush team to go back
to the same spot again tonight. Charlie and I had the same fighting hole as
last night. It was around 20:00 hundred hours and again the ambush team
headed north to the same place as the night before. When all of us heard
that, we all knew that they would hit the N.V.A. again. Word was passed
that the whole company was to be on 100% alert tonight. The night went
by slowly for us; something was on Charlie's mind. I whispered to Charlie
asking what it was and he said that he was having that same feeling coming over him again, that he was going to get wounded under his arm and
his shoulder. Charlie said that the feeling was very strong this time and he
knew that it would happen. He told me that there was nothing I could do
to stop it. I told Charlie that nothing was going to happen to him but in his
voice, I knew. As I looked at him, he said that he would get wounded but
would be going home.

It was 02:30, again the ambush team opened up; all of us were in our
holes and waiting to see what was going to happen next. The ambush went
on for about ten to fifteen minutes and then, it got very quiet. It was a repeat
from last night. Lieutenant Libutti came by our holes to make sure that we
were ready. He looked at me and I just nodded to him that we were ready
and that everything was all right here. As I looked into Libutti's eyes, I
could tell that he would like to have me next to him but he knew that he was
on his own. I just hoped Sgt. Lefefe was next to him when the shit hit the
fan. As he left to the next fighting hole. I thought he was the only lieutenant
in our platoon that really cared for his men. I knew that he was working
very hard at it. Our last platoon officer, Lieutenant Ervin, didn't even check
us on the perimeter every night like Libutti did. Ervin didn't have the balls,
and when he stepped on the booby trap he cried like a little baby in front of
the guys in our platoon. Charlie told me after he left that Lieutenant Libutti
really cared about us guys. I agreed with Charlie. As I was thinking to
myself, I thought that I made him into a damn fine officer and that the men
in our platoon would do anything for him. I knew that Lieutenant Libutti
was still a little green around the edges but I knew that he could still handle
himself when the shit really hit the fan, not like the first time when he was
out in the field at Phu An in the bottom of the fighting hole with his hands
over his head while we were getting hit by N.V.A. mortar rounds. I knew
that deep down inside of me that when we got into a fire fight and the bullets
flew all around that he would be able to handle himself. I just hoped that
Lefefe would be around to help out.

Again we all were on one hundred percent alert and still the N.V.A.
didn't come. Morning came and again the word was passed that we were

going to stay here for the day. About two hours later, word was passed that we were moving out but none of us knew where. We gathered all of our gear and started moving in a staggered column east toward Market Street. Captain Hutchinson made sure we had flanks out on both sides of the column. When we got to the cross section in the road at Market Street, the staggered column headed south toward The Strip. Captain Hutchinson decided to set up our perimeter along part of The Strip around a large open field away from the hedgerows. We were setting up here for the day. As the company made the 360 degree perimeter, word was passed that we were getting re-supplied. Charlie Horton and I took off our fighting gear but made sure that we could get to it very fast if we had to. The guys were watching everything all around us except from The Strip since there was a wide-open area of 600 meters to the south side. The word was passed that Lieutenant Libutti wanted to see me. I told Charlie that I better get up there and find out what the hell he wants. As I walked past the other guys along the perimeter, none of them said a word but just watched out in front of their positions.

I finally reached the platoon C.P. and walked over to Lieutenant Libutti. He looked at me and said when the choppers come to get on them and that I was to go on my R & R. Again I told the lieutenant that I wanted to stay because I knew that the N.V.A. were ready to hit us and I didn't want to miss out on the fun. Libutti told me that they were going back to the rear to Dong Ha the next day for seven days and when I came back, I would be with them back at Dong Ha. Libutti told me, "Hammer, you are to have a great time in China." I could tell that he was really going to miss me and I just hoped that nothing would happen to him and the guys while I was gone. I just nodded and slowly walked away back to where Charlie was. I knew that I wasn't getting out of not going on R. and R. Captain Hutchinson made sure of that.

I sat down next to Charlie and he asked me what our lieutenant had wanted and I told him that I was to get on the choppers when they arrived. I said that the last two nights were very, very unusual because in all of the ambushes we never had had two straight nights of hitting the N.V.A. Charlie said that he felt the same thing. We all knew that Hanoi Hannah had been telling us that they were going to wipe us out all together, playing those three songs, everyday. I told Charlie that tomorrow the rest of Charlie Company was going back to Dong Ha for seven days. Bravo Company was to take over the north side of The Strip patrolling around Market Street. Charlie had a smile on his face when I told him that the company was going back tomorrow to Dong Ha and the feeling that he had of getting wounded should go away. Charlie didn't say anything.

Around 10:30 in the morning the choppers came. All of us were getting on our combat gear and really paying attention out in front of our positions.

Captain Hutchinson called for "Hammer up!" to see him. When I got to him, he had a Chinese machine gun and told me to make sure that the machine gun was in his tent back in the rear. The first chopper landed, the C-rations and ammo were taken off and it left. The second chopper came down and landed. The captain then told me to have a good time on R. and R.

I told him that I would have a couple of drinks on him. He just smiled and then left and went back to his C.P. area. I walked over to the chopper which had landed on The Strip and I put the Chinese machine gun in the chopper first and I got in. I looked back out the door and Lieutenant Libutti and Captain Hutchinson were looking back at me. They were glad to see me go. Some of the guys that were close to the chopper were also looking at me and they were happy that I was leaving this place. I then moved back inside the chopper and sat on the floor of the CH-34. I could feel that I wanted to stay with the guys and wished that someone else had gone. The engine of the chopper started picking up more speed and then we went off the ground and headed up into the air heading southwest. I remembered what Lieutenant Libutti said, that the company would be back tomorrow for seven days at Dong Ha.

I looked out the door of the chopper and we were about 1000 feet in the air. I could see for miles and the chopper started heading south and in a couple of minutes there was Highway 1 and Dong Ha base. Dong Ha was ten miles from Con Thein. Looking down out of the chopper, I saw a lot of hardbacks in the base and that the base was really changing almost every time I came back. The chopper started coming down to the area where all of the supplies were stacked up for the outfits out in the field. Finally the chopper landed and I picked up the Chinese machine gun and walked up to the door and got out. I walked down the dirt road down to our battalion area. The guys that were at the chopper pad were loading up the chopper with supplies for another outfit out in the field.

Chapter Twenty

I went on over to our company tent and reported that I was back and I told the gunny that the Chinese machine gun was to be in the captain's tent and that he expected to see it there when he came in, a couple of days from now. The clerks told me that I was to change clothes and to leave as soon as I turned in my rifle and magazines and put on my khaki uniform. I knew that I better take a shower to get all of the dirt off me. The clerks told me that when I did all of that that they would have my order ready to go to China today. I left the tent and went over to 2nd platoon area tents, took off my combat gear and put it under my cot. I then went on over with my rifle and magazines to the supply tent. When I got there Sgt. Thomas was still there; I couldn't believe that he was still here. I thought he had been gone a while ago. I told him that I was turning in my rifle and sixteen magazines since I was going on R & R. I told him that I wanted my sea bag and he went in the back to get it for me. When he came back, I told him that I wanted all of my sixteen magazines back when I come back in a couple of days from now. I told him when I got back that if I didn't get all sixteen magazines that he and I were going to get into it. Thomas told me that I should hand him over the .38 cal pistol Chuck Knight had given me when he got wounded. Thomas said that he would be leaving in a week and he would make sure that Chuck got the pistol back when he got back to the States. I thought about it for a couple of minutes and Thomas insisted that he would get it to Chuck and that I didn't have to worry about the pistol. I told him, "You make damn sure that Chuck gets back his pistol." Again Thomas insisted that he would turn it over to Chuck when he got back in a couple of days. I told him all right, and I opened up my sea bag and handed the pistol on over to Thomas. Again, I told him that he better give it back to Chuck. I took my sea bag on back to the tent and took out a towel and my khaki uniform. I went on over to where the showers had been but they were gone. There was a new place to take a shower but it took only one person at a time. They had a 50-gallon drum high over head and you were under it in a four by four foot area. There were wooden walls on all three sides and on the fourth side there was a door to get into it. I finished taking my shower and went back to the tent and put on my khaki uniform. I took my sea bag back to the supply tent and went on over to the clerk tent to get my orders.

I opened up the flap of the tent where inside were all of the clerks of our company. One of them gave me my orders and told me to go on over to the terminal and get down to Da Nang as soon as possible. I then turned and walked back outside the tent and as I got outside, I stopped to look at the order. The flaps of the clerk tent were down and they didn't know that I had stopped to look at the orders. I could hear the clerks talking about me, taking the Captain's R & R. I couldn't believe that I was taking his R & R. I could hear some of them being upset with me. They didn't understand why the captain gave me his R. and R. I then went back into their tent and said that I just heard you guys talking that I'm taking Captain Hutchinson's R & R. and nobody in the tent said a word. I then looked at the clerk that gave me the orders and asked him if I was taking the Captain's R & R. and he just nodded, yes. I told them they better get the captain here so that he can take his own damn R. & R. I gave the order back to the clerk and went to my tent.

I got back to my tent and I started changing my khaki uniform back to my jungle clothes. The gunny came into the tent and told me that I was going on R & R and that I wasn't going back in the field. I told the gunny that I wasn't going and he said, "Oh, yes you are." The gunny told me that the captain wanted me to take his R & R and that I deserved it. The gunny said that they were prepared to make sure that I got on the C-130 to go to China, and that a jeep would be here in ten minutes with two M.P.s to make sure that I got on the C-130. The gunny said that he would be back in five minutes and that I better still have on the khaki uniform when he came back. He came back in five minutes with two M.P.s; he told both of them to make sure that I was on the C-130 and in the air before they left. The gunny then smiled at me and told me to have a good time in China. I was told to get in the jeep by the M.P.s and taken over to the terminal. When we got there one of the M.P.s made sure that I had a boarding pass to go down to Da Nang. Both M.P.s were on each side of me not talking at all. It was about thirty minutes and the plane was coming down and I told both of them that I would get on the plane; both of them just looked at me. The plane finally stopped and the guys that were in the plane got off first and the Marine in the terminal then called out our numbers and when my number was called both M.P.s walked with me to the back of the C-130 and made sure I was on the plane. Both of them then went back to the terminal and waited for the plane to start up its engines. I got up but they were still there at the terminal. I knew there was no way for me to get back out into the field. I remembered what Captain Hutchinson and Lieutenant Libutti told me that the next day the whole company would be back here at Dong Ha. I then sat down and hoped that they were right. I didn't like being away from my platoon and the captain.

The C-130 flew a couple of thousand feet in the air and we headed east to the ocean and then headed straight south to Da Nang. This was one sure way of not getting hit by the V.C.

It took about half an hour and we started coming down and finally land-

ed at the Marine terminal. As I walked on over to the other Marine terminal, I really felt naked without my rifle and combat gear. I didn't like walking around without any fighting gear, especially my rifle and magazines.
When I got there, I went on over to the desk and told them that I was going
on out of country R & R to China and the Marine there told me to go over
to one of the hardbacks and get some sleep and that tomorrow he would tell
me what to do. I left him and went over to one of the hardbacks and found
an empty rack and I just stayed there for the evening. It was time for chow,
which was around 18:00, and I got in line with the other guys that were
there who looked like they were from my battalion. When I got my food, I
went on over to where they were and asked them if they were from 1/9 and
all three of them said yes. I told them that I was from Charlie Company and
then each of them told me their names and which company they were with.
James Toy was from Alpha Company and as soon as they said their names,
I forgot them. I told them that the guys call me "Hammer." When we finished eating, one of the guys said that they were going on over to a beer tent
and have a couple of cans and wanted to know if I wanted to come along.
I told them that I would love to go. We went on over to where the beer tent
was at and all of us had a couple of cans of beer. It was cold and it tasted
great. When we were finished drinking the beers, we all headed back to the
hardbacks. James and the other two guys were in the same hardback that I
was in. The sun was almost gone and darkness was coming on fast. All of
us felt somewhat insecure not having our rifles with us. It must have been a
couple of minutes and I was off to sleep.

Morning came and I got up and the rest of the guys were also getting
up as well. James Toy looked at me and said it must be time for us to get on
over to the terminal to find out where we were to go to get onto the airplane
that was going to take us to China. The other two guys from our outfit went
with us to the terminal and when we got there they told us to make sure
that we had our orders and to get on the bus so that it could take us to the
terminal where we were to board our plane. All of us then walked to the
other side of the terminal and boarded the bus. After a couple of minutes
the bus started up and took us on over to the other side of the airfield. When
we got there, they told us to get off the bus and to have our orders ready. As
we were waiting for the commercial airliner to arrive, we saw there were
a lot of Vietnamese people that were dressed up for leaving the country, as
well as military officers. One of the military guys there told us to show him
our orders going to China and in return he would give us a boarding pass
for the plane. About forty-five minutes passed and the commercial airliner
arrived. Then the military guy told us when we heard our number to board
the airplane. My number and the rest of the guys' numbers were called and
all of us boarded the plane. I got onto the plane and sat down and James
Toy sat next to me. None of the guys said a word. As I sat in the chair, I

couldn't believe how great it felt to sit in a nice chair. All of us put on our seat belts and waited for the plane to take off. Still none of us said a word but just watched the other people get on board. After what seemed like a half hour, the plane started up its engines and then started moving down toward the runway.

As I looked out the window, I saw the individual hangers had the jet fighters in them that were stationed here. We were on one of the two long runways ready to go. Then the plane started to move and I knew that we were off. As the plane built up speed and was getting close to the end of the runway, it started going up into the air. At the end of the runway there was a B-52 that had crashed and burned. Someone on the plane was talking about the bomber and said that it crashed a couple of months ago. The plane was heading west and then started a long turn to the ocean by heading north and then northeast. We were over the ocean and heading for Taipei, Taiwan. The plane kept on climbing higher into the sky. After a couple of minutes the seat belt light went off and the stewardess got up and went back to the end of the plane. As she was walking past us, James and I just looked at her. She was the first American girl we had seen in some time. Both of us kept our eyes on her and we couldn't believe how pretty she was.

As I sat there in my chair, I started to get a wonderful feeling over my whole body because I was free and no one was going to kill me. It was a great feeling, but I was still not sure. I could tell that James was feeling the same thing. The captain of the plane got on the speaker and told us that we would be in Taipei, Taiwan in about five hours and that we would be having lunch on the plane. A couple of minutes went by and as I looked out the window, I heard a female voice tell me to put down my table and without saying a word, I did. She handed me the tray of food and asked if I wanted a Coke. I only nodded my head and she handed me a can of Coke. I looked at James and he was eating his food and looking at her as she passed out the food to the rest of the passengers on the plane. James and I were watching the other guys on the plane and they were trying to look up the girls' dresses as they went by. Some of them would see us looking at them and they would start behaving like soldiers. There was a vast difference between a guy that had not seen any combat compared to the guys that had. The guys that had seen combat were more mature and didn't act like assholes while the guys that were back in the rear played games and never grew up and tried like hell to get the girls to make out with them.

I asked James Toy what was he going to do when we got to Taipei. He said that the first thing he was going to do was take a hot shower for about half an hour, then go out and get drunk and then get laid. He said that he was going to get a suit made so he would look sharp when he got back to the States. I thought about getting a suit for myself as well. I looked at James and he was pointing at one of the guys who was acting like an animal to one of the girls and without saying a word slowly moved his head in a "no" movement. I looked at whom he was pointing and now there were two of us looking at him and boy, did he turn around and not say another word to the girls on the plane. One of the girls saw us looking at the guy and came over and asked us if we wanted something to drink and James only said Coke and I just nodded in agreement. She came back and gave us a can of Coke each. She then told us, "Thanks for helping me."

Then the captain got on the intercom and said that we would be landing in about twenty minutes and to buckle our seat belts for the landing. I looked out the window and all I could see was the ocean, but no land. I was starting to get a little excited, but not like the rest of the guys who were yelling and carrying on like idiots and couldn't wait for the plane to land. The plane started to come down and still James and I were quiet, not saying a word. I looked out the window and now we were over land. The rice paddies here were on the sides of the hills. I noticed that the land was not flat but had rolling hills. The next thing we heard was the landing gear coming down and we knew that we would be landing shortly.

The plane landed and there was a loud cheer from the guys that were on the plane. The plane stopped and in a couple of minutes the door opened up and then we left the plane. When we got to the bottom of the steps there was a bus waiting for us military guys. We boarded the buses and they took us on over to a terminal for a short briefing. When we got there, we got off the buses and went inside. On the intercom a person was telling us that we had three days of R & R.; then they gave us a short talk about V.D. and told us to make sure that we used rubbers. After the short talk about V.D., they told us that they would change our currency over to Chinese money. They told us how many Chinese bills (which was seventeen), equaled one American dollar. The last thing they told us was we had a free taxi ride to our hotel and on our last day a free ride back here to the terminal to go back to Vietnam. They told us that we were now on our own and to have a good time.

All four of us from the 1st Battalion 9th Marines went outside the terminal and got in a taxi. There were only three hotels for us to pick from. The guys asked the taxi driver which was the best hotel and he told us that it was the New Taipei Hotel. We all agreed and he took us there. As we were driving there, one of the guys asked him how far it was from the bars and girls and he said that it was only a mile away. We finally reached the hotel and it was ten stories tall. It was a new building and was the only tall building for about a mile. We paid the taxi driver and off he went. All of us went into the hotel with our little handbags that held an extra set of clothes and other things for our needs. All four of us had our own rooms. My room was on the third floor. James was on the second floor; Bob was on the fourth floor and the other guy was also on the fourth as well. We told each other our room numbers so that everyone knew where everyone was.

I then left the guys. I wanted to get to my room and take a long hot shower and just relax. I went on over to the elevator and went up to the third floor to my room. As I opened up the door to the room, I slowly walked in and saw how clean it was. I dropped my bag just inside the door and looked at the chair and desk. There was a mirror on the wall. I stopped and looked at myself and I couldn't believe how thin I was. I could tell that I had changed since I had been in Vietnam and it showed on my face. As I was looking at myself, I could hear someone knocking on my door. I went to the door and there was this short Chinese guy about 5' 4" tall. He asked me if I wanted him to made suits for me and I said "yes." I asked him the price and it was very cheap, so I told him that I wanted two suits made and for him to ship them back to the States for me and he said that he could do it. He then took out his tape measure and started measuring me, from head to toe. I could tell that he knew what the hell he was doing and in about thirty minutes he was done and asked what colors the suits that I wanted and he showed me all the different colors. I picked out two and he said that he would be back in two days to show me the suits. He politely excused himself and went to the other guys in the hotel to see if they wanted suits made as well.

After he left, I looked at the light switch on the wall and I started turning it on and off. I turned the lights on and then I would turn them off. I would do this a couple of times and it was fun. All those months in the bush and I had forgotten the little things in life. I went farther into the room and saw I had two beds. There was a blanket and sheets on the beds. I walked on over to the bed and sat down on it. It really felt very nice. I started thinking about back in Vietnam when I was out in the field sleeping on Mother Earth and when we went back to the rear we slept on a cot with no sheets or blankets. I got up and went on over to the end of the room and looked out the window and could see for miles around. It was nice to be inside and out of the weather. I then slowly went back in the room looking for the head, which is the bathroom, and I found it. I walked into the bathroom and there was a tub and a shower and a toilet. I went on over to the toilet and flushed it a couple of times and watched the water leave. I went on over to the tub and turned on the hot and cold water and it was great. I came back out and went over to the window and played around with the air conditioner and wanted it colder in the room. I was like a little kid in a candy store looking at everything. I couldn't believe that I had missed all of the little things that we took for granted back in the States. I then decided to see James and see what he thought of his room.

I went down to the second floor and knocked on James's door but he was not in his room. I went down to the first floor and got something to eat. It was evening time and I knew that when I finished eating that I was going back up to my room and take a good hot bath and get under those sheets and get a good night's sleep for the first time in a very long time.

When I finished eating, I went back up to my room, took off my clothes and turned on the warm water in the bath tub and slowly got into it. As I laid in the warm water covering my body, I could feel myself getting relaxed. It was the first time that I had warm water for a bath. I started remembering back in Vietnam where I took my bath in the rivers and cold streams, sometimes with my jungle pants on. I soaked for about twenty minutes and my hands were starting to shrivel up. I got out of the tub and dried myself off. I walked back to where the beds were and looked at myself in the mirror. I just couldn't believe how thin I was. It looked like I must have weighed about 150 lbs. I started remembering about when I was getting ready to go to Vietnam and I saw how thin all the guys were getting off the planes. Now, I was one of those guys. I could feel my spirit going down and I was starting to get depressed. The sun was down now and I got under the sheets. It really felt great getting under them and I could feel the tightness in my body starting to loosen up. I just hoped that I could go to sleep without any problems like having not to think about the N.V.A. and worrying that something was going to happen to me. Half of me was happy to be here and the other half of me wished that I was back with the rest of the guys in the outfit. The next thing I knew I was sleeping. About half way in the night I woke up and thought for a second that I was back in Vietnam. I could tell that my hands had been holding my rifle but I didn't have my rifle. At first, I didn't know where in the hell I was at. I really felt lost. It took me a couple of minutes before I could tell myself that I was in China and I again went back to sleep.

When I got up in the morning, I could tell that I was not in Vietnam. I could still feel the sheets over me and I just laid there thinking about the guys back in Nam. The air conditioning was on and it was very comfortable not being in that hot and humid weather. I was tying to relax but I couldn't get myself to relax at all. I still felt that I was in Vietnam. After about twenty minutes I knew that I better get out of bed. I got my clothes on and went down to James's room. There was no answer and I went back to my room. When I got back to my room I decided to take a taxi cab and just ride around the city. After a couple of hours, I had the taxi cab stop me in town and I just walked around from store to store. The people were going on about their own business as usual.

Chapter Twenty-One

I got back to the hotel around six o'clock and went to the dining room and got something to eat. After I ate, I went up to James's room and again he was not there. I went back to my room. As soon as I got back to my room I decided to go and take a long bath. I took off all of my clothes and went into the bathroom and turned on the warm water for the bath tub. I got into the tub and just relaxed for about twenty minutes. I could tell that it was time for me to get out and as I was drying myself off my mind went back to the guys back in Vietnam. I was hoping that nothing was going on and they were back in the rear doing nothing themselves.

I opened up the door and walked out into my room with nothing on and there sitting on the bed was this young Chinese girl waiting for me. I asked her what was she doing here and she told me that I was hers for the night. I went on over to the other bed and put on my pants and told her that I didn't want her and that she should leave. She told me if she left before morning that she would lose faith from her people. I knew that I was going to be stuck with her for the night but I was not going to have any sex with her. I never had had any sex with any girl in my whole life. I remembered about what they told us about venereal disease and that there were six known ones that they could not cure. The girl started taking off her clothes and I asked her not to and to leave her clothes on and she could have that bed by herself for the night so she would be able to show face with her people. I told her that I was tired and that I didn't want her for the night but that if it was all right to just talk. She agreed and we talked for the rest of the evening and I asked her why she was doing this type of job and she was telling me that she needed the money to help her parents who both were in the hospital and that she had to take care of her younger siblings, two brothers and a sister. I told her there had to be better jobs out there for her to make more money than trying to sell her body every night. I tried to convince her that she should try to get a better job than doing this. She told me that she would try to look for a job. It was getting late and I was getting tired. Both of us went to sleep in separate beds. Morning came and I got up and looked over to see if she was still in bed but she was gone. I just hoped that I told her the right thing. I knew I was not in the States and over here they don't make the money we do back in the States.

I heard a knock on the door and it was James and he asked me if I was ready to go out for the day. James asked me if I liked the surprise last night; I told him yes. I told James that I would meet him downstairs for breakfast.

I got dressed and went downstairs to the restaurant. As we were eating, one of the guys came over and introduced us to a very young girl, who looked like she was 17 years old. Both James and I looked at the girl who had fallen for this sergeant and was in love with him. Both James and I could see this girl was not a bar girl but how the sergeant had found her was a big surprise. The sergeant told us that she was very good in bed and was looking forward to having her again. The sergeant didn't care about her at all and was just using her for sex only. James told me that the sergeant didn't deserve her. The sergeant and the girl left and both James and I felt sorry for what was happening to her and she didn't know that she was being played. When James and I were done, I told James that I was going back up to my room for awhile and just rest. James said that he would come by later in the evening for us to hit the bars. The other two guys went off on their own and James and I never saw them again while we were there.

James came over to my room and we left the hotel and went down into town for the rest of the afternoon. James said that he was half Chinese and half American and seemed to be very proud of it. We took the cab down into town and walked for a couple of hours; we could smell the food that was being cooked out on the streets. There was chicken, fish, duck and goose that were hanging and waiting for someone to buy them. Some of them were still alive, while others were gutted. It made me think of back home in Cincinnati down at Market Street where all of the vendors would have their little stands selling different produce. Here in Taipei, they were doing the same thing.

James and I came across a massage place and both of us decided to get a massage. The girls inside told us that it would be ten dollars and we were to take our clothes off and get into the hot box. James and I decided to do it. So we took our clothes off and the girls put us into these steam boxes and we stayed in them for about fifteen minutes. Then the girls took us out and put us into a bath tub and washed us down. After a couple of minutes they told us to follow them and they put us on the tables and told us to lie on our stomachs. Both of us did so and they started working from our toes to the top of our head. Both of us had one girl each. My girl was taking her time and making sure that I got a very good massage. When she got to my back she stood on top of me and massaged my back with her toes from the lower part up to my shoulders. She was a little thing about 4' 11" tall and must have weighed about 85 pounds. She was telling me to relax and not to get up tight. After a couple of minutes, I started to fall off to sleep. Another ten minutes went by and she woke me up and said that I was finished. I slowly got up and really felt relaxed for the first time in a very long time. The girl did one hell of a massage job on my body. James came over and we both left and went back to our hotel. James told me that he really enjoyed it and had his girl perform a little sex on the side.

We got back to the hotel around 16:30 hours and both of us decided to go to the hotel bar for a couple of drinks. The bar was in the same place as the dining area. We thought that we would have a couple of drinks before we went out to the bars and pick up some girls for the evening. We went into the dining area but sat at the bar. I told James that I was going back out to the front desk to ask for a bartender. I got to the desk and asked the man there if he had a bartender and he said yes and that he would be there shortly. I went back into the dining area and sat at the bar with James and in a couple of minutes the guy that was at the desk came in and said that he was the bartender. So we asked for a couple of beers and started drinking them. As time went on, we were buying the bartender drinks also; the three of us were having a great time. A couple of hours went by; it was going on around 19:30 hours. The bartender made a phone call and told us that he had invited some girls to come over. He then asked us if we wanted anything to eat and we both said yes and he had the cook make us steaks. We ate the steaks and went back to drinking beer with the bartender. We were still drinking and it was going on around 20:30 hours when three girls and an older woman came in and sat down at one of the tables in the dining room. James and I didn't really notice them and the bartender told us that he was the owner of the hotel and he wanted to treat us for the night. He said that we could have any of the girls at the table. The owner told us that he thanked us for buying him drinks and said that he had a very good time. Both of us turned around and the girls were very pretty and sharp looking. Both of us knew they were not cheap. James and I told the owner that it was nice of him that he wanted to do something in return for us buying him drinks. Both of us knew that it would have been a slap in the face if we didn't pick a girl for the night. James got up and went on over to the table and picked one of the three girls and the mama-san agreed with his choice. Then I got up and went on over to the table and as I was about to pick, one of the girls got up and said that I was hers for the night. I looked at the mama-san and she was grinning and also agreed. The owner came over from behind the bar and told both of us to have a great evening with the girls and that it was on the house. Both James and I thanked him and he left.

James and his girl left and we were right behind them. I knew that this time I would have to have sex and I was scared. As we got up to my room and I opened up the door she walked right in and told me that I was a "Cherry Boy," and that she was going to teach me about sex and how to love a woman. As I closed the door, she went over to the rest room and took a shower and after about five minutes, she came out in a robe and then told me to take a hot shower. I went into the bathroom and got into the tub and took a hot shower and while I was in there I was kind of hoping that when I came back out that she would not be there. I dried myself off and wrapped a towel around my waist and came out. She was in bed and was smiling at me and told me that she wasn't going to bite me. She told me to get into bed with her and to relax. She told me not to say a word and that she was going to teach me about how to love a woman. She started kissing me and touching my body and as she was doing this she was talking to me at the same time. After she kissed me and touched my body she had me touching her body and showing me how to be kind to the opposite sex. I was getting excited and I could tell that I was not getting up tight about the whole thing. She really made me feel comfortable in having sex with her. Her movements were very slow and deliberate, and I wanted to go at a very fast speed. She told me to go the same speed with her and that I would feel the pleasures of making love. When we were finished, she got up and went to the bathroom and took a shower. When she came out, she told me to take another shower before I came back to the bed. I did as I was told and when I came back out we were at it again. After each time we would go and take a shower I felt refreshed. We went about five more times and after the last time I was drained and very tired and wanted to go to sleep.

When I came out the last time from the shower I almost crawled to the bed. I got under the sheets and she just smiled at me and I fell off to sleep. When I woke up, I looked over to see if she was still there, but she was gone. As I lay in bed, I was thinking that if I died over in Vietnam at least I had made love to a girl. I was glad that I had sex and now I had done everything in life. I knew that we would be going back in a couple of days. I got up and went down to see James and when I got to his room he came out and said that he was hungry and that he was going down to the dining room. I told him that I was going with him and that I was hungry as well. We ate and when we were almost finished, both of us saw the young girl that had been with the sergeant the other day. She came over to us to asked if we had seen him. We both told her that we had not seen him since yesterday when they were together. She said that if we saw him that she would be in the lobby. After she left, James told me that he had brought some Spanish Fly from one of the taxi cab drivers the other day. James wanted to see if it worked and told me that he was going to call up one of the girls from the other day to see if it worked. We both went back up to his room and he got on the phone and called one of the girls and he told me that she was on her way. James then got out a glass and filled it up with pop and then took out these small pills. He put two of them into the drink and then put it on the small table that was next to his bed. About twenty minutes later there was a knock on the door and James let her in. He introduced her to me and asked her if she wanted something to drink and she said yes. We were all drinking pop and both of us were watching her drink but after a couple of minutes went by, there was no effect. Then she sat in James' lap and started kissing him and I knew that it was time for me to get the hell out. I got up and told James that I was going back to my room. When I reached the door,

I looked back and she was half naked and really working on getting James naked as well.

I got back to my room and about a hour later I got a knock on the door and the tailor told me that my two suits were finished and wanted me to try them on before he shipped them back to my home back in the States. They fitted well and I told him that I was pleased and he was very pleased himself. A couple of minutes later James came up to my room and came in. I looked at him and he said that he couldn't get the girl to stop making love. She wanted it as long as he was up. He told me that he was not going to do that again. When I was listening to James I started laughing at him and I told him that he got what he deserved...sex, more than he wanted. James and I decided to go and get another massage like we had the other day. Both of us needed to be relax again.

It was going on evening and James and I decided to go bowling so we took a cab and he took us to a beautiful two story building that was made of glass and steel. I had never seen any bowling alley like this back in the States. It made all of ours pitiful looking compared to it. We went inside and went to the second floor and there were only two people bowling at one end. The person there gave us a lane in the middle and James and I got our bowling shoes and looked for bowling balls. We were getting ready to bowl when a young girl came up and told us that she was going to keep score for us and I told her that we didn't need anyone to score for us and James told me they had people do the scoring for the people bowling. The girl told us that we were two crazy guys but we were having a lot of fun. James and I started drinking beer while we were bowling and after a couple of hours we decided it was time for us to go back to the hotel.

We left the bowling alley and took a cab into town. The hotel was just down the street about two miles. We had the cab driver drop us at one of the bars and we decided to pick up some girls for the night. The time was 01:30 in the morning and I knew that we would not be able to pick up girls at this time of the night. As we went to the next bar, getting close to the door, I saw this Navy guy with his arm around the girl I had the other night. She smiled at me and told me that I didn't need her and I was on my own. She whispered into my ear and said to make sure that when I got back to the States to show American girls how to love. She also said to treat them as you would like to be treated. She was so much wiser than her age. And then she was gone into the night with the Navy guy. I knew that he was going to be a very lucky guy for the night. James and I went into the bar and there were very few people left and that all of the girls were gone. James and I decided to have a couple more drinks and then head back to the hotel.

We got word that the bar was closing for the night and it was last call. We went outside to get a cab but there were none to be found. James and I decided to walk back to the hotel. Both of us were swaying back and forth as we walked down the street. There were no cars at all on the street at this time. As we walked, we decided to walk down the middle of the street. All of the lights from the bars, businesses and homes lit up the road that we walked down. Then James started giving cadence and the both of us started marching down the road. There were a few people from their homes that were clapping their hands and liked what they were seeing. Two Marines that were drunk, giving cadence and marching down the middle of the street. We were coming up on a large intersection and there was a policeman in the middle of the intersection and as we got closer he gave us a military wave to go through the intersection. We finally got to the hotel and both of us went straight to our rooms.

I got up in the morning still not used to the sheets and blanket and the air conditioning. I could tell that I was starting to get a little civilized and I didn't like it. I knew that I would lose my edge when I got back out into the field in Vietnam. I got out of bed and went downstairs to the dining room for breakfast. A couple of minutes later James came down and I told him that I was going to the Air Force P.X. to look around. James decided to go with me. We took a cab and spent a couple of hours there looking at some of the cameras and stereo equipment in the P.X., besides other merchandise. I heard that Nikon was the best 35 mm. camera on the market but James and I decided that we didn't have enough money left and it was time to go back to the hotel. I made sure that I still had two hundred and fifty dollars left to spend on the guys. When we got back to the hotel, I decided to take another shower for the day. I told James that I felt that I had the dirt from Vietnam in my skin. As I was taking the shower, I remembered the other day when we took a massage and I knew that I wanted to take another massage before I went back to Vietnam. It must have been a half hour later and James came over to the room and asked me what I was going to do next, I told him that I was going out to get a massage and he said that was a great idea. It would get rid of the hangover from last night. James said after that he was going to have a girl for the evening. Both of us knew that our time was almost up and that we would be going back to Vietnam.

I got dressed and both of us left for the massage parlor. As I lay on the table, I was thinking about the guys back in Nam and was hoping that they were back in the rear doing nothing but drinking beer if they could get it. For some reason I couldn't get my mind off the guys. I knew that the next day, I would be going back to Vietnam. As the girl walked up and down my back, almost putting me to sleep, I still could not get my thoughts away from thinking of the guys. Today was July 3, 1967. The next thing I knew I was finished and left and went back to the hotel. James went into town to pick up a girl for the evening and I knew that he was going to make the best of it until we left tomorrow. I just wanted to be by myself for the rest of the day. I didn't even want a girl, but I knew that I had better write some letters back home.

I got to the hotel and went straight to my room and got out some papers and started writing back home. I wrote to my brother, sister, mom and especially to my father. I told them I was in China having a great time on R. and R.. As I wrote to my father I told him that I didn't know what the hell was going to happen in the future, but I knew that I was coming home alive. I knew that he understood what I was trying to say. When I was finished writing all of the letters to everyone, it was evening and I went to dinner by myself. I ate what I could eat since my stomach was still very small. I knew that I couldn't stretch it because if I did when I got back out in the field I would be having trouble again like when I first got over to Vietnam. I ate very little but I did a lot of drinking while I was here. Then one of the Marines came into the dining room and told me that the 1st Battalion 9th Marines got "Wiped Out." I asked the guy, "Are you sure?" and he said that it was coming from the air terminal.

I went back upstairs and went over to see James. As I got close to the door, I could hear him talking to a girl in his room. I knew that I had to tell him what I heard. I knocked on the door and as he opened it, I said that our outfit got wiped out. I just heard from one of the Marines a couple of minutes ago but I didn't know if it is true or not. The look on James's face said it all for the both of us. I told James that I was going back to my room and that I couldn't wait to get back to Vietnam. When I got there I looked outside the window; the sun was going down and it was very pretty. I had this strange feeling coming over me again but I started thinking about the guys in my outfit. I hoped that the guy was wrong about my outfit getting wiped out. I decided to get under the covers for the last time in my room. As I lay in bed, I still couldn't get the thoughts of my buddies back in Nam out of my head. I was thinking about Lefefe, Lieutenant Libutti, Frank Bignami, Whitey, Dale, Maxwell, Kenny Fulton, Van, Lugar, Ron Francis, Duvall, Charlie Horton, Jerry Moore, Kenny Fulton, Speedy Gonzales, Boni, Sullivan, Bradley, Hughart, Robbins, Ritivan and the rest of the guys but somehow I fell off to sleep.

I got up very early and as I did I looked out the window and saw the sun coming up over the mountains that were near by. I made sure that I got all of my gear in my duffle bag and went down to have my last breakfast at the hotel. A couple of minutes later James came by and sat down with me. Neither of us said a word but only ate our breakfast. The owner of the hotel came over to us and told us that he was buying us breakfast and that it was on him. He told both of us that he had had a great time with us and to take care of ourselves. He also hoped that nothing would happen to us when we got back to Vietnam. He told the waitress about us and not to charge us for the food and that we could have anything we wanted. He then left and went about his business. As James and I were eating , someone came into the dining room and said that he heard the 1ˢᵗ Battalion 9ᵗʰ Marines got wiped out. It was a different Marine this time.

James and I just looked at each other and asked the guy where he got the information. He told us that he heard it at the Air Base. That was all he knew. The other two guys from our battalion came into the dining room. They saw us and said that they heard that our outfit got wiped out. All of us got up from the table and went to our rooms and grabbed our duffle bags. We told each other to meet at the front desk and turned our keys in and thanked the owner. The owner of the hotel could see in our eyes that something bad had happened. The owner of the hotel called for a cab to take us to the airport. As we got into the cab and headed to the air base, none of us said a word; you could hear a pin drop as we drove to the airbase. All we wanted to do was to get more information to see if it was true or not about our outfit. The cab driver got us to the base and we then went into the terminal and were asking guys there if they had heard of anything of the 1ˢᵗ Battalion 9ᵗʰ Marines. No one that we asked had heard a thing. James and I were starting to relax a little. The other two guys from our outfit were at other places in the airport also trying to find out if our outfit had gotten hit or not. When we all got together we still didn't know for sure who got hit back in Vietnam. One of the guys mentioned that today was July 4ᵗʰ.

An Air Force guy got on a stand and said to get on the bus outside when he called off our names. The bus would take us to the other terminal for us to get on the plane. I hoped that nothing had happened to our outfit. I knew that the other guys felt the same way I felt; none of us said another word until we found out for sure. We all got on the bus and it took us to the other terminal. Everyone was talking about how they had a great time here. All four of us were quiet, wondering if our outfit had gotten wiped out. I remembered how Hanoi Hannah had told us for sixty some days by playing the three songs everyday for us that they were going to wipe us out. She had named a couple of days when they were going to hit us but nothing had happened. I then remembered the three songs; "Nowhere to run, Nowhere to hide; We Got to Get Out of This Place" and "Wipe Out."

The bus stopped at the terminal and all of us got out and went inside. There were guys that just had come in from Vietnam. James and the other guys were asking the guys that came in if they had heard about the 1ˢᵗ Battalion 9ᵗʰ Marines and all of them said that the outfit had gotten "Wiped Out." As they were telling us what happened, I wouldn't accept it and I knew deep in my heart that the guys were still alive. I told myself that our outfit was not wiped out. I looked at James and the other guys and each of them felt the same way I felt, that we were not "Wiped Out." The sick feeling was coming over me again, I wouldn't accept that our outfit got wiped out.

We boarded the commercial plane and after about twenty minutes in the plane the captain told us that we would be leaving shortly and that we would be in Vietnam in five hours. At 11:30 hours I knew that we would get to Vietnam around 18:00 hours. The plane started moving and then we were up in the air. Those five hours went by very slowly, but in that time none of us said one word. All of us were thinking about our buddies and how we had not been there with them, if they had gotten hit by the N.V.A. I was thinking that I had taken my Captain's R. & R. and I hoped that nothing had happened to him. I would never forgive myself. My insides were twisting but there was nothing I could do. I never felt so helpless in my whole life. I looked out the window and started saying the 23rd Psalm to myself for all of my buddies. I must have said it a couple of times slowly, with feeling.

The plane was starting to descend and a couple of minutes later the captain came on the intercom and told us that we would be landing in about twenty-five minutes. I kept looking out the window and could see that we were coming down the coast and saw Da Nang in the distance. The sky was a pretty blue with a few white clouds hanging around. My body was getting excited and couldn't wait to get down on the ground so we could find out for sure whether our outfit got hit or not. None of us said a word and all of us couldn't wait to get off the plane to find out what had happened. Finally the plane touched ground and went on over to the terminal where the civilians and military personnel would fly out of the country. We got off the plane and the buses took us on over to the Marine terminals.

We got off the bus and all four of us were asking other Marines there if they had heard of the 1st Battalion 9th Marines but no one there knew. We started walking up to the other Marine terminal to get a boarding pass to go up north where our outfit was. We got about half way to the terminal when I saw one of the guys from my platoon and he called out to me, "Hammer, they're all dead." He started crying and, again started saying, "They're all dead, all dead." The other three guys that were with me gathered around and just listened. None of us could believe what he was staying, and the way he was carrying on. James asked about Alpha Company and again he told all of us that the whole battalion was dead. The tears were running down his face as fast as they could come and he couldn't stop crying. It was uncontrollable and he started rambling on that they were all dead again. I knew that we couldn't get anything more out of him and we let him go. Two of the guys went up to the terminal to get a flight to get up north. He was with our platoon for about a month and was a runner for Lieutenant Libutti. James looked at me and said that he was going on over to the P.X. and get some goodies for the guys in his platoon. I thought about it and I decided to go with him and both of us went on over to the P.X. and I grabbed a cart and started getting cigarettes, candies, soda, juice. I spent about two hundred dollars and took the stuff back to the first Marine Terminal and stayed there for the night. James came over to me and said that he was in one of the huts and there was some room for me so I followed him and we stayed there with the other two guys from our outfit.

Morning came and all four of us headed to the other terminal to get on the first C-130 to go up north. We received the first four numbers and waited until it was time for the first plane to arrive. The time was 09:30 and they called our numbers and I grabbed my goodies as well as James and the other guys and we boarded the plane. The date was July 5, 1967. We finally reached Dong Ha and the C-130 landed and we got off. We walked down to where our outfit was, James went over to where Alpha Company was and the other two guys to their company, Bravo and Delta. I reached my platoon tent and laid the goodies on my rack and went over to the company tent where the clerks were. I went inside and all of the clerks were quiet. I asked where the Top was and they told me that he was up front. He was the highest ranking sergeant in the company. One of the clerks called the Top and he came in and just looked at me. He knew that both Captain Hutchinson and Lieutenant Libutti were both hit but he didn't say a word to me. I asked him how bad both of them had gotten it. He said they were both wounded but not too seriously. The N.V.A. had almost gotten all of us but there were still a few guys left. I told him that I wanted to get out there today and he said that he would try to get me on the chopper. I told him that he better do more than try. I left and went on over to the supply tent and Sgt. Thomas was still there. I told him that I wanted my rifle and magazines. He went to the back of the tent and got my rifle and only eight magazines. I looked at him and I had told him that I dropped off 18 magazines and was getting only eight. I said, "You better give me more then eight, or I'll kick your ass." He knew that I was not in any mood to fool with and went in the back and came out with six more magazines. He told me that while I was gone we got in more new men and he had to give them some of my magazines. I told him I wanted two bandoleers; a bandoleer holds six boxes of ammo for the M-16. I then gave him one hell of a look, and he knew that he had fucked up with me. When I left Thomas I knew that he hadn't gone out in the field to help the guys when they were getting hit by the N.V.A. He didn't have the guts to be with the guys.

I then went back to my tent and when I got inside there was one guy lying on a cot. I went to my cot which was at the end of the tent; my goodies were in sandbags but were not there on my cot. I asked the guy where my goodies were and he said that the guys in the next tent had them. I asked him why he didn't stop them and he said that they threatened him if he got in the way that they would beat the hell out of him. I put the bandoleers and all but two magazines on my cot. I took my rifle and two magazines with me over to the other tent.. I locked and loaded my rifle and put a round in the chamber and then put the rifle on semi-auto. The young guy just looked at me and didn't say a word. I told him that he had nothing to worry about.

They would not beat the hell out of him. I walked on over to the other tent and as I was outside, the record player was playing one of the Motown songs and the Negroes were singing along with it, inside the tent. I went inside and stood about four feet in their tent. There were twelve of them and all of a sudden they stopped singing. I looked half way down the tent and saw my sandbags with the goodies in them. One of the Negroes was getting ready to take a bite out of one of the candy bars. I pointed my rifle at him said that if he didn't want to die he better put that candy back in the wrapper and get all of the sandbags back on my cot that he took or none of them was going to see the next few minutes alive. I pointed my rifle at all of them. They knew that I was not playing around and I meant business. Some of them were from other companies. I told them that if they ever set foot in 2nd platoon tents again that I would blow them away. Just looking at them made me sick and I wanted to blow everyone away. I was hoping they would give me a little excuse so I could kill them. The Negro got up and quickly picked up the three bags of goodies and took them back on over to my cot. When the Negro came back, I told them all if they did anything to the young guy in my tent that I would personally come over here and "Kill you assholes. Do you assholes understand?" and they all shook their heads. I told them the only way you're brave is when you're together and pick on one White guy especially when he is 5'8" tall. I then said, "None of you have the balls to be out in the field with the rest of the men in our outfit that are fighting the N.V.A. Now that I'm here, if you want to try me out I will be next door waiting to kill every damn one of you." I told them if they didn't belong to Charlie Company that they better get their sorry asses out of here now and for good. I looked into each and everyone of them in their eyes and I could tell that they didn't have the guts to fight me. I slowly walked out of their tent and went back to my tent. I got back to my cot and sat down. I was still pissed and I was hoping that the stupid asses would, take me up and come over to my tent. I put my rifle on my cot in case the bastards wanted to take me on but I knew that they wanted no part of a guy that is 6' 3."

I opened up my sea bag and took out my jungles clothes and changed. I took the bandoleers and took out the ammo which were in the boxes. I grabbed the magazines that didn't have any ammo and started filling them back up, fifteen rounds each. The guy in the tent was watching me and asked me who I was and I told him that everyone called me The Hammer. He then walked down and sat on the cot next to me and said that he heard about me. He told me that I was a bad son-of-a-bitch in this outfit. I was thinking to myself "I'm a bad ass? When did this happen." He had black hair and was about 5' 7" tall and looked just like the leader of the Bowery Boys in the movie; he could have been his twin brother. I asked him what his name was and he told me that it was Glenn Gangware. I asked him if he was new and he said, "Yes." He came out to the field the day I left on R.

& R., which was June 30th. Gangware then said that he should have been dead but played dead to the N.V.A He told me that a grenade went off and knocked him out and after a couple of minutes he awoke and could hear the enemy checking on the Marines that were lying around, shooting each one and when they came to him Gangware said that he played possum. He had blood coming out of his mouth and also his ears. They looked at him and went on thinking that he was dead and didn't have to use up one round on a guy that was already dead. I knew that he couldn't tell me about the rest of the guys in the platoon since he had not been with them that long. I had finished loading the rest of the magazines with sixteen rounds each. I put the magazines into the bandoleers. I just hated these magazines because they felt cheap and they were easy to jam as well as the M-16 rifle. I was just about ready and then made sure that I had all three of my canteens filled with water. I could feel the heat and humidity rising and I was feeling almost at home. I told him to watch my stuff and that I had to see the Top; Gangware told me that he wanted to go with me back out in the field with the other guys. He said he was ready to go. I got up and went on over to see the Top. I went inside the tent and he said that if I wanted to get out there to get on over to the chopper pad. I told him that Gangware was going with me and he was all right with that. I went back to my tent and grabbed the sand-bags of goodies and headed up to the chopper pad. Top came out and looked at what I had and he told me that I couldn't take it out in the bush. I then told Top, "Who's going to stop me?" Top knew that he couldn't argue with me anymore and also knew that he owed me big time. Top also knew that me passing out the goodies would cheer up the guys that were out there.

Gangware and I got to the chopper pad and I told the guys there that we had to get out to the bush where 1st Battalion 9th Marines were. They told me that right now they needed to deliver food, ammo and supplies before they could get us out there. The choppers were coming and going as fast as they could getting loaded with supplies to the outfits. The rest of the day went by and the weather got hotter. I went on over to the choppers but they told me I couldn't come yet. I got up every time the choppers landed and each time the pilot would wave me off. It was going on late evening and the last chopper came back and was down for the night. Both Gangware and I slowly walked back to our area and went back into 2nd Platoon tent. The tent seemed so empty without the guys and I felt so far away from them. I got to my cot and just lay there thinking about Dale, Whitey, Libutti, Lefefe, Van, Horton, Moore, Sullivan, Boni, Bradley, Bignami, Francis, Lugar and the rest of the guys and how they were holding up. I could hear the mosquitoes flying around over head of me. I knew that it was time to close the flaps of the tent and to turn on the light inside. As I lay there in the cot, I couldn't believe how helpless I was not being out there with the guys. My mind was racing over the hard times in how many times we were out of water and food and always patrolling the D.M.Z.

I looked over at Gangware and he was writing letters back home. I couldn't write any letters until I knew that my buddies were all right. Somehow during the night I fell off to sleep and morning came. I got up and it was July 6, 1967. I went on over to the chow hall and got something to eat (which was very little) and went back to our tent and grabbed the sandbags of goodies and headed back up to the chopper pad. Gangware went with me and he was proud to be with me. I started wondering what the hell the guys had told him about me but I wasn't going to ask him. Again we sat there and watched them load up every chopper with supplies and each time I would walk up to the choppers, the pilots would wave me off each and every time. I knew that my battalion didn't need that much supplies. As the day went by I asked the chopper pilots if they could get us out to my outfit in the field now. They all shook their heads and told us that it would be impossible. I looked at Gangware and told him that we better get back to our tent for the night. Both of us walked slowly back to the tents. Not saying a word to Gangware, I went on over to my cot and put the sandbags of goodies on the ground. I then laid on my back on the cot and wished that I could have gotten out there today. I really was all alone and I needed to be with my buddies, whoever was left out there. I just didn't know who was alive or dead. My mind was starting to play tricks on me and I felt all alone in the whole world.

After about an hour lying on my cot, I got up and walked outside of the tent and looked up north to Con Thein. Everything seemed to be all quiet up there. I went on over to the company tent and asked the Top if he had heard of anything and he told me, "Not a word." He was also concerned as well for the guys. Top said to me that if he heard of anything that he would let me know. I slowly turned and walked back to my tent and laid down for the night. Gangware watched as I lay down on my cot; he knew that I was really worried about the guys up there at Market Street.

Around 21:00 hundred hours, I could hear flares going off over their position in the distance. I got out of my cot and then the alarm went off at our base signaling an attack and the Top came over to our tent and told us to get to the bunker. I looked at the Top, and only shook my head showing that I was not leaving here and that I was staying. I couldn't believe what I was seeing in front of me. Everyone at the base was scared and it really showed from our clerks in our battalion. I knew that the Top would be scared, as old as he was. He then left and didn't say another word to me. I told Gangware that he better go with the First Sergeant. I went outside. It was dark out and up north, there were about six to eight flares in the sky overhead making sure that it was like daylight. The word was passed that we might get hit with rockets from the N.V.A. here. The guys that were clerks didn't want to go out in the field to help the guys out there because they were scared to death. And these guys called themselves Marines. They acted so tough when the new guys come into the outfit but at the same time they didn't have the guts to help us guys out in the bush when the shit hit the fan. What old timers that were still in the outfit were still out in the field but there were none back in the rear getting ready to leave for home because their time was finished. If there were any back here, I knew they would have been out there on July 2nd. I sat down on the ground and just watched what was going on up there in the D.M.Z. I was hoping that they would tell the rest of these chickens back here in the rear to saddle up and that we were going up there. I had my gear ready and was hoping they would call these guys so we would be going. At 03:00 in the morning there were between six to eight flares still protecting the guys.

Then the alarm was called off and they could stand down at the base. Our clerks were very happy they could stand down and they all went to their tent and went to bed as though nothing had happened. The rest of the guys at the base were happy to get to their cozy little cots as well. My buddies were getting hit up there and the only thing that was keeping them alive were the flares that were going off overhead. Morning came and I still couldn't sleep. I had been up all night and the sun was coming up and now the flares had stopped. I went in my tent and just lay down in my cot for a couple of hours, before the chopper pad opened. I knew that the N.V.A. would not hit them now and that they had time to rest up there.

The Top came over to the tent and told me it was time to get on over to the chopper pad if I wanted to get out there. I gathered all of the sandbags and Gangware gathered his fighting gear and both of us headed on up to the chopper pad. When we got there the guys told us that the choppers were coming in about ten minutes and to get ready. I sat down on the ground and waited. In a couple of minutes the choppers were coming and one of the guys that was loading the chopper waved for us to come. I got up and grabbed the sandbags and headed off to one of the choppers. I got on and sat on the edge of the door with the door gunner and Gangware got on the other chopper. As I sat on the edge of the door, the door gunner was talking in his headset to the pilot that we were ready to go. I couldn't wait for it to take off and then we started up and again just like the day before, we almost landed, but this time we were off and the chopper started to climb. The chopper turned and started heading north and after about five minutes we started heading northeast. We were heading for Market Street. The chopper was about 500 feet high and as we were getting closer, I saw combat gear all over the place. Then the choppers were starting to come down and we landed on the north side of The Strip where the road led due north into the D.M.Z. and Market Street. The chopper landed and I got off with my sandbags, and as I did, a couple of Marines came over to the chopper and get the supplies off of it.

After a couple of minutes, the chopper I was on left as well as the other one and Gangware came over to where I was. I picked up my sandbags and asked this one Marine where 1/9 was and he looked at me. He was a sergeant from another outfit and he told me that they were all dead. I just looked at him and again I asked him where was 1/9 at and again he gave me the same answer. I pointed my rifle and was getting pissed off with the sergeant and told him that he better not say it again that 1/9 was dead because I was 1/9 and that I wanted to know where my buddies were. A corporal came over to his sergeant and told me what was left of my outfit was over near the tree line about 100 meters north of here. The corporal then pointed and we slowly left them. I gave the sergeant the dirtiest look I could give him with his shitty attitude toward me and my outfit. We headed about fifty meters inside the tree line. I came across some of the guys from 1/9 and asked them where Charlie 2nd Platoon was. The guys asked me what the hell I had and I told them nothing. They told me that they were over there by the tree line. As we walked on over to the tree line, Dale Davis saw me and yelled out to the rest of the guys in the platoon that Hammer was back and the guys were happy to see me. As I looked at all of them, I knew they had gone through hell. I could tell that they were hoping that Hammer had some goodies for them like the last time. I asked Dale who got it and he told me to follow him and he would tell me what the hell had happened up here while I was gone.

I told Dale that I wanted to pass out the goodies to the guys in the platoon first and Dale said there was not many of us left. I then gave Dale his cartons of smokes, candy and juice. Then I went down the line to the rest of the guys in the platoon. I came up to Whitey, Boni and Sgt. Lugar and gave them whatever they wanted, I went down the line to Maxwell and Speedy. Then Keeley, Hughart, Bignami and then Lefefe. I still had goodies left and I went to the rest of the guys in our battalion and gave them whatever I had left as well. Every one of them that I looked at when I passed out the goodies were just beat and had no life in them.

I went back to the fighting hole where Dale was and sat down. He told me that Sullivan and Gary Duvall were killed the same day I left for R. and R. but it was in the evening. Dale told me that the next day they were moved back to Dong Ha in reserve to rest. Bravo Company took over where we had been, which was on the north side of The Strip at Market Street and Alpha Company had the south side of The Strip. Dale said on the morning of July 2nd which was Sunday, Bravo Company walked down the road that led down to the river into North Vietnam.

Dale told me that where the road started going down and the sides of the road were about three to seven feet high was where they got it. He said the Captain of Bravo Company didn't want any flanks out at all and that he had just joined Bravo Company. Dale told me that about 09:30 Lieutenant

Libutti told Dale to get the guys out of church and to get their combat gear on and that Bravo Company was being hit. Dale went over to the church and told the guys to get back to the area and get their combat gear on and that Bravo Company was getting hit. When everyone in Charlie Company was ready, they went on over to the chopper pad and got on the choppers that were ready for them. Dale said when they landed up on the north side of The Strip next to the road that lead to Market Street, the snipers were firing at the choppers, trying to knock them down. Dale said when he got off the choppers that the N.V.A. were firing at them from the hedgerow that was next to The Strip. Most of the guys in our platoon made it inside the hedgerow and were separated from each other. Word was passed to get down to Bravo Company and help them out. Dale said that our platoon was the only platoon to reach Bravo Company and carry back their Captain. Charlie Horton was the first guy from our platoon to reach Bravo Company. As Dale was talking to me, I saw equipment lying all over the place from us and the N.V.A. Dale said that Maxwell killed about 200 N.V.A. out in the open field as they tried to take his position and he never moved one inch. I told Dale that you don't ever want to mess around with him, he's a bad ass Marine. I asked him about Lieutenant Libutti and he said that he got hit four times but we got him out of here. I then asked Dale about Captain Hutchinson and he said that he also got wounded a couple of time but he was all right. I told Dale that when I got back to the rear for my R. and R., I found out that I was taking Captain Hutchinson's R. & R. Dale looked at me and in a stern face told me that he and the rest of the guys were glad that I missed this fire fight. Dale said that our X.O. 1ˢᵗ Lieutenant Dixon got wounded up at Con Thein, on the 2ⁿᵈ. There was nothing I could have done being with the guys. I looked at Dale and told him that when the guys needed me I wasn't there to be with them. Dale again told me not to be hard on myself but I couldn't help it. It was on my mind and was eating at me. Dale said, "Thanks for the carton of Marlboro cigarettes, six candy bars and some juice and soda." Dale said that our company had about thirty guys left. I wished that I had more goodies for all of the guys.

As I listened to Dale, Whitey came over and sat along with us. Both guys told me that when they came up here on the choppers, that the snipers were shooting at them from the tree line that was right next to The Strip. The snipers picked off the guys when they were getting off the choppers. Whitey said that one of the choppers got hit about fifteen feet in the air by a R.P.G. round and killed the guys in the chopper from our sister platoon. Most of Charlie Company had to jump out of the choppers on the north side of The Strip because of the snipers. The N.V.A. were all mixed in with the Marines from the tree line down to Market Street and down to where Bravo Company got hit. It was hard to know who was who. Dale said that it was the first time that they gave them gas masks back at the rear. Dale also said that for the first time in a fire fight that the N.V.A. used flame throwers, firing their 152 mm rifles in on top of them as well as the Marines of 1/9. The N.V.A. really wanted to "Wipe Out" the 1st Battalion 9th Marines.

Dale said that yesterday, July 6th, what was left of the 1st. Battalion 9th Marines, was about 100 men between Charlie Company and Alpha Company. The two Marines Battalions that were there, 1st Battalion 3rd Marines and 3rd Battalion 9th Marines told what was left of 1/9 that they were going out with the recon teams. Dale said they were to go out with Recon and set up a small perimeter about 1000 meters to the North. Whitey and Dale said that around noon, they went out with three recon teams. They went down the road from Market Street heading north. The three recon teams told them to setup on the top of the hill, left of the road while the three recon teams went down into the D.M.Z. in three directions, northwest, north and northeast. While the recon teams were looking for the N.V.A. the guys in our battalion started digging their fighting holes. Lefefe told everyone where to be in the perimeter and Alpha Company had part of the west, north and part of the east of the 360 degree circle and Charlie Company had part of the west, south and part of the east of the perimeter. About an hour later the three recon squads ran back to them and said that the N.V.A. were right on their heels. The three recon teams went back to where the other battalions were which was next to The Strip. The guys - what was left of our battalion - didn't move and just waited for them to attack.

Dale and Whitey said they didn't dig the holes deep because they were only to be there for a couple of hours and headed on back in with recon but that had changed. When recon got back around 19:30 it was too late to get the guys to saddle up and get the hell out of there. Recon left the guys there and went back to where the other two battalions were. Our battalion decided to fight it out where they were. They said that the N.V.A. didn't hit them until night and when they did they were throwing grenades at them and in return we were doing the same thing. Whitey asked if I remembered James Stuckey, the corporal that had come last month to our platoon and I said yes, but I never talked to him. Whitey said that he was picking up the grenades that were falling into their fighting hole from the N.V.A. Stuckey was throwing them back while Horton was firing his rifle. The last grenade that Stuckey was about to throw went off and blew his hand off. I then asked if anyone got killed last night and both of them said that about fifty guys had gotten wounded yesterday but no one had gotten killed. There was only one green lieutenant and about fifty guys that were left from out here between Alpha and Charlie Companies of the 1st Battalion 9th Marines. Whitey and Dale said that Van, Charlie Horton, Jerry Moore, Kenny Fulton and a couple of others had gotten wounded, but didn't know how bad.

I asked if the two battalions helped us and both of them looked at me and said, "Hell, no." I asked, "What the hell did they do?" Both of them said "Nothing." They said what was left of us had to pick up our dead and wounded guys in our battalion from July 2nd and of course, this morning, by carrying the wounded men back here to get medievaced. The two battalions just didn't want to move into Market Street for fear of the N.V.A. that were around but yet they wanted the 1st Battalion 9th Marines to protect their asses. The two battalions told what was left of 1/9 to go on the patrol with Recon yesterday; they didn't want to leave from this secured area. All of the officers in our battalion were either killed or wounded by the N.V.A. with the exception of a green lieutenant who just joined our battalion. Whitey said there were three battalions of Marines on the south side of the strip and they were told not to cross over to the north side. They were to make sure that the N.V.A. didn't go down to Cam Lo, but, all of us in our battalion knew that the enemy was only out for one thing and that was to kill all of us from 1/9. Dale said that from July 3rd to the 5th they were picking up the dead men from our battalion and on the 5th they had to use their gas masks so as not to smell the rotten flesh of their buddies. The hot sun and humidity caused the bodies to decompose very quickly. As I was listening, I started smelling the death of our buddies as well as the N.V.A. that had been all around us. I said that it looked like the two battalions that were here to help us made sure what was left of us protected them while they were on the north side of The Strip. They were afraid to go after the N.V.A. and everyone knew that the N.V.A. only wanted to deal with us. Both of them said that they hadn't moved since they landed by choppers from the first day until now. I just shook my head in disbelief.

I asked how many of us were left in our platoon and they started saying off the names of the guys who were still alive, Whitey, Dale, Sgt. Lefefe, Sgt. Lugar, Bignami, Boni, Keeley, Speedy, and Hammer. The guys that were wounded and might be back were Van, Charlie Horton, Gerry Moore, Hughart, Kenny Fulton, and Maxwell. I told them when I left six days ago, there were twenty-four of us in the platoon and now there were only nine. Whitey said there was one more guy in our platoon and he left carrying one of the dead Marines back to a staging area and the next thing he took off on a six-by with the dead men. Dale said that it was Larry Robbins and I knew that he came from my home town. I told them that if I saw him that I would kill him for running out on the guys. Both of them told me that I had to get behind them because they we going to kill him first.

Whitey said that I would have been proud of Dale because he saved the guys in his squad by moving up front and killing the N.V.A. machine gun in-placement that was in the tree line. As the other N.V.A.'s were trying to get to their machine gun, Dale was knocking them off with disregard to his own life. Whitey said I had been right saying that someday Dale was going to save their sorry asses. Whitey said that he had a lot of respect for Dale and he was very proud to know him. As I listened, I could tell Whitey really trusted Dale and knew that he was with two guys that would give their lives for the other guys in the outfit. Dale said that he saw one of the guys from another platoon getting hit about seven times and while he was killing the N.V.A. to save the rest of the guys around him, he slowly fell to the ground and died. Whitey and Dale said how proud they were of the guys in our battalion because no one retreated and everyone fought side by side in upholding our name, "The 1st Battalion 9th Marines," with the exception of Larry Robbins who took off and never came back. Both of them said that the M-16s had jammed on most of the guys while trying to kill the N.V.A. on July 2nd as well as on the night of the 6th.

I knew that this was the best damn Marine outfit in Vietnam and the other outfits couldn't match up to us at all. I was proud to be with what was left of the guys and know them. As I listened, both of them were looking at me and could tell I wished that I had been here. They both told me there was nothing I could have done if I was here on the 2nd or the 6th. They were trying to make me feel good but I knew deep inside of me that it was going to stay with me for the rest of my life, missing the fire fights of the 2nd and 6th and not being here for them when they were getting hit.

It was getting close for the sun to go down and the three of us had a fighting hole for the night. What was left of us had the northern part of the perimeter that connected with the other two battalions. If the N.V.A. was going to attack, they would be going up against us and not the other two battalions. We were to take on the enemy if they attacked. Both Dale and Whitey were very tired and really needed to get some sleep. I told them that they had the first two watches and I would take the third. Whitey took the first watch and Dale took the second watch. I laid down under my poncho and had my rifle ready in case we got hit. I just laid there thinking about Lieutenant Libutti and Captain Hutchinson and I knew that I would never see them again. I knew they were alive but I knew that they would never be back out in the field especially with this outfit. I just looked up at the stars until it was my turn. Dale was about to kick me at the bottom of my foot and I quietly got up. I whispered to Dale, "O.K." before Dale kicked me for my watch. I sat up and Dale got under his poncho and quietly went to sleep. About fifteen minutes later someone was coming toward me from the other fighting hole and I quietly called out, "Halt!" Lefefe called to me and identified himself; I whispered to him to come on in. He came up to me and whispered to me that he was glad to see me and asked if everything was all right here and I told him, yes. He then went to the next hole and was checking the perimeter to make sure that everyone was all right.

As I was sitting next to the fighting hole I thought about everything Dale and Whitey had told me. The heat of the day easing up and it was starting to get a little cooler. I could still smell the rotten flesh of the N.V.A. that were around us and feel the loneliness of having missed out on this fire fight with my buddies. The guys that were not here but back at some medical building being taken care of would be going home for good and out of this place. I felt that I had been left out and I wasn't with the guys when they needed me the most. Oh, how I wished that I hadn't taken the R.& R. that the captain made sure I took. It was his R & R. and he should have taken it. I then remembered all of the times when Lieutenant Libutti first came over here and pissed off the guys in the platoon and how he made a deal with me to help him become a damn good leader of 2nd Platoon. I remembered that he told me he was married but did not say much about his wife. I remembered every night he would ask me how he was doing and I told him that he was doing a damn good job and to keep it up, making sure that he would check each of the men at their fighting positions everyday in the field. I also remembered he didn't have to remind us that he was the officer; we all knew he had the bars. I also knew that Lefefe was not around the C.P. group when I was helping out Lieutenant Libutti. Lefefe thought that Libutti was just like the last lieutenant we had in our platoon, another dumb ass. I knew that I was really going to miss him and I hoped that someday I would be able to see him again back in the States. He was like a brother to me and I was very proud of him.

I then remembered Charlie Horton and what he had said to me about getting his second purple heart and how he was going to get it. He told me he was going to get it under his arm and that it was his ticket home. He was one hell of a nice guy and I was sure going to miss him but I was glad that he was going home. I then started thinking about Jerry Moore and I also heard that he had gotten wounded and was being sent home as well. I remembered how Boni tried to mess up the radio that night up at Con Thein when Jerry was acting fire team leader. I then started thinking about the two battalions on the north side of the strip and the three battalions on the south side of the strip and none of them helped out my battalion when we were getting hit on July 2nd . It made me mad because it seemed that no one wanted to be near us especially the other Marines outfits and of course the N.V.A. It seemed to me that every Marine outfit was afraid of us because of our name, "1st Battalion, 9th Marines" and when we got hit, no one really wanted to help us because they knew they were in for one hell of a fire fight. It seemed now that Hanoi Hannah had gotten rid of most of us. I looked down at my watch and I had been up for two hours. I could feel the tears running down my face. I just wished that I could have been here in the fire fight with the guys.

I looked out in front of me and the N.V.A. were watching but they had had enough of our battalion. They knew that they got most of us but still there were a few of us left. I could sense that they were watching but didn't want any more of what was left of us. I looked at my watch and tried to think of home but my mind wouldn't go there. It seemed like my home was here in Vietnam with what was left of our battalion. Home back in the States seemed not to exist anymore. I knew that what was left of us might not be able to make it back home alive. Death didn't seem to scare me anymore and I would welcome it if it came to me. I just hoped that the rest of the guys would be able to finish their tour of 395 days. I looked at the watch and the time was getting close to 05:00, time to get the guys up. I knew that they would be pissed at me but they needed the sleep. I kicked Whitey at the bottom of his foot and said that it was 05:00. He went over to the fighting hole and shortly after that Dale got up and they knew that I stayed up the whole night so they could get a good night's sleep. I covered myself up and looked over to where Whitey was and the Playboy pennant that was attached to his M-16 rifle. Whitey looked a couple of times behind him to make sure that no one was sneaking up behind him. The sun was up and everyone around was getting up as well. I fell off to sleep and the next thing I knew Dale woke me up and both he and Whitey looked at me and wanted to know why I stood most of the watch and I told both of them that they needed the sleep. I could tell that they were mad at me but they understood why I did it and we all ate our breakfast.

Late in the morning the word was passed that we were going to stay here for a few more days. We didn't even move for the next couple of days and the other battalions had us do the dirty jobs by picking up all of the combat gear from both the N.V.A. and from our guys that had gotten wounded and killed. The two battalions never helped us - they just watched us while they lay around. We didn't have any officers to tell off the other battalions to do their own jobs. We only had a green 2nd lieutenant that took orders from the other battalions, and did as he was told. We finished picking up the equipment that was lying around and put them in piles. The word was passed that we were going to move next to The Strip and set up there.

It was July 12th - my birthday I was now 21 years old and I was a man. I stood up and yelled out that I was 21 and I had made it as a man. Dale and Whitey both started laughing and thought that I was really funny, but I was serious. After a couple of minutes standing with my arms up I then sat down with Whitey and Dale and they both told me that the Hammer would never change and someday some girl was going to be the luckiest girl in the world. I looked at them both and they were both very serious. Then Dale said that I was the only guy in the whole battalion that thought about the other guys first and then himself second. Dale said that I did more than my share in this outfit and Whitey agreed. Whitey said this was the second time that I spent money on the guys in our platoon. I couldn't take what they were saying to me and I got up and walked away from them and sat down by myself and started crying. I didn't want to hear anymore about what they were saying about me. All I wanted to do was to make the guys happy over here and to make life a little easier for them. I knew that both Dale and Whitey knew me very well and knew what I was doing for the guys. I got up and went back to them and I asked them to not say anything. They both knew that they had gotten to me and decided to drop everything and just went about doing nothing the rest of the day. We hardly talked since there was not much to talk about. The weather was very hot and it had to be somewhere around 110 degrees out with the humidity. I started thinking that our battalion would never be the same anymore. Most of the guys in the battalion were wounded and most of them had two, three or four Purple Hearts and that they would be going home for good. I knew that there was only going to be nine of us in 2nd Platoon, Charlie Company. All of us lost really close friends and now there were only a few of us left to keep our battalion going. The nine of us had deep scars and all of us had changed mentally. The next two day dragged by very slowly The word was passed that we were moving out.

At 06:30, the word was passed that we were moving out and that we were heading south. What was left of our battalion got saddled up and there were about fifty of us left out of the whole battalion. Sgt. Lefefe told us to get into a staggered column and took charge of all of the guys including the green lieutenant. We headed across The Strip down the dirt road on the south side and got to the village and passed it. We made sure that we were spread out good enough to make the N.V.A. think that we had a large company on patrol. We were heading west down toward Phu An. It took us about two hours and all of us knew that the enemy was nowhere around. We finally reached the road that lead from Con Thein straight south to Cam Lo. Lefefe passed the word to stop and set up a perimeter until the six-bys came to pick us up. Whitey, Dale and I set up facing east from where we had come from but did not dig any fighting hole since the trucks were on their way to pick us up. Speedy, and Maxwell were next to us setting up the machine guns. We sat down and had our rifles ready just in case we got hit again. Dale asked what the hell are they going to do with us since we have almost been wiped out from the N.V.A.? There was only about fifty of us left. We didn't know how many men were left from Delta company and we knew that there were only a handful from Bravo Company. Whitey said that they could take us back to Okinawa like they had with other outfits to receive new men and get retrained. I knew everyone of us wondered what the hell they were going to do with us guys from the 1st Battalion 9th Marines. We could see in the distance the six-bys coming up the dirt highway to pick us up. We had been waiting for a good hour. The trucks drove past us and went up to Con Thein and turned around and came back down and stopped and the word from Lefefe was to get on the trucks.

After everyone got on the six-bys, they started off kicking up the dust off the dirt road and flying all around us. It was almost hard to breathe with the heat and humidity of the day. I knew that all of us were happy to get the hell out of here for awhile. I was thinking about our sister battalion, 3rd Battalion 9th Marines and how they were afraid to help us when we got into a fire fight. I just hoped that we wouldn't have to help them when the shit hit the fan for them. It just seemed that we always ended up helping other Marines outfits when they got into the shit. But heaven's sake, when we needed help, no one wanted to help us, and it showed when we got hit at Market Street.

We reached Cam Lo and some of the mama-sans, young girls, and little children were having fun with the Marines who were guarding the bridge there. The two little boys who had helped Van and me with our bunker and fighting hole were talking to the Marines stationed there. We drove past Cam Lo and reached the blacktop one-lane highway, which went straight north and south and we turned south toward Dong Ha. As we were getting closer to Dong Ha, the six-bys then turned right on Highway 9 and headed west. We got to Camp Carroll and the six-bys took us there. We got inside the gate and they told us to get off. We got off the trucks; they left and Lefefe came by and said that we were going to be here for a little while. Lefefe left and in a short while later he came back with Bignami and Sgt. Lugar and they told us to follow them. They showed us where we were to be and placed the guys from the north section on over to the east section of the base. When it came to the guys in 2nd Platoon Charlie, they were placing one of us guys to a fighting hole. Whitey was first and then it was me and Dale had the next hole. There were two guys that were already there. As I took off my gear, one of the two guys asked me if I was from 1/9 and I just nodded. They told me that they were assigned to our battalion. I went over to see Dale and he told me that the guys at his hole were also assigned to 1/9. Both of us then went over to Whitey and he said the same thing. Then Frank Bignami came over and said that he was the first squad leader and that us three were under him with two guys each. None of us wanted to take care of any of these green horns but Frank said that all of us were stuck and he didn't like being the squad leader. We knew that if we didn't take the job these green horns would definitely get us old guys killed. Frank told us to get the new guys and teach them what was expected of them. Frank also said that we would not be going back to Okinawa to refit the outfit but would remain here and be going back out on patrols. We asked him why and he said that the Marine Corps didn't want us to leave but to show the N.V.A. that they were unsuccessful in wiping out the 1st Battalion 9th Marines. The Marine Corps was telling Ho Chi Minh that the 1st Battalion 9th Marines was not dead and they didn't wipe us out. All of us knew - what was left of us - that the Marine Corps had just signed our death warrant, again. All of us then went back to our fighting holes and I asked the two guys if they were new and both of them said that they had come from other Marines outfits, and were cooks, clerks and other noncombatants, plus new men that had just come. The guys I had were a cook and an M.P.

Both guys told me they heard that we really got hit up there in the D.M.Z. and asked if it was as bad as what they had heard. They said that other Marines outfits were really afraid of us now because they hadn't come to our aid when we got into a fire fight. I just sat there listening to both of them and said they didn't want to be assigned to this outfit. One of the guys was a Mexican and asked him his name and he said "Perez." I asked him if what I smelled was him. He said yes. He was on the heavy side and that the sweat was pouring down the sides of his face. I told him that he would not make it out in the field with his body odor; the N.V.A. would be able to smell him for miles. I told Perez that he would be losing a lot of weight and some how he would have to do something with the smell. I asked him what he did here and he said that he was an M.P., Military Police.

I then told both of them there were certain rules out in the field, they had to follow if they wanted to stay alive: First, do not talk. Use all of your senses including your sixth sense. Second, do not sleep on your watch. The N.V.A. would kill your buddies but would keep you alive. Third, pick your feet up when you walk. Don't shuffle your feet even when you're tired, you may set off a booby trap. Fourth, stay as far away from the guy in front of you as well as the guy behind you, even if it was hilly or thick with jungle, just so you see him at all times. Fifth, if you get hit, don't call out for the corpsman. You crawl back to the corpsman but you should never call for him to come to you. The N.V.A. just love killing corpsman. Sixth, always have your rifle ready in case we get hit. I told both of them that I didn't want to know anything about their home lives back in the States; they both understood. I asked them if there was anything else they wanted to know. Both of them said no and I told them both to take it easy while we are back here at the base. I told them that I was going on over to the next hole and would be back in a little while. I walked over to see Dale and he was also finished talking with his two men. Both of us just sat together and I asked Dale how he was feeling. He looked at me and said that we would never leave Vietnam until all of us were dead or got wounded. I looked at Dale and said that I still didn't have a Purple Heart and if I made it back to the States, no one would believe me that I was with the 1st Battalion 9th Marines. I told Dale that I came here March 11th, and here it is in the middle of July and I don't have a Purple Heart. Dale told me that I should be happy that I don't have one. I then asked Dale what happened to our corpsman and he said that Doc Dodson got captured by the N.V.A. on July 2nd and they hanged him and castrated him and stuck his balls and cock in his mouth for us to see. After that we both just sat there saying nothing, just thinking to ourselves.

Word was passed that we had mail call and to come on over to the C.P. tent. Both of us walked on over to the tent and they called out our names and we picked up the letters and packages from home. I had three boxes and a handful of letters and Dale and Whitey both had a large handful of letters from home as well. We all went back to our fighting holes and I sat next to Dale and both of us read our letters from home. Whitey went over to Bignami and Lugar and they sat together as well and read their letters. I was glad to get my letters from Mom. I had a letter from my sister Starr and one from my brother Ryan who was getting ready to go back to school his senior year. When I was finished reading the letters, I then opened up the three boxes and shared them with Dale, Whitey, Lugar and Bignami. I knew that I should have had more than three boxes from my mother. I knew that the clerks back in the company area were stealing some of my boxes.

We had hot chow there at Camp Carroll and I knew that the guys were happy to get it. Again they passed out the rice and Spam for dinner. I didn't eat the rice but I ate the Spam. I knew that it was going to be the closest thing to steak I'd have for a while. The old guys were passing up the rice and ate the other things that they made for us.

Chapter Twenty-Two

The next day came and the guys that were with Alpha, Bravo, and Delta Company were shipped out on six-bys to other places to get their new people as well. As each day went by, a patrol went out during the morning heading north and came back in later in the afternoon each day. The word was being told that they were getting the new guys used to going out on a patrol and learning what to do while out there. We also got a new 2nd lieutenant but he never came out to see us. Us old guys didn't care if the lieutenant came around or not. We all knew that he would be scared and wouldn't know what the hell to do when the shit hit the fan. It would be up to us old timers to get the guys through the shit.

A little over a week went by and Frank Bignami came over and said that we were going out on our first patrol the next morning and made sure that our gear was ready. Frank looked at me and said that I was to carry the radio because I was the only one that knew what to say on the radio. I nodded and he then left. There was one other guy in our platoon that knew the radio and that was Keeley and he was now our platoon radioman. I told both guys that when we went out tomorrow to make sure that their canteens were full of water so that they didn't make any noises, when we went outside the perimeter of the camp to put their rifles on semi-automatic and to make sure that they stayed as far apart from each other. Both of them were getting a little nervous. I knew that we were going north like all of the other patrols going down the hill. I went over to see Dale and he said that we should do all right since there were no N.V.A. on the hill.

We stood our watches for the night and in the morning the guys were getting a little nervous but yet looking forward to going out on their first patrol. Frank came over with the radio and handed it to me and called Whitey and Dale over and the four of us discussed where each of us were going to be in the squad. Frank told Whitey to take the point team and Dale had the rear team; I was to be behind Frank just in case he needed me or I needed him. We all agreed to make sure that we taught these guys how to handle themselves. Frank said there shouldn't be any N.V.A. around but to still keep a sharp eye out in case we could hear or see them. We then broke up and I told the two guys that were with me that one of them would be with Whitey and the other one would be with Dale and do whatever they say. I went back to Frank and he told me that we had four checkpoints and the first one was at the tree line just north of us, the second one was at the bottom of the hill, the third was at the top of the hill and the fourth would be 100 meters from the perimeter. I nodded and Whitey's and Dale's teams came over as well. I took the antenna and bent it down so that the N.V.A. couldn't tell that I had the radio. Frank told Whitey to move out and as he did, I called on the radio to the platoon radioman, Keeley, and told him that we were leaving the perimeter. Frank looked back at me and I just nodded to him that I had just told them that we were leaving the perimeter. We walked north up to the tree line and Frank stopped them with his hand. He then walked up to the point team and talked with Whitey and told him where we were going next. As Frank walked back to me, I called in and told Keeley we were at Checkpoint One. We were in the tree line and were heading east down the hill. At first it was not too steep but the foliage was getting thicker and the trees were all over the hill. We looked like a snake going down the hill. All of a sudden we stopped and the word was passed that the point team was almost at the creek bed. The first team was down on the dry creek bed and set up cover for the rest of us coming down the hill.

Frank was carrying a M-79 grenade launcher and started going down the fifteen foot drop and he got about half way there. I was on the edge of the fifteen foot drop when his M-79 went off and the round hit the rock bed but did not explode. My heart went right up to my throat and Frank looked back at me and the fear in his eyes told me that his heart had gone to his throat as well. The guys at the creek bed were thinking the same as us. Neither one of us moved but just looked at each other. It took us a couple of minutes to realize that we better get the hell out of there in case it decided to go off. I started going down, hanging onto the small trees to keep from falling. I began to fall but Frank caught me and made sure that I didn't fall the rest of the way. I told Frank thanks but we still had about seven more feet to go. I told Frank to make sure that he didn't touch the round that was lying there in the creek bed. Neither of us wanted that thing to go off on us. The guys behind me were watching and were hoping that I could get down to the creek bed without damaging the radio. Frank made sure to really hang onto the small trees that were around us and he made it to the creek bed; now it was my turn. Boy, if I didn't have the twenty-five pound radio and five pound battery on my back I could get down with no problem. I started to go down the rest of the way hanging onto the small trees and Frank was down there waiting for me. He then leaned back up to where I was coming down to get a hold of me. I finally made it and both of us again looked at the unexploded round and we then waved to the rest of the guys to come on down. They didn't have as much trouble as me. I called back to our platoon radio and told Keeley that we were at Checkpoint Two. I told Frank that we better move down the creek bed about twenty meters and take a break. He passed the word to move out and take a ten minute break. Frank and I got off our feet and neither of us said a word about the M-79 going off. We didn't even want to think about it. I then remembered that the M-79 shell couldn't go off until it went past thirty meters to be activated.

Frank then quietly told the guys that they were still making a lot of noise and were too close to the guy in front of them. I knew as well as Dale, Whitey and Frank that it was damn near impossible to not make noise as well as being this close to each other, but none of us said a word to the green horns. They really had to work hard to not make any noise. To be in this outfit you had to do it right or the N.V.A. would kill us. When it was time to leave, Frank told Perez to take point and that he was to take us back to the camp. Perez found an easier way of getting back up the hill. I noticed that Perez had a great sense of direction being out in the bush. The heat was rising as well as the humidity and most of them were sweating except for us old guys. Perez looked like he had taken a shower. The green horns were all wearing their jungle shirts while us old guys, Frank, Whitey, Dale and me didn't wear our jungle shirts. We finally reached the top and I called in that we were at Checkpoint Three. Frank called for another ten minute break and all of the green horns took off their jungle shirts and drank the water that they were carrying. Dale, Whitey, Frank and me just looked at them. This was a very small patrol. What would happen when we go out and walked for two to four hours out in the bush? They had a lot to learn being out in the bush. Us old timers didn't take a drink of water, but watched them and we knew there was a big difference between them and us. It was time and Frank got up and was telling them from the point man on back to stagger their rifles so that the guy in front of them was looking in one direction while the next guy looked in the opposite direction; one rifle facing left, the next rifle facing right and back to left and so forth. These were basic things that they didn't know and I didn't realize that they had never trained for this. But I remembered when I first came over here no one ever told us on how to do the simple things. It was the guys in this battalion that taught the new guys on what to do. Frank got up and said that it was time to finish up on our patrol. We moved westward until we were at the edge of the tree line and then stopped. I got on the radio and called in and they told me to pop the green pop up. I told Frank to pop the green star cluster and he looked at me and said that he had forgotten it. I could see the look on his face that he forgot about the red and green pop-ups. Frank had so much on his mind that it was the only thing he didn't think about. I then reached down in my jungle pants and showed him the red and the green pop-ups and he started smiling and was glad that I had both of them. He took the lid off the green one and used the heel of his hand, pointed it in a 75 degree angle and popped it. The green star pop-up went off and they told us to come on in. The red star pop-up was used for N.V.A. Frank told the guys to move out back to the perimeter and as we got inside all of us went back to our fighting holes. I gave Frank the radio and said that I hoped that I didn't have to carry this damn thing any more. Frank knew that I didn't want any part of the radio from now on. He knew that for now there wasn't anyone qualified on the radio in our platoon with the exception of Keeley, who was our platoon radioman.

When I got back to our fighting hole, I told Perez that he did a hell of a job of taking over point and knowing where to go. He said that he was good at knowing what direction to go. I told them that when we go out on patrols they are usually two to six hours long at time, and this was a very short patrol, they should not have taken a drink of water. I know that the weather is very hot and humid but there's going to be times that they wished they had water. I also said that during the day the water in the canteens would be very hot and they would not be able to drink until sometime during the night. I also told them what Frank said about being too close to each other is a sure way for the N.V.A. to kill more than one guy. You have to concentrate all of the time being out in the field. It is very easy to get lazy out in the hot and humid weather by dragging your feet and the next thing is you would set off a booby trap and your buddies would die. You have to be alert at all time, even when you're dead tired. The last thing is to try as hell not to make much noise out there.

Two and a half weeks went by. It was around the first of August and we hadn't left this place at all. New guys were coming in almost daily and some of the old timers that were wounded were also coming back, such as Van, and Boni. I was glad to see that Van was back here. I wasn't too happy to see Boni but what the hell. All of us old timers were getting bored but then again we didn't want to go out in the bush with all of these new men. Dale came over to me and said there was a lieutenant that wanted to see me and I asked Dale who it was and he said that it was Libutti. I got a lump in my throat. I didn't know if I should see him or not but deep down inside of me I needed to see how he was. Dale said that Libutti was talking with all of the old timers that were left and that he was waiting for me to come over to him. He then told me to get the hell up and see him. I got up and both of us walked on over to the lieutenant. As we walked closer I could see that he looked great. Dale stopped and stayed away from us. I kept on walking toward Lieutenant Libutti. He was thin but looked very old before his time. My mind went back in time when he first came over here and how he got all of us pissed off at him because he thought that we didn't know how to handle ourselves out in the field. I remembered when we were at Phu An and we got motor rounds hitting us and he was at the bottom of the fighting hole while I was sitting on the edge, telling him to take it easy. I remembered the look on his face when we got hit and he was so scared to death and yet he had a platoon to take care of. I remembered that we made an agreement, that I would teach him everything I knew out in the field and how he should handle himself with the guys in the platoon. I was about five feet from him and stopped. The rest of the guys knew that we should be left alone. They all slowly walked away, including Whitey. I stood there not saying a word and just looked at him and he was doing the same thing. After what seemed like a long time but was only minutes, he said that he was being shipped back home. I replied that I was glad that he was leaving this place alive and I hoped that he would never forget us guys, what was left of us. I could tell that he wanted to say something else but couldn't get the words to come out. I stuck out my hand and we shook and I told him that he was the best damn officer 2nd Platoon ever had or would ever have. As we shook hands, I wanted to hug him but I knew that Marines don't do that sort of stuff. He then turned and headed back to one of the tents and left. I slowly walked back, I had a couple of tears in my eyes and I was glad that he was getting out of here alive.

I got back to the fighting hole and stayed to myself for awhile. I remembered the times when Captain Hutchinson would tell me that he knew that the lieutenant would fall asleep on his radio watch but couldn't prove it. The captain always knew that I was covering up for the lieutenant but never pushed the matter any farther. Now, both Captain Hutchinson and Lieutenant Libutti, both two of the most outstanding officers this company and platoon would ever have, were gone. What was left of us now in the whole battalion depended on green officers at the company and platoon level. It was now left up to what was left of all of the old timers in all four companies to keep this outfit alive at all costs. I knew they didn't want us to leave this country because we had made a name for ourselves and it made a lot of other Marine outfits feel safe that we were still here in Vietnam.

Chapter Twenty-Three

For the next couple of days I really kept to myself, I didn't even go and see Whitey or Dale. I didn't talk to anyone and I could tell that I had changed. Dale came over to me after the third day Libutti left and told me that he didn't like what he was seeing of the Hammer. I told Dale that I just didn't feel like smiling anymore and wanted to be left alone. Dale then sat down beside me, not saying a word and stayed for awhile. Then Dale said that he understood and felt the same way. I turned and looked at him and could see in his eyes that he had had it also; he was tired of this war as well. I told Dale that it was hard to smile when you find out that you took your Captain's R.& R. and then come back and find out that your outfit got damn near wiped out plus losing our wounded Lieutenant Libutti, Charlie Horton, Jerry Moore, Sullivan, Doc Dodson, Gary Duvall, Van, Boni and some of the other guys that got wounded as well. I looked at Dale and said that I was damn glad that he, Whitey, Maxwell, Van, Bignami, Speedy, Lugar, and Lefefe were still here. Our club was getting very, very small and I didn't want anything to happen with the rest of us. Dale said he was glad that I wasn't at the fire fight and then told me he remembered the time when I was the only radioman in the company and I called in choppers for one hour to get all of the dead and wounded men out of Phu An, plus kept the company intact. Dale said that I deserved a silver star for that and I told him that I didn't want any medals. All I wanted to do is just take care of myself and my buddies. I told Dale that he was trying to make me feel better and that it was not going to work. I then cracked a little smile and he saw it. Dale knew that he got me back and then got up and said that he had to get back to the guys.

A week went by and every day was hot and humid and very boring. Whitey came over and said that Maxwell got his orders to go back home. I was happy to hear that Maxwell made it. One day as I came back from the mess tent I felt a stone in the bottom of my right foot. Getting closer to my fighting hole I could feel the pain getting worse. I then sat down and took off my combat boot. It was the first time I had taken off the boot in over three weeks. As I turned the combat boot over I used my hand to hit the boot so that the stone would leave but nothing came out. I rubbed the bottom of my foot and it really hurt right in the middle. I put the boot back on and went over to our new corpsman who took over for Doc Dodson. He was Doc Robby and he checked it out. I told him that I had a pain in the bottom of my right foot and it felt like it was getting worse. He told me to take off the boot and sock and looked at my foot and said that nothing was wrong. He then pushed the bottom of my foot and I jumped. He told me to go on over to the Battalion Aid Station. This time I just put my foot into the boot and did not tie it up and walked on over to the Battalion Aid Station. As I walked on over, the pain got even worse and I was now starting to limp. I repeated myself to the corpsman and doctor there and took off my boot and again they both said that there was nothing wrong with my foot. The doctor started pushing in on the bottom of my foot and I told him that it really hurt. He went into another part of the tent and a couple of minutes later came back and gave me pills and told me to stay off my feet, with the exception of going to chow, and not to walk around at all. I was told that I was to stay in the bed and keep my foot elevated. I went back to the company tent and told the C.P group that the doctor told me to stay off my feet unless I was going to chow. I went back to our tent and lay in the cot.

The next three days went by and the pain eased up a little each day. I remembered that the doctor told me that I had to elevate the foot all day. One of the guys came over and said that we were going out on a company patrol. Sgt. Lefefe came over to me and said that the platoon was going out on a ten day patrol and that we were not going back up to the D.M.Z. Lefefe told me to get well and that they would see me in a couple of days. Lefefe said that they were going down the road a little and patrol near Dong Ha Mountain. I then sat up and I thought that I could go but as I laid my foot down on the ground I could feel the pain coming back although not as bad as before. I knew that I couldn't be any good to anyone if I tried to go out with them.

I then elevated my foot back up and watched from inside the tent as the guys were getting on the six-bys. The six-bys started off and they were gone. It was lonely being the only one left behind but I knew that at least they were not going back up to the D.M.Z.

A couple of more days passed and my foot was really starting to feel better. A new sergeant came into the tent and asked if this was 2nd Platoon tent and I told him yes. He then asked me which cot he could have and I told him that he could pick any one he wanted. He seemed to be a easy going guy but I just watched him. He had all of the 782 gear that they had issued him back at battalion area in Dong Ha. I knew that he had never seen combat. I asked him, "What the hell are you going to do with all that shit?" He looked at me and said that he was going to use all of it. I said, "Do you know just where in the hell you're at? The weather is over a hundred degrees and very high humidity and you're going to carry all of that shit? Good luck." I told him that he would be losing a lot of weight when he went out in the bush. He looked at me and asked if I was all right and I told him that I was getting better. The sergeant had brand new jungle clothes on and my jungle clothes were brown compared to his, which were green.

Another Marine came into the tent and stopped at the front of the tent and waited for one of us to say, "Attention." The sergeant looked up and called it and stood up but I just laid there looking at this new 2nd lieutenant. The green lieutenant came into the tent and asked why I didn't get up; the sergeant said that I was on bed rest. I then looked at the lieutenant and told him that I was ordered not to get out of the cot with the exception of going to chow. I just looked at him and his eyes meet mine and he knew that I had been here for awhile, because of the way I looked and talked. He turned around and walked back out of the tent and we never saw him again. I couldn't believe the games being played around here.

I asked the sergeant where he came from and he said that he signed up to come to Vietnam where the action was. He said that he came from India and was stationed there doing embassy duty. The duty there was very boring and I just shook my head and told him that it would not be boring here. I told him that he would see a lot of action with this outfit, "You got your wish." He then asked me my name and I told him that the guys called me "The Hammer." He then asked me how long I had been over here and I told him that I'd been here since March '67. Later that morning around 11:30 across from us we saw this one Marine having the shit detail. The sgt. asked me what was he doing and I told him to just watch and he would see what he was going to do. We watched the Marine go over to the back of the head (which was the outhouse) and open up the side panels and take out the barrels that were cut in half and replace them with empty ones. He took out the five gallon can of kerosene and poured it into the half barrels of shit . I knew that by now the sgt. knew what he was going to do and that was to burn the shit from the head. There were four barrels that had shit in them and the Marine got out his lighter and lit it. He took the long stick that he had which had kerosene on it and lit it. He put the stick into each of the barrels and that was how he lit them. But somehow he had gotten kerosene on his jungle pants and he was also on fire. Both the sergeant and I called for him to roll on the ground but he started to run and both of us ran after him and tackled him and put out the fire that was burning his jungle pants. We both checked him to see if he was burned and he was not; he was lucky that both of us were there.

The next day came and the sergeant told me that he was going out to the bush with the outfit. I didn't say a word and watched him saddle up all of his gear and leave on a six-by. Every day I reported to the Battalion Aid Station. I knew that within the next couple of days I would be able to join up with the guys. Around 21:00 hundred two guys came into the tent and went to the far end away from me. One of the guys I had seen before in the company but didn't know his name but the other guy I had never seen before. Both of them were smoking and having a great time. About twenty minutes went by and they were laughing a lot. I then turned over on my side to see what the hell was so funny. One of them would take a long drag on the cigarette and then hold his breathe and then hand the cigarette over to the other guy and he would do the same thing and he would hold his breathe as long as he could. After they would hold their breath, they would then begin to laugh like a couple of crazy guys. After about fifteen minutes I could smell something funny in the air and I knew that it had to be pot. I had never seen anyone smoke pot before and these two guys were really out of it. I turned on my back and closed my eyes. A couple of minutes later I could hear them coming toward me not saying a word and went outside the tent. They then split up. One of them went one way and the other went the opposite direction. I somehow fell off to sleep and the next morning came, I got up and walked down to the other end of the tent. The butts of the cigarettes were on the ground and I knew that they were hand made. I picked them up and took them down where I was at and dug a little hole and buried them.

I had just come back from the mess tent, and as I got off my feet about half an hour later a officer came into the tent and asked me if I had been here last night. I told him that I had and he asked if there were anyone else and I told him that there were two others. He then asked if there was anything strange about them and I told the officer there was nothing unusual. I told the officer that they were having a great time and laughing a lot. He then asked me where in the tent were they at and I pointed to the pole at the other end of the tent. The officer then went down to the other end to look around and after a couple of minutes he asked me how long were they here and I told him about half an hour and they left in different directions. They did not come back after that.

A couple of hours went by and the 1ˢᵗ sergeant who is also called Top called for me to his tent. I went on over to see him and he asked me almost the same questions that the officer asked me earlier. He was studying me as I spoke. I knew that he had a feeling that they were smoking pot. Top told me that one of them went on over to the Commander's tent and called him all kinds of names and was trying to get himself in trouble and was also trying to get the other guy that was with him in trouble. I told Top that they split up outside the tent and that they were never together the rest of the night. Again, Top asked me if they smoked pot in the tent and I told him they were smoking cigarettes but all they were doing was laughing and having a great time. I told Top that I had never seen anyone smoke pot before and I don't know what it looked like or smelled like. He knew that I was telling him the truth. He told me that I was dismissed. I walked back to the tent and I knew that I could be going out in the field in a couple of days. I was ready to go back out.

I went over to the Battalion Aid Station and asked if I could go back out in the field and they said that I could. I then went back to the Top and said I could go out tomorrow back in the field. He told me there was a six-by taking out supplies to the company and I could go out in the morning when it left.

Morning came and I got out of the cot and got all of my gear ready to go out. I went over to the mess tent and got something hot to eat before it was time to go. I got back to the tent and put on my fighting gear and walked on over to the six-by and they were loading it up with C-rations cases for the guys. Top walked up to me before I got on the six-by and asked if I knew they were smoking pot last night. He asked if I was protecting the one guy in our outfit. Top said he didn't blame me for protecting him. I told Top that I was glad that he understood, and yes they were smoking pot. Top said that he would cover for the guy in our company. He smiled and I got on the back of the six-by and sat down up against the cab. I then laid my rifle across my lap and waited for the six-by to leave. It was around 09:00 in the morning and the six-by started up and we were off. The six-by reached Highway 9 and turned left going west toward the mountains. The six-by passed the small bridge we had to protect for a short while and the highway curb between the hills. We were on the highway for about ten minutes and the six-by stopped and the driver inside the cab told me that we were here. I got up and got off the six-by and asked one of the guys where 2nd platoon was at and he pointed on the north side of the highway. I walked on over to the north side and the C.P. group and Keeley was lying on his side resting by the radio. The C.P. group was about fifty feet from the road on the top of the hill. I saw Sgt. Lefefe and asked where first squad was at and he told me down the hill. I walked down the side of the hill and there was a large valley with low rolling hills around. I finally reached the bottom and came across Dale and he told me that he was glad that I made it out here. I asked Dale if there had been any action and he said hell no, it was very boring doing nothing. Dale had a cigarette hanging out of his mouth and I asked him if he was trying to sun bathe out here and he started laughing. Both of us knew that he had a very good tan being here for some time now. I asked Dale how had the green horns been and he said that they seem to be getting very cocky thinking they are as tuff as us old timers. But they would not talk back to us; they knew that if they did they would really pay for it. I asked him if he had been sitting on his green horns and he said you better believe it. I then asked him where Whitey was and he said that he was down by the stream . Dale told me to follow the stream and I should be able to spot him.

As I walked along the shallow stream which was about eight inches deep, and going around the hill, I saw Whitey under a large tree and with his rifle lying across his lap. I walked up to him and he was in very deep thought. I looked around and saw the rest of the guys. They were down away from him about fifty feet. I sat down beside Whitey and not saying a word, waited for him to respond to me. I just looked at the stream and for some reason I knew that something was on Whitey's mind. I decided to wait for him to say something first. I didn't want to come out and ask what the hell was going on. So I just sat there.

After a couple of minutes went by, Whitey turned and looked at me and said that he was thinking about writing to his girl, Roxann, telling her he wanted to break off their relationship. I didn't know what to say so I just let him keep on talking. A couple of minutes went by without him saying another word. Whitey then told me how he had met his girl. Whitey began by saying that he had been driving home from the movies one evening and as he did he saw Roxann walking down the streets of Southern Chicago. He knew her from school and drove past her and went around the block and slowly came up to her again. Whitey said that this time he called out her name and asked her if she needed a ride home. Whitey said that it started to rain a little so she got into the car. They were talking about school since she was going to be a senior and Whitey was on leave before going over to Vietnam. Whitey said that she went to the same school that he had just graduated from. Whitey said that they went out almost everyday before he left for Vietnam. I could tell that he was in love with her and that she was in love with him from the way he was talking about her. He told me that he was going to write her and tell her to go out with other guys and not to think about him. Then Whitey stopped and looked me right into my eyes and said that he was going to die over here and he had had that feeling all day. I asked him, "How in the world do you know that you're going to die?" and he said that he knew. He seemed so sure that he was going to die. A couple of minutes passed and neither one of us said another word, but kept looking at the running water that was in front of us. I just looked straight ahead and said that nothing was going to happen to him while I was out in the field. Whitey slowly looked at me and he knew that I meant what I said. I slowly looked at him and he showed in his eyes that he knew I was not going to let him out of my sight when we were out in the bush. Whitey then had a little smile on his face but I knew that deep down in his soul he somehow knew that he was going to die. I started thinking about Charlie Horton, Michael Poisson, and

Chuck Knight because they all knew that something was going to happen to them. I had that feeling that somehow I was going to make it out of here alive, but I knew that I couldn't tell the guys about it. I just hoped that Whitey's feelings were wrong. I had to get him from thinking about dying over here and I decided to talk about his family.

I asked Whitey if he had any brothers or sisters and he said he had two sisters and that Midge was very close to him in buying him beer when he was younger and helped him out in school. By the way he was talking about her, I knew that she was very, very close to him. Whitey loved his father and mother as well. After he talked about his family he got quiet again and I told him to snap out of it and he looked at the stream and said that he could not shake off the feeling that was over him. I told him that nothing was going to happen to him but still he told me that he couldn't shake off this feeling. I said to Whitey to think about Roxann or his family, but none of that was changing how he felt right now. Whitey said that the feeling was not leaving him and he couldn't shake it off even if he wanted to.

I started thinking about Charlie Horton when he told me that he knew that he was going to get wounded and that the feeling would not leave him. Horton said that the feeling stayed with him for a couple of days and would not leave. He said that he had to tell someone about him getting wounded. Then I started thinking about Michael Poisson and what he told me when he said he knew what guys were going to get wounded and killed over here. I knew that when you get the feeling there was no way of getting rid of it. I remembered the strange feeling that came over my body when I was back at Phu An and it stayed with me for a few minutes during the fire fight. So I just sat there next to Whitey not saying a word but just looking at the stream. It was a good half hour that went by and Whitey got up and said he was going on back to where the rest of the guys were at. He told me not to say what we talked about to anyone; he made me promise him. I watched Whitey walk back very slowly like an old man. I could tell that something was with him as he walked away - I could sense it. I got up and went back to where Dale was and sat down with him and he looked at me and said that I had a funny look on my face and I only told Dale to really keep an eye on Whitey while we were out in the field. Dale looked at me and knew that something was up. Dale made damn sure he kept an eye out for Whitey. I found Perez and the other guy and took off my fighting gear.

A couple of hours later a runner came by and said we were going back to camp the next day and I looked at Dale and told him that I should have stayed back in the rear and he started laughing. He said that it served me right to come out here and then go back the next day. I told Dale that I hoped that nothing would happen to him, Whitey, Lefefe, Bignami, and Speedy. I couldn't tell Dale what Whitey had said to me earlier because he had made me promise not to say anything about it to anyone in the platoon. Night came and as I stood my watch I said a little prayer and asked God if he would make sure Whitey would made it back to the States alive. I said to God that Whitey was a good man and that he shouldn't have been over here in the first place and had already been through enough hell and that he needed to go home alive. I was finished and just sat there looking at all of the stars in the sky and wished all of us could get out of this damn place of death. I knew deep down in my soul that God couldn't get us out of here but only we had to get ourselves out of here to be able to go home. July 2nd changed all of us in the platoon because we knew that we were not going home.

Chapter Twenty-Four

Morning came and we were told that the six-bys were on their way here. Us old timers were making sure that the green horns didn't show the enemy that we were getting ready to leave the area. We made them sit there at their holes with their gear ready to put on until we got word that the trucks were here. A couple of hours went by and we could hear the six-bys coming for us and went past us and turned around and came back. Then we saddled up and got on the six-bys. We got on the six-bys and after about fifteen minutes the lead six-by started off and we headed back to Camp Carroll. Again it took us about ten good minutes before we arrived there. When we got off the trucks and went over to the tents, we were told that we were going to be here for a short while.

I went on over to the tent and grabbed one of the cots next to the end of the tent so I could get out fast if I had to. The rest of the guys were having a good time being with each other. What was left of us old timers just watched them and stayed to ourselves. We all knew that when these guys got into a fire fight and saw their friends get either killed or wounded that they would change very fast. All of them would not be as cocky and as sure of themselves, when the shit hit the fan. Us old timers didn't know how they would handle themselves when we got in a fire fight. As I watched them I remembered that before July 2nd our outfit had been very tight and that the guys knew just what to do when the shit hit the fan. Each of us knew how to watch each other's back and to take care of each other during a fire fight, but we were never as cocky as these guys were. All of us old timers retreated within ourselves and didn't talk to the green horns. As I watched them I didn't like what I was seeing. The green horns were trying like hell to really get to know us and to be one of us. I didn't want to be around them and be their buddy. I just wondered just how they would be able to handle themselves when the shit hit the fan. One of these days they would encounter the whore of war. The rest of the day I just laid in the cot and thought about nothing and tried to get some sleep in.

The next day came and the word was passed that we were getting a new Lieutenant for 2nd platoon. The lieutenant was new from the States. I got to a point that I didn't give a damn if the 2nd lieutenant screwed with us or not, I didn't give a damn anymore. The rest of the old timers also said the same thing and that included Lefefe. A couple of days went by and the word was passed that we were moving to Delta Five. Ted Van Meeteren and Boni came into the tent and said that they were back. Whitey, Dale, Speedy,

Fulton, Bignami, Hughart, Lugar, Lefefe, Keeley, and me were happy to see them. All of us had breakfast and when we had finished, we all walked back to the tent and there waiting for us was Sgt. Dodge. I wanted to talk to Van but I knew that it would have to be later. Lefefe asked Dodge what the hell was he doing and he said that he was assigned back at battalion as a driver to deliver hot chow to us at Delta Five which is an old triangle French fort, about 2000 meters south of here. Dodge told Lefefe that he was needed up at our C.P. Dodge said to the rest of us that he would be bringing down hot food two times a day, lunch and dinner.

Lefefe came back and told us in the tent to saddle up and that we were moving out. We followed Lefefe to the back of Camp Carroll. The second lieutenant was going with us and didn't say a word, Lefefe pointed down the hill to where Delta Five was, a very small outpost down the hill about 2000 meters and about 1300 meters from the village. The fort was built like a triangle; there were only three sides to the camp. Lefefe told us to move out in a staggered column and to head off down to the camp. Lefefe ran the platoon and the 2nd lieutenant just followed him. It took us about thirty minutes and when we stopped for a break, there was this water buffalo looking right at us. I made sure that my rifle was on semi-automatic and pointed my rifle at the animal. The animal looked like it was pissed off with the little boy on its back. It seemed like the animal did as the boy told it and the water buffalo walked out of the water and on over to the vill. Lefefe told us to move out and we did. We reached the outside of the camp and just before we got to the door of the camp, there was a trench about four feet deep and about ten feet wide and at the bottom were punchy stakes sticking upward. They were all very sharp and I knew that the N.V.A. or V.C. didn't want to end up there. There was also Clay Moore Mines and barbed wire in front of the trench about thirty feet just to slow down the enemy if they tried to attack. The walls of the camp were dirt about six feet high. At the top of the walls were fighting holes. In the walls were the bunkers.

We then went inside the camp and Sgt. Lefefe told the three squad leaders what part of the camp they had to protect. Bignami had 3rd squad, Sgt. Lugar had 2nd squad and Van had 1st squad. Boni, Whitey and Davis were also fire team leaders for 2nd squad. I was in Van's squad. Speedy had his own machine gun team. We had the west wall and the large mountains that were a couple of miles away from us and they were very large. Around 17:00 hundred hours the word was passed that Dodge was coming down with hot chow. Dodge came down with his jeep and a small trailer.

I was happy that Van was back with us and wanted to talk to him about what happened to him on July 2nd and 6th . The old timers in the platoon were being fire team leaders or squad leaders, but so far I didn't want any part of it but only to be left alone. Van came over to me and told me that our squad had the west wall of the fort. I introduced the guys in the fire teams and told them that Van was the squad leader. All of us went on over to get the hot food that was in the containers keeping them hot. After we all ate, Dodge then packed up everything and headed back up to Camp Carroll. All of us old timers could see that he couldn't wait to get back up to Camp Carroll. Lefefe came over and told us that we had the block house detail and we were to protect the chief people of the village. They were the mayor, police chief and a school teacher. We then saddled up and headed out to the block house that was about seven hundred meters from the camp and about five hundred meters from the village. We were to stay there for a few days and then another team would take over for us.

There were three strains of concertina wire around the block house. One of the green horns had the radio and Van told me to get on it and tell them that we were here. I went to the radio and took the receiver out of the hand of the green horn and called back to the platoon radioman and told him that first squad was at the fort. I made sure that the radio was in good shape and told Van everything was all right. Around 19:00 hundred hours there were five people coming from the village. One of them was a woman, who was the school teacher. They came inside the gate and went straight inside the block house. No one said a word. Van told the guys to go on over to the two fighting holes that were against the building. From the concertina wire to the block house was only fifteen feet.

The block house looked like a "L " shaped building. There were two small rooms on the first floor and one room on the second floor. The whole building was made out of concrete. I could tell that this was not a very good place to protect the chief villagers but there was nothing any of us to do to change the situation. When morning came (around 07:00), the village people would leave and go back to their vill. They would eat rice for breakfast around 06:00.

Nothing happened the next three days and it was time for us to be replaced by the next squad. When they arrived, we told them to have a nice day. We went back to the old French fort; when we got inside, our squad started working on the fighting holes. For the next couple of days, all we did was work on our fighting positions by filling new sandbags. The rest of the time I spent with Whitey and Dale and we did nothing or hardly said anything to each other. Just being together made each of us feel comfortable.

Frank came over to Van and said that he was taking over the squad and that Van was back to being the fire team leader. Bignami said that we were going out on a patrol and that he wanted me to take one team and Van the other team. Lefefe told him that Recon had spotted a couple of thousand N.V.A. west of here and wanted us to check it out. We looked at each other; we all knew there were only three of us that had been in a fire fight and the rest of the guys hadn't seen shit. Frank told Van and me where we were going and that it was going to be very interesting if we could spot the enemy or not. We told the rest of the guys to get their gear on and we were going out on a patrol. As we walked on over to the gate, which was on the east side, I saw Lefefe looking at Frank, Van and me, I could tell in his eyes that he knew something would happen to us out there but there was nothing he could do about it. Dale and Whitey came over to us and told each of us to watch ourselves and just stared at us as we walked out of the gate. They were also hoping that nothing would happen to us. I knew they could not leave the fort and that we were on our own. When we got outside the gate, Frank told Perez to head west on this red dirt road and we moved out in a staggered column. We followed the road for about two hundred meters when it started sloping down about fifty feet. As it did, the road turned into a small trail and the squad was now in a single column. Frank passed the word to spread it out and not to get too close to each other.

When we got to the bottom of the small hill, the guys crossed a stream and then started going almost south. There were some rice paddies next to the guys. At the stream, the foliage started to get thick and it was almost hard to see the guy in front. We traveled for about five hundred meters and then we turned right and started heading west again. We were going up on a small hill which was about six hundred feet and went on over to the other side. When we got to the bottom of the hill, there was a stream that was going north to south. We headed south down the middle of the stream which was about six inches deep. I could feel the water getting inside of my jungle boots and my socks were getting wet. Again we traveled for about five hundred meters and Frank used his hands to "break" something and the guys knew that it was break time. Frank then showed ten fingers and waved the guys to get out of the center of the stream. Frank then motioned to Van and me to come up to where he was; when we got there he whispered to us that we were going about two hundred meters down the stream and then start heading southeast then east and back to the fort. Frank told Van to take the rear point team and I was to take the point team but have Perez at point man to take us back to the fort.

When the ten minute break was over, I motioned to the team to take point and as they headed up to the front, they were scared to death. Frank told Perez to remain at point man for the squad. Perez pointed to me that it was time to go up the hill heading southeast. I nodded and he started going up the hill. I looked back and pointed to Frank that we were heading up the hill. We got to the top of the hill and I pointed to Perez to start heading more eastward. He agreed and started off. We had walked through a lot of brush and then we reached a small hill close by the fort. Perez stopped and I walked up to him and asked him what was wrong. He said that we were in a mine field. I told him not to move and that I would be right back. I went back to Frank and told him that we were in a mine field and what the hell did he want to do? Frank said there were only three of us that knew what to do and I told him that I would take point, make sure that everyone picked up their feet, and toes to get out of here all right. Frank agreed and I walked back up to where Perez was and I told him to walk where I walked. We passed the word to everyone to make sure that they walked the same place as the guy in front of them. I told Perez to stay about fifty feet from me. I then turned, knowing that I really had to watch my step. I started out slowly and took short steps and made sure that the ball of my foot landed on the ground first. I really kept my eyes moving back and forth to look for the trip wire. I must have moved about twenty feet when I came across a trip wire. I slowly raised one foot very high and then the other foot the same way. I then waved for Perez to come up to me and I then pointed at the wire; I made sure that he saw it and then moved out and he did the same thing as I had done to get over it. He waved the next guy up and repeated what I had done to him and everyone did the same thing.

I went another fifty meters and I out of the mine field. I waited for the rest of the squad to get out. In front of me was a dip that went up about fifty feet. I waved for Perez to come up and to take over the job of being the point man. The trail was starting to lead into where the red dirt was. I pointed to Perez to stop and I would be right back. I went on my own down into the dip and back up the hill and when I got to the top, saw we had made it to the fort which was about six hundred meters ahead. I went back and waved to Perez to come on up. He started moving and came up to me and I told him to keep on going until we all reached the fort.

As we got to the entrance of the fort, Frank told the guys to put their rifles on safe and to take the round out of the chamber. As we walked inside, the old timers were happy to see us back and that we hadn't run into the N.V.A. Lefefe was happy that we came back and went back to what he was doing. I went on over to our fighting hole and put my gear down and made sure that it was ready in case we got hit. I made sure that I had everything ready and that was also my grenades. The guys in the team watched what I did when I got back inside and did as I did with their fighting gear.

Dale and Whitey came over to me. I told them that it seemed that the N.V.A. were just watching us from a distance and didn't want to engage with us at all. They talked with me for a couple of minutes and then they both left. I took off my boots and socks so that my feet could dry out from walking in the streams. I didn't want to have what I had a week ago. I made sure that my socks were empty of the water they were holding and I laid them across my boots so they could dry. I walked around without any boots on the rest of the evening. I knew that it wouldn't take too long for both my boots and socks to dry out in this weather. It was kind of nice to walk around without having my socks and boots on. I put on my socks and boots on when it was time for our watch at 21:00 hundred hours.

The next day the word was that the N.V.A. was still coming toward our fort. Our mortar team fired their tube for about an hour. Lefefe told the platoon to saddle up and that we were going out to look for N.V.A. again. The rest of the guys in the camp got to their stations including the two Army Anti-Aircraft tanks that had twin 40 mm. guns. One of the tanks was facing east from the village southward. The other tank was facing north. Frank came up to me and told me that I was to be the rear point man for the platoon. I nodded, grabbed my gear, headed to the gate of the fort, sat on a couple of sandbags and waited for the rest of the guys to move out. As the guys walked past me, I told them to have a good time out there in the field. Most of the new guys had a puzzled look on their faces at this but the old timers were cursing me. I just smiled back at them and acted like I wasn't going out with them. Dale and Whitey's fire teams were coming and when Dale came I told him to have a nice time, I said the same thing to Whitey. Both of them just looked at me and didn't know what to say.

The whole platoon was outside the gate in a staggered column and we started going down the red dirt road that went west toward the mountains. We were going the same way we had gone the other day. I waited for about fifteen minutes before I left since I was the last man in the platoon. I told the other two guys that were in front of me to stay as far from me as they could. I was a good seventy-five meters from the last guy. We were following the same path that we had the other day. We went over the one hill and down into the stream and moved about almost the same distance. Then went southwest for a little bit instead of going southeast. As I watched both sides and behind me, I kept on looking for blood trails that indicated we might have hit them. Then the word was passed to stop for ten. I looked at the green horns in front of me and they were soaked in their jungles clothes. All of the green horns wore their jungle shirts and all of us old timers didn't have them on, just our flak jackets. They got out their canteens and drank as much water as they could get into themselves. I looked at myself - I only had a few drops of sweat on my forehead. I had a little spot of sweat on both of my knees. I then turned around and looked out the back to made sure that no one came up our backside. I didn't even feel like drinking any water. As I sat there for those ten minutes I thought about when I had first come over here and how scared I was when I was out in the field and getting hit that first night. I could feel the heat of the sun hitting all of us and I knew that most of them were finding out just how tough it is to be out in the bush. I knew that the green horns would have to learn on their own on how to save energy out in the hot sun with the humidity as high as it was. I knew that the slower I moved the better I was in the heat.

I could hear the word being passed to move out and although everyone was getting up, I just sat there. I knew that it would be another five or six minutes before it would be time for me to move out. I really kept my eyes open and ears listening to see and hear if the enemy was coming up behind us. I looked back every couple of seconds to make sure if the team started moving out. When it was my time to start moving out, I got up and slowly and quietly started walking. We had started changing direction and now we were heading southeast. We must have moved about one hundred meters and then we had stopped. I could tell that something had happened. The foliage was getting thicker and the word was being passed that we were going through elephant grass, about twelve feet high. I remembered a couple of times before when we had walked in it and how sharp the edge of the grass was, cutting our skin. It was worse than a razor blade. When it was my turn to go through the grass, I tried like hell to keep from getting cut, although it was hard to avoid. It cut my jungle pants into shredded wheat. My jungle pants went down to my knees.

Finally we got out of it and we were going up on this small hill. When we got to the top of the hill, the word was passed to stop for ten. Again I looked back to make sure that no one was coming up from behind. I knew that in the distance the N.V.A. were watching us on our patrol. Then the word was passed to get ready to move out. One of the guys took a picture of me with my jungle pants that were cut from the elephant grass; I looked like I had shorts on. Gangware took out his lighter and started burning the grass that was about a foot high. I couldn't believe that he did it because I knew that it was a good chance for the enemy to know where we were. I looked around and still I could tell that the enemy was watching us from a distance. The next thing I knew, we were back on the dirt road that led into the camp.

Later that day the word was passed that Frank Bignami was going home and that he had to get his gear together and that Dodge would pick him up. The word was passed that Van was going to take over the squad. I was cleaning my rifle when both Dale and Whitey came over to me and said that I would make a great fire team leader. I told them that I didn't want to take care of anyone but myself. I just wanted to be left alone. But both of them said that I didn't have any choice and that I was going to be one. I got up and went on over to see Sgt. Lefefe and he said I was to take the first fire team of first squad and that Ted Van Meeteren was the squad leader. He said, "Hammer, you're not getting out of it and now you have to take care of three other guys besides you." I said, "I don't want the job." "Tuff, you got it."

I walked back to my gear and both Dale and Whitey laughed at me and said that I would make a great fire team leader. I told them that if it weren't for them, I wouldn't take the damn job. We could see choppers coming toward us landing just outside of our camp. A couple of us were watching and I grabbed my camera and went up to where the choppers were coming down. They were landing between the camp and the small concrete building that protected the village people. I got up to the top of the wall of the camp and started taking pictures with my Nikon 35mm camera. I was taking the pictures as the Marines were getting out of the choppers and setting up a perimeter for the rest of the choppers to land. It took about half an hour for the rest of the company to arrive. Word was passed that it was our sister company, "Bravo." All of these guys had new jungles uniforms and there were only a couple of them that had on dirty jungle clothes. I knew that they were the few that made it through the 2nd and 6th of July. They were going west, the same place we were the other day. I just hoped that they didn't run into any of the N.V.A..

Dale and Whitey were there waiting for me when I went back and sat down next to them and told them that I still didn't want the job of being a fire team leader. Then Dale said, "Remember the time when I had all of my nerves shot and Jerry Moore wanted me to go out there with him on his very first fire team mission out on the strip?" I nodded, remembering how I had gone out there as sick as I was to help him and ended up taking care of the team for him as bad as I was. "Everyone trusts you, Hammer. Everyone knows that you care about all of the guys, not just a couple of guys, but all of the guys in the platoon." I knew that they were right and I knew that I couldn't argue with them. I told both of them that I needed to be left alone for awhile and they got up without saying a word and walked slowly back to their teams. I watched both of them leave and deep down inside of me I knew that I had to be a fire team leader even though I didn't want to be.

I then went on over to my team and told them that I was their new fire team leader and that what I said they would do without question. They nodded and I told them who had what watch and time for the night. I sat down and started thinking about when I had first come over here, the squad leaders were sergeants and the fire team leaders were all corporals. Now the squad leaders were now corporals and fire team leaders were all lance corporals. We were supposed to have a staff sergeant as the platoon sergeant but we had Lefefe who was just a Sergeant. Now, it was just what was left of us old timers to take care of this new 2nd Platoon. We had a green 2nd lieutenant and all of these new guys that had joined us just after July 15th. I then started thinking about Frank Bignami; when Dodge came with the hot chow and when he left, the rest of us old timers came over to Frank and told him that we were glad to see him get the hell out of this place. Frank said that in two weeks, he would be home back in California. All of us had smiles on our faces. Now, we were down to ten old timers left.

I stood my watch for the first time with my own fire team and I asked the Lord for his strength in taking care of these guys and I hoped they would not die under me. One of the guys was eighteen years old and had blond hair, with two other guys that were new to the platoon. I knew that the next day I would have to tell them the laws of combat so when we went out into the bush they would know what to do. I looked up into the sky and could see all of those stars. It seemed like they were on top of each other. I had never seen so many of them.

I called the guys over after breakfast and told all of them what I expected of them when we went out in the bush. I told them not to talk, to stay far away from each other, to not call for the corpsman if they got hit but try to get back to the corpsman, pick their feet up when they walk, stay as far away from the guy in front of them as well as behind, and keep their rifles on semi-automatic and ready to fire. I made sure that they all understood. I told them when we were back in the rear - like a camp - all of us would be doing jobs that needed to get done and that no one including me would get out of work. I could see that they all agreed with that. I told them that I would be watching them very closely when we were out in the field, and if they saw the N.V.A. to open up first so that the rest of us knew. I wanted to make damn sure that they understood me and each of them gave me the O.K. sign.

A week went by and word was that our squad had the concrete block house duty. I told the guys to get their gear on and that we were headed over to the block house. When we got to the block house, our squad settled in for the evening. Van was our squad leader and Lefefe came along with us. It wasn't until 19:30 when the village people came into our small area for us to protect them. I told my team to set up by the fighting hole while the other fire team set up inside the building. It wasn't until around 19:45 that the Vietnamese people were cooking their food. I told my team that I would take first watch for the night, and I informed Van. Everyone settled down and I decided to talk to the Vietnamese that we were protecting. It was around 22:00 when Van came out of the block house and jumped all over me. I couldn't believe what I was hearing from him. I just looked at Van and told him that I didn't need to be told what to do here. I couldn't believe that the power of being a squad leader got to Van's head; he was really acting like a prick. I walked on over to him and told him that I wanted to talk to him in the block house away from the guys who were sleeping. As Van turned around inside the block house and looked at me, I told him to never, ever talk to me like I don't know how to handle myself with the Vietnamese people. I told him that if he did that shit again, I would knock the shit out of him and said, "Do you understand me?" He just looked at me and knew that he had gone too damn far. Van was almost as tall as me. After we got done talking, I left him and went back outside and finished my watch. We never said another word to each other while we were at the block house. I looked at Van and could never understand why he jumped down my throat like he had. I really liked Van and I always got along with him and we never had had words until now. Each day we laid around doing nothing but clean our rifles or fall off to sleep or write letters. Each evening the village people could come to be protected by us at night time. Each morning they would eat a breakfast of rice and maybe some meat mixed in with it, then leave back to the village. When our four days were up and we headed back, another squad from our platoon took over the block house.

When we got back to the fort, orders came for Ted Van Meeteren to go home because his tour was finished. After we had lunch, I watched Ted and Frank Bignami get into the jeep from a distance but didn't say goodbye. The rest of the old timers were happy that he was getting the hell out of this place. Dodge took Van and Frank back up to Camp Carroll. As they left, I kept on wondering why he had jumped down my throat. It seemed strange that the two of us ended off on the wrong foot and not saying goodbye to each other. Some of the guys were playing volleyball outside of the fort. There was one person from the village that was playing volleyball with the guys and it looked like everyone was having a great time. I watched the Vietnamese guy serve the ball by hitting it overhand, and saw that he was very good at it. I went inside the fort and set my gear up and made sure that my team did the same thing before they did whatever they wanted to do for the rest of the day. There was a group of guys in our platoon that were talking about getting all kinds of medals and they were going to win this war over here. They were calling for me to come over to where they were and I told them that I wasn't interested. I went on over to where Dale was, writing home to his girl. I then went on over to see Whitey, who was inside his fighting hole reading Playboy magazine. I asked if he was reading the articles or just looking at the centerfold and he said both. I laughed and sat down and told Whitey that some of these green horns have big ideas about how to win the war and getting a lot of medals. Whitey stopped looking at the magazine and shook his head at me and both of us knew that when the shit hit the fan out there in the field, they would find out that they were not as brave as they thought they were. Whitey then looked back down at the magazine and I just sat there thinking about nothing and just relaxed. I started thinking that these guys would find out how hard it really is being in a Marine infantry outfit in with the pain, hardships, getting hit by the enemy that was trying like hell to kill all of us, the loneliness, getting no mail while out in the field, and death hanging over us at all times. I got up and told Whitey that I was going back to my team to keep an eye on them.

One of the guys had a small transistor radio up loud and I could hear the rock and roll songs that the Armed Forces Radio was playing. For the first time I heard the song, "Blue, Blue, My Love is Blue," then another new song called, "San Francisco," and then another new song, "Give Me A Ticket For An Airplane." They all had a great beat and the words were great. The new guys knew the words of the songs and were singing along with the music. Dale finally came over and sat down next to me and took out a cigarette and started smoking it. I looked at him and said, "One of these days, you're going to die from them." Dale looked at me and started laughing like hell and I started laughing with him. Dale said, "Hell, the N.V.A.

can't kill me and this cigarette is just pure pleasure." I shook my head and smiled. Dale also said that he had to have some bad vices. I told Dale that I was a little concerned about Whitey in the way he looked when I had seen him earlier today and Dale said, "Hammer, do you still think something is going to happen to him?" and I said, "Yes." I told Dale not to say a thing about it but I could see it on his face. I again told Dale to keep a sharp eye on Whitey.

The next couple of days, most of the guys played volleyball and were becoming fast friends with the old timers in the platoon. The new guys showed that they wanted to be your friend. We got word that the whole platoon was going out on a two day patrol. I told my team to make sure that they took C-rations with them for at least three days. This was going to be their first time out in the bush for real. I told Dale to really keep a sharp eye out on Whitey; he said that he would. Lefefe came over to me and said that there would be no squad leader for first squad until they could get someone, which might take sometime. I knew that I was acting squad leader. He also had new jungle pants for me and said that I really looked like a sorry ass Marine. I asked Lefefe if he didn't like my jungle pants and beautiful legs. He just shook his head and walked away.

The word was passed that 1st squad would take point for the platoon and 2nd squad behind them then the C.P. group with mortars and then 3rd squad. I had my team take the point and the second fire team was behind me. Again we headed in a staggered column until we reached the trail at the bottom of the hill and then went into a single file, heading southwest for a couple of hundred meters and then going west toward the mountains. We walked down a stream that was going west and after about 800 meters the word was passed to stop. I raised my hand and told the guys that we were taking a ten minute break. I told them to get off to the side of the stream but stagger the side so that no two guys were on the same side of the stream. I got off to the side and of course there were two very large hills on each side of the stream and as I looked up the side of one of the hills, I could see there were freshly dug fighting holes about half way up. I got up and went to the other side of the stream and looked up the side of that hill and again about half way up the hill were also freshly dug fighting holes. A cold feeling ran down my back and I then waved for Sgt. Lefefe to come up and as he did I told him to look up the side of the hill. I told him there were also fighting holes on the other hill also. He looked at me and said he was glad that the N.V.A. were not here right now; if they were we would all would have been dead. Lefefe said, "Hammer, we are going about another 600 to 800 meters ahead. Look for a small hill off to your right side about 150 meters high; we're set up there for the day." He went back to where the C.P. group was and about five minutes later the radioman in our squad told me to start moving out. I got up and went to the middle of the stream

Con Thein perimeter, with Bill Gonzales (Speedy) standing, looking east down the strip. April 1967 – picture by Bill Gonzales

Con Thein 2nd platoon going out on patrol. From left to right Ted Van Meeteren (Van), Kenny Fulton, Randy, Gary Kasten (Hammer), and the rest of the guys getting ready to move out. April 1967 – picture by Bill Gonzales

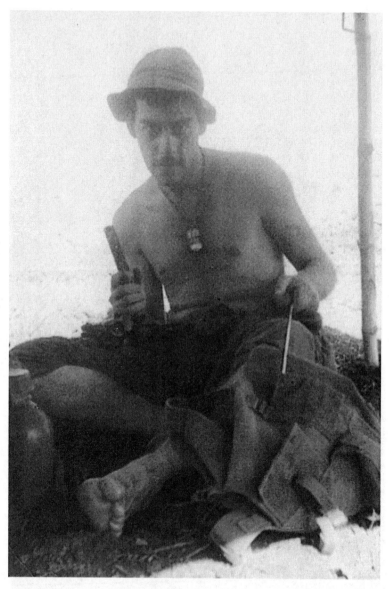

North side of The Strip near Market Street, taken a couple of days before
Charles Sullivan was killed on June 30th.

North side of The Strip near Market Street. From left to right Jerry Moore and Frank Bignami. Late June 1967.

Delta Five, Triangle Fort with Punji sticks, concertina and barbed wire. Middle of August 1967.

Block House between Delta Five and the village. Protected the village chief, teacher and other high ranking people.

Hot chow from Camp Carroll, George Hahner (Whitey) with his back to the camera with his Jungle shirt on: next to him is Gangware. Late August 1967. – picture by Gary Kasten

Delta Five eating C-rations. Right is Gangware. Late August 1967.

At Delta Five, Gary Kasten (Hammer), picture taken by Dale Davis on my camera. Late August 1967. – Picture by Gary Kasten

Delta Five, From left to right, Dale Davis and Doc. Robby
– picture by Gary Kasten

2nd platoon on patrol west of Delta Five, looking for 10,000 N.V.A. Doc
Robby getting ready to take a picture of me. Late August 1967.
– picture by Gary Kasten

2nd platoon on patrol. From left to right, Gangware and one of the guys in his fire team. Late August 1967. – picture by Gary Kasten

On patrol after going through elephant grass, which was about fifteen feet high, ripped my jungle pants. Late August 1967.
– picture by Gary Kasten

and told the guys to move out, quietly. I also told the guys to keep a sharp eye out with ears listening for any signs of the enemy. All of my senses were very sharp now that I had seen the fighting holes on both sides of the stream. We finally reached the small hill and I pointed to the point man to head up to the small hill. Luckily, the water in the stream was only about 4 inches deep at the most. When the point man reached the top of the hill, I told him to stop. Lefefe came up and told me to take my first squad and set up on the northeast side of this very large crater that one of our planes had dropped not long ago. I told the two fire teams to move off the crater and down about fifty meters and set up our two fighting holes. I had my green horns dig the fighting hole and then showed them how to set up interlocking fields of fire. I grabbed two small sticks and put them on the mound of dirt so that they would tell us how far over to the side we could fire our rifles without shooting the guys in the holes on either side of us. Those two sticks were our guides. I then went on over to the other hole and also showed them about the field of fire so they wouldn't shoot at us at night time. When the guys were finished with the fighting holes, I told them that it was time to eat. I could see that they were looking forward to eating, since they hadn't eaten since morning and now it was going on around 18:00 hundred hours. I told them to keep silent and to just listen while we were here. I made sure they knew where their combat gear was and that it was ready in case we got hit. About an hour later Robby, who was our corpsman, came over to us and asked how everyone was. He then left and went on to check the rest of the fighting holes in our perimeter. I knew that he was making sure that he knew where the fighting holes were so if we got hit he would know just where they were located.

As the night was coming up on us, I told each of them when they had their watch that they better not go off to sleep or I'd cut their throats. I was thinking about the bomb crater hole and how big it was. It was about 75 feet deep in the middle and the diameter was about 150 feet. It was made by a 2000 pound bomb. Then I started thinking about how these guys were going to handle being out in the bush with no one around but the N.V.A. I told them all to stay very close to the fighting hole in case we got hit, and when they woke up the next guy, to kick him at the bottom of his foot, and not touch him - they understood. Night was coming early and I laid down and covered myself with my poncho. I was thinking about Whitey and Dale and how they were doing. I could hear the sounds of the insects that were around us. I couldn't sleep and when I did I would wake up and just check to see how the guys were doing on their watch. So far they were doing their jobs right. Then it was my turn and I got up and went on over to the fighting hole and sat down and I could hear there weren't as many insects making noise as there had been earlier. I looked to my left and also to my right side to see if the guys were at their fighting holes as well. I then looked up into the sky and again I could see thousands of stars. It looked so peaceful up there - then down here where we were it was different. I thought about Whitey and I wanted to make sure that nothing would happen to him on this two day patrol. My watch was over and now it was the second turn to watch for the night. I laid down and I didn't have my watch until 04:00 in the morning. I knew that if the N.V.A. wanted to attack us that from 04:00 to 05:00 in the morning was one of the best times to hit us.

I took my last watch and could almost tell that we were not going to get hit by the enemy. When 05:00 came I started waking up the rest of the guys in the team and told them to eat their breakfast and to get their gear together and to get ready to leave around 06:00. They didn't want to get up but to just lie there. I told them that they were not back in the States but here in Vietnam and that the N.V.A. would hit us at this time in the morning. I told them to get up so that they could watch the birdie catch the worm. They didn't like my little joke. Finally they got up and did as I said. They ate their breakfast and got their gear ready to move out. The runner came by and said that we would be moving out in ten minutes. My team had point this morning.

I told them that it was time and to follow me. I took them back up to the crater and I met Sgt. Lefefe who told me to go back down to the stream and still head west. He asked me who the radioman was and I told him one of the green horns. He asked if I would take the radio and stay in between both fire teams. I nodded and grabbed the radio from the green horn and told my team to move out; I followed them and the other fire team followed behind me. We reached the stream and headed west. I got on the radio and told them that we were in the stream and heading west. I had the guys in a staggered column.

About thirty minutes had gone by and I heard on the radio to stop and I then passed the word up to the point man. Then I heard on the radio that 2nd squad was to take over at point and that we had rear point for the platoon. I was told to hand over the radio to 2nd squad when they got to me.

As 2nd squad came up and passed me, Sgt. Lugar came up to me and I asked him if I could carry the radio for his team. He said that it was all right with him. I waited until he passed me and got in between both of his fire teams which were with Whitey and Dale. I got on the radio and said that Charlie 2-2 was moving out and about ten minutes later I got word on the radio for the squad to stop. I told the guys to stop and then a couple of minutes later Sgt. Lefefe came up with the lieutenant and asked me why I wasn't with my team. I told him that I heard from Sgt. Lugar that we were moving up the hill and setting up for the rest of the day. I told Lefefe that my team was all right and that we were just going to the top of this hill that 2nd squad was now starting to go up. Then Lefefe told me to go back to my team and that nothing was going to happen. I still insisted on being with

2nd squad on going up this hill. Sgt. Lefefe said that nothing was going to happen to the squad and all we were going to do was get to the top of the hill and observe for a few hours. Then I told Lefefe if that was all we were going to do, to just let me go with 2nd squad up the hill. Then the lieutenant told me to get back with my squad. Lefefe then said, "Hammer, nothing is going to happen to the guys, I will make sure of that." I looked into his eyes and I knew that he would make sure that nothing would happen. I then regretfully gave in and handed the radio to Keeley and even he told me that it was all right. I watched Whitey and Dale go past me and told them to watch themselves going up the hill. I slowly walked back to where my team was and then in a couple of minutes we started off again.

My squad was just starting to go up the hill and I looked back to make sure that no one got too close to each other. We must have taken about twenty steps when all of a sudden a very large explosion went off. I knew that someone had tripped a booby trap. Everyone just froze in place and didn't move a muscle. As the seconds were going by I thought about Dale, Whitey, Sgt. Lugar and Keeley. I started calling out for Dale, Whitey, Sgt. Lugar and Keeley over and over. Ten minutes had gone by and I looked up the trail and Sgt. Lefefe looked back at me with a strange look and told me not to move but stay where I was at. I quickly told my team and the other team to start looking outward in case the N.V.A. would hit us. I looked back at Lefefe and he told me that he would let me know but I was to stay right where I was. He then went up the trail and it seemed like hours but it was only minutes before the guys brought down one of the dead men. Dale and Keeley were helping carry down one of the guys from their squad. All the while I was calling out for Dale, Whitey, and Sgt. Lugar. I could see now that Dale was all right but I didn't know anything about Whitey. Keeley had a first aid pack covering one of his ears. I looked at Dale as he and the other three guys were getting close to me, and he and Keeley both said that it was Sgt. Lugar. As they got next to me with the dead sergeant in the poncho, I looked in and I saw two large holes in his chest and a great deal of blood.

I looked at Dale and asked if Whitey was O.K. All he said was that he was still up the hill. I then started going up the hill; as I was walking, I could see the scared faces of the guys in our platoon. I was calling out for Whitey and the guys were pointing on up the trail. I finally got up to where 2nd squad was and there was one of the guys lying on the ground on his side. I couldn't see his face, so I got closer to him and as I did I could see a rifle with the Playboy pennant on it. I then stopped; I couldn't believe that Whitey was gone. I then said," Oh, My God...No!" I started calling out to Whitey to get up and quit playing games. Still he didn't move and I took a step closer. Again I told Whitey to get up and not play this game. I knew deep down inside that he was gone but I still didn't want to believe it. I was standing right next to him and started looking to see where he had got it but I couldn't see a thing. I knelt down next to Whitey and turned him on his back. As I did I could see that he hadn't gotten hit in the legs, arms, or chest. I then looked at his face and saw a couple of very small shrapnel pieces, one of which was just above his left eye and the other one in his right cheek. Whitey looked like he was sleeping and there was nothing wrong with him. He had a smile on his face. I looked on the right side of his face and saw the back of his head was gone from just behind his left ear and the back of his head was gone. I could see his brain. It really hurt like hell to see him this way. The tears started coming but there was nothing I could do. I started thinking that I had told him that nothing was going to happen to him out in the field and I had failed him. I started telling Whitey that I was sorry. A couple of minutes went by and no one came up to where I was with Whitey and I knew that I had to get him down off this hill and on his way back home to the States. I got out his poncho and by myself slowly made sure that I got all of Whitey into the poncho and had not left anything behind. I got up and called for a couple of guys to help me get him down off this hill but they didn't move. A couple of them told me that they were told not to move and that the enemy was going to hit us. I looked at them and told them that the N.V.A. were no where to be found and that it was safe but still they didn't move. I went half way down and asked for help and not one of them even moved. I then went up to where Whitey was and I covered his body and I grabbed the end of the poncho where his head was and lifted that part and then started dragging him down the hill. As I went past the guys I still kept on asking for help but all they did was just look to see where he had got it but I denied them by making sure they couldn't see his body from head to toe. Whitey was getting very heavy to drag down the hill but I was determined to make sure that he was going home. I got about a third of the way down and Dale came up and not saying a word, knew that I had Whitey. Dale then got to the other end where his feet were and lifted that part of his body. We then carried him on down the rest of the hill. The middle of the poncho was starting to rip apart and Dale grabbed a poncho from one of the green horns and we again covered Whitey's body in it. We lifted him but both Dale and I were getting tired. Whitey was getting heavy on us. I gave up asking for help from the guys in our platoon and Dale had also had it with them.

We finally reached the bottom of the hill and then Keeley and Lefefe came over and helped us carry Whitey over between the stream and a flat piece of land where only a chopper could land. The piece of land was about three feet higher than the stream. We laid Whitey down next to Sgt. Lugar. The rest of the guys were bringing down James Cools, the green horn that tripped off the booby trap and laid him with Lugar and Whitey. Dale and I both sat down next to Whitey and waited for the chopper to come to pick up the guys. I looked at Keeley who was wounded from the shell. His left ear got hit but he said that he was all right. Dale didn't say a word while we were there. Dale was looking at me and could see that it really affected me that I told Whitey that nothing was going to happen to him out in the field. About twenty feet away Sgt. Lefefe looked at me and knew that I was really pissed off at him and the platoon. He knew that something was going to happen. He kept his eyes on me as each minute went by. I was getting madder at the whole platoon because they didn't have the "guts" to help me carry Whitey down off the hill. Finally, after about thirty minutes, we could hear a chopper coming and one of the guys popped the smoke and the CH-34 landed. Dale and I helped get Lugar, Whitey and Cools onto the chopper. Keeley got on as well to go back to the med station. Then it lifted off and it was the last time Dale and I would ever see Whitey again. I watched the chopper as long as I could until it disappeared.

I then grabbed my rifle and started saying, "Those assholes didn't want to help carry Whitey down off that hill." I put my rifle on semi-automatic and put another magazine in my flak jacket pocket and got up and started walking toward the assholes that hadn't wanted to help carry Whitey down off that hill. Dale started yelling to Lefefe that Hammer was going after the platoon and that he was going to kill all of them. Dale grabbed my arm and started telling me that "It's not worth killing those assholes," but I just kept on walking closer to the hill. The guys that helped carry the rest of the dead men down off the hill got up and came after me. By the time I reached the stream Perez, Speedy, Dale and Lefefe were on me. All of them were between the heights of 5' 6" to 5' 10" and trying to stop Hammer, 6' 3". I walked across the stream and the guys were trying to get me to go back to the flat area where we put the guys on the chopper. They were doing their best to stop me but I was carrying and dragging all of them with me to the hill. I reached the bank and started up the hill to the first guy and was about fifteen feet away and started pointing the rifle at him and Dale was trying like hell to move the rifle away from the kid. I was yelling out, "They all need to die and leave their bodies to rot here."

All of a sudden I pointed my rifle down and at the last second decided that it wasn't worth it, killing them. I then walked back to where we had put Whitey and Lugar on the chopper. Lefefe told Dale to stay with the Hammer and to make sure I didn't walk off into the field by myself. I could tell that Lefefe, Dale, and Speedy had been affected just as much as me in losing Whitey and Sgt. Lugar.

Then the word was passed to get ready to move out. Dale stayed with me and took over my team and what was left of his team. I then picked up the rest of Whitey's gear and not saying a word, got ready to leave. The lieutenant said that we were moving back to the fort. The whole platoon was quiet and they couldn't wait to get back to where it was safe. They had got- ten a little taste of what it was like being out in the field and now they were all humble and didn't like being in the infantry. I really didn't care how they felt about what happened now; they showed me that when the N.V.A. hit us that they would end up dead. I carried half of Whitey's gear and after a couple of hours we finally reached the fort. I walked inside and Dale helped me get off some of the gear that I was carrying. Dale looked at me and said that he was going back over to his hole and to check on his men. I just sat there for about an hour and the guys in my team were really afraid of me and knew to stay away. After about an hour I decided to go on over to Whitey's bunker to see what was there that was his. I knew that I had to make sure that whatever was Whitey's should go home to his parents. I walked on over to Whitey's fighting hole and saw all of those Playboy magazines. I knew that his parents didn't want them. Dale came over and he found a lot of pictures that Whitey had taken over the past couple of months and as we were looking at them, the guys that were in this platoon were watching us. I told Dale if he remembered this guy and that guy and both of us laughed over a couple of them in what had happened to them. There were some pictures of Whitey with his rifle and the Playboy pennant. Dale and I said that anything with Whitey in it went to his parents and the others went to the guys if they were still here. The only guys left were Keeley, Bill Gonzales, Dale Davis, Boni, Hughart, Tony Lefefe and me. Then the word was passed that Dodge was coming down with hot chow and when he got there I just stayed away from the whole platoon until they all got their food. Dale came over and asked if I was going to eat and I told him that I would but I didn't want to be around these shit heads. I got up and went on over to where Dodge was and not saying a word, grabbed some hot chow with Dale. Both of us went over to Whitey's fighting hole and sat down and ate. An hour went by and the word was passed there was going to be a platoon formation. Dale got up and everyone but me went over to the area where the platoon was assembling. Dale went on over there and then came back to me and said that we had to go and I looked at Dale and said that these guys don't give a damn about us and right now I don't give a damn about them. I'm not going. I told Dale that he should do what he wanted to do. Dale got up and went on over to where the rest of the platoon was. The lieutenant looked at me and told Sgt. Lefefe to leave me alone and then started talking to the guys in the platoon. I didn't give a damn what the 2nd lieutenant said to them. Then the lieutenant told Dale, Speedy and Lefefe to leave and that the lieutenant wanted to talk with the rest of the platoon. The lieutenant then really jumped into them by telling them they were not Marines but a bunch a chicken shit, that they didn't deserve to wear the uniform of the United States Marines. I couldn't believe what the 2nd lieutenant said. I knew that he should include himself with them. I knew that he hadn't helped us either. I really didn't give a damn about any of them and I couldn't care less if they died because I was not going to carry them out so they could go home. I didn't give a damn if they rotted over here; they didn't deserved to be buried.

Dale came back over to where I was at Whitey's fighting hole and he didn't say a word to me. He was watching the lieutenant really jump into them and making them feel like shit. I told Dale that if any of them got killed over here that I was going to leave their rotten bodies here in Vietnam. I was not going to pick them up and have them sent home so they could be buried back in the States.

I looked at Dale and I told him that he was the only one left that I was very close to and that I didn't want anything to happen to him. He then looked at me and said, "Hammer, I'll take care of you." I started to laugh and told him that I took care of him when he had heat stroke and the other time when he stepped on a booby trap and blew himself up. I carried his sorry ass out of the minefield. I could see in Dale's eyes that he was just as hard as I was and I knew that he was going to make it out of here alive, even with two Purple Hearts to his name. I knew that if he got one more Purple Heart that they would send his sorry ass back to the States. I told Dale that someone should write to Whitey's parents and tell them that he didn't feel any pain when he died. Dale said that he couldn't do it and said that I should write the letter. He said that I wrote to his parents when he got wounded and when he had heat stroke. Dale said they were glad they got the letters from me telling them that he was all right. I told Dale that I had never written a letter telling his parents that their son died. It was getting late and I told Dale that I had to get back to my team and Dale said the same thing.

I got back to where my team was; they were afraid to talk to me and knew that I hated everyone in the platoon for what they hadn't done out in the field. Then one of them got up the nerve and asked who had what watch for the night. I called out their names in the order of their watch and I took the first watch of the night. They all bedded down for the evening and as I sat there looking west out toward the mountains where Whitey and Lugar had gotten killed, I quietly started crying and wished that they hadn't died. If only that green horn had picked up his feet and not shuffled them, Whitey and Lugar would still be alive. I quietly said a prayer that God would watch over them and also the other guys that I knew had gotten killed. I then said their names; James Fowler, Benny Houston, Sergeant Lugar, Gary Duvall, Gerald Vizer, and of course George Hahner known as "Whitey." I really missed these guys and wished that they were still alive. I could feel the emptiness inside of me and felt like a shell of a man. I looked at my watch and saw that it was time for me to get the next guy up for his watch.

I kicked the next guy and he got up and I then covered myself up and fell off to sleep. I stood my second watch and the loneliness was still with me and I couldn't get Whitey and Lugar out of my mind. For some reason I could almost tell that they were with me, sitting next to me on my watch and telling me that they were all right. It was time to wake up the next guy again and I tried to sleep for the rest of the night. When morning came, the guys came over to me and asked if I was all right and I just nodded. They told me that I was calling out "Dale", "Whitey", and "Sgt. Lugar" all night and when I wasn't calling their names that I was crying in my sleep. I could see in their faces that they were really worried about me. I went on over to Dale and asked him if he had any paper and he said that he was glad that I was going to write to Whitey's parents. Dale gave me some writing papers and walked away from me. I sat down on a couple of sandbags and started writing.

Dear Mr. & Mrs. Hahner, Sept. 2, 1967
I am one of your son's buddies from 2nd Platoon and I have something to tell you. This is very hard for me to write to you and tell you that your son died. I want you to all know that Whitey did not feel any pain and that he had a smile on his face.
Whitey was a very close buddy of Dale Davis and me. Dale and I carried Whitey so that he could make it back home to all of you. I hope that this letter will ease your pain and again, Whitey did not feel any pain.
I pray to God that he takes care of all of you. I wish that there was something that I could do or help. If there is, let me know. Well, I better go, I'm very, very sorry that Whitey passed away.

Sincerely Yours.
Gary "Hammer" Kasten

I showed Dale the letter and asked him if I needed to say anything else and he said that it was very good and to send it. Dale then gave me a envelope and I addressed it to Whitey's parents from one of the letters that Whitey had at his fighting hole. I wrote, "Free" in the upper right corner of the envelope. I took the letter on over to the mail pouch and put it in there for Dodge to pick up later.
After I wrote the letter and mailed it, I still felt very low and wished that Whitey was still alive but I knew that he was gone from us. Dale said, "Hammer, you got to let it go and if Whitey was here, he would tell you the same thing." I agreed with Dale but it was still very hard to let go. I told Dale that if anything ever happened to him I don't know if I would ever be all right. I told him that nothing better happen to him. I was getting a little tired of watching over him and taking care of him and began to smile at Dale while I was saying it. Dale then told me that he was tired of me taking care of him and that he was still mad at me for getting his girl's picture wet when he had heat stroke. He started laughing and said that he was very thankful for me at that time for throwing the water on all six of them that

were down with heat stroke. If it weren't for me doing that, all of them probably would have either died or never would have been the same again. Dale
knew that I was the kind of guy that would help everyone in the outfit and
care about them first rather than myself. I told Dale that I better get back to
my team and give them their watches for the night.

Chapter Twenty-Five

The next morning came and I asked the guys this time if I had talked in my sleep and did any crying. They again told me that I was still calling out "Dale," "Whitey's and Lugar" during the night but this time I didn't cry as much. After breakfast I told my team that I was going to talk to them about what I wanted out of them while we were over here. I again told them the rules: if they wanted to live over here and regardless of how tired they were out in the bush, that they should never drag their feet. I told them if they made a mistake out there in the bush that I would leave their bodies there to rot. They would never go home. I looked into each of their eyes and they all knew quite well how important it was. All three of them said, "We understand, Hammer, and you can count on us." I told them to take it easy for the rest of the day and also to make sure that their rifles were clean since I still didn't like the damn M-16 rifle. I still remembered how these damn rifles all had jammed on us when we went out into the field with them for the first time. I wished that we still had our M-14 rifles. I stayed away from my own team as much as possible and stayed to myself everyday.

Three days went by and the word was passed that we were going out on another patrol, but this time we were going to have tanks with us. I went over to Dale and told him to watch himself out there with these ass holes and he said that his team was ready and I told him that my team was ready also. Both of us knew that at least eight guys in the platoon were ready to face the enemy and were not afraid to fight. The platoon waited until the tanks came; there were two of them. The tanks were outside of the fort and then the word was passed to saddle up and to move outside the gate. As we got outside of the gate, the word was passed to get into a staggered column. We were going to the same area we were a few days ago. After a couple of minutes the tanks started up their engines but they started moving out going southwest and we moved out going west down the dirt road as usual.

My team was rear point and I was in between the guys in my team and I was using hand singles to let them know if they were too close or too far away. I really made sure that they were picking up their feet. It must have been about ten minutes in the patrol when I heard about six to eight very large bees that were about an inch long and about half an inch thick going just over our heads and then in a minute, the column stopped and the word was passed that Perez had gotten stung in the neck by the bees. The word was passed that a chopper was coming to get him out of here because he was starting to swell up. At least the rice paddies were dry at this time so the chopper could come and get him out of here. That was the last time we ever saw Perez. All of the guys knew that I would be watching to see if they were picking up their feet when we started moving back out. We moved west for awhile and headed south and then southeast. When we were going southeast, the tanks were waiting for us. The word was passed that there were about 10,000 N.V.A. heading toward us and all we had was a platoon. Only Speedy, Boni, Hughart, Dale, Keeley, Lefefe and Hammer were left of the old guys in the platoon.

I could hear in the distance that the choppers were coming and as I looked up to see where they were going, they hit a small mountain that was about 2000 meters away from us with rockets. There were four choppers really giving it to them and I was happy that they were getting it. The lieutenant told the platoon that the enemy was coming after us and they were still coming and that we had to get the hell out of here. The word was passed to get on both tanks and boy did the green horns get on them quickly. My team and Dale's team were still on the ground and we told them to get on the tanks. Both of our teams took their time in getting on the tanks without showing that they were afraid of the enemy if they were out there watching us. Then the tanks started up and we moved back to Delta Five area which was our base camp.

We got back to the camp, got off the tanks, and went inside. I told my team to put their rifles on "safe" and to take out the round in their chamber. The guys in my team were proud that they acted like Marines out there and not like a bunch of guys that were afraid of the enemy. They looked at me and said, "Hammer, we did good out there, didn't we?" I just looked at them and didn't say a word. I said, "We'll see how you guys do under a fire fight with the N.V.A." I then got up and went on over to see Dale. I just sat down next to him and didn't say a word. It seemed that most of the time we never said a word - just being next to each other we felt comfortable. I remembered in the past that all of us old timers never talked much but were always next to each other. All of the guys in the past were very close to each other; all of us were from different backgrounds but when the shit hit the fan, we all watched over each other and took care of each other. All of us were going through hell over here and no other Marine outfit knew what the hell we were going through. We knew that no one wanted any part of us or to be near us. This included the N.V.A. as well as the other Marines and Army outfits that were in the D.M.Z. area.

A week went by and the word was passed that Sgt. Lefefe got orders to go home. Dale came over to me and said, "Hammer, Lefefe got his orders to go home; his tour is up." I looked at Dale and I was glad that he was getting out of here. I remembered when Lefefe argued against me, trying to stay with 2nd squad and said that nothing was going to happen to Sgt. Lugar and Whitey. I knew that I would always remember the argument that morning of Sept.1st ,1967 for the rest of my life. I looked at Dale and said that the next one that will be leaving will be me and that will be some time yet; Dale nodded in agreement.

Then Dale and I started talking about Lefefe and how bad a shot he was and both of us laughed until we had tears in our eyes. Both of us knew that he cared about each of us in the platoon and yet both of us were glad that he was leaving and getting out of here alive. Dale said that he had taken care of the whole battalion when we got hit back at Market Street on the 6th of July. I told Dale that we better get on over there to where Lefefe was and say goodbye to him. Both Dale and I saw that his seabag was ready and Lefefe would be leaving in a couple of days. Dale and I slowly walked back and sat down and didn't say a word. As I sat down, I remembered the time when Lefefe told me that he was going to save my life and he then pulled a Lifesaver out of his pocket and gave one to me and said, "I told you that I was going to save your life." I had a smile on my face and remembered that we had walked all morning that hot and humid day. Those were hard days for our company as well as our sister companies in the battalion. I got up and told Dale that I would see him later. I went back to my fighting hole and sat down by myself and started thinking about when I first had come over here and all of the shit that had happened to our battalion all the way up to July 15th. I remembered how proud I was to be with the guys who gave up their own lives to be with us when the shit really hit the fan and how we never asked for anyone to help us get out of a fire fight. I remembered that when the shit hit the fan no one was screaming or yelling when we were firing our rifles at the enemy. The only time we got help was with our own sister companies within our battalion. The only help we got was from the Marine artillery, Army 175s, and the Marine jets, and that was all. The N.V.A. were afraid of us and it took some 40,000 of them to try to wipe us out and they damn near did it. To this day there is a handful of us throughout the battalion that are still here. I knew that everyone had heard about 1/9 now.

I told Dale that it was time to get back to my team. I left and sat down by myself and thought about Lefefe. I remembered a couple of days before when Whitey got killed and I argued with the Lieutenant and Sgt. Lefefe about staying with 2nd squad with the radio. I remembered that Lefefe and I argued for a good couple of minutes and he told me that, "Nothing was going to happen to the guys and that we were only going up to the top of the hill." I remembered the look on Lefefe's face when he came back down and looked right at me and he couldn't come to grips to tell me that Whitey was dead. He just walked past me with his head down. It hurt losing Whitey and Sgt. Lugar and now it hurt losing Lefefe but I was glad that he was going home alive.

The next day Dodge came down with our hot food. Dodge had with him a Staff Sergeant who was our new platoon sergeant, taking the place of Sgt. Lefefe. We just sat around doing nothing and the new staff sergeant, who was a heavy set man and was almost as tall as me, came over and said that the squad I was with was going out on an ambush tonight. He then turned around and walked away and I could tell by the way he walked and carried himself that he had never seen any combat. Again we had another green horn who was in charge of the platoon with the green Lieutenant and that spelled trouble for what was left of us old timers in the platoon.

I told my team to get ready and to get some sleep before tonight and that we were setting up an ambush. Dale came over and said that he heard that my squad was going out on an ambush and said that I was the only one with any combat experience in the squad. I told Dale that I would be all right and not to worry. Dale sat down and without a word stayed till evening. It was time for the squad to leave, I made sure everyone knew what the hell to do out there. I also made sure that I had the red and green star clusters with me.

Staff Sergeant West came over to me and had a scope with him and he gave it to me and said that this is a Star Light Scope and told me to take off the caps at both ends when the sun was totally down for the night. He said that the light from the stars would light up the scope when I or the other guys looked through it. He said that everything would be in green. I nodded my head to let him know that I understood. I told my team to saddle up and that we were about to leave. I told both teams about the Star Light Scope and how to use it. I then told everyone what time they had their watch and what order to be in when we left, which was the same. I could see that the other team was ready. Just before we left, the lieutenant came over to me and told me where we were to set up for the night. He also told me that I was to take charge of the squad for the evening. I didn't want any part of it but I also knew that there was no one that could handle it. I made sure everyone knew that I would be the one that would start firing my rifle first if the enemy came. It was going on 19:30 hours and the sun was getting low in the sky. The squad started out in the same order of their watch for the night; I was in the middle. We headed west down the road and when we got close to the bottom of the hill I pointed to the lead man to go south along with the stream which was north - south in direction. We went about 100 meters and I raised my hand to stop. This would be a great place to hit the enemy if they came. On the other side of the stream was a path that went up about five feet west and then it went into three directions. The one direction was still heading west on a gradual slope and the other path went along with the stream on the other side. I looked at our position and we had small bushes that were about two feet high and the grass was around us was about 12 inches high as well. I looked behind me and saw that we were on the side of the hill that led up to the camp where the rest of the platoon was. There was no way for the N.V.A. to see us, even when the stars come out.

I went to the point man and pointed to him that he had this spot and we would be watching the stream and trail on the other side. I also made sure that he took his time in taking off his combat gear but also make sure that he could get to it fast if we had to get out of here fast ourselves. I went down the line and saw that everyone was trying to be as quiet as possible. I gave the radio and the Star Light Scope to the first guy that had watch for the night. The sun was gone now and it was very hard to see the stream and trail on the other side which was about fifty feet away.

It was my turn for watch and the guy gave me the Star Light Scope and radio; I looked through the scope and boy, did it light up everything in front of me. I could see a good couple of hundred feet in front of me. I knew that if the N.V.A. were around here that we would be ready for them. I kept looking through the scope and hoping that they would come. I could tell they were not going to show up and it was going to be a long night. When my turn was up, I woke up the guy next to me and handed him the scope and radio and covered myself up. I looked at the guy that I had just woke up and he was sitting and looking through the scope for the enemy. He didn't want to see the enemy at all. I knew he was scared like the rest of them. I looked out in front to where the trail was, on the other side. The moon was coming out and it started lighting the place up and I knew right there and then they would not be that stupid to be out in the open on the trail, with the moon out. The next thing I knew, one of the guys woke me up and said that it was time. I looked at my watch and it was 05:00 and the sun was just starting to come up over the hills. I told everyone to saddle up and that we were getting ready to move out. I pointed to the rear point man that he was now the point and to take us back the same way we came in last night. When we got to the road I told them to stop and called in the camp and told the platoon radioman that we were ready to come in and fire the pop-up. The radioman told me to shoot the pop-up and I took the cap off the top of the green star cluster and put it on the other end and then hit it with the palm of my other hand and it went off in a 75 degree angle, toward the camp. The word was passed to come on in and I pointed to the point man to move out and head back to the camp.

We finally got inside the camp and I told the guys to clean their rifles and to relax for the rest of the day. Dale came over to me and said that Lefefe was leaving us today. Dale also said that Lefefe had told the new staff sergeant about us old timers in the platoon. I looked on over to where the big bunker was that was in the middle of the compound that housed the C.P. group. The size of the compound was twenty feet wide and sixty feet long, but I didn't see Lefefe. I knew to myself that I had to play a joke on Sgt. Lefefe for his joke on me when we were down at Quang Tri City. I went over to see Dale and asked him if he had a roll of Life Savers on him and he said that he did. I told Dale that I would like very much to have that roll and he went into his fighting hole and gave it to me. He asked me why I needed it and I told him that it was a joke on Lefefe.

A couple of hours passed and it was time for lunch. Sgt. Dodge came down with the hot food. Everyone was finished with lunch and Dodge was cleaning up and putting the containers that carried the food back into the trailer that was behind his jeep. Sgt. Lefefe went over to the jeep and as he put his sea bag in the back, I came up to him, Dale was watching, I told Lefefe that I was going to save his life and that I had something for him on his way back to the States. I told him to open his hand and I put a Life Saver in it and he looked at it and then gave a big grin. I then gave him the rest of them. Dale started laughing and so did I and then Lefefe got into the jeep and without a word, Dodge drove off back up the hill to Camp Carroll. The loneliness started coming over me and I felt a part of me had just left. Dale felt the same way. Both of us went back to our areas for the rest of the day.

A week went by and the platoon pretty much stayed in the camp. There were no patrols but only the block house detail, which was between us and the village. I could feel what seemed like a rock in the middle of my foot again and I knew that I was going to have trouble with my foot. I went over to Robby, who was our new corpsman, and told him that I was having the same problem as before. He asked me to take my boot off. It was the first time in about a month that I had taken off my boot. Robby looked at my foot and said that he couldn't see anything wrong. I told him that if he put his hand under my foot in the middle and pressed inward that that was where the pain was. As he pressed inward I felt the pain and boy, did I jump. He couldn't believe it and told me to go on over to the C.P. bunker and find a cot and get in it. Robby told me to take the other boot off and let my feet air out.

The next day Robby came over to me and he could see that my right foot was giving off a clear fluid between my toes. Robby told me that it was impossible to move me and that he was going to give me a shot of penicillin three times a day and when my ass was too sore to take the shots that he would put them in my thigh. Robby said that I had trench foot. On the first day he told me to roll over on my side and he gave me my first shot. As I looked at my foot I could see that it was giving off more fluid than before and all of my toes were sticking to each other. It looked like the fluid was wrapping around the toes. As each day went by, my toes turned black and it looked like someone had burned them. Now they were all together and it looked like I didn't have any toes at all but a stump. Dale came over and asked how I was doing and I told him I wished that my toes would heal up. I had been taking three shots a day from Robby and so far nothing had helped. This was the third day and I hadn't gotten off this cot.

My cot was right next to the opening of the bunker and I knew that there was no way I would make it if a round would come in the door. I saw there were clouds in the sky and I could tell that the weather was changing and that the Monsoon season was getting close. I felt the dampness in the air and knew it would be almost any day now for the rains to start.

As each day went by, Robby gave me the shots. Almost any day now, the rains would start. The sky was getting more and more cloudy and the temperature was dropping a little each day. Robby came in and said that it was time for my next shot and told me to roll over on the other side; he then slapped my cheek and gave me my shot. I was glad that he did because the right side of my ass was getting very sore from the shots. I thought to myself that I hoped I would lose my foot so that I could go back home. I would be out of this damn place. But then I remembered that I made a promise to the guys in my platoon that when I got back to the States that I would go out for the Quantico Marines football team. They all told me that I would not have any trouble in making the team. I looked at my foot and wondered if and when this foot would ever heal. I wished that I had never made that promise to the guys in my platoon about playing football. I remembered when I looked into each of their eyes that they knew something that I didn't know. I thought to myself that I only had two years of football in high school but was unable to play my senior year because of my age.

Just then, Dale came in to looked in on me and asked, how was I doing. I just looked at him and said that my ass hurt and that my foot hadn't changed at all. Dale looked at my foot and said that it looked like it was starting to heal and that I would be as good as new in a few days. I told Dale to quit lying to me and that my foot didn't seem to be healing at all. Then Dale told me to quit feeling sorry for myself and to get my act to gather. Dale than said, "Where's the Hammer that I knew?" I then looked at him and said, "O.'K.' , I'm all right" and both of us started laughing. It started to rain and Dale said that he had to get back and get his gear covered up. Just before Dale left he told me that I had mail and he gave me my letters and quickly left. I had three letters from Mom and one letter from Dad. I looked at the postmarks on the letter and put the three letters in order and put Dad's last.

I read the first two letters from Mom and she made me feel like I was back at home and that everything was all right. Then I opened the third letter and she said that the word back at home was that I was either dead or missing and that our outfit had gotten wiped out and was missing. I knew that when I got done reading the letters that I better write home quick. Mom said in her letter that a lot of the kids from high school that graduated with me had heard that I was dead. I couldn't believe how in the world they would know that I was dead but I just looked at myself; I was far from being dead. I started to laugh and I knew that I had to tell Dale about this. I realized that I hadn't written home in a month and the only letter that I wrote was to Mrs. Hahner about her son being dead, which was just a couple of weeks ago.

I looked at my Father's letter and slowly opened it up. I knew deep down inside of me that he knew what I was going through. His letters were very short and he only talked about the house and what he was doing in fixing it up. He would also say that my sister and brother were doing fine. That would be all to his letters. I put the letter down on my lap and looked out the door. The rain was coming down lightly, and the water was coming into the bunker. I remembered back when I was about 12 years old and was out in the woods when it started to rain and I was soaked. I knew that when I got home that my Dad would be waiting for me and that I would be getting one hell of a beating. When I opened up the door he was right there and told me to go straight upstairs and take a shower and to make sure I dried off good. When I got out, I was waiting for him to say that it was time for the beating, but this time he looked me straight into my eyes and said, "When the hell are you going to grow up and be a man?" He would always say it after a beating. I remembered that my last beating was when I was sixteen and I asked to be hit. What had happened was that my younger brother Ryan and sister Starr decided one day to burn the bag bugs that were on the bushes around the house. Ryan got some gas and poured it into a small coffee can and lit it to burn the bugs. I was there but I let him use the gas. Dad came home and saw what was going on and knew that we used the gas to burn the bugs and he was mad as hell and all three of us were going to get it. When we got inside he took us downstairs and told all three of us we had two options; first was three swats with the belt or not watch T.V. for a week. Both my brother and sister said that they didn't want to watch T.V. for a week. When it came to my turn, I decided to take the three hits from his belt. I remembered what he said - that I became a man and took my punishment as a man and he was proud of me. I remembered that my ass didn't feel good about it. I am really glad that my father was very tough on me because I don't think I could have done some of the things over here in Vietnam. I know that I wouldn't have made it my first two months for sure.

Chapter Twenty-Six

The next day came. My foot was healing up and I knew that in about a another week I would be up and around. Today the skies were gray and the rain was coming down - not hard, but steady. I got out my writing gear and wrote to my parents and told them that I was still alive and kicking.

Around 19:30 hours, one of the squads came into the bunker. Dale's team was going out for the night on an ambush. The rains had stopped for the evening and the clouds were breaking up and there were some stars out. After the meeting with the lieutenant, I called Dale on over and told him to watch himself out there. Dale looked at me and said, "Don't I always?" I told him that, "I'm not going to be out there to help you this time, you little fart," and the both of us laughed.

Dale left with his fire team and squad and as he left, I started thinking of the times before when I ended up taking care of him out in the bush. I knew that this time I didn't have to worry about him because he knew how to take care of himself. Dale had it very hard here with the guys; they stayed away from him because of Boni. The only thing I was worrying about were the green horns in the squad and fire team that he was in. I remembered the day back in Con Thein when Dale walked up to a group of us that sat on the bunker with sand bags and passed the word from our C.P. group, and when he left how the guys laughed at his Southern drawl and of course how he wasn't going to make it over here. I remembered I told all of them that one day would come that he would save all of their dumb asses, and he did. I was very proud of Dale and what he had done in keeping us alive. I knew there were a lot of times when he was all alone in the platoon, and the guys wouldn't give him the time of day.

A couple of days passed; my foot was starting to heal and the black crust was starting to break up. I was able to see some of my toes. Dale came in and said he heard that the platoon was getting ready to move out and we were going back up to Dong Ha. I asked Dale when and he said he didn't know for sure but it sounded like in a couple of days from now. The guys in my fire team would check on me each day but I made sure they were always ready for combat. Robby came in and said that it was time to start shooting me in my thigh. My ass was sore, and he knew it. Two days passed and the word was that the platoon was moving out and to get our gear. The lieutenant came over to me and said that I was to stay here until I was able to get up and move around. The lieutenant told me that he didn't expect to see me for at least another week. About an hour later Dale came over to see me for the last time and as we were talking, a 1000 footer crawled down the pole that was supporting the top of the bunker. Both Dale and I were watching it and as it got a little closer to me I asked Dale what the hell he was going to do and he said, "I want to see if it likes you, Hammer," and I told him I didn't feel like sleeping with the damn thing. As it got closer to me I saw it was about 15 inches long and a good 1 ½ wide, and it had a hard shell for its back. A couple of the guys come by and said that it was poisonous. Dale got out his E-tool and cut it in half. The 1000 legger still came down the pole, and about two feet away from my cot. Dale started cutting the 1000 legger into smaller bits and finally it started dropping down on the ground. At first I thought Dale was not going to be able to kill the damn thing. Doc Robby came into the bunker and told me that I was finished with the shots and I should be able to join the platoon within a week.

Dale heard the lieutenant tell the platoon to saddle up and get ready to move out. Dale said that it was time and that he would keep an eye out for my fire team while I was here. I told Dale thanks and he turned and went out of the bunker. After a couple of minutes, I decided to see the platoon off so I got out of the cot and went out side. The sun was out and there were a few clouds. I went on over to where Whitey's fighting hole had been. The platoon was ready to go but the other platoon that was to relieve us wasn't here yet. Dale came over and didn't say a word; both of us were thinking of Whitey. Dale asked if I got a letter from his parents and I told him that I was not expecting any letters from them. Dale missed Whitey as much as I did. Finally the other platoon showed up. We saw that the two lieutenants were talking and my lieutenant was pointing to me, showing the other lieutenant that I was staying here until my foot was all right. My green lieutenant told our platoon to move out in a staggered file up to Camp Carroll. I waved to Dale and he was gone. The other platoon came into the fort and I went back to my cot and laid down.

Three days passed and my foot was back to normal. I went over to the lieutenant and told him that I needed to get out of here and to get back to my outfit. He told me that I could not leave. I went back to my cot and was starting to get mad. I knew that he better let me go tomorrow or I would give him a lot of hell. The next day came and I went over to him in the morning and told him that if I didn't get out of here today that I was going to show him what hell was like. He looked at me and knew that I wasn't a green horn. He told me that at lunch time the driver from Camp Carroll would be down here with food and that I could go back with him. I went back to the cot and got my gear ready.

As I was waiting for lunch time to come, I started thinking about this place and how I had lost two very close friends, Whitey and Sgt. Lugar. Frank Bignami, Sgt. Lefefe, and Ted Van Meeteren got their orders to go home while we were here. I started thinking about Van and how we got into an argument over the Vietnamese people at the block house. For some reason it hurt me deep that we had separated on a bad foot. I still liked Van but I knew that I would never see him again if he made it back home alive. I remembered how the rest of the platoon would not lift a hand to carry the dead men, Whitey and Lugar, off the hill but they didn't mind looking at them as they were being carried down. God, how I hated the green horns in our platoon and how it had changed overnight. I felt like I was being left out and the only true friends left were Dale, and Bill Gonzales known as "Speedy."

When lunch time came the driver was still Dodge. I couldn't believe that he had gotten out of the field and was not with our platoon. We didn't have any squad sergeants at all. Just a couple of green horn corporals. When lunch was over, I got into the jeep and went back with Sgt. Dodge and didn't say a damn thing to him. I knew that he was skating and I could tell that he knew and not a word was said while we went back up to Camp Carroll.

I thought about Sgt. Lugar and Whitey and how I would miss them. Dodge drove me on over to where the platoon was. We had the north side of the base again. He stopped in front of one of the tents and said that this was where the platoon was. I got out without a word and went inside the tent. Dodge drove off and that was the last time I would see of him. I knew that he didn't have the stomach to go out in the bush with this outfit, even though the majority of the old outfit was dead or gone.

I saw Dale sitting on the cot and I called out to him and asked what the hell was wrong and he looked up and said, "Nothing, Hammer." He smiled and said that we had perimeter watch again. Dale said that I could take that cot over there; no one had it. I took off my gear and told Dale that I better inform the lieutenant that I was back with the platoon. I left and reported to the lieutenant and he told me that I had two new men in my fire team. I turned around and left the tent.

When I got back to Dale, I told him that the lieutenant had two new men in my fire team. I told Dale that I better go and check them out. I went into the other tent and I saw one of my men with the other two new guys. All of them were sitting talking to each other. I came up to them and asked the new guys their names and they told me. I then took out the small notebook which I used as my radio book and wrote down their names, services numbers, and blood type. I told them they could call me, "The Hammer." I told them what I expected of them while they were over here. I started out by saying that while we were back at any base camp that they were free to do whatever they wanted to do, but when we went out in the field that I had a few rules that they had better follow if they wanted to live; not to talk out in the bush but only listen to what is around you; always have your rifle on semi or automatic; stay as far away from the guy in front of you as well as the guy behind you; never drag your feet, I don't care how tired you get; and finally, if you get hit out there, don't call for the corpsman but get yourself back to him without a word. I then told them the reason was that the gooks liked to hear the word "corpsman up" and they would start shooting at him, trying to kill him. The gooks don't care about you, just the corpsman. And, I told them that the gooks hate this outfit and if they had their way they would like to wipe us off the map, and they almost did a couple of months ago. I told them if there was a work detail back at any base that all of us would take a turn and that included me. I could see that they liked that part.

Something was going on between the two new guys and I asked what the hell it was. One of them said that he was Jewish and the other one said that he was an Arab. I asked so what? They told me that there was another war going on between the Arabs and the Jews. Both of them asked me if I had heard of the Seven Day War and I told them that I was too busy trying to keep alive over here to worry about another war. Both of them were rooting for their side and I told them they could have this little argument between themselves but when we went out in the bush that both of them better be like brothers and watch out for each other. I told them that if they didn't care for each other out in the bush that there was going to be another war and that war was going to be with me and I told them that they didn't want that. I reminded them that they were American and the N.V.A. didn't give a damn if they were Jewish or Arab. I told them they better not piss me off. I then left them and as I did, I could hear the blond guy telling them they better not piss me off. He told them what happened about a month earlier when this platoon wouldn't help me carry one of my best buddies down the hill. I was going to kill the whole platoon. He told them that it took about six guys to calm me down and hold me back. He told them please don't get The Hammer mad.

I got back into the tent with Dale and I told him that the other guy was making me out as hell on wheels. Dale just laughed and we both just laid on our cots not talking for awhile. I told Dale that I couldn't believe Sgt. Dodge and how scared he was not to be with us. He really liked driving from Camp Carroll down to the Delta Five area with the hot food and going back to Camp Carroll. He was like Sgt. Thomas in that he couldn't handle the shit out in the field. I told Dale that he was happy to be around us when he had the hot food and then when it was time for him to go back to Camp Carroll, he couldn't wait. Dale agreed and said that he didn't have the stomach to be with our outfit.

As I laid in the cot, I realized that I had better get my ass in the other tent with my fire team. I told Dale that I better move my gear on over to the other tent and keep an eye out on them. Dale knew that I had to move on over to the other tent. I got up and gathered my gear and went over to the other tent. There was a empty cot and I took it. I didn't say a word to the guys; I just laid back down and stayed to myself. All three of them watched me but didn't say a word and after a couple of minutes they went back to talking. I could hear them talking but I really didn't pay any attention.

A couple of hours passed and Dale came into the tent and had my mail. He told me that I had a letter from Mrs. Hahner, Whitey's mom. I also had a couple of boxes from my mother. I told Dale to go ahead and open up the boxes. Dale sat down and as he opened up the boxes, I could tell that he wanted me to open up the letter. I looked at it and I began to open it slowly. My mind was going over that day Whitey died and Dale and I carried him off the hill and onto the chopper to go home. I felt myself getting tight all over my body. Dale sat down on my cot, and I began to read the letter. It was typed out on a typewriter. The first thing that Whitey's mother said was they first got word that their son had died from my letter. I stopped reading and I looked at Dale and told him that my letter got to their home before the Marines came to inform them that their son had died over in Vietnam. Both Dale and I got sick to our stomachs. I told Dale that I couldn't believe that my letter got to their home in just four days; it normally takes seven to ten days. The Marines came to their home the day after my letter arrived. She wrote that the Marines were really surprised that she and her husband knew about Whitey before they could tell them. I went back to reading the letter and as I read more, I started to cry. Dale could see that I was starting to cry a little but he still didn't say anything. Mrs. Hahner told me that the whole family was glad to know that their son did not feel any pain when he died and that it eased their minds a lot. At the end of the letter she said to thank Dale and me for carrying out their son so that he could go home. When I was finished I handed the letter to Dale and as he read it he also got tears in his eyes. When Dale was finished with the letter he told me that I better write to them again and to let them know that I had received their letter. I looked at Dale and said that I would.

Dale then asked me if I remembered the time when I wrote to his parents and told them that he was all right and had only gotten wounded. I said yes. Dale said that I was the greatest friend anyone could have had over here. He said that I cared for all of the guys and never put anyone down. I told him to stop with all of this and that he was making me feel really bad. I didn't feel like crying any more and wanted to be left alone. I told Dale that I had to get out for awhile and that I would be back. I got up and took my rifle with me and walked around the base. I just needed to be alone and as I walked, I thought about all of the guys I knew that had died in our platoon and battalion. I started thinking about Benny Houston, Whitey, Duvall, Sgt. Lugar, Vizer, James Fowler and all of the others that died in our outfit, not counting the ones that got wounded and went home, Chuck Knight, and all of the others. I could feel my heart swelling up with tears and I wished that none of us had ever been here. Then I started thinking that if we were never over here I would have never met these wonderful guys. I could hear in my mind the Marine Corps Hymn and how proud I was to be with the 1st Battalion 9th Marines and what we had done. I knew deep down in my heart that we had made a name for ourselves and I didn't give a damn if anyone knew it or not.

I could feel my insides becoming empty again and wished that all the guys were still alive. I walked by the big Army 175mm guns that had saved us from being wiped out a couple of months ago, along with the Marine 105s, 155s and 8 inch guns, plus air power. I thought of the Hahner family and how much they would miss their son. I wished that I had not written the letter because I felt bad that my letter got there before the Marines could notify them that their son died in Vietnam. I remembered what Mrs. Hahner said that she was glad that word came from his buddies first rather than from a Marine who did not know him. About an hour went by and I just looked all around me. I could see Dong Ha Mountain, which was on the other side of Highway 9 and then looked north up at the D.M.Z. and saw the road that led from Cam Lo straight to Con Thein and how everything was changing from month to month. I could see part of The Strip. Then I started feeling very old because the only really close buddies left were Dale and Bill Gonzales. I sure didn't want anything to ever happen to them. All I wanted to do now was to be left alone but I had a fire team just like Dale that I wanted no part of because they did not help me carry Whitey's body down off of that hill. If the old timers were still in the platoon I would not have had any problems in getting guys to help carry Whitey. It was time to get back to the tent.

I got back to the tent and just lay down and stayed to myself for the rest of the day. It was getting close to standing watch for the night and I informed each of the guys what time their watch was. We started our watch at 20:00 hundred hours every evening.

The next day came and I told the team that we were going to rebuild the fighting bunker and also the fighting hole which was next to the bunker. For the next couple of days the team did as I said. Everyone worked very hard. On the third day it had rained all day and I saw that our fighting hole was filling up with water. We needed a little trench to let the water run off. The temperature was in the low nineties, so I decided to take off my jungle shirt, boots and socks and take my E-tool and dig a small trench so if the enemy did hit us we could get into the fighting hole without having water up to our necks. I walked over to the fighting hole and started digging since we were on the side of the hill the water was running down into it. The rain felt great and as I was digging I somehow slid and fell into the fighting hole. I had water up to about half way up my chest. I knew that I could only dig a little bit more but that was going to be all. I also knew that when three more guys got into the hole that more of the water would leave. When I was finished I tried like hell to get out of the fighting hole. When I finally made it, I started laughing to myself about the number of times I tried to get out of the fighting hole.

The next day came and as I lay in the cot I started thinking of home for the first time in a couple of months. I started thinking of Mom and Dad and knew that Dad would be fixing up the house. I thought about my younger brother Ryan, and that he was a junior in high school and that it was basketball season for him now, and wondered how he was doing. My sister was in air line school, and I wondered how she was doing. Then, I remembered that my sister got married to a guy in the Air Force and his name was Michael. I remembered when I first came over here how I thought of home everyday and now I didn't. I couldn't believe how much I had changed. Now, I wasn't thinking of home at all. Home did not exist anymore.

Chapter Twenty-Seven

Two days passed and Dale asked if I had written to the Hahner family and I told him that I was going to write them today. I got out of the cot and went on over to the P.X. to get some writing paper. There I saw these tapes that I could use to talk to my parents so I decided to get a couple of them and use one of the small tape recorders, from one of the guys in my team. I went back to the tent and wrote my letter to the Hahner family which was very difficult but before I had finished, I told them that Dale Davis was the other guy that helped me carry Whitey down off the hill. I asked the guy with the tape recorder if I could use it. I took one of the tapes and put it into the machine and left the tent. I looked around for a place where I could talk in private and decided to talk in the hardback that was used as a "Head," restroom. I went inside and sat between the holes and started talking so my parents could hear my voice for the first time in months.

When I was finished, I took the tape and put it into the small container that it came in and on the flat side I wrote the address of my parents and in the top right corner I wrote, "Free" for postage. I took both the letter for the Hahners and my tape for my parents on over to the mail tent that took care of the letters in our battalion. Bill was working in the tent and I asked him what the hell he was doing here and he told me that he had been wounded twice out in the bush and that now they had him back in the rear doing the mail for the battalion. I told him that I was glad that he didn't have to go out into the bush and he asked how I was doing and I told him a lot had changed in our platoon. Bill nodded and knew what I was saying - that it wasn't the same platoon as when both of us joined it back in March. I told Bill that I still hadn't gotten a Purple Heart and every time I tried to get one, it seemed that the N.V.A. were getting worse at killing me. Bill looked at me and said, "Why in hell do you want a Purple Heart?" and I told Bill that no one back in the States would believe me if I told them that I was with this outfit and I hadn't gotten wounded. Bill said that I had a good point but he was still glad that I didn't get wounded. I told Bill I better leave because I had to get back to my team.

The next day came and again the sun was out and was drying out the ground. I was just coming back from lunch and decided to lie in my cot for a short while. It must have been about fifteen minutes later when I could hear two guys arguing, and I decided to see who the hell it was. As I looked out of my tent, I saw a sergeant and a corporal talking to each other in between the tents. The sergeant told the corporal that his team had shot gun duty on the six-bys; the corporal was telling him the hell with that, that they were not going to do it. The sergeant was a green horn in Alpha Company and the corporal was one of us old timers from before July 2nd. The sergeant told the corporal that if he didn't go on shot gun duty that he was going to the brig. I could see that the corporal, Tom Pierson, then look at him and start laughing and said, "Go ahead." He looked forward to going to the brig. I started laughing at the sergeant and thought that that was the dumbest thing to say in this outfit, especially to one of the old timers. Then the sergeant gave up and left and I saw the corporal laugh a little and then go back into his tent to his team. The guys were behind him all the way.

A couple of hours had passed and it was time again for chow - it was almost the same as lunch, Rice and Spam. There was a trench that zig zagged like the old World War I trenches, for the guys to get into if we got hit. It was about 25 feet in front of our tent and almost 100 feet long. There was some water but not that much. As the day went by, at 19:30 hours two of the three guys in my team asked me if they could ask me some questions about what to do when we would go out in the field. We were right next to the trench and as they were asking me the questions and I replied, I could hear "pumping sounds" in the background. The next thing I knew, all of us were in the trench and a couple of seconds later the rockets hit. Everyone else that was in the tents came over to the trench and got in it. I asked the three guys that I was with what the hell had just happened. They said that I had the strangest look on my face and then my arms came out and pushed all of them into the hole and I followed after them. They asked me how in the world I knew that we were getting hit. I told them that you always listen to sounds around you, even if you are back at a base just like this one. You never know when the enemy will hit you. They then knew that they had someone that would take care of them while they were over here. I heard in the distance three more pumping sounds and I told them to keep their heads down and that we were getting hit again. I knew that I had to get to my tent and get my gear. I told the three guys in my fire team that only two of us would go to the tent and get our combat gear. I looked at the blond headed guy and told him to get ready and he said, "O.K. Hammer." I then told him to move and both of us got out of the trench and headed for our tent. I grabbed my gear, which I always had ready, and I saw that the blond guy was having trouble getting his gear since he had it scattered all around his cot. I yelled at him to only get his magazines and rifle and get back to the trench. As he did I heard in the background three more rockets and told him to get to the trench now. When we got to the trench, I then told the other two guys when I told them to move out to only get their magazines and rifles and get back here as quickly as possible. I told both of them to get ready and again I heard the rockets coming in, but now everyone could hear them. As soon as the rockets hit, I told the guys to hit it. Both of them got out of the hole and went into the tent and got their magazines and rifles and were back very quickly. I told them to get ready and that we were going to go on over to our bunker. The guys were really scared and they didn't know what in hell to do. I told the blond guy that he was first and the other two guys were going to be behind him and I would be last. Everyone had to be about 40 feet from the guy in front and when they heard me yell out, "Duck" they should hit the ground where they were at. When you hear me say "Move out," you get up and run like hell to the bunker. "Does everyone understand?" and all three of them nodded and I told the blond guy to get ready. I listened for the rockets to be fired at us. Then I could hear the three sounds of rockets heading toward us. The rockets hit near our tents and I told the blond guy to move out. When he got about forty feet I told the next guy to go. I then told the third guy to move out and I waited my turn to move out. It was my turn and I got out of the trench and got about forty feet when I heard three more rockets coming in and they sounded like they were coming at us. I yelled out to hit the ground and everyone of them stopped and hit the ground where they were. I looked back at the trench; the rest of the platoon was in the trench and they were all afraid to move. Dale was having his men get their magazines and rifles and get back into the trench.

As soon as the rockets hit, I yelled to move out; the guys got up and headed as fast as they could to the bunker. The guys were at the bunker and I was about fifty feet away - then I heard the rockets coming. I told all three of them to get inside the bunker. When I was about twenty-five feet away I knew that I couldn't make it and I saw that they were coming right for me. I then dove for the ground. I knew that I was going to get it and I could almost feel my name on the rockets, coming right for me. The first rocket hit behind me about twenty feet. The next one was also twenty feet away but the last one was about fifteen feet away. I got up and I looked back at the holes that the rockets had made. I couldn't believe that I didn't get any shrapnel. I walked over to the bunker and told all of the guys to make sure that they had their magazines in their rifles and to put a round into the chamber, but to keep their rifles on safe. I told one of them to keep a sharp watch out in front. I then sat down calmly - they were watching me and wondering how I could be so calm about the whole thing.

I got up again and told them to stay there and went back out and sat down in front of the bunker next to the fighting hole. I looked back down from where we had come from to see what the rest of the platoon was doing. I really didn't give a damn if they all stayed in the trench. I saw Dale and his team going to their bunker. The rest of the platoon didn't know what the hell to do. The spotter that was having the rockets hit the base went back to where our tents were and began hitting that area. The N.V.A. spotter had to be on Dong Ha Mountain. I just shook my head and didn't give a damn if the platoon got it or not. The spotter had the rockets come back to our position a couple of more times to try to hit our bunker and kill my team. I told the guys in the bunker that if I told them to get the hell out of the bunker to get out now; they understood. Then the spotter had the rockets go back to where the rest of the platoon was at in the trench line. I remembered what our platoon did for Whitey, they didn't have the balls to help carry him off the hill. I didn't give a damn if the platoon got it or not. I paid more attention to what was out in front of me and I knew that the N.V.A. could rush us while we had our heads down. Dale and I knew that this was one of their favorite tricks. After about an hour of being hit by rockets, it got very quiet. I told the guys inside the bunker to get ready and to keep a sharp eye out. The sky was getting cloudy and that night was coming sooner than later. After a couple of hours went by, our platoon lieutenant and sergeant came over to the bunker and told us to keep a sharp eye out and that S-2 said we were going to get hit tonight, no shit. I just looked at the lieutenant and nodded. Both of them were scared to death and had no idea of what might happen next. The lieutenant and platoon sergeant, who was with him, left and went to the next hole. I couldn't believe the look on the lieutenant's and platoon sergeant's faces. They couldn't lead men into battle. I knew that it was going to have to be up with Dale and Speedy to make sure that our teams were able to help each other out, when the shit hit the fan. Stateside Marines acted tough over here but they didn't have the guts that us old timers had and knew what the hell to do.

It was getting close for the first man to stand the watch for the night. I told the team that I would take the first watch and then I also told them that if they heard or saw anything to wake me up. They all nodded and I told them all that they better go and get some sleep in now. They were all still scared as hell. As they were bedding down, I told them when they stood their watch to get into the fighting hole so that they would not make a big target for the enemy if he was out there. I then went outside and saw that it was getting close to 21:00 hundred hours and for me to stand my first watch.

I went outside of the bunker and walked in front of it and sat down and put my back against the sandbags. I laid my rifle across my lap and began looking out in front of me. I could feel that the enemy was out there watching us and I knew that if they would hit us that they would try it just before dawn. I also knew that just after them hitting us with the rockets that this was also a great time for them to hit us as well. I saw that the fog was starting to come in and it was hugging the ground as it came toward the base. I could feel that the enemy could crawl in and check on our perimeter. I then looked down at my watch; it was now 21:05 and I had been on watch for five minutes. I knew that within the next two hours the N.V.A. could hit us and with this fog coming in, it would be ideal.

I started thinking about the fog and remembered a long time before there was this large pure white cloud of fog coming from the west heading to this base camp and when it got to us how hard if was to see our hands two inches from our faces. It was really weird because you couldn't hear anything or see. You had to wait it out until it passed.

I started thinking about the rocket attack at first. I remembered that I could hear the rockets going off in the distance and I remembered the first night in the field back in March, when we got hit by mortar rounds. They almost sounded the same when they were being fired.

I kept my eyes moving out in front of my position. The barbed wire or concertina wire was about sixty feet out in front of our position and there was a clear open field for about 100 meters and then a tree line. I knew there was another twenty feet before it started going down off the hill. I wondered what would happen if the enemy did hit us and how these green horns in our platoon would handle it. In a way, I really didn't care what happened to them. I was still hurting from losing Whitey and how my platoon would not help in carrying out his body.

I looked down at my watch and I saw that it was time for me to wake up the next guy in my team. I got up and walked around the bunker and went inside and woke up the blond headed guy and told him that it was his watch. I told him if he saw anything to wake me up. I watched him get his rifle and magazines and headed on over to the fighting hole and sat on the edge of it. I then went on over to where he was and whispered in his ear that he better get in the hole or I would shove my foot up his ass. He got into it and I then gave him the watch and went over to the side of the bunker and laid down. I just kept an eye out to make sure he was doing what I wanted him to do. Somehow I fell off to sleep.

The next thing I knew the last guy in my team was finished with his watch and he kicked me at the bottom of my foot. I got up and he handed me the watch. He went back inside the bunker with the rest of the guys. I got up and went around to the front of the bunker and sat up against it just as before. The fog was a little thicker; it was about three feet high in some places and two feet in other areas. I looked up into the sky and saw that the stars were out. There seemed to be thousands of them. I looked back down and saw some kind of animal about 80 meters straight out in front of me. I looked at it and at first it looked almost like a cow but it had large teeth sticking out of his mouth. It stood almost as tall as a cow. Then I saw that it was a wild boar. It was twice the size of any wild boar I had ever seen. I knew there were some animals over here that were larger than other places in the world. I thought to myself that I was seeing things so I looked away; I would come back to it and it would not be there and when I looked back at the same area it was still there. I looked away a couple of more times and again it was still there. I knew that it was for real. I looked away again and when I looked back, it was gone. I could tell that the enemy had left and they were not going to attack the base. My watch was up and I kicked the bottom of the foot of the blond-headed guy and he took over. I went over to the side of the bunker and went to sleep.

Morning came and after a couple of hours the word was passed to stand down. I told the guys to get their gear and head back to the tent and to make sure that they had their gear ready in case we got hit. We reached the tent and this time they got their gear ready first in case they had to get it fast. I thought to myself, they were starting to learn what the hell to do. I knew that the little things were the big things over here, if you wanted to survive.

I went over to the other tent and I asked Dale if he had seen a wild boar out in the open field last night and he said he hadn't see a thing. I told Dale that I saw the biggest wild boar in my life on my second watch last night. We were told to take it easy for the day.

The next day came and the word was passed that both Dale's team and my team were to go over to the L.P. or O.P. and set up flares around that position. There was a dirt road about 60 meters going northeast of the base to a little knoll where we had a team doing the O.P. during the day and L.P. at night. When we got there Dale said that his team would take west to north and my team would take east to south. I told my team to make sure they pulled the pin out about half way and to make sure they didn't pull it all the way or it would to go off and blind them. I grabbed about five flares and went over to the concertina wire and started setting them up. I was on my third flare when it went off on me, I quickly turned away and was very lucky. The guys asked me if I was all right and I told them that I was and to go back to setting up the rest of the flares. I was putting the last flare on the wire when it went off. This time I could see a bright white light and that was all. I closed my eyes and one of the guys in my team yelled out that Hammer couldn't see, the flare went off on him. The rest of the guys from my team came over to me and took me out of the concertina wire and sat me down. As I had my eyes closed I could see thousands of small white dots in front of me. One of the guys took out his canteen and they poured water over both of my eyes. I heard one of them tell one of the other guys to get our corpsman.

I sat there on the ground waiting for the doc to come. Even though my eyes were closed I could still see the bright white light in front of both of my eyes. Robby came and he asked me to try to open my eyes and I told him that I couldn't yet. I felt the water in my eyes coming out as though I was crying. Slowly I could feel my eyelids starting to open up but I still could see the bright light out in front of my eyes. Robby looked at me and said that I would be all right but it was going to be a couple of more minutes before I could see again. Dale came over because he heard that one of the flares went off on me. I could tell that he was a little concerned but when I started seeing him without the bright light and all of the little dots that looked like stars, I told him he was still as ugly as ever and I wished the stars were back. We stayed there for about ten minutes before I could see without the dots. Both of us laughed. Then all of us went back to our tents for the day.

The next day came and they told us to saddle up because we were going back up north. I told my team to gather their gear and to get ready to move out when the six-bys come. Dale came over and told me that our outfit helped make "Leatherneck Square." I asked Dale what the hell was he talking about. He showed me the, "Stars and Stripes," and on the front page it talked about the Third Marines Division making Leatherneck Square. The Leatherneck Square consisted of Con Thein, Gio Lin, Camp Carroll and Dong Ha with Cam Lo in the middle of our four bases. Dale said that 3/3 and 2/4 also had had a big hand in making Leatherneck Square. I told Dale that I hoped that we didn't have to go to Con Thein again especially with all of these green horns. Dale agreed and said that he had to get back to his team and the six-bys were coming.

I told my team to stay where they were until I told them to get on the trucks. I saw that the rest of the platoon was gathering around the trucks and the guys in my team wanted to get over there with them. I told them with all of those guys being in one place, one rocket could kill most of them so it was all right with me if they wanted to go on over to the trucks. They knew that it made sense to stay here. They sat back down and waited for me to tell them to get on the trucks. The lieutenant told the squad leaders which teams to get on the trucks. When my squad leader got word, I told the guys to get up and on the truck. Dale's team was also away from the trucks and then he was telling his men to get on the truck to which they were assigned. The rest of the platoon was so green that they didn't think about the rockets from last night. The N.V.A. could have had a field day hitting us.

As the guys in my team got onto the truck, I told them to face outward on their side of the truck and to have their rifles ready in case we got hit on the way up there. The truck driver came around in back and put up the gate. I sat down in the back end of the truck in the middle and made sure the guys in my team did as I said. Then the trucks started up and we were heading back down off of Camp Carroll. I had a funny feeling that this was the last time that I would see this base again. When we reached Highway 9, the trucks turned right and headed east toward Dong Ha. After about fifteen minutes I saw we were coming up on Highway 1. I saw that Dong Ha base was getting even bigger than before. There were a lot more hardbacks being built and the tents were almost all gone.

The lead truck turned north on Highway 1 and off we went. About fifteen minutes later, there was a split in the highway where Highway 1 went northeast to Gio Lin and northwest went to Cam Lo and then to Con Thein. When we reached that part in the road, we went to the northeast to Gio Lin. As we got closer to Gio Lin the rice paddies were on both sides of the road.

There were six mama-sans out in the rice paddies; one of them was peeing in the middle of one of the paddies.

We were getting closer to Gio Lin and Highway 1 started to go uphill slightly. We came into a small village that was on both sides of the road. The mama-sans and children were not very friendly up here. I could tell they were cold by the way they acted toward us. The rest of the guys in the platoon didn't see the difference in how the mama-sans and children acted. The mama-sans stayed inside their huts and some of the children were asking for, "Chop-Chop." They didn't like us Marines up here. As soon as we got past the village about 600 meters was The Strip that headed due west from here to Con Thein. I looked on the east side and saw the large Marine base. The trucks did a very large turn around and stopped just outside of the gate. All of us got off the trucks and were told to get in the camp. The trucks rode off back down to Dong Ha.

Inside the camp, the lieutenant told the squad leaders where we were to take up our positions in the camp. We had a fire team at each bunker with a fighting hole on the south side of the base. The squad leader told me my team had this bunker and I told the guys to take off their gear and to make sure they had their fighting gear ready at all times. I told them that we were at the D.M.Z. and we were the first line of defense if the N.V.A. attacked from the North. I told my team that a short distance from here was North Vietnam and boy did their eyes get big. They all knew there were no games going on up here - just life or death. They really got scared. I told them to really pay a lot of attention to the sounds around them and not talk much up here.

Around noon time the word was being passed that chow would be ready in about half an hour. They told us that half of us would go while the other half stood their watch. The word was passed that my team could go to lunch and I told them to take their rifles and magazines with them as well as their pots and flak jackets. We got about half way there when we started getting hit with air burst from northwest of us. It was coming from the D.M.Z., so my team ran back to the bunker and got inside. I kept on going up to the mess hall and I saw they had cooked six large beef roasts. One other Marine was grabbing a roast and a loaf of bread and milk. I grabbed a cardboard box and then grabbed three of the beef roasts. I grabbed about 12 loaves of bread, and cartons of milk. While the air burst was still going on, I walked back to the perimeter of the base to our platoon and asked how many were in the bunker. I then passed the bread and cut part of the roast and gave it to them and I then gave them the cartons of milk. I went to the next hole and all this time the air burst was all around me and the shrapnel was hitting next to me. The guys told me to get under cover, but I just kept on feeding the platoon. I could hear the shrapnel just missing me by inches but I went to the next hole and went about my business of feeding my platoon. When

I was done, I went back and sat on top of the bunker but the air burst had stopped for the day. The word got around that we would get hit every other day up here.

As I sat on top of the bunker eating the roast beef and bread, I just couldn't believe that I didn't get hit from the shrapnel. In a way I was hoping that I could get hit so I could get a Purple Heart. The next thing I knew Dale came over to me and asked me what the hell was I doing feeding everyone and not getting under cover. He looked at me and knew, didn't say another word, and sat on the bunker with me. After a couple of minutes Dale asked me again why in the hell did I feed the guys in the platoon and I told him I wanted a Purple Heart that's why. I didn't really give a damn about the guys in the platoon.

The rest of the day was quiet and of course at night time I could tell that someone was watching us along the perimeter. The village was only a couple of hundred meters in front of us. My bunker and fighting hole was on the south side of the base facing the vill. For some reason I felt that the village people were watching us twenty-four hours a day. I couldn't believe that on our first day up here at noon time we got hit.

In the morning I saw people from this village walking across The Strip about 2000 meters away going north into the D.M.Z. I saw they were carrying baskets. I could tell they were all girls and were all wearing black pants. I knew that they must be the ones that were firing the 57mm recoilless rifle the other day at us. I went on over and told Dale that I knew who was firing at us. I asked Dale if he saw the girls and he also came to the same conclusion.

Around 18:00 both Dale and I saw the girls were coming back from the north side of The Strip. Both of us could tell that they didn't have anything in their baskets. When they got to the south side of The Strip, they went into the tree line that was going parallel with The Strip and we lost them. We knew that they were coming back to the village.

Early the next morning Dale and I watched the girls going across The Strip and felt that today would be the day for them to fire their 57mm recoilless rifles at us. As noon time was approaching, Dale and I told our teams to get ready for an air burst. As soon as we told our teams, the rounds started coming in on us. It was time for them to harass us. The air bursts lasted for about fifteen minutes. Most of the bursts were coming to the south side of the base where we were located. The rest of the day was quiet.

I just sat on top of my bunker; a few hours went by and Dale and I saw the girls coming back from the north side of the D.M.Z. Again the time was 18:30 hours. Dale and I got their routine. The girls would leave every morning with their baskets empty at 07:00 and walk on the south side of The Strip between the hedgerows and The Strip. They would walk about 4000 meters and then in a single line would walk across The Strip to the north side carrying ammo for their rifles. At noon time they would fire air bursts for fifteen minutes at the camp every other day. Then at 18:30 they would walk back the same way they would go every morning bringing back their empty baskets.

The word was passed that I was to go up to the C.P. because they wanted to talk to me. When I got there the squad leaders and all the other fire team leaders in our platoon were there. The lieutenant told us that we were going out on a two day patrol. We were to go south into the vill and then head east, then go up north and set up for an ambush. The lieutenant said that S-2 had information that the N.V.A. were coming down from the north. The lieutenant told us that was all, and we left. The squad leaders said that we would be leaving in the morning. I went back to my team and told them to get their gear ready and to make sure they had C-rations for two days. I told them that it was time that they earned their combat pay. As each of them got on their combat gear, I saw how nervous all of them were getting. When they were all finished I told them to remember what I told them about being out in the bush; keep your mouth shout and your eyes and ears open. Make sure that you stay away from the guy in front of you as well as the guy behind you; always have eye contact. I told them when we got outside the gate to make sure there was a round in the chamber and that their rifles were on semi-automatic.

When they were ready and I told them to move on over to where the other team was. We would be moving out shortly. The squad leaders said that it was time and he told the team to move out. I looked back at our bunker and I saw other guys in the base taking over our bunkers. When we got outside the gate and I told my team to, "Lock and Load." The other teams had no idea what to do so they followed what my team did. The squad leaders didn't say anything since they were as green as the rest of them. I was the only one besides Dale's team and Speedy's machine gun team who knew what the hell to do up here and no one questioned what we said or did. We started out going down Highway 1 into the vill and when we got to the edge of it the platoon turned left going east along the side of the vill.

As we walked along the side of the vill, we got the nasty looks from the mama-sans and children. I had my rifle pointing at them; they were not moving about inside their huts but watching everything we did as we moved through their vill. I kept an eye out on my team to make sure that they were doing what I expected them to do and so far they were doing a very good job. The guys were more afraid of me than anyone else. We finally got through the vill and were now in the bush. We kept on going for another 1000 meters and then we headed up north. When we did, the squad leader called, "Hammer up." I walked up to him and he told me that we were going about 500 meters and set up for the night. I nodded and saw that he wanted to get my approval. I just turned around and he pointed out to the point man to move out and the squad moved out slowly. I watched my team walking up to me and I kept a sharp eye out on each one to make sure he was doing his job right.

We finally got to where we were supposed to be for the rest of the day and we set up our platoon ambush for the night. As the evening went by, we dug our holes and everyone was on alert at all times. Not a word was said out there from anyone. Around evening I pointed to my C-rations indicating that it was time to eat. The guys got out their food and cooked it but stayed very close to their rifles. Dale's team was on my back side and I knew that I didn't have to worry about the N.V.A. coming in from my rear. Speedy's machine gun team was on my left side. When night time came, we all just listened. Everyone stood his watch. We knew that the enemy were watching us but they didn't want to attack. It was time to stand our watches for the night. This time I was the last to stand my watch for the team. On my first watch of the night it was 00:15 in the morning and everything seemed to be strangely quiet. I could almost tell that we were being watched but somehow they wanted to know how we were handling ourselves out here in the bush. On both of my watches I had the same feelings that they were studying us. The next day came and we headed back to Gio Lin.

When we got to the gate I told my team to take out the round and put their rifles on safe. We went inside the base and relaxed for the day. Two days passed and the word was that we were going out again in a platoon operation, this time toward The Strip.

Morning came and the word was to get on over to the gate to get ready to move out. The rest of the platoon with the exception of Dale's team and mine stayed where we were. Speedy's machine gun team also stayed away. We three knew that you didn't do the same thing twice up here in the D.M.Z. I told my team to move on over to Dale's team. As we got there, the word was passed that Dale's team had point. I told Dale to watch himself and his team left for the gate and started moving out heading south toward the vill. Then the rest of the platoon followed behind Dale's team. I was told that I had rear point for the platoon. As Dale's team got very close to the vill, they turned and headed west parallel along with The Strip. I told my team to make sure to keep their eyes open and listen to everything out here. As we headed west, there were scattered pineapple plants along the way.

As we moved westward parallel with the strip the lieutenant called for flanks out. I knew that we were going to cross The Strip, but where? I just hoped that we wouldn't get hit on this patrol. We went about 3000 meters when the word was passed to halt and to take a ten minute break. I told my team to face outward on their side of the staggered column.

Then the word was passed for "Hammer up." I got up and headed up to the C.P. group and the lieutenant told me that my team was to take point and we were going to cross The Strip from here and when my team got half way across to stop; a machine gun team would come up and cover for us the rest of the way across. I went back to my team and I told them that we were going to take point and I was going to be the point man for the team and told the rest of them who was to be behind me and so on and to make sure they all stayed as far away as possible if we got hit. The fear showed in their eyes that we were going to cross The Strip for the first time. I told them to move out and as I walked up to where Dale's team was I told him that we were going to cross The Strip from here.

Dale looked at me and he saw that I was going to be the point man for the platoon. Dale said, "Watch out for yourself, Hammer." I just smiled and then headed toward The Strip itself which was about 200 meters north. When I got to the edge of The Strip I felt my heart drop down to my feet. As I looked up and down The Strip, I saw that it was clear of anything on it. I looked back at one of the guys in my team and pointed to him that I was going to start moving out and to let the platoon radioman know. I then turned around and looked straight out in front of me and knew that it was time to go. I started moving out of the hedgerow that went parallel along the side of The Strip and now I was all alone in the open on The Strip. I moved out in a zig-zag movement. I would look back to make sure that the next guy was about fifty feet from me. The only thing on The Strip was the barren earth itself. There was no grass anywhere on The Strip - just dirt. It was only six hundred meters wide and I remembered when it was only 200 meters wide when I first got here in March. Everything was changing up here. As I got about half way across The Strip, I stopped and knelt down and waited for the machine gun team to come up. I could tell that the N.V.A. was watching us. I looked back and the rest of my team was also kneeing down where they were at on The Strip.

It was Speedy's team and he placed the machine gun on the ground next to me and got behind it and said, "O.K. Hammer, you're up." I got up and waved for my team to get up and we started moving out. I felt my heart in my throat as I took every step. I finally got to the other side of The Strip and waited for the rest of my team to get across. As each of them got to me I told them where to be and to watch out in front of them. The rest of the platoon got across and the lieutenant told another team to take point; we headed north for about 500 meters deeper in the D.M.Z. and then turned right heading east. I knew we were about 3000 meters from Market Street, where we had gotten hit back in July. The three of us old timers knew that if we got hit, there was no way for anyone to help us.

The lieutenant was talking out in the bush to the S/Sgt. and I wanted to be as far away from him as I could. I couldn't believe what I was hearing out here, but none of them knew how bad it could be at anytime. I looked over to see what Dale was doing and he had his team always on the alert and ready to fight. Speedy's machine gun team was also keeping a sharp eye

out as well. I had my team watching out in front of them in case we got hit.
The rest of the platoon just sat around not paying any attention out in front
of them. The platoon moved out going northeast toward the trees. As we
got close to the trees, we came across railroad tracks. They only went about
100 meters and that was all, east to west. We made a perimeter around the
railroad tracks and I told the guys to make their dinner. I also whispered
to them not to talk. I then sat down and laid my rifle across my lap and
just didn't feel like eating. I kept looking around me while we were out
in the open and the lieutenant and S/Sgt. going over to the tree line about
200 meters north of where we were. I couldn't believe what I was seeing.
Both of them acted like they were back in the States playing war games. I
wondered if they really knew just where the hell they were in Vietnam. A
couple of hours went by and then the word was passed to saddle up. As I got
my team ready to move out, I knew that the N.V.A. was no where around
and if they were, both the lieutenant and S/Sgt. would have been the first
two to get killed.

Everyone got on their gear and we moved out again in a staggered column. We moved over to the tree line and then set up our perimeter. It was
getting too close to night time for us to dig our fighting holes. I was really
getting worried now. We were next to the tree line and didn't have any
cover at all. I couldn't believe what the hell the lieutenant was doing to this
platoon. I knew that the N.V.A. were watching us and knew just where we
were. I knew they were going to hit us in the morning since we didn't have
any cover.

Night came and I knew that they were still watching us but didn't do
anything. Morning came and as soon as the sun came up the lieutenant
told the platoon to saddle up and that we were moving out. We went back
to the railroad tracks and then made our perimeter and he passed the word
to eat our C-rations. Most of the guys were finished eating when we could
hear shells coming in at the tree line where we had been an hour ago. The
N.V.A. was really pounding the hell out of where we had been. As the platoon watched the shells coming in, they were glad not to be there. I felt that
we were being used as bait to see what the N.V.A. would do to us out here
in the D.M.Z.

I had my flak jacket off and also my helmet as I sat there watching the
fireworks. I tried to think of home but it felt like home didn't exist any more.
I couldn't picture in my mind what my home looked like. All of the things I
had done as a kid seemed to disappear in my mind. The only world I knew
was this world of Vietnam and the N.V.A. We stayed for a few hours and the
word was passed that we were moving out again. I couldn't figure out what
in hell the lieutenant was trying to do. It seemed like we were the bait for
the enemy. We moved east for about 400 meters and made a perimeter and
were told that we would be here for a few hours. Most of the day went by

and the word was passed to get our gear ready and that we would be moving out again around 19:00 hundred hours. I told my team to get ready and the word was passed to saddle up, we were moving out. We headed west back to the railroad tracks and the lieutenant pointed for each team to set up for the night. We were setting up an "L" shape ambush at the railroad tracks. Again we didn't have any cover. Doing this the past two days was going to make the N.V.A. figure out just what the hell we were doing.

We were about half way into the night when the lieutenant got scared and passed the word that we were moving out in fifteen minutes. I woke my men and quietly told them to get their gear on, we were moving out. The moon was out and boy did we stick out like dummies in the open. The platoon headed east about 400 meters where there was some cover. For some reason, I knew that we were going to get hit where we had been in the morning. The platoon then reset up the perimeter for the rest of the night. When morning came again the N.V.A. hit where we had set up earlier last night at the railroad tracks, but this time only a few rounds came in. The word was passed to saddle up and that we were going back to Gio Lin. I was looking forward to getting back to the base. This cat and mouse game with the N.V.A. was not getting it with a green platoon.

We finally reached the base and the word was passed throughout the platoon to put our rifles on safe and take out the round in the chamber. When I got to the gate, I went on over to our bunker and took off the flak jacket and helmet and put on my soft cover. I sat down and relaxed. Dale came over and said that we were getting another new lieutenant for our platoon. I looked at Dale and asked what in hell was going on with this outfit. I told Dale that this made our fourth lieutenant since we've been here. Dale said that he wished Lieutenant Libutti was still our lieutenant and I agreed with him. Both of us really missed him and wished that he was still with us and had never gotten wounded. But both of us were glad that he had made it back to the States alive.

Dale and I knew that this was one hell of a place to be for a green lieutenant to take over 2nd platoon Charlie Co. The day went by and all the platoon did was lie around. I looked at the base and saw that it had two towers, one on the north side and the other, which was only about fifty yards from my bunker, on the south side. I was glad not to be the guys that were up there in the towers. The word was passed that the squad leader wanted to see us fire team leaders. I went over to the squad leader and he told us that we were going out on a squad patrol. We were going to set up an ambush. He told us that we would be going through the vill and head east out of it and then head north and set up the ambush for the night. When he was finished, I saw that the other fire team leader and of course the squad leader were scared. The squad leader said that we would be taking along with us a machine gun team and he mentioned Speedy's team. I was glad that I had Speedy going out with us with his experience in combat. He said that we would leave tomorrow right after lunch. I went back to my team and told them to get their gear ready and that we were going back out on another patrol.

The next day came and we had our lunch, I told the guys to saddle up and that we would be moving out shortly. I again told my team what they were supposed to do and to not make any noise while we were out there. They all understood. The squad leader called for first squad to meet at the gate. Speedy's team was there waiting for us. I passed Dale and he told me to watch myself out there. My team was to start out as rear point team and Speedy's machine gun team was to be in the middle. The other fire team was to take point and then we started out toward the vill.

As we headed south on Highway 1 through the village, I saw there were not many mama-sans. The squad spread out like we were a company going out on patrol. There were hardly any kids. It seemed strange that there were not many kids in the vill. I was thinking to myself about Cam Lo and how all of the kids and mama-sans would come out and talk to us and wave to us as we would go on patrols around their vill. They would tell us if the N.V.A. were around. Here at Gio Lin the mama-sans were very cold and would not talk to us or even wave at us. Even the kids wouldn't come up to us and talk. I knew they were on the side of the N.V.A. The point man started heading east along the side of the vill. There was a small trail that went through the rest of the vill. I passed a couple of mama-sans arguing over something but when they saw me they stopped and just stared. Throughout the vill were pineapple plants and banana trees. We were just leaving the vill and were still on the path heading east and must have had gone about 600 meters when we started heading north onto another small path.

We went about 400 meters and the word was passed to take ten. The word was, "Hammer up." I went up to where the squad leader was with Speedy and he told us that we would set up the ambush here for the night. I looked around and saw that it could be a good place to have one. I told the squad leader that we should go on up this trail north for another 800 meters and rest for the day, and to make the N.V.A. know that we were setting up for the night. The squad leader thought that was a great idea and Speedy agreed. It was time for the patrol to move out. The squad leader passed the word, "Move Out." I just waited for my team to come up to me and wave them past me.

When the last man passed me I started out. I stayed as far away from the last man as I could so I could hear if anyone was following us. I could barely see the guy in front of me but yet I could hear my own squad making noises. Finally, I saw that we had reached the place where we were going to set up for the night. We were going to make the enemy think that we were setting up here. The guys got out the C-rations and ate while I watched and listened for the enemy. Speedy's machine gun team was doing the same thing, watching and listening. It was starting to get late and I knew that it was time to move out again for the ambush. I whispered to my team that they had to be very quiet when we moved out. Everyone had their gear on, the squad leader pointed to me to move out. I started back down the trail to set up the ambush for the night. When I finally got there, I started putting the guys off the trail and into the brush. The rest of the team came down and Speedy's machine gun team covered the north part of the road and my team had the south part. The guys in the middle had what was between my team and Speedy's team. I gave each of my men what time their watch was and I just laid there thinking that I couldn't go off to sleep. I looked at the stars in the sky and also listened for any unusual noises that might come up. I just couldn't let myself go to sleep. As the night went on I got sleepy and my eyes would close but my ears were listening. The night passed by and nothing happened. The team got up when the sun was coming out and it was going to be another partly cloudy day. The guys ate and it was time to saddle up.

It was time to move out and the squad leader was happy to get back to Gio Lin. He came over to me and said that we were heading back up north until we came across a path heading northwest. Again he told me that my team had rear point again. I told my men to make sure they picked up their feet while we were walking. The squad started moving out back up north looking for the trail that went northwest. We went about 1000 meters, going to the northwest; I knew that we were heading back to Gio Lin. When I got on to the trail, we were going down on the side of the hill but could not see the base. We were now heading west and still couldn't see the base. The word was passed that we were getting close to the base and everyone was to take ten. I knelt down where I was and realized that the rest of the team was forgetting about being quiet in the field. Same with the rest of the squad except for Speedy's team which was trying to listen for any movement out in the brush that was around us. I kept on looking back from where we came from to make sure that the enemy didn't creep up on us. The word was passed to move out toward the base. Some of the guys in the squad started talking and letting their guard down. I couldn't believe what I was seeing and hearing. As we went up the hill, I saw the north tower of the base and we reached the top of the hill. We came in from The Strip. As we got close to the gate the word was passed by the squad leader to take out the round in the chamber and to put our rifles on safe. I was the last one to get to the gate before I put my rifle on safe.

When I got to my bunker I was really mad at my team and scared the hell out of them. I told them that the next time they talked out in the bush or took a round out of their rifles before they got to the base that I would shoot them. They knew that they had crossed the Hammer. I told them that if they wanted to die out here to do it on their time, not on mine. Just because we didn't hit anyone in our ambush doesn't give us the right to let our guard down and talk. I made sure they knew that when I told them to take a round out of the chamber that they obeyed me, not the squad leader or the lieutenant in our platoon. That also included when we would go out on a patrol. After I was done with them, I started thinking about the 57mm recoilless rifle that was out there. I knew that we had to be close to where it was but I knew that it was under cover. It was hard to even see it since it was on the side of this hill. There was no way we could see the smoke from the 57mm recoilless rifle when they fired it.

The rest of the day went by and we received mail. I got another letter from Mrs. Hahner, Whitey's mother. She started off by saying, "Son." That really hit home with me and I felt a pain in my heart that she would call me her son. The rest of the letter was that I was to take care of myself and also Dale. She also said that she was proud of us over here and to take very good care of ourselves. When I was finished, I knew that if I made it back to the States that I would go and see Whitey's parents. I told Dale that I got another letter from Whitey's parents and they told us to watch ourselves over here. Then the word was passed that we were going out on another patrol and that the new lieutenant wanted to see how we handled ourselves.

The next day came and just after breakfast the word was passed to saddle up and that we were going out for a couple of days. I got my team ready and made sure they listened to me. I would hit them in the head if they did something stupid out in the bush. I told them that I didn't care about the rest of the platoon. I put the fear back into them. Dale's team was also getting instructions from Dale. The platoon passed through the gate and as Dale's team and my team got to the gate we told them to, "Lock and load." The platoon headed south to the vill. When we got close to the vill the point team started heading west parallel with The Strip. There was a path that showed two tire tracks in the dirt, heading west. I knew that the road went to Phu Ox. We followed this for about 2000 meters and the word was passed to set up for the day. Our platoon then made our perimeter and I had the guys start digging our fighting holes. When we were finished I made sure that we had interlocking fields of fire in case we got hit.

The night went by quietly and when the next day came, we moved out again but only went another 4000 meters and set up at the vill where the N.V.A. had tried to starve us out at Phu Ox. The dirt road led north to Market Street, which was on the other side of The Strip, and we set up on the east side of the road. I went over to Dale and I saw that he was thinking back to when we were here a few months ago. I decided not to talk to Dale and went back to my team and made damn sure that we had the fighting hole dug and our interlocking fields of fire. The guys in my team could tell that I was acting strangely and keeping to myself. The word was passed that we would be here for a couple of days. I sat down next to the fighting hole and thought about when we were here last and how the N.V.A. tried like hell to starve us out by attacking the other Marine outfits so that we would be last to get supplies from the rear. It almost damn near worked. I also remembered there were only two of us at a fighting hole at the time because there were only twenty-four guys in the platoon. I looked at my team and they pretty much stayed away from me. They didn't know what to do or say to me.

The next day came and the word was passed that we were getting mail. Around 14:00 hundred one of the guys from Dale's team came over to me and said that Dale had gotten a "Dear John" letter. I asked the guy, "Are you sure?" and he said that Dale was now walking out in front of his position without his rifle hoping to get killed. I got up and went on over to his team position and saw that Dale was about forty feet out in front of his fighting hole. I walked up to him and said, "Just where do you think you're going?" Dale didn't even look at me. I could see that he was really hurting. I knew he was planning on getting married to her, but I knew that it was over. There was no life in Dale. Being in Vietnam drained everything out of you from day to day but to get a "Dear John letter" made it twice as bad. I knew just what he was thinking, "What's the use in keeping alive when you lose your girl?" I finally got him to head back to the fighting hole, but he still didn't say a word. I knew I couldn't say anything until he started talking first. I told him to sit down and told his team to get away from us. As I waited for Dale to talk, I could tell that his whole life was shattered right in front of him. There was no way for him to get out of here to go back home and talk to her. I just prayed that this day would have never come. I knew that when he started talking, I wouldn't know the words to help him. I prayed to God to help me in saying the right thing. A couple of minutes passed and then Dale asked, "WHY?" After all they had gone through together with her parents not liking Dale and them meeting quietly behind her parents' backs for years. I asked Dale what made her write the Dear John letter and he said that the college professors and students were against the war and said that we were killing babies and mama-sans. She also told him that he should not write to her any more. From what Dale was saying, it sounded like the anti-war protestors had gotten to her in college and had her thinking their way.

I told Dale that no girl was worth dying for, especially when they didn't know what the hell we were going through over here. I told Dale that our outfit had gotten almost "wiped out" from the N.V.A. and even they couldn't quite do it. I told him to look at what all of us who were left had gone through, in our battalion. I put my arm around Dale and I told him that I didn't want anything to happen to him now after what all of us had gone through. For about ten minutes, not a word was said between us. As we sat there together I was thinking of the time when the guys called Dale names and said that he wouldn't amount to much over here and what does he do?

He ends up saving their lives. I told Dale that I had walked through a mine field and carried his ass so that the corpsman could take care of him. I then said, "Do you remembered the time when you got heat stroke and again I took care of you and now you want to kill yourself? Not on my time will you kill yourself. I have too much invested in your dumb ass. Now, get your shit together and your team needs you and so do I." I also knew that after what Dale and I had gone through that we didn't need anymore surprises, especially from home.

Dale looked at me and said that he was all right and I could go back to my fire team. I just looked at him and he said that he didn't want to talk about her anymore. I could see the hurt in his eyes but now he was trying to forget about her. I got up and started to leave and he again told me that he was all right. I looked back and told him that I better not have to come back and go after him out in the bush again. As I walked past the guys in his fire team, I told them to get me in case he decided to go back out in the bush by himself. They all said that they would.

The next day came and the word was passed that we were going back to Gio Lin. After everyone ate in the morning we saddled up and got ready to move out. My team was called to take over at point and to get us back to the camp. We moved out in a staggered column and finally reached the base. As we went inside the base I told the guys to take out the round and to put their rifles on safe. My team went on over to our bunker and I took off my gear and sat on top of the bunker for the rest of the day. Around noon it was time for the air burst to come in on us. As soon as I told my team to get under cover, I heard the firing of the 57mm recoilless rifle. I just sat there on top of the bunker, wearing my flak jacket hoping that I would get hit by the air burst. The shrapnel was flying all around me and again I heard the pieces hit around me, missing me by inches. Again no luck. It was over with in about half an hour and I knew that we would not get hit until two days from now.

That evening Dale came over and told me that he was glad that I came over to him the other day. I told him that it was nothing and that I was glad to do it. I told Dale that I was getting worn out from taking care of him and that I needed him to take care of me for once. Both of us laughed and he began to get serious and said that I had done so much for the guys in this platoon that I needed a rest. Dale said that he was getting a little worried about me when we were getting hit with the air burst. I told him that I wanted to be with the rest of the guys in the battalion in that everyone had gotten one, two, three or even four Purple Hearts, and I didn't have one. Dale said that he was glad that I didn't have a Purple Heart, but he knew that it was weighing heavily on my mind. Dale then changed the subject and told me to tell Ma Hammer thanks for all of the goodies and to keep them coming.

Dale got up and said that he didn't want to see me again out there in the open trying to get wounded from the air burst. I told him that I wouldn't do it anymore. He went back to his team. It was around 20:00 hundred and the word was passed that the lieutenant wanted to see me. I went up to the bunker where our lieutenant was and went inside. The lieutenant said that I was to go on over to the radio bunker and I was to call home back in the States. I left him without saying a word and went on over to the radio bunker which was about fifty feet deep. I told the radioman that I was to call home and they told me to sit down and wait until they could get an operator back in the States. I sat there thinking about what I was going to say to my parents. I didn't want them to know that I was up here in the D.M.Z., and I knew that

I had to watch what I said to them. An hour went by and I couldn't believe that it was taking so long. One of the radiomen said that a general was on the phone calling home and he didn't know how long I would have to wait. I waited for another hour and the radioman said that it was too late so I got up without saying a word and went back to my bunker.

When I got back one of the guys was on watch and I told him that I was next. I couldn't sleep so I just sat there with the young guy. He started talking to me and asked me how bad was it up here and I told him that it was very bad. I said that if we headed north on the dirt road and crossed The Strip, that we were at "Market Street," which was where we almost got wiped out from the 40,000 N.V.A. that hit us. His eyes got very large and scared. I told him that we had been very lucky not getting hit by the N.V.A. so far. The only thing was that they hit us with artillery rounds a couple of days ago. I told him they were watching us very closely. After his watch was over I took over. I watched him go back into the bunker and go to sleep with the rest of the guys. As I sat there, I started thinking of the Dear John letter that Dale had gotten the other day and I started thinking of all of the guys that had died or had gotten wounded over here. A very large empty feeling came over me. As I stood my watch, the feeling never left me at all. I then started thinking about earlier tonight when I almost had a chance to call home but didn't get the chance. I knew that it would have been nice to call home and talk to my parents. I looked at the watch and I saw it was time to get the next guy up. I kicked him at the bottom of his boot and he got up. I just laid down on top of the bunker.

I wondered if the people back in the States really knew what the hell we had been going through over here. Somehow I fell off to sleep and the next day came. I got up and decided to go on over to see Dale and to see how he was doing and also to see Speedy. I could tell that Dale was slowly coming around from the Dear John letter. I told Dale that I was going on over to talk to Speedy and as I got there, he was sitting behind the machine gun cleaning it. I sat down and watched him clean his weapon. As we talked about home, we saw people crossing The Strip at 06:30. Speedy said that it was the girls from the vill. I asked him if they crossed The Strip about the same place and he said yes. He also had a feeling they were the ones that were firing the 57mm recoilless rifle at us every other day. They wore black pajamas and a white top and each of them had a basket that they carried with them. It was hard to tell if there was anything in the baskets. Both of us knew that today we would get hit by the 57mm recoilless rifle at noon. I told Speedy that I was going to inform the new lieutenant that the girls were the ones who were firing at us every other day. I got up and went on over to where the lieutenant was and informed him and the platoon sergeant. Both of them said that the girls were out picking up pineapples on the north side of The Strip. I said the same place everyday? I couldn't believe what the hell

I was hearing from both of them. I knew that neither of them knew what the hell they were talking about. I told them that they were stupid and that didn't go over well with either of them. The lieutenant said that he could send me to the brig for talking back to the lieutenant I told him, "Go right ahead, I need to get out of here." The lieutenant said that I better get back to my team. I turned around and left without saying another word. I went on over to Dale and told him what I had told the lieutenant. He asked me, "You told Billy Bum Scoop (which is a dumb ass) and he told you that you didn't know what you were talking about?" Dale said that the lieutenant wouldn't be with us long in this outfit, another Ervin. We would be carrying his ass out of here in a body bag. I told Dale that it was almost noon and that the girls would be firing at us very soon. I then went on over to my bunker and told the guys to get under cover. It was time for the air burst. Right at noon the fire works began and we were getting the air burst. Again it only lasted for about thirty minutes. I just sat on top of the bunker with my flak jacket on again, hoping to get hit.

The rest of the day went by quietly and just after dinner time, the squad leader came over to me and said that we were going out on a "L. P.", listening post. I knew that the lieutenant was getting back at me for what I had said to him. I didn't care about the L.P. - at least if the camp got hit my team wouldn't have to worry. I went over to the platoon radioman and asked for an extra battery and I wrapped it up so that if it rained that it would not get wet. I looked for both a green and red pop-up. I gave each of the guys in my team one of the items to carry for our L.P. I told the guys to lie down and to get some sleep in before we left for the night. The squad leader came over to me and told me there was a little zig-zag trail in between the barbed wire and claymores.

The sun was starting to go down and I told my team to saddle up. I took my team over to where it began and saw where we had to go to get through it. The squad leader came over to me and told me that he was not going - the lieutenant wanted him here in the perimeter. I told him no problem. I told my team to follow me and I headed over to the break in the wire. Dale came over to us and didn't like what the lieutenant was doing to me and my team. I told Dale that I didn't give a shit. I told my team to be very, very quiet and not to make any noise. I then told them to follow me and started off going into the barbed wire and zig-zagging. I went to where the end of the barbed wire and whispered to the guys to set up here for the night. I knew that if we had to get back in the camp in a hurry that we didn't have to go very far. We didn't have any cover. The guys then slowly and quietly took off their gear, trying not to make any noise. I pointed to each of the guys and showed each of them what watch they had for the night, by showing one finger or two, three or four. I took the last watch. As the guys covered themselves up under their ponchos, only the one guy was listening and watching. I couldn't believe that if we got hit it was because we were between the guys at the base and the enemy and there was no way for us to get back alive. I didn't want the guys in my team to know that we were between a rock and a hard place.

It was my time for watch and I got up. As my eyes were getting adjusted to the darkness around us, I saw the guys were all sleeping. It was somewhat light out and we stood out like sore thumbs. As I was listening and watching out in front of us, I started thinking about what I had said to the lieutenant and how stupid he and the staff sergeant were. I started thinking about Lefefe and if he were here that he wouldn't believe what was going on with this platoon and how it had changed. The C.P. group was staying as far away as possible from the rest of the guys in the platoon. The three of us old timers could only teach our teams how to handle themselves out in the field - as for the rest of the platoon they had no one to show them what the hell to do. I had known that this platoon would never be the same anymore after July 13th when we got all of these new men into our battalion. My first watch was over and I woke up the next guy and I settled down under the poncho. As I did, I was still thinking about our platoon and that there were only Dale's team, Speedy's machine gun team and my team that were making sure that the guys we had under us would be able to take care of themselves when the shit hit the fan.

The next thing I knew it was time again for the last watch of the night. I wanted to made sure that I got the guys up around 04:45 and to get back inside the base before the sun got up. Half an hour went by and I called in on the radio that we were coming back in. I got the rest of the guys up and told one guy to get the green pop-up ready to fire in a 60 degree angle. The word came back on the radio to pop the flare. I told him to pop it and as it went over the base I told the guys to get up and that we were going back in. We zig-zagged back through the wire and went back to the bunker and the guys all went inside and went back to sleep. I just laid on top of the bunker and got a little sleep in. I saw the clouds going by and in between the clouds the sun came out.

Dale came over and said that we were going back out on a platoon patrol going on the south side of The Strip heading west again. I asked him when we were going out and he said sometime in the late afternoon. I told Dale that I was beginning to dislike the lieutenant and that he better watch out or someone just might get a bullet in the head. Dale looked at me and asked if he knew who was going to do it. I just laughed and didn't say anymore.

The word was passed for the platoon to saddle up and to meet at the gate. I got my team ready and headed over to the gate and we sat down. Dale's team came over and they also sat down next to us. Then the rest of the platoon arrived and the lieutenant then passed the word there would be no round in the chamber of our rifles and they were to be on, "Safe." This order had come over from the States. I looked at Dale and he looked at me and both of us knew that that rule just went out the door with us. I told Dale that they were really trying to get us all killed. Just who in the hell, back in the States, came up with this? Dale said to me that, "That son of a bitch hasn't been up here in the D.M.Z." Both Dale and me told our teams to put a round in the chamber when we went out of this gate. We could see Speedy going crazy and he also put his belt into the machine gun and cocked it to be ready in case we got hit. The squad leader came over to me and said that I was to be the point man and to move out. As I walked out the gate I put a round in the chamber and put the rifle on semi. I looked back and as each of my men walked out the gate they did as I told them.

I walked south to the edge of The Strip then headed west along the southern part of The Strip. As I walked the 3000 meters, I saw the girls were coming back from the north side of The Strip with their baskets. They were walking toward me as I was walking toward them. I got about 100 meters from them and stopped the patrol. I then looked back at my team and told them to face outward and down on one knee. A couple of minutes later the lieutenant and staff sergeant came up and asked what was going on and I pointed to the girls, who were coming toward us. Both the lieutenant and staff sergeant looked at the girls and they also stopped about 100 meters from us. The lieutenant told me to stay and he and the S/Sgt. then walked up to the girls. A couple of minutes passed; they were talking, but nothing was getting done. I walked up to where the lieutenant and S/Sgt. were with the girls. I could hear that one of the girls was talking in Vietnamese and either the lieutenant or S/Sgt. talked Vietnamese. I finally got about three feet away from one of the girls who seemed to be about 16 years old. All five of the girls' faces showed that they didn't like us Marines. I could feel the hatred they had for us. I told the lieutenant they were the ones that were firing the 57mm recoilless rifle at us at Gio Lin. The lieutenant looked at me and told me I didn't know what the hell I was talking about. I told him, "Can't you see on their faces that they don't like us?" and he replied, they were frightened of us. I then pointed my rifle at the girl who was next to me, the 16 year old, and moved the selector switch to fully auto. She knew what I was going to do next. Then she started talking like a bird in Vietnamese. She was telling us where the recoilless rifle was at. As she was talking, the girl next to her hit her in the ribs to shut her up. The lieutenant and S/Sgt. didn't see the girl hit the other girl. The other girls started getting frightened from the 16 year old telling us where the recoilless rifle was. I told the lieutenant that the young girl had just told us where the recoilless rifle was. The lieutenant looked at me and said that I had frightened them by putting my rifle on fully auto. I was not getting anywhere with the lieutenant and knew that I better get the hell away in case we got hit. Just before I left, I saw that they didn't have a damn thing in their baskets. I couldn't believe that the lieutenant and S/Sgt. wouldn't listen to me. I knew right there that it was no use in talking anymore.

I left and went back to the rest of the platoon. When I got back, I got on one knee as I watched the lieutenant and S/Sgt. still talking to them. I started thinking about the first lieutenant I had over here, and this son of a bitch was acting the same way he was, "I have the bars and you don't know shit as an enlisted man." Lieutenant Ervin was the same way and he took Chuck Knight with him by stepping on a booby trap and didn't listen to the squad leaders at the time. Here we were in the southern part of The Strip in the D.M.Z. out in the open and these two stupid sons of bitches thought that they were back in the States. I was hoping that the N.V.A would knock them off for the platoon. I knew that they would get killed by the N.V.A. because they were so stupid. I also knew that we didn't have to kill them, the N.V.A. would do it for us.

Then the lieutenant let the girls go and they walked off The Strip, heading east toward the vill. The lieutenant and S/Sgt. came back and both of them walked past me with their noses up in the air. As they walked past me, I told them, "You dumb son of a bitch."

The word was passed to go back to Gio Lin; now I had rear security. We finally reached the base and went inside. I went on over to my bunker and I took off my gear and just sat there. The sun was starting to go down and I then told the guys what time they had watch for the night. I told them that I would be first. I started thinking of the past, about when I first got over here and how Lieutenant Ervin would always be one of the guys back in the rear but when we would go out on a patrol, he would separate himself from all of us and act like he was now the boss and we didn't know a damn thing out in the bush. I remembered the day when he stepped on the booby trap and none of us in the platoon, including the corpsman, helped him at all. It seemed that none of the lieutenants that we had were Marines. They may have worn the uniform but they never went through boot camp like us enlisted men, who were Marines. Then I started thinking about Lieutenant Libutti and when he first came over and how he too had been an asshole. I could tell that some idiot back in the States, wasn't telling the officers how to treat their men in Vietnam with respect. I remembered one night when Libutti asked me for help in winning the guys over in the platoon and he listened to me and ended up being the "Best Damn Lieutenant of 2nd Platoon." The lieutenant we had now was almost like Ervin but now when we got back in the rear he stayed away from all of us. Then I started thinking of the S/Sgt. and I couldn't believe that he was a Marine and how he got into the Marines - who knows? I knew that if Sgt. Lefefe knew how this asshole had taken over the platoon, he probably would have beaten the shit out of him for acting the way he was with the enlisted men.

The next day came and Dale came over to me and asked what the hell went on out there and I told him. Dale couldn't believe what I said and he said, the lieutenant let them go? I told Dale that our outfit was going to hell in a handbag. Dale told me that he heard that the old timers that were left in our battalion who had two or more Purple Hearts were going to be shipped out of the battalion and back to a rear security outfit. I told Dale that I still didn't have a Purple Heart and it looked like I'd be the only one left out of the old outfit that was still here. Dale just looked at me and didn't say a word. I envisioned myself being all alone over here in the outfit and all of the old timers with Purple Hearts would be back in the rear. I was glad for them.

I asked Dale what the hell was happening to our Marine Corps? It seemed that we were getting people that were not acting like Marines; even some of the enlisted men were not acting like Marines. I told Dale that all of the lieutenants and captains, with the exception of Lieutenant Libutti and Captain Hutchinson, must have gotten their bars in a Cracker Jack box. Then Dale told me that it was up to us and Speedy to get this platoon back to where it used to be, taking care of each other and watching each other's backs.

Later that evening, I got word that the lieutenant wanted to see me. I went up to his bunker and went inside and he said that I was to call home tonight and to get on over to the radio shack. Then he asked, "How long have you been over here with this platoon?" and I told him, "Since March." He had a surprised look on his face when I told him. He didn't know that I was the oldest guy in the platoon. I told him that Dale was the second oldest and Speedy was a couple of weeks before me in the platoon. I turned and started back and the lieutenant said something, but I just kept on walking out of the bunker.

I got on over to the radio bunker and told them that I was to call home and again I had to wait. I waited for a couple of hours and I told them to hell with it. I got up and went back to my bunker for the rest of the night. When I got back it was my turn for watch and as I sat there looking out in front of me, I started thinking about the guys in my platoon who had died or had gotten wounded and how much this platoon had changed. I started thinking of Benny Houston, James Fowler, Duvall, Whitey, Charlie Horton, Chuck Knight, Vizer, Sullivan and the rest of the guys. I started thinking of Dale who was here almost as long as I had been here. The tears started running slowly down my face. I couldn't get myself to stop. I was trying to get myself to stop but the more I tried the more the tears kept coming. I felt the pressures of being over here and the fact that there were damn few of us left in the platoon to make the rest of the new guys understand what the hell was going on. Now, there was this new law from the States about not putting a round in the chamber and keeping our rifles on "Safe." Who ever in hell came up with that idea should be shot. I felt that the Government already had a policy about not going into North Vietnam, Laos, Cambodia or Thailand. It just seemed that they were tying our hands and letting the enemy do or go anywhere without us going after them. What a screwed up war this was. The tears stopped and my watch was over. I got up the next guy and I then laid down on top of the bunker and slowly went off to sleep. I did my second watch for the night and finally morning came.

Later in the day the word was being passed that we were going to be leaving this place and going back. One of our sister platoons was going to take over for us. I went on over to Dale's hole and he said that they had something in for this platoon. I told Dale, "Just so we get out of the D.M.Z. with this lieutenant." The word was passed that we were going to saddle up and to get ready to go out on The Strip. I went back to my team and told them to get everything ready and that we were leaving Gio Lin. It was around 16:00 hundred and I got my team over to where Dale's team was and we waited for the word to move out.

The word was that we were leaving and that we again were not to put a round in the Chamber and to put the rifles on "Safe." When I got to the gate of the base, I pulled back the hammer and the round went into the chamber of my rifle and put it on semi. I looked back at my team and each one of them did the same. Dale's team was doing the same thing. The platoon headed south toward the vill and I saw the point team heading south going parallel with The Strip heading west. Then the word was passed that Hammer and Dale's teams were to come up to the C.P. group. When both Dale and I got up to the C.P., the lieutenant said that he wanted us out on flanks about 100 meters from the platoon. The lieutenant told Dale that his team had the north side and my team had the south side of the platoon. Both Dale and I went back to our teams and told them that we were going out on flanks. I told my guys to make sure they were about 100 meters from each other. I then led them out there about 100 meters from our platoon, which was in a staggered column. When we got out there the lieutenant told the platoon to move out. We went about another 400 meters and the platoon stopped and I knelt down and faced outward looking south and west. I looked back at my team and each of them were facing southward. We stayed there for about an hour until we heard the six-bys coming up Highway 1.

The lieutenant got up and started the platoon back to Gio Lin. I then got up and pointed to my men to get up and start heading back. As I came in, the lieutenant told me that we were missing someone in the platoon and he wanted Dale and me to go back and see if we could find him. I looked at Dale and couldn't believe that we had left someone out in the bush. So both of us started heading back out in the bush and we must have gotten about 100 meters when one of the guys came up to us and said that they had found him. We then went back to the platoon which was just outside the gate and the six-bys were facing south and ready for us to board them.

The word was passed to get on the trucks and I told my team to get on the truck and to face outward. I told them to put their rifles on "safe" but to keep the round in the chamber. We boarded the trucks and they started off. The drivers were not happy to be this far up north, especially in the D.M.Z. The people were watching us as we went through the vill. The six-bys took us back to Dong Ha and when we got there, I told the guys to take the round out of the chambers. The trucks took us on over to our battalion area. The truck stopped and I told the guys to get out and I went over to the platoon tent and the rest of my team did the same. I grabbed the dusty cot at the end of the tent and took my gear off, then laid down and watched the rest of the guys.

The sun was starting to go down and the guys in our tent took down the flaps of the tent and turned on the lights to write letters back home. I didn't feel like writing home, all I wanted to do was to get some rest. I was just happy not to stand guard watch for the night. Somehow, I fell off to sleep and the next day came and the word was passed that we were to stay here for the day. The word was that we could take a shower around 10:00 and I stripped down and went out back of the tent. The showers were still there as before. I started thinking about when I last had taken a shower and it was some time ago when I was in out of country R and R. It was now very early in October. I was happy to get the dirt off my body.

When I was finished, I went back to the tent and Dale told me that the supply sergeant for our company was Sgt. Lefefe, so both of us went on over to see him. He looked the same and had that big grin. He was just as happy to see us as we were to see him. Dale and I asked him when would he be leaving and he said that he had about two more days and he would be gone. Lefefe could see by our faces that the platoon was not the same anymore, then he said he had something for both of us and this was the last time that he was going to save us. I started laughing because I knew what he was going to do. Dale had no idea and when Lefefe gave both of us a roll of Lifesavers, he said that this was the last time that he was going to save us. Even Dale started laughing.

The word was passed that we were moving out again tomorrow and that this time we were going out with our other sister platoons. As I got my gear together, Dale came over and said that we had another new lieutenant. I told Dale that I didn't give a damn anymore with these new second lieutenants that we had been getting. I asked Dale if he knew where we were going and he didn't know. We got our gear on and soon the trucks came and the word was passed that we were to get on them.

As my team got on the truck, we had gotten more new guys in the platoon. Our new captain and our new lieutenant for second platoon were riding in the cabs of the trucks. The six-bys were heading back up north. There was a new road that led straight up to Con Thein from the south.

On each side of the road the Seabees had cleared the foliage away from the road about 100 meters on each side. We were at the point where we either went straight up north or went northeast toward Gio Lin. This time we headed straight up north. I knew that we would be going though Cam Lo and it would be good to see the people of that vill again. As we started going though Cam Lo, the mama-sans and young teenage girls came out with the little kids. The mama-sans and teenage girls were selling pop and Vietnamese bread. I took out some money and bought a loaf of bread and pop from them. They remembered me and one of the mama-sans refused to take my money and told me no. Some of the kids came up and talked to me in broken English. I remembered a couple of the boys that helped us when we were here protecting them. As we went through the vill, the trucks moved very slowly and when we got to the end the artillery base had gotten even bigger than when we had been here. Everything was changing. Then the trucks started picking up speed. The dirt road was now straight; it had been winding around the hills before. At the bottom of the hill a new camp being built. We moved on and again about 5000 meters we came across another new camp, called Charlie Five; then the dirt road started slowly going up to Con Thein. As we were going past the new camp, the guys were putting up three strands of concertina wire side by side and two strands on top of them and one strand on top of the two-strands. This was being done for the perimeter around the new base. The concertina wire was the new stuff that had come over from Germany. Some of the new guys had seen it and said that it was easy to get into it but very difficult to get out. Actually, there was no way of getting out of it at all.

We finally reached the outside of Con Thein on the south side and the word was passed to get off the trucks quickly. I got my men off the truck and I had them facing outward looking east into the foliage. Our sister platoons went up to Con Thein first but they were not going inside the base. They were going over to the east side of the base and setting up outside of Con Thein. As our platoon got closer, the captain told our lieutenant that we had the west side. Our platoon didn't go into the base either. As we walked over to the left side of Con Thein there was only one strand of concertina wire that was our perimeter. Who ever had this place didn't have it protected very well.

There was a lot of concertina wire that was piled up, waiting for someone to use around the perimeter. There were also spools of barded wire. The platoon started going inside the perimeter that we had been assigned by the captain. As I got inside the perimeter, the squad leader told me that I had the 2nd bunker on the north side of the perimeter. I told my team to follow me and we walked on over to the bunker. There was a trench that was about twenty feet long and about five feet deep that ran from the bunker to the fighting holes that were in front of the trench. I told the guys to make sure they put their fighting gear in a place to get to it quickly, in case we got hit. The guys in my team knew that I was very serious about what I was saying to them. I then jumped into the trench and went inside the bunker and it was big enough for four guys to get into.

When I came out of the bunker I looked out in front of our position and there was barbed wire that was 10 inches off the ground and criss-crossing about 30 meters around the perimeter but that out in front was only one strand of concertina wire. There were a couple of claymores that each of the fighting holes had; they were also around the perimeter. The last platoon that had this perimeter was still working on the perimeter defense. I knew that we were going to finish getting the perimeter in shape.

I told the guys that I wanted to talk to them and I wanted to make sure that they knew just how important it was to follow my instructions. I then began to tell them the rules first: You will have your helmet and flak jacket on at all times. If you go to another fighting hole to talk with other guys in the platoon, always take your rifle and magazines with you. Always listen to any noises, such as artillery rounds that would be coming in from North Vietnam. Always make sure that the grenades were in our two fighting holes and ready to be used. If you go anywhere, always make sure that you tell me where you are going, so I know where to get you in a hurry. If you don't plan on going anywhere, stay very close to the trench and bunker. There will always be one man on duty in the fighting hole during the day. If we go out on patrol - make damn sure that you have a round in the chamber and the rifle on semi.

I told the guys that a lot of men in the past up here have died for this ground. I told them that they had the day off and that tomorrow we would be working on our perimeter so if they wanted to write home or just get some sleep to do so now. I then told the guys that this was the hottest place in all of Vietnam. The N.V.A. had tried in the past to hit this place with rockets, 152mm artillery rounds and even human wave attacks.

After a couple of hours, the word was passed for all fire team leaders to come up to the C.P. and get C-rations for their team. I walked toward the middle of the perimeter and the rest of the fire team leaders were there. The new lieutenant wanted to talk to us and tell what he expected from us. Dale looked at me and he started shaking his head as we listened to what he was expecting us to do up here. They were the wrong things to do. He wanted us to work on getting the perimeter in better shape than what it was now. He also said that there would be work details inside the gates of Con Thein itself. He was more worried about doing a good job and pleasing the captain and didn't fully understand how bad it really was up here. When he was finished he told us to pick up the C-rations and to take it easy for the rest of the day.

I walked back to where my team was and handed the C-rations out to them. It was going on 18:00 hundred hours and the squad leader called for all three fire teams. He began by saying that he was Corporal Curry and that he was our squad leader. This was the first time that I had a Negro as a squad leader. He began to say other things that I didn't care to hear. Another new guy was right next to him a, Negro PFC., and he was enjoying it because he was a good friend of the corporal. Then the last thing Curry said was that he would not be standing watch at night time and to only wake him up when there was something going on out in front of our position. When he said that, he just pissed me off. I told him that he would be standing watch every night while we were up here. He told me that he was the corporal and didn't have to stand watch and I told him in this outfit everyone stands watch and that included squad leaders, even if you are a sergeant. Everyone was watching him and me get into an argument. I told him that he had third watch for the night and if he didn't, I was going to drag his sorry ass over to the fighting hole. He then got up and said that he was going on over to the lieutenant and tell him what I said to him and I told him to go right ahead, but he was still going to stand watch.

As he left, the new guy who was with the corporal was smiling and I told him that he better wipe off that smile before I knocked his teeth out. I told one of the guys to wake up the corporal and if he didn't stand his watch to wake me up and I would take care of it. The guys in my team could see that I was pissed and he said that he would wake me. Curry came back from seeing the lieutenant and told me that the lieutenant wanted to see me. As I got up, I told Curry that he had third watch and that he better stand it. He told me that he was not going to, and I told him that we would see.

I walked over to the lieutenant and he told me that I didn't have the right to tell a corporal that he had to stand his watch. As he talked, I thought that I would just let him talk and let him scare me by throwing his weight around. He told me, "Do you understand?" and I just nodded and he told me I could leave. I gave a hard look at the other guys that were in the C.P. group and they just looked at me and didn't say anything. I then left and went back to my team.

I walked back to my team and I was really pissed. No green horn, especially a corporal from the States, was going to tell me that he was not going to stand his watch. Night was coming on and I laid down on the ground next to the bunker while the rest of the guys in my team were in it, except for the guy that had the first watch. The next thing I knew, I was getting kicked at the bottom of my boot. When I got up the guy in my team told me that the corporal wasn't going to stand his watch. I got up and told him to get some sleep. I went over to the next bunker and could see there were two sets of feet sticking out and one of them was larger that the other. I knew that the smaller one was not the corporal so I grabbed both of his feet and dragged him out of the bunker and on down to where our fighting hole was. I whispered to him that he better not move. I then went back to his bunker and grabbed his rifle and went back to him. I then whispered that he would stand his watch for one hour and that he better not turn the watch up and cut his time or I would skin him alive. I told him that when his watch was over, that he was to wake me up and that it would be my turn. He was really scared and the whites of his eyes were very large in the dark. I went back behind him to where my poncho was and laid down. I knew that I had scared the living hell out of him. He was not going to use States-side bull shit on me over here. I kept my eyes on him for about twenty minutes to make sure that he was standing his watch. Then he woke me up and gave me the watch and he quickly went back to his bunker for the rest of the night.

Morning came and I knew that Curry would be running over to the lieutenant and telling him what I had done to him. I went over to Dale's hole and told him what I had done to the corporal and Dale started laughing. Dale said, "You dragged his sorry ass over to the fighting hole and put his rifle in his lap and made him stand his watch? I would have loved to have seen that." Then the word came that the lieutenant wanted to see me. I told Dale that it was time for me to tell the lieutenant off as well. I was starting to get pissed with the lieutenant. I walked over to the lieutenant and he was inside his poncho; I told him that Hammer was reporting. The lieutenant then told me to wait. That really pissed me off with the lieutenant. I told him that if he wanted to talk to me that he better get his lazy ass out of that poncho. He stopped what he was doing and came out of the poncho. He asked me if I dragged the corporal over to stand his watch last night and I told him, "YES." He asked me who in the hell gave me the right to do it? I told him that I had the right since I've been here in this platoon since March. I asked the lieutenant if he stood his radio watch last night and he didn't say a word and I told him that he better stand radio watch tonight. The new radioman was listening to me and he had a smile on his face. I then told the radioman that if the lieutenant didn't stand radio watch from now on to get me. I told the lieutenant that if he didn't stand the radio watch, I'd find out about it, I would drag his sorry ass out of the poncho that he was under and make him stand radio watch. He asked me if I wanted to go to the brig and I told him, "Hell, yes. I need to get out of this chicken shit outfit." The lieutenant knew that I was one that couldn't be scared. He also knew that I was one of the very few guys in the platoon that knew what the hell was going on. He needed me as well as the other two old timers when we got into a fire fight with the N.V.A. He could see in my eyes that I knew what the hell I was doing. I said that Curry would be standing watch every night while we were out in the field. The lieutenant then told me to leave and he never messed with me again.

As I left, I made sure to see Curry. Curry saw me coming and had a smile on his face. When I got up to him, I told him that the lieutenant was also in trouble and that he would be standing watch with the rest of the squad. His facial expression changed and I told him that he hadn't proven to me he had that right not to stand his watch. I told him that he had not proven himself to the squad that he could handle himself in a fire fight. Until then, he would stand watch with the rest of us. I told him that States-side rules didn't qualify him for not standing watch over here in Vietnam. I told him that everyone in this outfit from the captain on down to the Pvt. stands watch, no exceptions. I finally told him that he better be on work detail just like the rest of us. He told me that my team was to put up more concertina wire out in front of our bunker. Curry said that the lieutenant wanted two concertina wires side by side and one concertina wire on top of the two that were side by side for our perimeter.

I left him and went on over to my bunker where my men were. They were worried about what had happened to me with the lieutenant. I told them that everything was O.K. and that we were to work on the perimeter putting up the concertina wire. I told a couple of them to go on over to where the pile was and grab two rolls and to bring them over to the bunker. They did as I asked and I told one of the green horns to stay at the fighting hole to keep a watch out in front of our perimeter while the rest of us worked on the perimeter. I told the rest of the guys to make sure that they had their flak jackets on and to have their rifles and magazines with them while we worked out in front of our position. We walked out to where the one concertina wire was and had the guys unroll one of the concertina wires and put it next to the one that was already out there. I made sure that they tied it with the other one so that they could not be pulled apart. I told one of the guys to go and get a spool of wire and that he and I were going to string it inside the concertina wire to make it very hard for the enemy to lie on the ground.

It took us most of the day but we finished sometime around 17:00. Everything was starting to look great out in front of us. I told the guys to come on in and as they did, I saw that Curry was working with the other fire team. I started thinking about Benny Houston and Maxwell and I knew that if they were here they would have gotten on the corporal. I knew what Benny would have said to him, "Don't pull your black States-side shit over here." Maxwell would tell him, "Kept your black ass away from me until you treat your men right." I really didn't know many black men until I came into the Marine Corps where I knew one black guy in our boot camp by the name of Bell. I remembered back some time ago in the rear of our battalion area where the black guys would play their soul music and really treated harshly other blacks who couldn't sing and wanted no part of them in the group. In fact, they didn't want them anywhere near them at all. The blacks that were in the rear were afraid to go out into the field and would go out and get the clap, or some other kind of venereal disease. This was how they tried to keep from going out in the field. They didn't have the stomach for fighting, but they sure let the rest of us know that they were treated harshly back in the states. I remembered Benny telling me that a lot of them couldn't see that all of us over here were in the same boat and that no one was any better than the next guy - we were all the same, regardless of our background. I knew that Benny had a very hard job in explaining to the rest of the blacks that we were all in the same boat.

Curry came over to me and said that we were going to have only one fighting hole for night watch and that both fire teams would watch from the same hole. I knew that everyone would only have to watch one time during the night and that included Curry. Then Curry told me that the lieutenant wanted to see me. I went over to the lieutenant and he told me that I was getting another man in my fire team. I told him that I already had a full fire team of four guys and he said, "Now there are five men in your team." The lieutenant said that he didn't want to hear about it, he was mine.

I walked back and as I did, I decided to see Dale. Dale already knew about the new guy. Dale told me that the new guy was a shit bird and that he had been passed around the battalion and had caused all kinds of problems. Dale said that he had been caught stealing from the guys in the outfit. I asked Dale, "How in the world do you get the information before I get it? Do you know someone in the C.P. group that is telling you what the hell is going on in this outfit?" Dale just smiled. I told Dale that I was going back to see the lieutenant. When I got to the lieutenant I told him that I had just found out that the guy had been from one fire team to the next in the battalion. The lieutenant looked me in the face and said, "Hammer, he is yours and you get him squared away." He told me I could argue all I want but he was still in my fire team. I didn't believe this shit was happening to me.

When I got back to my team, the new guy that nobody wanted was waiting for me. He was sitting on top of the bunker. I could tell that the guys had told him a little about me. I asked him his name and service number. I told him about the rules when we went out on patrol: they were to keep your mouth shut, eyes and ears alert, to stay as far away from the guy in front of you as well as the guy behind you, to pick up your feet when walking out in the bush, and to keep your rifle ready at all times. When we were back in the rear or at camp you can do whatever you wanted, with the exception of work details. I asked "Do you understand this?" and he said that he did. I remembered what Dale had said to me about him stealing from the guys in the battalion. I told him that I had one more thing to say and that was he better not do any stealing in this platoon; right now his slate was clean with me; I asked, "Do you understand?" He said, "Yes." I then told him to put his gear next to one of the fighting holes and to take it easy for the rest of the day.

I gave everyone their times for watch, including Curry. I enjoyed telling

Curry that he had to prove himself out in combat to prove he could handle the job of squad leader. There were small groups of guys staying very close to each other, and sharing information about their home life. I felt sorry for them when the time came when we would get hit hard from the N.V.A. because they would see their buddies getting killed or wounded. I knew that if I tried to tell them not to say much about their backgrounds so that their feelings would not get hurt if something happened, they wouldn't understand because being human, it must be our nature to know the people who are around us. I covered myself up with my poncho and just lay there next to the bunker and trench. I watched the guy in the fighting hole just sitting there looking out in front of our position. I was wondering what he was thinking about. Before I knew it, it was my turn for watch and I went over to the fighting hole and sat there looking out in front of our position. The sky had some clouds moving by with the stars in between them. There was a little wind and the grass that was out in front of our position was waving around. I started thinking back when we had been up here a few months ago and all of the shelling that the N.V.A. did to us. I remembered that the guys called it "Time in a Barrel." I also remembered when all of my nerves were shot and lying on top of the bunker not being able to move while the 152mm rounds were coming in from the North. I knew that I had aged over here but I couldn't tell how much. I then looked at my watch and my time was up. I got up and woke up the next guy.

Chapter Twenty-Nine

Morning came and the word was passed just after breakfast that we were going out on a patrol. I started thinking that we'd be going out on a patrol with a green lieutenant and 95 percent green horns and if we got hit, wondering what the hell everyone would do under a fire fight. I told my team, including the new guy, to get their gear on and to get ready. I also told them that when we went out of our gate to lock and load their weapons. I reminded them to stay as far away from the guy in front of as well as the guy behind. If you get hit, not to call out for a corpsman , but to get yourself back to where the corpsman was. I asked if everyone understood and they all shook their heads.

The lieutenant came up. He was very excited about going out on this patrol, his first one. He told the platoon that we were going out in a staggered column heading south down the dirt road that led us up here when we arrived a couple of days ago. When the whole platoon was outside the gate, the lieutenant wanted flanks out. Curry pointed to me to take my team out on the flanks. I pointed to my team and I took the point and the rest of my team followed. I walked almost to the edge where the dirt ended and the foliage started, which was about a good 100 meters from the road. When I got out on the flank, the team on the other side of the platoon was ready also. I could tell that it was Dale's team and he was also the lead point guy for his team. Then the main body started moving out and I got up and started off. My eyes and ears were listening to and watching for any unusual sounds or movement. I could feel the hairs raising up on my back, and I knew that the N.V.A. was watching us.

The platoon finally reached the bottom of the hill, which was about a 1000 meters and started moving east. When the platoon got to the edge of the foliage, they called for the flanks to come in. I raised my hand and pointed to the guys that we were moving back in to where the rest of the platoon was. Once both flank teams were in, the platoon started out heading east. Now we were in a single column walking on a small trail. I knew that the trail would take us to Phu An, where we had some hellish fire fights. We reached the vill and then started heading back up north. I had the new guy in front of me because I wanted to see how he did out in the bush. So far he was doing O.K. As we were heading north, he was starting to drag his feet and his rifle was pointing down into the ground. His head was down not watching where he was going, and he was getting very close to the guy in front of him. The word was passed to take a ten minute break.

I walked up to him and as he was sitting down, I knelt down and whispered that if I saw him drop his head down , drag his feet and point his rifle down toward the ground that I was going to use the butt of my rifle and hit him in the back of his head. I asked, "Do you understand?" and he said, "Yes." I went back to where I was and sat down and took out my canteen and drank some water. I just hoped that I scared him enough to do his job right.

The word was passed to move out and he got some distance from the guy in front of him and he was doing what I told him to do. It wasn't but ten minutes later and he started doing it again, dragging his feet, pointing his rifle down toward the ground, dropping his head down and not staying his distance from the guy in front of him. I moved up quickly without his knowing it and took the butt of my rifle and hit him in the back of the head hard. His helmet flew off of his head and he almost fell to the ground. He looked at me and could see that I was really pissed at him and he knew that the next time would be worse. The guy was as tall as me. I got over him and whispered in his ear that when we got back to the camp that I wanted to see him. He got up and grabbed his helmet and moved out. The platoon got to the edge of the strip and we then headed west back toward Con Thein.

We finally reached the base and as we got inside the camp, my team headed for the bunker. I got to the bunker and told the new guy to get inside, I took off the rest of my gear and the guys in my team could see that I was really pissed and I told them, that whatever they heard, not to come into the bunker. I asked them, "Do you understand?" and they all said, "Yes." I also told them that included the squad leader and lieutenant. I went inside the bunker and the guy was just sitting there looking like he was down. He looked like he didn't have any life in him what-so-ever.

I sat across from him and wanted to know why in hell he had done what he did out in the field. He didn't even look up at me. I could see that talking wasn't doing a damn thing. I could tell that everyone that had him must have talked to him about his actions out in the field. I knew that the only thing that might get to him was giving him a beating. I asked him if he had a girlfriend back in the States and he said no. I knew that I had to do something and started slapping him in the face. He still wouldn't look at me so I kept on slapping him in the face and started calling him worthless. It was paying off; he didn't want me to slap him anymore and then he pulled out his bayonet. I looked at him and asked "What the hell are you going to do with it?" and he just looked at me and I saw there finally was life in his body and eyes. I told him, "Are you going to use it or just show me that you have a bayonet?" I still kept on slapping him in the face and finally he got so mad that he lunged at me with the bayonet. I got out of the way and took it away from him and started beating the shit out of him. When I was finished, I told him never again would he ever do what he had done out in the field or the next time we got inside this bunker that I would really beat the hell of out him, I asked, "Do you understand?" He told me, "Yes."

Just before I left the bunker, I told him again that I didn't ever want to see what he had done out in the bush. I told him that if he thought that he had gotten one hell of a beating, he hadn't. I told him that he better stay in the bunker for a little bit and think about what I told him before he came out. I got up and left him. When I got outside, the guys were just outside the bunker and I knew that they had heard everything. By the look on all of their faces, I had really gotten to them as well. I could sense that they never wanted to cross the Hammer, and they all knew that they had better do their jobs as well. I told the guys that I was going to see Dale and to get away from my team for a little bit.

When I got there, I told Dale that I wished that I could get rid of the new guy and I knew that I was stuck with him. I told Dale that this guy was going to kill me and my team. Dale just sat there listening to me. He knew that I was really pissed. After I got it off my chest he said that it was a pretty day. I looked at him and then began to laugh. Dale asked "Are you happy that you got it off your chest?" I told him, "Yes." We both just sat there and didn't say a word to each other for about twenty minutes and I told him that I had to get back to my team.

I again gave everyone their times for watch and covered myself up for the night until I felt someone kicking me at the bottom of my boot. I got up and went on over to the fighting hole and sat there. I was thinking about what I had done earlier to the new guy to see if he had some life in him because before he hadn't showed any life at all. I just hoped that the beating that I gave him woke him up. About twenty minutes later someone came over from my right side. I called out, "Halt, who goes there?" The lieutenant said his name and I told him to come on in. I asked him "What in the hell are you doing?" and he said that he was checking the perimeter I told him that he better be standing his watch so that the platoon radioman could get his sleep in as well and he said that he was. The lieutenant asked me where the next fighting hole was and I pointed off to my left and said about 50 feet. He then left and that was the last I saw of him for the night.

Curry came over to me in the morning and said that three of the guys in my team had word detail in Con Thein for the day and the other two should put up empty cans with rocks inside so they made noise when the enemy touched the concertina wire in front of us. I told the new guy and two other guys in my team that they had a work detail up at Con Thein and to make sure that they took their rifles with them as well as their bandoleers. The blond guy and I worked on putting up the cans in front of our position. The first thing both of us did was to get all of the cans that were empty and gather some small rocks. I told him to take his time because we were not going anywhere in a hurry.

That evening the guys came back from Con Thein and I went on over to see Dale. He told me that his mother wanted to thank me for writing to her when he was wounded. I told Dale that I was not planning on writing to her again because he was not allowed to get wounded again.

The next morning came and our platoon had, "road sweep." The lieutenant told the platoon to get saddled up and to move out. As we got outside the gate, the engineers came out from Con Thein and all four of them started waving these machines just about three inches above the ground to check for any booby traps or mines. Our platoon got behind them and again we had to put out flanks. We headed south down the dirt road down to where Charlie Five base was at about 3000 meters from Con Thein. It took us about three and a half hours to get there and when we got there the word was passed that we could go and take a bath in the stream if we wanted to. I decided to take a dip into the stream and I remembered that I had done so a long time ago, in the same stream. I sat down and remembered how cold it was and it was still cold. But it felt great taking off the dirt and dust off my jungle clothes. I didn't want to use any soap because it gave off a smell that carried for miles. When I was finished, which only took a couple of minutes, I got out and just sat down and let the sun dry me off. Then the word was passed that we were moving out and heading back up to our base.

When we got inside the camp, the word was passed that we would be going out on the road sweep every third day. The days that we didn't go out, our sister platoons would be doing the road sweep. I was pleased with the new guy in how he handled himself like a Marine out in the bush. About an hour later, Curry came over with more things for us to do out in our perimeter. He had a little smile on his face as though he didn't have to do a damn thing. I told him that he still hadn't shown me that he earned those stripes, and he still would be standing his watch with the rest of us. Curry left and I got my team together and told them that we had to put up flares and more cans on the concertina wire. I told the guys to take their time and that we were not in a hurry to get it finished. I told the guys that the lieutenant would find something else for us to do.

As evening approached I told the guys that we were finished for the day and to go back to the bunker and get something to eat. As the guys got out their C-rations and settled down to cook their food, I just watched them. They were talking about the States and what they were going to do when they got back there. A couple of them were talking about their girlfriends and thinking about getting married. I knew deep down inside of me they would not get married to them if they stayed in this outfit or even made it through 395 days. Some of the things they were talking about were funny and put a little smile on my face. As evening turned into night, I told the guys what watch they had for the evening and then went on over to Curry and had the satisfaction of telling him what time his watch was. I enjoyed telling him every night when his watch was to be, including his friend that hung around him like a puppy dog so he wouldn't have to do any work. I then went back to my bunker and could hear the guys inside talking and I just stayed outside and covered myself up and looked on over to the fighting hole and the first guy on watch.

The next thing I knew someone was kicking me at the bottom of my foot and I got up and went on over to the fighting hole with my rifle. As I sat down and looked out in front of me, I started talking to God and telling him that I needed a break and that losing a lot of good men was really working on me. I started saying their names slowly: Benny Houston, Duvall, Sgt. Lugar, James Fowler, George Hahner known as Whitey, and the rest of the guys in our battalion. Then there was Chuck Knight who was crippled for life when the lieutenant stepped on the booby trap by not listening to the squad leaders. I started thinking about the time that I was lying on top of Chuck and telling him that it was all right and that nothing was going to happen to him. Boy was I wrong. I told God that I had met some great men over here and wished that all of them were alive to go home instead of going home in a body bag. I could feel the loneliness deep in my stomach. I had never felt so all alone over here. I started thinking about Dale and he was the only one except for Speedy who was left over here and they would be leaving the platoon soon because of their being wounded. I didn't want to make any more new friends and watch them getting killed. I was getting very tired and really needed a rest. I looked down at my watch and saw my time was up and I woke up the next guy. I then got under my poncho and fell off to sleep.

Morning came and the word was to get ready for the road sweep. The guys all got up and ate breakfast and then we saddled up and moved out for the patrol. I watched the new guy to see if he was getting better at doing his job of walking like the rest of us and doing his job right. He was doing a damn good job and I knew that beating the hell out of him did the trick. We reached the base of Charlie Five and headed back up to Con Thein. I was pleased with the new guy because he was doing his job right again. I could tell that he was starting to act like the rest of the guys in the team. When we got back to our camp, Dale came over to me and said that a lot of personal gear was missing from most of the guys in the platoon. I asked him what kind of gear and he said wallets, rings, watches, and other stuff that all pointed to the new guy. I told Dale to go back to his bunker and if the new guy had the stuff that I would hand it back to him. Dale agreed and went back to his bunker. I went on over to our bunker and told the new guy to get inside and that I wanted to talk to him. Again, I told the guys not to come in and to stay outside. I saw a puzzled look come on their faces because they had no idea what was going on. I went inside the bunker after the new guy and looked him in his eyes and told him that he better give me all of the stuff that he had stolen from the guys in the platoon. He didn't move or look at me and I told him that I would say it one more time, and that I was going to beat the living hell out of him until he did. He knew that I meant business and then he pulled one of the sandbags over and under it was another sandbag and inside of it was all of the rings, watches, and wallets. There seemed to be more stuff than from the guys in our platoon, but the whole battalion. I couldn't believe what I saw and I told him that if he stole again that I would be beating the living hell out of him, and said, "Do you understand?" He nodded. I got up and left the bunker and took the sandbag on over to Dale. I told Dale to say that he found it, so that the rest of the guys wouldn't go after the new guy. Dale agreed to tell everyone that he found it and that the guy didn't have it. Dale looked into the sandbag and couldn't believe his eyes in what he saw. He said that it looked like he stole from everyone.

I let the guys rest for the rest of the morning and after we had lunch, I told them to get back out and work on the perimeter. A couple of the guys were putting up trip flares and one of them called for me and told me that he was stuck. As I got over there, I told him not to move because the flare was about to go off but as I bent over to grab the flare, it went off in my eyes. I couldn't see anything but small white dots. My eyelids were closed and my eyes were watering. I could hear someone call for the corpsman and he came over and asked if I could open my eyes and I told him that I couldn't. My eyes were watering and I told the corpsman that it was very hard to open my eyes. After a couple of minutes went by, I started to open them a little, but I was still having trouble seeing. Ten minutes went by and the corpsman asked how I was doing and I told him that everything seemed to be getting back to normal. I went back to our fighting hole and sat there while the rest of the guys went back to work. The guys in my team asked how I was doing and I told them that I was all right.

The guys in my team went back to work on the perimeter, making sure that it was harder for the N.V.A. to get through to us. Around 16:30 hours I told the guys to come on in for the day. Curry came over to me after my team had eaten and said that my team was going out on an L.P. for the night and to go on over to the lieutenant and he would tell me where we were to set up. I saw the lieutenant and he said that he wanted us to go out southwest and set up. I nodded and left him and grabbed a radio from one of the other squads for us to have on our L.P. I then headed back to my team and called all of them together and told them to get their gear ready because we were going out for an L.P. tonight. I told the guys that we would be leaving around 20:30 and that now they better get some rest before we went out. I watched all four of them get their gear ready and then lie down and try to get some sleep in before we left. I sat down next to the bunker and as I did, Curry came over. I told him that he better stand his watch while we were out on the L.P. I knew that he wasn't going to do it and he was going to get a whole night of sleep without standing watch.

Three hours had gone by and I looked at my watch and saw it was time to get the guys ready for the L.P. I called them to get their gear on and to get ready to leave. I gave the radio to one of the guys and gave a red flare to another guy and a green flare to someone else. I told the guys to just sit there until I told them that it was time to leave. I told them if they saw or heard anything on their watch to wake me up. They were ready and scared at the same time. I then told them to, "Lock and Load," and told the guy with the radio to tell the platoon radioman that we were leaving the I.P. I told the guys to get up and to move over to the gate. When we got there I again told them to stay close and don't drag your feet and try to be as quiet as possible out there. I took the point and the rest of them followed me. We headed just outside the perimeter toward the tree line which was about 600 meters from our perimeter. As I reached the wooded area, I went in about another 100 meters and found a very good defensive position from where, if we got into trouble, we could defend ourselves, and also we could observe. I placed each of the guys in my team and told them their watch for the night. I took off my fighting gear and had it ready in case anything would happen for the night. I put my poncho over me and I just laid there listening for the enemy. I stood my watch and as I looked at my team, I just didn't want anything to happen to them. But I knew that the enemy didn't care about what I was thinking.

Morning came and I got all of the guys up and ready to move out and to get back to the base. We moved back, I was the point man again and when I reached the edge of the tree line, I had my team stop and told the radioman to call the platoon radioman that we were ready to come back in. We waited a couple of minutes and the word was passed to pop the flare. I told the guy with the green star pop up to pop it about 60 degrees toward the perimeter. A couple of minutes passed again and then the word was passed for us to come on in. I had the big guy take point to take us back into the perimeter. I then told the rest of the guys to make sure they stayed as far away from the guy in front of them as well as the guy behind. I was the last one in and I was proud of them doing it right; as they came into the perimeter I told them to take the day off.

The next day came and Curry came over to me and told me that my team had to work up at Con Thein for the day. He and the lieutenant were out to screw with me and I just laughed to myself. I really looked forward to getting away from the platoon. I told my team to saddle up and only take their fighting gear with them and we had the work detail up at Con Thein. The guys were griping and didn't want to go. I told them that I was going with them and that it was not going to be as bad as being here and working out in front of our position all day. So I took the guys on over to Con Thein and we all had our rifles and magazines with us as well as our canteens in case we needed to drink. I took the guys over to the supply area and they told us that they needed two of my men on perimeter watch and two of us here at the supply area. I told Bill to stay with me and that we would be here at the supply area and the other three guys would take over one of the perimeter positions. The sergeant at the supply area said that a CH-53 was coming in with supplies sometime later in the morning and that we were to take it easy and wait for further word. I told Bill to take off his gear and to sit down where we were. Both of us saw that our platoon was out working on building up our perimeter. I told Bill that as long as the lieutenant and Curry keeps fucking with us, and thinking that they are making us work more than them, that we were getting out of work more than the rest of the platoon. Bill looked at the rest of our platoon and saw that they were all working with the exception of Curry, the lieutenant and the C.P. group. My buddy Dale was working right with the rest of his fire team. Speedy was with his machine gun team making sure everything was ready in case we got hit. I knew that without the two machine gun teams and Dale's fire team the rest of our platoon was green and all of the other guys had never seen combat or knew what to expect up here. What was left of us old timers knew without being told what to do. All of us had gone through a lot of shit together and we were not going to let the N.V.A. get the rest of us, even though the rest of our platoon had no idea how bad it really was.

A couple of hours later the sergeant told us that the CH-53 was on its way and should be here in about thirty minutes. Bill and I watched back down south from the very large hill that we were on and could see the dirt road leading straight south of here for miles. Both of us saw a chopper in the distance coming this way with a net underneath it with a cable attached to the net at the bottom of the chopper. When the chopper was overhead of us and about fifty feet in the air, the sergeant guided it to where to lay down its load. When it got lower, the wind from the blades of the chopper made the dust around us start flying into the air and get into everyone's eyes. Finally the net landed on the ground and the chopper unhooked the line and left as fast as it could before the N.V.A. could open up its large 152 mm guns. The sergeant called for everyone to get a line started and unload the net as quickly as possible. All of the cases were C-Rations for all of us up here at Con Thein. Both Bill and I got into the line and helped out moving the cases. It took about fifteen minutes and everyone went back to where they were at and rested until the next chopper could come. Bill and I went back to where our fighting gear was and sat down again.

The sergeant came over and told us that the next chopper would not be here for a couple of hours and that we should take it easy and go get a couple of C-rations boxes. We got a couple of boxes that we wanted and cooked our food there. After we were done, Bill asked me how long I had been over here and I told him that I had been here since March 11. Bill waited a couple of minutes and I could tell that he wanted to talk to me about what it was like in our outfit. Then he asked me if I had seen a lot of shit over here and I just replied, "Yes." He said, "You must have seen a lot of guys come and go." This time I didn't say a word. I kept looking at the dirt road that left from Con Thein leading straight south. I knew that he wanted me to tell him much more about being over here. I thought that he really wanted to know about this outfit of ours and what the guys in the outfit had done before he came over here.

I knew that he needed to know about our outfit and what the guys had gone through. I told him that the dirt road that he saw that headed south from here was not here a couple of months ago nor were the new bases. I told him that the old road went south to Phu An; from there the dirt road would zig-zag along the top of the rolling hills that led to Cam Lo. From here to Cam Lo was around 8000 meters. As I started telling him about when I first got over here, he could feel the pain of what I was saying. I told him that the first time I walked down the dirt road, I saw a lot of dried blood. The old timers were telling me that they were there a month before and all hell had broken loose then. They were trying to get to Phu An but fell short. We tried three more times and each time we got closer and closer to Phu An, the N.V.A. would keep us from getting there each time. We lost a lot of men. The one thing about this outfit was that we watched out for everyone of the guys in our battalion. I told him that we got to the edge of Phu An and the enemy had hit us and we withdrew and as we did, everyone was checking to make sure that we all got everyone out of there. The word was passed though that Sergeant Singleton was missing back in Phu An. We called for air strikes and after that the whole battalion went back in there and our fire team found him and we made sure that he went home. Sergeant Singleton had saved his squad by giving up his life for them and the battalion went back in to get him out so he could go home.

As I kept looking south on the dirt road, I couldn't believe how much had changed in such a short time since I'd been here. I started thinking about all of the guys in this battalion and how each of them watched over each other and how close we were to each of our sister companies. We had very few officers that were good men in our battalion but Charlie Company had had two of the best in Lieutenant Libutti and Captain Hutchinson. I could feel the pride coming deep within me and overtaking my whole body. Bill didn't know what else to say so he sat next to me and waited for the next chopper.

A couple of hours passed and the sergeant came over and said that there were no more choppers for the day and we could go back to our platoon. The other guys in my team were coming over to us. Before we left I told the guys not to say anything but that everyone should complain about working up here at Con Thein. We all left and diddy-bopped together back to our base. The guys were all laughing and hoping that we would get sent up here tomorrow. We finally reached our perimeter and went straight over to our fighting position. Curry came over and the guys really told him how bad it was up there. I saw a smile on his face and I knew that he would tell the lieutenant about what the guys had said. He left and I knew just where he was going. I went on over to see Dale and as I got there Dale told me that he had seen Curry talking to the lieutenant. I started to laugh and I told Dale that I told my boys to tell Curry that we worked our asses off up at Con Thein and Dale started laughing.

The word was passed that we were getting mail. I told Dale that I better get back to the guys. When I got to my fighting hole the word was for Hammer to go to the C.P. and pick up his mail. I went over to the C.P. and I saw the lieutenant was lying on his side reading one of his letters. The platoon sergeant showed me where the mail was and I saw that I had a couple of boxes from my mother as well as letters for the guys in my team. I walked back with the mail and passed out the letters. The tall guy, the one who screwed up in the bush and who had stolen stuff, received only one letter and he sat down on top of the bunker and read it. I went about reading my letters as well as the rest of the guys. I looked up and saw the tall guy slowly get up. It seemed that all life had drained out of his body. He laid the letter down on the bunker and slowly walked away. I got up and went over and picked up the letter and started reading it. The letter was hand written from his mother and I could tell that she didn't have much of an education. It was somewhat hard to read but this was how it started out:

Dear Bastard,
    I have been waiting these past few months waiting for my $10,000 and that I need it soon. I need the money soon so would you hurry up and die. I can't understand why you haven't gotten killed by now.

She said a couple of more things but it was hard to understand. The letter made me mad and sick at the same time because I never knew a mother could be so cold and hateful to her son. Now I knew why he was trying to get himself killed over here. If the enemy couldn't kill him maybe someone in the outfit would kill him. I knew deep down inside of me that I had to get him back in the bunker and maybe beat the hell out of him and to get him back to his senses. I called for him and as I did, I put his letter in my pants pocket. He stopped and turned around and headed back toward me with his head down looking at the ground. I knew to myself that I really had a lot of work to do and that I was the only one that could really help him.

The rest of the guys asked me what was going on and I told them that it was nothing but that no one was to go into the bunker while the tall guy and I were in it and if they heard anything, not to come in the bunker. They all knew that something really bad had happened, but didn't know what. I told the big guy to get into the bunker and he did. As I looked at the rest of the guys in the team, they were all puzzled and had no idea what was going on. I knew that there was no way I could tell them; we were trying to make it from day to night and back to day. I went into the bunker and saw that he was sitting down still looking down at the sandbags.

I asked him what was wrong. I was watching him to see if he would respond to me. I was hoping that he did. He just kept on looking down at the ground. I knew that I had to get him to forget about what his mother had said to him. He was playing right back into her hands in giving up on life. I asked him again, and this time he'd better give me an answer. Still he didn't say a word and I then grabbed his jaw and had him look me right into my eyes and I said it again; "What is wrong?" His eyes looked away from my eyes and knew that I would have to start slapping him. I told him if he didn't answer me that I was going to slap the hell out of him and I still didn't get any reply. I started slapping him and he just kept taking it and I knew that it was time to tell him that I had his mother's letter. I took the letter out of my pants pocket and showed him and he looked at me but still didn't do or say anything to me. I went back to slapping him and I told him that I'll be damned if his mother was going to get his 10,000 dollars. As long as I was over here and he was in my fire team that he would not die.

I could see that even while I was slapping him he really didn't care. He just gave up living and wanted to die for his mother so she could get the 10,000 dollars. I did one of my father's techniques and that was to grab him and pull him to about two inches from my face and talk to him. I told him, "As long as you are in my fire team you will deny your mother's wish. The other guys depend on you keeping them alive and they are keeping you alive. We all have to depend on each other over here. Do you understand?" He started nodding his head. I told him that he was old enough to do things on his own without his mother telling him what in the world to do. I told him that it was time that he stood on his own two feet and started acting like a Marine. I told him that when he got back to the States, he didn't have to see his mother at all and could live on his own and make a new life for himself. He was starting to look alive again. I told him that he had been doing great the past couple of days and that I wanted him to keep it up. I reminded him when we go back out in the bush on patrol that he better remember what to do out there. I told him he could go and that I would keep the letter of his mother.

He got up and went out of the bunker and I just sat there thinking about his mother's letter. I knew now why he was trying for the guys in the battalion to kill him. With a war going on, no one had time to know why he was doing the stealing and not doing the right things out in the bush. I got up and had to talk to someone about him and I decided to see Dale. I got out of the bunker and the guys in my team just looked at me and I told them to keep an eye out on the tall guy and to let me know if he went back to his old ways.

I walked on over to Dale's fighting hole and sat down next to him and he was reading a couple of letters from his mother. I remembered that I had a couple of letters that I had not read. Dale looked at me and saw that I had something on my mind and I told him I know why the tall guy was stealing and not doing what he was told to do out in the bush. I then gave Dale the letter of the guy's mother and he opened it up and read it and just looked at me and said that if I didn't keep a close eye on him that he would get the whole platoon killed. I told Dale that he was not to tell anyone else in the platoon what he had just read. Dale promised me that he wouldn't say a thing. I told Dale that I had to get back and finish reading the rest of my letters and I told him that I had gotten a couple of boxes from "Ma Hammer." He said that he would be over in a little while.

I went back to my letters and saw that I had a couple from my Mom, Ryan, Mrs. Hahner and a girl named Joy. I read the letter from Joy first and it was a girl friend of my sister who had gone to airline school with her in Kansas City. She told me that my sister asked her to write to me as a pen pal. I thought about it and decided I would write her a letter but I wasn't going to tell her anything about what the hell was going on over here. I opened my brother's letter and he said that he was on the Varsity Basketball team and was a starter. He said that he scored 33 points in his first game. I remembered back when I was playing basketball on the reserve team and my brother told me that he didn't want me to play basketball any more so I only played football, where I made a name for myself, and ran track. He said that he would only play basketball and cross-country. I remembered that we made a pact. I was very good on defense in basketball and showed him how I got down on the little guys and defended against them. I remembered how Ryan would play basketball all summer long from morning to about 02:00 in the morning, every day. Wherever he went he would always have a basketball in his hands and would play against anyone who wanted to play basketball. I knew he was one hell of a shooter and he could shoot the threes. (Although at that time there were no three pointers) Ryan could dribble, shoot and play very good defense.

I looked at the letter from Mrs. Hahner, and as I was opening it up I thought about Whitey and how I missed him. I just wished that he had never gotten killed. I thought about the green horn that shuffled his feet and tripped the booby trap which was one of our 105 rounds. I started reading her letter; she wrote, "Son, I hope that you are well." She told me how the family was doing and everyone was in good health. She told me they were all looking forward to seeing me when I got back from Vietnam. Dale came over and I told him to get whatever he wanted from the boxes. I told Dale that I got another letter from the Hahner family and each time I read it I would get this lonely and sick feeling inside of me. Dale said there was nothing that he or I could do when the guy tripped the booby trap. I told Dale that I had argued with Lefefe and the lieutenant about keeping the radio and staying with them as they went up the hill. Dale looked at me and was glad that Mrs. Hahner was not writing to him because he couldn't handle it. I told Dale that Mrs. Hahner wanted my parents' address so she could write to them. Dale said that you better give her the address of your parents. I thought about it and I told him that I would let her have it. I told Dale that every time I read her letters, I would get tears in my eyes. Mrs. Hahner's letters would reach my heart and I felt so helpless because I couldn't do anything more for her son. Then I remembered that Mrs. Hahner wanted to tell my parents that they had raised up a good son.

Dale's eyes were starting to well up and he said that he had to leave and would see me tomorrow. I saw how the whole platoon was getting very tired from all of the work being done each day here. At night time some of the guys would fall off to sleep on their watch. Corporal Curry would stay away from me and only stayed with the one black guy in the other fire team. Curry just didn't want to be around the white guys in the platoon. We had now about five to six Negroes in the platoon and all of them were green. I saw that most of the green horns, besides Curry, stayed around only certain guys in the platoon. I noticed that the platoon was not close at all and I just hoped that we would not get hit. I just wondered if they would take care of their buddies if they got hit, and, make sure that the ones that got killed made it back home, or would just leave them here to rot. The whole battalion was green and I knew that it was not the same old 1/9, with what was left of the old timers who were still in the battalion.

The guys were very tired from working out on the perimeter and I knew that some of them were falling off to sleep. I told each of them their watch times and just after evening, the rest of us laid down and went off to sleep. One of the guys woke me up and said that it was my time and I got up but I was still very tired as I sat next to the fighting hole. After about twenty minutes, I heard someone coming from my right side. I knew that it was the lieutenant and I didn't challenge him as he came up to me. I just wanted to see what he was going to say. He got about two feet away and I looked at him and asked, "What the hell do you think you're doing?" and he said that he was checking the perimeter to see if anyone was sleeping so he could write them up. He asked why I didn't challenge him and I told him that he made too much noise when he came over here and that the N.V.A. would never come up within the perimeter from the right or left, not with all of the shit we'd been putting out in front of us. I told him that he would cause the whole platoon to get itself killed over here with his States-side bullshit, by working the guys everyday and making sure that they just didn't lay around. The lieutenant asked me if I would like to go to the brig and I told him,

"Where do I sign up? I would be glad to get out of this chicken shit outfit."
Boy, did I stop his bullshit. I then told him, "Do you know where in the hell
you're at right now?" he just looked at me and didn't say a word. He knew
that I was the oldest one in the platoon besides Dale and the two machine
gun teams and that he needed us in case we really did get hit. I told him
that my team would be taking a couple of days off from perimeter work to
get our rest. I told him that he better check and see if Corporal Curry was
standing his watch and not sleeping all night. I said, "I hope that you are
standing radio watch every night as well." The lieutenant left and went to
the next hole and boy did he make all kinds of sounds when he walked over
there.

Morning came and the word was passed that we were going out on a
patrol around noon. I got the guys up and told them that we were not doing
any more perimeter work and that we were done for good. They were all
happy. I told the guys in my team to make sure that their gear was ready
for the patrol and when we got outside the gate of our perimeter to lock and
load and to put their rifles on semi or fully automatic. It was around 11:00
in the morning and the word was passed that from now on we were to police
up the area when we were out in the bush and that included picking up the
empty rounds that we had fired at the enemy. I couldn't believe what the hell
I was hearing. I told the guys in my team I wouldn't be surprised if the next
thing we would have to spit shine our combat boots.

I looked at my watch and saw that it was getting close to that time for
the patrol. Dale was getting his team ready and they were just sitting on
their bunker; I had my team saddle up and we were sitting on our bunker.
I knew that if the N.V.A. spotters saw most of our platoon lining up at the
gate of our perimeter that they could call in the 152 mm rounds on us. I told
my team if they heard any incoming rounds to get inside the bunker. Curry
told me that my team had rear security. I saw that Dale's team had the point
and each of the machine gun teams were behind Dale's team. It was the first
time since I had seen Kenny Fulton before I went on R. and R. It made me
feel great to know that both of our machine gun teams had old timers running the teams. I saw that we were heading east just on the south side of the
strip, and going along the old dirt road that went to Phu An. We were heading southeast for about 1500 meters and I was watching the tall guy who I
had in front of me and so far he was doing a good job. We were close to Phu
An and the word was passed to take a break for about fifteen minutes.

Then the word was passed that the lieutenant wanted Hammer up, and I
got up and went up to the lieutenant. When I got there I saw that Dale was
there also. The lieutenant said that he wanted both of our teams to take the
flanks and that we were heading due west until we hit the dirt road that went
straight up to Con Thein. He told us there was supposed to be a battalion of
N.V.A. around here. I looked at the lieutenant's face and he was scared to

,death about being out here, and that he needed Dale and me to get his ass back to the perimeter. Dale and I knew that we had to tell the two machine gun teams about what we were going to do and for them to be ready for anything. Kenny and Speedy told us good luck and they would watch our backs.

Both Dale and I left the lieutenant; we had about ten more minutes. I came across the machine gun team and told them what the hell was going on but I didn't have to say much to Kenny Fulton. I just told him that there might be a battalion of N.V.A. around here. Kenny said that his team was ready and I told him that my team was going out on the flanks and Dale's team on the other side. Dale saw Speedy and told him also what we were going to do. Ten minutes went by and the word was passed that Hammer's team was to take the right flank. I told my team to get up and to follow me. I went out about 75 meters and saw the rest of the platoon. I had the tall guy behind me and the other three guys behind him to keep an eye out on him. As I passed the tall guy, I whispered to him that he better not make one mistake or I would really beat the living hell out of him. I could tell that he was O.K. We moved about 1100 meters and finally I saw the dirt road and the large clearing on both sides of the road. I headed up right along the side of the tree line, heading toward Con Thein. We reached the top and I motioned to the guys behind me to come up to where I was and as each of them got to me, I told them to head to our gate and go on over to our bunker. I saw Dale's team well on the other side of the dirt road and the main body of our platoon on the dirt road itself. Everyone was heading back into the perimeter and saw the lieutenant and staff sergeant were very happy to get back inside.

As soon as I got inside the gate, I went on over to our bunker and took off my gear. I watched the guys in my team taking their gear off as well. The tall guy looked at me and saw that I was watching him to make sure that he didn't go back to his old ways. I still couldn't get over how his mother wanted him to die so she could get the 10,000 dollars. It was about 15:00 and I told the guys to take the rest of the day off.

Around 18:00 hundred the word was passed that the lieutenant wanted to see me. I was trying to figure out what the hell he wanted this time. I got up and slowly walked on over to where he was; as I got there, I saw the staff sergeant was sitting on the ground eating and the lieutenant was doing the same. The lieutenant said that I was going on R and R In-Country, and that I was to leave tomorrow. The lieutenant told me that if I wanted to take a couple of extra days off the book, to do so. He then said, "Hammer, you need a rest." I just looked at him and told him that I don't want Curry messing around with my team while I was gone. The lieutenant told me that my team would be left alone. I left and went back to my team. As I was walking back, Dale called me over and said that he heard that I was going on in-country R. and R. Dale also told me to take a couple of extra days , down there at China Beach and that I needed it because of the tall guy and what our platoon had been doing, working everyday on the perimeter. I left Dale and got back to my men. I told them that I would be leaving tomorrow for China Beach and that I would be back within a week. The tall guy was happy that I was leaving for the week. I told all of them to keep an eye out on the tall guy and if he screwed up while I was gone to let me know. The smile left his face and he knew that he still had to be on his toes with the rest of the guys in the team. We all stood our watches for the night and the next day came.

It was 10:00 in the morning and the day again was cloudy I knew that it was time to go on over to Con Thein and get on the six-by that was coming up to take us back to Dong Ha. I put on my gear and the guys told me to have a good time down at China Beach and watch out for the girls. I just smiled and walked on over to Con Thein and asked where the six-by was to pick up the guys to go to Dong Ha. It was the same area where Bill and I unloaded the chopper a couple of days ago. As I sat down, I looked at where our little perimeter was and saw the guys were finished working on it and they were all just lying around talking to each other.

I looked down at my jungle clothes and couldn't believe how brown they were and how they had changed from green to brown within a couple of months out in the bush. I saw how dirty my hands were but I knew when I got to China Beach that I could take a shower and get cleaned up. The word was passed that we might get hit today from the N.V.A.'s 152mm rounds from North Vietnam. Everyone went about their business as usual. I knew that the guys up here didn't think much about getting hit from the N.V.A.; they were used to it.

A six-by was coming up from the south on the dusty road that led to Con Thein. We had to get on the truck as quickly as possible and the truck was going to leave as quickly as it had come up here. The way the driver had the six-by moving and causing all of the dirt to fly up into the air made it easy for the N.V.A. to open up with their 152 mm guns. There were two more guys also going back down to Dong Ha. The six-by had mail on the back of the truck for the guys up here and I knew that I wouldn't be seeing my mail until I got back. The truck came over to where we were and the three of us got on the truck and helped get the mail off. I sat down against the cab. The driver said to hold on and that we were leaving. He was really scared and that he wanted to get out of here as quickly as possible. The driver wanted to get the hell out of here as fast as he could. As soon as all of us sat down, he started up his engine and we took off. As we got outside of the gate, he really put on the gas. The tires of the truck were kicking up the dust on the road and you could see us for miles around. Then, as we were about half way down the hill, the N.V.A. rounds started coming in on Con Thein and the guys were hitting their bunkers for cover. I knew that if the driver had come up here slowly and not have caused the dust to fly into the air that the N.V.A. wouldn't have hit the base.

I remembered the times before when our outfit was up here and we would get hit from the 152mm rounds from the enemy. I remembered when I couldn't move and the guys put their flak jackets over my whole body from my feet to my head. I remembered the shrapnel flying all around me and hitting the ground. As I looked back at Con Thein, I saw how much it had changed since I'd been here. I remembered the three small knolls at the top of Con Thein and now they were gone. I saw that the hill had taken a hell of a beating by the N.V.A 152mm rounds in the past. Then I remembered one time when I was up here and we were being shelled from the N.V.A. and a Marine was running to his bunker and when he got to the doorway, the round followed him inside and killed him.

As we were getting farther away from Con Thein, I saw that the dirt road was moving to the right a little and we were on the old road that lead to Con Thein in the past. I remembered all of the times that we used to walk down this road and how we'd encountered the N.V.A at Phu An.

We were getting close to Cam Lo Bridge and I started remembering the mama-sans and young girls and of course the kids there. The six-by was starting to slow down and I looked over to my right side and could see the artillery base just outside of Cam Lo vill. It was larger then ever. There were a lot more artillery pieces there than a couple of months ago. The dust off of the road was coming up, landing in the back of the truck. The dust was flying all over and landing on each of us. The banana trees and plants next to the road were all covered with dust. As we went past the artillery base and into the vill, the truck stopped and as it did, I looked over to my left side and saw the old one room school house. I remembered when our platoon was here for a short while and Van and I were with the two boys and they showed us their school house. Then, I thought back how the old school house had looked! It had been hit with bullets from the AK-47s and there was only one chalk board and part of it was hit and cracked and lying on the floor. There were a few books around and a couple of old wooden desks. The boys didn't have a teacher because the enemy had killed her. The boys would asked Van Meeteren and me to talk about our country and what it was like in the U.S. I remembered back when I was in history class and didn't think too much about what the teacher had asked us, "What would happen if someone from outside the U.S. would ask you to talk about the history of the U.S? What would you say?" I remembered how hard it was just to tell them about what we had back at home: toys, cars, dating, let alone the history of the U.S.

After a couple of minutes, the truck started to move and then we turned to the right; I knew we were getting ready to cross the bridge. As we went over it, I saw there were some kids swimming down in the river with some of the Marines that were here. I then looked over to where our old bunker and fighting hole was and it was still there and had not been changed since we redid the place. I knew that the Marines that were here had it made. The people from the vill made the Marines feel welcome, plus they were protected by the them.

When we got to the other side of the bridge, a M.P. stopped the truck and gave our driver a ticket for driving fast on the dirt road. I laughed to myself and we took off. As we got a couple of miles down the road, I looked into the cab of the truck and the driver took the ticket he just got and threw it out the window. I just smiled to myself. We finally reached Dong Ha and the six-by took us on over to one of the P.X.'s and dropped us off. I got up and off the truck and he took off to where he was stationed. I had to walk a little way to get to our battalion area which was over by the airstrip.

I finally got to our battalion area and went straight over to the company tent. I told the clerks there that I was going on In-Country R. and R. and they gave me my pass and it showed that my time on R. and R. was starting tomorrow and ended five days later. The guy gave me the pass and said that I could leave right now for Da Nang if I wanted. I went back to my tent and put my combat gear next to my seabag and I told the guys there to make sure that no one touched it. I put my magazines inside my seabag and locked it so that no one could get to them. I left and went on over to the airport and when I got there, I got a boarding pass that had a number on it and saw there were about 40 people before me also going down to Da Nang. In the terminal there were also ARVN Officers, (known as South Vietnam Army Officers), going on different airplanes.

As I looked at the other Marines and ARVN Officers in the terminal, I noticed that everyone had on clean uniforms and jungle clothes. I looked at myself and I didn't fit in with anyone; I really stuck out like a sore thumb. My jungle uniform was brown and my jungle boots didn't have a spot of black on them. Everyone was looking at me and couldn't believe how dirty I was. None of them had the guts to tell me that I was dirty. I wanted to get out of the terminal and didn't feel like being inside of it in case we got hit. As I got to the door of the terminal, the word was passed on the loud speaker that we were expected to get hit by the N.V.A. and when the plane got here to be ready to get to it fast. I knew that I was the only one in the terminal that was in the infantry and was not scared about getting hit here. I saw that some of the Marines and Vietnamese soldiers were worried about getting out of here. When I got outside of the building I knew just where to go in case we got hit and I knew that I would be safe.

About twenty minutes went by and I saw the choppers flying in and out taking supplies out to the field for the Marines Infantry. The wind was blowing and the dust was flying all over the place. I saw there was a C-130 coming in and on the loud speaker I could hear that everyone going to Da Nang was to get ready to board the plane in a couple of minutes. I went back inside and saw that everyone here was ready to get to the plane. They were all at the door and I knew there was going to be a mad rush to the C-130. I stayed back away from all of them because I didn't like being pushed around trying to get to the plane. Then the word was passed to go on over to the plane. As I got to the door leading to the plane, everyone before me was running like crazy to the back of the C-130 but when they got there, they had to wait for the Marine to take their boarding pass. I just laughed to myself as I slowly walked on over to the plane. By the time I got to it, all of them were inside of the plane and sitting down. They couldn't wait for the plane to leave. The engines of the plane were still on and the plane was about to leave. I enjoyed my 100 foot walk to the back of the plane and gave my pass to the Marine and he looked at me and smiled and told me to enjoy my flight. I nodded back and got on the plane. All of the officers and enlisted men watched how I was taking my time getting on the plane as though there was nothing going to happen. A couple of minutes went by and then we left for Da Nang.

As we were heading south, I remembered that we might be going to Phi Bai first and in a way I hoped that we did. I wanted to see how much it had changed and before I knew it we were heading back down and then we landed. The plane door opened up and after a couple of minutes the word was passed for those getting out here to do so. There were just a few soldiers getting off and there were other soldiers getting on the plane. The old hanger that had been hit was not being used anymore and there was a new terminal and it was very large. From the runway, I noticed that the base had changed from all tents to all hardbacks. The base was even larger than before when I first got over here. It seemed that everything had changed a lot since March and now it was November. After about ten minutes the back door of the plane started closing and we were off again.

Before I knew it, we were landing again and this time, it was Da Nang. I got off the plane and headed over to the terminal. When I got there, someone on the speaker was telling the soldiers if they were going to China Beach, there was a bus just outside to take them there. I walked outside of the terminal and went on over to the bus and asked the driver if he was going to China Beach and he said yes. I then got on and went about half way into the bus and sat down. I looked outside the window and the sun was out; down here it seemed that the temperature was in the 90's. Ten minutes went by and the driver of the bus started it up and we took off. I was the only one that was going to China Beach. I asked the driver how often was there a bus from here to China Beach and he said, "There is a bus every hour from China Beach to the base, from 08:00 to 21:00." I looked at my watch, it was 13:00. The driver took me right into the city of Da Nang and as we went through the city, I could see the small one-way side streets and it reminded me of downtown Cincinnati. Then, we went over a one-way bridge that was very old and right next to it, about 100 feet away, was a new bridge and it also was going one way but going north while we were going south. When we got to the other side of the bridge, the bus took a left-hand turn and I noticed that we were heading toward the ocean. About ten more minutes had passed and there was a sign right in front of us that said, "Welcome to China Beach." There was an M.P. stationed there and he waved us through and the driver took me to the main building and told me to go inside and register. I got off the bus and thanked the driver and he nodded and then left. I headed toward the building which was a large hardback. I went inside and the soldier there told me to sign in and asked to see my pass. I showed him the pass and he wrote down the days I was to be here and then told me to go over to building number five and get my bed linen. He told me that I would be in building number thirteen while I was here. He told me where the P.X. and snack bar were. I left and went on over to building number five and got my bed linen. The guy looked at me and said that I needed to get cleaned up, I told him no problem. I headed on over to building number thirteen and it was right next to the ocean. I went inside and was about half way down it and noticed there were only a very few beds that had sheets on them. I was about in the middle of the barracks and there was no one around me. I made up my bunk. All of the bunks in the barrack were double bunks, one on top of the other. I took the bottom bunk. When I was finished making the bed, I decided to go back outside and go on over to the ocean. At the end of the barrack, there was a shower room and bathroom. As I walked outside, I thought about the bed and linen and bathroom and shower room. I wasn't used to this type of living; it felt strange to have these things, even having a light switch in the barrack.

I walked on over to the beach and as I did, I saw a couple of picnic tables there and I headed over to them. There were also a couple of trees there that gave some shade. I sat down and took off my boots and socks and it felt really great to take them off. I started thinking about the last time that I had taken off my boots and it was back at Delta Five base which was behind Camp Carroll. That was when I had trench foot and almost lost my right foot.

The sand was warm and felt good between my toes. I put my boot and socks on the picnic table and decided to walk on the beach and into the ocean a little. As the waves came in running over my feet, I could feel the coolness of the ocean. I went a couple of hundred feet and headed back to the picnic tables and there were other soldiers around but they were going to the snack bar. I finally got back to the picnic tables and I sat down and looked at the waves coming in. I started looking over the horizon and knew somewhere east was the United States but it didn't seem real anymore. It seemed like it really didn't exist. I started thinking that I had been over here so long, that I had lost all sense of reality and that I didn't know what it was like being normal. I remembered that when I first came over here that I had not seen death and didn't know what it was like being out in the field going through hell and confronting death every day and every night. I had now forgotten what I had done as a kid back at home and all of the games we played against each other in school.

Chapter Thirty

I knew that I had to forget about home and get my mind on other things, such as the music coming from the snack bar. I could hear rock-n-roll music from inside the building. I put on my socks and boots and headed on over to the snack bar to get something to eat. I went inside and there were a few soldiers there, mostly Doggy, Army boys. I went up to the counter and ordered two cheeseburgers and some fries. At the end of the counter, there was a person taking your money and also getting you the type of soda you wanted. It was like being back in the States again. I got a large Coke and paid for my food. I went over to a table where no one was close by and sat down. I just wanted to be alone and didn't feel like talking to or being close to anyone. There were a couple of guys by the music box punching the different numbers so they could hear their favorite songs.

I began to eat my food and I was having some trouble eating the two cheeseburgers and fries. I ended up eating most of the burger but left most of the fries. I sat there for awhile and just listened to the songs that were being played. It seemed that with every song that came on, I started remembering what I was doing when it first came out in the U.S.A. It was starting to make me home sick and I knew that I had to get out of there. I got up and went outside and went over to the small P.X. and got some writing paper and went on over to the picnic tables. I sat down and there was a slight wind blowing but it was very nice out here. The waves were slowly rolling in on the beach and again there was no one around.

I started writing to my mom and then to my brother and then to my father. After I wrote to him I wrote to both pen pals, Jennifer and Joy. The last letter I wrote to was the Hahner family. In the past couple of letters, Mrs. Hahner said she wanted me to come to see them in Chicago when I got done with my tour over here. I remembered Sgt. Dodge saying when his tour was done that he was going to see the Hahner family. I knew that he was going to tell them that he was with their son all of the time when actually he was up at Camp Carroll eating hot chow, while the rest of us, including Whitey, were at Delta Five going out into the bush. Even Dodge was afraid to go out into the bush with the platoon. He was just like Thomas in a lot of ways. I knew that I had to go and visit them when I got back, and I told Mrs. Hahner that I would see them. I finished writing all of the letters.

Around 16:00 hundred, I got tired of writing letters and I had to do something so I went back to the P.X.. I made sure that I wrote , "FREE" in the upper right hand corner of the envelopes and dropped them off in the mail bag. I went back outside and went on over to where the bus picked up and dropped off the guys and decided to get on the bus and go on over to the big base. I sat just behind the driver and after about ten minutes, he started the bus up and we left. It was just the driver and me going back to the main military base at Da Nang.

The driver noticed my dirty jungle clothes and asked what outfit I was with and I told him the 1st Battalion 9th Marines and he looked at me in the mirror for a couple of minutes. He said he had heard that my outfit really had gotten the shit kicked out of us from the N.V.A. I looked at him in the mirror and told him that it was the other way around that we kicked the shit out of the N.V.A. He asked me how long was I going to be down here and I told him that I had three more days and I had to get back. We finally reached the base and he dropped me off just outside the Marine Terminal and said that he would be here at the top of every hour up to 21:00. I got off the bus and looked for a ride to go on over to where Freedom Hill 327 was at and to check out the P.X. and snack bar there. A six-by came up to where I was and the driver asked if I needed a ride to Freedom Hill and I told him yes.

I climbed onto the back of the six-by and sat down on the floor of the truck and we took off. The truck went outside the main gate and we went through, "Dog Patch." I had heard that this was the place if you wanted to have sex. There were all of these small huts and young girls just outside of them calling for the G.I., "You want to have good time, just ten dollars." I remembered the guys in my battalion talking about these girls down here having razor blades in their pussies and when you stuck your penis into them that you would have a split dick. I wasn't going to play around with these girls because I also had heard about the "Black Syphilis." The guys said that if you got the Black Syphilis that the doctors would send you to the Philippines for the rest of your days until you died from it. What happened is that the disease would work on your spinal cord and eat away your nervous system. You also had other systems that were affected with it but the attack off the spinal system was the main thing. Most of the Negroes from my outfit would come down here to pick up the clap so they wouldn't have to go out in the bush. They took a big chance in picking up the Black Syphilis. The truck went through another gate and we were now inside the base where Freedom Hill 327 was. The driver took me up to the P.X. and said that we were here. I got up and jumped off the truck and he took off.

I went inside the P.X., which was huge, and went over to the electronic tape players, radios, cameras, and other stuff. As I walked around, I noticed that everyone was looking and staring at me. I could feel that none of them wanted to be around me. I noticed that everyone in the building all had clean jungle clothes on and black jungle boots. I really didn't give a damn what anyone thought of me and I just stayed to myself and looked at the electronic gear. After about an half hour, I decided that I better get something to drink, so I left the P.X. and went next door to the snack bar, which also was huge, and went inside. Again everyone was looking at me but now I didn't really give a damn what anyone thought of me. I knew that all of these guys were not in the Marine Infantry but were stationed down here inside this huge Marine and Army base. I was getting a lot of looks from the officers and I knew that they wanted to tell me to get cleaned up.

I went up to the counter and asked for a Coke and looked for a place to sit down. Again, there were guys around the music box picking songs that they wanted to hear. I found a table that was empty and sat down and again the Marines that were living down here were looking at my jungle clothes. They were playing songs from The Monkees, the Mamas & Papas, Motown, and the new songs that were coming out; "San Francisco," "Blue, Blue" and others. I took my time and finished my drink and I knew that I better get the hell out of this place. I knew that I had them all wondering just where in the hell I came from. I got up and went out the front door and walked on over to the Red Cross building and saw there were a lot of Marines and Army guys talking to the girls there.

All of the guys were trying to get the American girls to go to bed with them. Even the officers were after them. I decided to see what was inside the building and as I did, I saw there were ping pong tables and a couple of pool tables. There were also cards tables for the guys that wanted to play cards. There were tables for the guys to write letters on. I went over to where there were chairs and sat down. There was a guy next to me and I told him there sure was a hell of a lot of guys trying to get the Red Cross girls to go to bed with them. The corporal said that if you were a enlisted man that the girls charged you fifty dollars and the officers one hundred dollars. I leaned back in my chair and couldn't believe what I just heard. The corporal said that the girls had a racket going on over here and were making money like crazy. He said they had been here now for a couple of years and didn't plan on going home since they were making a hell of a lot of money off of the guys and officers. I sat there looking at a couple of the American girls, one of whom had red hair and the other had blond hair. The girls were very pretty and very attractive and it was the second time that I had seen them since I had been over here. It sure was nice to see a round-eyed American girl with a beautiful body. I knew that if I wanted to get one of them that they wouldn't get near me because of my jungle clothes. I looked at myself and realized I was so skinny and very thin-looking. After about half an hour, I knew that it was time to get back to the main base and to China Beach. I got up and went back outside and as I did, I saw there was a huge theater and they were showing two shows. I told myself that tomorrow I would take in a show.

There was a pick up point for the guys to go back to the main base and

I went on over there and got on a six-by. As I did, I saw a notice saying that Bob Hope would have his Christmas Show next month. I knew that I would not be able to see it and I also knew that all of the 3rd Marine Division Infantry outfits would not be able to see the show either. I started thinking when I was back in the States and they showed the Bob Hope Christmas Show, everyone in the audiences had clean jungle clothes on; they were guys that were stationed here and did not do any fighting but only support work, such as clerks, cooks, air wing, mechanics, truck drivers, chopper pilots, supplies men and others. The guys that really needed to see the Bob Hope Christmas show would never see him or the girls he always had in his show.

Finally, I got back into the main camp and the truck driver dropped me off just outside the Marine Terminal. I waited for the bus to come by and pick me up. Around 19:00 hundred the bus pulled up and opened the doors and I got on again. No one was on the bus. I got on and again I sat behind the driver and he asked me if I had a good time over at Freedom Hill and I told him that it was sure nice to see an American girl. I told him that I had never seen so many enlisted men and officers going after them and he just laughed and said that the girls had one hell of a business going on over there. After about ten minutes, he said that we were leaving and heading back to China Beach. We finally got there and I got out and told him that I would see him tomorrow.

We finally reached China Beach and the driver let me out. I walked on over to the picnic tables next to the ocean and I just watched the sun go slowly down for the day. I thought of the guys that were after the girls working for the Red Cross. It seemed to me that it was like being back in the States and that there was not a war going on. I couldn't believe how the guys were acting toward the girls; all they wanted was to have sex with them. Then, I started thinking that the girls working at the Red Cross were making money off of the guys. If the guys wanted to pay for it, the girls hit a gold mine here. I could see why the girls didn't want to go back to the States, the money they made over here was tax free. They sure had a good business going for themselves.

I started thinking to myself that I had changed so much because I couldn't play these games that they were doing down here at this very large base: making sure that your jungle uniform was clean and your boots were black... the officers and enlisted men paying the Red Cross girls money to have sex with them... and the biggest thing was that here at this base it didn't seem like there was a war going on. Everyone was going about their business as if nothing was going on at all over here.

I started thinking about Dale and I hoped that nothing was going on up there at Con Thein. I was also thinking of my men in my team and I just hoped that the big guy was not doing what his mother wanted him to do by getting himself killed. After sitting there for almost a couple of hours, darkness was coming toward me from the east and it was time to get back to the barracks and take a hot shower for the night.

I got to my rack after taking the shower and just lay down on top of my sheets and as I did, about ten minutes later I could hear a couple of guys outside the barracks getting after each other. They weren't fighting but only yelling at each other. Then, they came into the barrack and still they were yelling. I looked to see what the hell was going on and was getting a little pissed at them. This young Army guy and the old man who was in the SeaBees were having one hell of a disagreement.

As I listened, the young guy was saying that the Army did all of the fighting over here and that everyone else was doing jack shit. I started laughing to myself, because that was the dumbest thing I had heard. The Army guy had clean jungles clothes on and I also noticed that he hadn't been out in the field by the way he looked in his face. The old man told the kid that he had been in the Army, Air Force and now in the SeaBees and also was in WW II and Korea. I could tell that he had some miles on him but I couldn't tell if he had ever been in an infantry outfit.

There were about six other guys that were around both of them to make sure that they didn't get into a fight. I could also tell that both of them, including the other guys, were all drunk. Now, they were about ten feet away from me and I then got out of my rack and looked at all of them. Someone said that we better get out of here and let the guys get their sleep. Finally both of them agreed to get out of the barracks and go back to drinking. A couple of the guys told me they were sorry that they came in here making such noise. I didn't say a thing and I took off my clothes and got under the sheet and went to sleep.

Chapter Thirty-One

The next day came and I got up and went outside to see the sun but I knew that up north in the D.M.Z. it was cloudy and the monsoon season was about to start. I went on over to the beach and sat there for awhile, watching the tide coming in. It was so peaceful sitting here with no one around just listening to the tide. After a couple of hours I decided it was time for me to go on over to the main base and take in a movie. I walked on over to the bus and got on and the driver said, "Hello." I sat behind him and again it was just the two of us. He started up the bus and we took off and again he dropped me off just outside the Marine Terminal.

I got onto another six-by and he took me on over to Freedom Hill 327 and again dropped me off and I was right in front of the Red Cross building. I walked on over there and as I did one of the girls that worked for the Red Cross came over to me and she noticed that I was different from all of the other guys by my jungle clothes. She was a red head and very pretty. She asked me if there was anything she could do for me and I quietly told her, "No, nothing." She said that if there was to make sure to see her. I left the Red Cross building and went around it to where the theaters were in, in which there were two shows. One of the shows was a Bruce Lee movie and I decided to see it. I paid and went inside and sat in the back close to the exit in case we got hit.

When the movie was over I got up and went back outside and I saw where Bob Hope would be performing. The stage was built into the side of the hill. It was very large and the seating was for a couple of thousand men. I knew that none of the guys that were in the 3rd Marine Division Infantry Battalions would ever see the Christmas show. I just hoped that the guys in the 1st Marine Division Infantry outfits down around here would be able to see the show.

I walked back to where I could get on one of the six-bys and get back to the main base. I was getting tired of being bored down here. I knew that I needed to get back but I still had a couple of days to go. I finally got back to the main base and went inside the Marine Terminal and it was time for chow. I went over to the chow hall and got into line and got fed. When I was finished, I heard there was a beer tent about a hundred feet from here. I decided to sit in the terminal for awhile and just relax and stay to myself. A couple of hours passed and I decided to look for the beer tent.

I found the tent and went inside and as I did, I noticed there were a couple of empty crates with a couple of long boards over them for a bar top.

There was a Marine behind it and he was serving the beer. All of the beer was in cans. I went up to the bar and asked, "Bud, please." All of the beer was in tubs with crushed ice. The Marine said that it was fifty cents. I gave him one of my military one dollar bills and he gave me fifty cents in paper money. I took my time in drinking it and boy, it was surely cold. One of the guys that was in the tent called out my name, "Kasten. Do you remember me?" I turned and looked at him and before I could say anything, he said his name and that we had been in the same boot camp platoon. I smiled at him and asked how was he doing and what was he doing now. I knew he was in the infantry also since I remembered our D.I. saying that all of us were going into the infantry. He told me that he was stationed here at this base and didn't have to go out in the bush. I was glad for him and I asked him if he knew where Bell was and he said no. I told the guy that I wondered what happened to Bell since he was the only one that was black in our boot camp platoon. I told him that if he didn't know, that was a good sign that he wasn't dead. Then, he asked me what outfit I was with and I whispered to him, "1ˢᵗ Battalion 9ᵗʰ Marines." As soon as I said it, he yelled out my outfit name and said, "1ˢᵗ Battalion 9ᵗʰ Marines." He quickly took a couple of steps away from me. The Marine that was behind the bar came over to me and handed me another Bud and said that it was on him. Then, the guy from my boot camp bought me a beer and the rest of the guys in the tent bought a beer for me also. I had about thirteen cans of beer. I couldn't believe that he would yell out my outfit and again he said, "1ˢᵗ Battalion 9ᵗʰ marines." I told him that I just wanted to blend in down here and not for anyone to know that I was with the 1ˢᵗ Battalion 9ᵗʰ Marines. I asked him how he heard of our name, and he said that our name had been around here for a long while. He said that every time they brought dead men down here on six-bys from the north, it was our outfit that was getting hit. He said "You guys are like, "legends." Even so, he backed away from me a little. He said that everyone feared us down here and didn't want to be anywhere near us. I asked him how long had he heard the name, "1ˢᵗ Battalion 9ᵗʰ Marines" and he said the past few months.

I had about ten cans of beer and I asked him if he wanted a couple of them and he said that he would help me drink them. Then, he asked me how long I had been with that outfit and I told him since I first had come over here in March. He told me that it seemed that my outfit really got it from the N.V.A. and they were after us all of the time. I told him that the N.V.A. dwindled us down quite a bit but we killed a hell of a lot of them. Most of the guys had two to four Purple Hearts and had been shipped home. He asked me if I had been hit and I told him that I was the only one with the exception of Smithy in Delta Company who had not been hit as far as I knew.

The bartender said that it was last call and I knew that I didn't have to worry about getting another beer since I had at least ten unopened cans in front of me. My buddy from boot camp said there was going to be a movie shown at 21:00 hundred and asked if I wanted to go with him and I told him, "Yes." As we left the tent, I thought about my outfit and wondered when they first started calling us that name and I knew it had to be before July 2nd. We walked a little way and I saw on the side of one of the building a large white board attached to the building painted in white. He sat down on the ground and I sat next to him. I knew that it was too late to go back to China Beach and that I would have to stay here for the night. I asked my buddy where I could get a bunk and he told me I could stay with him and his buddies. We watched the movie and drank our beers. I ended up drinking only about two more of the cans and gave the rest away to the other Marines around us.

When the movie was over, he told me to follow him and that I could have one of the cots in the hardback that he was staying in. As we walked to the hardback, I asked him not to tell his buddies what outfit I was from. When we got there, he pointed to one of the cots and I went over to it and sat down. As I sat there, I started thinking of when I first came over here until now. I remembered when Richard McBride and I first got here and when we got our orders, the only thing on the back of the yellow envelope was written 1/9, (the 1st Battalion 9th Marines). This Marine had come up to us to see what outfit we were going to and said, "Good luck, you're going to need it."

I remembered the very first night when I joined my platoon and we got hit by mortars about an hour after I joined the guys and the dead men that were covered up by a poncho. I remembered the 8,000 meter walks to Phu An and getting hit by the N.V.A. and of course down at "The Street Without Joy" and the French author who came with us after being here twenty years ago with the French. He had also lost his life being with us. Also the pounding that we got up at Con Thein when the N.V.A. would hit us with their 152mm. artillery from North Vietnam.

I started thinking of the guys that we had lost in my platoon; James Fowler, who got killed the second night in the field; Benny Houston, who stepped on a booby trap and lost his leg. (I remembered Benny telling me that when he got off the patrol that he was going to trim the growth under my nose); Duvall, who got killed right after he came back from out of country R & R.; Sergeant Lugar, who with "Whitey," got killed by a green horn who dragged his feet and tripped over the trip wire and caused their death as well as his own. I thought about "Whitey," George Hahner, and I remembered him and Dale setting me up as a fire team leader. I thought about Charlie who got hit by us two times, coming in from L.P., and all of the other guys that we put on choppers when hell broke loose out there in the bush. I knew that there was a lot more to war than just killing people. It was seeing your own buddies getting killed or wounded in front of you.

Somehow I finally fell off to sleep and the next thing I knew I felt the sun hitting me in the face. I got up and saw that everyone was starting to get up. I told my buddy that I had to go and went back over to the terminal and waited for the bus to take me to China Beach. This was my last day and I wanted to spend some of it at the beach for the last time. The bus came and I got on and again I was the only one on it and again he dropped me off and I went over to the picnic tables next to the ocean. As I sat there, the empty and lonely feeling came over me and I knew that I had to get back to my team. I started thinking about home and how it felt like it didn't exist. The hours passed and I went over to the snack bar for the last time and got a cheeseburger and Coke and went back to the picnic tables that were outside and ate my food by myself with no one around. The flies flying were around trying to land on my cheeseburger but I wouldn't give them a chance.

I just couldn't write any letters and all I wanted to do was watch the waves come in from the ocean. I looked at my watch and I knew that it was time for me to turn in the linens that they had given me here. I went over to the barracks and took off the linen and turned it in to the supply sergeant and left back to the beach where the picnic tables were. I started thinking about how much time I had before I left for the United States. It was the first time I thought about it since I got over here. I knew that it was November but I had to go to April and it seemed like a long time to go. I quickly forgot about it. I remembered what the guys said; when you start thinking about home is when you will get killed. I knew that I wasn't worried about dying over here so I decided not to think about it again, or even count the days. Around 16:30, I was tired of this place and I knew that it was time to leave. I got on the bus for the last time and headed back to the main base. The rest of the day I just stayed there at the main base and slept in the terminal that night.

The rest of the day I went on over to Freedom Hill 327 and took in another movie and visited the Red Cross building, looking at the girls but just staying to myself. That evening, I went to the beer tent and got a couple of beers for the evening and went back to the terminal for the rest of the night. I lay down on the bench and I knew that I was going back to my outfit the next afternoon. I knew that I had to bring goodies back with me, and I better get some smokes for Dale.

It was 02:30 in the morning and I heard knocking on the wooden benches around me. I got up and there were about ten M.P. Marines telling the guys to get up and get in line. I got up and got in line with the rest of the guys that were in the terminal. I was the seventh guy in line and after a couple of minutes a door opened from one of the hardbacks that was next to the terminal. The M.P. told the first guy to go into the hardback and a couple of minutes later he came out the other end of the building being guarded by two M.P.s As I got closer to the building, I could hear someone inside saying, "AWOL, Brig; next." All six guys in front of me went to the brig. I was looking forward to going to the brig and it looked like the lieutenant was going to get his wish. I waited outside until the person told me to go in and said, "Next", I walked in and went in about half way into the hardback and there was a desk and a Gunny sitting there and he looked at me and asked me for my Pass. I took the pass out of my jungle shirt pocket and handed it to him and he looked at it and a couple of minutes went by and said, "Do you know that your pass has expired?" I told him, "Yes, Gunny!" Again he kept on looking at the pass and he looked up at my eyes for the first time and looked at my jungle clothes and he said, "You know that you are AWOL and that you could go to the brig for having an expired pass?" Again I said, "Yes, Gunny." Then he asked me how long I had been with the 1st Battalion 9th Marines and I said, "Since March. He leaned back in his chair and it was though he couldn't believe I was with them that long, that was the impression he gave me. He asked me when was I going to go back and I told him that my lieutenant told me to take a couple of days off the books and to try to have a good time. I said, "I was going back today, after I went to the P.X. to get some goodies for my team." He then gave back my pass and said, "If I see you here tomorrow, you will go to the brig," I told him, "I will be gone by the afternoon, Gunny." Then he told me to go back to where I was at and told the rest of the M.P.s to leave me alone.

As I went back to the bench, I noticed that the M.P.s were whispering to each other about my outfit. They were staying away from me. The rest of the guys in line, about thirty of them, went to the brig with the exception of a couple of others who had good passes.

Morning finally came and I got up and went to the chow hall and got something hot to eat. The sun was having a little trouble getting out from some of the clouds. After chow I went back to the terminal and sat down for awhile. I watched the other Marines that were stationed here on their daily routines and boy did they have it easy. I noticed that they all had to be in clean uniforms and their boots had to be black, but not shined. I knew they were starting to play stateside Marines. I didn't want any part of it. It was getting a little bad out in the bush but all of the new guys as well as the lieutenant and staff sergeant hadn't seen any combat yet. I knew that when they had gotten in a fire fight they would stop with their bull shit with the guys. There were only the four of us left; both machine gunners Kenny Fulton and Speedy, and Dale and me.

Around 10:30 I knew that the big P.X. was open and it was time for me to go on over there and buy the goodies for the guys. I got on a six-by and went on over there. I went inside the P.X. and went on over to where the candy, smokes and juices were. I bought what I could with what was left of my money and grabbed a couple of empty sandbags to carry the goodies in. As I walked out the main doors of the P.X., I noticed there were about ten officers just outside the doors talking and as I got close to them, I said, "By your leave." I kept on walking and none of them paid any attention to me. As I was walking away from them I saw this new second lieutenant coming toward me in his State side uniform who must have just gotten here. I had a feeling that this dumb ass was going to make me salute him. As I walked past him, sure enough he called for me to stop and as I did, I slowly turned around to look at him. At that same time the other officers that were just outside the doors also stopped talking and were looking at us. All of them watched to see what was going to happen. The second lieutenant had his back to the other officers and he started telling me, "Why aren't you saluting me?" I didn't say a word and he said, "Your uniform is dirty and your boots are not shined." I started getting a little pissed off and noticed one of the officers telling the rest of the guys that he would be right back and came toward us. I kept quiet and the major came up behind the second lieutenant and said, "What's going on here?" The second lieutenant turned around and was ready to salute when the major told him that he better drop his arm and not salute. The major asked him if he knew where the hell he was at and the second lieutenant was again puzzled by what the major said. Again the major told him that we were in Vietnam and the enlisted men don't have to salute. "But, if you want him to salute, he would be glad to and you will be getting a round between the eyes." The second lieutenant was telling the major how disrespectful I was and also had a dirty uniform. The major turned to me and asked what outfit was I with and I slowly said, "1ˢᵗ Battalion 9ᵗʰ Marines." The major said, "Oh, my God!" Then the major told me to leave and that he would take care of the situation. As I left, I heard the major really ripping into the second lieutenant and telling him, "Never pick on guys that have dirty uniforms, especially from 1/9." The major said that when you see guys like me that had dirty uniforms and no black on their combat boots usually it meant they were in the infantry. As I walked away, I remembered that the major said, "You had to pick on someone from that outfit."

I finally got to the six-by and got on with my two sandbags of goodies and he took me on over to the terminal. I then went up to the other Marine Terminal and got a boarding pass for Dong Ha. After I got the boarding pass, everyone in the terminal was looking at my jungle clothes, at how dirty they were. But I just stayed to myself and looked at them. I wanted to see if they had any backbone, but not one of them would look me in the eyes. About an half hour went by and there was an announcement that the plane for Dong Ha would be late. Dong Ha was being hit by rockets from the N.V.A. The guys that were going up to Dong Ha were getting worried. I kind of smiled to myself and sat on one of the benches, waiting for the plane.

Finally the word was passed on the intercom that the plane to Dong Ha was being boarded and to make sure that we had our boarding pass. The Marine at the gate called out each number and my number was called and I gave it to the guy and slowly walked on over to the back of the C-130 and boarded it. I sat down and buckled myself up and just looked out the back of the plane and watched the rest of the guys getting on. Everyone had on new jungle clothes with the exception of me and everyone was looking at my dirty uniform. We didn't get new jungle clothes in our outfit because we were never back in the rear to get new ones. We were always out in the bush. No one said a word, but as I looked at them, they would turn away and look elsewhere. No one wanted to ask me about my dirty uniform. Then the plane started up its engines, and we started moving toward the runway. As the plane was going over to the runway, I could see the F-104 jets in their hangers.

The C-130 started taking off and the back door started closing as we were going down the runway. I closed my eyes and just rested. I knew that we would be stopping at Phu Bai first, before going to Dong Ha. After about a twenty minute ride, the plane went back down. I knew that we were landing at Phu Bai. The plane stopped and the back door opened up and some of the guys got off while others were getting on. I had my eyes closed and was trying to rest as much as possible. I could hear some of the guys on the plane talking about Dong Ha being hit and they were all worried. The plane started back up and we were off again and I knew that this time we would be landing in about ten minutes. The Air Force sergeant on the C-130 told us as soon as the plane stopped and the door opened up to quickly get off; they were going to be leaving as quickly as they could.

The plane was coming down and I opened my eyes and noticed that everyone except me was getting nervous. I never knew there were so many Army and Marines that were scared about getting hit by rockets from the N.V.A. The plane hit the runway and we came to a stop about 100 meters from the terminal and the back door started coming down. As it did, the guys got out of their chairs and headed to the rear of the plane as quickly as they could. As soon as the door of the plane hit the ground they all started running to the terminal. I slowly got up and walked down the ramp of the door while Army, Marines and Officers were getting on the plane. I took my time going over to the terminal and I noticed there was some smoke that was near the runway. I could tell it was one of the places that had gotten hit from the N.V.A.

I went through the terminal and out the back of it to get to where my battalion was station. I got to my tent with the two sandbags filled with goodies for my team as well for Dale, Speedy and Kenny. I went on over to my cot and dropped the sandbags onto it and I went over to the supply tent and got my rifle. I told the sergeant that he was a good boy and I left.

I smiled to myself as I did. Sgt. Lefefe had finally left for home and I was glad that he made it out of here. I went back to my tent and saw that there were some new men in our platoon. I went over to the clerk tent and told the guys there that I was back and that I wanted to know when I could get back with the platoon. They told me that it would be a couple of days and there would be a convoy going to Con Thein. I asked them if I had any mail here and they said that all of my mail was up at Con Thein. I told the clerks that they better not be opening up my packages or I would skin them alive. I left and went back to the tent. I got out my rifle and magazines and started cleaning them. As I was cleaning my rifle, I was listening to the new men talking. They came over to me and asked me about the outfit. They could tell I had been here for awhile and one of them said that he heard about this battalion. I asked them where they heard about us and they said from everyone over here in Vietnam. Another asked if it was true about what they heard about this outfit getting wiped out by the N.V.A. and other battles. I just looked at them, and in their eyes, it showed they were really scared and they didn't want to die over here. I knew that whatever I said to them, I had to make sure that I didn't cause more fear and really cause them to worry more. I said "If you did your training back in the States the best that you could do, you have a very good chance of making it over here." I said, "Listen to your fire team leaders or squad leaders and do as they say; you will make it." Then one of them said there were not many old timers in the outfit. I didn't say a word and I knew that he was right. I didn't want to tell them that almost all of the guys in the battalion were all green and hadn't seen any fire fights.

Word was passed that it was time to eat and I got out my mess gear and went with the green horns over to the mess tent. When I got there I saw they were giving the guys Spam and Rice and I decided to go back to the tent and heat up "C" rations. I went over to the supply tent and asked for a box of "C" rations and the sergeant handed it to me. I went back to the tent and opened up a B-3 can of cookies, cheese and cut holes in the bottom of the can so that the air could go through and help the fire cook the meat. I took out the small can of cheese and the can of meat and opened both of them up. I got the "C" 4 and put it in the bottom of the cookie can and lit it and put the can of meat over it and as it was cooking I put the cheese onto the meat and had both of them cook together as usual. I had done this many times out in the bush. I was tired of the rice that we got every time we came back to the rear. I knew when the battalion was out in the bush, the cooks and clerks would have the steaks and other goodies that we never got.

As my food was being cooked, the green horns came back from the chow hall and said that the food was great. I looked up at them and said, "What?" They said that the Rice and Spam was great. I told them that every time we came back in from the field that the cooks would feed us rice all of the time. I told them that they would be getting tired of it very quickly. When my food was finally cooked I ate the meat and cheese. The green horns were just watching me and couldn't believe that I only ate three pieces of meat from a small can and I was done. They asked me if I was going to eat anything else and I told them that I was done. I took out my canteen and drank some water and I was finished. I knew they were puzzled by what I had done while they were going to the chow hall and getting all of the rice and Spam they wanted to eat.

They all had a lot of baby fat on them and they would soon be losing it fast over here just like me when I first had come over. I remembered how thin Sgt. Thomas and other guys in the platoon had been. But now, when these guys went out in the bush and met the rest of the guys in the platoon there would only be four of us that were very, very thin.

Then one of the guys asked me more questions about the outfit and I told them that I didn't feel like talking any more. One guy asked me how long I had been over here and I said, "March". They started talking among themselves, saying that they had 395 days to go before they could go home. I laid down on my cot and just looked at the top of the tent. I started thinking of when I first got over here and I remembered that one of the guys had 17 hours to go before he left Vietnam and there I was with 395 days to go before I could go home. I remembered it made me sick inside and I knew that these guys were also sick knowing that they had 395 days to go before they could go home. I also knew they didn't realize that they might not make it their first two months and if they did, they would have to worry about out-of-Country R. and R. and then the last two months of their tour.

I knew that I had changed quite a bit and was more to myself than a lot of guys. The only guys I stayed close with were Speedy, Kenny and Dale. I knew that the four of us kept each other going over here. I knew that it was bad to know more guys in case they either got wounded or killed. It took its toll on everyone that had seen combat. I started thinking of my father because I had told him that I liked eating rice when I was a kid. He didn't like it at all when he was in the Army in WW II. Now I knew why he hated it - because I slept in it, walked in it and ate it when I first came over here and now, I didn't want any part of it. I knew that my dad had done the same thing in WW II.

The word was passed that there was going to be a movie just behind our area and it would start sometime just as the sun went down. I got up and went over there by myself. I sat down on one of the benches and waited for the movie to start and I could hear someone sitting behind me. Then I heard this voice saying, "Excuse me, are you a Marine?" I didn't turn around and I thought that he was talking to someone else. Again the guy said, "Excuse me, are you a Marine". I turned around and looked at the guy and saw that he was in the Army. There was a Army patch on his left arm and he was a corporal. I told him, "Yes". He told me that he wished that he was a Marine and not in the Army. I asked him why, and he said that the last couple of times that they would go out in the bush the N.V.A. would hit the point squad and the rest of his platoon would turn around and DiDi, meaning getting the hell out of there quickly. He said they would leave them there to die and not go back to help them. I looked into his eyes and told him that I can't believe that any outfit would leave its men to die to the N.V.A. He told me that it was true. He said that he was thinking of going over the hill, "AWOL" so he could go to the brig and be safe. He asked my outfit name and I told him, 1st Battalion 9th Marines and he said that he heard that we never left our men to the N.V.A. He said that if he was with my battalion he knew that he would be going home to be buried back in the States if he got killed because the guys would make sure he went home. I started thinking about Sergeant Singleton and how our whole battalion went back in and found his body among the N.V.A. and I helped in carrying his body out of there for him to go home, even though we got hit again and lost more men - but everyone got out of there. The guys in my battalion were very close to each other. I wished that none of them were gone but were still here. The whole battalion felt strong against the N.V.A. and we never felt they were better than us. It seemed like when we first got those damn M-16s they never told us anything about how to clean them and how many rounds we could put in a magazine. When we went up against the N.V.A. we ended up using our bayonets to kill them and lost a lot of men in our company.

The movie finally started and I turned back around and didn't say anything more to the Army guy. When the movie was over I got up and he was gone and I went back to the tent. The next day, I didn't do a damn thing but just lie in the cot and think about nothing. I just couldn't wait to see Dale, Speedy and Kenny. I hoped that the lieutenant and Corporal Curry didn't mess over my team and the platoon. I knew that the lieutenant loved me being as far away from them as much as possible so they could screw over the guys. The day went by slowly and I knew that tomorrow I could be going back out into the field with the rest of my platoon. I had a good night's sleep.

The next day came and I went over to the clerk's tent and asked them where I should go to get up to Con Thein and they told me there was a convoy going up there and I was to go over to the P.X. to where the trucks would be. The clerks said that they would be leaving sometime around 10:00 hundred. I looked at my watch and it was around 09:30. I went back to the tent and got my combat gear on and the rest of the guys there were also getting their gear on and were told to go with me. I grabbed my two sandbags of goodies and headed up to the P.X. with about five of these green horns following me. I didn't say a thing and looked at all of them and they were ready and I left the tent and headed up to the P.X.

When I got to the P.X. there were four six-bys and I came up to the first truck and asked the driver if he was going to Con Thein. He said no but the truck behind him was going there. I went to the next truck with the green horns behind me and asked the driver if he was going to Con Thein and he said to get on. I put the two sandbags onto the truck and got on myself. All of the green horns got on also and were watching what I did next and I sat down on the floor of the truck and they all did the same. I thought to myself that they were getting scared and just didn't know what to do. I told them to sit outward and when we got outside of the gate to put a round into the chamber and make sure that their rifles were on safe. I just didn't want any of them grabbing the trigger and shooting me if we got hit. I had my clip in my rifle and I put a round into the chamber. A few minutes went by and the trucks started up their engines. It was an overcast day. There were seven trucks that were going up to Con Thein, that was a lot. We got out the gate and I put my rifle on semi, and laid it across my lap. I sat up against the cab of the truck and watched the green horns. All of them were watching me.

The trucks turned left and headed north. After a little bit, I knew that we would be turning off to the right to go through Cam Lo. As we got closer to the turn off, we kept on going straight north. I knew that the driver said that we would be going to Con Thein, but I just wondered if there was a new route to get there. We traveled another ten minutes and we came into a large base and as I looked over both sides of the truck, I saw hardbacks all over the place. There were 105 mm batteries, a lot of them. Our truck turned around and stopped. As I sat on the truck I asked the driver how long we would be here and he said just a very short while. I got up and saw in the distance a single line of men walking from east to west into the mountains. I asked one of the guys there at the base who that was out there and he said the N.V.A. and I asked him "Why aren't we shooting at them?" He said that we can't because they are in North Vietnam. I said to myself, "States-side bull shit, again. The N.V.A can go into Laos, Cambodia, but we can't go to those places or even fire at them. What a screwed - up war."

The truck started up and now there were only three trucks heading back down south on this highway. Again, I saw the turn off and this time the truck turned toward Cam Lo. The other two trucks still headed down south. The ground was somewhat wet from the rains they had had the past couple of days. There was gravel on the road so we didn't have to worry about the mud. We headed up the large hill and I told the guys that we were almost there. The truck went into the perimeter of Con Thein and then stopped. I told the guys on the truck to get the supplies off as quickly as possible. I told them to get off and grabbed my two sandbags of goodies. The truck left and headed back to Dong Ha. I told the guys to follow me and that I would tell them where the lieutenant was. Mud was all over the place. The mud was about eight inches deep but I walked as those it wasn't there. I could hear the green horns behind me having some trouble walking in it.

We got to our perimeter and the ground didn't have the mud as much as up at Con Thein. I told the guys to go straight on and that they would run into the lieutenant. I went on over to where my team was and they called out "Hammer is here!" and waited for me to get to them. They saw that I had a couple of sandbags with me and there were goodies for them.

I put the sandbags down and told them that I would be back in a couple of minutes. But, before I left them, I asked them if they got screwed over with while I was gone. They looked at each other and didn't say a word. I knew what had gone on; I left them and went over to the lieutenant. I saw that now he had a small bunker for himself and the staff sergeant and radio-man. I called out for the lieutenant and he came out of his bunker and asked why I hadn't come over to him. I told him I had to unload my gear first. He looked at me and was surprised that I came back so soon. I told him I kind of knew that you would screw over the platoon as well as my men. I told him again that we were not back in the States and that we were in the D.M.Z. trying to survive. I knew that he wouldn't understand until we got hit by the N.V.A. I told him that I was going back to my team. As I walked back to my team, I made sure that I would go past Corporal Curry's bunker, which was at the other fire team. I told Curry that his sleeping all night was over with and that he would be taking the fourth watch tonight. I told him to make sure that he woke me up when his time was up. The look on his face quickly changed from being happy to being pissed off at me. I loved it and didn't give a damn.

I went over to my fighting hole. When I got there Dale was there. Dale asked me what I had and I grabbed a carton of smokes for him with candy and juice. I passed out the rest of the goodies to the guys in my team and I looked at the tall guy and asked the rest of the team if he had behaved himself. The guys told me he did good. I then gave him some of the goodies and everyone was happy. The guys said that I had mail and that it was in the bunker and one of them got it for me. I asked Dale if the lieutenant screwed with the platoon and he said only a little. Dale said that the platoon was tired of working out in front of their perimeter. The lieutenant said there would be no more work details on the perimeter. The rest of the day and evening went by slowly.

Night came and I assigned everyone their times for watch and I told Bill to wake me if he couldn't get Curry over here to stand his watch. I was awakened by Curry and he went back to his little hole with the one black kid. I knew that when the time came if he needed the rest of the guys to help him in battle that they wouldn't, because he only associated with his soul brother. I knew that he was making a huge mistake by only staying with the one black guy that was in our platoon. Curry made his feelings well known among the guys in the platoon. I thought we had not been hit up here for awhile and it was time for us to get hit again.

The next day came and it moved slowly. One of the guys, Bill, came over to me and asked if he could dig a hole about six feet long and three feet wide. I asked him why and he said that he wanted to lie in it so that the enemy wouldn't shoot at him. I asked him how deep he was going to make it and he said about eighteen inches deep. I told him to go ahead. Bill got out his shovel and started digging it and I watched him. The other guys in the team were in the bunker resting for the day. As he was digging it just behind our fighting hole, I noticed that he was making it six feet by six feet. It took him a couple of hours and he asked if I wanted to join him and I looked at him and decided I would. I got up and went over to one side and laid my rifle just outside the hole so I could get it in a hurry. I then laid down into the hole and he was next to me and started asking me some questions about being over here. I told him to forget it and he started singing one of the Righteous Brothers' songs called "Unchained Melody." I joined in with my bad singing voice. When we were finished singing that song, we then sang another of their big hits. The sun came out for a couple of hours and went back behind the clouds. I told Bill that it was time to get out and to eat and get ready for our night watches.

The night was over and the next day started off slow again, the guys just lying around talking about home. The next thing I knew the guys were going inside the bunker talking about something but I just stayed outside at our perimeter, making sure that the enemy didn't come sneaking up on us. It sounded like the guys were having one hell of an argument inside the bunker. I jumped into the hole and went inside the bunker and the guys stopped talking and asked me, "Hammer, do you believe in the Bible?" I looked at them and after a minute I told them, "No." I walked back out of the bunker and sat in the fighting hole. I couldn't believe that the guys were having a discussion about the Bible, of all things. The blond-headed guy came out of the bunker and said, "Hammer, then you don't believe in God." I looked at him and said, "I do believe in God." I told him that I didn't believe in the writings of the Bible since it was written by man and not by God. I said that the real translation had been lost a long time ago. He understood and went back in and told the rest of the guys in my team.

About 10:30 in the morning I could hear in the distance, from North Vietnam, artillery being fired. The guys up at Con Thein were running for their bunkers and the 105s were getting ready to fire back. I yelled to the guys in the bunker to stay there and not to come out and to make sure they had their fighting gear on and be ready to get out of the bunker when I told them. Then, one of the guys came out and it was the blond-headed guy. The 152mm rounds just started hitting Con Thein and the shrapnel was flying all over the place. Some of the pieces were coming toward us.

I was standing up and had my legs apart about 18 inches and then I heard this shrapnel coming toward me and I knew that I couldn't move. It hit the ground right in between my legs and I looked at the blond-headed guy and slowly told him to get inside now and boy did he move back in the bunker. I knew he saw the look on my face and knew that I could have killed him. It seemed that the N.V.A were really letting us have it with all of their 152mm artillery pieces. The 105mm artillery pieces at Con Thein were shelling as fast as they could back at the N.V.A. The N.V.A. rounds were getting closer to our perimeter and I knew the enemy liked to sneak up on us while we were under ground waiting for their artillery to stop. I looked over to the northwest corner of the base and there was no one in the fighting bunkers. I looked behind me and Dale was in his fighting hole while he had his men in the bunker. I looked over to both machine gun teams and Kenny and Speedy were manning them. I knew that I had to get over to the corner bunker and tell them to get two guys outside in their fighting hole while we were getting hit. I called out for Bill and the blond-headed guy to come out with their combat gear and to get into the fighting hole. I told the rest of the guys to stay in the bunker until I called for them.

It took a couple of minutes for the two guys to come out and I was still standing on top of the fighting hole. I pointed to them to get into it and told them that I would be back. I started running over to the northwest corner of our perimeter. I ran past the fighting hole of our sister fire team and all of them including Curry were inside, I told them to get a couple of guys out and in their fighting hole while the shelling was going on. I picked up my speed and tried to get there as fast as I could. I was about fifteen meters away when I heard a round coming right at the bunker at the northwest corner of our perimeter. I knew that I couldn't get there fast enough and I had to dive for the ground. As I hit the ground, the 152mm round just missed the bunker. The ground shook and I was bouncing around and my ears were ringing from the explosion of the round. I got up and started walking like a drunken sailor to the bunker and jumped down into the trench that led into it. I went inside and as my eyes were trying to focus on the guys, I saw they were all at the other end of the bunker together. They didn't know what the hell to do while the shelling was going on. They were picking each other up from the blast and I called out if anyone was hit and they all said, that they were all right. Everyone was complaining that their heads hurt from the blast.

I told them to get two guys out into the fighting hole in case the N.V.A. tried to sneak into our perimeter. As I looked at them, they were all scared to death of what was going on with the artillery rounds hitting all around us. They told me that they would get a couple of guys out there and I left them and walked back to my team. My head was still ringing and I knew that all of them in the bunker were feeling what I was feeling, ringing in their heads. The 152mm rounds were still hitting more at Con Thein than our perimeter but you just never know if a round is a long round - that's where the round went farther than it should. I got up out of the trench and started walking back to my fighting hole. As I ran past Curry and the other fire team, I saw they still hadn't gotten anyone out of the bunker while the artillery rounds were hitting up at Con Thein and here. I knew that he didn't have the balls to do his job and it showed. I got back to my team and called out the rest of the guys in my team to get out and into the other fighting hole. I told the guys to make sure that they had their rifles on semi and to get the grenades ready, if there was a ground attack.

As we watched and listened to the rounds coming in on Con Thein, the shrapnel was hitting all around us and the other small perimeter that was on the other side of the road that led south. Our sister platoon had the other perimeter and our third platoon was in Con Thein. The N.V.A. artillery was slowing down and our 105s were still hammering at them. I started looking to see if the lieutenant or the staff sergeant was running around the perimeter but I didn't see either of them. I looked behind me to see how Dale's team was doing and saw that Dale had his men ready in case we got hit from the ground. Both machine gun teams were ready but the rest of the platoon was still inside their bunkers waiting it out and that included Curry. This was the N.V.A. hitting us with only their 152mm artillery pieces and my platoon was inside their bunkers waiting for the shelling to stop. Us four old timers had our teams ready in case the N.V.A. would have hit us while the artillery was being fired on us. The lieutenant and the rest of the platoon would have gotten killed by being in their bunkers. I couldn't wait to see the lieutenant's face when it was over.

The N.V.A. artillery was finished and our own 105s had also stopped firing. Everything got very, very quiet. I told the guys to relax and to put their rifles on safe. It didn't look like the N.V.A. was coming this time. The guys in my team asked me why I was so calm and I told them that I had gone through this many times before up here and that in time they would be getting used to this also. They all said, "Hammer, we can't take the quietness." I told them that in time, they would. I knew that they didn't like being shelled at and there was nothing they could do to get back at the enemy; it was very frustrating. I told them it was time to get some rest in before our night watch begin. I told them to go and relax and I would stand watch while they cooked their meals. I went over to where the lieutenant was to see the look on his face and as he came out of the bunker with the staff sergeant - the look on both of their faces told the story. They were both scared to death and I said that this was just a small part of what the hell it is like over here and I walked back to my team.

It was getting close for the guys to stand their night watch and I went over to Curry and told him that he better stand his watch tonight with the other fire team. I told the fire team leader to let me know in the morning if

Curry hadn't stood his watch. I told Curry that what we went through today
was nothing and he better get ready for the worst that would be coming.
He looked at me and didn't say a damn thing. I could tell that the 152mm
rounds put the fear of God in him. I left and went back to my team. As I was
walking back, I knew that he wasn't the big man he thought he was.

One of the guys woke me up and I went on over to the fighting hole and
sat down. I laid my rifle across my lap and started thinking of what had happened today. All of the green horns in our company got an education from
the N.V.A. artillery. I knew that it was nothing compared to a fire fight with
them. The only thing was that no one got killed or wounded. I knew when
they saw their buddies getting wounded and killed that they would change
very quickly. They would know if they had it or not. I started thinking about
boot camp and all of the training I had and remembered that I hadn't had
enough. I remembered what my head D.I. said to me in boot camp, that he
would be proud to have me in his team in Vietnam. I remembered he also
said that I was the only one that they couldn't break in boot camp and the
reason was my father. I knew that my father had shaped me into a damn
good soldier as I was growing up. The night was getting cooler now and all
of the stars were out again as usual. I felt the loneliness coming over me
and thought of the guys that used to be in our platoon. Chuck Knight came
into my thoughts; if he hadn't argued with me about taking over the radio
for the platoon, I would be the one that was home now, instead of him, with
a Purple Heart.

I looked down at my watch and saw it was time for me to wake up the
next guy in my team. Morning came and I went over to the platoon radioman and asked him where in the hell the lieutenant and staff sergeant had
been yesterday, when we were getting hit. He told me that both of them
were in their bunker and didn't want to come out at all. I said in a loud
voice, I just hoped that our great lieutenant and staff sergeant would get us
through a fire fight, if and when it happens. The radioman showed me a big
grin and I told him that I'd see him later. I then went on over to see Dale.

As I started walking away over to Dale's bunker, I remembered the time
when Lieutenant Libutti first joined the platoon and we went out on a patrol
with the rest of the company and got hit with mortars by the N.V.A. at Phu
An. The word was passed that Hammer should go up to the C.P. and when I
got to the hole, the only thing I saw was the radio standing, with the lieutenant in the bottom of the hole with his hands over his head. I remembered the
look on his face and that he was scared to death and now he had to take care
of his platoon, as well as take care of himself. I knew that this lieutenant
had just gone through what Lieutenant Libutti went through a few months
ago, which seemed like years. I just wished that he was back with the platoon - actually I was glad that he was home, away from this damn place. I
knew now that this lieutenant realized that he needed what old timers that

were left in this platoon to keep him and the rest of the green horns alive.

I finally reached Dale's fighting hole and he was sitting on the edge of the hole reading a letter back at home. I asked Dale if his ex-girlfriend had written to him after the Dear John letter and he said a couple of times but he just threw the letters away. Dale told me that he had two things to say to me and I asked him what and he said that he was getting the Silver Star, in a couple of days from now and that he had to go down to Da Nang to receive it from the President of the United States, Johnson. I looked into Dale's eyes and told him that he should have gotten the Medal of Honor for what he did to save the guys in the platoon on July 6, 1967. I asked him what was the other thing was he going to tell me and he said that he would be leaving the platoon shortly and going back to the rear with some other outfit. Dale said that he would not be going out into the field because of the Purple Hearts, that he had. Dale said that all of the old timers that had two or more Purple Hearts were to leave this outfit and be stationed with some rear outfit. Dale looked at me and knew that I was the only one that could not leave because I didn't have one Purple Heart. Dale said, "It wasn't right, Hammer, that you can't leave with the rest of the guys. I didn't say a thing and I told Dale that I had to leave and get back to my team.

I slowly walked back to my team and for the first time in my whole life I felt completely all alone in the world. I was not going to see Dale, Speedy and Kenny, when the word came for them to leave. I finally reached my fighting hole and sat down and just didn't want to talk to anyone. The guys in my team could tell that something was wrong and knew that I needed to be left alone.

The word was passed that we were going to get hot chow because it was Thanksgiving. A six-by came over to our perimeter and the guys unloaded it and put the hot containers on make - shift tables. The word was passed to come over and get our hot chow. Everyone was running over to the hot chow and got into line and I just slowly took my time and wasn't in any hurry. Dale came over and joined me and didn't say a word. He knew that I was feeling very low about what he had told me earlier. Both of us could see that there was turkey, dressing, corn and gravy. As soon as I got the food, I found a place and Dale sat down next to me. As both of us ate in silence, I looked up to the sky; it was a cloudy, gray day. After a couple of minutes, Dale told me that he felt bad about what he said about the old timers leaving. I told him that I was glad that they were getting out of this outfit because it wasn't the same anymore. I looked Dale in the eyes and said I was really glad that he was getting out of this outfit and I knew at least one of us would make it back to the States. Dale went back to eating and said that the food was really great.

One of the guys came over to us from the C.P. and said to Dale that he had to leave tomorrow morning for Da Nang, to get his Silver Star. I told

Dale to have a nice time down there at China Beach, it was great there.

It was my time for night watch and the time was 01:00. I sat there next to the fighting hole. I could hear the lieutenant coming and didn't say a damn thing to him. He looked at me and I could tell that he was changing from being a shit head to somewhat of an officer. He just looked at me for a couple of minutes and without a word went on over to the next position in the line. I watched him leave and started thinking of everything that I had done over here and what I had seen. I made Lieutenant Libutti into a great officer, by teaching him for two weeks out into the field and taking care of him. I had had a great Captain, Hutchinson of our company, who always wanted to know if Lieutenant Libutti stood his radio watch and did a great job out in the bush. I started getting a smile on my face just thinking about the captain, and I surely missed him also. Then I started thinking of all the guys I knew in our platoon who had gotten killed or wounded and the one guy who had a brother in Vietnam in the Army and was a truck driver so he could go home and out of the combat field. I was starting to feel better and I was especially happy for Dale, Speedy and Kenny to get the hell out of this battalion. I remembered that they called this battalion down at Da Nang, "The Walking Dead," and how everyone got scared when they met someone from this outfit. I knew that I better tell Dale tomorrow about what they called this outfit and I knew that he would get a good laugh out of it.

Chapter Thirty-Two

Morning came and I went over to Dale's hole and told him that in Da Nang they know all about our outfit, "1st Battalion 9th Marines." Dale told me he would see me after he got his medal and had his In-Country R. and R. I told him to have a good time down there and not to worry about us up here. He left and went on over to Con Thein and waited for the six-by to take him back down south. I went back to my fighting hole. Some of the guys in our platoon were going over to the shittiers, fifty gallon drums (they are cut in half and used as a toilet, with two boards). As I watched a couple of the guys running to the shittiers, one of them stopped because he had the runs. His jungle pants had a large wet spot running down his legs. I started laughing because as the hours went by more and more of the guys were getting the runs. Almost all of the guys were stopping and shit would run down their legs. The guys that did make it to the shittiers were sitting there for some time. I could hear some of them telling the others to get off so they could get on it. It wasn't until later in the day when some of the guys in my team started getting the runs. I told them to run like hell or DiDi, laughing at them. When they got back they said "Hammer, we can't wait for you to have the shits," and I told them I knew just what to do when the time come. The rest of the day came and still I didn't get the runs and I knew that it was only time before I did. The only reason for the guys to come down with the shits was the hot Thanksgiving chow they sent out here in the field.

The next day came and it was around 13:00 and I could tell that my insides were hurting and that it was almost time for me to go to the shittiers. The guys in my team said "Hammer has the shits," and they were betting that I wouldn't make it in time and that it would be running down my pants. I got up and slowly started walking over to the shittiers. When I knew that I couldn't make it, I stopped and dropped my jungle pants and squatted down and shit like the Vietnamese people do when they are working in the rice paddies. After a couple of minutes, I was finished and pulled up my pants and went back to the guys and they were all disappointed. I told them that I wasn't dumb like them, letting it run down my legs.

The next day came and the word was passed that we were moving back and to saddle up. I told my team to get all of their combat gear and to get ready to get out of here. The word was passed that we would be leaving around 12:30. It was that time and the lieutenant told me that my team was to take point and to walk on over to the road and to get on the east side of it and start heading down it about 100 meters. I told the blond-headed guy to take the point and we started out of the perimeter and went past the road, got about 100 meters and then headed south parallel with the road. We were right next to the tree line. We went about half way down the hill and the word was passed to stop. I told the guys to face into the tree line and to get down. As we sat there, the rest of our company came out of the other perimeter as well as from Con Thein. It was a partly cloudy day. We waited for about 45 minutes and the six-bys came toward us from the south. I wondered if 3rd Battalion 3rd Marines were going to relieve us or 2nd Battalion 4th Marines. Both were damn good outfits.

The six-bys were getting closer to us from the south and finally they reached the bottom of the hill, went about half way up, and then stopped. The troops on the back of the trucks got off and spread out along the side of the road. The Marines had new jungles clothes and everyone was green looking. I looked down at my jungle clothes and mine and a few other old timers in our company had brown jungles clothes, even our flak jackets were brown. Most of the clothes in our company were between brown and green.

As soon as the guys got off the trucks, they started up and went up to the top of Con Thein and turned around and came about half way back down and then stopped. The word was passed for us to get on the trucks. I waved my hand and my team walked toward the trucks and we boarded them. Everyone in our company was boarding the trucks and the trucks started up their engines. I heard one of the guys in our company call out to the other company that was relieving us, "What outfit?" The reply was "1st Battalion 1st Marines." I couldn't believe that the first Marines Division was coming up here to relieve the 3rd Marines Division. The 1st Marine Division was up here in 1966 but couldn't handle the job so they replaced them with the 3rd Marine Division. The 1st Marines Division was sent down around Da Nang to protect the large base there and the surrounding areas.

Then one of the guys from the 1st Battalion 1st Marines asked who they were replacing and one of the green horns yelled out, "1st Battalion 9th Marines." I saw in their eyes that they didn't want any part of replacing the 1st Battalion 9th Marines. I heard one of them say, "Just great; 1/9, of all of the battalions up here we had to replace them." I knew that the word had really gotten around about our battalion in Vietnam.

The trucks started moving and at the same time the 1st Battalion 1st Marines started walking up the hill and taking over our two small perimeters as well as Con Thein itself. I knew that they hadn't yet been hit by the N.V.A. 152mm artillery rounds but I knew that they would be getting hit very soon, since the N.V.A. had to see us leaving and see a new group coming in. 1st Battalion 1st Marines was going to see what it was really like being up here getting hit by artillery and also getting into fire fights with the N.V.A. and I knew that this was going to be a new experience for them.

This place was far different than down there. I knew that they would not like getting shelled at from the N.V.A.'s 152mm artillery pieces from North Vietnam.

The trucks picked up speed and as we headed south back to Dong Ha, the weather was becoming worse each mile as we were going south. The skies were getting thicker and thicker with gray clouds. We reached Dong Ha and the trucks were still on Highway #1 and heading south and I started thinking of where we could be going. The only place left was Camp Evans, or down south where the 1st Division was located, around Da Nang.

We came into a large town called Quang Tri City and I remembered the one large beautiful Catholic church there, and of course, the Vietnamese girl that came out of the church. She was so beautiful and very clean looking; she was half French and Vietnamese and her very long black hair came down to her waist. Just past the city, we came up on the road where there was an old iron bridge that crossed the river and the trucks slowed down to get through it and we zig-zagged through to the bridge. There were a couple of bunkers that were guarded by the ARVN solders. As we crossed the bridge, we saw the ARVN soldiers squatting down and eating their rice out of small bowls. They looked at us and we did the same by looking back at them. The trucks started back up and I was getting a little tired of sitting on the floor. I hoped that we would go to Camp Evans and after about ten minutes, I saw that the lead truck was turning to the right heading west into the mountains. I knew that we were heading to Camp Evans and that we had about 4000 meters to go and we would be there.

The trucks went inside the base and everything had changed since I was here back in April. There used to be tents here and now everything was all hardbacks. At least we would be out of the weather when the rains came. The trucks stopped and they told us to get off; my team got off and after a couple of minutes the trucks moved out and we waited for further word. Then the lieutenant came over to us and he told the platoon to follow him. As we did he pointed out to one of the hardbacks and said that first squad had it and my team walked over to it. We were right next to a very large hardback that was about 100 by 75 feet and it was the mess hall. We got inside the hardback and the only thing inside of them were cots. I grabbed the cot right next to the door, in case I had to get out of it in a hurry. I told the rest of my team to take the one side and that the other two fire teams would take the other side. Curry went to the other end and I went to the other side with the other fire teams. It didn't make any difference with me. I really didn't give a damn what he did. I watched the lieutenant point to the other hardbacks for the rest of the platoon. He left and went to his hardback. I took off my combat gear and set it up in case I had to get to it in a hurry. I told the rest of my team to do the same. The other fire teams and Curry just watched and didn't do a damn thing. I told my team to take it easy for the day. I got off my feet and laid down on the cot until we got further word from the lieutenant.

As I lay there on my cot, I watched the other fire team and they all just put their combat gear under their cot in a mess and I knew that if we got hit that they would be having a hell of a time getting on their gear. I looked at my guys' gear and they had it almost the same way I had my gear so that they could get it on in a hurry without spending much time in trying to find out where this was and that was. I was proud of my men and I knew that every little thing I did would help keep them alive a little bit longer.

Then the word was passed to go to the mess hall. The guys got up and headed across our hardback to the mess hall which was about 100 meters from us. Inside there was a long rail and on the other side of the rail were the cooks and the hot foods. Again they had rice and Spam and some vegetable. I took the Spam and vegetables and had water for my drink. There were picnic tables inside and I sat by myself and ate. The rest of the guys were eating and having a good time. I knew that this was too good to be true and they were giving us a day off before they had something shitty for us to do. I was finished and went out and decided to go up to the P.X. and see what they had. It wasn't very large, but they did have a lot of things. I went back to the hardback and laid down on my cot and the word was passed that our seabags were coming down here to us.

A couple of hours later, the word was passed to get our seabags. I went over to where they had them stacked up by platoons, and I grabbed mine and went back to the hardback. I put my seabag up against the corner of the hardback and went back to lying down on the cot. The word was passed that tomorrow, and every day after that, the showers would be open to the troops from 18:30 to 20:00 everyday. I remembered back at the P.X. they had these very large pink towels and I went back there and bought three of them. I put two of them in my seabag.

The next day came and the lieutenant called the platoon out and said that he was going to show us that we had perimeter watch here at the camp. The whole platoon followed the lieutenant and we went to the gate of the camp and took the north part and went around the perimeter, northwest. As he was telling each fire team which fighting hole they had, the rest of us had to follow him like a bunch of idiots. I was telling my men not to get too close to the other guys in the platoon and to listen and keep their eyes moving around outside of the perimeter. We were coming up to one of the towers. There were only four teams left; I knew that we were going to be the last team to get assigned to our fighting bunker. About fifty feet away was another tower and our sister team had the hole to the left of the tower and the perimeter started heading downward on the large hill. We were about 100 meters from the tower and the lieutenant pointed to our fighting hole. The lieutenant told us that during the day we were to have one guy on duty and at night that the whole team would stand night watch. I knew that we were not going to have it good down here. The lieutenant then went back to his hardback.

I looked at the guys and told them that since we had one more guy than the other fire teams, it would be a little easier on all of us. I told the guys that I would take the first watch for the day and spend two hours before the next guy would take over and I told each of them what times they had their watch. They all agreed to what I said and I looked at my watch. It was 08:00. I told the blond-headed guy that he was next and to replace me at 10:00. I told all of them to get back to the hardback and to get off their feet and relax for the day. As they left me, I sat down on the edge of the fighting hole and looked out in front of me. There were hills all around us. I was looking straight out in front, which was straight north. I knew that it would be very hard for the enemy to sneak up on us because of the small shrubs that were on each of the hills, about 18 inches tall, and about 12 inches wide. The hill that we were on and our fighting hole was about a couple of hundred feet from the bottom. I knew that it would be hard for the N.V.A. to attack us. Down here, there were more V.C. than N.V.A.

I looked to my left and the perimeter started back up and our fighting hole was the lowest spot on the whole perimeter. I knew that at night time we could see their silhouettes, but no one could see us. I knew that our fighting hole had some good points as well as some bad points. The fighting hole could take only three guys and we had five guys in my team. I knew that two of us would have to be out of the fighting hole on either side. I sat there for the rest of the time just thinking of nothing and before I knew it, the blond-headed guy was coming toward me. I got up and left. I went back to the hardback and as I went back, I looked up into the sky and the weather was the same as it had been yesterday, with very heavy, low gray clouds and it looked like it was trying to rain. I felt the winds blowing a little and the humidity was getting heavier. It was just a matter of time before it started raining everyday and night.

The next two days went by just like the first day. Then on our third day, it started raining lightly. Even the winds were blowing harder, between five and fifteen mph. All of us used our ponchos when we had our time for perimeter watch during the day. When night came, we went to our perimeter and I told the guys to put two of the ponchos together for a tent and that way everyone could try to keep warm and dry. It was my turn for watch and I got out of the tent and went on over to the fighting hole with my poncho on me. My clothes were getting wet and damp in places. As I sat there watching, I knew that the N.V.A. was not stupid enough to be out in this weather. The winds were really blowing now and I remembered a couple of the guys would say, "The Hawk is Out." This was the first time that I heard of the wind being called, "The Hawk." I kept my eyes out for anyone coming down to us from either side. I just hoped that on the other side of the camp the guys were watching out as well. I knew that some of these green horns would try to cut corners by being inside somewhere. I never knew that a person could be so miserable being out in this kind of weather. Then I started thinking of the guys that fought in Korea, and WWII and the winters they had to go through, especially at the Chosen Reservoir. My body was starting to shake and there was nothing I could do. I was getting colder and wetter, and the weather was not letting up.

I looked at my watch and it was time for me to get the next guy up for his turn. I then got up and kicked the bottom of his boot and he got up and went on over to the fighting hole. He sat down next to the fighting hole and I knew that he was going to be just as miserable as I was on watch. I looked inside the tent and the rest of the guys were right next to each other trying to keep warm. I decided not to get in with them and I just laid down right next to the tent. As I laid there, I could feel the water running underneath me, since we were on the side of this large hill. I would fall in and out of sleep during the rest of the night.

When it was morning all of us got up, and it was the big guy's turn for his daylight hours of perimeter watch. The rest of the guys gathered their combat gear and headed back to our hardback. I told the tall guy that in two hours, one of the guys would be taking his place. As for the rest of us we headed back to our hardback and the guys were complaining about how cold and wet they were. I was behind all of them and I just shook my head thinking that they only had this to complain about. I knew that this was better than being attacked by the enemy. We finally reached our hardback and I took off my poncho and got into my cot. I just watched the rest of my team. The other teams in our platoon were also coming back in from their night watch. It was time for breakfast and I told one of the guys to take perimeter watch as soon as he got done eating so the tall guy could get some hot chow.

As I walked on over to the chow hall, the winds and rain settled down. It wasn't raining as much as it had during the night; even the winds died down during the day. After chow I went back to the hardback and just lay in my cot. Parts of my jungle clothes were damp. I took off my boots and let the air dry out my feet because I sure didn't want to have any more problems with them. I went into my seabag and got out another pair of dry socks and my field jacket. I didn't put the socks on until my feet were dry, which took about thirty minutes. I used some baby power on my feet first before I put on the socks. This went on for the next four days. Every other evening, I would go and take a hot shower to warm up my body. Everyday was the same in that it would rain lightly and the wind blew between five to ten miles an hour. Every night it seemed to rain a little harder and the winds would blow between ten to twenty-five miles an hour.

One day as I was walking back from the chow hall, I came across one of the old timers who was working as a clerk now in our battalion. We were walking back from the chow hall and he asked me how I was doing and asked if I knew about what was going on with the old timers in the outfit, and I told him I didn't know for sure and he said that within a month they would be out of the field for good if they had two or more Purple Hearts. He looked into my eyes and said that I was the only one in the battalion that didn't have a Purple Heart that he knew of. I asked him if there was some way I could get out of here and he said that there might be. I asked him what. He said, "Hammer, I don't think you would want to do this." I asked him what it was and he said they had been forming a new outfit since WWII. I asked him what new outfit and he said, "Echo Company, Reconnaissance." I thought about it for thirty seconds and I told him that it couldn't be any worse than this outfit and he said, "I agree, Hammer." I asked him to go ahead and put me in for it. He said that he would and we parted and he went on over to where our battalion was now living. I went back to my hardback and didn't think any more about it. I remembered what he said that he would try but didn't know if they would take me.

Word was being passed that the company was going out on a patrol and for everyone to saddle up. My feet hurt again and I called for the corpsman to see me and he said that I wasn't going out in the bush and to get off my feet again. He saw that I was getting trench foot again. I called Bill over and told him that he had the team and to make sure that the guys kept their distance, especially the tall guy.

The company left and went just outside the camp and walked around the hills for at least eight hours and they came back in around 16:00 hundred hours. As the guys dropped their gear, they said they were all pissed off at our lieutenant and captain. They were all saying that the enemy wasn't out there and that the weather was so bad that the enemy wasn't stupid enough to be out in this kind of weather. I just laughed to myself, and knew that I had to get out of this outfit. I started thinking about Dale and how he was doing getting his Silver Star from the President of the United States and his In-Country R and R. I knew that he would be coming back within a couple of days.

As soon as the guys got back into the hardback and took off their gear, I told them that I would go out on the perimeter and to relieve me for evening chow. I put on my poncho and headed out to the perimeter. The weather was getting worse each day and of course the winds were blowing, although not so much during the day as when it was night time. The rains were more like a mist during the day and harder at night time. I reached the fighting hole and sat down looking out in front of me. I knew that the enemy wouldn't be out in this weather. The guys relieved me for chow later that day and around 20:00 hundred hours, all of us headed out for our night time watch. Again I assigned everyone what time they had watch. One of the guys kicked me at the bottom of my foot and I got up and the rains were coming down harder than during the day. As I got up, I looked at the rest of my team and the guys were all huddled up in the two ponchos they made as a tent. I looked at my watch and it was 23:05 and I sat down next to the fighting hole while the wind and rain made the night worse.

My feet were getting wet again and knew that there was no chance for them to keep dry during the night time. I started thinking about my team; I knew they were having a hell of a time being over here and so far they really hadn't seen much combat. I knew when my watch was over that one of them had to get out of the tent they made. They didn't feel "The Hawk" hitting them. They were all inside the ponchos and couldn't feel the wind blowing.

About twenty minutes later I saw that someone was coming from my right side and I knew that it was the lieutenant by the way he was making noise coming toward me. I could see his silhouette against the hill and I knew that if the weather wasn't bad that the enemy would be able to shoot his ass. As the lieutenant got about twenty feet from me I told him to, "Halt," and to tell me who he was. He kept on coming and I told him if he took one more step that I was going to blow his ass away. He stopped and called out his name and I told him to come on in. I just loved it when I made him stop and say who he was. When he got about two feet away and asked me how things were and I just looked at him and then said, "Shitty." I asked him "How would you like being out here in this shit, knowing there was no one out there in this shitty weather but us dummies?" He didn't say anything and was getting ready to leave and as he was about to do so, I told him that he should hurry up and get back to his hardback and keep warm and dry. I knew that he got pissed but also knew that I was right. I knew that he didn't give a damn about his platoon.

I looked down at my watch and it was time for me to get the next man up. I knew that they all had a hell of a day walking around out in front of this base for about eight hours and now standing night watch. I decided that I would watch a little longer. I thought about Dale and how he was doing down south. I hoped that he was taking his time and enjoying himself down at China Beach. I knew that he would be back in a couple of days. As I sat there thinking of Dale, the winds were going crazy and the rain was miserable. I could feel my body shaking and parts of me were wet and other parts of me were damp. I looked at my watch and I had been watching for two and a half hours and then I saw someone coming down the hill again and I could tell that it was the lieutenant coming again. Again I told him to stop about twenty feet away and he stopped and I asked, "Who in the hell is it?" He said his name and this time I waited before I answered him. A couple of minutes went by and he started to move and I told him that I was going to open up on him. Boy, did he stop in his tracks and wait for me to tell him to come on in. I told him to come in. When he came up to me, he asked me why I was standing watch and I told him that my men were wet and cold and didn't get much rest during the day because of the patrol they had to do. I told him that if he was out to catch his men sleeping while on guard duty that was the lowest anyone could do to his troops. He asked me why I kept him there waiting for a couple of minutes before I asked him to come on in. I told him that I wanted him to see what it was like when someone played games, and asked how he liked it. He didn't like it at all but as long as he was going to play games with the men in his platoon that I was going to play games with him. He asked me if he hadn't stopped coming to me, what would I have done and I told him that I would have opened up on him and he would go home in a body bag. I told him that he wasn't going to play games with me. I'd been here too damn long. I told him that every time he came to this fighting hole during the night he better stop if he knew what was good for himself; when someone told him to stop. I said that he better get his ass out of here now.

I looked at my watch and it was 02:00 hundred in the morning and I couldn't stand my watch any longer. I got up and went on over to the tent and woke up the next guy. As he got up I told him that I stayed up for three hours and that each of them had only one watch each. He understood and just before he left, I told him that the lieutenant was hoping to catch anyone sleeping on watch. I told him to challenge the lieutenant when he comes and make sure to tell the next guy that goes on watch and he went on over to the fighting hole. I laid down just outside the tent where the guys were in.

The next three days went by and everyone was just miserable because of the weather. Even some of the writing gear was getting damp and the pens wouldn't write on the paper. During the day most of us just laid in their cots and either fell off to sleep or just thought of home. There was just nothing to do here.

Curry came over to me and said that my team was going out on a patrol and that the lieutenant wanted us over to his hardback in ten minutes. I told the guys to get their combat gear on and that we are going out on a patrol. I was glad that we were going out in the bush just to do something. As soon as the guys got their gear on we headed on over to the lieutenant and he came out and said that my team and Kenny Fulton's machine gun team were going out with two ducks. Both Kenny and I looked at each other and had no idea what the hell the lieutenant was talking about. The lieutenant told us to follow him and I knew that we were not going to be walking out in the bush. We went over to the main gate and there were two vehicles waiting for us. The lieutenant told us that we were going out in the field to supply one of the outfits in the bush. He told us to get into the ducks and we went to the back of them and each of them could hold eight guys. Kenny got his team in one of them and my team got into the other. The ducks held cases of C-rations for the guys out in the field. The ducks were vehicles that had tracks and were a two man team, a driver and gunner, with a 50 cal. machine gun. We kept the back door open so we could see where we had been.

Both vehicles started up and we took off heading north. After about three miles, we were out of the rolling hills and the area was flat. The ground had grass and there were puddles of water all around. We went about another mile and the ducks stopped. The gunner said that we were next to a stream and that we were going to cross it and if the water started coming in to close the back door quickly. We looked out the back and now the ground was covered in about two feet of water with just the top part of the grass showing. We started moving and the front of our vehicle went downward and I told the guys to make sure if the water started coming in to close the doors quickly. We were in the stream and the duck leveled out and the current was moving very quickly and I told the guys to close the door until we got to the other side of the stream. I could tell that this was no stream but a river. As soon as the guys closed the doors the water hit up against them. I didn't like being in this situation but there was nothing I could do. Everyone would have to be on their own if we sunk. It was a hell of an empty feeling that came over me and I just didn't want the guys to know that I was just as scared as they were. No one said a word. Then the duck got to the other side of the river and we went upward on land. The guys gave a sigh of relief. I told the guys to open up the back door and as we did none of us could believe how wide the stream was - it really was a river. We went about another mile and we ended up at the outfit. My team helped in unloading C-rations to the outfit and after about thirty minutes it was time to leave. The guys here were all soaked from head to foot and they even looked miserable just being out here. I really felt for this outfit. There was no way these guys should be out here and all of us knew that the N.V.A. weren't this stupid to be out here in this kind of weather.

It was time for us to leave and to get back. I remembered the stream and that we had to cross it again. We reached the stream but this time the driver told us that we were to get out of the vehicles and that we had to cross the stream on our own. As both teams got out of the vehicles the lieutenant told us there was a bridge but it had been hit by artillery. Only one side of the bridge was just out of the water and the iron bars were at least something to hold on to. The lieutenant told me that my team was to go first and I told Bill to take point and that I would be behind him. I told everyone to take their time and to make sure that they had good footing and to hold on tight. Bill started out first and I was right behind him as we went down on the iron bar that was about six inches above the water. I stayed close to Bill in case he fell in. Bill got to the middle of the bridge and the iron bar was just below the water about six inches. I told Bill that he really needed to hold on the iron bars that were about five feet above the water while we slowly slid our feet across the iron bar that was under the water. The water raced past my feet and was trying to take my feet with the current. The water was moving very fast and I knew that if I slipped that it was all she wrote for me. When Bill was out of the water heading up to the other side of the bridge, I passed the word to the other guys in my team to really watch themselves when they got to the middle part of the bridge. When I got to the top of the other side I made sure that I grabbed each of the guys in my team so they could get to the other end of the bridge. The lieutenant came after my team and then Kenny's team. Kenny was carrying the Machine gun on his shoulders. I knew that he would have a little trouble and I went back down to where he was trying to cross the middle part of the stream.

Kenny got to where I could grab him and I said, "I got you." As soon as I got him, one of his legs left the iron bridge. I told him that I still had him. I was glad that I did, because he would have drowned. When all of us were on the other side we watched the two ducks come across the stream. As we watched, the current was so strong that the drivers of both ducks had to almost cross upstream to keep from going downstream. Both of them finally made it and we all got back inside of them and headed back to Camp Evans.

As we went back, we had the doors open and it seemed that the water was higher now than before. The driver said that off on each side of the road that the water was six feet deep in some places. All you could see was water and only the tops of the grass in some places. We finally reached the camp and got off of the ducks and headed back to our hardback. It was around 14:30 hours and I told the guys to take it easy for awhile. The lieutenant told us that we didn't have to stand guard duty until tonight.

The word was passed that we were going to have mail call and I was looking forward to having mail since we hadn't had any in about five days. The green horns that had been here now for about twenty days still didn't receive any mail and I really felt for them. Their mail hadn't caught up to them yet. I remembered how hard it was not getting mail but how do you tell these guys to hang on a little longer? I knew that it was tearing them up inside and to tell these guys to hang in there was hard. I took my mail and went back to my hardback to read my letters.

One of the guys in my team got the Stars and Stripes newspaper and asked me if I wanted to see it and I told him yes. I had only seen about eight Stars and Stripes since I'd been here. It was just like any home town newspaper with news around the world, sports and the local news which was what was going on over here. At the back of the paper they would have a list of the men who died during the week as well as the wounded from all branches of our military.

When I was finished with the newspaper I gave it back and just lay on my cot and thought about my time over here. I remembered how the weather was when I first got here. In the morning hours, the skies were cloudy and by noon the clouds would break and the sun came out with the blue skies. The temperature would climb during the day. As summer came, the weather was very, very hot and we couldn't drink our water in our canteens until sometime during night. I also remembered how close the guys were to each other and our battalion. I remembered really how close we were when we got into it with the N.V.A. and everyone was watching out for everyone else in the battalion. I looked at the men in my fire team and they were close to each other but that was as far as it got. I knew that the platoon was not the same any more and wondered how this platoon or even the whole battalion would handle itself in combat. I knew that I just didn't want to be around when it happened. Before I knew it, it was time for us to take our perimeter watch for the night. I told my team to get their gear on and that it was time to get to our hole.

When it was my time for watch, I had a feeling that the lieutenant would be coming by to check on us. About ten minutes later, I saw him coming and I told him to stop and he stopped. I told him to come on in and he approached but this time didn't say a word and went on.

The next day came and the lieutenant told me to get new jungle clothes and to get rid of the ones that I had. I went over to the supply tent and told the sergeant that I needed new jungle clothes. He gave me a shirt and pants and I went back to the hut and changed my clothes. It felt good to get rid of my old ones since they were brown with a lot of body oil mixed in with my sweat.

At lunch time I took out a can of soup that my mother had sent to me and I cooked it instead of going to the chow line. We were getting more new guys into the company and the ones that were here just after July were being sent to other outfits. It was like playing musical chairs. Curry came over and said that three of my men were being replaced and that I was getting new men. I told the three guys that they were leaving and to gather their gear and to go on over to the clerk's tent and they would tell them where they were going. I told them good luck and they left. About an hour later Curry came over and said that these new guys were in my team. I had the big guy still and he had been doing great and it looked like he was not thinking about his mother at all and that he was thinking about his own future.

The word was passed that we were having a platoon formation and that the lieutenant was going to talk to us. We got out and were in formation and the lieutenant began by saying that while we were at this base that our boots were to be black but they didn't have to have a shine to them, just be black. We were to march in a platoon formation when it was time for chow. I couldn't believe what I was hearing and Dale wasn't here to hear this. I looked over to where Kenny and Speedy was and they were rolling their eyes as if to say, "To hell with you." The three of us had been over here long enough to know that this was pure bullshit.

The lieutenant dismissed us and everyone went back to their hardbacks. I decided to go over to the lieutenant's hardback to have a talk with him. I got over to his hardback and the lieutenant came out. As I got close to the hut. I asked him if he knew where in the hell he was? I again reminded him that we were not in the States. The other officers were listening to us talk. I just didn't care what they were thinking. I told the lieutenant again that we were in Vietnam and the enemy didn't give a damn about us and the guys didn't need this kind of bullshit while trying to keep alive. I told him that since the weather was bad I hoped that it stayed that way for awhile so the enemy couldn't hit us. I also told him that he better watch himself if he kept giving us stupid orders because someday he might get a round in the back while we were out in the field. I told him that I would not be the one to do it. I said that I would not be shining my boots or marching to the chow hall. I didn't feel like getting killed with the other guys in my platoon when we marched to the chow hall. I told him that he could send me to the brig if he wanted to - at least I would be safe from him. I left and went back to the hut. I told my guys that they didn't have to shine their boots and also didn't have to march to the chow hall.

The weather was getting worse everyday and each night the winds would blow harder, and the rain would come down like needles when it hit us. As I lay down on the cot, my mind wandered off and I thought about the past. My mind jumped back to boot camp and I remembered what the head D.I. said to me the day before graduation - if he was back in Vietnam that he would have me in his team. My mind would jump again and I remembered that I didn't want any rank but to just do my job and not worry about anyone but myself. Boy, was I wrong, I got promoted to Lance Corporal by Lieutenant Libutti and I was given a fire team which I didn't want. They also gave me another guy to take care of since everyone in the battalion didn't want him. And, now I had five guys and we were supposed to have only four in a fire team. That in itself pissed me off. And to top everything off, I lost my lieutenant and captain on July 2nd although both of them got multiple Purple Hearts. Captain Hutchinson received two Purple Hearts and Lieutenant Libutti received three Purple Hearts.

Then I really felt bad when I remembered that I took my Captain's Out-of-Country R. and R. and there were two M.P.'s to make sure I left for Dong Ha. I wished that the captain had taken his R. and R. instead of me. I really felt that I had missed the biggest battle over here and that I wasn't with my buddies when the shit hit the fan. I remembered how Dale and the rest of the guys that were left said they were glad that I wasn't here. I remembered how the guys really looked forward to when I passed out the goodies that I brought up from Da Nang. As I thought about it, I could feel my heart being torn apart because I missed being with my buddies in that fire fight.

I had never felt so low in my whole life as I did now. Dale was down south getting his Silver Star and taking his In country R. and R. I knew that he would be back any day now and it was hard not to have him here. I got up from the cot and decided to see Kenny Fulton and I went over his hut and asked for Kenny. His team said that he just got his orders and that he already left about an hour ago. I could feel my spirit going down and the loneliness coming back in.

The rest of the day went by very slowly. Night time came and we went back out on guard duty for the base. Around 20:00 hundred hours, the skies became very dark, darker than the other nights had been so far. The guys quickly made their tent and all of them got inside of it. The winds were picking up and I could tell that we were in for a very cold and wet night. Around 21:30 hours, the winds really started to pick up. The winds were blowing between 25 to 50 miles per hour. The rains were coming down a little more than usual, like bees hitting my skin. I knew that I couldn't wake the guys up at this time and I could hear them moving around inside the tent of theirs. I knew they were all miserable being here and trying like hell to keep warm. I knew that I better stay up a little longer if I could, so they wouldn't have to be out in this weather. Around 23:30 hours, and the winds were blowing between 50 to 70 miles per hour and the rains were really coming down hard. I knew at this time there was no way for anyone to be out in this shit. It was just impossible to be out in it at this time.

The winds were howling and I saw that someone was coming down from my right side again. I thought that it was the lieutenant because the winds were blowing him around and as he got closer to me, I told him to stop and he didn't. Again I yelled at him to stop and this time he was about ten feet from me and I asked him who the hell he was and he told me that he was the captain. I told him to approach. As he walked toward me he was having trouble trying to walk straight. When he was about two feet away he asked me what I was doing and I looked at him and said that I was on guard duty. He told me that everyone on the perimeter was inside their tents and I was the only one that was standing his watch. I said, "What, I'm the only one that is standing watch around the base?" and he said, "Yes". I told him that is just great. Now, I knew that I had to look out for my back side in case the enemy sneaked up. The captain said that he heard me talking to the lieutenant earlier today and said that he was the one that gave the orders. I told him that we were not back in the States but if he wants his men to fight for him, he better not have the guys in the company do those things he said. I told him that 95 percent of these guys had not been in combat and that the ones that were, were leaving the company because of the Purple Hearts they had. I told him there were no staff sergeant or sergeants left in the company that had any combat experience to advise him on how to handle themselves in a fire fight. I knew that I got to him and made him think about the orders that he told his second lieutenants. He told me that he was going to go around and check the rest of the perimeter. As he left, the winds were pushing him around while he was walking.

I sat down and put my rifle under my poncho and turned my face away from the winds so that I wouldn't get stung from the rain. I felt miserable from the wind and rain and to top it off, I felt very low. This had to be the worst day of my life over here. It was going on 01:00 and I couldn't take it any more so I woke up the next guy and told him that it was his turn. I could see that he was shaking and cold. This weather wasn't helping the guys out at all. He got up and went on over to the fighting hole which had been filled with the rains and sat down along the side of it. I lay down and just watched him and I could tell that he was shaking under his poncho. I made sure that my pot was still on my head so that I wouldn't get hit from the rain. As I laid there on the cold wet ground I would watch the guy and at times I could feel myself shaking. I lay there thinking there was no way we should be out in this miserable weather and I thought about the guys before me in other wars and what they had gone through. I knew that I wasn't any better than them.

Somehow I had fallen off to sleep and before I knew it, the guys woke me up and said that it was time to go back. I told all of them to saddle up and all of us were going back in. The winds were dying down about half. The rains were still coming down but lightly.

When we got back to the hut I took off the poncho and lay in my cot and as I did I could feel my body still shaking. Half of my clothes were either damp or wet. It was time for breakfast and the word was passed that we didn't have to go in platoon formation. I knew that the captain got the idea that if he wanted to have a damn good company he had to think about his men first. I went on over to the chow hall and when I got there, Dale was there eating. Dale came over to me and I asked him if he had a good time at China Beach and he said that he loved it. I asked him if he got his little medal and he said yes and that he had to go down to Saigon to get it. I said to him, "You're kidding," and he said no-that he had had to go all the way down there. Dale said there were six of them that got a medal. Most of them were Army.

As we sat down to eat our food, he asked me how everything was and I told him that the other day the word was passed that we were to shine our boots black and to march to the chow hall in a platoon formation. Dale looked at me and exploded and I told him that the captain canceled the orders. I told Dale that Kenny had gotten his orders and was gone. Dale told me that it won't be long for him to leave also. Dale didn't want to leave me and I felt the same way about him leaving. I also told him that we got a lot of new men in the platoon and some of the other guys that were here after

August had been moved to other outfits.

The next day came and it was around 10:30 hours and I got word to report to the clerk's hut. When I got there, the clerk came out and said, "Hammer, I have some news for you." I looked at him and without a word waited for him to speak again. He than said that my orders went through and that I was assigned to a new outfit that had been formed after WWII. He said the name of the company was 3rd Recon "E" Company and that I was to leave at noon. He told me to get my seabag and to turn in my combat gear and to report back here at 12:00 noon.

As soon as I left the clerk and started heading back to the hardback to turn my gear in and to get my seabag, the lieutenant came up to me and asked me to stay. I told him that it was time for me to leave this outfit. The lieutenant started getting desperate and said that he would make me corporal and that I would be with the C.P. group when we would go out into the field. I just looked at him and couldn't believe what I was hearing from him. As I was listening to him, I was thinking of all the times when we were up at Con Thein and he would work the whole platoon to death in building up the perimeter there. I remembered how the guys were so tired that some of them would fall off to sleep during their watch at night time. I also remembered how he and Corporal Curry would try to get me in trouble and they would screw around with my team.

I blasted the lieutenant about what he had done to my team up at Con Thein - how Corporal Curry got away with murder by not sleeping at night time and him threatening me by telling me that I would go to the brig. He didn't like it when I told him that he had to stand radio watch at night time as well. I also told him that I didn't want to be around when they got hit from the N.V.A. and the only taste he had had was the little bit of their shelling at us up at Con Thein. I told him that I couldn't find him when the N.V.A. did hit us with their shelling. I told him all he wanted me for is when the shit did hit the fan, he could ask me what in hell we should do. I told him "I'll be damned if I am going to take care of the whole platoon." I also told him that I didn't want that kind of responsibility. That was not my job. He was almost in tears because when I left, there was no one left in the platoon that had any combat experience.

I finally got to the hut and just before I walked inside, I knew that the hardest thing to do was to say good bye to the guys in my fire team. I knew that they would be all right and could handle most of the shit from the N.V.A. as well as from the lieutenant and Corporal Curry. I opened up the door and went inside and as I did, I started getting my combat gear together and left without saying anything to them. They all just watched me as I turned in my gear. I went back and grabbed my seabag and as I did, Dale came over and said that he heard and was glad that I was leaving. Dale looked at me and said that he would be leaving in two days himself and didn't know where he would be. I told Dale that I was assigned to the 3rd Recon, "E" Company, (Echo).

As I locked up my seabag and looked at my watch, I told Dale that it was time for me to go. Dale and I had become as close as brothers. Dale said that he had to go and we shook hands and he turned and left. I knew that the both of us were about to cry. The rest of the guys in my team told me they were glad that I was leaving and they would be all right while I was gone. I shook hands with each of them and when I got to the big guy, I told him that he better not let his mother win and that I wanted him to start a new life of his own when he got back to the States. He told me that he would not give up. I told all of them to watch each others' backs and always be there for each other. I turned and walked outside of the hardback and headed back with my seabag to the clerk's hut.

Chapter Thirty-Three

When I reached the hut, the clerk came out and said, "Hammer, here are your orders. Go on over to the main gate and get on the six-by heading south on Highway 1 to Phu Bai." That is where the 3rd Recon is stationed. The clerk said that he sure was going to miss The Hammer and then said good luck. I left and headed over to where the six-bys were. There were six of them and all of them were heading down to Phu Bai. I asked one of the drivers if he was heading down to Phu Bai and he nodded and I got on the back of his truck and sat up against the back of the cab. I put my seabag right next to me. Other guys were getting on the trucks as well as the one I was on. A couple of minutes later another guy got on board and also sat next to me up against the back of the cab. I noticed that he also didn't have a rifle with him. He also had papers going to another outfit and I asked him where he was going and he said 3rd Recon and I told him I was going there also. Both of us were going to Echo Company; I asked him what outfit was he coming from and he said the 1st Battalion, 9th Marines, Bravo Company and he in turn asked me where I was coming from and I told him that I was from 1st Battalion 9th Marines, Charlie Company. He asked me my name and I told him that the guys called me the "Hammer," and he said that he had heard of me. I said that I hoped that what they said was good and he smiled and said yes. He told me that his name was, "Bob or Robert"; I asked him how long had he been with 1/9 and he said since early May. I said, "You went through July 2nd ?", and he said that he didn't get hit that day but his company was hit very hard within one minute and thirty seconds. I told him that I took my captain's R. and R. and wanted to know just what had happened that day. Bob said that they got on the road from Market Street and headed north down the road. Bob said that the lead platoon stopped and was getting ready to put out the flanks and the captain said no. The N.V.A. hit them on both sides of the road. Bob said that half of the guys' rifles jammed on them and that was where most of them got it. Bob said, "The fuckin M-16s were a piece of shit." Both of us stopped and didn't say anything more. I knew that both of us could still feel the pain of losing a lot of men in our battalion. I looked up into the skies and the overcast was very heavy but it wasn't raining.

After about twenty minutes, the trucks started up their engines and I knew that we would be leaving very quickly. I knew that both of us were happy to get out of here. The other guys on the trucks had their rifles with them and I knew that Bob and I were thinking the same thing that if these guys got hit or wounded that both of us were going for their rifles.

The trucks started to move and we just looked back at our companies. I was glad to get away from my platoon but at the same time I didn't want to leave Dale although I knew that within two days he would be leaving as well. I did care for my team and hoped the guys would watch over each other. I was glad for Dale because he would not be going out in the bush again. I watched the guard close the gate after the last truck left. I looked over to Bob and he was thinking the same things I was thinking about. The trucks slowed down and I knew that we had reached Highway 1. The trucks turned right onto the highway and we were now heading south. It was the only paved road that went north and south in Vietnam. After about fifteen minutes I could feel my ass getting sore from riding in the back of the truck. I would turn to one side or the other so I wouldn't get sore. Bob was doing the same thing. I would look out on both sides of the highway and the little villages were different from the villages up north. These homes were made out of concrete even though they were the same size as the homes up north. All of the homes up north were made out of straw and wood. The skies were getting a little lighter as we went farther down south.

Our truck slowed down and we could tell that we were coming into a large city. As we went around the corner, there was a Catholic church with a large statue of Jesus with his arms outreached to us. It was made out of white marble and boy, was it beautiful. The church had beautiful stained glass windows and the walls of the church were made out of large stone. There were some things over here that were so much different than the rest of the country. It seemed like the Catholic churches were the best thing that they made over here, better than their own homes. As we got to the other side of the church, the road came together again. The north-bound traffic went to the right of the church and the south bound traffic went to the left of the church.

In the middle of the town, there was a market area where the Vietnamese were selling their goods to other people who lived in the town itself. Past that, the trucks turned right and we were now heading toward Phu Bai, which was west. The weather down here was not like where we were at up at Camp Evans. It looked like the sun was trying to get out from under the clouds. Bob asked the driver how much farther and the driver said that it was not long now. I looked at my watch and saw we had been riding for an hour. The trucks turned again and we saw that we had reached Phu Bai. The truck driver got us inside the gate and took us about a quarter of a mile inside the base and stopped and said to get off.

I grabbed my seabag and Bob did the same and put them on the side of the truck and both of us got off the truck and then grabbed our seabags and went up to the driver and asked him if he knew where 3rd Recon was. The driver said that he didn't know but told us to go over toward the large building and someone should tell us where it was. Bob and I both thanked him and he took off. We carried our seabags over to the large building and as we did, both of us saw that Phu Bai had completely changed because now all of the tents were gone and now everything here were hardbacks. We finally reached the large building and we saw a sign that said 3rd Recon. area. We both walked up to where one hardback was and went inside it and the clerks there asked us for our orders and without saying a word, we handed them to the clerks. After a couple of minutes went by, they told us that someone from Echo company would come for us. The clerks, after looking at our orders, saw that we came from 1/9 and didn't mess around with us. A corporal came inside the hut and the clerk said that these two go to Echo company. The corporal told us to follow him and that he would tell us where we would be housed. When we got there, both of us asked the corporal where we could get our rifles and he was a little surprised. He said that no one would be getting a rifle and ammo. Bob looked at me and I didn't like that answer. The corporal said that we had the rest of the day to ourselves. We could do whatever we wanted to do for the day and he told us where the chow hall was and the bar and P.X. were. He said that the rest of the guys should be here within the next couple of days.

The corporal left and both Bob and I put our seabags next to the cots and both of us lay down; I was thinking that today was December 15th. I looked at my watch and it was time for evening chow. I got up and Bob came over and both of us went on over to the chow hall which was just across the street. It was the large building that we came to first when we got here earlier. Both of us went inside and got in line and this time there was no rice and I was just happy not to see it. They had all kinds of foods and we could pick what we wanted to eat. So this was how Recon ate, better then the infantry.

When Bob and I got back to the hut, one of the clerks came over and said to go on over to the supply tent and pick up a blanket for our cots. We went on over to the supply tent and told the Marine there that we were to pick up a blanket. As the evening wore on, it was getting time for the movie to start. Both Bob and I saw a large white board that was attached to the mess hall and there were benches for the guys to watch the movies. I went over to where they were going to show the movie and it was a Western. When the movie was over, I went back to the hut for the night. I was glad that I didn't have guard duty on the perimeter. As I was lying on the cot, I started thinking about the old outfit and what they were doing up there at Camp Evans. I just hoped that Dale would get his orders and leave the outfit and get to another outfit so he didn't have to go out in the bush anymore. I felt the empty and lonely feeling coming over me. I looked over to see what Bob was doing and I noticed that he was also lying in his cot thinking about his buddies in Bravo Company, what old timers were left. I noticed that each day that went by I was staying mostly to myself. I knew that I had Bob to talk to if I needed him and I was there for him.

Somehow I fell off to sleep and got up very early in the morning and looked over to see if Bob was up and he was also moving around in his cot. We went on over to the chow hall for breakfast and came back. When we got back there were some new men in the hut. They were talking to each other and both Bob and I went to our cots and sat down. We pretty much stayed to ourselves and watched the green horns shooting off their mouths to each other. About an hour later the corporal came into the hut and told us to go on over to pick up our rifle, magazines and rounds. Both of us got up from our cots and headed on over to the supply tent and Bob was just as excited as I was in getting our rifle and ammo. The rest of the guys followed us over to the supply tent to pick up their blankets as well as their rifles and ammo. The supply tent gave us other gears as well. Some of the gear Bob and I didn't take. They did not pass out flak jackets. We went back to the hut and I put my gear together and started putting the ammo into the magazines. Bob was doing the same thing. As we finished we watched the other guys in the hut putting their gear together and noticed that they were not used to having live ammo. They also were changing their State side utilities for the new jungle utilities. Both Bob and I made sure we had four canteens. We both were not used to not having a flak jacket to wear.

When they were finished, they started talking about how many people they were going to kill and get all kinds of medals. They were really bragging to each other about how tough they were. Bob looked over to me and shook his head a little and then laid down. I went to my seabag and started writing letters to my parents, Mrs. Hahner, my brother and sister and the two girls. At the end of each letter I gave them my new address, which was 3rd Recon, Echo Company, 3rd Marine Division. I couldn't get myself to be with the rest of the guys in the hut. I knew that I had to stay to myself and not say a word to them. I didn't want to know anything about them. I just wanted to be alone. I knew that Bob felt the same way. The rest of the day went by very slowly and it seemed to just drag on.

The night came and I tried to get some sleep, but the other guys were drinking beer and playing cards. Somehow I fell off to sleep and the next day came and again Bob and I went over to the chow hall with the other guys in the hut. When we got back there were more new guys in the hut and every cot was taken. It was around 10:30 in the morning and someone called for everyone in Echo Company to fall in on the street. Everyone hurried up in getting out into the street and Bob and I were the last two to get with the other men in the company. The captain called all of us to attention and then to at-ease. He introduced himself and called out the three lieutenants; who would have their own platoon. He also named his fourth lieutenant but he was a first lieutenant and he assisted the captain. The cap-

tain handed over the talk to the first lieutenant and he took over. He had the
gunny call out our names and we lined up in the platoon to which we were
going to be assigned.

Again I was with 2nd platoon and Bob was assigned to 3rd platoon. At
least I knew where Bob was. The 2nd platoon lieutenant was as tall as I, but
he was very muscular. He had been with Force Recon in the States before
coming over here. I told myself that I would hold off judgment until I found
out what kind of officer he was. Each of the lieutenants told their platoon
that tomorrow we would be doing exercises in the morning and some recon work during the day. Just before they dismissed us the sun came out.
I looked at myself and couldn't understand why I had to do exercise since
I didn't have any body fat on me what so ever. I knew that I had to weigh
somewhere between 160 to 170 pounds. I knew that Bob weighed around
145 to 155 pounds.

The next day came and they called out our platoon to get into platoon
formation. All of us got out onto the street and the staff sergeant marched
us to an area to do our P.T. We did jumping jacks and other exercises for
about forty-five minutes. When we got done, we ran for about two miles inside the base. The lieutenant was right with us when we ran. When it was all
over we had the rest of the morning off and around 13:00 a sergeant came
into our hut and said he wanted to see first squad. The sergeant said that he
was our squad leader and that we would be learning things from him. The
sergeant was a Mexican and took out his little note pad and took down all of
our names and service numbers. There were six black guys and two white
guys in the squad. He asked if anyone had come over from another outfit
here in Vietnam. I told the Sgt. I did and was the only one. He asked me
what the name of the outfit was and when I told him that I had come from
1/9, he looked at me and could tell that I had seen more combat than him.

They called for our platoon to get into platoon formation and that we
were going somewhere. They marched us to another part of the base and
there was a staff sergeant there and he told us about the M-16 and that we
could fire the rifle from anywhere on our body. He put the butt of the rifle
in his neck and laid his chin on top of the rifle. He began to fire his rifle. He
explained there was no recoil when you fired the rifle. He talked for about
twenty minutes while shooting his rifle in various positions. I didn't like
the damn rifle and wished that I still had my M-14 rifle back. The M-16
jammed on me my first night out in the bush and we lost a lot of men in our
company. The word was passed to march back to our hut and that we were
off for the rest of the day.

The next day came and again we did our exercises and our run, and
were off the rest of the morning. Just after lunch they called us to take our
combat gear. We were going to learn to call in artillery. Our platoon went
outside the base and went up on one of the hills around the base and when

we got to the top of one of the hills, we could look down back to the base and see how large it was. The base was huge. We looked north of where we were and could see other hills but not as large as the one we were on. As I looked down, still looking north, there was a very small trail that went from east to west in a zig-zag pattern. There were no trees or bushes on the hills or in the valleys between the hills. As I looked west, the hills ran into the large mountains in the distance. The black guys in my squad had their sunglasses on and were really hamming it up while the other guys in the squad took pictures of them. I just sat away from them and kept my ears and eyes open in case the NV.A. would hit us. I just hoped that we wouldn't get hit. Half of the guys in our platoon were standing while the other half was sitting down. The lieutenant and staff sergeant in our platoon gave each of our three squads an artillery mission.

Two of the squads had a map and the lieutenant gave them a fire mission. The squad I was with was still hamming it up and taking pictures of each other and the countryside. One of the squads yelled, "Shot out!" They were looking north and I knew that it had to be on one of the hills that was north of us. I looked back at the base and one of the 105s fired a round and in a couple of minutes the Willy Peter round hit the hill. The team said on the radio to move it 100 right up 50 and fire for effect. I saw that the four guns in the battery fired their 105s and in a couple of minutes the four rounds hit right where they wanted the rounds to be. The other squad plotted their fire mission and as they were getting ready to call in the coordinates, there was a person walking from west to east on the trail well below us. A couple of other guys in the platoon saw the person as well. The lieutenant told everyone to wait until he was out of there and then we would go on with our learning how to call in artillery.

Ten minutes went by and the Vietnamese person was gone and we went back to calling in the artillery. The lieutenant gave a map to the sergeant and the black guys got around him with the white guy and I watched all of them and it was almost funny in the way they went about calling in the arty mission. When we called out for a W.P., the guys went crazy and carried on like a bunch of idiots. I thought to myself, what in hell did I get myself into? I had left my old outfit because of the petty bullshit and no combat experience from the officers as well as the green horns in the outfit. Here were all these green horns from the States and they didn't know what in hell they got themselves in for over here.

We were finished and went back to the base. I was glad that we were going back and I just wanted to be alone and away from the rest of them. When we got back, it was time for evening chow and I went to the chow hall and saw Bob eating and sat down with him. I told Bob, "I just hope that we get out of this country alive with all of these damn green horns," and he said that he didn't give a damn what in hell they did, just so they didn't screw with his life. I told Bob that we only had a few months left over here and I just hope that we wouldn't get killed by these green horns.

I knew that the green horns were getting to Bob as well as me. I knew that when they would get into a fire fight that their attitude would change in a heart beat and they wouldn't be as cocky as they were now. I got up and went back to my hut for the evening. A couple of more days went by and it was Christmas Eve. The sun came out around 10:30 and the word was passed that the Vietnamese College Kids from Hue would be singing Christmas carols to us. If we wanted to go, we should be at the outdoor stage at 11:30. I thought about it and at least it would be nice to hear kids singing to us. All of us knew that Bob Hope and his people would not come up here because of the danger. I grabbed my rifle and magazines and went over to where the outdoor stage was. When I got there, there were only about twenty Marines sitting there in the middle row of the theater. There was a middle section and two side sections and it held about a couple of thousand guys. I sat in the middle section about the tenth row back and next to the aisle in case I needed to get out of there in a hurry.

I also had my camera with me and I was taking shots of the stage where there were two rows of chairs on both side of the stage. Around 11:00 there were cars and busses coming over to the theater. There was a tall wooden fence around the theater about 12 feet high. There were more Marines coming to watch the show and as they were coming in a couple of teenage Vietnamese girls came in and started passing around papers with songs on it. When I got my paper I saw that, "Silent Night" and "O Holy Night" were on the program. The theater was starting to fill up and it looked like it was going to be a packed house. It was about twenty after eleven and the elders from Hue came in and went up on the stage. After they came on stage, the high ranking officers of the Marine Corps and Vietnamese Army came on the stage and sat on the opposite side of the elders of Hue. In the middle of the stage was a very large Christmas tree that was about fifteen feet tall. Above the tree was a large north star.

Then came in the college students, a few boys but mostly girls, and they were all dressed up and went in front of the stage and were about four deep. They began singing Christmas carols to us. There were other Marines doing the same thing, taking pictures. Most of the Marines were thinking of home and I could tell that they wished they were home with their families. The young girls were very attractive and most of the guys were watching them. The show went on for about forty-five minutes and one of the college students told all of us to sing "O Holy Night" and after that "Silent Night" together.

The guys started singing "O Holy Night" and it seemed that everyone was really into the song and when we all started singing "Silent Night" I noticed most of the Marines were weeping as they sang. Even I had tears in my eyes. There was so much feeling in the song that it was very hard not to cry. When the song was over the college students filed out and got onto the busses and headed back to Hue. I just sat there thinking about the show and how nice it was of them to take their time out and sing Christmas songs to us Marines. There were a lot of cute girls and I took pictures of a lot of them, so I could remember this day if I made it back home when my tour was up. I wiped away the tears from my eyes and slowly went back to my hut.

When I got back there I lay down in my cot thinking about the show and I really felt so all alone over here. What was left of my buddies was being transferred to other outfits. The only guy I could talk to was Bob; I really didn't know him that well but he was from my old outfit and being around him made me feel good inside.

As the rest of the day went by slowly, I decided to go over to the beer hall and have a couple of beers. I stayed there for about an hour and had about four beers and left. I headed back to my hut for the night. I felt good and when I got to the hut and laid down on my cot, I was thinking of home and wondering if they had gotten snow. I almost forgot about how nice and white the snow would be. I fell off to sleep.

Morning came and I went on over to the chow hall for breakfast. When I came back there were a couple of packages on my cot as well as the other cots in the hut. I sat down and opened up the small package and inside was a pen. On the pen it read, "FMF PACK VIETNAM 1967." I picked up the larger box and under it was a letter. I opened up the larger box and inside it was a face cloth and soap with some writing supplies, there was again a small little Bible about 3 inches long and about 11/2 inches wide. There was some candy, also. I looked at the Bible and remembered my team talking about if everyone believed in the Bible and I told the guys that I didn't and that was when the N.V.A. fired their 152 artillery pieces at us up at Con Thein. But I believed in God. I opened the letter and it was from a high school girl back in Michigan. She had all of these questions about what it was like over here. I knew that I couldn't tell her much because it would be difficult for her to understand. I took out some paper and wrote to her and only said that the country over here was beautiful and the people were happy that we were protecting them from the V.C. and N.V.A. I mailed the letter back to her. I just laid on my cot and was thinking of when our mail would be catching up with us.

As I laid in the cot, I started thinking about this day, it was CHRISTMAS. I never felt so all alone in the world. I looked around in the hut and there was no one here. The rest of the guys were out keeping busy by going on over to the bar and drinking. I was wondering when we would be getting our mail, if and when it would catch up with us. The feeling of being so all alone over here was sinking into my body and soul. I almost wanted to cry to let it out but I couldn't. This lonely feeling was not going to let go of me and I felt myself getting very depressed. My mind started going back in time when I first came over here and one of the old timers was saying that he had seventeen hours left before leaving Vietnam. I had 395 days to go. I thought about the guys in my platoon that died in the field starting with James Fowler, Benny Houston, Vizer, Duvall, Sgt. Lugar, Sullivan and finally Whitey. Each and everyone of them were like brothers to me as well as the other old timers who were in the platoon. Then there were the guys that got wounded and were sent home from the war; Chuck Knight, Charlie Horton, Jerry Moore, Parrillo, Poisson, Lisinski, and other guys in our platoon. I started thinking about Captain Hutchinson and Lieutenant Libutti. I remembered how the captain and the lieutenant really cared for me. It was playing in my mind in that I missed being with them out in the bush went the whole battalion got hit from the N.V.A. on July 2nd. I just wished that the captain had taken the R. and R. instead of me. I started thinking of Lieutenant Libutti and I got a couple of tears about how I took care of him and coached him so the guys would respect him out in the field and how great he became with the guys in the platoon. I thought about the last time I saw him when he got out of the hospital and picked up his seabag and left Vietnam in September. I was the last old timer he saw before he left and how both of us couldn't speak but just looked at each other and both of us knew that we were very close to each other and would never see each other again. I could feel myself sinking deeper into depression and to top everything off I started thinking about, "Whitey." That was it, I started crying and I couldn't stop. The letters I was getting from his mother and how she called me her son were just too much for me to handle. CHRISTMAS was really getting to me and all I wanted to do was just be alone. Each hour went by so slowly during the day that I felt I was dying inside. I had the fear of being all alone again and there was nothing I could do to change it. I wished Christmas had never come!

After about ten minutes I thought of all the crazy things I had done for the platoon and company. I remembered I carried out the body of Sgt. Singleton who gave up his life for his squad and received the MEDAL OF HONOR and I remembered his arm hitting me in the back of my calf muscle, letting me know that he was going home. I remembered all of the guys in our battalion that were short and had only a couple of days left before they went home. When we got hit they came right back out into the field to fight along side with the rest of us. I was very proud of the 1st Battalion 9th Marines in what we did over here. We gave the N.V.A. more hell then any other Marine outfit with the exception of maybe 3rd Battalion 3rd Marines because we exchanged some men from each other's outfit. The rest of the day went by very slowly.

Word was passed that Hugh O'Brien, the movie actor, was here and if anyone wanted to see him to get on over to where the Mess hall was. I got up from the cot and went on over to see the movie star. I remembered how tough he acted in the movie and when I saw him in person, I saw in his eyes that he was totally scared. I was about five feet away from him and he had on his cowboy guns that he used in playing, "O.K. Corral". He stayed with us for about fifteen minutes and had to get back down to Freedom Hill 327. Never have I seen anyone so scared to death. I only stayed there for about five minutes and headed back to the hut. I told myself that at least he came up here and stayed for fifteen minutes - it was better than nothing at all.

On the 26th, our platoon went back to exercising up until the 29th of Dec. The word was passed for Echo Company to fall out with their seabags and combat gear on. We were going back to Okinawa for training on Recon. The sergeant for our team came over and said he would be staying here while the rest of us learned how to be Recon. The sergeant came over to me and told me to watch and see how the others handled themselves back at Okinawa. The black corporal was to be our team leader and I was just happy that it wasn't me. All I wanted was to be alone and not to worry about any one. We went over to the terminal and waited for the C-130 to come in and take us to Okinawa.

Around 10:00 in the morning I saw two bright lights from a C-130 coming down to land. In the distance there was another C-130 behind the first one. The lieutenants from all three platoons told us to saddle up and to get ready to board the planes. Both planes taxied over to the terminal and the rear doors opened up. I grabbed my seabag and the lieutenant told us to take the second plane. I got on and sat down with my seabag in front of me. There were other men getting on the planes as well and I knew that we were going down to Da Nang.

The planes started up and we were off. In fifteen minutes we landed again at Da Nang and were told to get off the planes. The whole company was told that the planes had to get refueled before we left and that we had about an hour here. The captain passed the word not to get too far from the terminals. There was a small snack bar next to the terminal and the officers were getting something to eat and drink. I laid my seabag down and also got something myself. When I was finished, I took my Nikon camera out and started taking pictures of the captain and my lieutenant. I also took pictures of the first sergeant and our staff sergeant. I started taking pictures of Freedom Hill 327 where Bob Hope just had his Christmas Show. The word was passed that the plane was ready and to get our gear on.

Again we boarded the plane and I put my seabag in front of me. This time the whole company was on one plane. It was a little after one o'clock and we were heading to Okinawa. As I sat in the plane, I could feel the temperature dropping and it was getting somewhat cold in the plane. Our jungle clothes didn't help keep us warm. I laid my head on my seabag and tried to get some sleep. I could feel myself falling off to sleep in the plane, but it was not a deep sleep. I could hear things around me. The plane started to descend and as we were getting lower, I opened up my eyes and waited for the plane to touch down.

The wheels of the plane touched the ground and we waited for the plane to stop. The word was passed to get our seabags and to get off the plane. As I grabbed my seabag and walked out the back of the plane, the sun was almost gone for the day. I looked at my watch and it was around 19:00 hundred hours. The captain told the company to follow him and we went over to one of the terminals. We got inside and the word was passed to hang out in the hallway and that our transportation was coming. I got off my feet and knew that we would be here for awhile. As I sat there in the hallway the guys were saying, "Hurry up and wait, that's the Marines Corps, hurry up and wait." Ever since I got to Vietnam, I had gotten used to, "Hurry up and wait." I again tried to close my eyes and get some rest. The other guys in the company were getting upset and wanted to get out of here and get into the barracks and get to bed.

I thought to myself that Vietnam broke me of, "Hurry up and wait" when we would go out on patrols and there would be days where we wouldn't hear a damn thing and then there would be days when all hell would break out. You learned to not hurry and just take your time doing whatever you were doing, at a very slow pace. A couple of hours went by and the word was passed that the cattle trucks were here and for us to put our seabags on the two six-bys. I slowly got up and again slowly went on over to the six-bys, and of course, all of the green horns were trying to be the first ones to get their seabags on the trucks. I watched them pushing and shoving each other around. When most of them were finished and there were only a few of them left, I went up to the truck and handed the guy my seabag and got into one of the cattle trucks and about twenty minutes later the trucks started off. Again the green horns were all upset and saying, "Here we go again, hurry up and wait." I just laughed to myself and we were off.

As the trucks started off, most of the guys were carrying on like a bunch of idiots. It must have been about forty minutes later and we were coming into a small town. I got up to look out the small window and as the trucks were slowing down, I wondered if we were going to Camp Hanson, which was a Marine base. I remembered when I first came over by airplane that we landed here before going off to Vietnam. But the trucks kept on going and I began to sit back down and was wondering just where in the hell we were going. Another forty-five minutes later the trucks were slowing down and I got up again. Most of the guys in the truck were sleeping. The lead truck turned to the left and there was a Marine M.P. waving us through. We went past the first building on the right and then went past the second building on the right and all of the trucks stopped and the word was passed to get off. Everyone got off the trucks and all of the cattle trucks started up again and left us. The only trucks left were the two six-bys with our seabags on them. The captain told everyone to get their seabags and line them up on the side of the road. I grabbed my seabag and put it on the side of the road and waited for the rest of the guys to get theirs.

The captain passed out the orders that we were going to get something to eat. The mess hall was open for us and we went over to the second building that had all of it lights on. It was the first time in the whole day that we had something to eat. I got in line with the rest of the company and we ate. As we were eating, the word was passed to get out on the street and grab our seabags and that we would go over to our barracks. It was going on around midnight and after everyone was finished, we walked over to our barracks, which were a couple of blocks away from the mess hall.

There were three barracks; in two of them you saw only the one end. There was one barrack that showed the entire length. The captain and officers took that barrack and the rest of the company took the other two barracks. As I got inside the barrack, I went about as close as you could to the shower and bathroom. I laid my seabag on the bottom bunk and went outside to get our linen and blanket. One of the Marines that was stationed there showed us just where the building was to get our sheets. I just couldn't get used to what was happening to me. I had been in the jungle so long that I had forgotten how nice the sheets felt since Out-of-Country R and R.

As I walked back to the barracks and got inside, I couldn't believe there was a bunk with springs, so you wouldn't feel like sleeping on the ground. I made my bed for the first time in nine and a half months. It felt strange. When I was finished, I went over to the bathroom and shower room and just looked at the toilets and sinks. I went over to the sink and turned on the water and just watched the water come out. I turned on the hot water and it really felt great. I went on over to one of the toilets and flushed it and watched the water go down. I went into the shower room and couldn't believed how big it was. I went back to my bunk and opened up my seabag and took out one of the large pink towels that I bought at Camp Evans. I also grabbed a bar of soap and took off my jungle clothes and went to the shower room to take a shower, a real shower. I must have stayed in there for a good twenty minutes and then came out and went on over to my bed. There were a couple of us taking a shower and Bob was one of them.

Most of the guys were still up and were starting up card games. I went to my bunk and got into my bunk naked and felt the clean white sheets covering my body. It just felt great and as I lay there, I was thinking about Dale, Speedy, and Kenny and what they were doing back in Vietnam. Somehow I fell off to sleep.

Morning came and the word was passed to get out on the street for company formation. The word was passed from the captain that we had three days off and that training didn't start until January 3rd. The captain said there was no liberty for off the base at this time. He also said there was a movie theater, bar, P.X. and other things that were on the base. He dismissed us and most of the guys went back inside and started up their card games. I went back inside and fixed my rack for the day. I went outside and there were a couple of picnic tables, I decided to go over to them and just sit down and relax.

After a couple of hours I decided to write some letters to let everyone back in the States know I was now in Okinawa. I went back inside and got my letter writing gear and went back outside again and wrote to everyone. It was time for lunch and I decided to go on over to the mess hall to get something to eat. I knew that I still couldn't eat much but I made sure that I didn't eat more than I had to because I knew that I would be going back to Vietnam in a couple of weeks.

I walked down to the mess hall and I saw the flag pole that was at the intersection and the American flag was flying. I looked at Old Glory and it was the first time that I had seen my flag since March of 1967. I went inside the mess hall and ate. When I came out I walked across the street and there was another building but it had two purposes. Half of the building was the P.X. and barber shop and the other half was the bar and dance floor. I went back out and headed back toward the barracks. I got to the cross roads and again I looked at the American flag and this time I decided to lie on this small hill and just look at the flag. As I laid there and the flag was blowing around by the wind, a lot of things were racing through my mind. Just the colors of the flag really got to me. I started tearing up and I knew deep down inside of me that a lot of guys in our country had died for that flag, all the way back to the Revolutionary War. I knew that I was now part of all of those men. I knew that all of the guys in the past didn't die or get wounded for their country but for each other and what they had gone through together. I also knew that all of the guys before me and after me believed in our country, regardless if it was right or wrong and mainly the freedom that we had and cherished so deeply. There were a lot of guys that joined because their fathers had fought in World War II.

I started thinking about my old outfit and all of what we had gone through in Vietnam and so many of the guys that gave up their lives for their buddies. The only down side was that most of the black guys in our battalion didn't have what it took to be one of the guys in taking care of each other. I remembered how they treated each other horribly - if you didn't fit in with the rest of them you were not one of them. I remembered that if you were black and couldn't sing with them that you were an outcast. I remembered how Benny Houston, being the old man in our platoon, tried like hell to get them to be a part of the rest of the guys in the platoon and I knew that it was tearing him up inside. When Benny stepped on the booby trap, none of the black guys that called themselves his buddies would carry Benny on the chopper for him to go home. The only black guy was Maxwell and he always was a loner but when the shit hit the fan, you could count on him, he was right by your side. I had a hell of a lot of respect for Maxwell. I somehow felt close to him and he seemed to be close to me. I remembered just after most of the guys in our battalion got killed on July 2nd and I had just got up to the rear area and put my sandbags filled with candy, smokes and juice for what was left of the guys in our platoon.

I still kept on looking at the flag and couldn't believe how beautiful it was. Some of the guys walked past me but didn't say a word. Bob came by and sat down next to me and, not saying a word, also looked at the flag. I looked at Bob and I could see that the flag meant a lot to him also. I knew that he was thinking about July 2nd. Then I got up and he did also and both of us walked back to our area without saying a word.

Later that day I decided to go and get a hair cut and I needed it. I was still dry shaving and I didn't want to stop. My skin was tough and it really didn't hurt at all when I dry shaved. I had been dry shaving ever since I joined my old outfit. I remembered that I had my hair cut a couple of times when I was with the old outfit; I always had it cut very short.

The evening and was the time for the bar to open and the girls to arrive. I slowly walked over there and as I did, I could smell the flowers and trees. I went inside and sat down at one of the tables and the band was playing the hot rock-n-roll songs of the day. The guys from my company were doing their smooth talk with the girls and the girls were handling it and throwing it back at the guys. It was funny how everyone was playing the game. One of the songs that was being played talked about the games people played. I just laughed to myself and went about drinking my beer. Then it was 24:00 and everyone said "Happy New Year." Everyone got up and started kissing everyone around them. I didn't feel like doing any of that stuff. I lifted up my beer can and quietly toasted the guys of 1st Battalion 9th Marines. I toasted the men that had died in my old battalion and toasted the guys like Chuck Knight, Chadwell, Charlie, Quick, Von Bargen, Grear, Kenny Fulton, Maxwell, Dale Davis, Speedy, Poisson, Charlie Horton, Jerry Moore and the guys in my fire team. I just hoped they were still alive. I also toasted the guys that had died in my platoon and finally my Lieutenant Libutti and Captain Hutchinson.

I must have had ten beers after I toasted all of the guys in my old outfit. I knew that it was time to get back to the barracks and I slowly walked back and enjoyed taking my time and didn't have to worry about someone hiding in the trees to take a shot at me but still I looked into the woods that were around us.

I got in bed and I stayed there for the next day. I just didn't feel like getting out of bed and there were a few guys besides me that were also in bed with big hangovers. There were some guys playing cards and having a good time. I got up and took a hot shower and really enjoyed staying in there for about twenty minutes. When I was finished I went back to bed and just laid there for the rest of the day. It was nice to just lie in bed and do nothing. I really didn't think about anything.

The next day came and it was Sunday. I heard someone say that if you wanted to go to church that it started around 09:30. I couldn't make myself go and saw that Bob didn't have any intention of going either.

Monday came and it was our first day here being trained as Recon. That morning we worked on learning how to read the compass and map. After that, we went out on our first squad patrol. Each team in the company had to go on a two thousand meter patrol by using a map and compass. The corporal was in charge of the team I was with and boy the rest of the black guys were happy that one of their own was in charge. I was happy that I didn't give a damn about them and I didn't want any responsibility. All I wanted now was to be all alone and finish my tour. Our team took off and I was the last man. The guys in the team were making a lot of noise when they were walking and were not taking this seriously about keeping quiet. I worked on not breaking any twigs or bushes so that the enemy wouldn't know that we came here. I stayed away from the rest of them when we walked, just in case we got hit by the enemy. When we would take a ten minute break the guys in the team would talk and carry on as though this was a waste of time. I stayed to myself and kept lookout in case someone would come up on us. The corporal came over to me and told me that we were in Okinawa and there were no N.V.A. I didn't say anything to him and he went back with the other guys.

We reached our objective and headed back to the base. Again the guys were too close together as we went back. I stayed as far away from them as I could. We were at the end of our patrol and all we had to do was walk up the side of the hill and we were finished. There were some guys up at the top of hill looking at us and yelling at us that we were all dead. They were pointing to all of the guys that were in front of me and I knelt down in the brush. I knew they were counting the guys in the team and could hear them say there were only seven of them and they were missing the eighth one which was me. I knew that if I kept myself down and stayed away from the guys in front of me that I had a chance of getting up the hill without being spotted. I made it up to the top of the hill and they asked me who in the hell was I and I told them that I was with them.

The word was passed that someone had drowned and all of us that were up at the hill were told to stay here until further word. A couple of hours passed and still no word. I knew that the guy was gone if it was taking this long. The word was passed that some of the guys had on scuba gear and were diving to try to find the body. They told us that we should go back to the barracks and wait to hear further word. We got back to the barracks and most of the guys were waiting to hear who it was and than the word came and they said his name. I knew that it had to be one of the green horns that came over to Vietnam.

It was time for dinner and all of us went to the mess hall to eat and as we were eating, I noticed that the blacks were all together talking about something and I just stayed to myself. I had a feeling that the guy that drowned was a black guy. As I went back to the barracks the word was passed that they still hadn't found the body and they were still searching. What I didn't know for sure at the time was that it was one of the black guys that had drowned.

The next day came and the whole company had more classroom instructions and patrols. As the week went on, they finally found the guy's body and the word was passed by the captain that on Sunday, if you wanted to pay your last respects to the guy that drowned, the service was to be held at 13:00. I didn't know the guy, but he was one of us in our newly formed company and I had to pay my respects to him. It was a shame that he died drowning instead of getting killed by the enemy - at least it would have meant something. As the week went by, the blacks were staying away from all of the white guys in the company and the undertone was that us white guys let him drown and we didn't do a damn thing to help him. I could feel a split between the Negroes and Whites. I knew this was not good for the company.

The word was passed there were only white divers looking for him but couldn't find him. All of the blacks were using it as their biggest complaint that the white guys didn't do a damn thing for him when he went down. They made him cross the stream, knowing he couldn't swim. As the week went on, the blacks didn't mess with Bob or me and even though they didn't talk with us, they for some reason stayed away from us. I think they respected us since we were the two oldest guys in the company with combat experience.

Sunday came and at 13:00 I walked down to the chapel to give my last respects. As I walked through the doors, I noticed that the blacks were on one side of the church together and the whites were scattered on the other side of the church. I walked down to about the middle of the church and sat on the edge of one of the aisle seats. All of the black guys were watching me but didn't give me a dirty look, like they had been giving the rest of the white guys when they came in. All of the officers were at the back of the church and everyone was on their own praying to themselves. There were a couple of blacks that were praying and giving their last respects as well and the Preacher in our squad. There was something about the Preacher I liked and for some reason he was not like all of the Negroes in the company. Some of the guys spent twenty minutes before they left. As I sat there looking forward and thinking to myself, I remembered when my buddy Benny Houston had stepped on a booby trap and lost his one leg and ended up dying these two black guys in our company were yelling at us white guys about not helping Benny, yet when the chopper came in and it was time to get Benny on the chopper, they didn't have the guts to carry him. I also remembered that both of these two black guys wanted to see how Benny looked in the poncho but didn't want anything to do with him. I just couldn't believe what I was seeing and how they were acting toward us.

I started getting a couple of tears in my eyes and I prayed that Benny, Whitey, Sgt. Lugar, James Fowler, and the rest of the guys in our battalion who died were in heaven being taken care of by God. I was really thinking about my old outfit and the hell that all of us went through. I remembered that when I first got to my old outfit, there were a few blacks guys in the battalion and as each month passed after March, there were fewer and fewer black guys in the battalion until July. We only had one black guy in our platoon and he was Maxwell and even he didn't associate with the other black guys in the battalion. I looked at the blacks and most of them were only thinking about the white guys in the company and not paying any respects to this black guy who drowned. They were looking for an excuse to blame the white guys, not realizing they would be going back to Vietnam shortly. I got up and left the church and went back to the barracks. As I was walking back to the barracks, one of the guys who was in the squad with the black guy that drowned said to me the black guy insisted that he could swim and took the point. As he got about eight feet from the bank he went straight down and never came up. Two of the guys dived in to get him but he went down like a rock. He had all of his gear on as he started walking into the water and the next moment he was gone. All of them thought the water was not that deep and were surprised.

Monday came and the word was passed that we had mail. One of the guys said that all over Vietnam everyone was getting hit. It was called the Tet Offensive. Someone called out for mail call and all of us got outside to receive our letters and packages. I knew that the mail had finally caught up with us and I was looking forward to getting letters from home and from the Hahner family. When they passed out the letters, everyone had at least three to five letters apiece. I had a couple of boxes and at least a dozen letters. Most of the letters were from Mom and there was one letter from Mrs. Hahner. The letter from Mrs. Hahner was on a piece of paper that was 4 inches wide and 8 inches long; there were a couple of pages and it was typed, front and back. Here is that letter that she wrote:

12/28/67
Memo: Dear Gary
From: Whitey's Mom

Just had to get a note off to you with the hope it will reach you before you go to Okinawa and with the further hope that you have not and will not be talked into signing up for another month - two - four - six or whatever anyone may try to talk you into. Your life and future, Gary, are far more important than a purple heart etc. You have done your share being in Viet Nam as long as you have and seeing and experiencing all you have and now it is time for you to come home, adjust again and live a better and fuller life and through what you have learned and experienced the past month help make where ever you go or live a better place just because you are part of it. I suppose I sound like a preachy "Mom," but I would talk this way to "Whitey" if he were you and I feel he would want you to come back home now and try to live a normal life and a good life. We feel you are a son to us too and want the best for your future.

Enough of this for now, but give it thought and we are all anxious to you come to Chicago and be with us even if you can only manage a short time as we know your folks will anxiously be awaiting for your return home.

God be with you and take care of you. Until later, take care and enjoy yourself in Okinawa, but remember your three C's, Calm, Cool, Collected. Also your three P's (those are my originals) Prayer, Prudence and Patience - and all will be well with you.

Love from all the Hahners

P.S. Excuse the paper and typing but am getting this off to you from work. Have a good meal and a drink or so on us while in Okinawa

There were a couple of letters that were dated just before Christmas. And I was glad that Christmas was over because I never knew how lonely Christmas could be without loved ones. I just hoped that I wouldn't go through Christmas again like I had in Vietnam. Now, I knew how it really felt when you are far away from home and someone is trying to kill you. All of the guys that fought in the wars before me had gone though what I went through, and boy it sure isn't pleasant.

The weekend was here and I went to the club on base and did some beer drinking for the evening. When Sunday came I just laid around and rested the whole day. When Monday came we started on rappelling, learning how to use a Swiss seat and using the D ring. Most of the day we were on a low rolling hill and rappelling. The next day came and they took us to the edge of the ocean where there were cliffs and on this one cliff there were three to four anchors in the ground where you tied the ropes. I knew that I would have to do it, go over the side of the cliff and rappel down. When it was my turn I was the first one in my team to do it. I grabbed the rope and put it through the D ring a couple of times and the instructor told me to start leaning backward and make sure that my brake hand was in the middle of my back. I did as he said and let go of my brake hand by moving it out to my side and away I went. I loved it and I stopped about half way down and took in the sights around me. The ocean was on one side and of course the cliff that I was on. This was fun and I went on down to the bottom of the cliffs. I waited down at the bottom for the rest of the squad to come down. A couple of them gave all kinds of hell to the officers and said they were not going. Finally everyone that was in the company did it except for a couple of the blacks guys in my squad and a couple of other guys.

The next day came and we went back to the cliffs to spend the rest of the day there doing more rappelling. When we were finished, the word was passed that we were going to rappel out of a chopper tomorrow. The next day came and they called us out onto the street and marched us over to a large field at the base and we waited for the choppers to come. We could hear the choppers coming, two of them. Both of the choppers landed about 200 feet from each other and the word was passed for 2nd platoon to get on the choppers. The squad I was with got on one of the choppers and the rest of the company watched our squad rappel. The chopper went straight up about 200 feet and the door gunner threw out the rope. The lieutenant looked at me and said that I was the first to go. I stood up and tied the rope in the D ring two times and faced inward and stepped out of the chopper on the ledge. The lieutenant looked at me and said to give myself about ten feet of slack before I left the chopper. I was now ready and jumped out backward away from the chopper and fell about ten feet and with my brake hand in the small of my back let go and boy did I slide down the rope. I bounced about ten feet from the ground. I could feel that I had burned my side from the rope but still it was a lot of fun. I loved it and I had a big smile on my face and the rest of the guys came out of the chopper. When our whole squad did it we went back to our platoon and sat down and watched the rest of the guys in the company do it. They asked if some of us wanted to do it again and I went on it one more time. It took most of the day and the word was passed that we had the rest of the day off.

The next day came and it was Friday and they told us we were going to show the rest of the company how to cross a waterway. The staff sergeant of our platoon told us that we had mostly black guys in the team with the exception of two white guys, and that we were going to show the whole company how to cross a stream. When he left, I started thinking about the black guys in my squad. They didn't want any part of the demonstration. As I looked at the fear in their eyes, I knew they would rather watch than show the rest of the company how to cross the stream. They were talking to each other, to show that they were tough and not afraid to do it.

I knew I had to stay away from them as much as possible and hope that my time over here was done. All of the feelings were coming back again and I wanted to stay away from the rest of the guys in my squad and not to say anything to them. I just didn't want to know anything about them, I'd been hurt too many times from my old outfit by the guys I knew that got wounded and killed. I knew these guys were green and when we got into combat, they would not be dependable under live fire.

The next day came and it was Saturday morning and the platoon staff sergeant came over to us and told us to get our gear and that we are to report down by the small lake that was in between the steep large hills that surrounded it. The S/Sgt. told us when we were done that we were to be off for the rest of the weekend. That made the guys happy. We were to get ready by 08:30 and to show the rest of the guys in the company how to cross the stream.

It was getting close to 08:30 and I left to go to where we were to report. The other guys in the squad got their gear and also headed down to where we were to meet. I just stayed by myself as I went on down the road. The sky was very cloudy and it looked like it was going to rain. Everyone in the squad arrived and all of us just sat there waiting for further word from the S/Sgt.

About ten minutes later, we saw there was a small row boat coming over to us from the other side. The S/Sgt. came out of the boat and had a large rope with him. He asked us who in this squad could swim and the young white guy said he could and I was the other one. So the S/Sgt. told the other guy to tie the rope around the white guy's waist and for him to swim across to the other side. The S/Sgt. told me that I was to tie the rope around my waist, being the last guy to come across the lake. All of the other guys, who were the black guys in our team, were to slide along the rope with their hands and to tie their boots and put them around their necks. The S/Sgt. said to get ready and all of us took off our boots and got ready. The S/Sgt. yelled out to the captain and he had everyone watch us learn on how to ford the stream.

The S/Sgt. got back in the boat and told the first guy to go across. The young guy started swimming across and as he was doing it, the captain was pointing out that the first guy had the rope tied around his waist while he was swimming with his boots around his neck. He finally got over to the other side and tied the rope around the tree. The rest of the guys in the squad, one by one started holding onto the line and as each one got into the water, there was fear in their faces as they held on to the rope with their hands.

Then it was my turn and I untied the rope from the tree and tied it around my waist. I put my boots around my neck and I slipped into the water without making any noise or splash. As I swam on over to the other side the boat was about ten feet away from me to make sure I didn't go under. I told the S/Sgt. that I was all right and didn't need anyone to help me. I finally got to the other side and then untied the rope around my waist. I put on my boots and the S/Sgt. told me that our team could go back to the barrack and get ready to go out on our weekend passes. I heard from a distance the captain told the rest of the company they were now on weekend liberty. Most of them were running back to the barracks to change their clothes and go on liberty.

I walked back by myself to the barracks and as I did I started thinking about the Preacher in my squad and what he told me in church the other day. I remembered that he was the only one in my squad who sat close to me in church as we were paying our respects to the guy who drowned. I also remembered what I said to him - that the rest of the black guys in our company and squad would be chastising him for sitting next to me in church and not with the rest of the black guys. He told me that he didn't care what they thought and he knew how to handle them his way. I thought to myself that he must know what he was doing.

When I got to the barracks most of the guys were already gone and chasing after the girls in town and of course going to the bars. I didn't feel like going out like the other guys. The only thing I wanted was to be left alone. The barracks were very quiet with a couple of groups of guys playing poker. I got into my rack and started thinking about the Preacher and I just hoped that he didn't get killed when we got back to Vietnam. He really seemed like a very nice guy and I just hoped that nothing would happen to him if they made stupid mistakes out in the bush. I hoped that he didn't pay for their mistakes like James Fowler did.

My mind drifted back to Vietnam, to my old 2nd platoon of 1st Battalion 9th Marines and the Negroes when I first encountered them. When I grew up, I never talked to or saw many Negroes. The only time I'd seen them was when my parents would take me downtown Cincinnati and that was the time I saw them but never talked to them. They seemed to be like anyone else that I've seen in the way they acted. Since I had been in Vietnam I saw this hatred toward the White guys in both outfits. The Negroes were letting us know that they were not slaves, and they were better than us. But each time that we got hit from the enemy the Negroes in our platoon seemed to get smaller and smaller out in the bush. When one of them would get hit, the rest of them would blame the guys in the platoon who were White and say that we let them get hit. The only two Negroes that were damn good

Marines were Benny Houston and Maxwell. Both of these guys were men in that they treated everyone in the platoon as equals. Unfortunately for Benny, when he stepped on the booby trap, the Negroes in our platoon would not help pick him up and carry him on the chopper so that he could go home. The Negroes were making all of us White guys hate them and not trust them. They were doing a great job of it.

As each day went by, I could see in this outfit that all of the Negroes were blaming the White guys for not helping save the guy who drowned. But it was the White guys that were risking their own lives in trying to find him. They finally found him about forty feet down under a tree, two days later.

I started thinking about all of the old guys in my platoon and wondered what was happening to Charlie Horton, Jerry Moore, Poisson, Ted Van Meeteren, (Speedy) Bill Gonzales, Kenny Fulton, Dale Davis, and the rest of the guys that got wounded and either went home or transferred to other outfits in Vietnam. I knew that there was no one left in our old 2nd Platoon Charlie Company. I knew that the 1st Battalion 9th Marines was not the same after August because there were all new men and they hadn't seen any shit before I left, on Dec.15th, 1967.

Chapter Thirty-Four

It was Monday morning and the word was passed that we were going to the ocean for rubber boat training. We got there around 10:00 and the rubber boats were there waiting for us and they showed us how to hold on using our legs. The waves were about two feet high and I knew that I was going to have some fun. The rest of the guys in the squad had mixed emotions since most of them couldn't swim but when the instructor told them they would not drown because of the salt that was in the ocean - they would be floating around - that eased their minds. The captain told the whole company to row out where the flag was (which was about an mile and a half), go around it and to see who would be back first. Everyone in the company was into it and when the captain said, "Go" the whole company took off into the rubber rafts and all of us rowed out to the flag. There were a couple of guys that fell into the ocean and the guys in the rubber raft would go back and get them. I remembered that the captain said that everyone in our squad had to be in the raft when we finished. Our boat got around the flag with about ten other rafts and all of us were heading back in. Our squad was really into it and as we were rolling faster and harder, a couple of the guys fell into the ocean. The rest of us went back to get them and as we did the other rafts were losing guys as well and there were only two rafts that were in front of us. We got everyone back inside the raft and were really working together as a team and we were about a half a mile out and in first place when we lost a couple of more guys in our raft and again we went back for them. By this time the guys were laughing and didn't care if we won or not. Again we got everyone in the raft and started off and this time I over did it and fell into the ocean and it really felt good. Everyone in our raft was totally wet from being in the ocean.

Finally all of the rafts made it back and we had more practice on how to get the rafts out into the ocean. The company spent the whole day there. When we got back to the barracks, I went inside and took my boots off and went into the shower room and washed my jungle uniform and myself. I made sure that I got all of the salt off my clothes and made sure I had all of the salt off of me as well. I got my other jungle clothes on and took the jungle clothes out in back and let them dry which would not take too long.

The next day came and word was for a company formation. We had never had a company formation in the morning - this was the first time. I could sense that something was going on. The captain asked if anyone in this outfit had combat experience to take a step forward. From the three platoons, about thirty of us had some combat experience. I knew that Bob and I had more experience than all of the other guys put together. The captain told the rest of the platoon that they were dismissed and that the rest of us were to stay. When the rest of the guys left, the captain said that we were on standby and when the time came that we would be issued Cold Weather Gear. We would be going to Korea to set up a perimeter next to the ocean and the other group would be going to the prison camp to get the prisoners. The captain said the prisoners were from our navy spy ship that the North Koreans had captured. The captain told us that this was going to be a one-way mission and those of us who didn't want to do this should leave now. Everyone looked around and no one left. The captain said "You know this is a very dangerous mission and you may not come back." The captain said that he was damn proud of us for doing this. I looked over to Bob but I could tell he wasn't excited. When the captain was finished, I went on over to Bob and said that this was going to be different. It was better than training with these green horns. At least it was something to do, some excitement. We went back to the barracks and waited for the rest of the day for them to call us on this mission.

When I got back to my rack, the Preacher was waiting for me and asked me how long I had been in Vietnam and I told him that I had been there since March of '67. He started asking me questions about what it was like being out in the bush. I remembered when I first got over to Vietnam and I also asked the guys what to do out in the field. I thought about what I should say about what it was really like. He might get the rest of the Negroes to quit being assholes and start being Marines in learning on how to be quiet out in the bush. So I decided I would tell him even if he was the only one that asked. He would have a good chance of making it back to the States. So I told him that the first thing is to be able to walk quietly while in the bush and to let your eyes and hearing do your job in locating the enemy, plus your sixth sense. There is no talking when moving and also to keep your distance from the guy in front of you. The most important part was to have your rifle ready at all times. At night time you should know where all your gear is so if you have to leave in a hurry that you would not make any noise. I also told him that sound travels faster at night than during the day. Never, never let your guard down for one minute when you are out in the field. The biggest thing is that all of you have to depend on each other. When I was finished, he could easily see why I was different from the rest of them. I made myself think I was still in Vietnam, even though we were in Okinawa. The Preacher said, "We thought that you were acting like a super Marine and now I know that you weren't." He said that every time our squad went out into the bush we should be like you if we don't want the enemy to hear or see us. I told him if you want to live you better do it. I also told him that my father told me one way to stay alive was to find an old timer who stays to himself and do the same things he does out in the bush. I asked him if there was anything else and he said, "No." As he walked away, I just hoped that he took my words to heart if he wanted to live. As far as I knew, most of these guys in our company were green and were having <u>fun</u> and not paying attention to the guys that had some combat experience and to learn off of them.

Around 19:00 hours the word was passed that we would not be going to Korea. I was hoping that we would go on this mission but it was not to be. I felt that we could have gotten the prisoners out if they called us. I thought about Mrs. Hahner and I knew that she would not have liked it if I went on this mission. But, it was over with and the next day came and the word was passed that we were not heading to the north country.

That evening as I stayed to myself as usual, I started thinking about the Preacher and I knew to myself that he would be one of the very few Negroes that would be able to stand on his own two feet and not blame the white guys in the outfit for everything. I didn't judge any man and that included officers until they handled themselves in the bush. I knew that once any man was under fire you would know how they would be able to handle themselves, especially when they would have to pick up the dead and wounded guys in the outfit. I also knew that before anyone would see combat that a lot of guys would be your buddy and eat your food and shoot the breeze and know your family, but when we got into a fire fight, they would change, either to fight with the guys or hide from a fire fight by staying back in the rear.

As I looked around the barracks, I saw that most of the guys were hanging onto each other in their little groups laughing, kidding, talking and lying to each other. I knew that when we did get into the shit, they would not be as close to each other as they thought they would be. All of the Negroes were together and the Preacher was listening to them and every once in a while he would look over to where I was, by myself in my rack. I could tell that he was thinking of what I had said to him. I knew that he had not seen any combat but he would quickly see for himself that they were not as brave as they thought they were.

The next day came and the word was passed for 2nd platoon to get out on the street. The tall lieutenant in our platoon told us that we were leaving this morning for the Northern Training Area before the rest of the company, with the supplies. He told us to get our gear and that we would be there for the rest of the week. I went back inside just like the rest of the guys in the squad and grabbed my 782 gear. I went back outside and waited for the six-bys to come and the word from the lieutenant was to get on the trucks, we were leaving. I got on the back of one of the trucks and just laid down on top of the supplies. The trucks started off and we were heading north up to the Northern Training Area.

As we were passing the different villages, there were some people that were walking up and down the road waving to us. Then we came into this one town and the people there seemed very cold to us as we went through. One of the guys said that the people there were Communist. My mind thought about Gio Lin and the vill that was around there where we would go on patrol and the people would not come out of their huts but would just stare at us and you could feel the coldness from them. You could tell that you should not turn your back on these people. I remembered the teenage girls from the vill who would go over to the north side of the D.M.Z. and fire the 57mm recoilless rifle at the base camp.

It took us a little over two hours to get there and when we did, we saw there were tents set up for us. The trucks stopped and we started unloading the trucks and it took about 30 minutes and the trucks left to go back and get the rest of the company. As we waited for the rest of the company to get here, I saw that the hills were more like mountains than hills. They looked steep, very steep. I started thinking about Vietnam and I knew that they had steep mountains but we never went on them.

The rest of the company arrived and the captain passed the word that we would be going to a class at 16:00 hours. When it was time for the class the whole company went to the building and all of us sat down. A sergeant came up on stage and began talking to us about the area up here and said when we go out on patrol tomorrow to stay on the trails and make damn sure that we did. The sergeant said that some Marines had fallen some 80 to 100 meters down off the hills here and ended up with broken legs and arms. We were to make sure that we watched where we were stepping and to stay in the middle part of the trail. I looked around and saw that most of the guys were not taking the sergeant seriously. I knew that someone in the outfit would get seriously hurt.

The next day came and the lieutenant told us that we would be going on two patrols, one in the morning and one in the afternoon. The lieutenant told the three squads which trail to go on and how far and to set up and observe the area and make sure to describe the area. The black corporal of our squad was the leader. I knew that with him in charge, the rest of the black guys would carry on as idiots. The young white guy in our squad was carrying the radio for us. The corporal would either have me as the point man or the rear point man but I didn't care one way or the other. We took off for the morning patrol - I was the point man. As we were going into one of the hills, I followed the trail and stayed in the middle of it. As I went further into the mountain, I saw how steep the mountain was becoming. I looked over the side and it was about 200 meters straight down and as I looked back, the rest of the team was not goofing off like they had done on other patrols. They were all scared to death and made sure they were walking in the middle of the trail.

We finally got to the area where we were to set up and observe for a while and as we did I started thinking about the Marines that had fought here back in WWII. I just couldn't believe how the guys that fought here in WWII had done. In the distance there was a pill box from WWII. There were some bullets holes in the concrete. There were very few places where you could get off the trail and set up and observe.

On our last day here, the word was passed that one of the guys had fallen some 35 feet. Someone had said that he had walked on some of the leaves that were on the trail but they were not on it and he fell through but only got bruised with no broken bones. That afternoon the trucks arrived to take the company back to our base. We were finished and the captain and lieutenants were happy with our observations and knew that we were ready to go back to Vietnam. All of us were hearing that the Tet Offensive was going in the way of the enemy. I knew that we would be going back to Vietnam very soon. When we got back to the barracks, they gave us liberty.

Chapter Thirty-Five

It was a little after 12:00 noon and I changed into my khaki clothes and went over to the main gate of the camp. There were a couple of cabs there waiting to take the guys into the different towns. A couple of the guys got into the same cab with me and all of us shared the price of the cab. The guys asked the cab driver to take us to the town across from the Marine camp called Camp Henson. It took us about twenty minutes and we reached the town and we paid the cab driver and he left. The guys then split up and went into different directions. Most of them were headed to the bars, but I wanted to walk around and see what kind of shops there were in town. There were a few shops that had a lot of silk and cotton fabrics. Some of the silk was very beautiful and had flowers printed on them. I knew that I would come back tomorrow and buy some for my mother. I went past a theater and they were playing a Kung Fu movie and Bruce Lee was the main actor. I knew that I would come back tomorrow which would be Sunday and get the fabric and go to the movie. Around 18:00, I knew that I better get something to eat. I really didn't need much since I had been back from Vietnam. I just wanted to keep my stomach on the small side since we would be going back very soon. I finished eating and decided to go to the bars and check out the Japanese Go Go Girls.

Inside the bar, there were not too many guys there drinking. I went up to the bar and sat down. I ordered a can of beer, "Bud," and slowly started drinking it. As time went on, the music started and the girls that worked at the bar were also the dancers. One of them started dancing in the middle of the floor and most of the guys stopped and watched her. The girls were around 5' 0" or shorter. They didn't have large breasts but they were in proportion to their body size. They would dance to our Rock -n- Roll. As each of the girls was dancing to the guys, they made them think about having them for the evening or night. I heard one of the guys say that if you wanted them that it would cost you fifteen dollars for the night or ten dollars for a short time. A couple of the girls would come up to me but I told them that I was not interested in them and they would go on to another service guy in the bar to get them to buy them a drink.

The bartender had a special bottle that only had tea in it for the girls when the guys would buy them a drink. I shook my head and started to laugh to myself. The funny thing was the guys knew that the girls were drinking tea but were paying whiskey prices but didn't care since they were going to buy them for the night.

Around 20:30 hours, this American girl came into the bar and the bartender paid her some money and she put a quarter into the juke box and pressed three songs. She was a red-headed girl around 5' 5" and as the first song started, she started dancing to it and boy did all of the guys in the bar stop and watch her. She took off a couple of pieces of clothing and that really got the guys going. It was even hard for me to keep my eyes off of her. She moved better than the Japanese girls and she had larger breasts than them. When the three songs were over, she went around to all of the guys and asked for donations and boy did the guys give her money. She had a racket going and was making a lot of money over here. After she had gone around, she left and went to the next bar and again danced to three songs and repeated the process all over again.

Around 01:00, this one Japanese girl came over to me and wanted me to go home with her. I could tell that she had been drinking quite a bit and wanted to have a man for the night. Finally the bar was closing and she was still with me and asked me if I would buy her a drink and I did. The bartender gave her a real whiskey and I paid for it. When both of us were finished, we left the bar. When we got out into the street, there was no one around. She was so loaded that she told me that she had to piss. I looked back and right in the middle of the street she squatted down and pissed just like the girls over in Vietnam when they were in the rice paddies. I laughed to myself and I knew that she didn't know where in the hell she was at. I got off the street and just watched her. She totally forgot me and headed home, walking like a drunk, all over the road.

I headed back to the main street back to where Camp Henson was. When I was across the street from the main gate of the camp, I called for a cab and it took me back to my base. When I got there, the cab dropped me off at the main gate and I showed the M.P. my pass and walked down to my barracks.

Morning came, and I went to breakfast and slowly walked back to the barracks. I went to my rack and just laid down there until around 12:00, I got up and went to the main gate and took the cab to town. When I got to town, I decided to go to the movie and watch Bruce Lee. As I watched the movie, they talked in Japanese but they had a sub-title in English at the bottom of the screen. After a couple of hours, the movie was over and I went on over to the linen store. About twenty minutes later, I picked this white silk with pink flowers on it for my mother. I gave the person there the address and money to send it back to the States. As I was leaving the store, I opened the door for this elderly lady. As she came in, she told me that she would like for me to come to her house. The lady at the store told me by opening up the door for her, she was obligated to give me her daughter in return for the good gesture. I looked at the lady in the store and asked her how could I get out of this mess without insulting her. She talked to the woman in Japanese and after a couple of minutes looked at me and said that she understood. I thanked her and nodded to the elderly lady in respect.

I looked for a cab to take me back to the base. When I got there, I decided that I better write some letters back home to Mom and to Mrs. Hahner. I had told Mrs. Hahner that I was thinking about extending over here so that my brother would not have to go to Vietnam. I didn't think about saying it to my Mother. It was going on evening and I went to chow. After chow, I went back to my bunk and just laid there thinking about home, Okinawa, and of course Vietnam. Some of the guys in the barracks were saying that the news in Vietnam was still bad in a couple of places and they were "Hue", "Khe Sanh" and of course the capital, "Saigon." I could feel that we would be going back to Vietnam soon, since all of our training was over.

In the evening I decided to go out the back of the barracks and sit down on one of the picnic tables and looked up at the sky. I knew that we would be going back very soon and in a way, I was looking forward to it. I was getting tired of the guys playing their little games on each other and making other guys look like shit. I knew that being in Recon was not like being with an infantry outfit where you would have guys watching each other's backs, especially if they had seen combat. I knew there would be some assholes in each outfit. In this company being formed for the first time since World War II, we had 80 percent green horns and about 20 percent that had some combat. I knew that in the team I was with, I was the only one with any combat experience. Until we got back to Vietnam the sergeant would be the only other one with some combat.

I still had that feeling with me that I would not get killed in Vietnam. I just wondered that if I extended, if I would still have this protection. I just didn't know but I knew that I didn't want my brother to come over here. It was getting dark out and I went back inside the barracks and went to sleep.

The next day came and they had us on the street and told us that we had a little more training to do. The trucks came and we got on them and they took us to an area where we would be doing rope crossing. When we got there, they told us that we would be walking over a small valley which was about ten feet high. One rope was at our feet and the other one was about shoulder high. We would slide over one rope with our feet and slide our hands along the rope that was at our shoulder height. We had to use only one rope this time which we would slide our body over the rope. There was a lake below us about thirty feet and after that they had us go to where there were three ropes, one for our feet and the other two for our hands in a "V" shape as we were walking across. A one hundred foot drop was under us as we went across. When the whole company did all of the different rope crossing they told us that it was time for lunch. They gave us for the first time a new type of meal where we added just hot water to the food. They told us we would not be using C-rations at all but these new kinds of ready-to-mix meals. The meals came in a foil with the other stuff such as gum, smokes, toilet paper, matches, and heat tab, cookies and crackers.

We were finished eating and it was good. I had noodles and chicken and it wasn't that bad. They told us that it was now time to have fun. They marched us to the top of one of the hills and said that all of us were going to take the quick way down. We were going to hang onto this pulley and when we would get to almost the bottom the gunnery sergeant would wave the red flag and we were to let go with our feet hitting the water first, not our head or body. The staff sergeant said he would be the first to go down it so that the rest of us would be able to see how it was done. He put the pulley on the wire and took a running start. Everyone in the company was cheering him on and then at the bottom the gunnery sergeant waved the red flag and he let go and hit the lake with his feet. Everyone cheered and couldn't wait to do it themselves. It was a long way down to the bottom, about a thousand foot drop. As the first platoon was getting ready to go, their lieutenant was telling the guys to make sure that you hang onto the pulley and to drop when you see the red flag. When the first guy left, again everyone was cheering him on and then he hit the water. Most of the guys were really getting a head start by getting a run off the hill.

There were a couple of the guys that didn't hit with their feet and boy did they tumble in the lake. They were not hurt but still I knew that they were feeling some pain. Then it was my turn and I also took a running start and boy was I having fun going down to the gunnery sergeant; when he waved the red flag I let go and made sure that my feet would hit the water first, which they did. When I got out of the lake, I felt great and wished that we could do it again but the captain said that we were finished for the day and that we had to get back to our barracks.

The next day came and after breakfast the word was passed that the company was to stay in the barracks until they called for us. They called us out into the street and told us that we were getting new jungle clothes and jungle boots. The word was passed for the company to go to lunch and to get right back to the barracks again and not to go anywhere. They did tell us that we had one classroom instruction left for the company. After lunch and when everyone was back at the barracks, the word was passed to get on the street, so everyone in the company went out into the street for the company formation. The captain said that we had one more lecture in the classroom. So this time the captain marched the company to the classroom and when we got there he told us that our training was finished and that we were going back to Vietnam tomorrow evening. He told us when he dismissed us, we were to go inside the classroom. He told us that tomorrow we all had liberty and that we had to be back here by 19:00 hours. Then he dismissed us and the company went inside the building and waiting for us was beer for the whole company. Everyone grabbed a couple of beers and the music was on and the guys were all drinking beer including me. The officers were at one table and the guys from the three platoons were toasting them and thanking them for the beer that they and the gunnery and staff sergeants paid for. Everyone was having a great time and no one was leaving for liberty until later. One of the guys in 2nd platoon came over to me and asked if he could sit with me and drink his beer. I told him to go ahead and he had a great time.

Two hours had gone by and I had drunk about 12 beers and was getting tired. I was feeling good and there were not too many guys left. The officers had already left and most of the guys in the platoon were gone as well. I got up and left the building and headed over to the movie house. I got a ticket and sat there and watched the movie, "To Sir With Love." I had a large Pepsi and popcorn while I watched the movie. When it was over with, I got up and went back outside. The sun was out and most of the sky was blue. I headed down to the ocean and sat on the edge of the rocks that were next to the beach. As I looked out into the ocean, it was very beautiful. There was a greenish-blue color from the shore to about a hundred feet out and the deep blue took over. It was just beautiful. The waves were coming in at ease and going back out slowly. I just sat there, not thinking of any one thing but just day dreaming. It felt great just looking at the ocean and sky. After awhile I looked around and could not hear any sounds of cars, trucks or even people talking. It was just silent and peaceful; it felt great. Time was moving very slowly as though there was no pressure to do anything. After sitting there for about an hour, I knew that I better get on back to the barracks and get my seabag packed.

I got back to the barracks, and most of the guys were out on liberty and making it the best time they had. There were a few guys in the barracks that were playing cards. I could feel the loneliness coming back and just lay down in my rack. As I laid there, I started looking around and knew that I would miss the things that I was used to, like taking a hot shower and using the toilet bowl and turning on the switch so that the light would come on, the clean sheets and blanket, clean clothes, getting a hair cut, being able to shave with soap. I knew that I would not be having these things again until I left Vietnam.

The word was being passed that anyone in the company that had under 60 days didn't have to go back. I started thinking about how many days I had; it was a couple of days beyond the sixty. I started thinking about Bob who was from my old outfit, 1st Battalion 9th Marines, and wanted to see if he had the time. So I got up and went over to his barracks. As I reached him, he was also lying down in his rack. I asked Bob if he had the time and he said that he had more than sixty days. I sat on the rack across from him and asked him about July 2nd. Bob looked at me and said that it was the worst day he had ever gone through. I asked him just how in the world did the N.V.A. catch us without us knowing they were there. Bob said on the morning of July 2nd they were told by the new captain of Bravo Company that they were going to go down Market Street and on down the hill toward North Vietnam.

I told Bob just before I left for R. & R. that our company had had two ambushes the last two days before I left and that we had hit the N.V.A. I told Bob that when I left the field, I was taking back with me a Chinese machine gun that my captain told me to put on his rack back at Dong Ha. I asked Bob if Bravo Company knew that we had two ambushes and had hit the N.V.A. He looked at me and said they didn't know that we had hit the enemy.

Bob told me that as they were walking on the road down the hill that the point team stopped the column and passed the word to send out flanks and when they were getting ready to do it the captain told them there were not to be any flanks out. They were only going down the road a short way and were heading west parallel with the strip. Bob said that's where the N.V.A. were on both sides of the road; the banks were about five or six feet high. He said that most of the guys had a strange feeling that something was not right but didn't see anything. All of a sudden the shit hit the fan and word was passed to get over the bank of the road to the left side which would be the west side. One of the platoons made it but the rest of the platoons were still on the road getting chewed up by the N.V.A.

As Bob was talking, the horror in his face and in his tone of voice told me that he could see in his own mind his buddies dying right in front of him. Bob said that within two minutes most of the company was dead. He said that most of the guys died because the damn M-16 rifles jammed on them. He said that a couple of tanks came down to where they were on the road and the wounded were getting on the tanks to get the hell out of there. As the tanks were withdrawing, the N.V.A. fired R.P.G.'s at the tanks and the guys that were wounded on them ended up being killed. Bob said that he was one of a few guys that got out of there without getting wounded or killed.

He was finished and both of us just looked at each other and we could feel the pain that each of us had. Both of us had lost buddies that day who were killed or wounded. I knew that both of us would live with this for the rest of our lives and there was no way for anyone to really understand just what the hell all of the guys from the 1st Battalion 9th Marines had gone through that day. It was twice as hard on me since I had taken my captain's Out-of-Country R. & R. and wished I had been with the guys that day. I started thinking about what Dale said to me that he and the rest of the guys were glad that I wasn't there. But, it was eating at me everyday, and there was no way to get away from it. I knew that James Toy from Alpha Company and the other two guys also from Bravo and Delta also missed the fight. I knew there were four of us that would remember it for the rest of our lives.

I asked Bob, "Are you ready to go back to Vietnam?" and he looked into my eyes and said he was ready. I almost felt that he didn't give a damn if he lived or not when we got back to Vietnam. I got up and told him that I would see him later in Vietnam and he gave me a half hearted smile. I got up and went back to my barrack.

As I walked back to the barrack, I was thinking how Bob looked when he told me about July 2nd. I knew that he had lost a hell of a lot of buddies in his platoon, not counting his whole Company. As I reached my rack, I just laid there thinking about Vietnam. I was wondering what was happening to Kenny Fulton, Dale Davis and Bill Gonzales who were supposed to leave Charlie company and to go to another outfit back in the rear somewhere. I was wondering how in the world would I be able to find them. I started thinking about Sgt. Lefefe, Charlie Horton, Ted Van Meeteren, Perez, Chadwell, Charlie, Maxwell, Ski, and Chuck Knight. I was wondering how these guys were doing back in the States.

I started thinking about, Benny Houston, James Fowler, Sgt. Lugar, Vizer, and George "Whitey" Hahner. These guys were really great men and they had lost their lives in Vietnam. All of the guys in our platoon really missed the old man of the platoon who was Benny Houston. It seemed that he kept the whole platoon together and he was going to trim my mustache the day he stepped on the booby trap. Then, James Fowler got killed his second day out in the bush and I can still remember him telling me that God was with him and that nothing was going to happen. In those two days that was the only thing he said to me and he knew that I was worried about him. And then, when Whitey died, the new guys in the platoon wouldn't carry his body down off of that hill when the green horn "Cool" had dragged his feet and tripped the booby trap. The only one that helped was Dale who came back up the hill after he helped carry Sgt. Lugar's body down the hill.

The next day came and the word was passed to take our seabags outside for the two six-bys. They said there would be two laundry hampers for the bed sheets to be put into. The blankets were to be folded and put on the table by the restrooms in each of the barracks. There would be a formation at 19:30 hours for the company and that shortly after that we would be leaving by cattle trucks tonight. When they were finished, the company had the rest of the day to themselves.

I left and went on over to the P.X. to get some more writing gear and other stuff. When I was finished, I went back to the barracks and put the writing gear into my seabag and locked it up and took it on over to the truck and the driver stacked it up with the few others that were there. It was going on lunch time and I headed over to the mess hall for lunch. When I was finished, I went on over to the bar. I had a Pepsi and some potato chips and just sat there watching the rest of the guys in the company getting drunk because they didn't want to go back. It seemed they didn't have any backbone. Here they were all tough guys wearing the Marine uniform and acting tough. They were trying to get so drunk that they wouldn't feel anything by the time they got to Vietnam. A couple of the guys in my platoon came over to me and asked if I needed a drink and I told them that I had one. They left and here came Bob and he asked me if he could sit down and I told him that he didn't have to ask me for permission. He sat down and said these guys were not ready for Vietnam and I told him now that training was over, they wished they paid more attention in the classroom as well as out in the field. I asked Bob how the team he was in was and he looked at me and said he was worried a little about them but said if they got into combat that that would be the time to see how they handle themselves. Bob asked me about my team and I told him that I had one greenhorn White guy and six greenhorn Negroes and none of them had any combat at all. He shook his head and said that he felt sorry for me. I told him they thought they knew everything and they were going to kick N.V.A. ass. He told me that I was in serious trouble. The hours went by and it was time for dinner and both of us went over to the mess hall and ate our last good cooked meal for awhile.

We walked back to the barracks and said that we would see each other later when the company would be getting out in the street. I went into the barracks and just laid down in the rack and just before 19:00 hours, I would put the sheets into the hamper and fold up the blanket. As the guys came into the barracks, most of them were really drunk. I was shaking my head and laughing at them. There were a few of them that were playing cards and having a good time.

I looked at my watch and saw that it was time to tear up my rack. I took the sheets over to the hamper and folded up the blanket. I slowly walked outside of the barracks and there were a few of us waiting for the word to be sounded. Bob was also there waiting for the word. The word was passed to get on the street. I got to my spot in formation with the few of us that were not drunk and the rest of them were walking from side to side and trying to get in formation. The officers were also a little tipsy as well. The word was, "Attention." The captain told the company when the cattle trucks came to be ready to get on them. I could tell that he was a little tipsy as well. I knew that if this was an infantry outfit that we would really be in trouble. He told the guys to make sure that their seabags were on the two trucks. He dismissed us and most of them went back inside to get their seabags.

Finally the cattle trucks came and there were seven of them. The captain told the platoon commanders what trucks to take. I was laughing and couldn't believe this outfit. After about twenty minutes, the trucks started off and headed to Clark AFB.

As soon as the cattle trucks started off, most of the guys were already sleeping in the trucks. Being drunk, they really didn't care where they were going at this time. This was their way of facing up to going back to Vietnam. I looked at my watch and saw that it was a little after 2300 hours and we had just passed Camp Hanson. I knew that we had about another half hour to go before we got to Clark AFB.

We finally got to Clark AFB. We got out of the cattle trucks. The word was passed to get our seabags and to wait inside the building for the C-130 to take us to Vietnam. As I got my seabag and went inside the terminal, I found a spot and sat down and just closed my eyes and started thinking when we first got here we came under darkness and now we were leaving under darkness. I had a feeling that we were not going to leave for a little while. I tried to get some sleep but couldn't. I tried to relax but I could hear the guys around me. Some of them were starting to sober up but there were some that were too far gone.

The word was passed to get our seabags and it was time to get on the C-130 for Vietnam. I slowly opened my eyes and got up and grabbed my seabag and walked on over to the door. I looked at my watch and it was 01:00 in the morning. I walked over to the C-130 and walked up the back of the plane. It was cool out and I knew that in the plane we would get cold since they didn't have heaters. We piled all of the seabags in the middle of the plane and sat on both sides. The C-130 started up its engines and the back door started to rise. We started to move and after about ten minutes we were off the ground heading to Vietnam. About ten minutes into the flight, most of the guys were sleeping again and I could feel the coolness creeping over us. Since we all had on our new jungle clothes and they were very thin, it didn't take long for some of the guys to get cold. The hours went by and I knew that we would be in the air between five to six hours before we arrived in Vietnam.

In some weird way, I felt like I was going home. I looked on the other side of the plane and saw Bob and he was awake and giving me the thumbs up. I could sense that Bob felt the same way. I closed my eyes to just relax but after a couple of hours in the plane, I was ready to get out of it, but I knew we had a couple of more hours to go.

I opened my eyes and looked out the small window of the plane and could see that the sun was up and I looked at my watch and it was going on 06:00. It wouldn't be long now before we landed. I was thinking that we would be landing at Phu Bai, since that was where 3rd Recon was located. The plane was heading down and I was getting a little excited about being back in Vietnam. I looked at my watch again and now it was a little past 07:00. The wheels of the plane hit the ground and then taxied on over to the terminal. The back door came down and I looked out the back of the plane to see which airport we had landed at and it was the first time that I had been to this area. I knew that we hadn't landed at Dong Ha, Phu Bai, or Da Nang. Our lieutenant told us to get our seabags and to get out of the plane. I grabbed my seabag and walked out the back of the plane and went over to where the lieutenant was and he told us to leave our seabags here and not to get too far away when he called us.

I dropped my seabag and walked on over to the terminal to see where we were. The sun was out and there were only a few clouds around. As I got closer to the terminal I saw that the 1st Cal was here. I got to the front of the terminal and it read, "Quang Tri Terminal." There were about sixty 1st Cal. Soldiers and I looked on the other side of the terminal and there must have been about 20 some Hueys on the ground with their insignia on the front of the chopper. I was thinking that the Marines still had the old CH-34's from Korea.

I thought of my Uncle Bill and wondered if he was with this part of the Army outfit. I knew that he was over here since my Dad told me that he was. A couple of the guys from the 1st Cal came over to me and could tell that I was one of the Marines that came off the C-130 and with my new jungle clothes and asked me if I was new over here. I told them that we had just landed here. I asked them if they knew a Bill Kasten and neither one knew him. They told me that the Marines had called for the 1st Cal to help them up here. I asked them, "Is it really bad up here?" Both of them said that the Marines were really getting kicked around and needed help. They told me that since I was new over here that it won't be bad since the 1st. Cal was here. More Hueys were flying in for the 1st Cal. They told me that we were really North and that we were next to the D.M.Z. I started laughing to myself and couldn't believe the bullshit that these guys were trying to hand me. We were about 20 miles from the D.M.Z. I finally had enough of their bullshit and asked them how long they had been in Vietnam and one of them said two and a half months and the sergeant said five months. I told both of them that I had been here eleven months and asked them, "Just where in the hell were you when the 1st Battalion 9th Marines got hit in July, if you tell me that the Marines couldn't handle themselves up here now?" I said, "Back then, even the other Marines outfits wouldn't help us and now, you're telling me that the Marines are asking for your help? In your dreams, buddy." I turned around and headed back to my seabag.

Around 08:00 the lieutenant had some ammo and told us to fill up only one magazine. Finally the trucks came to pick us up and still we didn't know where we were going. As soon as everyone got on the trucks, we headed down Highway 1 and about a half mile we turned into this new base, which was called Quang Tri. I knew that a few months ago this was not here and now there were a lot of tents and a few hardbacks here. The base was very large and the trucks took us to 3rd Recon area. We got out of the trucks and they told us where our company area was to be. Our lieutenant took our platoon and showed us three tents and each squad had their own tent. There were two rows of tents; each row had six tents but the rows of tents were about 75 meters apart from each other. Each tent was about ten feet from each other.

My squad's tent was right next to the company tent. When the lieutenant assigned us our tent, I went inside and put my seabag next to the rack at the end so I could get out of the tent fast if I had to. The monsoon season was over with up here and it was starting to get hot. When everyone in the company settled in, the captain called for a company formation and all of us got out in-between the two rows of tents. The captain said that we would not be going out on any operations for a couple of weeks, so in the mean time, we would be filling sandbags and putting them up around the tents on both sides and also make a large wall in the middle here between the two rows of tents. I knew one thing: we had plenty of sand and it was here. When the formation was dismissed, the sergeant from our squad came back to us and called for me.

Both of us walked around and he asked me how the guys did back in Okinawa. I told him they thought that it was a joke and just had a good time. I told him that the Negro guy called "Preacher" was the only one beside the White guy that tried to understand the purpose of this training. I told him that they made a lot of noise when we would go on patrols back in Okinawa. He asked me if I took out this team, who would I have as point man, rear point man and backup radioman? I told him, of course, he would be the second man behind the point man. The point man would be the Preacher, the main radioman would be the White guy and the rear point man would be me. The Preacher would also be the rear point man and I would be the point man for the first few patrols before the rest of them snapped out of it and started acting like Recon. I did tell him if we got hit that I couldn't count on these guys getting the wounded and dead men out of the bush. I could see that he was concerned. He told me thanks and both of us went back to our tent.

Both of us went with the other guys in our company filling sandbags. I knew that the sergeant was happy not to go out in the bush right how. As we were filling sandbags, I asked him what the hell had been going on over here and he said that just shortly after we went back to Okinawa that the N.V.A. hit all of the bases in Vietnam as well as the large cities. He said from Camp Evans on up to the D.M.Z. did very well in holding off the N.V.A. but at Khe Sanh, the N.V.A. had almost surrounded the Marines and were trying to make it like another Dem Ben Fu. He said that the Marines there couldn't wait for the N.V.A. to try to wipe them out. He told me that the Marines there at Khe Sanh were really pissed off and were waiting for the N.V.A. to attack them. The sergeant said they were cut off from Highway #9 and the only way for them to get supplies was by C-130's. I told him that it sounds like they need more Recon units up in the mountains and he smiled and I knew that we would be going soon.

After a couple of hours the word was passed that the mess hall was open. I left and went back to our tent and picked up mess gear that was waiting for all of the guys in the company. I headed in the direction the rest of the guys were going and found our mess hall. It was a tent with the cooks serving out the hot food. The next tent was for us to get our drinks and picnic tables for us to eat our food. When I was finished, I went out the back of the tent and on over to wash out my mess gear. There was one can for the food that you didn't eat and after that there was a can where you dipped your mess gear in it and used the brush. Then you put the mess gear into another can of hot water and you were done.

The food being cooked wasn't bad here. I was just happy that they didn't feed us rice. I went back to the tent and put my mess gear away under my cot. I went back to filling up the sand bags. At least it was something to do for the day. All of the guy in the company went back to filling the sandbags. There were a lot of sandbags that were filled and the lieutenants in our company wanted all of us to make bunkers next to our tents in case if we got hit by mortars or rockets from the enemy. So that was what the guys did also.

At 16:30 hours we were finished for the day. I went back to our tent and just laid down for the rest of the day. Around 17:00 hours the word was passed that we had mail call. I remembered we only had a couple of days back in Okinawa that we had mail call. I knew when we were in Okinawa that our mail first came here in Vietnam before they sent our mail to Okinawa when we were being trained as Recon. I knew that my mom didn't have to sent me any more packages since I was with Recon. I remembered that I wrote to her when I first left my old outfit. The sergeant from our squad went on over to our company headquarters tent to pick up the mail. He came back and started passing out the mail by calling our last names. I ended up getting about fifteen letters. As for the rest of the guys in the squad, they didn't get any where near as many as I got. But they all were happy to at least get a letter.

I had a couple of letters from Mrs. Hahner and a few letters from my mother. I had a letter from my brother and one from my sister. I opened up the letters from my mom first, starting with the oldest postmark. I came across a letter from my Father and I was going to read his letter last. It was nice that my mom wrote all of these letters as though she was talking to me each day as if I was home. On the last letter I read from mom, she said that Mrs. Hahner had called her on the phone and both of them were talking and Mrs. Hahner told my mom that I was thinking about extending over here in Vietnam. I could tell that my mom was a little up tight about it and also told me when I got back here to make sure that I would see the Hahners up in Chicago when I got back.

I read both of Mrs. Hahner's letters and she was really getting on me about extending over here. She told me that I did my job and it was time to come home. She told me that "Whitey" would want me to come home. She also told me that the whole family wanted me to come home and to come and see them when I got back. I could really feel their pain because they were worried if I extended that I would get killed. At the end of both of her letters she told me to get that notion out of my head and come home when my tour was up.

I read the letter from my brother and sister. I also read a letter from Diane Grogan who was in high school with my brother. Her brother and I hung around together, with Bruce Knox. I was down to the last letter which was from my father and I opened it up. There were two pages and this was unusual for him to write this big of a letter.

Hi Son,

I thought I had better drop you a line or two. While I have the time. We are all fit as a fiddle, and I sure hope this letter finds you in the best of Health, and your buddies.

We got your tape and also got your box you sent with the pictures and the silk, Mother really likes it and I think its beautiful. So does Alma and Herbie. They said hello and their sorry to hear you're back in Vietnam. By the way, Gary, we can hardly wait till April when you get home. Colerain lost again Friday night. So that just about put them out of the running. There isn't too much of anything going around here. I'm still doing O.K. down at the warehouse. I've been kept pretty busy the last week or two. Since the glass strike, and we aren't getting any bottles in. I've been shipping out to the plant 6 to 8 loads a day, and my warehouse is getting to look mighty empty.

Donny is still working at P. & G. He is working over at Ivorydale as a Janitor. I guess he is going to wait till they Draft him.

So my boy, I'm out of news so I might as well close for now. Wishing you and your buddies the best of everything.

Love,
Dad, Mom and Ryan

P.S. May God watch over you all and Protect you

Three weeks had gone by and still everyone in the company was filling the sandbags. One evening it was cloudy and I saw Bob and asked him if I could take a picture of him. He said that it was all right and I went to get my Nikon 35 mm camera I told him to show me how he felt over here. He looked right into my camera without a smile or any feelings and I took the picture. After that we talked for a short while and he said that his team was going on a mission. I told him to watch himself and that I wanted to see him when he got back here. He just nodded and left. I went back to my tent and I knew that we would be going out very soon.

Chapter Thirty-Six

The next day came and the sergeant came into our tent and said that we were going out on a eight day patrol. The look on the guys' faces was worth a million dollars. They were all scared because now it was the real thing. The sergeant said that we would have a briefing in half an hour and to start getting our gear ready. I grabbed my rifle and made damn sure that it was clean and that I had 16 rounds in each of the magazines. All four of my canteens were filled to the top. I also had a pack for the first time so I could carry my food in it. I made sure that I had my D-ring with a nylon rope. I had it attached to the straps that held up my cartridge belt. I went on over to the tent to get eight days of dry food to which I only had to add hot water.

I laid down on my rack and watched the other guys getting themselves ready for the patrol and they were all worried. The sergeant said that it was time to go on over to the tent for our briefing. All nine of us went over to the tent and got inside and sat down. The S-2 officer came in and told us that we were to go up on Mother's Ridge to see if the N.V.A. was still around Khe Sanh. We were not to engage with the enemy. The officer told us that the choppers would be here within the hour. Our team left the tent and went back to our tent to get our gear. The sergeant told the guys to make sure that they didn't make much noise out there and to keep their eyes and ears open. The sergeant told me that I was to be the rear point man and that the Preacher was to be the point man for the team. He said that when the choppers came that I was to be in the second chopper while he was in the first chopper. All of us left the tent and went on over to where the choppers were to pick us up.

The hour was almost up and we could hear the two Ch-34's coming and they landed and both groups went to each chopper. I got in and sat next to the door and had one of my legs hanging out the chopper. Then both choppers lifted and headed up north to Dong Ha. When we got close to the base, the choppers then headed down Highway 9 going west toward Khe Sanh. We were about 800 feet up in the air. The door gunner was keeping a sharp eye out for snipers. In the distance, I saw the Rock Pile and knew that we would be landing shortly. The lead chopper was starting to go down and there was a new base next to the highway. I told the guys in the chopper that we were getting ready to land and to get ready to get off the chopper.

The chopper landed and I got out and so did the rest of the guys with me. Both choppers left and headed back to either Dong Ha or to Quang Tri. The sergeant told us to lock and load. He waved his hand and the Preacher started out walking across the highway heading north. The Rock Pile was on the north side of the road and it ran north/south. Just looking at it was something. It was very sharp with jagged rocks. You could tell that it was very difficult to attack. Lengthwise it was long and narrow, not like the rest of the mountains over here.

We were heading north off to the left, which was west, of the Rock Pile about a thousand meters. We were on the floor of a large basin. Off in the distance and in front of us about 2000 meters were the large mountains that ran east to west to Khe Sanh. The grass was very tall and stood about five to six feet tall. It was a little difficult to keep quiet but the team did the best they could. They were a little too close to each other in case we got hit. The guys needed to know that we had to look more like a platoon going out on a patrol instead of a Recon team. If the N.V.A. were watching us, we had to make it look like we were a company going out on patrol. About a thousand meters into the grass, the sergeant called for me to come up and he asked me if we were making a lot of noise and I told him that the guys were doing the best that they could and I said that we had to spread out as far from each other so that if the N.V.A. were watching us that they would think we were a Marine platoon on the move. He said that it was a very good idea; he passed the word to spread out as far as we could without losing the guy in front of you. The next thousand meters we did it and finally reached the base of the mountains and we stopped there for a break. As we did he told the guys that when we started up the side of the mountains to really keep their eyes open for any noise or if we saw any N.V.A. around to keep it close.

It was time to go and the Preacher got the word from the sergeant on where he was to be heading. He started off and up he went. The sergeant was right behind him and the rest of the guys followed. I stayed back as long as I could without losing sight of the guy in front of me and I didn't hear anything and knew that we were not being followed. I got up and started up the mountain with the rest of the guys. We went up, almost to the top of the mountain before we headed west. I knew and the sergeant knew that if we were at the top of the mountain that the enemy could see us quite clearly. We had to use the rest of the mountain to cover our figures as we walked westward.

We walked westward to Khe Sanh for about 2800 meters on a single trail that went along the side of the mountains. I didn't like it but I knew that we would make more noise if we were not on the trail. It was getting on around 1830 hours and the sergeant had the Preacher off the trail and about fifty feet down from the trail. He waved the rest of us to come in and make a perimeter and he told the guys to go and cook their food. I didn't like the idea of cooking out here because it would give us away. There was to be no talking but we were only to listen and to keep our eyes open. The sergeant pointed to me and both he and I went back up to the trail and he said that we would make the enemy think that we would stay here for the night but when darkness came that we would move about 200 meters to the west and then set up for the night and day.

Both of us went back to the rest of the guys and ate our food. The sun was now down below the mountains and the sergeant told the guys to saddle up and that we were moving out. This time, I took point and the rest of the guys followed me. I went a good 200 meters and headed off the trail and now it was getting a little difficult to see where I was going. I found this little area where there were a lot of small trees around and it was a very good place to observe the enemy for the next day or so. The rest of the team came in and the sergeant told everyone where they were to be for the night and also who had what watch. Everyone took their time in getting off their gear so that they didn't make much noise.

I had watch at 01:00 in the morning and I had to listen for sounds all around us, not like in the infantry, where you only had to worry from both sides or in front of you. The only sounds were of insects. My time was up and I woke up the next guy and made sure that he was awake before I fell off to sleep. At least in Recon you only stood one night watch for only an hour.

Morning came and everyone got up on his own and the sun slowly lightened up the mountains around us. Some of the guys made breakfast from the dehydrated food that we had. I didn't feel like eating. As I sat there listening and looking out around me for the enemy, I could smell the food that the guys were cooking. I couldn't believe how much the smell moved in the air. At least there was no wind. I knew that I was the only one that could smell if the N.V.A. was around. I knew how they smelled out in the bush. The sergeant looked at me and told the rest of the guys to pay attention around them and let him know if they saw the N.V.A. For the whole day the team just sat there looking out for the enemy. I really didn't like staying in one spot for most of the day. I knew that we had to leave this place before night time to set up at a different place. If we stayed here for one more day the N.V.A. would know where we were.

As the day wore on, I just wasn't used to staying in one place all day hidden from the enemy. When I was with 1st Battalion 9th Marines we made a little noise and we moved during the day so that the enemy would hit us. I had to get used to this type of war. Instead of fighting the N.V.A. we now had to hide from them and not make contact, and not let them know that we were out there watching them.

I only ate at evening time and saved the rest of the food for later in case I really needed it. I remembered in the past that I hadn't had any food for nine days out in the bush. The sun was starting to go down and the sergeant told the guys to get their gear on and that we were moving out about 200 meters to set up for the next day. Most of the guys were having trouble getting their gear on. They had it spread out and it took them a little time in getting it together. This time the sergeant took point and the rest of us followed him. We went about 200 meters and he found this spot just off the trail about 30 meters where you couldn't see through the bushes. There was a nice little area inside the bushes where no one could see in but you could see out.

This time we stayed here for two days and again we couldn't hear a thing or see any of the N.V.A. that were supposed to be around Khe Sanh. We were told from S-2 that the N.V.A. were supposed to be on Mother's Ridge. We could tell being out here that the N.V.A. had given up on Khe Sanh and that it was not going to be like what they did to the French back in 1954. I knew since the Marines had been over here we were not like the French but we looked forward to kicking the hell out of the N.V.A. I remembered when I first came over here a N.V.A. soldier came over to the South Vietnamese side and told us how the North had a lot of trouble in fighting the Marines. He said that the Army was much easier to fight against than the Marines. Then, I remembered the young Army guy that told me how his outfit had left him and the point team in the jungle with the N.V.A. and never came back to help them. I remembered how he was really scared about going back to his outfit, and that he wished that he was a Marine instead.

We stayed out in the bush for seven days and now it was time to head back in to get picked up. We went back a different way and again the sergeant told me that I had rear point and to make damn sure that no one came up on us. I stayed away from the guy in front of me as far as I could from the terrain. As we got out more in the clearing, I stayed farther away from the guy in front of me. I would squat down like a Gook and just listen and watch the guy in front of me. About thirty seconds later I would get up and slowly walk to where the last guy was. I could tell that no one was watching us or following us and I knew that I could catch up with the rest of the team. When I finally reached the rest of the team, they were just crossing Highway 9. The sergeant told the guys to sit down next to the road and that our transportation would be here in a little bit. Again two choppers came to pick us up and again I got into one chopper and the sergeant got into the other chopper and off we went. As I looked out the door of the CH-34 I saw how much the Northern area had changed from Dong Ha up to Con Thein.

We finally landed back in our area and they told us to get rid of our gear and to go over to the debriefing room. When I got on over to the tent, they told us to sit in this one area and they would call each of us when it was our turn. I was the last one to be called and they asked me what I did and what I had seen, heard, or even smelled out there. I told them that the N.V.A. had not been there for some time and the area seemed very quiet. There was no movement at all from the surrounding mountains of any N.V.A. I could tell that the Marines inside Khe Sanh and outside on the surrounding hills of Khe Sanh were going to be all right. They told me that I could go, I went back to the tent. I got into my cot and just rested for the remainder of the day.

The next day came and we went back to filling sandbags for the company. We did it for the next three days and after that, we were finished with the sandbags for good. The next day, I went to chow at noon and when I got in the chow line, I saw this one guy who was not with our company and it was Kenny Fulton. I got my food and went into the other tent and sat down with Kenny. He was by himself and he looked up and couldn't believe that it was me. I asked him who he was stationed with and he said that he was here at Quang Tri. Kenny said that he was doing the rest of his time here until it was time for him to go home. I knew Kenny had a couple of Purple Hearts. I asked him if he knew where Dale had gone. He didn't know. Kenny said that he left a couple of days before I left the platoon. He did say that Speedy was still with the platoon and the battalion was up on one of the mountains around Khe Sanh. I just shook my head and both of us ate our food quietly. When we were finished, I told him that I was stationed with 3rd Recon "Echo" Co. 2nd Platoon. We both left the tent and cleaned out our mess gear and he walked away to where he was stationed here. I was glad that Kenny would be going home sometime soon. I knew that at least he didn't have to go back out in the bush.

Around 14:30 hours they told us that we would be having perimeter watch while we were back here at the base. One of the guys from our company came over to our tent and said to follow him. I grabbed my rifle and magazines and followed with the rest of the guys in my team. We walked about a good 200 meters and started walking through a small graveyard and then up on a small hill that went up about 20 feet. When we got back to the other side, I saw that the perimeter of the base was here. The guy took us over to this one large hole that could handle about ten guys and he left and the guys that were here told us this was the main hole and there were a couple of radios here. One of the guys there said there was an 81mm motor tube about twenty feet behind us and the lieutenant would come out here every so often and would fire the damn thing and that the rounds would fall all over the place. The rest of the guys there said that is when you have to take cover when that idiot is here. I couldn't believe what I was hearing. The one guy said that we in Recon had four holes that we had when we were here.

I looked out in front of us and there was at least 400 meters of rice paddies and after the paddies was a ridge line of trees. At least we would be able to see the N.V.A. if they tried to attack us. We left and went back to our area for the rest of the day until it was time for us to take our watch for the night. The sergeant told us which watch we had and which fighting hole we had for the night. Our team had two fighting holes and that meant that we would be standing watch twice each night. The rest of the day I just laid in my cot and tried to get some sleep. The rest of the guys would be doing their thing and each one was playing his own game against his friends.

It was time to go out to the perimeter for the night. I grabbed my combat gear, which was only my rifle and magazines and headed out to the fighting hole. I felt at home by being to myself. I knew that the rest of the guys in my squad still didn't like me and wanted no part of me with the exception of when we would go out in the bush, then they really depended on me. But, when we were back in the rear, they wanted no part of me because I was white. That was all right with me in because I didn't want any part of them and their bullshit. I got to the fighting hole that the sergeant told us to be. The rest of the guys shortly came and everyone saddled in for the night.

About a half hour later, an officer came out and I knew it had to be the lieutenant that didn't know how to shoot the motor tube. The lieutenant came over to our hole and grabbed one of the guys and told him to go with him and he wanted the guy to take the rounds out of the containers that they were in and he would fire the tube. The lieutenant said, "Fire in the hole!" and slid the round down the tube and off it went and where it went no one knew and the next thing I knew was that someone said, "Duck." The round hit and it was about 100 meters in front of our hole. I couldn't believe that this nut was doing this and no one had the balls to tell him to stop it. He fired two more times and he was done for the evening. The lieutenant went back to where he came from.

The rest of the night was quiet and at 05:30 in the morning we were relieved of our watch on the perimeter. I got my gear and headed back to our tent. When I got back there, one of the guys from another squad in our platoon had some papers with numbers on it and he asked me if I was getting short over here and I told him yes. He told me that I needed one of these papers and all I had to do was draw a line from one number to the next number and as I did that it showed a naked woman. He also gave me another paper with a naked woman on it. You had to color each part of her body by numbers from 1 to 395 days, depending how long you had been over here. The last two days were her nipples.

I went back to my tent and just laid down for awhile until it was lunch time. After lunch, one of the guys passed the word around that a CH-53 had gone down and 19 Marines who were short timers were on their way home when the chopper went down. All of them were killed in the crash. I knew that the only way to get out of Vietnam was in a pine box. You hardly heard of anyone making it out alive from over here. I thought to myself that it seemed we didn't have a chance to go back home from here, you either got it out in the bush, back in the rear or if a plane or chopper went down. You just didn't know when you were going to get it.

Chapter Thirty-Seven

I went back to my cot and just laid there and I started wondering what Dale was doing and if Speedy was still with 1st Battalion 9th Marines or not. I knew that Kenny would be going home unless he would get it here at Quang Tri. I remembered that the Negroes back in the rear would sing this one song from my old outfit, the 1st Battalion 9th Marines, most of the time. The song went like this:

> The Whole world is a stage
> And everyone is playing the part
> The stage is set, the curtain goes up
> It's the scene of a broken heart

Their minds were on home and not over here in Vietnam. They wanted no part of being out in the field. They just didn't have the guts to fight along side with the rest of the guys in the battalion. Now, I'm with these guys in Recon and the Negroes in my team wanted nothing to do with going out in the bush. My mind went to the Preacher and I felt sorry for him since he was between a rock and a hard place with the other Negroes in the team.

I started thinking about Benny Houston and Maxwell and those two guys from the old outfit of the 1st Battalion 9th Marines were hell on wheels. Benny was the old man of the platoon and everyone respected him and cared for him. Maxwell didn't take any shit from anyone, Negroes or White. Benny and Maxwell were so much different from all of the other Negroes over here and the Preacher was just like them. I knew that the Preacher had to walk a tight rope to fit in with them. I knew that someday he would end up staying away from them when they got back in the rear from the patrols.

I didn't want to think about home and I knew that I was getting very short over here and knew that I had to keep my mind on this place. The sergeant came into the tent and told us that we would be having perimeter watch every other day, so tonight I could sleep in my cot. Around 01:00 in the morning we started getting hit by mortar rounds from the V.C. The rounds were hitting very close to our tent. The guys got up and started running out of the tent on over to the bunker we had made when we first got over here. I just laid in my cot and rolled over to the side and landed on the sandy ground. After about ten minutes, the lieutenant came into the tent while we were getting hit and told me to get into the bunker. I told him that he better and I was safe right here where I was. He told me to move and I told him that I could take care of myself. He left and went into the bunker. As the mortar rounds were hitting, it seemed strange they were hitting only a very small area inside the camp, 3rd Recon area. I knew that a Vietnamese person knew our area.

When it was over with, about half an hour later, the word was passed that everyone could go back to their tents. The lieutenant called me over to his tent and told me that the next time we got hit to get to the bunker and I told him that I had been over here longer than him and that I could take care of myself better than he could. The captain heard me talking and didn't say a word and I left and they knew that I had been in this country longer than them and knew how to handle myself.

Three days later at about 01:30 in the morning while I was sleeping in the tent and not having perimeter watch, a grenade went off in one of the tents of our sister companies. Now what the hell? I then went back to sleep. Some of the guys in the tent got up and didn't know what the hell was going on. Morning came and the word was being passed around that some of the guys in one of the sister companies were trying to kill their captain in his tent while he was sleeping. Some Marine was pissed off at the captain. I'm thinking to myself what kind of outfit this is when the guys are trying to kill the captain? It looked like the captain was fucking with the troops. It seemed like almost every other day a grenade would go off sometime during the night. After a couple of times I started laughing in my cot when it happened. I remembered I would say, "I wondered if they got him tonight or if they missed again?"

About a week and a half went by and the word was passed that our squad was going out on a ambush just outside our perimeter that we watched every other night. The lieutenant wanted our squad to get in an ambush while we were back in the rear. I didn't care one way or the other. The sergeant came in and told us that we were going out tonight and that all we needed was our rifle and magazines with grenades. He told a couple of the guys to make sure they took a green and red star cluster with them. The sergeant told all of us what time our watch was during the night and again my time was at 01:00 in the morning. The sergeant told whoever was on watch to make sure they woke up the guy next to him and to make sure we didn't let the enemy know just where we were. "No sound, got it?" Everyone nodded and the sergeant told them to go about their business for the rest of the day and that we would be leaving around 19:00.

I wrote a couple of letters home and to Mrs. Hahner and after I wrote the letters, I just laid in my cot for the remainder of the day. I went to chow at 17:30 and went back to the tent and rested. As it got close to 19:00 I knew that it was about time to get my gear together. The sergeant passed the word to the guys to get on their gear and to get ready to move out. I could see that they were getting a little uneasy but still the idea of going outside the perimeter played a big part on their minds. They still had not seen any combat but when they did it would be big for them. I just didn't want to be around when they did get into the shit. I knew that they would not help each other but only worry about themselves when the shit hit the fan.

Our team went on over to where we stood our watch on the perimeter and told the guys on the perimeter to make sure that the lieutenant didn't shoot the mortar tube tonight. The sergeant told them we would be on the other side of the hedge row that was about a good 400 meters in front of them. The sergeant told the Preacher to take point and I was to be the last guy to go out there. We were walking between the rice paddies on the area that separated each of the rice paddies. We finally got to the hedgerow and went inside them. As we got inside the hedgerow, there was this path that went the length of our perimeter with the hedgerow and rice paddies in between. The sergeant was pointing to the point man to follow the path going parallel with our perimeter. On our right side was a stream about thirty feet away, also going parallel with the path. The sergeant pointed to the point man to go over the stream and to the other side. All of us walked through the stream and got on over to the other side. Again there was a hedgerow that was above the stream by about ten feet and on the other side of the hedge row was a small hill with only a foot high grass on it. There were two small trails, one again parallel with the stream, and the other one leading away from the base. This other small trail went to the top of this small hill. The sun was going down fast and I knew where the best place was to have the ambush and the sergeant passed the word to go back and follow him. As we went back to the stream where we had crossed it, the trail led us to cross over to the other side. The sergeant passed the word by hand we were to set up for the night time. I knew that the sergeant was thinking the same thing I was. It was a damn good spot and very hard to see us with the hedgerow over us. We had a great field of fire and there was no way for the enemy to get out of it.

Everyone settled in for the night and made sure they had everything ready in case the enemy came. As the night went on, I couldn't sleep well; the next thing I knew that it was my turn for watch. As I lay there watching and listening for the enemy, I started thinking about the old timers from 2nd Platoon Charlie Co. because we looked forward to hitting the N.V.A. and getting a lot of payback. I started thinking about what the guys were doing back in the States as well as what Dale, Speedy, and Kenny were doing here in Vietnam. I looked at my watch and my hour was up and I woke up the guy next to me and gave him the watch and as I laid there, I was still thinking about the guys from the old outfit and wondered what they were all doing now.

Morning came and we didn't get any N.V.A. to come into our ambush.

It was going on around 07:00 and the sergeant told us to saddle up and we were going back in. The sergeant told the radioman to call in and let them know that we were ready to come in. The sergeant told me to shoot off the green star cluster and I fired it back toward the base, about 70 degrees. The radioman told the sergeant that we got the O.K. and the Preacher took the point and we headed back in. Again I was the rear point man.

Ever since I had been here, it seemed that the N.V.A. had their own way of fighting us on their terms rather than on our terms. It was very frustrating most of the time. By the time we reached our tent, it was time for breakfast. When I was finished with breakfast, I went back to the tent and a couple of minutes later one of the guys came over and said there was a guy looking for me earlier. I asked him what the guy's name was and he said something like "Dale something." I said, "Dale Davis" and he said, "Oh, yes… that it." I asked him, "Where is he?" and he said that he had perimeter watch. I grabbed my rifle and magazines and headed out to the perimeter. When I got to the perimeter, I started walking from hole to hole asking if anyone knew Dale Davis. I had gone past four holes and came up to the fifth one and there was a couple of guys in the hole looking outward and as I approached them I asked if they knew Dale Davis and one of them turned around and it was him.

I got a smile on my face and I felt relieved that he was still alive and I was really glad to see him. I felt whole again and I told him that I saw Kenny Fulton about a week ago and he was stationed here also. I asked Dale when he got off perimeter watch and he said by noon and I told him that I would come back and he told me to meet him by this tent that was about twenty feet away from here. I left and I couldn't wait to talk to Dale and find out what was happening to the old outfit.

I got back to my tent and just laid there on my cot until lunch time and when I was finished, I headed back out to where Dale wanted to see me. I got to the tent and sat down under the tent. A couple of minutes later Dale came out from another tent and came over to me. I could see that big Texas grin on his face. I told Dale that I had a lot of questions about the old outfit and he said that he left the 1st Battalion 9th Marines three days after I left. Dale told me that the old outfit was ordered to Khe Sanh on one of the hills there. I asked Dale if there were any old timers left in the platoon and he said that he thought that "Speedy" was still with the platoon but was not sure. I asked Dale if the tall guy that was stealing the wallets and watches from the guys was still alive and he said that the fire team leader wasn't taking care of him and didn't care if he died or not. Dale said that he heard but wasn't sure about the guys in the platoon but there were some of them that got wounded up at Khe Sanh.

Dale looked at me with a straight face and said that he was glad that I got out of the outfit in time. He said that the lieutenant probably would have gotten me killed up there in Khe Sanh with some of his stupid orders. I told Dale that I was not in much better shape here in Recon. Dale looked into my eyes and could tell I wasn't lying to him because I was in trouble. I told him that I'm in a squad that has a Mexican sergeant with combat experience in Recon. There was one other White kid that was green and six Negroes of which five of them acted like assholes and were green also. They didn't want anything to do with a White guy. I told Dale that the one Negro's name, "Preacher " was a caring guy but he was between a rock and a hard place with the other Negroes in the team. They didn't want him to talk to me or any white guy or Mexican. I told Dale that I already went on a mission up on Mother's Ridge with these guys and you should have seen them out there in the bush. Their eyes were bigger than the rest of their faces. You could see how scared they were, being out in the bush where there were N.V.A. around. They listened to the sergeant and watched me to make sure that they were doing it right out there. I told Dale that if we had gotten hit these guys would have run like hell out of there in a second. And if anyone had gotten hit they would have left him to die out there, even their brothers. But as soon as we get back to the rear, they would go back to being prejudiced to everyone including their own kind.

I told Dale that I had never been prejudiced in my whole life, but these Negroes that were in our old outfit as well as in Recon were always blaming us for them getting wounded or getting killed. They would always stay away from us, especially when we were back in the rear. I told Dale when we had gotten hit on July 2nd and 6th I had three sandbags of goodies for the guys out in the field and the Negroes back in the rear stole my stuff while I was getting my rifle and magazines. I asked Gangware, who was watching the sandbags! "What happened to my goodies?" He told me that the black guys took them and I went over to their tent while they were playing their soul music and gave them one minute to get the goodies back over to my tent or they would be dead. There were thirteen of them and only me, but I was going to kill them all if they didn't get the goodies back over to my tent. Dale told me I was like an angel, in passing out the smokes and candy and, of course, juice.

Dale told me to wait here and that he had something for me. He got up and went over to his tent and a couple of minutes later, he had a piece of paper and a pin and came over to me and sat down and wrote something on the paper he had and then he handed it over to me. As he handed me the paper, Dale told me that he wanted me to have it because I had saved his life a few times and that I deserved this more than him. I saw that the paper was typed and on the top of the paper it read, "SILVER STAR " I read what he wrote on the top left side of the paper.

To Gary,

The best guy and buddy, which I will never forget as long as I live. We ran through a lot together. God Bless you always. Your buddy Dale

I then read the citation:

SILVER STAR

Private First Class Edward Dale Davis, United States Marine Corps, is cited of extraordinary heroism for action on 6th July 1967, at Quang Tri Province, Republic of Vietnam, for which he is awarded the Silver Star Medal.

Company "C", First Battalion, Ninth Marines, operating against a numerically superior North Vietnamese Army Force, was pinned down by heavy machine gun fire. With complete disregard for his own safety, Private First Class Davis unhesitatingly moved across the fire swept terrain and, throwing hand grenade and firing his rifle, charged the hostile position killing four enemy and destroying the machine gun emplacement. When the enemy attempted to penetrate the marine perimeter, he again fearlessly stood up and delivered accurate fire against the attackers and prevented them from over-running his squad's position. By his steadfast courage and selfless devotion to duty in the face of extreme personal danger, Private First Class Davis upheld the highest traditions of the United States Naval Services.

When I was finished, I told Dale that he should keep it and he said, "NO." He began to tell me that I had done so much for the platoon and all of the guys in it. Dale began to tell me the reasons why he wanted me to have this paper. Dale said, "Remember the time at Phu An when all of the radiomen that were with the captain were wounded including Bill, you were the only one around that had a radio and the captain had you call in all of those choppers to get the wounded and dead men out of there?" I was the only radioman that wasn't hit from the three platoons. Dale went on when our platoon had only 24 guys and went on this milk run for the day and we ended up running into a reinforced N.V.A. bunker complex and it was so damn hot that no one had water and six of the guys including Dale got heat stroke and while the guys were coming down with heat stroke, we had an arty F.O. lieutenant fighting against Lieutenant Libutti on running his platoon. I, being the platoon radioman, called in choppers to get the heat stricken guys out of there the temperature being somewhere around 120 degrees with high humidity, telling Lefefe to listen to the radio and I went over to where the guys were sick and asked the corpsman what I could do and he said that he needed water and there was a small stream that was polluted and I took my helmet and separated the liner from the pot and carried them over to the corpsman and both of us poured the water over the guys and as we did they would flop around like fish out of water. I told the guys not to drink it and to just lie there. I made about ten trips and even the corpsman was coming down with heat stroke and I even threw water over him. Dale said that I saved a lot of lives that horrible day, including his life.

Dale told me about the time when we were at Gio Lin and we got air burst and I went over to the tent where we were going to get fed and while I was going from hole to hole, I fed the guys while the air burst was hitting all around me. Dale said "Do I have to go on?" and I told him no. He was making me realize that I really cared for the guys, even the assholes. Dale said that I did more for the guys in 2nd platoon Charlie Company than anyone else. Dale said that I should have gotten at least two silver stars and I told Dale that I didn't do anything extra. Dale said that I saved his ass a couple of times and also the other guys that were wounded by the N.V.A. as well as the guys that had heat stroke. He said, "Remember the time that you picked me up after I stepped on a booby trap and carried me back to the platoon through the mind field?"

I told Dale that I didn't want to talk about it any more. I told him that I would take very good care of his citation. I really felt horrible while Dale was telling me how much I did for the guys in the platoon as well as taking care of him when he needed help. I had never felt this way before, being empty inside, and I told Dale that I didn't want to hear anymore about the silver star and to talk about other things.

I asked him if he had heard from his ex-girlfriend and he said that he didn't hear anything from her. I told him that I was glad that he didn't think about her but to just make it back to the States. I asked him how many days he had and he said something about 30 some days to go and he would be home for good. I told Dale that I was going to get a tape recorder from one of the guys and that we should talk about our time over here. Dale said that it would be all right. So the rest of the time both of us just sat there under the tent for a couple of hours without saying a word to each other. Just being with Dale and not talking was great. I knew that he felt the same way. He took out a cigarette and smoked it while we just sat there together. It was time for chow and I told Dale that I would be back tomorrow with the tape recorder.

That evening, we had perimeter watch and as the night came, I was thinking about Dale and how glad I was to see him again. It had been a couple of months since I had seen him. I couldn't believe how much we missed our old outfit, the 1st Battalion 9th Marines, Charlie Co. 2nd Platoon. Deep down inside of me, I knew that the battalion would never be the same after July of 67. I just wished that the guys were still alive. I knew that me and the rest of the guys that made it after July would never ever be the same the rest of our lives. I also wondered if I would ever see these guys again. I remembered that I made a promise to the guys in my platoon that I would try out for the Quantico Marines football team, and they told me that I better make it or they would all kick my ass. I took out the citation that Dale gave me and put it into my seabag so that nothing would happen to it.

I had eighteen days left in this country and it was starting to feel strange about going back to the United States. As soon as I started thinking about the States, my mind went back to the guys in 1/9.

The next day came and the sergeant came into our tent and said that we were going out on another patrol and that we would be leaving the next day. I told the sergeant that I had 16 days left and that I would not be going out with them. He looked at me and said that he needed me, but that he didn't blame me for not going and told me to see the lieutenant and to tell him. The sergeant said that he had a couple of more months to go himself. He couldn't wait for his time was up so he didn't have to go out in the bush. I went over to our lieutenant and told him that I had sixteen days left and that I didn't have to go back out in the bush. He said O.K. and that I would be put on mess duty for the rest of my time over here. I told him that was all right with me and I would be starting tomorrow when the team went out on the patrol.

I went back to the tent and asked the Preacher if I could use his tape recorder and he said O.K. I went over to where Dale was and we sat down under the tent and started the tape recorder and started talking of when we first came over here. Dale said that he came about thirty some days after I had been here. Dale said that he first joined the outfit when we were at Cam Lo bridge and then went to Phi An. We made two tapes and it took a couple of hours and at times both of us were still not sure which places came first or second when we were here. When it was over, we just looked at each other and couldn't believe all that had happened not to us two, but to the rest of the guys that were here before me and the guys that came just after Dale. All of the guys in our old outfit had seen a lot of shit and stupidity from our side and now the N.V.A. used flame throwers, calling artillery and even using gas on us besides trying to overrun and kill everyone of us. Dale said that all of the guys in the 1st Battalion 9th Marines should get the Silver Star for all of the shit that we had gone through and done. We knew that no other Marine outfit could have done what the battalion went through, especially when we asked for help and they didn't want to help us. They knew it had to be really bad if we asked for help.

As I looked at Dale and him doing the same to me, we had that empty feeling inside of both of us. There was nothing either one of us could do. Dale said, "Tell Ma Hammer, thanks for all of the goodies." Dale broke out with a big Texas laugh and made me laugh as well. I told him that she really had helped most of the guys in the platoon with all of her goodies, didn't she? Dale still had that big grin on his face. Just by him saying that lifted both of our spirits.

Dale started talking about our country and our government. We had been hearing that most of the people didn't care about this war and wanted us to get the hell out of here and our government was making money on us. I told Dale, wouldn't it be great if our country had another "Pearl Harbor Day?" Then everyone would get behind us and untie our hands and let us go to Hanoi and kick the hell out of Ho Chi Minh. This war would be over with within a year. But most of the people in our country didn't give a damn about us or what we were doing over here. The only people that really cared were the people of South Vietnam. The South Vietnamese knew that if we pulled out that a lot of them would die for helping us. But, the people back in the States didn't care or know. I told Dale that some day someone will hit the United States at home and then we would see what the American people would do. Dale said that the college kids from Berkley in the U.S. were supplying medical supply to the North Vietnamese. I told Dale that we are over here fighting and dying and our own people are providing medical supplies to the N.V.A. Dale remembered that we found those two N.V.A. backpacks full of medical supplies from the University of California at Berkley. Dale said that the college kids had sent two ships of medical supplies to North Vietnam. I said, "Remember when the guys in our platoon came down with heat stroke?" Dale said that he remembered it well. We both knew that in some way we would end up losing this war with the Communists because that was the same day we found the medical supplies in the two packs. We were doing something right for the South Vietnamese and people in our country were helping North Vietnam. Both of us started to feel low again. It was as though our country didn't really give a damn about us over here. I told Dale that I had to get back to the tent. I told Dale that I would be back in a couple of days.

As I got back to the tent, the guys were getting their gear ready for the next patrol. I just laid down and watched them. A couple of them came over to me and asked why I wasn't getting ready to go and I told them that I was not going and that my time over here was finished. A couple of them were getting pissed off with me and I didn't really give a damn how they felt. It was time for chow and all of us went to the chow hall. After chow, all of us went back to the tent. Around 13:00 hours the guys were getting their gear on. The Preacher came over to me and said that he was glad that I had finished my tour over here and that I was going home. I told the Preacher to watch himself and not to do anything stupid out there for these guys. I told him to listen to the sergeant and he would be all right. I shook his hand and he smiled and left with the rest of the guys.

They went over to the debriefing tent and went on over to where we would test fire our rifles to make sure that they were working properly. I watched them get on the choppers and they left. I hoped that the sergeant and Preacher would not get into any trouble out there. I knew that the rest of them wouldn't help at all. After they left, one of the guys came over to me from the company tent and told me that tomorrow I had mess duty until I got my orders to go home.

Chapter Thirty-Eight

I went back to my tent and just laid on the cot and started thinking about home. It felt strange about thinking of home. I couldn't believe how much I had changed over here in that Vietnam felt more like home than the States. My mind was racing overtime when I first got over here. I remembered the first time when I got to my old outfit, and this black guy in the platoon had only seventeen hours to go before he left for the States. The rest of the guys were back in the rear were laughing and happy for him to get back to the States. I remember thinking that I had 395 days to go before I would go home. The other guys that were back in the rear had two to five days before they were heading back home themselves. I remembered that I was thinking of home a lot when I first got over here and how scared I was of not knowing what was in front of me.

Somehow I fell off to sleep that night and again a grenade went off around 02:00 in the morning I started laughing to myself that they still didn't get the captain. All I knew was that the captain must be one hell of a prick to his men. Morning came and I got up and went on over to the mess hall and told them that I had mess duty and the sergeant there told me that I had the garbage cans to keep clean. He knew that I was a short timer and made sure that I had it easy. Most of my time, I could do what I wanted and I only had to put in about one hour during each meal.

A couple of days went by and I went over to see Dale and to see how he was. I told Dale that I would be going home very soon and that I wanted his home address and phone number. I also gave him my address and phone number. Dale told me that he had a older brother and two sisters. I also told Dale that I had a sister and a younger brother. I told Dale that I hoped to see him back in the States when all of this was over. I had to get back and it was almost time for chow.

The next day came and just after evening chow the word was passed that one of the teams out in the bush got hit. I knew that it was my team and I went over to the radio shack and asked what the word was on the team that was getting hit and they said they were being hit as we spoke. I asked the guy what the name of the team was and as soon as he said the call sign, I knew for sure that it was my team. I just hoped that the sergeant and the Preacher were all right. I went outside the tent and sat on the wall of sand-bags, waiting to hear who got wounded out there. There were about fifteen radios inside the tent, large radios as well as the Prick-25's. My lieutenant was inside the tent and came out and saw me and said that a couple of the guys were wounded but they were trying to get them out of there so they could get medievaced. He saw the look on my face and said that he would tell me more as it come in.

He went back inside the tent to hear what was going on. Around 22:30 the lieutenant came out of the tent and said they were on the choppers and coming back in. They were all alive and only a couple of them got wounded. I just wondered who was wounded. I got off the sandbags and headed back to my tent to get some rest for the night.

The next morning I went over to the mess tent to get ready for my job. I started getting the water into the garbage cans and lighting up the little boilers on each of them to heat up the water. I went over to the sergeant and told him that I needed more soap for the one can. He took me over to the tent with the supplies and said that from now on that I didn't have to ask him to get the soap or anything else but to get it on my own. While I was at the mess hall working, the guys came in. I didn't see who got wounded in our team until I got back a couple of hours after they had come in. When I got back to the tent, Bob was waiting for me and said that he thought that I had gone out on the patrol and I told him that I hadn't. I only had a few days to go before my orders came. Bob told me that he was glad that I didn't go out there. I asked him how much more time he had and he said that he would be leaving soon himself but didn't know actually when. It had to be within thirty days. Bob left and said to take it easy.

I went inside my tent and there were only a couple of guys lying on their cots. The rest of them were in another tent having a good time listening to their records. Two of the guys were being treated at the hospital. I went over to the Preacher and asked him if he was all right and he turned around and said that what I said was true and that he couldn't depend on these guys out in the bush. I only shook my head and left him alone with his own thoughts. I knew that he had to have some time to himself to get himself together. I went on over to the sergeant and asked if it was that bad and he said the N.V.A. were waiting for them and that we made a lot of mistakes out there in the bush. I asked the sergeant how he was and he said that he hoped that he wouldn't go through that again, ever. I told the sergeant that I hoped that they all would grow up and start acting like Marines and quit playing this States side bullshit on the rest of the guys and themselves. As I lay in my cot, I watched them and they were watching me. I knew they wished they never screwed around back in Okinawa when we were being trained as Recon. Now, all of their screwing around had cost their buddies to get wounded.

I knew that they still didn't understand what the hell was going on over here and that every time they come back in from a patrol that they would go back to their old selves again, still playing games with the other guys, especially to themselves.

Toward evening, all of them were in the tent getting ready for sleep. All of the guys except for the two that were wounded and the Preacher gave me a dirty look. They wished that I was out there with them to help their sorry asses. They didn't want any part of me and I felt the same way about them. I told them all that they better start taking care of each other and quit putting each other down. I told them that if they wanted to say something to me to say it in front of my face, not behind my back. I could tell they didn't want to hear what I was saying but they knew that I was right. I told them when we were back in Okinawa being trained as Recon that you assholes didn't take the training seriously and screwed around. On this last patrol you paid the price and got into trouble and if it wasn't for the sergeant and a couple of the other guys, most of you wouldn't be here now. So, don't put the blame on me. If and when you make your 395 days over here and it is your time to go home, let's just see who will be going out on a patrol when they have fifteen days left over here. I laid down in my cot and fell off to sleep. The rest of the guys didn't say a word for the rest of the night.

The next day came and I left for my mess duty. I got half way there and realized I forgot something back at the tent. I turned around and headed back and as I did I could hear a heated discussion going on between the Preacher and the rest of the Negroes in the tent. The Preacher was defending me and the rest of them were ganging up on the Preacher. When I got to the tent they all stopped talking about me and I quickly left and this time I made sure I stayed away. I was very proud of the Preacher for standing up for another Marine while the rest of them were trying like hell to put him down as well. He was doing a hell of a job getting back at them and everything that he said was the truth and I knew that it hurt the rest of them, badly. They just didn't want to hear it from their own. I knew for some reason that the Preacher was going to make it out of here alive to go back home. I was proud of him standing up against them and I knew that it was very hard for him to do it.

When I was finished with my mess job, I went on over to see Dale because I needed him to calm me down. I was still pissed at the guys in my team with the exception of the sergeant, the white guy, and the Preacher. I just needed to be with Dale. As I walked on over to Dale's tent, there were some Vietnamese people at the cemetery digging up the remains of their relatives. I finally got to Dale's tent and called for him to come out and he came out and again we went on over to the tent with all of its; sides tied up so that the wind would come through. As we sat down, Dale looked at me and could tell that something was on my mind. He didn't say a word and about twenty minutes went by and I told him that the guys in my team hated me and they thought that I was a chicken for not going out into the bush with them. I said that the Preacher defended me and understood why I didn't go out there with them. I told Dale that I was damn proud of the

Preacher for sticking up for me.

Dale waited until I was finished and after a couple of minutes of silence, he said that I didn't have to prove to anyone that I wasn't afraid of going out in the bush. Dale said that I better get that out of my head right now. My mind flashed back when I came back from Taiwan and the guys just about got wiped out and I and James Toy from Alpha company missed the big one. We hurried back to see if we could get out in the bush as quickly as possible. Then on the 6th of July the guys got hit again and again I'm at Dong Ha watching the flares going off all night up while the guys were getting hit and again I couldn't do a damn thing but just watch the whole night, finally getting out there on the 7th and passing out the goodies to whoever was left in our battalion. Dale said he was glad that I wasn't there. I told Dale that it would always be on my mind because I had never, up to that time, missed any firefights. I told Dale that I was mad at the captain for giving me his Out-of-Country R. & R. Dale said that the captain thought a hell of a lot about me and what I had done for our platoon that I warranted it. Dale said that the captain knew me better than all of the other guys in the company.

Again I told Dale that I could never forget about not being with you guys on July 2nd and 6th. It was silent again and this time both of us were thinking of the past. I knew that both of us were thinking of the hard times we both had over here. I started thinking about how the guys would made fun of Dale in the way he talked, that Texas drawl and his look. I knew that Dale really had it ruff in our platoon because the guys wouldn't be his friend. Then, both of us looked at the Vietnamese digging up their relatives and putting them into these large glass jars that were almost the size of a water bottle about 18 inches tall. We watched them for about 45 minutes and I told Dale that I was leaving and it was almost time to go back to the mess hall. I got up and left Dale and this time I walked along the perimeter away from the Vietnamese who were digging up their relatives.

I came across a grenade that was on the ground that didn't have a pin in it. I reached down and grabbed the grenade and carefully and slowly walked over to about 150 meters to where a hole was dug for the rest of the duds. As I got closer to the hole, a couple of the guys were asking me what I had and I told them that I had a grenade with no pin and boy did they get the hell away from me. Finally I reached the hole and got down in a prone position and slowly put my hand on the edge of the hole and let it roll down into the hole. I knew that if it went off that I would have one hell of a hearing problem. After lying there for about thirty seconds I got up and quietly left. I told myself that I was a little crazy in carrying a grenade that didn't have a pin in it. I only had a couple of days left before I went home, I must be crazy.

The next day came and I went on over to the mess hall and the sergeant called me over and said that I was going on a beer and soda run. He said that we would be going down in three trucks and that I was to ride shotgun. The sergeant said that we were going down to Da Nang to pick up the stuff. I went back to my tent and grabbed my rifle and magazines and came back. About a half hour went by and the three six-bys came. The sergeant and two of us got into each cab of the trucks and we headed down south on Highway 1. This was the first time I ever sat in the cab of the truck. As we headed south, I remembered some of the places I was at with the 1st Battalion 9th Marines and also some of the landmarks, such as the church with the very large figure of Christ that was about thirty feet tall. Finally we reached Da Nang and went on over to the warehouse that housed the beer and soda. The trucks pulled in backward and stopped. I got out of the truck to see this warehouse that housed the beer and soda. All of the beer and soda were on skids and they were stacked four high and as long as the building. Two of the trucks carried the beer skids and one of the trucks carried the three skids of soda. It took about half an hour and we got back into the trucks and headed back up north on Highway 1.

The trucks finally reached our company area and stopped at this one tent and waited for some of the guys that were there to help unload the beer and soda. I got out and was helping and one of the guys said that the sergeant didn't care if we took a couple of cases for our selves. My tent was about four tents away and I grabbed two cases of beer and took it on over to my tent and put it under my cot. I told the Preacher not to tell anyone in the team about this. I went back and grabbed a couple of more cases of beer and took it back to my tent and told the Preacher to start digging a hole under both of our cots so that we can bury the beer. I told him to dig another hole for the soda. I went back and helped unload the beer and we started unloading the soda and I was going to get two cases of Pepsi and one case of Coke. I grabbed the two cases of Pepsi and again the Preacher had the hole dug and put the Pepsi into it. I told him that I would be back with Coke and he asked if he could have a case for himself and I told him that he could have two cases of beer and a case of Coke and boy, did he have a grin on his face. I went back and when we got to the Coke, again I grabbed two cases and took them over to our tent. I went back to finish up unloading the trucks and all of the cases were inside the tent that housed the beer and soda.

I went back to our tent and asked the Preacher if he got his two cases of beer and case of Coke and he smiled and said, "Thanks...Hammer." I had two cases of beer and two cases of Pepsi and one case of Coke buried under my cot. The Preacher had his buried under his cot, two cases of beer and a case of Coke. I told the Preacher that I would be back with some ice so we could drink our soda with ice. For the beer that was in the ground, the sand and water that was about three feet deep would keep the beer and the rest of the soda cool.

When I went back to mess duty the rest of the day, the mess sergeant told me that I better not say where I got my beer and soda and I told him that he didn't have to worry about it at all. I was finished with evening meal and I went back to the tent and when I got there I grabbed my camera and decided to take some pictures of the place. It was getting cloudy out and it looked like it was going to rain. I got outside of my tent and went around and took some pictures of the sandbag wall that was about four feet thick and almost six feet high.

I went on over to the bunker and sat down on it and felt the loneliness coming over me. I felt all alone in the whole wide world. I knew that I couldn't see Dale right now. I just didn't want him to see me this way. I then started thinking about the beer that I had buried under my cot as well as the soda. I knew that I couldn't drink all of that stuff. I made up my mind to tell the sergeant and the Preacher to pass it out to the rest of the guys in the team after I'd gone. I didn't give a damn if they had it or not. I started thinking about what month it was and it was March but I didn't know what the date was. I got up and left for the tent; it was getting late.

The next day came and I told the team sergeant about the beer and soda that was buried under my cot and I told him that when I got my orders to leave that he could pass out the beer and soda. He said that he would but in the meanwhile the Preacher was passing his beer and soda out to the guys.

Another week went by and as each day passed the sun was coming out more and more after 11:00 in the morning. It was just like when I first got over here when the sun would come out and then the temperature would go up about fifteen to twenty degrees. Not much was going on around the base with the exception of it enlarging. You could hear the bulldozers working over by the perimeter.

The mess cook called me over to talk to me and said that the guys were coming down with dysentery, the shits. He said that I might want to clean out the cans with soap and water and I told him that I had them cleaned after each meal with soap and hot water. I went back to the cans and looked at them and I washed each one with a scrub brush and soap. The only cans I didn't clean out were the cans that held the food that the guys didn't eat. Both of these cans were almost full and boy did they smell. I watched the guys as they dipped their trays and canteen cups into the hot boiling water and rinse them in the next can and off they went back to their tents. Still, the guys were coming down with the shits. It was either the food that was being cooked or the cans they were putting the food into.

A couple of days went by and this old dump truck with Vietnamese came in. There were a couple of guys and two females that were with them. One guy was in the back of the truck and both females got out and went over to the two cans that had the food in them and were scooping them out with a large dish pan and handling it to the guy on the truck. He would put it into the cans that were in the bed of the dump truck. I was in my tent watching them from about 150 feet away. The guy that was on the truck when not putting the garbage into the cans was looking at the mess tent area and also where our beer tent was at for the battalion. I thought to myself that I better watch this son of a bitch, just because of the way he was looking around and by his body language. I knew that we were going to get hit tonight at the two areas that he was judging. They were finished and they left and I went over to the mess sergeant and told him that we were going to get hit tonight at the mess area and our beer tent. He looked at me and asked how I came to this conclusion, and I told him that I was watching the Vietnamese getting the garbage and one of the guys was looking at the mess area and the beer tent area. He said that he knew them and that nothing would happen and I told him that it would. He looked at me and said that he knew these people very well and that nothing was going to happen. I said O.K.

I left and was shaking my head and knew that I couldn't tell anyone else, because everyone here knows everything. I went back to my tent and that evening I told the guys in the tent that we would be getting hit tonight and that the area would be the mess area and the beer tent area. I told the guys to just stay in your cots and if the rounds came over here to just get out of the cots and hit the ground right where you are at.

When it came at 01:00 in the morning, I heard the mortar rounds coming in and they were hitting the mess area and the beer tent area just like I told the guys. Most of them got out of their cot; and ran over to the bunker and only a couple of the guys stayed in the tent with me, the Preacher was one of them. The lieutenant came over and told us to get to the bunker and I told the lieutenant that they, N.V.A. or VC were only hitting the mess area and beer tent area. We were safe here. He left and went to the bunker as well. It lasted for about half an hour and it was all over with. I just hoped that the mess tent with the hot stoves didn't get hit.

Morning came and the word was passed that the lieutenant wanted me over to the company tent. He started getting on me for not telling them about this. When he was done with his bullshit, the captain was watching to see what I was going to say back to the lieutenant. I said to the lieutenant that if I came up to you yesterday and told you that I watched a Vietnamese eyeballing the mess area and the beer tent, you would have said the same damn thing the sergeant in charge of the mess area said to me and that was he knew the Vietnamese people and they wouldn't do that. I said when we first got back here from Okinawa that our area got shelled, and I wouldn't be surprised if it was this same Vietnamese person doing it then. I told the lieutenant in front of the captain that your problem is that you don't listen to your enlisted men and think we don't know a damn thing over here. The only thing you know is that you know everything and we don't know a damn thing. I said that a lot of damn good Marines get killed because you don't listen to your own troops. I said that it was funny that almost every other night a grenade is set off by one of the men trying to kill the captain of the other recon company. Does that give you guys a hint? The lieutenant said that I could go. I left and went back to my tent.

Chapter Thirty-Nine

It was time to do my mess duty and after I ate, I got the cans lit and the water hot for the troops to wash their mess gear. The mess sergeant came over to me and I told him that I know what he was about to say and I said that I didn't want to hear it. I just told him that he had some great Vietnamese friends. He told me they would not be on this base again and that from now on they would have a couple of Marines watch them to make sure they only get the garbage and leave. He knew that he had made a big mistake in not listening to me. I told him there would not be a next time.

I went back to my job and I looked at the two cans that had the garbage and both cans were covered with about half an inch of food that was caked on. I got out two new cans for the guys to put their garbage in and I started cleaning out the other two cans. I first put very hot water in one of them and after a couple of minutes I took a large scrub brush and started scrubbing the one down. The smell was unbearable but I knew that someone had to do it. The rest of that day I worked on the one can and finally got it clean.

I walked back to the tent and laid down on my cot and started thinking of the time there was this one N.V.A. that got hit by one of our tanks and was lying on the side of the road and the smell of a dead person was just unbearable. We were about fifteen feet away from the dead N.V.A. and the smell ended up on our jungle clothes and in our noses and we could not get rid of that smell. I remembered that I would rather smell egg farts or any other bad smell, even shit didn't smell as bad. I knew that the smell from the garbage cans wasn't that bad. It didn't come close.

I started thinking about the lieutenant when we had gotten hit and the look on his face when the rounds were hitting about 150 feet away. I thought about Lieutenant Libutti and his first time out in the bush when we got hit in Phi Ann and he was at the bottom of the fighting hole about five feet deep, when I was first told that I was now the platoon radioman from Boni. It was there that Lieutenant Libutti realized he didn't know as much as he thought he knew in taking care of his men and that it was up to me and Lefefe to help him along. I was very proud of Lieutenant Libutti because the guys ended up liking him.

I got up and went to morning chow. I went to my job cleaning out the last garbage can. I was half way inside the can scrubbing when I heard someone calling out my name: Lance/Corporal Kasten. I stuck my head out and told him that I was him and he came over to me and said that my orders came in and that I was going HOME today and to get over to the company tent. I didn't believe him and I slowly walked over to the company tent and went inside and the lieutenant told me that my orders came in and that I was going home today and to turn in my rifle and 782 gear. I was numb and I still didn't believe what I was hearing. I was thinking to myself that this was a game they were playing and I still had a little time left over here.

I went over to my tent and the guys there heard that my orders came in and just watched me, not saying a word to me. I grabbed my rifle and magazines and the rest of the 782 gear and headed over to our company tent and turned in my gear. I took out my toothbrush and gave it a quick clean and I turned in the rifle and magazines and the supply sergeant looked at my rifle and told me to clean it again and I told him that if I cleaned it again "There will be a round in the chamber and you are going to receive it, do you understand? You're not going to play games with me." He took it and I went back to my tent and when I got there, Bob was waiting for me. He gave me a chi cong grenade and told me that it was a present for me. I took the grenade and put it into my seabag. I told him that he would be the second guy to be going home shortly from this company. He told me that he didn't have to go out in the bush anymore himself. I shook hands with him and then grabbed my seabag and looked at my sergeant and the Preacher and nodded to both of them and left. No one in the tent said a word to me. I went back to our company tent and they told me that I had to go on over to the battalion tent and there was a driver to take me and another guy to Dong Ha and on our way home.

I went on over to the battalion tent and the clerks there inside were doing their thing and I told them that Lance/Corporal Kasten was reporting for his papers to go home. They told me to relax and that it would be a couple of minutes before me and the other guy could get our papers. I sat down on a couple of sandbags and while I waited I still couldn't believe that I was really going home. It was like a dream, just like that. I looked back at my company area and I saw our tents and all the sandbags that we made. It seemed so strange to hear that I was going home. It had been a long time in coming to hear those words, "You're going home."

As I was sitting there, my mind was thinking of all of the guys of 2nd Platoon Charlie Company, 1st Battalion 9th Marines: The ones that had lost their lives, all of the guys that got purple hearts, the ones that were like me waiting for their orders to go home, and the ones that had been lucky enough to get their orders and go home before me. I could feel the tears coming and I didn't want anyone to see me like this. I had to get myself ready to get the hell out of here. I should be happy but I was numb, I still couldn't believe. Finally the other guy came and the clerks gave us our orders and said that a jeep would be coming to take us up to Dong Ha. The jeep came and both of us got into it and I sat in the front seat with the driver and I asked him if I could hold onto his rifle and he said O.K.

The jeep started and we were off; the other guy was happy and he had a big smile on his face. As we left the main gate and got on to Highway 1 heading north up to Dong Ha, which was about seven miles, I had the rifle lying across my lap, pointing outward in case I needed it fast. I thought about Dale and I couldn't say goodbye to him and I just hoped that he would understand. As we were driving up to Dong Ha, I saw the girls were out in their rice paddies working as though there was nothing like a war going on over here.

The driver asked us if we had heard about how Khe Sanh got relieved by the Army. Neither of us in the jeep had heard about it and the driver said that yes, the Army had come up to help save the Marines at Khe Sanh, but what no one knows was a Marine Battalion spear-headed the column to Khe Sanh and the Army was behind them. All of us got a smile on our faces when the driver told us about it because the Army didn't want anyone to know that a Marine battalion was the point.

We finally reached Dong Ha and went inside the main gate and the driver took us on over to the airfield. He stopped at the terminal and told us that he was glad we were going home. We both told him thanks and he went back down to Quang Tri. We grabbed our seabags and went inside to get our boarding passes so that we could get on the plane. We got our numbers and waited for the plane to come in. The day was starting to get hot; I was glad to get the hell out of here.

The C-130 came in and we watched the plane land and grabbed our seabags and waited for the Marine to call our numbers. When our numbers were called, we both headed to the back of the plane and dropped off our seabag at the end. The Air Force guy tied our bags so that they wouldn't leave the plane. We grabbed a seat and strapped ourselves in. I was thinking about the time when I had first come over here and that the weather was just like it was now and how the dust was flying around. The back door started closing and the engines of the plane started and I knew that we would be leaving soon. The plane started to move and the next thing we were off.

The plane headed down south to Phu Bai. About fifteen minutes in the air we started heading back down. As we landed, the back door started coming down and as I looked out the back of the plane, I saw we were at Phu Bai. When the plane stopped, some of the officers and enlisted men got off and went on over to the base here. There were other guys coming on the plane that were also going down to Da Nang. I looked at the base and I couldn't believe how big it had really gotten. I remembered the first time I came here and joined my outfit that the base was all tents and half the size it was now. The base was now all hardbacks with hardly any tents at all. Even the roads going into and outside the base were paved. I was starting to feel like an old man because everything over here was changing everyday.

The plane started up again and this time we were up in the air and heading down to Da Nang. As I looked at the other guys in the plane, I noticed that most of them were not in the infantry and half of the guys were in the Army. I could see just by looking at them that they didn't have that stare like me and the guys from my old outfit. As I looked at them and they looked at me, they would shift their eyes away from me and look at someone else. I knew that I made all of them nervous. It seemed they didn't measure up to my standards.

I started thinking back when I was in the C-130 for the first time going to Phu Bai that we got shot at and a round just missed me by about two feet. I remembered that I could hardly hear the round hit the plane because of the noise of the engines. I remembered that I hadn't gotten my feet on the ground and, not having a rifle and ammo, I could have been killed or wounded before I got to my outfit. That wasn't right. I knew that in a short while we would be landing at Da Nang and from there I had to go to the hardback that did the processing of Marines coming into and going out of the Country.

No sooner I was thinking of Da Nang when the plane started to go down. The guy next to me was smiling and couldn't wait for us to land. The C-130 landed and went on over to the Marine Terminal and the back door came down and everyone was trying to get off the plane at once. Even the guy that was going home with me was trying to get off the plane. I slowly got up and took my time in getting my seabag and when I got off the plane, the guy with me was already gone. I thought to myself that this would be the last time I would be getting on another C-130 over here and the last time I would be in this terminal again. As I walked through the terminal and out the other side, I saw the other Marine terminal about two hundred meters away and again my mind raced back to when I had first got over here with Richard McBride and we both first got our orders and that this Marine with jungle clothes came up to us and asked us what outfit we were going to and when we told him 1/9 he told us that we both were going to need luck and said he felt sorry for us. Richard asked him why and he told us that that outfit always got the shit kicked out of them. I told Richard at least we were getting into an outfit that wasn't afraid of getting into a good firefight with the enemy.

I finally got to the other terminal and went on over to the hardback that had a sign on it: Processing In and Out of Country. I went inside and gave the clerk my orders and he said that I was to take my seabag and myself over to hardback Number 14 and wait for further orders. I went over to the hardback that was Number 14 and sat on a cot and there were other guys also there waiting and after about an hour, a sergeant came in and told us to follow him and that we were to take our seabags with us. We followed him out the back of the hardback and there was this open area where he told us to get into two lines twenty feet apart and make sure that our seabag was in front of us. When we got into the lines he told us to face each other with our seabags in front of us. The sergeant told us to take everything out of the seabags and to spread all of what was inside the seabag out in front of each one of us. I took out everything, including the grenade which I had gotten from Bob and put it into my jungle pants pocket. The sergeant looked at each and everyone of us and as he passed he told us to put everything back into the seabag. When he went past me I started putting everything back in and took out the grenade and put it in the middle of the rest of my clothes in the seabag. When the sergeant got to the end of the two rolls he came back and put a seal on each of the seabags and told us not to open them up until we got back home.

He told us to pick up our seabags and to follow him and as we did, there was a guy that had a six-by ready to take our seabags onto the truck. We handed them to the guys and were told to get on the buses on the other side of the terminal. We got on the buses and it took us to another part of the airport that I hadn't seen before where there was a commercial jet. When the buses pulled up to it, the sergeant in the bus told us to get out and that we were getting on the plane.

All of the guys in the buses got out and there was a staff sergeant who had a clipboard and told all of us that he would call our names to board the plane. He started off by calling the officers to get on the plane first by calling their last names. When the last officer was called, he then told the rest of us to listen for our names and to get on the plane. I was the fifteenth guy to be called. I slowly walked up to the steps of the plane and when I got to the top, I stopped and turned around and looked back at Da Nang for the very last time. The empty feelings came over me once more. I went inside the plane and sat down. As I walked past the officers, I saw that these guys hadn't seen any combat and they were mostly talking to each other as if they were going to another base.

I slowly got into my seat next to the window and put on the seat belt and watched the rest of the enlisted guys getting on the plane. It seemed to me that most of the enlisted guys were like the officers who had never been in the field. There were only a few of us that had seen combat who had that distinctive combat stare on our faces, besides being very thin and looking very old before our time. I stayed to myself and didn't talk to anyone and that included the guys sitting next to me. I sat next to the window and looked out at the airport. Everyone there were going about their business as though nothing was going on. Guys were still coming onto the plane and I felt that I needed to get back to my buddies but my buddies were now gone or with other outfits. I could feel deep inside of me that I would never see my old outfit, the 1st Battalion 9th Marines again. I started thinking about Bob and I knew that within a couple of weeks he would be going home himself. I knew that Kenny Fulton had gone home a couple of weeks ago. Then

I started thinking about Dale Davis and I felt like I had run out on him and didn't let him know that I got my orders. I knew Dale had about thirty days left before he would be going home and I was glad. Then I thought about my old outfit the 1st Battalion 9th Marines and all of the fire fights our battalion had gone through and how the rest of the Marines outfits didn't want to help us and how it was up to us to get ourselves out. It seemed to me that the other Marine Battalions didn't want to be in the type of firefights we were in because they didn't want to get killed themselves. I knew that the 3rd Battalion 9th Marines and a couple of other outfits in the 3rd Division wanted no part of us when we asked for help. I remembered the tanks wanted to be with us when we got hit but after we did get hit they had their fill of a firefight. It seemed the only people that helped us were the artillery and the F-4 fighter bombers. I could feel the hatred deep inside of me because no other outfit had wanted to help us but everyone was quick to tell other Marine and Army outfits that we got the shit kicked the hell out of us.

The jet plane started up its engines and the girl stewards were making sure that we were buckled up. Again some of the guys on the plane were grabbing the girls' asses as they were walking by. The plane started to move and I just kept looking out the window and most of the guys in the plane including the officers were cheering. The more they cheered the more I kept to myself. I didn't think that we were really leaving Vietnam and the plane would just fly around and then come back down here. The plane got onto one of the two long runways and as we were about to leave, I could see the two Marines terminals and there was a C-130 being loaded with Marines going back up north, either to Phi Bai, Dong Ha or other bases. The captain of the plane got on the intercom and said that we would be leaving in a couple of minutes when the F-4s were gone. They were in front of us taking off.

The plane engines were getting louder and louder and it started to move. Most of the guys were cheering and as we got off the ground, I felt my heart sink. My body got very tired but I still kept looking out the window. The plane made a 360 wide degree turn and we went right over Freedom Hill 327 and everyone was going about their business in Vietnam. The plane started going up northeast over the ocean. The guys in the plane settled down and most of them were talking about how they couldn't wait to get home. One of the guys asked the other guys what the date was and they told him that it was April the 1st. April Fool's Day, 1968. Some of the guys were laughing and kidding each other that we were going back to Vietnam and this was just a joke.

I started feeling very lonely and tired and didn't feel like talking or being with anyone. I looked out the window and all I could see was the ocean and after about twenty minutes I knew that we were going to Okinawa. I knew we would be there for five days to get our shots and our uniform plus our other seabag that was stored there. I closed my eyes for the rest of the trip to Okinawa, and tried not to think about Vietnam and my buddy Dale for now. I never really knew how tired I was until now. My body was still tense and my mind was still thinking that the enemy would be shooting at us, even though we were not in Vietnam. I remembered when I first came over here how some of the enlisted guys looked so old and now I knew I was one of them. I wondered how much I had changed in my appearance and my reactions. I felt off to sleep.

The next thing I knew, I heard the guys in the plane telling each other that we were getting ready to land in Okinawa. I still kept my eyes closed until we landed on the ground. I felt the heat from the sun coming through the window. We landed and I opened up my eyes and I still couldn't believe how large this airbase was for our military. The plane took us over to one of the terminals there and then someone came onto the plane and said that the officers would be getting off first. There were buses for them and the cattle trucks were here for us. We were to load onto them and they would take us on over to Camp Henson. The officers got up and started off the plane. It was our turn and we got up and walked off the plane. We walked in a single file over to the cattle trucks and got inside them. The last of the guys got on the trucks and they all started off together to Camp Henson. I remembered that it was a thirty minute trip to the Camp.

The trucks finally reached Camp Henson and they took us over to the area for processing to go back to the States. As soon as we all got unloaded from the trucks, the sergeant there told us to go on over and get our bed linen for our stay and after that we could go to chow. He told us that these barracks were the barracks that we were to be in while we were here. He took us over to the building to get the linen and told us to go back to the buildings that were going to house us for the next five days. The sergeant left and we were on our own. I grabbed my linen and went back to the area and went inside one of the barracks and grabbed one of the lower bunks. I made my bunk and left for chow. I remembered that I had not eaten for the day and I was a little hungry.

The rest of the evening I just stayed to myself and laid in my bunk. I looked around and there were a few of us that just stayed in our bunks while the other guys were having fun and playing card games. Some of them even went across the base over to the little town that was across the road. I felt very tired and couldn't see having any fun.

The next day came and they called for us to get into the street in formation. A staff sergeant told all of us that we were going on over for the day to the hospital to get some of our shots. There were over 170 of us and they marched us on over to the hospital. When we got there they told us to get into two lines and at the end of the hall I saw two corpsmen who were shooting their guns at us. When all of us got our first two shots, we got back into the two lines and got another shot but this time they used a needle. When we were finished with the second shot they told us to go on back to our barracks and that we were off for the rest of the day. Everyone could walk back by themselves.

I got back and all I wanted to do was just lie down in my rack and get some sleep. I knew that the shots had made us tired. The next day came and again they marched us on over to the hospital and again we got two more shots. When all of us were back at our barracks, they called us to get on the street and that we were going to get our other seabag that we had left here when we first came over. They marched us over to this very large building and I saw that it was some kind of supply building. When we got inside of it, I had never seen so many seabags in my whole life. There must have been thousands of them. It had to be every Marine in Vietnam and somehow they had them so that it was easy to find the seabag. The Marines there (about ten of them) started calling out our last names and when they did, we yelled out to them, "Here." They would give our seabag to us and we could take them back to the barracks. They called out, "KASTEN!" I said, "Here" and they gave me my seabag and I took it back with me to the barrack. When I got there I opened it up and everything was still there the way I had packed it, even the records that I had from boot camp.

On the third day we went to the hospital for the last time for our shots and while I was in one of the lines, I looked at this one guy and he looked like someone I knew. I saw that he was also looking at me while we were waiting for our shots. He called out to me saying, "Hammer, is that you?" and I said "Yes" and I told him that I couldn't remember his name and he said, "Bill." Bill said that we went to high school together and I had a little grin on my face. I had the nickname "Hammer" since junior high school and the day before the song came out, "If I Had A Hammer." The nickname has been with me throughout high school. I couldn't believe how small this world was. Here I was meeting Bill from high school for the first time since I had gone into the Marine Corps. When we got our last shot, Bill and I walked back to the barracks together and talked about our friends from our old high school and wanted to know about some of the guys we had hung out with in high school. From what Bill was saying most of the guys were in the Army and were all over the world. Bill was in the same barrack as me but in the opposite direction.

The next day came and someone in the barrack called for all of us to gather around and said that he wanted to talk to us. He said that since most if not all of us had lost a lot of weight in Vietnam, we were going to be given a khaki uniform and to go on over to the P.X. to get our ribbons. He told each and everyone of us what ribbons we were to get. When I gave him my name, he told me that I had gotten the National Defense Ribbon, Presidential Unit Citation, Vietnam Service Medal w/1 stars, and Republic of Vietnam Campaign Medal. I left and went on over to the P.X. with Bill with the paper that the sergeant gave each of us. I went over to the area of the fruit salad and grabbed the ribbons that I needed and the bars to put the ribbons on. I also made sure that I got the gold star that I deserved also. I went back to the barracks and put the ribbons together and my rifle badge on my shirt. I hung the shirt on the wall locker and just looked at my shirt with the lance/corporal strip with the crossed rifles and my ribbons. I couldn't believe that I would be wearing it a couple of days from now.

As I looked at my shirt with the ribbons on it, I couldn't believe that my outfit had received the Presidential Unit Citation. I just kept on looking at it. I looked at the other guys that were around me and most of them had only three ribbons. There were a couple of guys that had the Purple Heart which made it four ribbons just like me. I knew that if I had gotten wounded that I would have had five ribbons. None of the guys around me had the Presidential Unit Citation. The reality was sinking in that my outfit had done one hell of a job over here and without the help of other outfits, except for the artillery units and the 175mm of the Army artillery guns.

I thought of the times that we had it bad and that we were down to two guys in a fighting hole for weeks. I remembered that we had one guy who would turn the watch up almost an hour so that he wouldn't have to stand his watch at night. I remembered that Ted Van Meeteren and I had caught Hughart and told him that the next time he did it that we were going to beat the living hell out of him. The guy just couldn't or wouldn't stand his watch until we caught him. We had our share of idiots in our outfit but all of us in the battalion made damn sure that everyone toed the line with us. I remembered that one of the guys in our platoon got on a chopper with the dead men and never came back when the N.V.A. were trying like hell to kill all of us in the battalion on July 2nd and 6th.

When we were finished with getting our uniforms ready, the word was passed that we had the rest of the day off. When everyone was finished getting their uniforms ready for tomorrow, they started up their card games.

The next day came and the word was passed to get out on the street with our seabags and that we were going to seal them up until we got home. They also said to make sure that we had our small hand bag to change our jungle clothes when we changed into our uniform. I made sure that I had my handbag on my rack while my uniform was hanging on the wall locker. I grabbed my seabag and got outside and again we were told to get into two lines. As they came down to each of us they gave us the seal and told us to seal our own seabag. They didn't care what we had in our seabag but they also knew that we hadn't had the time to get off the base and pick up anything. When everyone was finished the word was passed to put them on the six-bys, the three trucks waiting for us. We were told that when we gave our seabag to the driver to go back inside and change our clothes for going home and that we were leaving within a couple of hours. I gave my seabag to the driver and went back inside and the word was passed to strip our beds and put our linen in the hampers that were inside. We were told to fold up the blankets and put them on the table to be picked up later. When we were finished with that, we were told to change our clothes. I stripped down to my underwear and slowly started putting on my uniform. I put my jungle boots and jungle clothes into my handbag and zipped it up. I went on over to the shower room where there were mirrors and looked at myself. I saw how very old I looked. I could tell that life had been sucked out of me, as well as from the guys in my old outfit, the 1st battalion 9th Marines. Now, I looked like those Marines I had seen when I first came over here. I knew that those guys had also seen combat as well but I also remembered there were more of the other guys that didn't look like they had changed at all. I knew there were guys back in the rear not seeing the shit that was really happening over here. They were never out in the field.

As I watched the guys also looking at themselves in the mirror, I knew deep down that these Marines who had never seen combat were going to lie when they got home and say that they were in the fighting. Some of them were laughing and carrying on like little kids who couldn't wait to go home. I left and went out the back of the barrack and there was a large group of new Marines that had come over from the States and they were getting processed before going over to Vietnam. I looked at them and saw they were all new to the game of hell. How many were going into the infantry, who knows? I felt sorry for those guys because they were the ones that were going to get very old before their time and there was nothing that anyone could do to help prepare them for it. They were either going to get killed, wounded or be one of the very few lucky ones that wouldn't get a Purple Heart, like me. I wanted to say something to those guys but I knew they wouldn't listen to an old man like me that didn't show any life in himself. I didn't think that they would understand me at all. I did know they had to go through hell to really understand what they were doing.

Bill came out and he looked at the green horns and told me that it was their turn and God help them. I looked at Bill and said that it is a shame that we couldn't get them prepared for what they were getting into. Bill came back and said the only way these guys would learn was to be in it. Teaching them doesn't cut it here. Both of us went back inside and sat down and talked for awhile. Bill did most of the talking and he kept on saying that he couldn't wait to get home. I told Bill that I had mixed feelings about going home and I would believe it when we touched down in Cincinnati. I looked on Bill's chest and he only had three ribbons like 95 percent of the guys that were going home with us. Bill asked me what outfit I was with and I told him the 1st battalion 9th Marines and Echo Company 3rd Recon. He stopped talking and started shaking his head and asked me how long I had been with "1st Battalion, 9th Marines," and I told him from March '67 to Dec.15th '67; from Dec. 15th to April 1, 1968 I had been with Echo Company 3rd Recon. He couldn't believe that I had been with 1/9 and said to me, "Is it true what he heard about that outfit? That the firefights were unbelievable?" I couldn't talk; it seemed that I couldn't tell him anything. I just shook my head a little and wanted to know what outfit he was with and he said that he was in the 1st Marine Division, 7th Marines.

When Bill said, "1st Battalion, 9th Marines," a couple of guys near us got up and walked away from both of us. Bill looked at them and couldn't believe they didn't want to be around us. I told Bill that the last couple of months with my outfit that wherever I went and said 1/9 everyone would leave or get as far away from me as they could. As I was saying this to him, I could tell that he almost wanted to get away from me as well. I told him that I tried not to say my outfit name but when I did, boy did they get the hell away from me like I had the plague.

The word was passed to get out on the street and that the buses were here to take us. I grabbed my little handbag and got on the bus to the airport, supposedly to be going home. Bill sat with me and I could tell that he didn't feel like talking, either. I looked out the window of the bus and knew this would be the last time that I would be over here. I made sure that I saw everything. There were a couple of buildings that still had the bullet holes in the building from World War II.

We made it to the airport and the buses took us over to one of the terminals and we were told to get off. Someone told us to go over to where the trucks were and we grabbed both of our seabags. There were about seven trucks which were fully loaded with seabags and each of the drivers would call out our names written in black ink on the strap of the handle of each seabag. One of the drivers called out, "KASTEN," and I said, "Here." I waited to hear for my name to be called the second time and again within ten minutes another driver called out my name and again I said, "Here." I took both of my seabags and small handbag and walked on over to the small trucks that loaded up the plane with suitcases and put both of my seabags on one of the trucks, and waited for the rest of the guys.

I went back to the terminal and sat down and waited for them to call us to the plane. As I walked to the terminal, the plane was being loaded with some of the seabags that we had put on the trucks. Finally, they were all finished and the word was passed for the officers to board the plane and the rest of us enlisted men were to wait at the bottom of the steps of the plane for them to call our name before we boarded. There were about 100 officers that got on the plane and the rank was from Full Bird down to Second Lieutenants. Most of the officers were Captains and First Lieutenants. I was the tenth enlisted man to be called to get on the plane and as I walked up the steps, I still didn't believe that I was really going home. I knew that somewhere along the line we would be going back to Vietnam. The first thirty rows of the plane were for Officers and we had the rest of the plane. I took a seat next to the window which was not quite in the middle of the plane. Bill got called and he sat next to me. I could tell that he hadn't seen as much as me over here; he had seen some fire fights but not as much.

The plane started its engines and then moved on over to the runway and stopped. The engines started getting louder and louder and then we were off. When we got into the air most of the enlisted men as well as the officers cheered. I just looked out the window and didn't say anything. I closed my eyes and as I was finally getting relaxed, the plane started back down. We had been in the plane for only about forty-five minutes and now we were going back down. As we landed, I opened up my eyes to see just where in the hell we were. I knew that we had never been here before and the captain of the plane came on the intercom and told us that we would be refueling here before we went home. He also said that we would be here for about an hour and we could go into the terminal until we heard that the plane was ready to take off. The plane taxied to the terminal and after a couple of minutes the door of the plane opened up and about 80 percent of the Officers and enlisted men got off the plane. Bill got up and left also. After a couple of minutes, I decided to get off and to find out just where we were. I slowly walked to the door of the plane and went into the terminal. On the front of the building it read, "Welcome to Japan." Inside the terminal, like any terminal in the U.S., there was a gift shop with these little dolls that were Japanese ladies dressed up in their native dress. I thought about it but decided not to buy one. I did pick up some post cards of the country and some of them were just beautiful, especially the flowers and plants. There were a lot of ARMY enlisted men coming into the terminal and I thought they were all new guys going to Vietnam. All of them had only the National Defense Ribbon and one of the Marines asked if they were going to Vietnam but they said they were going to KOREA. All 300 plus guys. There wasn't much talking between us Marines and the Army. They saw that we were going home from Vietnam and it seemed that they were happy to go to Korea rather than to Vietnam. In a way, I didn't blame them for not going to Vietnam; they were the few lucky ones. The guys were all over the terminal, some of them calling home to tell their family that they was coming.

I turned around and went back to the plane and as I got to my seat in the plane I started thinking of the times that I was to call home from the D.M.Z. and both times I couldn't get through because some high ranking officer had to call home. I remembered that it seemed a bad joke to play on a guy out in the bush; to be told they were going to call home and then have it denied after sitting for about an hour both times. I remembered that after the second time, waiting for about an hour, I got up and walked out of the radio bunker at Gio Lin and the radioman said, "Where are you going?" I told him that this was a joke and I'd been here an hour and I still couldn't get on the radio to call home, "To hell with it." I left and for 395 days, I never called home from Vietnam. They told me that everyone had one call home from Vietnam but it was for those guys that were back in the rear. For us grunts, it was up in the air pending if you made it through your tour. I knew that none of us guys that were out in the bush ever got to call home.

The guys were coming back on the plane and Bill came in and sat down and I could tell that he was excited about getting out of here and heading home. The plane started up its engines and again we taxied out of there onto the runway and then the engines started getting louder and this time we were off. After a couple of minutes, the pilot came on the intercom and said that we would be at 48,000 feet and would land at Travis Air Force Base in ten hours. I looked out the window and the sun was starting to go down. I could tell that we were heading east and darkness was coming toward us.

The guys that had the aisle seats were having fun with the stewardesses. Some of them were just talking to them and others were putting their arms around them and already telling them that they had been in the jungles of Vietnam and they hadn't talked to a round eyed girl in over a year. I knew that they had seen a round - eyed girl at the Red cross building at Freedom Hill 327. These guys were playing on the girls to feel sorry for their lazy asses. I turned around to looked at the back of the plane and a couple of the girls were sitting in the laps of the guys that had the aisle seats. The few of us that had seen combat stayed to ourselves. I then turned around and looked out the window.

Chapter Forty

I started thinking again about my tour from start to finish as I looked out the window. When I first got over here, saying to myself that I had 395 days to go and the first guy in my outfit had 17 hours before he was going home. I was going over everything that I had done and saw over there in 2nd Platoon Charlie Company. I remembered how a large piece of me had died when Benny Houston died, another piece when James Fowler who was in my Boot Camp platoon died and then Sergeant Lugar and "Whitey." They really took a large piece of me with them. I remembered Poisson, who told me that the guys in the platoon didn't want any part of him because they would either get wounded or killed by talking to him. I remembered Jerry Moore, who got a fire team up at Con Thein because I was still weak with all of my nerves giving me pain, and he wanted me to be with him on the L.P. Boni gave him all kinds of hell that night by screwing with the radio and it rained a little during the middle part of the night, and I fixed the radio, shaking all night out in the bush, helping him out so that back in the rear that they wouldn't think that he couldn't handle a patrol. I remembered all of my nerves being shot and they couldn't move me and within those ten days or so the N.V.A. were shelling us with their 152 mm rounds and the guys would cover me up with their flak jackets. I remembered the shrapnel flying all around me and hitting the sandbags that I was lying on.

I remembered talking to Charlie Horton in late June and we talked all night and he told me that he was going to get wounded and that it would be in his shoulder and under his arm. I remembered how he knew that he would get wounded but make it out of there. I started thinking about early August, talking to Whitey and he was sitting under the tree next to a stream and seemed to be far off in space and after a couple of minutes he told me that he was trying to figure out how to write to his girl, Roxanne, that she should be going out with other guys. I remember the look in his eyes when he told me that he was not going home alive. Whitey stunned me and for a couple of minutes, I didn't know what to say. I remembered saying that while I was out in the field he would not get hit by the N.V.A. But he still had that feeling and he couldn't shake it. I remembered Charlie Horton had that same feeling and I knew that I had to be out in the field so that Whitey would be going home. I remembered talking to Dale and he told me that I should write a letter to Whitey's parents and let them know that he hadn't felt any pain when he died. And now, supposedly going home, I would have to take a trip up to Chicago and be with Whitey's parents. I was scared to see them and to face them. I knew that they would ask me again how he died and other questions and I didn't know if I had the nerve to be able to talk to them, face to face.

The feeling of loneliness seemed to be covering my whole body, and I just wanted to be left totally alone and not to talk to anyone. Bill was sleeping at this time and I tried to close my eyes to see if I could get some sleep. The loneliness wouldn't leave me; it kept me thinking about all of the guys including the ones that were assholes in the platoon.

Then I thought of Sergeant Singleton, who got the Medal of Honor, and that Ted Van Meeteren, Frank Bignami, Al Quick, and me carried the dead sergeant out so he could go home and that our whole battalion went back in and got hit again by the N.V.A. and more guys got wounded, and how all of the guys in the battalion that day watched over each other and made sure that all of us got out of there alive. I remembered that my platoon set up relay teams of four men at a time carrying a wounded guy that only had one leg and the other one was blown off by our own artillery, and the guys patched him up and talked to him all the way back and out of harm's way. I was glad that I was part of the relay team while carrying the radio on my back. There were quite a few guys that made up the relay team every fifty feet.

Somehow I was half asleep but there were a few of the guys still taking to the girls on the plane. My mind raced back in time again and this time, I was up in Con Thein and we were getting hit by 152mm rounds by the N.V.A. from North Vietnam. I told the guys in my team to stay in the bunker until I told them to get out. The blond - headed guy came out of the bunker and I told him, "GET THE HELL BACK IN THERE!" and then, a piece of the 152mm round hit between my legs and I reached down and it was still very hot and I dropped it and looked at him and boy did he get back into the bunker. I then remembered the time that I fed the platoon up at Gio Lin with the air burst all around me and still I never got hit by the shrapnel. I remembered that I tried to get wounded but couldn't. I really did some stupid stunts and somehow got away with it. A couple of minutes went by and I remembered when we got to Phu An and we got hit and Sergeant Singleton was behind me and as I was lying on the trail in front of the dead sergeant , in front of me was Sergeant Thomas, my squad leader who was digging with his hands and feet. Then all of a sudden this feeling came over me from the end of my feet through my body and to my head. It was like a Guardian Angel telling me that nothing was going to happen to me over here in Vietnam. I knew that I couldn't tell anyone because no one would believe me.

The darkness kept coming and the stars were all over the sky. It seemed peaceful and quiet. My body was starting to relax a little more as time went by. Most of the guys including the officers were sleeping and only a few of the guys were still talking to the stewardess. The plane started going down slowly from 48,000 feet. We were on the last leg of our flight. In a little while we would be landing on U.S. soil. I still couldn't believe that we were really going home. It still felt like a dream.

I thought about Dale. He and I were very, very close to each other, like brothers. I knew that he had about three weeks to go himself before he got his orders to go home as well. The pilot of the plane got on the intercom and said that we would be landing shortly and boy was there a hell of a yell on the plane. Everyone was up trying to look out the windows of the plane to see if they could see land. I looked out the window and Bill asked me if I could see anything and I told him that I could see a lot of lights in the distance and it was like Christmas time with all of those different colored lights: red, yellow, orange, blue, green, and of course white. It was the first time in a very long time that I had seen so many lights. The pilot of the plane said that we would circle around San Francisco and then land. One of the guys said that it was going on 01:00 in the morning. It seemed to me that we were sneaking back into the United States. I remembered that we left the United States in the evening and now we were coming back into our country so that no one knew that we were here. The plane landed and I could feel the wheels touching the ground but still I kept myself under control. Then everyone yelled, with the exception of a few of us that had been out in the field who didn't show any emotions. Bill got a little excited and said that he couldn't wait to get back to Cincinnati.

The plane went on over to the terminal and stopped. The stewardesses opened up the door and they left the plane. As they did, one of the officers from the base came on and told all of us that before he let everyone go, to listen up on what to do once we got off the plane. He said that the officers would get off the plane first and then all of us enlisted men, when we got off the plane to pick up our seabags that were on the ground in front of the terminal, and when we got inside the terminal to go over to the pay window to get paid. Once we got paid there were cabs out front for the guys that needed to go to the San Francisco Airport to go home. The cabs were paid for so we didn't have to pay to go to the San Francisco Airport and they didn't open up until 06:00 in the morning, so there was no rush in getting out of here. He said, "Does everyone understand?" He told the officers to go ahead and leave. As soon as the last officer got up and got out, the rest of us by row got up and off the plane. When I got to the bottom of the steps, I went on over to where the grass was about some sixty feet away and knelt down to touch it; it felt great. I looked around the base and everyone there was sleeping since it was a little after 01:00. I got up and went over by the terminal to pick up my seabags which were laid out in a long single file. I found my two seabags and went inside the terminal to the pay window and I signed a release paper and they paid in American money instead of military money.

I looked for Bill and there he was, also in line behind me. I told him that I would wait for him and I pointed to him where I would be when he was finished getting paid. There were about fifty guys in front of him and both of us knew that we had plenty of time. As I was waiting for Bill, I saw seven Army second lieutenants walking toward me. As I looked at them: they all only had the National Defense Ribbon. I knew one of them - I couldn't believe that it was Larry MacAfee and as they were getting closer to me, I saw that Larry was telling his buddy something and I knew that he was going to try to make me salute him. Larry MacAfee was from my high school and played on the football team with me. Larry thought that he was the toughest guy in high school. I remembered he wanted to fight me and Rocky Sunshine. He took on Rocky and ended up getting the shit kicked out of him. Rocky and I in gym class put on boxing gloves and a couple of hundred kids watched the two meanest guys go at it and I ended up beating Rocky and that was how Larry decided to take on Rocky first. Larry knew that if he beat Rocky he had a chance with me. Now, this was the first time since high school since I had seen the asshole.

When they got about three feet away, I said, "Is that you, Larry, and he said Yes." He said "Aren't you supposed to salute me?" and I told him that I didn't salute second lieutenants, especially you. Boy, that hit a nerve with him. He started going off on me and as he was going off, I just smiled at him and that made him even madder. The rest of the Marines that were on the plane with me came over to where we were at and surrounded the second lieutenants. I still didn't raise my voice and I told him if he was smart to shut up. I asked him and his buddies where they were going and he said, "Vietnam." I asked him where, and he said, "Saigon." I slowly told him that he was going to do a pussy job and he was the right kind of guy to handle that type of job. I knew that he couldn't handle an infantry job because his guys would be shooting at him, because of him being so all-knowing. I really got him mad and I told him that he didn't want to fight me here because I would probably come close to killing him. I knew deep down inside of me he still thought that he could beat my ass in high school but Rocky Sunshine beat the hell out of him before I could have gotten to him. I told him that I had gone through hell over there and if he really wanted to know if he could beat my ass, let's go. Right here and now.

One of the Marines around the Army second lieutenant asked me when they could kick ARMY ass. I told the guys they were leaving in peace, if they knew what was good for them. Just as Larry was about to leave, I told him there were no games over there in Vietnam and that it was easy to get killed. Then we parted. The rest of the Marines who were there were really hoping they could kick the hell out of them if I gave them the word. Bill came over to me after getting paid and asked if that was Larry and I told him that it was and that he still hadn't changed. Bill said, "Let's get the hell out of here," and both of us headed out the front of the building to grab one of the cabs to take us to the San Francisco Airport. When we got outside there were some Marines with their families and of course their mothers were very happy and crying at the same time. There must have been about ten sets of parents, girlfriends and a few friends there to greet them. There were a couple of other Marines there and all four of us got into one of the cabs and put our seabags in the trunk and the driver took us to the airport. It was somewhere around 04:30 and now we were heading to the airport to get our tickets to go home.

None of us said a thing while the driver drove his cab. In the distance we saw the Golden Gate Bridge. As we got on it, I got a couple of tears and I knew that the other guys had a few tears as well. We came up on the Airport and the cab driver took us up to the front door. Just before we got out of the cab, we saw about ten young hippies and four of them were girls. None of us guys could believe what we saw. All of them were wearing T-shirts, including the girls, and blue jeans with holes in them. All of them looked like they hadn't taken a shower in weeks. The four girls were not wearing bras and they were smoking.

All of us got our seabags and went into the terminal and as we did, Bill and I knew that we couldn't get our tickets until they opened and that was about an half hour from now. It was 05:30. Bill and I just sat down and waited for the airport to open and one of the Marines there told us that they had told those dirty people if they came in here before all of us left that we were going to kick the hell out of them. As Bill and I sat there waiting, I couldn't believe that the young people back here in the States were looking like filth. I remembered back in Vietnam how the young teenage girls were dressed up and if they were not dressed up they wore clothes that didn't look like they were poor. Even the little kids had shorts and a shirt on even if most of them didn't have shoes to wear. But they were always clean. I was glad to fight for them because they really appreciated us protecting them. Here, back in the States the teenagers were protesting against the war and wanted our troops to come back home. I knew that people like Jane Fonda were helping the enemy with medical supplies. That included the University of California at Berkeley sending two ships loaded with medical supplies to the N.V.A. The more I thought about being back here in the States, the more I wished that I would rather be in Vietnam; at least the people there helped us and gave us information on the enemy. Bill told me that it was 06:00 and that we better go on over to the ticket window and get two first class tickets for Cincinnati, Ohio. We got our tickets and we were on the first flight to Cincinnati, which was 09:30. We headed for the gate and when we got there, sat down and waited. Bill got up after sitting for about an hour and decided to call home to let his parents know that he was coming in. I knew that I better do the same thing, so both of us went to the phones and called home.

Mom answered the phone and I told her that I was coming in today in the afternoon. I gave her the flight number and she was very happy that I made it home and said that she would tell the rest of the family. I also told her that Bill from my high school was coming home also and that I saw him in Okinawa a couple of days ago. I said that it was 08:30 here in San Francisco and that we would be boarding in an hour. I hung up and went back to the chairs. Bill and I heard the first call for our flight and both of us started walking up to the ramp of the plane. I thought that I heard them calling Bill's name on the intercom but I wasn't sure and I asked Bill if he heard them calling his name and he said no. We showed the stewardess our tickets which were 1st class, and we went on the plane.

I told Bill there were no signs here saying, "Welcome Home." As the people got on the plane, they would either look at us or wouldn't look. They didn't say anything like welcome home and they were proud of us. It seemed that everyone was going on about their lives as though there was no war going on. Both Bill and I stayed to ourselves by not saying anything. The plane started up its engines and we were moving and Bill looked at me and said that in three hours we would be home for good. I just nodded to him. The plane was off the ground and after a couple of minutes, the stewardess came over to us and asked if we wanted anything to drink and Bill said yes and asked for 7 and 7 and I said the same. A couple of hours went by and neither of us hardly said a word. The plane started coming down and as both of us looked out the window, we tried to look for certain landmarks. The pilot told us to put on our seatbelt and that we would be landing in a couple of minutes. We could see the Greater Cincinnati Airport and before we knew it, the wheels touched the ground. We were home.

The plane taxied over to one of the terminals and both of us got up and had our little handbags and then walked off the plane. When we got to the top step, our parents were down at the bottom away from the steps waiting for us. Bill got off before me and I was right behind him. As we got to the last step and went over to the side, both of us went to our parents. Bill's parents were there with other family members and my mother and father were there with my Aunt Alma. Mom came up and I hugged her and while I was hugging her, I was shaking my father's hand. He couldn't say a word but I knew that he was damn glad that I was home. After I hugged mom, I also hugged my Aunt Alma. I told Bill to take it easy and that I would see him later. There was a news person there with a camera taking pictures of both of our families. He took a picture of both Bill hugging his mother and me hugging my mother.

We all walked through the terminal and again there were no signs welcoming us back to the States. I picked up both of my seabags and went over to the car. Dad drove and I sat in the front seat with him. I didn't say a word in the car. Mom and Aunt Alma sat in the back. As we were driving up I-75 heading into Cincinnati from the Kentucky side, Aunt Alma asked me how many people I killed. I couldn't believe what I had just heard and Dad really got mad at his sister for saying it. He asked her, "What the hell is wrong with you?" Mom started talking and telling me about how Starr and Ryan were doing since I had been gone. I listened to Mom without saying a word.

Mom said that she had been talking with Mrs. Hahner and said they would like to see me while I was on leave. I said that I would go up there and see them. Mom said that it would be great that I would do this for them.

Dad pulled into the driveway and there was a sign that covered the whole door and it read, "WELCOME HOME, GARY." I started to choke up when I saw the sign and almost had tears in my eyes. I got out and helped Dad with my two seabags. Aunt Alma said that she had to go home and again said she was glad that I made it back. I kissed her and she left. I went into our little home and nothing seemed to have changed while I was gone for those 395 days. Dad took one of the seabags and went upstairs to my room which I shared it with my younger brother Ryan. Ryan came out from the other room and surprised me and I asked him why he wasn't in school and he said that he wanted to see me first. I saw that he was as tall as me, but was slender. I went upstairs with my other seabag and handbag and went to our room. Dad said to me that he was glad that I was home and I could see that he was very happy that I had made it back alive. He could tell that I had changed a lot since I'd been gone. Dad knew that I had gone through hell over there. He went back downstairs and watched T.V.

I looked around my room and I couldn't believe how small it really was. There was a desk that both Ryan and I shared and both of our beds were made. Mom always made our bed everyday and never complained about doing it. I walked over to my bed and just laid down and it was the first time since I was home on leave before I had gone over to Vietnam. It felt good and yet strange that I was lying in my bed.

A couple of days went by and I spent a lot of my time staying in my bed thinking about Dale still over there and couldn't wait for him to go home. I came downstairs and Mom said that I should watch T.V. to see what is going on in the world. So, for the first time I turned on the T.V. and the news was on and at this time, Mom was making dinner. The news men were showing pictures of the war in Vietnam and telling the American people that we were not winning the war over there. They were telling everyone back in the U.S. that we lost so many men over there that it was a losing cause. I turned it off because it was making me mad at the news stations. I asked my mother "Is that what they say on the news?" and she said they say it everyday, telling everyone that we were losing a lot of men everyday over there. I told my Mother that I didn't want to hear that garbage because that it was not the truth.

Mom said that I should go up to Chicago and see the Hahner family and that I should call them to see when they would like to see me. Mom gave me their number and said that she had talked to Mrs. Hahner a couple of times and they became good friends. Mom told me that Mrs. Hahner told her she was lucky to have a good son and that she should be proud of me; Mom said to me that she was proud of me. I got the phone number from her and called Mrs. Hahner. She answered the phone and I asked if this was Mrs. Hahner and she said yes. I told her that this was The Hammer and I had made it back. She asked me if I was coming up and I asked her when would be a good time and she said this weekend. I told her that I would call the airport to see if I could get a ticket and I would call her back to let her know for sure that I would be up there this weekend. I then hung up and called the airport to make a reservation to go up to Chicago on Friday and come back on Tuesday. Once I got a confirmation, I called Mrs. Hahner back up. She told me that the whole family would be waiting to see me on Friday and that Midge, Whitey's sister, and his father would pick me up at the O'Hare airport. The plane would arrive there at 1:30 in the afternoon. I told my mother in a way this was going to be very hard on me. Mom said that only I could ease their pain of losing Whitey. "I sure hope so, Mom," I thought.

For the next couple of days, I never left the house. I would wear my T-shirts and some of my old pants that were still large on me. Friday came and I put my uniform back on, since it was the only thing that I could wear and Dad took me to the airport and then told me to take it easy up there. He knew what I was about to go through. I nodded my head and left to get onto the plane. As I walked through the airport, people would stay away from me like I had some kind of disease. I didn't give a damn about the American people; they seemed to be too damn stupid or dumb to know what the hell was going on in the world. I knew they didn't give a damn about us service guys.

I got on the plane and it took us about an hour and a half to get there. While on the plane I was wondering what to say to the Hahner family. I knew they would want to know as much about what Whitey did over there in Vietnam and of course what happened to him the day he died. The plane landed at O'Hare airport. Everyone on the airplane wanted to get off the plane first. I just sat there getting this sick, scared feeling. Most of the people were off the plane and I grabbed my handbag and started walking toward the door of the plane. Each step felt heavy and I started walking up the ramp and as I was about half way there, walking slow, I saw this young woman that looked almost like Whitey himself. Her face was very close to Whitey's face and it was like looking at Whitey again. I got about ten feet from her and she called out my name, "Is that you, Hammer?" I told her, "Yes" and she hugged me and at the same time asked me if Whitey felt any pain when he died. I couldn't talk. She had caught me off guard. She put her hand around my arm and both of us walked into the terminal together and Whitey's father came up to us and said to me, "We're glad, son, that you are home from Vietnam." He hugged me and I ended up with a few tears. He had called me son, and I really felt uneasy.

Chapter Forty-One

All three of us walked out of the terminal without saying another word. We got into the car and Whitey's father drove us home but before we got there, his father asked if it was all right if we stopped at the bar that he and Whitey had gone to. I told him that it was all right and we got there and went inside and Whitey's father ordered three beers. There were a few people there drinking and Mr. Hahner told the bartender this is one of Whitey's buddies from Vietnam and his name was "Hammer, our other son." Again that got me and the bartender gave us another beer on him. He said that he was proud to know me because I was a great buddy of Whitey.

About a half an hour went by and Mr. Hahner said that he had to go to the restroom and would be back in a couple of minutes. As he got up and walked on over to the restroom, Midge, Whitey's sister, came over to me and sat down and looked me right into my eyes and again she wanted to know if Whitey had felt any pain. I looked right into her eyes and said that he had a smile on his face and didn't know what had happened, it was that quick. Whitey didn't feel anything, it was that fast. She told me that they had a closed casket and asked, "Was his face gone?" As I looked into her eyes again, I knew that whatever I said, she would know if I was lying or not. I again looked into her eyes and with a firm voice said his face was still there and he had a couple of very small cuts but that he had a smile. Midge told me not to say anything to her father to spare him the grief. I told her O.K. I saw Mr. Hahner coming back from the restroom and Midge said that she was going to the restroom and now it was the father and me.

Whitey's father waited until Midge was inside the restroom before he asked me, just like Midge had asked me, "Did Whitey feel any pain when he died?" As I looked into his eyes I could tell that he also wanted a straight answer and I had to tell him. Again, looking right into his eyes I told him, that Whitey didn't know what had hit him and that he had a smile on his face. I saw the tension leaving his face. Again the second question was because they had a closed casket on Whitey. He also wanted to know if his son had lost his face and again looking into his eyes, I told him no, his face was still there because he had a smile. The father was really glad to hear that. I could tell that the weight of the whole world had left his shoulders.

Midge came out and he said, "Is everyone ready?" We all agreed and then finished our beers. Again the bartender shook my hand and said that he was glad to know one of Whitey's buddies. We got into the car and this time it took only a couple of minutes and he parked the car on the street and all of the homes looked the same. Midge told me to get out of the car and all three of us walked up the steps of the home. As we did, I was getting scared because this was where Whitey had lived all of his life.

Whitey's father opened the front door and I waited for Midge to go in first and I went in after her. As we walked into the hallway there was a picture of Whitey in his dress blues with his ribbons. Around the picture were all of his ribbons and medals that our battalion had received in Vietnam. There was the Purple Heart that had a gold bar around the ribbon which meant that he had died in combat. After a couple of minutes looking at Whitey and the ribbons I went into the living room and there was Mrs. Hahner. She came up to me and gave me a big hug and kissed me and said, "Welcome home, Son." Then she told Midge to take me up to Whitey's room and that dinner would be ready in about an hour. Midge told me to follow her and the both of us went upstairs and she showed me Whitey's room which was in the front of the house on the second floor. As I slowly walked into his room and looked around, I told Midge that I feel that I didn't belong in his room. Midge told me that Whitey wouldn't have it any other way and that he would be offended if I didn't stay in his room. I saw some of the awards Whitey got in high school sports, I asked Midge to sit down with me and talk to me a little more about Whitey. She told me that he had been dating a girl who was a senior in high school and she would be graduating this spring. Her name was, "Roxanne." Midge said that tonight we would be going to the high school to see a play that Roxanne was in. Midge told me that she helped Whitey buy him beer behind their parents' backs and she began to laugh about those times. She also said that she helped him sneak out of the house. The main thing was that he was a very good brother and cared about people. I knew that Midge loved her brother very, very much and would do anything for him. Again I felt myself wanting to cry but I would hold it off.

Mrs. Hahner called us to come on down when it was dinner time. As we walked downstairs to the dining room, there was a large oxygen tank and a hand-held mask to put around the nose and mouth. I didn't say anything, but I knew that someone needed oxygen. When all of us were finished eating, Whitey's dad got up and went into the next room with the oxygen to use it. Mrs. Hahner told me to just call her "Mom." She told me that we were going to the high school to see a play that Whitey's girl was in.

As we left the house, I saw a small flag in the window with one star on it, meaning that the Hahner's son had died in Vietnam. We got to St. Regis, the same school Whitey had gone to. All four of us went and sat in the audience and watched the play. When it was over all of us went outside in the hallway and Midge gave me this large bouquet of long-stemmed Red Roses to give to Roxanne. As we waited for Roxanne to change her clothes, I was wondering what I could say to her. Midge came out with Roxanne and Mrs.

Hahner told me there she was and I walked toward her and as I got close to her, Midge dropped back a couple of steps so that we would be together. I asked if she was Roxanne and told her on behalf of Whitey and me , we would like to give her these flowers on a great performance. She gave me a kiss on the cheek and said thank you and that she had heard a lot about me from Mom Hahner. I smiled and the rest of the family came in and everyone was talking and telling her how great she was up there on stage. I just watched all of them and I knew they were trying to go on with their lives. But I knew that it would have been even better if Whitey was here to give the flowers to his girl.

When we got back that night and as I was in Whitey's room, I talked to him, telling him that I just wished he was here instead of me. I told him that I tried like hell in Vietnam that morning to stay with their squad, arguing with Lefefe and the lieutenant; I would still have been carrying the radio and he wouldn't had gotten killed that morning. I told Whitey that I didn't argue hard enough and I failed. As I was talking to Whitey, my eyes filled up with tears and I couldn't help myself from crying. For some reason I knew that Whitey was somehow in the room with me and telling me that it was all right. But still, I couldn't stop crying.

I remembered calling out Whitey's name that day and waiting and waiting until the old timers were bringing down Sergeant Lugar down the hill and then I went up the rest of the way up the hill and found Whitey on the side of the hill in a fetal position. I remembered sitting there looking at Whitey and telling him that I was sorry and telling him to get up. After a couple of minutes, I took out his poncho and put his body into it. As I did, I couldn't see where Whitey got it until I rolled him onto the poncho and saw that half of his skull was gone. I saw his brains and started saying, "No, No," out loud. I finally covered him up and called out the rest of the guys there to help me carry him down the hill. Not one of those bastards would get off of their lazy asses to help, so by myself I started dragging Whitey down the hill. I got almost about a third of the way down when the poncho started to rip. I grabbed another poncho from one of the green horns and again covered him up. No one could see him and then Dale came back up the hill and I told Dale that I got Whitey and I needed help and he looked at me and said that he was here to help me.

I stopped crying and somehow I fell off to sleep in his room. Morning came and I was up at 05:00 and went downstairs waiting for the rest of the family to get up. Mrs. Hahner got up and asked me if I wouldn't mind going up to Wisconsin and I asked her why and she said that Whitey's oldest sister would like to meet me. I told her that it was all right and in the afternoon Mom and Midge went with me, but Whitey's father couldn't go because he needed his oxygen. We left early in the afternoon and got up to Wisconsin in the evening and met Whitey's oldest sister. She looked more like her mother than Midge. Her husband worked for one of the T.V. stations up there. We finally left that evening for home.

On Sunday, I asked Mrs. Hahner if we could go to Whitey's grave if she didn't mind. I wanted to pay my respects to Whitey. We left sometime around noon and got to the cemetery and there was this stone wall completely around it. We drove over to where Whitey was buried and Midge stopped the car. Mom said that she couldn't go over there now and I understood. Midge said that he was over there and pointed. I told Midge that I had to be alone for this. I got out of the car and walked over to the area where Midge pointed and I found him. I knelt down and slowly read his stone, which said when he was born, "April 19, 1948" and that he died in Vietnam on "Sept. 1, 1967." I put my hand on his stone and started talking to him and told him that again I was sorry for not being with him when it happened. I took out a nickel and placed it into the ground in front of the stone and said that this nickel represented the guys from our platoon, Dale Davis, Ted Van Meeteren, Frank Bignami, Denny Lugar, and the Hammer, Gary Kasten. As I stayed there, I felt myself at peace but still felt that I hadn't lived up to my part in taking care of him. I got up and went back to the car and got inside and without saying a word, we went back home. Monday came and everyone just relaxed. Mrs. Hahner told me not to go back there to Vietnam and told me to make her a promise. She also told me that my Mother didn't want me to go back there, also.

As I watched Mrs. Hahner the whole day, I could tell that she was always keeping herself busy with no idle time. I knew that she was hurt deeply, even though Midge was around, because Whitey was not here, made it very difficult. I also knew that I was glad to leave tomorrow because the hurt would not be so strong. I knew that being there helped her but also made her feel sad at the same time. Mrs. Hahner said to me that she got word that Sergeant Dodge was coming to see them and he was a good friend of Whitey. I told her that he wasn't out in the bush with us but was always driving a jeep and bringing us hot chow everyday until Whitey got killed. I didn't want to make her think he was that close to Whitey, but he knew him. Then, Mrs. Hahner said that she had something to give to me and it was a small picture of Whitey in his dress Blues with his ribbons and on the back of the picture they had written: George L. Hahner, Jr., Lance/Corporal., U.S.M.C. April 19,1948 - Sept. 1, 1967 Quang Tri Province Republic of South Viet Nam.

"Talk to God as you talked to me. He will hear - Listen well and He will answer you."

Tuesday came and Midge was taking me to the airport and before I left them I gave Mrs. Hahner one last hug and kiss, then hugged Whitey's father and shook his hand and told both of them that I would always be thinking of them. Midge and I drove to O'Hare airport which took about forty-five minutes. I told Midge that the whole family was great to me and I appreciated it very much for what they had done for me. I said that I wished there was something I could do to ease the pain for everyone in the family. Midge said just coming up here meant a great deal to the whole family and her. She took me to the front of the terminal and I told her not to get out but to go on home. As I got out of the car, she got out also and came over to me for the last time and gave me a hug and a kiss and said that I really helped out the whole family and to take good care of myself. I told her that I would never forget them all.

Chapter Forty-Two

I got on the plane and sat down and just looked out the window and stayed to myself. I knew in some way that I had eased their pain and also they now knew that Whitey didn't die in pain. I took out the small picture that Mrs. Hahner gave me and just looked at Whitey and knew that I would read everything on the back again and again.

The plane finally got back to Cincinnati and my father was waiting for me and both of us went back home together. I got inside the house and Mom asked me if I had had a good time and hoped that everything went well. I told both of my parents that it was a little rough but they really gave me a great time while I was there; they had taken me in as their son.

I went upstairs and lay down in my bed. As I lay there, I knew that I would not be going back to Vietnam and my brother was still in school and I didn't have to worry about him. I had two and a half weeks to go before I was to report to my next duty station which was Camp Lejeune, South Carolina, 2nd Recon.

I WAS HOME FOR GOOD.

ISBN 142510646-3